ALSO BY JOHN KOBAL

Garbo
(with R. Durgnat)

Marlene Dietrich

Gotta Sing, Gotta Dance, The American Film Musical

Marilyn Monroe: A Life on Film

Rita Hayworth

Hollywood: The Pioneers
(with Kevin Brownlow)

Hollywood Color Portraits

Foyer Pleasure
(with V. A. Wilson)

The Art of the Great Hollywood Portrait Photographers

Hollywood: The Years of Innocence

PEOPLE
WILL TALK

PEOPLE WILL TALK

by John Kobal

ALFRED A. KNOPF

NEW YORK

1985

THIS IS A BORZOI BOOK
PUBLISHED BY ALFRED A. KNOPF, INC.

Portions of some of these interviews originally appeared in *Film* and *Focus on Film*.

Library of Congress Cataloging-in-Publication Data

Kobal, John.   People will talk.

Includes index.
1. Moving-picture actors and actresses—United States—Interviews.
2. Moving-picture producers and directors—United States—Interviews.
I. Title.
PN1998.A2K646   1985   791.43'028'0922   85-40121
ISBN 0-394-53660-6

Manufactured in the United States of America

FIRST EDITION

CONTENTS

ACKNOWLEDGMENTS

T HANK YOU TO ALL THE people along the way who helped, eased things, lent encouragement, and even those who didn't and by trying to obstruct me fired me up and made me prove that something that couldn't be done could. Wherever possible I name the people who helped me in the introduction to each piece, but there are some who were an enormous help when it came to the actual writing, and whom I'd most particularly like to thank, here and now.

William Kenly read the manuscript in its earliest stages—twice its present length—checking endless facts and dates; throughout the time I was writing it, he was ever available with his vast store of information.

Maxine Fleckner Ducy of the State Historical Society of Wisconsin allowed me to browse through the archives as well as loaning illustrations for this book.

I'm indebted to Peter de Rome for transcribing many of the interviews, a talent that required a good ear and a great deal of patience when voices overlapped or words were smothered by my yelps.

It was Kate Franklin who introduced me to June Duprez.

The French film critic and historian Bruno Villien, when he heard of the book, said that I had to meet and talk to his friend Arletty—and didn't leave it at that: he came along and translated for us. And back in New York, Carlos Clarens turned it all into English.

My colleague Kerry Kammer read and reread the book in its final stages, and made it easier for me to cut some interviews and drop others, sorry though I was to lose Bette Davis, Lil Dagover and the screen's first Jane of *Tarzan* fame, Enid Markey.

This book would never have happened if it weren't for my editor, Victoria Wilson. My writing it was her idea, and in the time that followed, her constant support, her always good advice, generous criticism and enthusiasm made it a cherished working experience.

Lastly I owe an enormous debt to Matthew Daniels. He not only typed the manuscript but came up with invaluable suggestions. Writing this book, remembering these people, was a wonderful experience, and I'm indebted to Matthew for making the writing time as much fun as the actual interviews had been.

John Kobal
July 5, 1985

INTRODUCTION

T<small>HIS BOOK IS A COLLECTION</small> of what were to me meetings with extraordinary people. Their work, whether behind the scenes or much celebrated, had been the best part of my life, my world until I met them, and for a long time after. They were the people who made the movies I seemed never to be away from. Even when I was home in bed, I was reading about them, dreaming about them. Those years of my childhood and adolescence are a blur. I'm not being sentimental. I paid for it, begging for money from strangers to pay for my obsession, and often failing my classes at school. What I had learned in movies came in handy in only two subjects. I could talk about little-known details pertaining to Marie Antoinette, or to Napoleon and Marie Walewska (the day I overrode my teacher to insist on Napoleon's affair with Greta Garbo remains a black spot of humiliating embarrassment). Literature required imagination, even though I failed grammar. I had the most extensive collection of comics and film fan magazines anyone in my neighborhood had seen.

One day I couldn't pass for a child anymore—the twelve-cent admission days were over, and even though I could now get in to see movies forbidden to children under twelve, the new admission prices brought their own problem. The next day I was fifteen—I looked older, I had grown fast and my skin was sallow from all those hours in dark rooms. I passed for eighteen and forged my way into the only Sunday screenings my puritan city allowed: a film society that met once a month.

The first foreign movie I saw without subtitles was Marcel Pagnol's 1931 French classic *Marius,* part one of the trilogy that later made up the Broadway musical *Fanny.* When I saw the later Hollywood version of *Fanny,* all rosy-hued and kitschy-pooed, I knew it wasn't as good, and my dislike of director Joshua Logan's work was born then.

Through the film society I saw Garbo in *Camille,* Cocteau's *La Belle et la Bête,* Arletty in Carné's *Les Enfants du Paradis.* Instead of an empty cinema, screenings were held in the lecture room of the Natural History Museum. The new location only confirmed my opinion that movies were something very special . . . to the left of some early Canadian dinosaur's fossil . . . whether Yvonne de Carlo or Henri-Georges Clouzot.

Then I read about Marlene Dietrich, who was in the news because of her triumphal one-woman world tour to places like Tel Aviv, Moscow and Berlin. Her picture made headlines when some Germans, who had never forgotten or forgiven her for entertaining the Allied soldiers fighting against her Fatherland, threw eggs and tomatoes at her when she returned to Germany. Now she was coming to the newly built O'Keefe Center in Toronto. Everything has to start somewhere. I knew I had to see this show: I had to meet her. Newspaper money I'd saved took me to Toronto; I told those in charge of the O'Keefe's press office that I was a journalist from Ottawa. The story I told them and the chutzpah it took to convince them came to me from all the movies I'd seen. I got a ticket in the front row of the 3000-seat auditorium; I assured the publicity woman that yes, I understood it would not be possible to arrange an interview with the star; that I wouldn't even be able to go backstage; that there was no way to see Dietrich later because after the show there was to be a party in her honor, invited guests only; and me nodding yes, yes, because one thing at a time, first see it and then . . .

I got backstage, where crowds of people were trying to get to the sweat-soaked, tuxedo-dressed woman leaning exhausted but beaming outside her dressing-room door; and to get myself noticed (my extreme height I then took for normal) I shouted to her across the room something flattering in German, the language I'd been warned was *taboo;* and she looked at me. I still remember the quizzical but amused expression on her face as she craned her neck up to see me better after she'd called me over to her; and the even more bemused, startled expression on the face of the publicity woman between us. I told Dietrich that I had come hundreds of miles to see her and I couldn't leave without seeing her again. She told me she would see me tomorrow and invited me to the party.

It's all very clear to me still, yet at the time everything took place in an emotional turmoil in which my stomach never stopped churning, and everything was a brilliantly lit haze emanating from Dietrich's presence and my nearness to it.

The party was almost over. Dietrich was in another room with just a few close friends, her secretary, her musical director, Burt Bacharach, her escort for the evening and one or two local people. I had missed my bus back to Ottawa; I had no money, no place to stay and no certainty about seeing her tomorrow without reassurance. I sneaked into her private dining room behind a waiter and planted myself next to a tree such as they usually put in corners of rooms for those occasions. Dietrich was talking, going over the evening; clearly, she still felt good; it had been an amazing occasion, with Canadians behaving like Cossacks, screaming and shouting and refusing to let her off the stage; she even gave encores (something she cut out completely in later years) and was forced back onstage to sing with only Bacharach at the piano to accompany her, though her voice was now a croak amplified to ear-splitting proportions. And still the audience had been wild. There in the room was a small band of musicians

Marlene Dietrich and *John Kobal,* October 24, 1960

serenading her. Her escort, a small actor I've never liked, the kind, all gray hair and pearl teeth, who on American TV plays self-satisfied English diplomats, saw me first and looked as if he'd seen a dropping. Marlene turned her head in my direction and she smiled, called me over, asked how I'd liked it. Fine, just fine. It wasn't what I said, it was the way my heart pounded in my voice. I sweated, and I still hadn't taken off my hat. It was new. It was Tyrolean. I'd never worn a hat before and I didn't want to lose it; besides, it made me feel more adult. She was smiling and turning to the others at her table and translating what I'd said because it turned out I was talking German to her and she presumed I spoke nothing else. Had dinner been good? she asked. I remembered to say thank you and that I'd forgotten what the food was like because all I wanted was to see her again. So she smiled again. Was there anything else I wanted? Yes, why hadn't she sung "Falling in Love Again" in German? She asked the lead violinist if he knew the melody, which he did, so she said, "Shall I sing it to you in German?"

I was down on my knees now because she was sitting and the strain of having to crane her neck even more to look up to me was beginning to tell on her. She was nearly sixty and even though she looked ageless onstage, she didn't look half her age to someone so close up. She could have been wearing a sandbag over her head and I would have thought she was everything wonderful rolled into one: Her cheeks were sunken, her teeth very white and pronounced, her eyes large with slow-flapping lids. Her head was and is very large, and the youthfully styled bouffant blond wig that I took for her own head of hair only made it seem more so. I remember she wore a plain gold-embroidered, two-piece outfit; the gold threads were like the strands of her hair, and the light from the candles on her table caught and leapt all over them with every gesture. She was the most vibrantly gorgeous thing I'd ever seen in the flesh. And she sang to me: "Ich bin von Kopf bis Fuss auf Liebe eingestellt . . ." Everything was spellbound.

When it was over, she asked about my mother, Did she know where I was? And where was I staying the night? Her interest was that of politeness and good feeling after a great success. I had no story made up. I hadn't expected to get this far. Instinct helped out. I said little or nothing and she understood. I know, these things only happen in movies, or when you are so young, so hungry, so dazzled that nothing can stop you. She took me back to her hotel, and when the desk clerk said very apologetically that he really had no remaining room in the hotel for her young friend but, giving me the once-over, he might get me into the YMCA up the road, Dietrich said no, and as long as I promised to be up early in the morning and out of her suite before she got up, she'd put me up in her living room.

Marlene Dietrich put me to bed on the couch in the living room, covered me with blankets, and I fell asleep with baskets of flowers at my head and more at my feet, so that I must have looked like a corpse laid out in state.

In the morning I did as she had asked, left quietly, and spent the next three hours walking up and down the street in front of the hotel, the door never out of sight. I wouldn't risk getting lost. I came back to her suite at noon. Had lunch. Talked with her. She was a tawny vision, wearing a then currently fashionable sack dress, a soft woolen version by Chanel, even so a shapeless garment Dietrich elevated to elegance. "You look like a lion." She accepted the naïve compliment with a slow smile. With all of the beige-carpeted living room as her stage, and with one enraptured fan at her feet, she sat, balancing the needlepoint tip of her high white heel on the floor with the exquisite delicacy of an aerialist above the center ring. She was famed for her legs, and this posture showed off the flawless curve of her calves. But her posture was as practical as it was flattering, and when she suddenly rose, that fragile-looking heel took and propelled her full weight, enabling her to glide up and out from the chair and across the room in one seamless gesture, as if she were beyond the law of gravity. She moved in her spike heels like a dancer in ballet slippers, ravishing me with her grace, her kindness, her elegant manner. And what a funny interview she must have thought it was, since it was all movie gossip about *The Blue Angel* and Emil Jannings.

"His fingers were around my throat and I suddenly realized he was really trying to strangle me." She shrugged matter-of-factly. I thought she was a great actress. "You should have done more dramatic roles." "They don't give you a chance," she said. "I wanted to play in *The Deep Blue Sea,* but the producer said, 'Marlene, the audience won't take you seriously trying to kill yourself because you have been left by a man. They know you need only go stand by a window and the streets would be crowded with hundreds of men.'" Another eloquent shrug. It was the price one paid for beauty. She was standing by the window overlooking downtown Toronto, the curtain screening her face from the full force of the noon sun, yet still bathing her in a spectacular glow. God, she could even enlist nature to enhance her illusion.

She wanted me to hear her latest recording, just arrived from Paris, "Marie," about a prisoner writing to his sweetheart. It was penned by her friend, the French singer-composer Gilbert Becaud. Burt Bacharach's arrangement for Dietrich's version was great; she was great. "You must hear Becaud," she chided, "no one sings it better." She wasn't going to convince me. She sang along with it, translating the French lyrics into English as she did so, looking at me, smiling wisely. Later she gave me a copy and sent me back home.

We would meet again the next week when she was performing in Montreal. Even if I'd never see her again, I'd been hooked—by her, but also by the world she represented and by the discovery that the people I'd so loved on the screen were just the same in person, powerful, magnetic, with thousands at their feet. Well, not all of them were like Dietrich. . . . But few of them were really ever disappointing. Most of them at one point or another became, right before my eyes, that which they exuded when lit, dressed and coached to perfection on the screen. Whatever it is that makes some people successful as movie stars is something they have in themselves—whether they're smart or naïve, whether legitimate actresses able to remember lines on a stage or personalities who shrink in person when you talk about anything except the specific details of their careers. It is this that led me years later to write about the Hollywood portrait photographers whose talent lay not in camouflaging the stars' defects, but in capturing with their cameras the quality that set these people apart.

It is customary to think that the stars of the '20s ". . . had faces then." So did the stars who came with sound. But far less frequently discussed is that those great faces also had voices every bit as individual and memorable. Garbo's voice, like a tugboat; Mae West's, like a vibrating bed; Davis, a hedge-clipper; Stanwyck, like the chink of a perfume bottle or the rap of a judge's gavel, or both; and Tallulah Bankhead, all voice when I met her, like a benevolent steamroller, safe and satin; Colbert had a voice like a velvet choker, as short as her neck. But even the less obvious ones had unforgettable voices. When one thinks of Rita Hayworth, first one recalls her beauty, but then a line of dialogue comes back, the words hesitant, girlish, yet self-assured: "Hate can be a powerful emotion, Johnny." Truly, they had great voices then. Think of current faces, like Farrah Fawcett, Raquel Welch, Tom Selleck—great bodies, nice smiles, but voices of one dimension. When I listen again to my old interviews with Joan Crawford, Joan Fontaine, and Anna Sten—as high and bright as a chandelier and as light as a breeze stirring the crystals—Joel McCrea, Miriam Hopkins and all the others, voices, like bodies of water, suddenly ripple and reveal all sorts of things hidden in their depths. Talk to a director, a cameraman, a choreographer or a screenwriter, and what you see is what they are, what you hear is what they say. Marvelous storytellers they are; men like director Henry Hathaway or the choreographer Jack Cole, or the musical producer Arthur Freed, or any of those brilliant Hollywood portrait photographers: forthright and gutsy men who can tell it as it happened. But, talking with film stars (as distinct from stage actors), it becomes not just a matter of transcribing what they actually said, but how they said it, the way they said it, the facial reflections and changes that accompanied what they said and set up counterpoints in mood to their answers. Often it was a facial expression that made me shift my questions, prompted me to strike out in a new direction, or realize that I'd missed the point and it was up to me to catch it, since they weren't about to entrust a perfect stranger with secrets or little-known facts they preferred to leave forgotten.

One time, with the wonderfully homespun, all-around screen pro Joan Blondell, we were rattling away about the old musicals. I was telling her some bit of gossip from a time back in the early '30s, and Joan broke in with "That's right, because he was going up to the cottage that weekend. I'd forgotten that. And I couldn't go. . . ." She stopped and looked at me with amazement. "My God," she said, "how the hell would you know? You weren't there! Why am I telling you?" But she said that laughing, and we kept right on.

———————

WHEN I FIRST SET OUT, in April 1964, in New York, a city born for spring, I had no plan. The excuse I used when I called a publicist to make an appointment for an interview was, had to be, the star's latest film. That's why studio publicists I badgered for introductions to Barbara Stanwyck, Bette Davis, Joan Crawford or the others who'd drawn me to America, naturally asked me to do interviews with the actors in the films who were of more interest to my London radio producer, which was why I went to see Faye Dunaway fresh from *The Happening;* Janet Margolin from *David and Lisa;* Natalie Wood, who was filming in Central Park some awful movie called *Penelope.* The only thing that interested me was why she should be getting $750,000 to make it; but she was hot at a time in the industry when nobody seemed to know what would hit, or why, and instead the desperately confused actor/star in a successful film was too often confused with the fluke that made it a hit.

A Carroll Baker vehicle like *Sylvia* provided a chance for great acting from a whole host of favorite stars in small parts, but instead of interviewing Miss Baker, I wanted to interview Viveca Lindfors, who had worked with Errol Flynn in *Adventures of Don Juan* and was happy to remember it. Later, when I'd learned a bit, when I had started writing and needed specific answers to specific questions, I knew how to ask questions that made it easier to understand what I was after. Finally I was writing about movies instead of living in them or trying to relive them.

I remembered Loretta Young as a star, still as gossamer pretty in her last few films like *Paula* and *Because of You,* when she made a fragrant mist of soft hugs and cheekful kisses. As a person, she is made of sterner stuff. And when she talked about movies, every aspect of them—from the clothes she wore and the way her hair was done, to fighting with her director *and* her co-star, her lack of say over scripts, the interests that dictated front-office decisions—I began to understand the nature of the film industry.

Bad films were a dime a dozen and Gina Lollobrigida was in town for one of them and sneered, saying, "You English always ask these rude questions!" (I thought I'd flattered her on her longevity, 1946–1965). Another Italian sexpot, Claudia Cardinale—long brown hair, husky voice, large brown eyes and melting smile—was a dream. Her film was bad, but for somebody like that one makes allowances. That led to another discovery: studios didn't bring the stars to town so you could moon over them, but so you would write nice things about their awful films, which (they knew better than I did) needed all the help they could get. Score zero for Gina in *Strange Bedfellows;* score ten for Claudia in . . . what was that film called?

I did get to meet new people like Robert Redford, sensational in three films I'd seen in the space of a couple of weeks: *The Chase, Inside Daisy Clover* and *This Property is Condemned.* I called Hy Smith at Paramount after that film and said I had to see people with *that* sort of camera charisma. Redford was about to leave town that same day, but they'd see if he'd mind. Would half an hour over at Paramount, then still on Broadway, be okay? Why not? He was small, compact, reddish blond, the kind of rough skin prone to boils but the type of man not to rest on his looks; he was dressed in jeans, a heavy black jacket, boots and a cowboy hat before they became a uniform, and we talked for hours about the nature of stardom and what he might have to expect, and what, he said, he had no intention of putting up with. And, by God, if everything he said he didn't actually mean, because that's what he did: take a trip around Europe before the fan of fame would hit him; then up to Utah, where he'd build a house with some Indians he knew; and come back when he was ready—four years, give or take one. The next interview I read on him was a cover story in *Life* four years later when he'd come back with a vengeance, the star of the '70s, and so hot and private they boasted of their "exclusive."

All of the aforesaid, whether I enjoyed them or not, had become part of my job. But they were an excuse . . . an excuse to talk to Barbara Stanwyck, to Tallulah Bankhead, to director Eddie Sutherland, who'd been married to Louise Brooks and had directed Fields, West, Crosby et al.; to Nancy Carroll. "Excuse me, you're Nancy Carroll, aren't you?" I was standing in front of St. Pat's Cathedral, thinking of going in, when she walked past with the rush-hour mob. "Why, yes, how did you know?" "Because you haven't changed. I'd recognize you anywhere. I've got hundreds of portraits of you and I adore you.

Can we do an interview?" Both of us were swept along by surprise. I had never seen her in a movie, just knew that she'd been in them. Later at her apartment she brought out scrapbooks. I did, to my eternal regret, a totally terrible, stupid interview, all generalities which even she, with all her goodwill, couldn't salvage and tie into a sensible bundle. I wanted to know about everything, all of it, all her films, all the items, all at once. Nancy sat there across from me, waiting her turn. She had worked with her daughter in summer stock and on TV. Her daughter now worked with an agency. The agency handled Tallulah Bankhead. That's how I got her number, and Nancy said, "Call her, you'd like her." You wonder sometimes. For instance, if I hadn't agreed to do an interview with nightclub comics Martin and Rossi to put Hy Smith in the mood to let me go through the drawer of yet one more filing cabinet outside his office, which was the one that contained the pictures of Nancy Carroll that turned me on to photography because I found myself fascinated by a woman I'd not yet even seen in a film, and if I hadn't then met her, would I ever have gotten to meet Tallulah Bankhead? And it was Tallulah who unlocked Hollywood for me.

One night she called George Cukor and said, "Dahling George . . ." and after they gossiped forever, she remembered why she had called him in the first place and said, "I have this diviihhhne young man here, and he's going to Hollywood and he doesn't know anyone and you know everyone; and he's really a most serious young man." She looked at me to make sure, and then mortified me by telling Cukor that I was broke "but presentable, dahling. And he knows everything about everybody's movies." When I started out, there wasn't much competition for what I was doing and my enthusiasm was usually accepted for knowledge. And off I was on my first visit to Hollywood.

"Without a car, you're dead in LA," I'd been told in London. I didn't know how to drive, but I rented a car two days after I got there. I drove carefully out of the rental lot and immediately got into the wrong lane and drove for the next six hours on a wing and a prayer, no longer sure of how to stop, shift, signal while trying not to panic in that frenzied stream of confident cars honking, speeding, overtaking all round me. I just kept my eye on the one ahead, praying, "Hail Mary, full of grace . . ." My first halt was on the freeway halfway to Palm Springs because that's where the car in front took me, then left me. It was late. The traffic had dropped to a few cars in the fast lane. The stars were out. I had no choice. I turned off, went under and back up on the other side, following the signs that said "LA" and a lot of other awful, confusing things. Remember Lana Turner in *Portrait in Black* telling Anthony Quinn, "I can't drive. I can't drive"? And he thought she was getting hysterical, and slapped her. (He played a doctor who loved her and helped her kill her husband and needed Lana to help him get rid of the body.) Lana, subdued, got into the car, still saying, "But I really *can't* drive." I knew what she must have gone through—only no police, no Quinn, no suspicious stranger . . . no one to help. That first time in a car I saw the desert, and before I was done I saw the Pacific Ocean, for that was where I ran out of freeway on the other side.

I arrived for my appointments always late; limp with fear and shiny with sweat; often near to blabbering. "I'm sorry, Miss Blondell, I got . . ." "Good God, kid, what's happened to you? Come in. Do you want to use the bathroom? Can I get you something?" "Oh, no, it's nothing . . . really. . . ."

Without even realizing it, I had begun to live, to become part of things going on around me. All of my childhood, while it was by no means a complete emotional vacuum, was spent inside movie houses, relating to people whose emotions were prescribed by the roles they played. It had been all one-sided. My interests outside the movies were in talking about what I had seen, what I had felt. This further restricted the circle of my friends, who were more interested as they grew up in what *they* were doing, the problems they had in getting dates, going to parties or making plans for the future. Nobody I recall liked school, but at least they were there to get an education that would prepare them for a job. I had no job in mind.

A career evolved by necessity, to justify my reason for seeing these film stars and filmmakers. With them I could speak freely on the only subject I knew anything about, the only topic that interested me and on which I could be interesting. Even talking about movies, I had to eat; had to learn how to get around, how to get what I wanted. It was survival and became my career. The movie star, that unique work of art made possible through the invention of the camera, man as a creative being in himself rather than expressed outside his own flesh-and-blood being as with a painter, a musician or a writer, had become the means to my own career in life.

If I can now write about it, it's because Barbara Stanwyck told a little boy (in *All I Desire*) never to forget that, no matter what he thought or what anybody said, she believed in him; she loved him. I felt she was talking to me. That quality she had on the screen and with audiences touched me; her voice caressed me and led me on.

PEOPLE
WILL TALK

Gloria Swanson, photographed by Preston Duncan, 1930

GLORIA
SWANSON

G LORIA SWANSON liked to think of herself as an ordinary woman, a "pint-sized pipsqueak"; she believed this and worked at it. Yet the very speed at which she spoke was extraordinary, unnatural, almost as if it were developed to counterpoint the image one has of silent-picture acting: gestures frozen in aspic. Gloria's gestures were not those of an ordinary woman, neither was her look. While pretending, possibly believing, that she was a Plain Jane (one should remember that this Plain Jane had six husbands, marrying her last one in 1976, when she was seventy-seven), she presented an appearance which would have arrested any passerby and made even an Outer Mongolian think that this *must* be a movie star.

Gloria Swanson swore against sugar and surgery, and became a health guru; she was holistic when it was first fashionable in the '20s, but kept at it while everyone else went back to meat and potatoes. She was back in fashion (as if she gave a fig for that) when a whole new generation discovered brown rice and vitamins. She presented her unlined face as the proof of the lack of pudding. Yet only to see her eyes—never small, but by the end of her life filling no less than half of her face—made you realize the intensity of her personality; you realized not merely how she had survived (and quite clearly thrived) in and out of the spotlight, but also why this "pipsqueak" had dazzled the world and had become the first symbol of Hollywood glamour. Gloria Swanson had been more than popular, more than the highest-priced movie star of her day: this Napoleon in skirts had focused everything that Hollywood stood for on and around herself.

Because Gloria was not mad, the pitiful implications in the lines said by Norma Desmond in *Sunset Boulevard* were not applicable when said by Gloria Swanson. The pity we give Norma when we hear her lost in her own illusions—unaware that she has long ago been derailed and shunted off to a side track—doesn't apply to Gloria: she was not pitiful, she had not been derailed, she was not a victim. But divorce those same lines from their pathetic context, and there couldn't be a better epitaph for her (though she herself said she didn't want to think of an epitaph, she wanted to live "now!"). Norma dreamed of a comeback as Salome; Gloria came back as Norma and at the same time scored a major hit on Broadway in a revival of *Twentieth Century*. Gloria could play Norma Desmond, but Norma could never have played Gloria Swanson. It was because she didn't need others to reassure her own ego that Gloria Swanson was able to command the hundreds of thousands of fans with stunning detachment when they thronged to her. When Pickford and Fairbanks first toured the world in the early '20s, they were overwhelmed and terrified by the millions who flocked around them wherever they went. Gloria was only bemused. Sometimes it was nice, sometimes a nuisance, but always manageable.

The fact that in the end there really were no roles for her to play comes down to just one reason: there wasn't a character in which she could immerse her own personality. There only was the character of Gloria Swanson: she had become larger than life.

GS: When people meet me, they expect me to bite them, I guess, because they expect I am going to be Norma Desmond and I'm going to have eyes popping out of my head and I'm not going to be normal. So it's not difficult to impress people when they find I'm a perfectly normal half-pint of a woman who couldn't care less about impressing anybody. A lot of people thought Norma Desmond was the story of my life. I'm not a recluse, nor am I out in the past. In fact, it's awfully hard for me to even talk about. That's one of the reasons I am never writing my life story, or have any intention of doing it . . . it's not interesting to me.* It's amazing to find so many people who I thought really know me could have thought that *Sunset* was autobiographical. I've got nobody floating in my swimming pool. I don't have a pool, for that matter, but there are some bathtubs around here [she made a swift gesture in the direction of other rooms in her New York apartment] and nobody is floating face down in them as far as I know! It was just nothing like me. The only thing that was actually a parallel was that I called Mr. DeMille "Mr. DeMille," and he called me "Young Fellow." Most everyone called him "Chief" or "C.B." or a lot of nonsense. I called him "Mr. DeMille." I don't think he quite knew why he called me "Young Fellow" either, except that I was never complaining . . . and I was never a tomboy! It was very difficult for the people who worked with him after I did . . . I was three years with him, I made six consecutive pictures, more than anyone else. He was forever calling people "Gloria" or "Young Fellow." I was so intent in what I was doing in my pictures for him that once, when my knees were bleeding, I was unaware of it. They wanted to call doctors, and I said, "Oh, come on, let's get on with it. Wipe them off." They got so frightened because only the day before there had almost been a real tragedy. One of the lions for the Babylonian flashback in *Male and Fe-*

---

* "A woman has a right to change her mind" and actresses even more so. Stars are nothing if not mercurial. Fifteen years after this interview Miss Swanson wrote one of the liveliest, raciest and most absorbing accounts of life in that era.

male got loose, jumped up very close to the couch I was on, and we stared at each other. Somebody came to get me, and before I knew it, I was thrown like a football off the couch. The set was a swimming pool made up to look like an arena and was entirely surrounded by wires and nets, like a circus, so that the animal couldn't get loose. Nor could we get out! And only the camera crew and the people who were really needed there to make the scene were permitted to be there. All the maids were standing there, nervous, and getting worried that something was going to happen.* When I had come back to continue doing the scene, going down steps with this animal, again he made a lunge at me [as Miss Swanson told this story, her cat paced around her and at this point, almost as if on cue, began meowing with insistence; the effect was chilling], only this time two trainers came in and stopped him. I didn't feel the reaction until the following day. Oh, I suppose at the time the hair stood up on my spine, but at the time I wanted to get on with it. The next day I was a little shaky from it. That's why Mr. DeMille didn't want to do the scene with the lion on my back which was the climax of the flashback scene. He just wanted to fade out with the assumption that the lion had got me. But this was to be a reproduction of "The Lion's Bride," a famous painting. I had seen this in my grandmother's home when I was a little girl. So I was actually disappointed that we weren't going to do it after all. I said, "Oh, please, Mr. DeMille," and he looked at me as though I should have my head examined. So he said, "All right," and they set up the scene. There was the cameraman, his assistant, two trainers, Mr. DeMille and myself, and Mr. DeMille had a gun in his hand in case the lion scratched me or something . . . if the lion had smelled blood, he would have torn me to pieces, because I was just entering a period and animals have a very highly developed sense of smell.

JK: DeMille seemed to specialize in asking his stars to do incredible things. Jacqueline Logan [Mary Magdalene in DeMille's *King of Kings*] told me that he asked her to do something with a panther and she didn't have the nerve to do it, then you told her this story and she said, "If Gloria can do it, I suppose I can."

GS: I'm surprised Mr. DeMille didn't tell her himself! Oh, yes, he was very hard on those young girls, he was inclined to say unkind things too, but he never said one unkind thing to me, ever. [Nor, she subsequently added, did he ever proposition her or invite her to his notorious Paradise Ranch.]

JK: And now he is eternally linked with you and you with him, not only because of your films together, but also because in *Sunset Boulevard* you said that line . . .

GS: Norma Desmond said the line.

---

*There'd been some problems earlier with a leopard that appeared in the shipwreck island sequence of the modern story.

JK: "I'm ready for my close-up, Mr. DeMille." Whose idea was the character of Norma Desmond? I know Wilder-Brackett wrote it, but did they come to you and ask for suggestions?

GS: No, they didn't know what they were going to do with it from day to day . . . they wrote every day. I had only twenty-six pages when I went on the set for the first time. Also, remember that it's far easier to play a character. Give me a wig and a lamb bone and I'll play Henry the Eighth. This is easy. The hardest of the arts happens to be comedy. This is very difficult. This is *the* essence of the art of acting, and very few people can do this. Anybody can be a dramatic actress, anybody can be a character actress, that's easy. But to play a perfectly normal woman in a drawing room is the hardest. What are you doing? You have no props to use, you're so natural that it doesn't mean anything, the girl-next-door type of thing. So you could talk like the girl next door, but it's a difficult thing to make an impression in that role.

But Norma Desmond . . . along comes the part of a woman who hasn't been out of her home, is a recluse, who lives in the past, who wants her career back, who's a nut in many ways . . . maybe not crazy but certainly an odd character . . . who has her ex-husband as her butler, who loves to live in a dream world and who lives in the past! This is a character who is fascinating. So you can do an awful lot with her, and it's very easy to do this. It just so happens that people think it's so great because there was no other actress available at that particular time to make it ring true. Suppose some young girl had to play it from the "now" period, and they had to make her up to look older. It might be good and she might give a great performance, but the problem is that it was so closely allied with me, the period of the whole thing, that it had a bigger impact emotionally because they thought it *was* me.

JK: But as for the body of your work on screen, which is so good . . . are you willing to forget that? Like a painter, would you forget about your early work because it was done when you were young?

GS: I don't think in terms of acting as you do. Painting is something you put on from a brush to a piece of canvas. Your eyes are involved and a spiritual and emotional thing is involved. In terms of acting, you sort of mock up a character in your mind. You may choose knowingly or unknowingly from people that you know—their walk, their mannerisms. I'm talking about myself—I don't know what other actors do, I have no way of knowing. I know this, that I get very cross, and I'm thinking of a certain actor who shall be nameless, but when I see this actor, or others who are always themselves, whether playing a cowboy or an English lord or an American businessman, it's them all over, who *they* are. I don't think that's real acting. If you play comedy with a very low voice, you're going to have trouble; if you're supposed to be a scatterbrain, for some strange reason a scatterbrain goes with a very high voice. I like to get mannerisms for the people I play so *I* don't show in this thing. I want the character to be it. I don't want my stamp on it. And since *Sunset Boulevard,* everything I've done I've said to the director, "If you hear one intonation or see one mannerism of Norma Desmond, for goodness' sake come and tell me—or smack me!" I don't want it, that belonged to Norma Desmond. My voice isn't even the same as Norma's, is it? [The question was rhetorical.]

When I first came out and there wasn't any script, I had friends such as George Cukor and another young man by the name of Alex Tiers, and they were all wanting me to make a picture. And when I walked on that film set, the love that was on that set, all the prop men, the electricians, the gaffers, the whole crew . . . I've known them all their lives . . . they hadn't seen me . . . it was like the prodigal had returned. They couldn't do enough to make me comfortable and happy. There was such an atmosphere of camaraderie, it made everything so easy.* I wasn't fighting upstream, I wasn't swimming alone, I had every bit of help you can imagine.

JK: You mentioned that you watch people for their mannerisms. You are a wonderful mimic as well.

GS: Yes, when we came to doing the impersonation in *Sunset Boulevard,* they wanted me to do someone like Douglas Fairbanks, and I said, "Why don't I do the Chaplin thing I did in *Manhandled*?" Mr. Wilder said, "Can you do that?" And I said yes, and that's how it happened. Now, my impersonation of Chaplin in *Manhandled,* which I must say they cut out and now they can't find it, came about because someone had left a derby hat around the set and in between scenes I put it on my head and started wobbling around like Chaplin, picked up a stick and twirled it, and it amused Allan Dwan [the director] so much that he said, "We have got to put it in the picture because you are doing impersonations of a Russian countess in the party scene, so why don't you just go from that into the Chaplin thing?" and I said, "Fine," and that's when I first did the impersonation . . . which, I might add, was far better than the one in *Sunset Boulevard* because I looked more like Chaplin, my face was rounder and in those days I had puppy fat. It wasn't an elongated face as it is now. I showed a photograph of my impersonation to Chaplin once at a dinner party, and he thought it was himself! He said, "Who is that man with me?" because he didn't recognize the person in the still with me! While I was a United Artists artist, so was Chaplin. I was never associated with him like I was with Mr. DeMille. I did a picture for Goldwyn and I was on the lot making a picture, and Chaplin and Mary and Doug were there. I saw him socially at Pickfair, at dinner parties and the Hearst house down on the beach. He was at my house one evening, a very amusing evening, when he entertained very early in the morning. He'd been out with Prince George, later the

---

*Wilder saw this and incorporated it into the script to become Norma Desmond's moving visit to the DeMille set with the reunion of "Hawkeye!" . . ."Miss Desmond!"

Duke of Kent. There were only about seven guests, including Prince George, but there was an orchestra of about fifteen people we had brought down from Fatty Arbuckle's house on the beach. Chaplin played every instrument and entertained for two solid hours . . . he did drama, comedy, everything under the sun, and it was a very memorable evening, very interesting. I knew him that way. When I moved away in 1938, I didn't see anything of him. Of course, I always adored his comedy. Then I saw him in the South of France some years ago and I remember the subject of communism cropping up, and somebody said, "Well, you're supposed to be a communist," and he said, "I'm not a communist, I'm an atheist . . . I don't believe in any government!" And sometimes I wonder about that myself. But Charlie is Charlie . . . he's his own government, I guess. He just wants to keep what he's made. I suppose he feels he has a right to. I don't know all the ramifications of what actually went on, but it's hard for me to believe that he would believe in pure communism.

JK: Do you believe there was a conspiracy among the big studio executives when sound came in to eliminate a lot of the big, expensive silent stars?

GS: My dear, to know what was going on behind those big desks, I have no idea, and I wouldn't really want to know.

JK: I am going to take a line that you said . . . that Norma Desmond said . . .

GS: "Get them in the front office, those masterminds"?

JK: No, not that one. "Faces, we had faces in those days." Do you think in your own right that this is true?

GS: I don't know how to make that comparison, it would be unfair of me to answer because I don't keep up with the pictures that much to know what is going on. I saw Ingrid Bergman on the stage, and that face is so beautiful and gorgeous, and what she does with it, what's inside the face, the thinking that's going on, and the acting, and her ability is unbelievable in an extremely difficult part. We could say that she is a Johnny-come-lately if you want to compare it to the period we are talking about. And then there is Sophia Loren, and if I start making a list, I'm going to omit somebody and it's going to be unfair. I'm not prepared to do this off the cuff. [Swanson had to struggle to come up with names, but when she did, they were both strong women, powerful women, survivors like herself.] I've seen some very good performances by people from the time I left California in 1938 and came to live in New York. But there is a tendency, I think, now, to put things on an assembly line. We do this with our babies in the hospitals too, they no longer feed at their mother's breast or are allowed to stay in their mother's room, they have to be put in a basket and look like an automobile on an assembly line. The tragedy that this brings about must be awful and nobody seems to think about it, certainly not the doctors. It's easy and convenient for hospitals, but certainly it's awful for the child to suddenly be without the warmth of its mother's body and heartbeat. Individual artists are few and far between today, even in art. I don't know whether you go along with all you see today on canvas, I certainly don't. Suddenly everybody has to have an upturned eye. I must say, when I was young, I felt my eyes were freakish, and I wanted my eyes to be like everybody else's, which seemed to be down at the temples. Then a certain kind of nose. Now, let's just think back to the days of Mary Pickford [and as she does so, Swanson dramatically lowers her voice and slows her speech], the Talmadge sisters; they had two different noses; and then we had the Gish sisters, and Corinne Griffith, and we had Garbo. But she comes a little later. Colleen Moore, Pola Negri, Barbara La Marr . . . they all had *different* faces. One did not look like the other. And then we didn't all have the same-shaped breasts, if I may be a little vulgar, all popping out of their dresses. They had different personalities, no one was like the other, even the sisters weren't alike. [Her voice rises without speeding up; her hands clench the air as she declaims the names and their virtues.] Take the Talmadge sisters, one was a comedienne, the other was a dramatic actress, one was blond and one was brunette. Certainly the Gish sisters didn't look alike . . . nobody looked alike.

Well, now they have me saying it as if it was my line. I didn't write that line; *I* didn't say it; Norma Desmond said it, "They don't have faces like that anymore." I said it *as* Norma Desmond, I never said it myself. But now they've got *me* saying it. I never believe *any*thing I read about *any*body. I'm starting to wonder if history even makes any sense. I don't think it does. Look at the political situation, we don't know the truth about situations. In fifty to a hundred years from now, who's going to be able to write about this period and know the truth if we can't know the truth right now?

JK: And this is what fascinates me so about you: there you are, the personification of the grandeur and extravagance of the '20s, and, on the other hand, you didn't care what they did with you.

GS: But I didn't, I didn't. I did it myself. I've never once in my life sat to be made up; and I've always done my own hair, except when I was with Mr. DeMille. He had someone called Hattie, and she—or we—used to dream up those hairdos.* So I was never putty in the hands of *any* studio department.

JK: You were, are, a natural. You would risk your life and not think about yourself for the sake of a scene, yet you came back from Paris and, in the

---

* "Those hairdos," Gloria says, feeling no need to enlarge on the outrageous elaborate concoctions of feminine coiffure DeMille felt to be height of fashion, those Madame de Pompadour might have thought were old-fashioned, the '20s arbiters of taste thought ridiculous and the public at large adored "their Gloria" for. Continuously photographed, continuously in the papers, Gloria could afford to give only two words to anything so trivial and so talked about that she would presume you remembered.

true style of what one thinks of as movie-star behavior, sent a cablegram
saying, "Arriving with Marquis, arrange celebration."

GS: No!

JK: Wasn't that you?

GS: No, of course it wasn't. I've never done this in my life. I've never paid
fifty cents for publicity.

JK: Where did that story come from? It's legendary.

GS: Where did they *all* come from? You don't suppose I ever called up any
newspaper and said, "Come over"? Do you think I would call up anybody
and arrange . . . ? There are so many famous stories. They say I was a Mack
Sennett bathing girl, but I was never a bathing girl in my life. I did light
comedies for Sennett. I never worked with a low comedian until my last
picture for Sennett, and that's why I left him. And we don't seem to have the
publicity people we used to have in those days, they were always dreaming
up things you were supposed to have done. I never had a press agent, so I
don't know what goes on. I never paid a five-cent piece for any kind of
publicity. When I was producing, we used to have photographs of the sets,
and the publicity department would send stuff out when they were advertising
the picture . . . for the theaters and displays and so on. When you are making
a picture for a studio and you don't have a press agent, they arrange for
people to come and interview you . . . and half the stars wouldn't see them.
I always did, because I feel that's your duty to the studio, or whoever is hiring
you, to do as much as you can for the exploitation of a picture. For you can
have the best product in the world, but if it's up on the shelf and no one
knows it's there, that's where it's going to sit! I don't think an actor's job is
really finished until that picture is in the auditorium and the audience are in
their seats. Then your job is over.*

JK: Did you have to fight much for what you wanted to do in a film?

GS: No. I didn't go, you see, from one studio to another. I made about nine
pictures with one director when I was at Keystone. When I was at Triangle,
prior to Mr. DeMille, I had maybe two or three directors. With DeMille, it
was always the same crew, the same director, same cameraman. So it was
like a big family, I imagine like circus people when they are traveling together
and living together. I used to get up at 6:00 a.m. and be on the set, ready, at
9:00 a.m., and sometimes we wouldn't go home till 7:00 or 8:00 at night.
And you did this week in and week out for quite a number of weeks, and you

*She was the most photographed woman of the decade. Every important photographer both in
Europe and in America took her portrait, making her as popular in *Photoplay* as in *Town and
Country,* in *Screenland* as in *Vanity Fair*. One could mount a survey of great early 20th-century
portrait photography and photographers using just her pictures.

got to know everybody, more or less, as if in school. When you met them at a party and somebody you knew as the prop boy is in black tie, you don't know who it is! Because he's suddenly somewhere else where you don't expect him, so it was a little difficult sometimes.

And then, after DeMille, I was with Sam Wood. We were together with the same writer for two and a half years, four pictures a year, which is ten pictures. Then I came to New York and worked in the Astoria, Long Island, studio with Mr. Allan Dwan, and with the exception of one picture there, *The Humming Bird*—and the *Madame Sans-Gêne,* the one in France—I made eight out of my remaining ten pictures with Allan Dwan . . . to finish my five-year contract. We worked together, the writer, the director and myself. When we were on one picture, we would be thinking about another, and we would meet, have dinner together and talk after dinner. Mind you, I was bringing up the family and I had children to get home to.* But we would talk about new ideas for a film . . . or sometimes, maybe the New York office would say, "We like the title *Manhandled.* Can you give us a film with that title?" This actually did happen. A man called Sidney Kent was head of distribution and they thought that would be a great title. Well, it was up to us to get a story for it. I said to Mr. Dwan, "I want to play a gum-chewing little clerk in a department store," and that's how it started. We'd meet, the writers and I, to talk, and the story developed out of it. So we worked *together* on a film. Everybody suggested things and threw ideas about. When a painter is putting something on canvas, he is the only one there, he doesn't have twenty-five different people standing behind him saying, "That yellow is too dark, why don't you put white instead?" You see, a picture is like a play. I often wonder how it gets there in one piece because you have so many minds working for one focal point. You can hope you're on the same track, but you can never know what's in another person's mind. I may be describing something to you and I may even have a pencil and paper out, trying to draw something for you. Yet your own ideas, obviously, if you are a creative person too, are coming into it and changing it while I am showing it. Maybe a straight line . . . you are making a curved line. So to get all these minds together and to put it together is really a chore.

After Allan Dwan, I went into producing my own pictures for UA, and I had various directors for various things: Raoul Walsh for *Sadie Thompson,* Von Stroheim for *Queen Kelly.* In the case of my first talking picture, *The Trespasser,* when I finished *Queen Kelly* and had to put it on the shelf, Eddie Goulding,† who was a director—also a very prolific writer, a fantastic mind for all kinds of music, he wrote songs and lyrics—there was nothing he couldn't do in the creative world, but the problem was to get him to put it on paper.

---

*By 1924 and 1925 Gloria had already been twice married.
†Goulding. See also Arthur Freed and Miriam Hopkins interviews.

So I went and got Laura Hope Crews, who was a first lady in the theater, one of our top actresses, for the dialogue part, to keep Eddie down in dialogue. And then we had a court stenographer and myself. The three of us took down every word that was uttered in this breakfast room of mine, and *The Trespasser* was written by the three of us, although Goulding's name was up there as sole writer of it. People get a funny kind of pride that they have. . . .* I have been so involved in the writing of stories on my films, and yet when an actress opens her mouth about having any ideas, everybody shudders, thinks you are temperamental and want to interfere. It's all right if a male actor does it, I guess, but just let a female do it and they really have a fit. But I have had to cut a picture, like *Sadie Thompson,* for instance. The man who was directing that, Raoul Walsh . . . he also played the Sergeant in it and he was magnificent—I really had to do all kinds of things to get him to play that part. But before the picture was over, he had to go back to Fox, and I had to cut it. And I have once or twice had to direct scenes. But I never do it in front of an audience. I always am very silent about it. The director must always have the last word on the set, and I don't like any kind of discussions or arguments. I want it all done beforehand, or, if you have something to say, you always arrange it so nobody else need know. You take a five-minute break and they presume you are going to powder your nose, and you get the director away and discuss something. But to make a scene in front of the rest of the cast and crew would be just like mutiny. It's just not fair to the director.† In the case of Allan Dwan and me, the way we used to make pictures before there were producers, everybody had their say. You would say, "What about this?" or "What about that?" and you would try something. Film is comparatively cheap, so if you look at it in a projection room and you say you like "this" better than "that," you've got it. Then later it sort of got into big business, like an assembly line. If a director changed one thing, all hell would break loose. Why do they pay a director $150,000 if he hasn't the right to change something? Why doesn't the producer come down and direct, or get a Western Union boy to do it if he can read? If that's all it took to direct . . . But if you are going to add something to the film—and directors do, and a good director and a good writer are more important than anything else, as far as I am concerned, because of what they can get out of an actor or what they can give an actor . . . and the actor takes all the bows for it . . . it's kind of sad in a way. And I've seen that phase of the industry too, where the directors got so angry at not getting proper credit, they wanted to be stars. They got their names up on the marquee and it didn't work, except for just a few, like Mr. DeMille. But there was a big movement in California about the early '20s to make the director the star.

---

*Miss Swanson moved on past her bemusement at other people's egos, possibly recalling that when she tried to remake *The Trespasser* for a comeback, she got nowhere and finally sold her rights to WB, who made it with Bette Davis as *That Certain Woman,* directed by Goulding.
† How did Von Stroheim get the news that it was all over with *Queen Kelly?*

JK: "James Cruze Productions," "A Marshall Neilan Production," etc.

GS: Yes, they insisted on that because they felt they were not getting enough credit. Then the writers also. Writers are the ones that have the most difficult time because they conceive, and it's their baby more often than not, before the actor changes or the director changes or both of them change it. I should think that they would be cutting their throats all the time.

JK: Let me ask you . . . Lillian Gish told me, "When sound came in, imagination went out." Do you think this is true?

GS: I don't quite know what she means, and maybe taking it out of context like that . . . What was that apropos of? Did she say they showed more emotion in their faces when they were silent? We have got to remember one thing, and I'm not disagreeing with Miss Gish, but we must remember that we have used up an awful lot of ideas since then. It's all well and good when you're starting an industry and you're going into this thing because you, well, everything you do is a new, fresh idea that hasn't been used a thousand times. Sure, it might have been in books or the Greeks might have done it, but those ideas were new to films. Now, to come by a new idea, a fresh character, a new situation anymore is practically impossible. Everything today is almost a rehash of everything we did in the early days, in the '20s.

JK: Was the '20s the most exciting period for you? As it clearly was for Miss Gish?

GS: Naturally it was! Now, had I been sixty years old, let's say, and looking at the youngsters of the '20s, I might not have had the same feeling. I don't know how I would have thought about us in those days. It seemed to me that everybody back then *was* twenty or thirty years old! With it all, there was a certain graciousness and good manners. At least, I felt it more. Today you could hold a door open for somebody and they would walk right through without even saying thank you. I think this is a kind of sickness that we have here. I think it's a "pill" sickness. I think everybody is not quite here, mentally or physically. This is not so much the fault of the period as what people have done to themselves, body and mind.

JK: Hollywood in the '20s was a beacon light to the developing world . . . but that beacon also shone on the Babylonian side. . . .

GS: I don't know. I'm sure Detroit was just as . . . [she giggles mischievously at this] . . . I was about to say something which would have been censored. No, but I don't believe this at all. Paris was different, Rome, Berlin, all places, London. . . . I can remember the Carlton Hotel, you could walk in there and the attendants all wore white wigs and silk breeches and silk stockings. It was a way of life. A different way of living. Now everything is plastic, all in a big plastic bag. I hear about it, but I don't want to see it! Living was a totally different thing then, and people had a sense of abandonment the youngsters can't have now because of the bomb business, which frightens them. There was a feeling then that we had had the war to end all wars. Then the disillusionment set in with the Second War, when they realized it wasn't so. I think this has affected them and maybe their attitude towards life: "We may be dead tomorrow, so let's do something today." But in doing "something" today, they may be destroying themselves sooner. It may not happen, you know? What I feel sorry for is the youngsters who want to live an entire sixty or seventy years before they are seventeen years old. What have they got to look forward to? They are going to be so bored, so satiated. What is left for them? My father once said that 95 percent of life is anticipation. Stop and think about that, it's absolutely true. You work, you strive, you dream for that first automobile . . . what happens? A month afterwards it's lessened and now you dream for a different one! Longer, bigger, faster, something else. It's true. If you want to take it down to physical fundamentals, it's also true that the poetry, the romance has gone out of life, out of living in life. There is no such thing now as a flirtation, I don't imagine, which is like poetry. They miss so much in wanting everything so soon and so quick. But this is part of it. We have had a lot of people with imagination, and look what happened. You do not know what they are trying to tell you on the screen anymore. So this, I think, is a great problem and it's going to get graver as time goes on unless we become different people and we go into another dimension. It's like style . . . what can you do? You're stuck with two arms, two legs, a neck and a torso. You tell me, if you possibly can, what can you do with a dress that hasn't already been done? Sleeve-wise, hemline-wise, neckline-wise, waistline-wise . . . We have had the waist down to practically the knees; we've had it up under the breasts and above the breasts. We have had square necks, long necks, round necks, boat necks, every kind of neck you can think of. Everything. We have had puff sleeves, mutton sleeves, tight ones, long ones, short ones, and no sleeves at all. It comes to a point when what are you going to do unless you start out in space with the astronauts? So, for Miss Gish to say that the imagination has gone . . .

I agree that the silent-picture actor really had to believe and feel a lot more than the stage actor. The stage actor can be convincing in a love scene or a tragedy by the intonation of his voice, because if you were in the tenth row you could not see his eyes, and you cannot see a muscle quivering from there. But in a picture everybody is in the first row of a motion-picture house. Because when they want to see what's really going on in the mind of that person, or emotionally, they come to a close-up. They don't give you a long shot, do they? I mean, you cannot be thinking about your income tax or if you'll be late for dinner when the scene is over. Yet on stage, out of the mouth of the person who can be thinking all kinds of things there are coming lines he has said a thousand times before.

Back then I'd often wonder why careers came and went, why the light that had shone so brightly for a person at one time should suddenly have turned off. Of course there were the obvious reasons; tastes change, new faces supplant old ones, people become smug, stale, too secure to be of any great interest; and sound came in and amplified a lot of these problems. But Swanson entered the talkies on a box-office success, *The Trespasser*. Her voice was hailed. Her personality still seemed to stimulate and excite interest even in a generation of new faces like Crawford, Dietrich, Shearer, Harlow, Lombard, etc. Came the talkies and Frankenstein's monster became the first screen robot to become a star; James Cagney heralded a "new" style when he shoved a grapefruit into Mae Clarke's puss. But Gloria, for all her powerful optical image, was no hothouse flower but as punchy a cockerel as Cagney; she'd taken pratfalls and pies in her face, she was resilient. And what was more, though high-priced, she entered the sound era with her own production company, which must have given her all the control over her fate any star would have wanted?

GS: That's what you would think! [she says, heavy with irony, and goes on to clarify]. In those days the high mucky-mucks, the higher-ups, the powers that be, whatever you want to call them, *didn't want* stars to make independent pictures, so they did *not* make it easy for you.* Now they can't wait for stars to make their own pictures. Now they rent them the space.

JK: Still, you produced some of your very best films, *Sadie Thompson* and *Queen Kelly*.

GS: *The Trespasser* was also a very successful picture. It had its premiere in London, and it was one of the first talking pictures to be made. I also wanted to make the first talking picture in England, I wanted to make a lot of pictures there. Also, in 1925 I was the first American to make a foreign picture. . . .

JK: *Madame Sans-Gêne* . . .

GS: And I'm still trying to find a print of it.

JK: On *Queen Kelly* you worked with Von Stroheim as your director, and then all those years later you worked as co-stars in *Sunset Boulevard*. Now, you walked off the set of *Queen Kelly*, but it was your own production, that was the end of the film, which was never completed. Why did you?

GS: Because, as a director, he was shooting a lot of film that would never see the light of day, and he wasn't sticking to the script. He had been shooting for weeks and weeks on what would be about a third of the picture, and we already had about 20,000 feet of film! Kind of nonsensical.

---

*I figure she meant MGM and Columbia, two studios that let her sit around cooling her heels, and the public's interest in her as well, by promising roles that never materialized beyond a session in the stills gallery.

JK: Hadn't you known about his working method before? There was enough publicity about him.

GS: Yes, but I was told that there was going to be two men who would hold him down, like supervisors or producers today. One who came over especially from MGM, the other was a friend, and they were going to watch over him on the set with an eagle eye. But a lot of the things he did escaped them, and I was conscious of what was going on because I have the eye and the mind of a detective. And, secondly, I was on the set and they were not. I could see it happening, so when I had spent $600,000, I got nervous and said, "The stuff isn't going to be on the screen, so stop it." Well, it cost me $800,000 finally. I just went and did another picture, *The Trespasser,* which got me out of the hole. It paid for all the losses and a lot more.

JK: You were one of the few big stars of that era who made the transition into sound without the difficulties others had, like John Gilbert, who I've heard did not have a high voice at all, but Mayer wanted to eliminate him.

GS: Well, we'll never know the truth about that one. Neither will he, because he couldn't see what was going on! You know, *they* [the masterminds] wouldn't have Jean Arthur because they said her voice wasn't good . . . so she came back to New York and made a tremendous success on the stage, and then of course they couldn't wait to get her back to Hollywood. You see, one thing is often forgotten, and shouldn't be: this is a business. And how anybody gets a job in business we'll never know. Sometimes it's influence, sometimes it's working hard from the bottom up, various ways . . . maybe it's a pattern of life, or fate. I don't know. Maybe because . . . But I *did* make the bridge from silent pictures to talking pictures, and some of them didn't. But, as you say, it's a possibility that the studios didn't want to pay the big-star prices and maybe I, who happened to be my own producer, went from one to the other in good pictures. Sound in those days . . . everybody's voice was much higher, everybody's voice was not quite normal, I don't believe. Even the singing voice—some of us had our own.

I sang in a picture and I can hardly believe I hit those high notes! I sang in a lot of my pictures, in *Indiscreet,* with music by De Sylva, Brown and Henderson. That was made by Mr. Sam Goldwyn, on the same lot at the same time I was producing, I did that one for him. And *Music in the Air** was later, in 1934, and that's more normal, but even then I couldn't believe I had that kind of operatic voice.† John Boles and I sang that together again just a year and a half ago [1963]. But that was how I made the transition, you see. Audiences make stars, either they like you or they don't like you. And if you are liked equally by men and women, you have a longer life than if you are just going to be liked by men. A woman will go out of curiosity once,

---

*The first of several publicized projects to actually get off the ground, it was her last Hollywood film (except for a 1941 RKO programmer) till *Sunset Boulevard.*
† Why didn't anybody think of Swanson for *Hello, Dolly!?*

but won't want Harry to go again because it's too sexy or something. Women who have enjoyed longer careers, female stars, were stars who were adored by men *and* women, where audiences could hold hands together and enjoy it. The realism that came into pictures after the war, the last war—hopefully the last war—was so realistic that I think it drove a lot of women away from the theaters. Then you got into the sordid things that children adore because they don't have the problems of living life or responsibility, so they get a vicarious kind of kick out of seeing somebody else suffer. But the young married couple, after they have had a day with the children screaming or knocking their second tooth out, or measles, or a mortgage on the house having to be paid, they want to be entertained, they want comedy, they want to laugh. And then you get the next category, the women who helped make the motion-picture business, who used to go into darkened auditoriums and dream dreams because there was no harm in wanting to be a millionaire then [Gloria had made and lost millions several times over and was shrewd enough not to end up poor]. Now it's just foolishness because you can't . . . but we didn't have taxes then. . . . So now they want romance.

The first real romance that came along in years was *Summertime* with Katie Hepburn and Rossano Brazzi. I was his escort to the premiere of the film in Venice, we went in a gondola to the theater and he was a wreck because he was sure it wasn't going to be any good, and I kept saying, "Now you see, this is wonderful," and he said when it was over, "Do you really think it is going to be an enormous success in America?" and I said, "I'll tell you two things. One is that you have brought back romance to the mature woman and you are going to become a star. And the other thing is that Venice is going to be ruined—tourism. You're going to find that for every one man there will be twenty-five women looking for you, or your equal." And years later we met and laughed about this, because it's exactly what did happen. But we don't have stories for the people who made this business, the women. I say women more than men, because most of the men died before the women, and it was the women who would say, "John, take me to see so-and-so," and he, being a nice gentleman, would take his lady to where she wanted to go rather than say, "Now you come to where I want to go, to see Bronco Billy"* or something. But it's also a difference of the times, as we said before, you see; it's the '20s versus today. Then everybody tried to do a better job than the next person because there was tremendous competition. Today we are talking about paying people who have less than $4000 a year and making up the difference. Work is one of the greatest joys in the world in life. I always say that I don't think I could stand Paradise for more than eleven months of the year, I would have to go to Hell for the other month.

JK: Fame has its own rewards and its own troubles. It's something I want to ask you: you have been famous for just about all of your life. Ten thousand kids

---

*"Bronco Billy" Anderson was the screen's first Western star.

scream for your autograph and just want to look at you. People stand in line for hours just to look at you on screen.

GS: Well, you see, it all happened . . . It's hard to remember other than a few little spots here and there . . . the first ten years of your life are rather spotty. From the time I was about fourteen and a half, I was catapulted into this business. I had no desire whatever to be an actress. I wanted to be an opera singer. In those days no one ever thought of becoming a motion-picture actress. It was like saying, "I want to be a burlesque queen." People in the theater looked down on that. Since I had a mature singing voice, I wanted to be an opera singer. I had nothing to say or do about this film career . . . there it was, I played an extra in a scene,* sitting as "atmosphere" one day, my second day at a studio. The first day I played a part. Well, there I was, it all happened, it wasn't me standing in line, I didn't come from the wrong side of the tracks, I wasn't hungry. Girls didn't have to go to college and I had had half a year of high school. I had an insatiable curiosity that got me into trouble and probably into pictures. I wanted to see how pictures were made. I had never seen any American pictures. I had only seen pictures that had been made in Sweden, all the places where my father was stationed. They were very black-and-white, not too attractive. This was not an ambition of mine. But when you talk about being a famous person, well, I don't know how you feel about it, but I don't feel anything.

I am just very grateful to Mr. Edison and Mr. De Forest, and all the people who had anything to do with an invention. It made it possible to put us all in tin cans, like sardines. We could have been bad actors, it didn't matter. It was the fact of volume . . . you were just shipped everywhere and people got accustomed to that face, like they would get accustomed to the emblem of a Rolls-Royce, that little statue of the lady on the hood. . . . I'm *not minimizing anything!* [She says the latter in a burst of irritation at my suggestion she might be making too little of the cost of thousands, the work of millions, the fortune she earned et al.] I don't say that I didn't grow up in the business, that I didn't learn and grow. I hope to goodness I did, because of my insatiable curiosity. I was hungry for knowledge. So I started, at the age of seventeen, just getting my hands on books. If I take you to my bedroom now, it's not so much that a storm hit it, we don't know what to do with all the books! I love books, books, books. I'd rather read a good book than go to any ball, or these invitations that come in for this and that. It's because I had no real teenage life. I was never an ingenue, I went from being a little girl, starry-eyed, in awe not of fame or of a career, but in sheer awe of life. I also wanted to have my cake and eat it too. I was the only child, so I wanted to have children, and I wanted to be married. As you know, I made several attempts, many attempts, but this wasn't in my nature.

---

*Gloria came from Chicago and began her film career with the Essanay company there.

There's a price to pay for fame, as you can well imagine. When a woman works and she wants children too, you cannot have your cake and eat it . . . so you get a lot of heartaches over this. If you have to turn your children over during the day to someone else, and then when you're home and they run towards you and they trip and fall, they turn around and run back to their nanny or whoever is looking after them, rather than to you. Those are the things you have to give up. About the only thing you do have of another individual or child is their babyhood and childhood . . . you can't claim anything else. I have been blessed with having three fascinating people for children, seven grandchildren, and no delinquents yet or beatniks, knock on wood.

JK: Your world appeared to have everything. You grew up in Hollywood, you had the kind of adulation that people live lifetimes trying to achieve without ever attaining.

GS: I never took it quite as seriously as some people because of my insatiable curiosity about everything. This is why the moment I finished making a picture, I left California as quickly as I knew how, on a train in those days, and used that time in bed all the way across the continent for reading, because I didn't have time to do it back there. I would see all the plays in New York, see all my friends and then maybe stay here or go abroad.

I went abroad, starting in 1921, every year until last fall, and sometimes I would go two or three times a year. I would use that period of time on a train or a boat as a rest period, where I could read or relax and didn't have to be onstage all the time. If I went to a place where somebody didn't know me, this was all right. But if you live in Hollywood and you put blinders on, you hear nothing but pictures, pictures, pictures. At a dinner party all the producers are talking pictures; then they would run a picture after dinner . . . What could you learn? You get an idea that California and Hollywood are the focal point of the entire world. It is *not*. This is where the big mistake comes. When the career starts to slide, it's very hard on some egos that can't take it. A lot of them come to New York and they feel hurt because there are only three people outside of "21" who want their signature; or they don't get the best table because they don't know the headwaiter as well as someone from an advertising agency on Madison Avenue; and this hurts them, because they are used to Chasen's, where everybody knows who they are, what their last picture was, their bank account, their house, how many servants they have got, etc., etc. It's all a status thing. It's hard for them to take it and they can't wait to get home again. Can't wait.

JK: You worked with Valentino while he was still being "built up," he worked with you in *Beyond the Rocks,* which Elinor (*Three Weeks*) Glyn wrote especially for you and him. Working with him, did you think there was anything special about him . . . to account for the endurance of the Valentino legend? For those incredible salaries stars like you and him commanded? Were you struck by him?

GS: People demanded and got those fabulous salaries because it was the product that people wanted to buy. If people would buy more of yours than somebody else's, then you got more money. That was all that happened there. Studios vied for people who would bring something into the box office. They tried to get away from the star system in pictures and the theater and TV, and they didn't succeed. I suppose it will always be thus. So much so that this whole thing has gone into so many kinds of businesses that even executives, presidents, chairmen and vice-presidents have their own PR men writing about them and building them up. What for? So they could have a shinier desk or a bigger office? No. So they could get more money in their paychecks. I wasn't to have had a co-star at this period, but I allowed Valentino to co-star even though it went against my contract. I did this because I wanted Paramount to do something for me that they didn't want to do . . . and because I liked Valentino.

JK: Are there any films in particular of yours that you're most proud of?

GS: There are only a few films. *Sadie Thompson* is the best "Sadie Thompson," but there's a reason for that. But I can't take the credit. It was a silent picture. You see, the two women who played it after I sold it to Schenk for Crawford . . . because I owned the play *Rain* and I owned the short story "Miss Thompson" . . . I knew they would have an awful time making it into a talking picture. If you remember it, it was a very violent play, insofar as language is concerned, and that was its impact on the audience. I could say those lines in a silent picture and then it would be cut and a title put in. But it's hard for a person to build up an emotional scene if you have to stamp your foot and say, "You cur!" Which is what poor Crawford had to do, because it was a talking picture. And that made the performance a little weaker and milder, whereas I was able to say every word that . . . um . . . uhm . . . what's her name?

JK: Rita Hayworth?

GS: No, no, no.

JK: Crawford?

GS: No, no . . . um, *Rain,* play, stage . . . Eagels, every word that Jeanne Eagels had gotten to say on the stage. Now, if you had to come with this bland whistle which they have sometimes for censorship on TV, and every time you come to a blasphemous word you had to whistle, you can imagine what the performance would have been like.

Then I did a thing called *The Coast of Folly,* an English thing, and I played two parts. I played the mother and the daughter. The mother was so characterized that nobody knew I was playing it. It was a very successful picture money-wise. People went in to see me and they saw me playing a small part, the daughter, and they didn't know that the other character was up there and me all the time. You see, in those days they used to come in the middle, they didn't just come at the beginning of a picture where they could have read the titles. Even then they wouldn't have believed it! I was like Lon Chaney up there. I was playing this strange old woman and I loved doing it. I loved that better than the young girl.

JK: Did you like *Queen Kelly*?

GS: No, because there was not enough of it. Just the character at the beginning.

JK: Thank you so much for your time. I'd better let you get to bed. [It was almost 1:00 a.m.]

GS: Not at all, my dear. I just get a little tired of talking about me.

1964

Colleen Moore, publicity photograph, circa 1926

COLLEEN MOORE

COLEEN MOORE was born Kathleen Morrison in 1902, and a lot of things happened to her while she was still in her teens, before she became a big star during the early '20s. Some books list her birthdate as 1900. It's not that Colleen Moore looks two years younger or older than her age, but rather that her energy is twice that of anyone with her.

In both 1926 and 1927 the young starlet was voted the nation's number-one box-office attraction by the Exhibitor's Poll. In the era when Mary Pickford was America's Sweetheart, Gloria Swanson the epitome of glamour and the screen's highest-paid star, Clara Bow the "It" girl, and Greta Garbo still only the new girl on the block, Colleen Moore was the most popular at the box office. She was earning $12,500 per week. There were little if any taxes then, and Colleen not only kept a lot of her money but later on, after she left the movies, made even more on the stock market. What she knew about stocks and bonds she later put into a best-selling book, *How Women Can Make Money in the Stock Market*.

Although hard-working, high-spirited and determined, Colleen's career moved at a steady but unspectacular pace for the first six years—until the day she cut her long, curly black hair short and had it styled into a severe Dutch-boy bob for her role as the flapper incarnate in *Flaming Youth* (1923), the story of an undisciplined young girl who discovers that there is more to life than good times and the pursuit of pleasure. The haircut gave Colleen definition. She wasn't a pretty girl or a glamour star; she was "The Modern Girl."

Overnight she was a whopping big star. There were Colleen Moore dresses and Colleen Moore dolls. The cartoonist John Held, Jr., who chronicled the behavior of the smart set, used Colleen as the prototype of his bird-brained flappers. Everybody cut their hair like hers if they didn't want to look old-fashioned, though perhaps no one ever looked as good with it as a starlet at another studio, Louise Brooks, who no matter how she subsequently cut, grew or styled her hair is remembered the world over for the look Colleen Moore created.

While making *Flaming Youth* she married the man who would produce most of her hugely profitable silent films, and to whom she stuck even as his alcoholism progressed to the point where he tried to strangle her. Their marriage was one of those classic laughing-on-the-outside, crying-on-the-inside Hollywood dramas, though only insiders knew it. One of them, her longtime friend Adela Rogers St. John, drew on this chapter in Colleen's life for her fictional movie-star couple in the original story from which—via *What Price Hollywood?* (1932)—*A Star Is Born* was eventually made. Even the film's unforgettable last line was something Adela overheard one time when she was visiting Colleen. Colleen, then the studio's biggest draw, knowing that the executive board wanted to unload her alcoholic husband, called an executive in New York and said sweetly, "Hello, this is Mrs. John McCormick." The studio got the point.

Colleen made six sound movies in all, including one that has gained significant cult status over the years, *The Power and the Glory* (1933), but by 1935 she was out of films. A whole new life began, and she never looked back until she met King.

Sergei Eisenstein visited Hollywood in 1931, hoping to set up a film project, and was wined and dined as the Russian genius who gave the world *Potemkin*. He met everybody and returned to Russia without having made a film in Hollywood. He gave vent to a lot of opinions on Hollywood and its people, among which he found Marlene Dietrich dull, Greta Garbo stupid, but Colleen Moore the only intelligent women he met there.

People were always saying that I didn't act like a movie star. I think other stars took themselves very seriously and they didn't have a chance to look at another side of life to find out that the Hollywood slice of life is a very small slice, instead of all of life. So many of them couldn't handle stardom. Mind you, I think the women took it much more in their stride than the men. [John] Barrymore, for one, took to drink. Today people are more adjusted. Another thing was that we were silent—that gave it an extra glamour. The stars were more unobtainable, more exciting, behind the gloss curtains. People made up their own ideas about them. I went to the cinema a lot in those days. I always hoped to be recognized. That was in the beginning when I first started out. Mr. DeMille and people like that had private screenings, but I never saw any of that until after I was married. Later on, of course, we went to Marion Davies', but she didn't come out to Hollywood until 1927.

When Garbo first arrived, she was only nineteen and a very young girl. We all used to give Sunday lunches which started at noon, and Jack [Gilbert] would have one, and she would be there and she couldn't understand why Jack wouldn't let her swim in the nude. Because that was what she was used to doing in Sweden.

When I first arrived in LA, I was met at the station, my grandmother and I, by Mrs. Brown. She was the studio chaperone. You see, we were all little girls. Because of the cameras, when you were twenty you looked like Mount

Vesuvius in a photo—until they discovered better lenses. Mrs. Brown took me to the studio and I was going to have a bit in a picture with Robert Harron and Mildred Harris, starting the next day. I had already been tested in Chicago to see if my eyes were all right. I had long curls, and I played a spunky little city girl while Mildred was a little country girl. It was only a small part, but they seemed to think it was all right. They gave me another part the next week where I played opposite Bobby. Then I had a part where I played the daughter of a railroad magnate. Monte Blue was the hunted bandit. Griffith's publicity man, Chet Withey, said, "With some good material this girl could be a star someday." Those were friendly days—we all helped each other. It was nothing for one of us to hear about a film being cast and to tell our friends about it—you know, "There's a great part in the new Tom Mix. I didn't get it, but go out there quick."

The publicity man sought me out and asked me to come to his office, saying he was a friend of my Uncle Walter's.* They wanted to send me to have some publicity pictures made, so they sent me down to Nelson Evans' studio. He was the top photographer. All the magazines at the time were filled with pictures by him. There was no such thing at this time as the Colleen Moore look to sell a specific product. The big thing was to be blond with long curls like Mary Pickford, or to have great big eyes and a little tiny mouth like Lillian [Gish] and run around shaking.

The first time my picture appeared was unforgettable. It was in *Photoplay* magazine and was the picture of me holding the dusty roses. I was so excited. I was down in a little corner, about $3'' \times 5''$—"Newest Griffith Find—Colleen Moore." It took me a little time to get used to the name because my own name, Kathleen Morrison, was still with me. But my uncle and Teddy Becker, who was the managing editor of the *Chicago Tribune*, got tiddly one night and decided that I should have a different name since mine was too long. The ideal name then had twelve letters because in small-town cinemas the marquee was only large enough for twelve letters, so if you wanted your whole name up, you got a name that fitted. If your name was Jeanette MacDonald, in so many small towns they could only fit "J. MacDonald." If there were two stars with more than twelve letters, it would end up, for instance, like "J. Macdonald and N. Eddy." So they worked it out by chopping off Morrison and changing it to Moore. My grandmother used to call me Colleen, as I was half Irish, so this became my first name.

One of Evans' favorite poses was with a lot of tulle around the head, making one look angelic. It was an innocent era and this is what people liked. The captions were very amusing. I was described as "The First Child of the World." Corinne Griffith was "The Orchid Lady." Corinne and Norma Talmadge were in the East at the time, producing their own films. Corinne didn't come out until just before First National was formed. First National picked eleven girls who might make stardom—they might and they might not. And that was the nu-

*Her uncle was Walter Howey, editor of the Chicago *Examiner,* immortalized in *The Front Page*.

cleus. They made a movie with each of us. I was lucky. I made *Flaming Youth* and became a star, and people were saying, "Ah, she's a star overnight," but I had been around for six years. There really is no such thing as an overnight star. I had learned my trade well in Christie comedies, in Westerns, falling off horses, in everything, comedy and drama, so that when the time came I was prepared. I was sixteen just before I came out.

When I arrived at [D. W.] Griffith's studio, there were Carmel Myers, Bessie Love, Mildred Harris and me. The Gishes weren't there. They had just moved back to New York. They were big stars, almost unapproachable. We girls were the tail end of the closing up of the company, which was still obligated for a lot of these little pictures. The company finally closed. We went to an agent, and there really was only one, Willis and Inglis. Mr. Woods, who was the head of the studio when I arrived, took me down there and introduced me, and Mr. Willis' sister took charge of me. She sent me out to Charles Ray to see if I could get a job and I did. I came out to Hollywood under contract to Griffith, but I never actually worked for Griffith. I didn't meet Mr. Griffith until I was a big star, when I met him in the lobby in New York at the opening of one of his films, and he came over and said, "I did a pretty good job of discovering you, didn't I?"

So I got the job with Charles Ray for two pictures, and then Mr. Inglis got me a contract with the Selig company, where I played *Little Orphan Annie* [1919]. It was very funny. I walked on the set to meet the director, Colin Campbell. He took one look at me and he said, "Are you the niece of Liberty Howey in Chicago?" I said, "Yes," and he said that he knew it, that he could see a resemblance; he turned to the cameraman and said, "I'm taking this one, she's hired."

I felt at home in LA before I ever got there! This makes me believe in the power of positive thinking. From the age of five I *knew* that I was going to be a motion-picture actress. The other girls would say, "When I grow up, I'm going to be a movie actress." I would always say, "When I grow up and *I am* a movie actress"—one of the few things in my life I was ever so sure of. I didn't have any preconceived ideas of what LA would be like. I did know something about it because my aunt used to come out sometimes to the Coronado Hotel, and she'd tell me about the orange and lemon trees. Of course when I got there, there weren't nearly as many as I thought there would be. I remember the train ride completely; when we came to Pasadena and we looked out to the snow-covered mountains, and orange groves with great big yellow oranges on them, I had such a thrill of excitement because I was "home." I was *never* disappointed. I was coming to a place that I always wanted to be in. I don't know why. Hollywood to me was always the enchanted land—even to the very end. Though it was a suburb then—a real suburb. Hollywood and Vine was an orange grove. The studio had rented a little tiny California bungalow for me and my grandmother, which was furnished, right near the studio, so that I could run to the studio. Bessie Love lived further down on the same block.

I wasn't a bit interested in anything to do with the LA social scene. The only thing that interested me was that one day I might see Mary Pickford. And I thought I might drop dead, but I might see her someday. None of the others, only Mary. She was such a queen to me and, I suppose, to all of us. She was the first and the big one, the one with all the publicity. I had pages and pages in my scrapbook of her.

I stood out a bit from the others then because I was tall—Lillian too, but we both came across as small for some unknown reason. I was 5'6" when the ideal height was 5'2". Mary Pickford, Gloria Swanson, Bessie and Mae Murray all were, while I was a big tall girl, but my bones were small and narrow and that's why I photographed small. The men were small too. I can't tell you the number of scenes I used to play with my shoes off so I'd be little for the leading man. Nothing could destroy my illusions. I was living in fairyland. I loved the work. I could hardly wait to get to work in the morning. Even after I was a star, when I had days and days off, I would always go to the studio because that was where the fun was and that's where my friends were.

I remember in the '20s when everybody thought Hollywood was all hell broken loose, and I went to New York and went to quite a few parties that weren't movie parties and I'd never seen such carryings on. I was only eighteen then and an aunt of mine arranged for me to go to some parties. I never saw such wild girls and boys. I thought how nice we are in Hollywood compared to these so-called social girls in New York.

In Hollywood there would probably be six of us, or a double date, and we'd go to the Cocoanut Grove to have dinner and dance. But that wasn't until I was eighteen. Before then I couldn't go out at night. Besides, Mr. Gardner, my tutor, would come in the evenings to keep up my schooling, because the family thought I would be going home and they wanted me to keep up with my lessons. Then on Sunday I would take my piano lesson. And none of us had a beau. We didn't even have a beau at the studio. We all nearly died of shock when Mildred Harris at sixteen or seventeen married Charlie Chaplin; but then we decided she was very advanced for her age! And then the next shock was when Winifred Westover, who was one of us, married William S. Hart. She was playing in a picture with him. None of us had a beau. None. In about 1921, around the time we formed the girls' club, we began going out with boys. Usually from the studio. I missed my youth. We all missed our youth: beaus, going to dances, all that. But if I hadn't had what I had, I would have grown up to be the most frustrated wife, the most pushy mother, trying to push her daughter into the movies, or something equally horrible. I would have been dreadful. Yet when the time came to leave, I didn't mind giving it up.

There were many contributing factors. The main thing was probably my very bitter first marriage, and the second one wasn't much better. I was still young, only about twenty-seven. I sat down—I'll never forget that night—I was sitting out on a swing—it was moonlight, reflected in the garden pond— well, I had gotten everything I wanted. I had been voted top box-office attraction for the third year running and I had a million dollars and I had a dream house—but really I had *nothing*. Upstairs in our dream house was my husband, a complete dipsomaniac, with a nurse around the clock. It was nothing but unhappiness. When I met Albert [Scott, her second husband] I wanted to get away from it all and went to New York with him, but that didn't work either because the jump was too great. When I met Homer [Hargrave, her third husband], who was very stable, very amusing, who was a powerful businessman and who couldn't possibly take the movies seriously any more than my family could, I knew I had found the right person. I could never take myself seriously at home with my family. They thought it was all a bit of a joke, even though I was fullfilling my daydreams, but they were never impressed. I was just always "little Kathleen," and they used to laugh about it.

If I hadn't been in the movies and had been able to go out with boys a lot—like my cousins who were going out with boys at the age of sixteen and seventeen—I might not have made all the mistakes I made in my marriages. But there were no boys at the studio. They were all men. The men at the studios were mostly old or married, or both. They were twenty-five, twenty-six and married; there was no one of my own age. Except Bobby Harron and Jack Pickford, they were the two young ones—but Bobby was going with Dorothy Gish and Jack was going with Constance Talmadge. My grandmother would take us to a movie downtown at Tolly's cinema, and then we'd stop at the Pig and Whistle, where we'd have a chocolate ice-cream soda, and come home. It was a very famous ice-cream parlor where they also served fabulous lunches. Oh, I remember those even now. We were hardly ever recognized when we went out because we were so little known. When we'd have time off, Carmelita, Julanne and my idea of a big time was to go down to the Pig and Whistle, have lunch and go to a movie. On Saturdays we would go to the Alexandria Hotel for tea. I can see those now—little tiny buns with ham and little *petits fours*. But we girls always went around together—like at high school, only we made movies.

We had to avoid getting klieg-light eyes and the only way to do that was by remembering not to look at them. If you looked at them, you'd get it. If you did, the cure was getting raw potatoes and scrape them and put them on your sore eyes and it would do the trick in about four hours.

Girls did not go out on dates at twelve and thirteen in regular life; at fifteen you could go to a children's party, and at sixteen, boys would be there and sometimes they would slip away and have a kiss. It was all very innocent. It was an innocent age. But I never missed boys until finally I remember I went to New York and I was working with John Barrymore [*The Lotus Eater,* 1921], and my mother went with me and we stayed with my aunt, who lived there, and one night Marshall Neilan, who was a director, asked my mother if I could go out on a date with a very nice boy that he knew in New York, as he thought that I was old enough to go out with boys. We were going out to dinner with Ben Ali Haggin, who did the sets for the *Follies*. And my mother said of course I could go, as she trusted me with Marshall to go anywhere. And he introduced me to this very nice boy who was going to Yale and he was my date for the evening and I had such a good time. I hoped that I had talked about the right things that *boys* would be interested in. And he was thrilled to be with Colleen Moore.

When I came back to California after the Barrymore picture, Marshall again invited me to go to a party and he said, again, that he had a very attractive boy for me to meet and he got permission from my mother. He was a nice Irish boy, a press agent for First National, and, I'll never forget it, I got into the front of the car with Marshall and Blanche Sweet, and he was in the back of the car with someone else. We made our introduction and we went to the Sunset Inn and had dinner and I thought he was the handsomest thing I'd ever seen in my life. And we were dancing, and he asked me to marry him. I just looked up and I thought he was nuts and I said, "Call me up in the cold gray dawn," a movie title. And in the cold gray dawn he rang and said, "Hey, my name is John McCormick, remember last night?" And asked me when I was going to marry him, "but before you marry me, will you have dinner with me tonight?" I refused, saying that I was busy, though I had no date at all. But I could go the night after, which happened to be my birthday, and he knew this from the studio autobiography thing. Every hour I received a present. A man came with a big bunch of balloons, and a monkey man came for me to shake hands with the monkey, and this went on all day long, and that was it, I married him! That was really the first time I had been wooed by somebody. He said, "This may seem sudden to you, but I've been in love with you for six solid months. If you don't believe me, come and look at my office, your picture is all over it."

Of course the day did come when I couldn't go out without being recognized, but that was after *Flaming Youth*. It made me realize that what I hoped was true *was* true. I was a star. I thought being a star meant for me to be able to pick parts. Only it wasn't true. In spite of the fact that my pictures made so much money, and money is power in the studio, I had to keep making comedies. I was getting desperate. And then the company bought *So Big* and I wanted to make it. I begged and begged and they had to let me do it. The best reviews I ever had in my life were in *So Big*. The picture made no money, so I had to go back to making comedies. It was directed by Charles Brabin, who was married to Theda Bara. I adored him. I used to call him Uncle Charlie. I didn't know Theda until I was working for her husband, when she had already retired. She was a very funny woman, and her best imitations were of Theda Bara. She used to poke fun at the vampire all the time.

In the early days we all went through phases of copying the established stars. I used to copy Theda Bara, but always in a burlesque form. The stars I copied in earnest were Lillian and Norma Talmadge. Then I would have my Mary Pickford days. At other times I was Grace Cunard and Marguerite Clark. I copied them all. Out of all this pretending I found me and me was exactly like the little girl I played opposite Bobby Harron in the first picture I made. We were very conscious that our careers were short. It had to be short in those days because of the camera, unless you wanted to go on and play grandmothers. Mine wasn't short [1917–1934] because along came the diffusing lenses, and so you could stand a close-up. It was always so interesting. When I was beginning, I remember one of the older character actors offering me advice. He said, "Now, little girl, be nice to everyone on your way up, because you'll meet them on the way down!" And another piece of advice was to be nice to your prop men because they might be your directors tomorrow, and I saw plenty of prop men turn out to be directors!

If Marshall Neilan hadn't been a drunkard, he'd have been a great director. He was a good friend of mine, I adored him. He directed me in several pictures. He was a man with a great heart. He had his own company releasing through First National, and I had a contract with him. Marshall went broke, but before he dissolved his company he took every single member of his company and got them a job. He sold me to Sam Goldwyn—poor Sam thought he was getting Sarah Bernhardt—for a year's contract. Marshall even got a job for the prop man, and then he took a job as a director at the Goldwyn company. You had to love him. He introduced John and me, so we always felt very sentimental about Mickey. When he was down and out, we hired him to direct me in a picture [Her Wild Oat, 1928], for which we paid him $50,000, which was more than our usual $25,000, because he was broke, and we tried to encourage him to put it in some kind of trust or something—because I saw him spend a million dollars. Anyway, Christmas was coming and we were in the middle of the picture, and this idiot—this idiot!—went out and bought gift certificates to give to everybody; all the men got them for Eddie Schmidt, the most expensive tailor in town, and he gave me the most beautiful jade bracelet. I just wanted to take that bracelet and cram it down his throat, I was so mad at him, and asked him why he did it. He replied, "Well, I like jade and I thought you'd like jade." When he was down to his last $2000, he gave a $2000 party. Champagne flowed, marvelous entertainment. Paul Whiteman's band. Mad—delightfully mad.

Hollywood and LA society hardly mixed at all then. So funny, really, when you think that today their children and grandchildren are breaking their necks to be with movie people. But then, in the teens, we were very separate. The Ambassador Hotel wasn't built because of us movie people, but because of the great influx of winter visitors, though we were just as mobbed when we went to the Ambassador as anywhere else. Finally, in the late '20s, we had our own dinner-and-dance club, the Mayfair, down at the Biltmore Hotel, which was just for the people in the profession. People would give dances and dinner parties there. They were great fun and *very* elegant. I was invited to a lot of the Los Angeles parties only because my mother knew a lot of the people giving them. Our eastern friends gave me that entree, but the people were very dull, they didn't have anything to talk about that interested us, and I suppose we bored them with our movie talk. I remember when [George] Fitzmaurice was married to Diane Fitzmaurice. She was always mixing the parties with a lot of private, social people and we had nothing in common with them. Our talk was all movies, that was all anyone cared about, and later on when the musicians came, it was music and movies.

The only rivalry between the stars at the studios was over publicity. Corinne Griffith used to complain all the time that I got too much publicity. And she was very angry because they built me a bungalow with a patio and a fountain. It had four rooms and a sunken tub in my bathroom. Corinne caused such a commotion that they had to build her one. Then Corinne—well, I think it was the gardener—planted a hedge between us which grew up *so* tall that the studio gossip said that it was the "spite fence." But we were great friends, we had nothing whatsoever to be jealous of each other about. She played the grand, gorgeous ladies and I was the *gamine*. But my pictures made more money than hers and that used to irk her. It could well be that because of the disparate social backgrounds of so many of the stars of those years, when they became stars they tried to marry into society for the security they never knew, and to many of them, those in the social scene were idols. Isn't that what happened in Newport? The Vanderbilts marrying their daughters off to those impoverished European aristocrats so that something would rub off on them? Same thing. Gloria [Swanson] brought the first title home, but I don't think Gloria married the Marquis Hank for any other reason than that she was in love with him. It was the studio who capitalized on this to a point where it became utterly ridiculous. I know they made it up, it just wasn't Gloria's way. It was the studio that made it a circus. One became a pawn of the studio's press agents from the beginning—the moment you arrived at the studio.

Now, here's the thing. The publicity people invented stories—they made everything up. For instance, when I was writing my autobiography [*Silent Star,* 1968], trying to get historical dates and facts from the studios, I ran into *more misinformation* than you can believe. Stories made up by press agents. I know that they're not true because I was there, I saw it happen. I have a very good reporter's memory, and it just wasn't so, any more than the one my uncle sent out about how I got into the movies. It was just invention, invention, invention, and the invention has become fact. I'd read everyplace that I was in *Intolerance,* [that] Griffith picked me to be in *Intolerance*. I was still in Tampa, Florida, going to school. It was *because* of *Intolerance* that I got into the movies. They couldn't get all those orgy scenes, etc., past the Chicago censors, and my uncle arranged it, and then poor Mr. Griffith said, "What can I do to repay you?" and my uncle said, "I have a niece . . ." and Griffith groaned and said, "Oh, not another niece," and my uncle said, "Yah." And that was it! So I tracked that fact down to show you just where that story came from. Daniel Blum got it from Dick Griffith, who was the head of the Museum of Modern Art film department. He knew me very well, so I called him up and he admitted that the story had come from him. So I told him that I hadn't been in *Intolerance*—I wish I *had* been! So I asked him why he hadn't checked with me to make sure that I had been in it, and he said that he had just guessed, so now it is fact!

Yes, there were some real extravaganzas that made good stories. But take

the sunken pool in my bungalow instead of an ordinary bathtub. The studio PR
did that to make a good story. They just took an ordinary bathtub and sunk it. I
thought it was hysterically funny. That's why I laughed when I said it. There
were some wild houses built in Hollywood, especially Tom Mix's, which had
neon lights out front saying "TM BAR"! I dreamed of having a big house, but I
knew exactly what I wanted and it was about like the one now. There were a
few people who became desperate and silly later on, like Mae Murray. And
Corinne Griffith, who, when she was being divorced by a much younger man,
denied that she was Corinne Griffith and said she was her understudy, but she
was senile by then—too bad, too bad. Pola Negri was another one who went a
bit mad. But you can think of ten who were pretty together. Look at MGM—
Jeanette, Norma, Myrna Loy, Garbo, Marie Dressler, Crawford, and they
weren't mad.

The '20s was the Scott Fitzgerald *Great Gatsby* time; New York was just
as crazy as Hollywood and so was Podunkia. Hollywood merely reflected this
time, it didn't start trends. I made *Flaming Youth,* the first flapper picture; the
flapper was already well established, but no one had portrayed her. I knew she
was an established type because these were the girls my brother used to bring
home from college, that's how I knew about them. It may have been the first
flapper picture, but I wasn't the first flapper, she was on every campus across
the country. In the picture I had to smoke, which was awful because I never
smoked; it was the perfect image of the flapper, but I haven't had a cigarette
since. I never even had a cocktail until I was probably thirty. A flapper I wasn't,
but I was the right age and looked the part and I had the "bangs" and I was it.

Louise Brooks, who came about five years later, copied my bangs. What
is fascinating about Louise Brooks is that I don't remember her very well, and
nobody else did either, and nobody thought she was very much; but you look at
her pictures today and she's awfully good. But she was nothing—nothing. She
was a Paramount starlet, that's all. But people who imitated me didn't bother
me at all. And we never met. One's social life was usually with the people from
one's own studio. Bebe Daniels was the only person I ever knew at Paramount.
Mostly we were just with our contemporaries. When I was married, we went
out with Irving and Norma. But most of my friends at other studios were ones
I'd known when we started out. Mae Murray was of a much older—to me, at
any rate—generation. I didn't know her at all.

When the scandals broke, the reaction in Hollywood was complete and
total shock. That Fatty Arbuckle, the hero of the kids and everybody else, was
carrying on like that. Nobody could believe it, nobody knew about him. Then
there was the William Desmond Taylor thing. A real shocker. I knew Mary
Miles Minter. Not long before that scandal broke, I had gone to a party at the
Cocoanut Grove with Mary and a young man from the East and Marshall [Nei-
lan] and Blanche [Sweet]. Mary was very simple, very pretty. I liked her. She
was supposed to be the new replacement for Mary Pickford at Paramount. I did
a lot of research on William Desmond Taylor with King [Vidor] because we
wanted to make a movie at one point, based on the Taylor murder, which is a

great story. But the misinformation on that story is unbelievable. For example, we spent one solid day tape-recording the detective who'd been put on the case by the DA. He had it all. Now, the papers came out with a good story that Mary Miles Minter's little nightgown was found with the initials MMM—but what was really found was a handkerchief in his drawer. The nightgown story ruined Mary Miles Minter's career. Mabel Normand's career was ruined because she was the last person seen leaving the Taylor house. They had no part in it, just innocent bystanders. But these two scandals coming one on top of the other immediately made Hollywood a city of sin. Sodom and Gomorrah. We were made terribly conscious of it. The letters came in. That was when, very cleverly, the motion-picture industry got in Will Hays. And I remember when Will came out, and in everyone's contract there was a morality clause—that if you had any sort of publicity of this type, your contract was immediately canceled. This didn't apply to the studio head. A scandal surrounding Louis B. Mayer wouldn't have hurt Garbo, but the reverse would hurt the studio.

My problem was that the public wouldn't accept me "grown up," like Mary Pickford. They wanted me to be their "dear little darling" who used to run around and clap her hands and say, "Papa, what is beer?" and then I found out what beer was, but they didn't want me to know what beer was.

Here's what my life was like. After each picture I had a four-week break— I made four pictures a year. Those four weeks went like this: The first week they are cutting the picture and we are going back for retakes; the second week I make publicity pictures every day, in the studio. The next week I'm interviewed, sometimes in the studio, sometimes at my house for lunch, and always the publicity man is there. I had my own publicity man then and his whole job depends on me. Once he got us a marvelous interview in the *Ladies' Home Journal;* this was considered extraordinary because they never had much about movie stars then. The last week was spent taking costume tests for the new picture, to see how they photographed and to be fitted for them. So I never had a vacation while I was a star. I rebelled. I reached a point when I said I wanted to go to Europe. Right after I broke my neck, after *Desert Flower,* about 1925– 26, John said okay. The doctor said I badly needed a rest and a vacation. This was supposed to be it. I was met on the dock by a tremendous group of reporters; I opened a new theater; publicity here and there. First National gave an enormous banquet at the Dorchester, inviting all the theater owners. I was *on, on, on.* I had to go to Dublin because I was Irish and open two theaters and was mobbed. In Dublin the papers reported that there were about 10,000 in front of this theater and I couldn't get out, and John, who was a big guy, put me on his shoulders and carried me out. I had just come from Paris, where I'd bought this darling little ostrich-feather cape, which the crowd picked at until it was almost bald, just to get a souvenir.

The adoration stopped about three years after I stopped making movies. I could walk down Broadway and nobody turned around—and I was delighted.

1975

Dorothy Gish

DOROTHY GISH

S HE WAS THE MARRIED GISH, the Little Sister, the comedienne, the one who
was 5′2″ and didn't take the world on screen or off quite seriously. Pratfall
poetry was appreciated only if it could mirror social roots, or assist reforms
with a kick up the backside. When comedy was anti-establishment, the establishment treated it as art, but when it wasn't—when it was just funny—it was
forgotten with the last laugh: vide Keaton vs. Chaplin.

Dorothy Gish was just a naturally funny woman, full of impish delight.
Pinch her, she'd shout; prick her and she would ball up her fist and punch the
offender; and if you snubbed her, she'd shrug it off and dance with the next boy.
A forlorn maid she wasn't. She may have had the long, long hair that Griffith
loved his girls to release in those moments of pursuit by enemy hands when the
sight of a woman in peril was naturally enhanced by the wild flurry of her locks,
but you could tell in Dorothy's eyes that she was a "flapper-in-waiting." The
villain could have her hair, *she* wanted it bobbed. You could imagine her climbing trees. With her sister, Lillian, Dorothy belonged to the first generation of
Hollywood, the teens, and even though they were themselves in their early teens
(born 1896 and 1898) when they started in movies, years when counted by
decades heap a stature of the sort that weighs the recipient down. It requires
great ambition to seem to be what that stature implies: greater, nobler, prettier,
lovelier. Whatever the adjective, it usually ended with an *-er.* With Dorothy, to
err was human, and to go where her heart led or her friends were was divine.
After she left America to work with sister Lillian in Italy on *Romola,* she went
on to Germany and England, which she loved, making movie after movie, silent
and talkie, playing *Madame Pompadour* and *Nell Gwyn,* co-starring with
Charles Laughton in *Wolves* (1930). Many years later, in America, Laughton
directed sister Lillian in the film that shows Laughton's fascination for Ameri-
cana *à la* Griffith, the Gothic cult classic *Night of the Hunter.*

Sound came into Hollywood without Dorothy, who was still in London.
When she came back, too many of her friends were too old with stature to wish
to struggle. Some—the uncrowned rulers, Pickford, Fairbanks, Swanson—
made talkies. They were acclaimed. But for personal reasons (dissolution of
indissoluble marriages, money lost on the "talkies" they produced) they left
while they could still enjoy basking in the glory they had.

35

Sister Lillian made her talkie, *One Romantic Night* (a Molnár play that has never been a hit on film under this title or its own, *The Swan*), and went to Broadway to play Chekhov and Shakespeare, for she had been the silent screen's acknowledged Duse. Dorothy, the comedienne, didn't even bother with sound—she'd been away from Hollywood for so long that in the panic of the moment her return didn't stir up a great fuss, and with even less fuss on her part she also went back onstage, where she had begun at the age of five, and went from one play to another. Her most famous was in a touring production of *Life with Father* opposite Louis Calhern, and connoisseurs of all the versions with all the different actresses said she was the jolliest of all the Mrs. Days. In the '40s she was back in Hollywood making a couple of movies, and if you hadn't known who she was, you would just have said that you liked that nice lady who played the mother in *Our Hearts Were Young and Gay* and *Centennial Summer*. Otto Preminger, who directed that film, also used her in what turned out to be her last film, *The Cardinal*.

She wasn't showy—not that the roles were, but somebody else, in a similar situation, might have tried to make more of it. She was content to be an actress, and what did it matter that in a story set in the '20s, about young flappers setting out for the Continent, Dorothy could have given the girls (Gail Russell and Diana Lynn) pointers on how to make a flapper tick? She played the mother hen with a knowing, tolerant but in no sense smug smile. It wasn't her film. I wonder now if the Misses Russell and Lynn knew who Dorothy Gish was, and if they asked her for pointers.

Dorothy Gish lived not very far from where I went to dinner most evenings back in those first visits to New York. Her apartment was decorous, the furniture and draperies a bit old-fashioned. She too was dressed in the style of—and with fabrics from—an earlier age. A polite, charming little old lady who served tea and, throughout my time with her, kept tugging away at the edges of a little white lace handkerchief. She wasn't the madcap hellion her movies might had led me to expect. Of course, she was no girl, she was seventy, but I'd met a lot of old people by then and one thing they had in common was their youthful memories. Her voice, frightened, small, almost inaudible at times, would come in and out with her memories. Dorothy Gish, who with Mabel Normand and Constance Talmadge had made up the most youthful of all her generation, had changed.

We were looking at albums of pictures. "Oh, *Annie Laurie*! I've got some lovely pictures from that film," I told her, and Dorothy said that "she [sister Lillian] used my little dog in *Annie Laurie*" (MGM, 1926). "This has disappeared, this picture," pointing to a still of her and Richard Barthelmess in a film, and so has the title of the film she's referring to. But she ended up doing all sorts of things, like *Pompadour,* and she laughed and said:

DG: Yes, they're kind of crazy, the things I did. But I feel so sorry about Mr. [Herbert] Wilcox [the producer-director of many of her British silent films], the problems he's been having. Oh, there's *Nell Gwyn* . . . the costumes were wonderful. Just wonderful.

There are loud yelps of discovery when we pass the pictures of her in *Life with Father* on stage. "Oh, yes, heavens," she said, passing quickly and quietly on. Then she added a little laugh. We were just going through pages, looking over pictures, and they couldn't have been in any order, or we each had a different one because one moment it was theater, the next a film she made in England or another one of Lillian's. "It's *The Wind,* isn't it? No, this is, that is . . ." "Oh, just a minute while I get my eye . . ." We were getting acquainted.

JK: When were you first conscious of the fame that comes with being a movie star?

DG: This was in Grand Central Station, when we had a Grand Central Station and we had trains. I started, and I ran. And I ran and ran and ran all the way across the station and up the steps of the depot and got into a taxi; and we were staying at the hotel right over here on . . . not the big one, but the other one, and I came into Mother's apartment and started to cry. She said, "What is it?" And I said, "These people followed me all around; and they touched my skin, and my hair, and my this," and everything was wrong. And she said, "Sit down. Now, if you had just kept on walking, they wouldn't have done anything. You must get out of that attitude. You make a lot of money; and you have a lot of things written about you. But you mustn't pay any attention to that," which is true. And she said the most wonderful thing to Lillian when *Way Down East* was done. Mother and I were over in Europe and we came back together, we'd been over in London . . . Mother loved England too. And we went to see the film. It was playing in one of the big theaters, they had a big orchestra and everything, and it was marvelous. And then we went over to the Ritz Hotel and had tea; and Lillian was getting kind of nervous, we were talking all about England and she finally said, "Mother, what do you think? How was I? Was I all right?" And Mother said, "Well, my dear, you're going to have to work hard to keep up performances like this." And I felt it was the most marvelous thing you could say to anybody. But she wouldn't let you get . . . big-headed. Always. That's why I feel so sorry for so many of those young people today. When you think even that little boy, what's his name now?—getting work all over the place, little Irish boy . . . he married everyone too. He's in his forties now.

My reactions had been a bit slow. "So he's not a little Irish boy anymore?" "Oh, no," Dorothy laughed. She was really quite sweet. She'd been talking about Mickey Rooney. "And look what happened to the one with the beautiful voice, who played Dorothy and sang all over the world. And that was one of the things that I saw very early in my childhood, on the stage. And Dorothy, you know, she gets blown into Kansas . . ." "Oh, *The Wizard of Oz* with Judy Garland." "Yes, and it's still going," she continued, quite unperturbed by my puzzled looks of confusion followed by loud exclamations of who and what. She was nimble, she was quick, she knew what she was talking about and I had better just try and keep up. "But look at her life; and her family; and her mother. What they did to her. The studio would give her pills; and then they'd wake them up and they'd do the next scene, and the next dance, and the next song. Oh, yes. It's frightening." But in fact we'd skipped again, and we were talking not about Judy Garland's similar problems at MGM, but about the studios back when Dorothy Gish was young and starring in films. She was talking of things she had seen firsthand. And it was quite a different image of silent movies than the one I had expected—I had thought she would have been part of the Pickfair crowd.

DG: No, because, you see, I was over in Europe all the time. That's why I missed knowing so many people. And I used to go—even when I didn't have a film to do, I would go on over, and I would stay probably for four or five weeks and then come back. They spoiled me when I was there. I loved the country. In a way, I was making up for the childhood I didn't have. I was thirteen years old when I made my first film. There [she pointed to a photo], there it is. [She and Lillian were sitting on a bench against a white bare wall that was the Griffith studio.] A lot of those early films were done with Lillian. . . . There's one thing that somebody's got, and some young man stopped me on the street and told me about—it was that I—I was showing off, really—I did a circus picture in which a villain was after me; and I was supposed to be put against a wall and knives were being thrown all around me. Well, they didn't get anyone to do it for me. I said, "I'm going to do that myself." Well, I was strapped up there, strapped up there, and . . . was circled right around with knives. Well, Lillian said that Mother had found out that I was doing that, and she was nearly crazy. I can't remember what the story was, which is terrible, but I do remember that, naturally. I'd love to see it, and there is a collector in town who says he has it.

My mother [her voice drops to an affectionate whisper] was so *marvelous* in her wisdom. And she had a feeling that she was going to die and leave us alone. With the result that when we got our salaries and things like this, Mother would go to a bank and ask about what was good and what wasn't, and she tried to make us safe and invest; sometimes we did, and sometimes we didn't know what to do about it. But that was why she did that, why she had to do that, because there was only us two children. And she had the feeling that she might . . . go . . . when we were still both so young. She was trying to train us to take care of what we had worked so hard for.

The girls' love for their mother could be felt whenever Dorothy mentioned her; the examples she gave of her mother's advice or astuteness don't convey the degree of affection that she would put into that word "mother." The close family tie wasn't disrupted when Dorothy married actor James Rennie. Though they'd been divorced for more than thirty years, she still referred to him as "my husband": "My husband is very ill now. He's married, he remarried very well, but he's sick at this time. But he's getting better." They had no children, but her side table was covered with photos in little silver frames which turned out to be her godchildren.

Another page gets turned. Another face. D. W. Griffith, the man who played what was probably the most important role in the lives of both sisters, regardless of those who came after. They began their film careers with Griffith. They grew with Griffith. They made their names with Griffith.

DG: Marvelous man. Marvelous. And it's so sad, to both Lillian and me, that things went so bad for him. I was in one of the Shaw plays at the [Theatre] Guild, and I hadn't seen Mr. Griffith for ages, and a telegraph boy came backstage and gave me this telegram. I opened it. It was from him, saying, "Would you come over and have supper with me after the play tonight?" [Her voice becomes inaudible, almost theatrical.] I sent the boy back saying yes I would, and I did. He was living over in that big hotel, it was the big hotel at the time, the Astor Hotel. I had my little dog with me, as usual, and I got over there, and they wouldn't let me upstairs with the dog into his apartment. So I called up to Mr. Griffith's apartment to say they wouldn't let me up, and he called the manager and it was finally cleared for me to go to see him. I went upstairs, and there was Mr. Griffith, with one of the girls who'd started out in the movies with him, and a trained nurse, and his nephew. And I had never seen him drunk before in my life. I didn't know he drank. And on the way home I cried all the way, and all that night. I couldn't believe it. Dorothy West was the woman with him. You'll see her name in some of those books. It was such a shock to me I . . . I couldn't believe it. He'd changed so much. He was depressed because of the way Hollywood treated him. And they really did treat him dreadfully. We, Lillian and I, worked for him at the old Biograph studios. There was one way uptown. We went out [to Hollywood] first. And, you know, we had all those white sheets above the set when we were working out in California. And they took a warehouse, when we got back after the first time we went out there, and they built a bigger studio uptown, and that's when he left the Biograph and went on with this other thing. That's when so many of these pictures crop up that I can't remember, like that circus story. I had friends of mine call up and tell me that I did a film in which I played a telephone operator. I said that's impossible, and this was with a big actor who married a very pretty girl, beautiful girl, and they were with . . . Oh it's so difficult to remember. I made so many of them, all those two-reelers. It's awful not to be able to remember.

She was so dear, trying so hard to recall names and places. Her unfinished sentences trailed whiffs of memory as precious as facts. And the books confused things. Too many memories, too many names, too many films, too much of everything. Better to begin at the beginning and follow logically.

DG: Well, honey, this is what happened. We were on the stage and we went to agencies that did just children completely. And the Pickfords, Jack, Mary and

Lottie—their names were Smith, Lottie and Gladys Smith—and they had outgrown their parts and we were sent out to the middle East here someplace and Mother told us our lines on the way out there, and we took their places. Well, Mother and Mrs. Pickford, or Mrs. Smith at that time, became devoted and corresponded the whole time we were out. And then Mother and Mrs. Smith took an apartment together. It wasn't in a very nice place, one of those railroad flats; and Mrs. Smith didn't know how to sew, and Mother taught her how to sew and things like that. So that's how we got to know them. And then we went off in different plays; and I went down to a school in West Virginia, I had a term there, and when I finished there, Mother and Lillian came down to pick me up, and we were going down to look for jobs in New York City, which we did, and which Lillian got right away. But on our way to New York we stopped off in Baltimore, where my father—he had an ice-cream shop there when we were children, a nice thing to have, you know, all the ice cream you could eat—had left my mother, and we stayed there for two weeks, it was called the Gish and Meisner confectionery store. So Lillian and I, we stayed there for two weeks, and we asked him for a nickel to go to the movies. And we went down and there was Gladys Smith in *Lena and the Geese*. We were shocked because, you see, we had been in the theater and we thought this was pretty low-down business, this movies goings-on. *Really*. [When Dorothy laughs, it seems nearly always to be at her own former naïveté. She was still incredulous.] Lillian wrote down the company. It was the Biograph studio. So when we came home, we told Mother what we had seen, we were so surprised.

Back in New York, we got a place with a lovely Jewish lady way up on Central Park West, two rooms, and we were looking for work. When I had gone out with this play, this manager who handled us from the time I first began in the theater, when I was four years old, and who had since joined up with the biggest theatrical manager of that time, David Belasco, well, he was managing. And I remembered his name. They didn't have *Variety* in those days, but they had different magazines, so we saw that he was with Belasco now, and we had been just nothing, you know—*Her First False Step* and things like that—so we came down this Saturday and asked if this man remembered me. "Well, of course I remember you." I suppose anybody as small as that and as young as I was would stay in his mind a bit. He took us right up to Mr. Belasco.

I lied a bit about my age, but he looked down at me and said [her voice is a whisper], "I think you'd better go back to school a little bit more, but I have a part for your sister, *The Good Little Devil*." We called Mother and told her that Lillian had gotten a job, so that was okay, and that we were going to call up the Biograph on the way home. Which we did. And said we wanted to talk to Gladys Smith. They said there's nobody there with that name. And we said, "Oh, yes she is. We saw her in a film. *Lena and the Geese*." With Lillian and I both talking into one telephone. And finally he said, "You mean

Mary Pickford." And we said, "No, we mean Gladys Smith." And the operator said to hold on and the next thing, Gladys Smith's *voice* came over the
telephone, and she said to come right down on 14th Street, across from
Stern's. So down we went. We weren't allowed to go inside the thing. It was
a brownstone house, and you went up a flight of steps and there was a cashier
thing there; and we had to wait while Gladys came out. It was really Gladys.
And she was *so* glad to see us.

While we were talking, there was this staircase that went up in this place,
and a man came down, got halfway down, and he saw Lillian and he saw me
and he saw Mary. Next thing we knew, a manager came up to us, with a little
waxed mustache and everything, looking very I don't know what, and he
wanted to know if we were actresses. We said yes. And he said, "Do you
want to work today?" We said, "Well, we'll have to call our mother and find
out." Mother came right down and . . . she let us go in. We worked overtime
and I think we got $17 apiece. We went in and sat in the audience—there
was a scene in a theater and we had to applaud the whole time. Well, we
wrote to the family that we were in the movie, although we *were* a little
ashamed. And all the kids we knew in Massillon, Ohio, when they heard
this, they lined up outside of this movie house in this small town. Of course,
all we did was to clap our hands, and it flashed past, but they had lines outside
the cinema, because they just wanted to see *us* and they couldn't find us
at all.

And from then on, we just kept on working. Mother guided us all this
time. She needed to. It was a tough business. I didn't realize this so much at
the time because of Mother's strength shielding us from the problems, and
knowing what was right and what was wrong. I had the most awful time after
Mother died. [Her voice drops to a whisper.] D. W. Griffith was a wonderful
man. He was so kind to the elderly people. I know every Christmas he would
want my mother to go down and find out what to get for all the character
women, and she'd pick out pins and things they might want. He was very
generous.

We used to rehearse the way we rehearsed plays, always. I tried to get
D.W. to take on Rudolph Valentino for a film. I was doing a Mexican picture
at the time, and I didn't think that Dick [Barthelmess] was good for a Mexican. Mr. Griffith was directing one of his big pictures at the time, the one he
lost all his money on, *Intolerance,* and when he could, he would come in and
see what I was doing and how things were coming along on my set, and I
said to Mr. Griffith to come and watch this young man who was playing, ah
. . . oh, what do you call a man who lives off old ladies? . . . a gigolo!—
and Rudy was playing the gigolo. Well, my dear, Griffith watched Valentino
in this scene where he was trying to find out if the jewelry of this old lady he
went out with was any good. Mr. Griffith watched this thing. He was interested. Very much so. Finally he said, "Wait a moment, let me show you
something." So he sat down by this woman who had these pearls that they

wore all around their necks in those days, and he said, "Now you just sit and don't be cute, just look at them and take these pearls and bite them, like this. [Really, she mimed more than she said, delicately biting a pearl on an invisible strand.] And that's the way you can tell if the pearls are real or not." But in the end he let Rudy go. Rudy was a wonderful man, really. Very quiet. We were going horseback riding in the evenings, up and around the place, and he took me to a tailor's and had my things made for me, my riding outfit. He used to call up at home and ask to come over. You know, women used to chase *him*. It was awful. They were *always* running after him. But he loved to come and visit, and there was usually cooking going on, Mother was a good cook and they got together and cooked things up, and he made spaghetti which was *so* good.

It was with Griffith that the Gish sisters first saw Europe, World War I and all, when Griffith went to make his emotion-charged propaganda film *Hearts of the World* in 1917; it wasn't the first American film to go abroad for locations, but it was probably the most famous to date.

DG: I wasn't in Germany, just Mr. Griffith was. We went to England. We were over there for six months. Did you see those pictures of Griffith in the trenches? But things weren't so different. We still did our own makeup, our own costumes. Oh, yes. We did these things, hats and things, for *Orphans of the Storm*. We got the ideas from things we'd seen at the Met. There again, it was our mother who took us when we were little kids. She got us into the Met as often as she could, but it was expensive and two little kids could only stand up so long . . . and years later I went with Peggy Wood and her husband and they took me right to the top, right in the center.

We were sorting out the plot of *Orphans of the Storm*, and, to be fair, I wasn't being much help. "You were the blind one?" "Yes, the woman got me. I was sent out begging." "So you and Lillian didn't work together all that much, just this and *Hearts of the World*, and the one she directed you in, *Remodeling Her Husband*, and there was the two-reeler where you tried to knife her. And there was *Romola*."

DG: Yes, we didn't make that many films together. And people are always saying that we look so much alike. I wish we did, but we don't. I don't think so at all. I have none of Lillian's traits, none at all.

I hazard to say that Lillian was the ethereal one, the one who floated, while she, Dorothy, was more realistic, walking the ground . . . which amused her no end. But . . . "Oh, you should have seen my aunt and my mother together. Mmmmmhhmmm. They tell me in Mother's hometown, Massillon, they still remember the two of them. They were so beautiful."

DG (looking at stills from *Hearts of the World*): It's so beautiful. It . . . oh, it makes you cry when you look at it. They really knew how to photograph a film.

We weren't in any danger when we were making the film in England. The Germans were flying overhead, but we didn't feel any of that. We were so busy then. Honestly, I can't remember things. Everything went *so* quickly. I didn't know what was going on around, outside us, in the world. The Germans, the idea that maybe they too had seen Lillian and me in films. I didn't know any of that. I didn't know that we were popular; not like Gladys—Mary—when she went on a trip around the world when she got married and she found all these people waiting for her. My dear, when we opened in Boston—I think this was with *Orphans of the Storm*—and we had people climbing all over us, grabbing at our clothes and everything! I used to get nightmares! That sort of adulation made me . . . I . . . I got sick. I couldn't take it. Others, I know, thrived on it. But they would—they'd come and pull things off your coat, buttons, trimmings, things like that. It was terrifying, terrifying! I know they haven't changed. I know. But at least they don't molest *me* any longer.

I went to England because Mr. Wilcox wanted me and asked me. Oh, and I also went into the war. I said, "The reason you feel that way is because you had a bad war on your grounds and we never had that, and I can understand that." But they were just marvelous to me after that. I just adore the British. *Nell Gwyn* was the first really sexy role I ever had, she was the King's mistress. Oh, there's a story about Helen Hayes. She wanted a part in one of these plays—and this was a long time ago when she was *very* young—and this manager with whom she'd worked before said, "Helen, it's not for you. It's not for you. It's a little sexy part." "Well," she said, "I'm *married*!" [and Dorothy burst into giggles]. When we were making *Hearts of the World*, I used to tease Mr. Griffith, because I said, "No Germans run after me. Why not?" But it was true. All through it I had to have this black wig on, and they went after Lillian's blond hair. I had to have this black wig because we were so much alike, *they* said, so they tried to make us look different by giving me the black wig. But in *Orphans* they tried to accentuate the similarity. In *Romola* I had long black hair, since I was playing an Italian gypsy type. She was more stupid than the girl I played in *Hearts of the World*. That walk that I used in there, when Noel [Coward] saw it first, he said, "You're over-egging the pudding with the way you walk." And he was right, but Mr. Griffith, Mother, Lillian and I had seen this woman when we were out one Saturday afternoon, and she walked exactly like this. And the war was on. And she was accosting every man that came along, with this awful walk. And Mr. Griffith said, "Now, that's the way I want you to walk when you get out there." It's a very amusing scene.

When we went to Italy to make *Romola,* the Italians were just marvelous to us. Of course we had to have so many Italians in the film . . . but there wasn't any problem with crowds chasing us. You see, Lillian went over first. She'd already made *White Sister* there. Mother and I had been in Italy before, but that was just for touring. When we got the actors and everything, they were marvelous. And the costumes and all that they did there were just won-

derful. And it didn't cost as much to make it on location as it would have cost
to make over here. And we didn't like California. No. It's just a dull, dull
place. And people are terrified out there. I remember when I was there making *Centennial Summer,* I'd been doing my own makeup for as long as I could
remember, and I'd been doing my own hair up since I was a little, little,
about-this-high girl. Where am I? I'm off the subject . . . oh, yes, *Centennial
Summer.* They came on and put some lipstick on me and put it down on the
table just before this scene around the breakfast table where I had to sing.
Well, I sang and I had difficulty, you know, coming right in on cue because,
not being a singer and all that . . . Well, anyway, the girl who did the hair,
when I finished and finally got it right, she was just standing there and looking at me, like this . . .

Her eyes grew larger, her mouth hung slightly open, her voice rarely changed
inflections except when ending on an exclamation, but her face and hands were
constantly miming things as she spoke, which is why I felt a greater sense of
continuity in her presence than I can find traces of on the tape now. I suppose I
thought I'd never forget the pictures she pointed to, and her facial expressions,
a whole alphabet of silent-screen gestures.

DG: And she finally came around. She had a handkerchief and she picked something off the table quickly. And, my dear, when I saw her looking at me, it
was sheer terror. She was afraid, this film being in color, and this lipstick
lying there, they would have to do this thing over again. That feeling of panic
all around me, that just terrified me.

   Those films I made at that time, like *Whistle at Eaton Falls,* they were
so terrible too. This man Louis de Rochemont, he would write everything
and you couldn't change a thing, not one word. Not at all like Mr. Griffith.
He would listen to you when you had something to say.

1964

OLGA
BACLANOVA

OLGA BACLANOVA was a Russian. A Russian is like no other creature in the world. Because they look Western, white-skinned, Christian and all that, one forgets that they are heathen barbarians descended from the Tartars and the Slavs; separated from their own kind, they become huge, shambling, melancholy bears, forever knocking things down and getting things wrong and laughing about things you'd have to spend a lifetime drunk to start to comprehend: Dagmar Godowsky, of the international jet set, whose speech was an ocean of commas and giggles; Anna Sten, who spoke in a series of semicolons and dashes, pauses that reflected the Russian soul of this half-Swedish actress who was the method in the eye of the method; and, of course, the adorable Olga Baclanova. There was nothing wrong with Olga's Russian; there was nothing wrong with her English. The two just met head on and their collision sounded like the clinking of jewelry—heavy jewelry. I met her in 1964, and she was an old woman, though full of huge, lumpen bursts of energy, at which her wrists of many bracelets jangled ferociously and her little dog barked and made the conversation incomprehensible. She was blond and big-boned, with large eyes and a large red mouth . . . and with her large wrists made for large baubles, she looked—well, she would have been exotic had she come from Kansas, but, coming from Russia, one expected "exotic," so "*strange*" would be the word. She was never a conventional beauty even back in the '20s. She was always too large in every respect, both physically and emotionally.

On screen, especially in her silent films, she played vamps, cruel ones, man-eaters, the kind who rested their hands on their hips (and you could almost hear those bracelets jangling in the silent films, ringing trouble for the hampered hero), as they threw back their heads and opened wide their mouths to make their laughter at the expense of the broken man even harsher. She starred in films with titles that told all—*A Dangerous Woman* and *The Man I Love*. And yet when one sees her in films like Von Sternberg's *Docks of New York* and Mauritz Stiller's *Street of Sin* (opposite Emil Jannings), you sense an actress of great passion with great reserves of rich emotions. On screen, she destroyed men. In life, she was a woman more dominated by them. She was such a child. She spoke like a child, just naïve, and in large, gulping chunks, always—and still—full of surprise and wonder at her story, her successes and her adventures.

45

Olga was a silent star of the kind that you heard fell by the wayside with the coming of sound because of, presumably, their heavily accented voices. In fact, that wasn't so. In *The Wolf of Wall Street* she spoke and sang, thereby establishing herself as one of the few foreigners to survive talking films. Most of the few casualties of "sound" were not foreigners, regardless of apocryphal stories to the contrary. The casualties were mostly Americans with regional accents but no voices. Olga made it into "sound," but "sound" didn't require and couldn't accommodate the larger-than-life personalities which the silent cinema had thrived on, and that is where Olga fell victim. There were only so many "temperamental opera star" and "temperamental vamp" roles to go around, and in the burst of realism brought on by the Depression, Olga began to appear anachronistic. A later generation would describe her style as camp, but she made enough talkies for her pleasingly melancholy voice to be heard. Instead of going on to become the Bride of Frankenstein or Dracula's Daughter or a reincarnated high priestess of the Pharaohs, she sang in nightclubs and on Broadway, and worked long if not spectacularly into the '40s. Olga's "talkie" career wasn't important enough to find much space in the books, except for one film: *Freaks*. If one had seen her only in that extraordinary picture, as most people who knew of her had, one would have gotten the wrong idea of this charming and warm Russian lady who'd already lived ten lives before coming to America.

I had remembered hers as a fascinating story ("I vas creation of Russian Revolution"). I had remembered her voice as heavy and dark as the Volga and always hovering near a full-stop, but it wasn't. I listened to the old taped interview again and discovered her richly accented voice bubbling like a turgid south-Russian river during the spring thaw. She was also very generous, in a real motherly Russian way. I was asked to stay for dinner, just she, her cook and I. The large dining-room table was truly laden. Just for me. You name it: caviar, lox, the works, it was all there. "Chust eattt . . . eet eze all forr eu-you. . . ." Olga kept bringing out sour cream and slicing meats and breads and putting them on plates; she talked about Joe (Von Sternberg) and her second husband (Richard Davis, the film producer and distributor, who started a whole chain of art cinemas in New York back in the '50s); she talked of the past, and of *Freaks,* and of all the people who were in it, how she was terrified and then she met them and they loved her. . . .

As I say, there are different sorts of Russians, but her sort makes you suffer through all the rest. After the orgy, there's balalaika and tears and regrets and snoring sleep, and the snow and the people in it sobering up, laughing like the howling wind. Olga was one of these.

OB: She [Pola Negri] was very jealous. Everybody was terribly jealous. Of each other. Of me. Because I didn't know anything. I came from Russia and I spoke not English and it was terrible. Why am I here? Why am I there? I am

Olga Baclanova, photographed by E. R. Richee (Paramount), 1928

only an extra, I am nothing. But they are very jealous of me, I don't know why. All those stars. Psheuww.

JK: But at that time at Paramount there was Pola, and Dagmar Godowsky and Jetta Goudal. . . .

OB: Jetta Goudal I don't know. Godowsky is a big, fat woman.

JK: She is now, but she was thin then. And Nita Naldi, all at Paramount.

OB: And now I tell you how it happened. I was at Paramount, I work twice, three times, and then I have to go back to Russia. So Selznick (Myron, the agent, David's brother) tells me, why don't you get married? They wanted to sign me to a contract, but I said, I can*not*. Because I have to go to Russia. And then I met my husband—that was the Red actor Nicholas Sussanyan. He was a very handsome man, he wasn't talented at all but very handsome, very tall. If I show you pictures of him, you go crazy. And he was there like extra, so I marry him. Because we went together and he fell in love with me and he had a son . . . that after, after I married Sussanyan, he had son who wanted to make love to me. . . .

JK: The son of your first husband! Oh, well . . . but you were discovered in a play at the Moscow Art Theater.

OB: I vas the youngest in Moscow Art Theater. I am the first one that sang in *Périchole, Madame Angot, Lysistrata* and *Carmencita* in Moscow Art Theater. It was musical studio in Moscow Art Theater. And my mother and father—well, my father died during the Revolution, but they would never allow me to do nothing, only if I go to Moscow Art Theater, and they have examination and they took each year three girls and three boys. There was 200 people there. They say, "*If* they take you as pupil at Moscow Art Theater, I will allow you, but nothing else." But I was so crazy, I wanted to sing, so I went and I was one of the three. And then Nemirovich-Danchenko started to get very, very interested in me. He says, "That's the most talented girl." Excuse me I say this, it's all gone now. "That's the most talented girl we ever have in the theater." So he got in love with me. And he taught me and I don't know what he did. He say, "Can you sing?" And my mother had beautiful voice, she sang in concerts sometimes, so I say, "I love to sing, but I never sing in my life." He say, "I take you to the teacher. If the teacher tells me that you have good voice, then I tell you what I am going to do with you." So I went to the teacher and I was so shy that I couldn't sing, you know, but I sing and the teacher say, "She has good voice. If she is going to do something with her voice, I tell you that she can sing." So Nemirovich-Danchenko ask her, "Tell me, please, how long she got?" "I tell you, I think she's very talented, so in two months she is going to sing." And he says, "I want to put her with soldiers in a new production of *Carmencita*. Do you think she can sing?" She say, "I don't know, but I think she is very talented."

So I study and study and study about six, seven weeks, and then they tell me that I am going to play in *Madame Angot*. That is the first operetta that came to the Moscow Art Theater during the Bolsheviks. And it was a very big success, and I sing it about twenty-five times. One day it [the Moscow Art Theater] was dramatic, then the other day . . . usually it was only dramatic, but during the Bolsheviks they open with musical studio too, so one day it was a play and the other day I sang. So I sang *Madame Angot* twenty-five times, and Nemirovich is cross with me and he always say I am creation of Nemirovich-Danchenko, and he was jealous of me and he was about sixty-eight years old then. And after about twenty-five times he brought me flowers, he brought me candy. I start in *Madame Angot* only from the second act, and I am told, "Don't move." They open curtain, everybody applauds, and Komisarjevsky, he was head of the theater,* he came out onstage and everybody got up and he start to make speech. And he say, "We are going to give great, great award, and a ticket for Conservatory for the best one that is here." And you know who it is? "Olga Baclanova." I got so fright I nearly cried. The whole theater start to yell, to applaud. I got an apartment. Well, the Communists take everything from my father, we had a house, everything they took. So I got an apartment. I have to go every second week to have a concert in Kremlin. Gertsa was there; Gertsa dance, I sing.

JK: Did you meet people like Lenin as well?

OB: Lenin, no. Lunacharsky, Inokitsky, they sit there every day at *Madame Angot*. They give me apartment, I didn't have to pay anything, because I am creation of Revolution. Everybody was sitting there all the time. And then they say we must show that Moscow Art Theater abroad. We have to sign in Kremlin a paper that in four months I have to be back. Now, I was the only one. My brother, who is now in Florida, he was an officer. He was arrested. He nearly was killed. By the Bolsheviks. And there was somebody from Ukraine took him out. He is now married and has son and lives in Florida. I have son and husband here. Big. I have three grandchildren: four, five, six.

JK: Tell me, going on to Hollywood, when you arrived there . . .

OB: Not one word of English could I speak. When I come here, not one word. Maurice Gest had brought the musical studio here from Moscow.† Musical studio went away after four or five months, and he said, "Stay here." He was a little bit crazy about me. "I think you have a possibility in Hollywood." I say, "Thank you, but they tell me I can leave country for five, six months, so

---

*Komisarjevsky was founder and director of one of the most brilliant little theaters of Moscow. He went to the US in 1923 to work for the Theatre Guild and then went to England to live, where he married the young Peggy Ashcroft.

†This was in 1925. Olga's acting was the talk of New York. Said *Vanity Fair* of her Carmencita, "She was the most Russian of gypsies and probably the most magnetic actress who has appeared on Broadway in recent years."

no more." He say, "I am going to Russians and I will see." So he come back and he say, "You can stay six months more." And he give me apartment and he tell me, "You study English." Because I speak French, German, Russian. And every day I study and study and study . . . for a week and a half. Then I get telegram from Maurice Gest. It says, "Tomorrow morning you are going to my sister to Hollywood to make a test." United Artists.

I went there with his sister and I make a test. I spoke blah-blah English. It was silent film, but I had to talk to somebody. I was there, in *The Dove* [UA, 1928], but I was an extra. Then they wanted to make a close-up of me, and Norma Talmadge did not allow it. "No, no, no, not Baclanova. Not Baclanova." You don't know how it was there. All the men were very helpful. All the women . . . By the way, I play one with Pola Negri [*Three Sinners*, 1928], she was Polish, and she had that Prince Mdivani, and he came and sat with me, so she was angry. "Baclanova, you go out," she say. She spoke to me in Russian. I didn't say a word. Then they give me a masseur, a man. Then, little by little I start to play here, and other studios, and then I bought a house, and I got a contract at Paramount.*

I never even thought that I am a star. I was in *Street of Sin* with Jannings. He shouted in German, "I will not play with her!" Because when the picture came out, there were big signs: "Not Jannings but Baclanova is the star." That was in Chicago, that was all over America here. And he say, "*Ich spiele nicht, spiele nicht*" [I don't play, don't play]. Stiller started out directing it, but Von Sternberg finished it. Stiller was crazy about Greta Garbo. He was her lover. She came with him, you know. She always say, "Hello, Olga. How are you?" [Olga imitates a deep voice.] And at Metro-Goldwyn, where I make some pictures,† her dressing room was near me.

JK: Did you enjoy working on *The Man Who Laughs* with Conrad Veidt? [Veidt had particularly asked for Olga to play the licentious Duchess.]

OB: I was crazy about him. He was crazy about me too.

JK: What do you remember most about that time if somebody asks you about working in silent films?

OB: I was happy they were silent. There were some love scenes there like hell. They gave me all the sex, sex, sex. . . . There is one picture of me where I am lying down on the bed, I am in black chemise made from lace, and Conrad Veidt comes . . . Oh, I like that picture very much.

JK: Did you enjoy working in movies?

OB: I did, because they pay very good, first. Second, I didn't care what I played. I liked it because I am an artist. I am born artist. I just study my part,

---

*Olga then appeared in picture after picture with outstanding and repeated success.
†These included *The Great Lover, Downstairs* and *Freaks*.

and when I start to play in talkies, I have very good memory. I memorize very quick, I work very good. I'm crazy about the theater. Absolutely magical. I like all of it. And I sing very much in clubs. I sing at the Algonquin when I play opera star in *Claudia.** Until I marry my husband, Richard Davis, and he does not allow me to sing anymore.

JK: Can you tell me about Von Sternberg?

OB: I don't say anything bad about him. He is very nice. I had some fights with him. On artistic points. And maybe he was absolutely right. He say he wants it that way, and I say I don't feel it. He say, "I don't care what you feel, you do what I tell you." So I did it, but I still like him. And I met him after that many, many times and I kissed him and he kissed me, and we were very good friends. I liked nearly everybody. I never hate anybody. I don't care if they dislike me. I never show them that I dislike them. I always say, "She's a very good actress." If she doesn't like me, she doesn't like me. I am very sincere. I will say she is a wonderful actress even if she insults me. I like very much Greta Garbo. I like now, oh, I forget all the names. There are so many. Dietrich I don't know at all. I played on the same set with her.† She play something with the trains [*Shanghai Express*] and I was on the set. And I see her and I say, "What a beautiful woman." She was with Von Sternberg.

JK: Why were you always cast as the evil woman?

OB: I don't know why. They decided that I have a temperament. I was very happy. Everything that I played I was happy. And everything that I played I wanted to do everything how I feel. And I studied everything. In a silent picture we still have to know what's going on.

JK: Did you go out much in those days?

OB: No. There is not time to go out when you make a picture. It is no good. I never was in the scandals. Six in the morning I got my car. And I went to the studio. And the man make up my makeup. And I study my script. You know, everything that was written, we talk. I didn't have any problems when sound came in, my accent didn't matter. Now they like even more an accent. I started to talk English very, very quick. I know four languages anyhow.

JK: Well, after *Cheer Up and Smile,* your most famous talkie was *Freaks*. How did you get that part?

OB: *Freaks* is at the Museum of Modern Art here. And it is showing all the time. That was the director that died now. Tod Browning. I loved him. He say, "I want to make a picture with you, Olga Baclanova." It was done at MGM, I think. "And you speak English, but I don't care *how* you speak

*She played the part in *Claudia* both onstage and in the film version (20th Century–Fox, 1943).
†Olga was making *The Billion Dollar Scandal* at Paramount that year.

English. You read that script and see if you like it or not." I said I like it.
"Now I show you with whom you are going to play. But don't faint." I say,
"Why should I faint?" So he takes me and shows me all the freaks there. First
I meet the midget and he adores me because we speak German and he's from
Germany. Then he shows me a girl that's like an orangutan; then a man who
has a head but no legs, no nothing, just a head and a body like an egg. Then
he shows me a boy who walks on his hands because he was born without
feet. He shows me little by little and I could not look, I wanted to faint. I
wanted to cry when I saw them. They have such nice faces, but it is so
terrible. They are so poor, you know. Now, after we start that picture, I like
them all so much. He takes me and say, you know, "Be brave, and don't faint
like the first time I show you. You have to work with them." [Her dog, a freak
in its own right, is growling. He's been doing that a lot. By the time he is
quiet, the train of thought has been broken. We move on.]

JK: I wish you'd come to England.

OB: I *cannot* on account of my dog. My husband goes every year there.

JK: Well, you've heard of the story of Mrs. Patrick Campbell? She had a dog
and she was living in America. And they told her she couldn't go to England
with the dog. So she hid the dog in her dress because she had very great
bosoms.

OB: This is very dangerous, you know. Because I know that is how dogs die.*

JK: But you were telling me about *Freaks*.

OB: I was working in black tights because I was the Queen of the Air. And
white here [she gestures to different parts of her anatomy], white with black.
Now, they started to love me so much, the midgets, they were just crazy about
me, and I was crazy about him. Because in the story the midget was a husband of mine and I married him because he was rich. I have forgotten his
name, Max or something, he was German, and he was thirty years old. And
I make him jump on my lap, and I treat him like a baby. But always he say
to me, "You be surprised!" [She laughs and says,] "Okay, you surprise me."
And I went with my husband to the circus when the circus was here much
later, and they say the midgets are downstairs, and I go down and they shout,
"Baclanova! Baclanova!" And they were just the same as when I make the
picture. But I tell you something else. There was a freak, half-man and half-
woman and half-gorilla sitting there. And she had always said, "Oh, Olga,
you are so beautiful, and your blue eyes . . ." And she talked to me all the
time and she said, "I tell you a very funny story about me." She say that her
husband always play the part of a woman, he was always dressed as a
woman. "I always play the part of a man," she say, "and we fall in love." You

---

*When Olga's dog died, stories have it, she hid him in one of her drawers. Olga was growing
strange then.

understand that? He was always like a woman, and she was always like a man. They fell in love and they married. And she says, "I was afraid when I heard that he was a man; I thought that my husband was a . . ." But she got married and she got pregnant and she look at me all the time and she say, "Miss Baclanova, I just want my child to have eyes like you. Excuse me, I just look at you all the time because I adore you and I want my child to have eyes like you." So she was with me the whole time through the picture. So when we finish, I give her my address and I tell her, "You write to me when you have the baby. You write me for sure!" So in two months I get the letter. I open it up and it say, "My dear Miss Baclanova, I'm happy, happy. I have a baby and this is a girl and she is like you exact." And I wrote her and I say, "I am so happy."

You know, I was sorry for all these people. There was a man who didn't have any arms or legs at all. He was like a bird, man-bird, walked in gloves. He was so handsome. And, you know, he looked at me all the time and I was so 'fraid of him, you know. And after, they tell me that he is crazy about me. And when I am in the circus ring, he put his head down like this and look at me all the time. And I always see that beautiful face, black hair, and he look at me all the time. It was like he hypnotized me. I got so fright . . . and when we finish that picture, he came and he gave me a present. And you know what?—he did it himself. He make a circus ring and he make it from matches . . . I don't know how he make it. It was like the circus we had, all the chairs we had, all about the circus like we had, and he say, "I make it in your honor." Can you imagine that?

It was very, very difficult first time. Every night I felt that I am sick. Because I couldn't look at them. And then I was so sorry for them. That I just couldn't . . . it hurt me like a human being. How lucky I was. But after that, I started to be used to them. But this one who was like a monkey, she go crazy sometimes and start yelling like a monkey; she tore everything and they put her in the closet and close the door. But she was half human being and half monkey.

JK: When I saw the film, what came across was this terrific sympathy and understanding that Tod Browning had, because he made you, a beautiful, normal woman, the evil one, and he showed them as they were—people, human beings, very sympathetic, and it came across. . . . Well, going to any other film after that surely must be trivial, because this must have been one of the most profound things in your life.

OB: This was a very good film, I like it very much. [Olga brings out a cache of pictures of her from the film.] When they offer it to me, I say, "If you think I can play it, I will."

JK: After 1943, after *Claudia,* in which you played the part you played on Broadway, you gave up films. You got married to Mr. Davis and that was that?

OB: After that, I was in nightclubs. My husband is a producer. He is owner of the Fine Arts Theater, and now, because he has to go to Europe to make a picture, he has to rent that theater. I am vice-president of the theater. I am still here. I don't go to the movies. I go only to our theater. Or I go to the opening. The opening of every new picture we show, that's all.

JK: I was going to ask what stars today had the excitement of people when you were a star.

OB: I don't think I was a star. I never believe it that I was a star. But I tell you, I don't see anybody better than I saw in Hollywood when I was there. No. Some of them were so good, I was ashamed. I thought I was rotten.

JK: How was John Gilbert to work with? In *Downstairs* [MGM, 1932]?

OB: I thought he was wonderful. He was crazy for that girl Virginia Bruce. I don't know why he died. Suicide or something, but everyone was crying when he died. He had a sex appeal. Terrific. No, his voice, his voice, no, but himself was wonderful. He was really very nice. . . . Garbo is a very good friend. I saw her when I was singing at all the clubs. She came to hear me. She was still in that hat, like that [she mimics a slouch hat]. Garbo was very sick. Very sick woman. I don't know why, but she was sick. . . . I like very many people in Hollywood. I forget every name. Conrad Veidt was wonderful. Adolphe Menjou was very good friend of mine. He was so-so as an actor, but he was very nice. And wonderful personality. Gary Cooper, wonderful. I'm just crazy about him. I saw him before he died, in Cannes. He is wonderful.

JK: Another film you made, *A Dangerous Woman*. Does that strike a bell?

OB: With who?

JK: With you.

OB: Who played it?

JK: You did.

OB: Who else?

JK: I don't know.

OB: I don't remember. . . . I go only to the studio. The weather was wonderful, the people are very nice to me and I was very happy to be in Hollywood. Very happy.

One evening at one of those tributes to Hollywood's yesteryears, this one at the Lincoln Center Library, writer-director Joseph L. Mankiewicz came on to deliver the opening speech. What the show was about and what he said about the people being honored doesn't matter now.* Mankiewicz, as acerbic as ever, started by reminiscing about the time he first arrived in Hollywood, a kid in his teens, wet behind the ears, and how, first thing there, his older brother, Herman, took him to a party at the home of a famous director. He arrived, walked in, and there was every name in town—writers, directors, poets, painters. But most important, and you could tell it from the way he savored it, these women, these stars—and he paused to heighten the effect, for Mankiewicz was a famed womanizer with a string of glamorous conquests. "And," he lowered his voice so we had to strain our ears, "there was Olga Baclanova." He allowed that to sink in before continuing.

1964

*Mankiewicz gave the speech at the DeMille Dynasty exhibition, April 24, 1984.

Dagmar Godowsky, photographed by C. S. Bull (Goldwyn Pictures), 1923

DAGMAR GODOWSKY

MORE THAN ANYTHING ELSE about Dagmar, more even than her ripe, billowing fatness, the first thing you noticed were her eyes. They were small, almond-shaped, with one pencil-sharp black line on the upper lid and one just underneath, so that when she smiled, which was often, they completely disappeared and looked like one line drawn across her face. Set carefully between large, round cheeks and the richly braided jet-black coronet of hair that had to be a wig but looked like a regal appendage to increase her stature, they twinkled, they glittered and they never missed a trick. She liked to give the appearance of being slow, of good-natured ambling, with much cheerful sighing and playful wheezing at the weight of age, but those eyes moved fast. She'd still be shaking hands in the doorway and enthusing about a concert the night before, all the time that those eyes sized up the room, the people in it and the best spot to sit, and never far from the food or the center of interest. She didn't have to take the center spot, it came to her, but if the guest of honor was other than herself, she made no attempt at upstaging, like one who has seen and known all of the world's great and can afford to stand out of the light—which of course only made her more interesting and inevitably brought the star of the evening into her orbit. Dagmar was to party-going what Perle Mesta had been to party-giving.

People who had never seen her before felt that they knew her—she looked so much like one of those people you've always heard about, or read about in published diaries, or seen in films about old-time films like *Singin' in the Rain* or *Has Anybody Seen My Gal?* that signaled their period and their atmosphere. Youthful copies of Dagmar—silent-film vamps, the long cigarette-holders, the outrageous spider-web costumes, scarlet lips the only color in otherwise ghostly white faces and eyes like Dagmar's eyes—were posing, they were copies.

Dagmar was born in Vilna, Lithuania, in the vicinity of 1897, so she must already have been sixty-seven years older when Kevin Brownlow was glad to introduce me to her as an old silent star I should interview. She'd been resident in America since her early teens, when her father, Leopold Godowsky, one of the world-famous pianists so numerous at the turn of the century, brought his family to the land of social-climbing opportunity, but until she died she kept her accent as thick as her ankles became. Her father, from whom his children got their passionate love for music and musicians, was apparently as shrewd as he was gifted, and possessed a formidable wit. The night of the violin prodigy Jascha Heifetz' spectacular debut at the Imperial Opera House in Vienna, Godowsky shared a box with a perspiring violinist who turned to him and complained about how hot it was. "Not for us pianists," said Godowsky. His son inherited the father's shrewdness, becoming part-owner of Eastman Kodak. Dagmar got the wit.

At some party Dagmar was regaling, a competitive matron who felt her money was more than a match for Dagmar's personality turned to her and frostily asked, "And how many husbands have you had, Miss Godowsky?" to which Daggie replied, "Two of my own, dollink, and most of my friends'." It became much quoted, probably by none more often than by the perpetrator. She didn't say anything else quite that memorable, but she made everything else she said sound as if she thought it was. She laughed at everything she said that was supposed to be funny, smiling before the story began, laughing to punctuate it as it unfolded and adding several flourishing rolls of chuckles to let you know it was over, give you time to catch on or just bob along. Her eyes twinkled, her cheeks dimpled, her jowls shook with amazement at her own experiences.

She was by nature and, later, necessity (she had known her share of lean years) a magical spinner of tales, for which her meager career on camera in silent films was an endless source of fabulous tales. Not unlike her borscht, which seemed never to grow less no matter how many servings she took from it. Rarely was the silent screen so voluble. She didn't co-star with everybody— two films with Rudolph Valentino ("I *introduced* Valentino. Nobody else. I don't care who discovered him, *I* introduced him!") and one film with Lon Chaney before he'd become known as the Man of a Thousand Faces. He taught her makeup, she said. I don't believe that one. There was also a film with the imperious Russian-born actress Alla Nazimova. Dagmar, a Lithuanian to her bones, was not fond of Russians, but Alla was one of the greatest stars in the firmament, and genius could always overcome Dagmar's prejudice.

Dagmar had also been married to a popular leading male star of the day, Frank Mayo, and she was in a few other films without ever attaining a prominent position. I think that was because Dagmar preferred people and parties to making movies. Movies were a means of making money easily, but she was never serious enough about them. But she did know everyone. She didn't have to tell you that in so many words; it was more like "Garbo was two or three times a week." Or, "Was lunch that day with Heifetz or Rubinstein?" she'd say, looking at you as if you might have the answer. She didn't make it sound like a big deal; consummate pro that she was, she asked the question and left *you* to make the deal. She didn't just know everyone there was to know in Hollywood in the ten years she lived there, but in New York, in Salzburg (every year, except for the war, there were the festivals), in London—"I must make a phone call; I'm supposed to be having dinner with Getty, but I'd rather have dinner with your friends," and this old warhorse would dimple like a child. "I've known him forever. You wouldn't like him; he's very boring," smiling, and nodding, and exclaiming appreciatively about the smells from the kitchen, with the phone to her ear; then suddenly you'd hear a high, reedy old voice piping up loudly from the other end of the line, as people did when the telephone was still a new invention and they shouted to convince themselves it worked, and she and Getty, who had known each other forever, would sort out the traveling arrangements to bring Dagmar from her hotel to his estate. "He's so stingy," Daggie would throw in as an aside with her hand on the mouthpiece and her eyes screwed up as if she were taking shorthand notes. "Small eyes have big ears," as Mr. Chan might say. They knew her in Paris. Vienna had changed too much. "It's so sad. Everybody is so old." By now she was into her seventies. When she knew Vienna, she had been a little girl, little enough to sit in an emperor's lap while her father played for him. Because people like to hear about big stars, the giants of finance, the painters, musicians and writers who had made their mark on the century from someone with firsthand knowledge, Dagmar talked about them to strangers as if they were old intimates; she had a way of telling stories as if they were naughty secrets while you'd be refilling her plate as silently as possible so as not to lose a syllable, and it wouldn't be till later that you realized she had told you nothing new, just with an accent.

Her amusing, anecdotal autobiography, *First Person Plural,* published in 1959, had scored quite a success for a book by a woman not widely familiar to the general public. If her facts were shaky and some of the most personal bits had to be left out due to the laws of libel, her ability to conjure up atmosphere, places and people was wonderful. She gave her readers what they wanted and expected from someone who had been a vamp when movies were young and silents were golden.

Her apartment was in the fashionable block on West 57th—the man downstairs to check you out before letting you in, the one in the elevator discreetly looking you over while taking you up and pointing you in the right direction. The place looked like champagne and caviar in the lobby, but the corridors were heavy with sauerkraut and kitty litter. Dagmar, swathed in flowing things, her turban off but her hair up, led me in, preparing me straight off for a view suited to a rummage sale, and swept my attention to the view outside her window. That's why she liked the apartment heaped with little pictures, knickknacks from a hundred different trips, and pointed to a place for the tape recorder only she could see beneath the pile of mantillas and silk scarves and books. How Dagmar found anything—well, she often did say that she couldn't find anything except for her makeup, which she carried in the bag always close to her. I avoided the kitchen. For one thing, I might have been tempted to clean up for her; for another, what you don't know won't upset you when you eat it.

JK: With the success of your book . . .

DG: I can't remember the title . . . it's the *worst*! I wanted to call it *Two Husbands Ago*, and Viking didn't like it, and then it got so late that the publishing date came up and we still didn't have a title. I didn't like the other one, *First Person Plural*, and I said so. I just got talked out of it.

    . . . If I'd been younger, I wouldn't have experienced those marvelous times when father was Head of Music, Austria-Hungary. There aren't many emperors whose lap you can sit on. Ohhhh, I loved him, old Franz Josef. . . .

JK: From Emperor to Valentino.* How did you get into movies?

DG: I studied acting. I was a protégée of David Belasco, who was one of the greats, and I studied at the American Academy. I remember when Mr. Belasco asked me into his office and asked me to stand on a block of something and made me turn around and I thought: "That's the way they buy a horse!" I was so shocked. But I studied there . . . and I played Ibsen at the Lyceum Theater. Oh, I was awful! I was *awful*!

    Then I went to Hollywood. Father had to go to Hollywood because he had master classes there, and I didn't think very much about movies . . . but Father's great friend was Chaplin. I was *dying* to see a film studio and he took us there. It was terribly confused, but it was much nicer than it is today. Now it's a factory—then it was cozy and fun. I don't think I was one hour on the lot when a woman, who was the casting director, said: "There she is!" This was at Universal . . . and I played opposite Art Acord.† I was a dance-hall girl with a rose in my mouth, and I had to dance. There were a lot of Western men and horses. Oh, it was terrific! That was the *first* picture I ever made. I can't remember the title, and the working title is usually different. That was my beginning, and I must say I enjoyed it very much.

    I didn't play vamps at first. I played opposite Lon Chaney in a film where I started out as a very young girl . . . in fact, I must have been twelve . . . and I was supposed to be eighty when I was dying, and Lon Chaney used to make me up . . . you know, aging. He was marvelous at that, and he was very nice. We had gone on location to Yosemite Valley, and I had a chaperone. She was so strict. I had this woman with me. But anyway, after we were there for quite a few months . . . it was one of those long *super* things [*The Trap*, 1922?] . . . and when we were all finished with the picture, Lon Chaney asked me to come and talk to him. When I went to see him, he had the whole cast around him and he said: "I want to say this in front of everyone. When you were cast opposite me, ohhhh, I didn't like it at all. I said: 'Dagmar Godowsky? No, no, no.'" Anyway, he spoke rather unkindly of me . . . but he wanted to say, in front of the cast now, that he got to love me. He said

---

* A salacious biography about the actor, *Valentino*, by Irving Shulman, had just been published and was being talked about.
† Acord was a star in Western pictures.

I was a real trouper. And I was so proud, touched, so touched. Wasn't that nice?

JK: Yes. I know Joan Crawford was saying that when she worked with him on *The Unknown,* she learned more about self-discipline from him than anyone.

DG: Well, I don't doubt it, excepting that I could never learn discipline. But he was wonderful with me. And he never took a day off. When he wasn't working, he was practicing different makeups. I played the ingenue with him— that's why I said that I wasn't always the vamp when I started.

JK: You were part of all that world, all those people. Did you read the Mae Murray biography, *The Self-Enchanted*?

DG: I don't think very much of it is true. No, I didn't like the book at all. Mine is the only honest one. But the trouble is you can't write everything, you see . . . many of the things I wrote have been taken out. There were so many lawyers, and they were always having conferences, saying: "You must take this out and that out because the great-grandson is living." It was ridiculous. For instance, I wasn't allowed to say that someone whom I mentioned quite a bit in the book had tuberculosis. Not permitted. Not allowed. This was Igor Stravinsky, and I shouldn't say it now either!

JK: You knew Stravinsky well?

DG: I did *more* than know him! I looked after him all the time he was sick. He was my great love. He was going to marry me. Then he got well and he married that other woman. [Daggie sighed—fate wasn't always kind.] So many things were taken out. It got so the only person that I could be sued by was myself!

Hollywood was an exciting place then, that is why I was so lucky. I was always in places where it just *happened* to be the height of excitement. Vienna—the end. It was beautiful. Then Paris. Ohhhh, Paris was divine . . . nothing like it now. This was in the '30s; it was wonderful.

JK: You knew Valentino very well?

DG: Oh, very well. He asked me to help him with his divorce from Jean Acker. He called me. He wanted me to be a witness at his wedding. But I was out that night. When I came back I found a message, and then he called me the next morning and said: "Dagmar, I've married Jean Acker last night, that's why I called. I wanted you to be the witness . . . but the marriage is over. She left me!" It was the quickest marriage ever! I had met Valentino in New York the first time I had been at a nightclub, with Mike Barrington and Enrico Caruso. Caruso knew him, of course, Italian-Italian, and so introduced him to us. He was then dancing, his name was still Guglielmi then. So when I went to Hollywood and I was an actress in a picture with Metro, and the head of Metro gave a dinner party at the Ship's Café, with May Allison and Jean

Acker, a lovely dinner, and suddenly who comes across the dance floor and greets me most effusively and was happy to see me because I was a face he knew from New York, was Mr. Valentino, who'd changed his name in the meantime. Just when I wanted to introduce him to Madame Nazimova,* she put her head down and wouldn't accept the introduction . . . and all the others followed. Wasn't that terrible? I was so shocked. And when he went to leave, she said: "How *dare* you introduce that unprincipled cur to me?" And that was because he had been mixed up . . . well, mentioned in a horrible society murder case. But he had had nothing to do with it what*so*ever. The woman had been in love with him; he wasn't in love with her. It was very unfair of Nazimova.

JK: I've heard that Mae Murray discovered him and put him in one of her films, and Dorothy Gish, and that Nazimova discovered him, because later on he made *Camille* with her, and that's how he met Natacha, who was working very closely with Nazimova at the time.

DG: Nazimova discovered him, but *met* him through me.

JK: And that fabulous screenwriter June Mathis, who put him in *The Four Horsemen of the Apocalypse,* was supposed to have discovered him.

DG: Nobody discovered him, but *I* introduced him, and there is no doubt about it, no matter what anyone says. I liked him, and he was very, very poor. A very charming, very well-mannered, rather shy man . . . and I could never understand his appeal. Could you? But one day I was at the Famous Players–Lasky, and Jascha Heifetz had returned from Australia with his sisters and his accompanist, Samuel Chotzinoff, the man who became head of the music at NBC, and Rudy passed me and said "Hello" and was walking down a spiral staircase when the two Heifetz sisters swooned and said: "Ooohh, who's that, who's that? Why, he's the most beautiful thing." I said: "Would you like to meet him?" and I said: "Rudy, come back here." I remember them being surprised. I thought what an amazing thing, he must have a terrific impact. That was the first time I was conscious of it . . . *never* before.

JK: How did Pola Negri fit into the scene? She really carried on something terrible all across America when he died.

DG: I don't know anything about it, dear. Rudy was my friend. I introduced him.

JK: You made two films with him?

DG: Yes—but, you see, the thing is this: I remember asking Rudy to my house, and I had invited Nazimova, and I had invited Natacha Rambova. I had to

---

*Nazimova was very high-hat, especially when it came to men.

work late that night, and I asked my mother to sort of take over until I came home . . . and when I came home, they had all met.

JK: You introduced him to all the wrong women in his life.

DG: Well, I don't know. I think maybe Rudy would *only* have met the wrong women . . . he was so sensitive. I haven't seen Jean Acker in very many years, but she had great charm. Of course, Natacha is a great personality.

JK: She dominated him.

I was trying to get Dagmar to talk about the emotion-charged relationships Nazimova had had with Jean Acker and, subsequently, Natacha Rambova, an exotic American heiress, born Winifred Shaunessy Hudnut, who'd gone to Europe to study ballet and design and came back with an exotic name and a lot of original ideas. It was known, apparently to everyone except Valentino, that Acker married Rudy to spite Alla, who had a thriving lesbian circle and had discarded Jean when she got involved with Natacha. The marriage to Jean lasted a day, but not the night. Valentino, who seemed fatally attracted to women who didn't want him instead of those who did, was clearly not turned off by Nazimova's refusal to meet him when Dagmar tried to introduce them. Instead, he even ended up playing Armand to her Camille in the film designed by Natacha. Having married one of Alla's girlfriends, he then fell in love with and married the even more mercurial, strong-willed Natacha. They looked striking together. Natacha then imposed her ideas for his career on him and all around him. It led to his falling out with his studio, Paramount, who were furious at her creative interference not only over the script, but over the sets, the costumes and everything else on his films for them. While he was in dispute with the studio and not earning any money, he and Natacha, both trained dancers, put together an act in which they tangoed to enormous acclaim across the vaudeville circuit, raking in so much money that the studio, seeing his star undimmed, came to terms. But his marriage to Natacha foundered when the films she controlled, like the costly and ravishingly beautiful *Monsieur Beaucaire,* failed. By the time he made his second film with Dagmar, Natacha was kept off his sets.

DG: When I made that picture with him here in New York, *The Sainted Devil,* I played the sainted devil. Nita Naldi* played a part in it, but I played the title role opposite him. She played a siren, I was the devil. I remember then that we always had two takes of each scene, one for the European consumption, for which he could make very much on-the-screen love to me . . . and the other for the American market, and Natacha was not allowed on the set. She was *barred* from the set. It was after they had all that trouble, and if he wanted to work, she couldn't come on the set. I don't know what she did . . .

---

*A rival vamp of the time and another crony of Alla's; she was really Irish, but adopted a name to suit her smoldering appearance.

but she was absolutely not on the set . . . which made it very much easier for us when we played those European love scenes. They were pretty hot. Compared to today, no. We were dressed. Rudy used to be . . . in the beginning he was such a lonely man. I used to give him a lift in my car to go up to the Universal company.* He would come and he loved cooking spaghetti; being an Italian, he was good at it. But what I remember, he was wonderfully kind. For instance, when I wanted to get a divorce, he went to his lawyer, Max Steuer, and he arranged everything for me. This was my divorce from Frank Mayo. He was very, very nice. I saw him the night before he was taken to the hospital, we were at the Colony restaurant. He wasn't a happy man. He was shy. He was a romanticist. He wasn't at all like the movies. He loved one woman, and that was Natacha . . . he really loved her.

Dagmar had earlier referred to Valentino's problems when he wanted to marry Natacha while his divorce from Jean wasn't yet final. Hollywood was going through its moral shake-up at this time, and Valentino and Natacha got caught up in the technicality that threatened to erupt around him. His studio was very worried. After all, Paramount, to whom he was under contract, was also the studio to whom Fatty Arbuckle had been under contract, to whom William Desmond Taylor and Mary Miles Minter were under contract, and for whom Wallace Reid had worked. The last thing that studio needed was one more scandal, no matter how innocent or how blameless the participants were. The finger was pointing at them and, having writ, just kept on writing and writing and writing. Jean was dragging her heels over the final decree, and Rudy, impatient to marry Natacha, slipped across the border to Mexico to marry her there, since Mexico would accept his divorce. Back in California, this smacked of bigamy.

DG: No, I don't think that was it at all—because, you see, Rudy and Natacha and Frank and I, we were married together, and it was I who told Rudy about getting married across the border, because I had been to see C. B. DeMille, and his lawyer, Neil McCarthy, was called in, and I was asking him about getting married to Frank. Though Frank had gotten a divorce, I didn't know when it would be final. He said that if we went across the border to Mexico we could get married. So that day I was in Santa Monica and I saw Rudy there, he had two beautiful big dogs, and I had quite a chat with him, and I said to him what McCarthy had told me to do. He was terribly excited and he called me that night and we decided to go to Mexico together. But Frank and I went to—what in the world was that place?—a little village, and Rudy and Natacha went to a little place next to it somewhere, and we both decided not to let the public know about our marriages.

Frank and I, with a friend of his and one of mine, went to Mexico and we found out that we had to have a health certificate, you couldn't get married

*Valentino was then playing supporting roles in films starring Carmel Myers and Mae Murray.

in Mexico unless you had it—so we got a health certificate and got married the next day. Well, we were taken all over the village, every bar was open, and when we were coming back to my parents' house, the garden was full of newspapermen and cameras . . . and here was our quiet entrance, we didn't want anyone to know about it! But Rudy couldn't contain himself when he got back before us. It was *he* who told it to the public—he told about our marriage too! There was a man running as District Attorney, his name was Woolwein . . . isn't it amazing that I remember this? Woolwein took Rudy's and my marriage as test cases. They said that we shouldn't have gotten married . . . I think the law then was nine months before you had your decree. I must say, maybe I was naïve, maybe I was so well protected by my parents. But I saw nothing wrong. So this thing happened and I got a note from the District Attorney to appear. Natacha got the same. Natacha left Rudy and went East. That's what she decided to do. I decided to stand by Frank. I didn't see why I should run away; after all, we had done nothing wrong.

JK: Jacqueline Logan said that you and Frank Mayo were one of the handsomest couples in Hollywood.

DG: I guess we were beautiful. He was amazingly good-looking. Amazingly. He was handsome, he and Wallace Reid. Anyway, what was I talking about? Oh, yes, so just before anything happened . . . we never got called, nothing happened . . . I went to McCarthy, but the DA never did anything . . . but Natacha left him.*

JK: It sounds mad, chaotic. . . . What was Chaplin like? He was forever marrying these very young girls, and you knew him very well?

DG: Yes. I met Chaplin the very first day I was in Hollywood. Chaplin. What can I say about him? You see, I've changed my opinion about him so much that I'm trying to recollect my feelings then. I feel completely differently about him than I do about Rudy because I was never emotionally involved with Rudy . . . whereas with Chaplin I was. I think Charlie was very fond of me, and I was very fond of him. But it was very difficult. My parents didn't approve. It was I who left and made a picture with my husband in the South Seas, and we were away for quite a while and we became involved. When I came back . . . no matter how much Chaplin called, I wasn't anymore to see him. And I remember, after I married Frank, Charlie would call me anyway. And when Frank was there, I would always say: "Oh, you have the wrong number!" Frank became so annoyed about it he went to the telephone company and said: "This has got to stop. All these wrong numbers. Something must be done about it." After I was divorced, in Paris, and then in Berlin, we would meet.

---

*Natacha came back. She and Rudy then married when everything had been cleared up.

But what was Charlie like? Peculiar. I don't think he was very popular in Hollywood, socially. He had his coterie of friends. But Charlie was amazingly talented, you know. The way he would act out little scenes . . . I don't know if I told you about the last time I was in Hollywood, he was there, and I broke my leg, I don't remember which one. But he was so strict with his children, it's amazing, and everything they do is wrong.

Dagmar was clucking over the fact that Charlie Chaplin's autobiography had come out and his first two wives got little space, with Mildred Harris, Wife #1, hardly any at all.

DG: She was very pretty, extremely pretty. She was the daughter of a wardrobe mistress. Charlie had seen quite a bit of her . . . and I'm sure with very much the consent of the mama.* I don't know her [the mother], but I do know that they went off on a trip across the state line. Well, one day Charlie called me and he was terribly upset. My family had moved to San Francisco and I was staying with friends, very rich, affluent people, and he called and said: "I want to see you immediately." He came over and Mr. and Mrs. Shein, my hosts, were delighted to meet Chaplin. He was so terribly upset . . . and he walked up and down and stayed till it got light, he was so desperately upset.

You can just about picture Dagmar, young, sloe-eyed, fetchingly dressed in black, standing inside the curtained window, looking out and watching the pacing Chaplin, suffering sympathetically on her own. This may be because while she spoke of it she would often look out of the window with a dreamy look and a philosophical sigh, and she had curtains over the windows in her apartment and I could imagine her standing there, gazing out, a pretty picture.

DG: He was saying: "What should I do?" He was telling me about Mildred. I remember that the last thing he decided on was that he would have to marry her. When he left, every step that he took, he would turn and tears would run down and he'd say: "I'm going to get married." For he thought he was in love with me.

JK: You seemed to be involved in a lot of other men's dramas.

DG: We had great publicity! We all believed everything we read about ourselves! And so we had to live up to it. I was the "greatest mistress" and I had to act it in life. It was a dream world. The people came and suddenly they had so much money—Charlie with his gold bathroom fixtures . . . and you had to go through three secretaries, and if you got to him, it was great luck! Little Mildred Harris did something that was so funny in those days. When she married Chaplin, she was really in love with Fairbanks. This was a whole "comedy of errors." It was the strangest thing. Well, anyway, it was a very short marriage. I think they had a child that died. I saw Charlie the day the

*Mildred, like Lita Grey later, was still under legal age when her romance with the comic began.

child died . . . I was being called always in an emotional crisis . . . I haven't seen him in quite a time, so I guess he hasn't been having any more problems. [She had a way of laughing as if to say "Aren't I terrible?" and she'd look as innocent as Buddha.] All this time I was working very hard. It wasn't work, it was play. It was play that I was being paid for—well, can one imagine anything nicer?

I was doing a film, and Rupert Hughes was the writer and director [*Souls for Sale,* 1923]. He had a son, Rush, who was very attractive, but I couldn't make Rush out very well, because . . . We were on location and we all lunched and dined together. Some days Rush would be so full of respect for his father: "Yes, Father, yes, Father." And other days he would call him every name. It was such a disrespectful thing. I couldn't make it out until I found out that Rupert was deaf in one ear, and it depended which side he sat on near his son!

I remember Florence Vidor.* I remember being at one of the big hotels with . . . who was it? Was it Heifetz? No . . . Artur Rubinstein it was. Florence was sitting at the next table and she looked very, very pretty, she was a beautiful woman . . . [Dagmar made "very pretty, very pretty" sound as if she were looking over the serving arrangements for a posh sit-down dinner with approval.] . . . and I introduced Artur to her, which was the first great musician she had ever met. Then she married Jascha, so she and Artur mustn't have gotten on that well . . . and I became known then as the Ambassadress of Music of Hollywood. Everybody called me that . . . because whoever came to town, of course, called me up and I entertained. My family didn't like me to go into pictures at all. They had to get used to it. They *never* went to my pictures. Only my brother . . . but my mother and father, never.

JK: You know, after seeing *Sunset Boulevard,* Mae Murray was supposed to have said, "We may have been crazy, but none of us were *that* crazy."

DG: But she was the craziest of them all. I'll never forget the party she gave, it was very, very swanky. At the end of the party the chef, with a big white hat, came in and demanded his money—it sort of took the glamour away. He was so annoyed that he had not gotten paid. Mae was *completely* mad. I remember Nazimova wanting to get off the train . . . in those days we used trains, five days—*five* days!—to come from New York to Hollywood, and she had bought a Rolls-Royce and wanted to get off the train in great style, as she was supposed to be the great star, and she was, and it cost her only $10,000 to bring the Rolls-Royce on the train. There were those sort of things.

Daggie opened a well-trained copy of Daniel Blum's *Pictorial History of the Silent Screen* to a picture of herself as a siren in *Altar Stairs* (it could also have

---

*The silent star, noted for her elegance and stylish presence in drawing-room comedies, who retired from films to marry Jascha Heifetz and never looked back.

been *The Temple Dancer,* and then it gets more confused, since she was calling it *Stronger Than Death*).

DG: I made a movie with Nazimova . . . *Stronger Than Death* [1920] it was called, and Charles Bryant [Mr. Nazimova] was the director, and I was the Temple Goddess. We had to learn Oriental dancing, and every morning before we went to work, Nazimova and I had a teacher who taught us a sort of seductive wiggling. It was for the temple, and we had a great time learning that.

JK: Nazimova was sort of the Garbo of her day, sort of a test run, wouldn't you say?

DG: They were *so* different. She was—oh, this is a bad word I'm going to use—she was Russian . . . *completely.* ["Russian" as she said it was a word meaning something black, purple, rotting and then some.] Was she beautiful? . . . She was remote. She was *extremely* intelligent. Extremely.

JK: Do you think Hollywood treated Nazimova well?

DG: Why do you ask if they treated her well?

JK: Because years later, long after the *Salome* fiasco, she was hard up and she was wanting to get back into films, to get a job . . .

DG: When that happened, that was a tragedy; and she told me that. I never knew about it. I had a little dinner at my house when I was married to Frank, and I had invited Nazimova and her husband, and Mae Murray and her husband, Robert Leonard. We were all going to the theater, and I had been at Universal that morning, and I liked very much the little office boy who got the appointments for the general manager, and I thought it would be nice if he would come too, and I asked him as I was going out. I said: "I cannot ask you to the theater because I haven't got enough tickets, but come afterwards and have supper with us." He was delighted. But when Mae Murray and Nazimova heard about it . . . "Office boys!" . . . they were *horrified.* And it happened to be Irving Thalberg. Well, it *seems* that Nazimova acted very badly in the way she treated him. He did not mention anything to me . . . we became *very close* friends; as a matter of fact, when he became general manager of Universal, I really could have had anything in the world I wanted, we were such close friends. I loved that boy. But Nazimova, when she was down and out and really had no money in the '30s, when he was at MGM, there was a part coming up that she wanted. It wasn't a leading part; it wasn't a star part. And she went up to see him—she told me this. He reminded her of that evening at my house when she completely and absolutely ignored him. It must have hurt him desperately because he wasn't a small person, that he couldn't forgive her that. And I was surprised that a man like Irving would carry that grudge . . . but I understand that that was at the beginning. Later, you know, she did make a picture at MGM with Irving's wife, Norma Shearer [*Escape,* 1940], but by that time Irving was dead.

JK: Didn't you also know Garbo?

DG: Ohhhhh, *very* well! What did she call herself? Oh, yes, she used to call herself Miss Green. I think that's what it was. I used to see her a great deal. She was very, very shy . . . terribly interested in astrology. . . . [She giggles.] Isn't it funny, you remember certain habits of people. What they liked to eat. She liked—what is it, that Southern vegetable? . . . Stravinsky loved pistachio ice cream. I can't see pistachio ice cream without thinking of Stravinsky, and . . . and Garbo loved *okra*! She could eat that every day. She loved it. We used to see each other a great deal when she saw Gaylord Hauser, a very old friend of mine, we were at dinner two or three times a week. I was a whole year on the radio with Gaylord Hauser when he had a program. . . . I think she is very shy . . . and she has a very hard time with insomnia. So she usually goes home rather early to prepare to be able to sleep as much as she can.

JK: But if she were to come into the room, so much has been made of her beauty, what would you think?

DG: I wouldn't know what I think because I know her so well. She is very sweet in this respect that she could say: "Dagmar, you would be the most beautiful of them all if only you got thinner!" And she watches me eat and she always spoils my appetite, which is very good, because she says: "Oh, you mustn't eat this." That's when she does talk. When she begs me to get thin. She's very sweet in that respect. She is very interested in *art* and likes to browse around museums and galleries. I really couldn't tell you if she was intelligent. I wouldn't know. She talks *very* little about herself. Practically not at all. I think she's amazed at the success she has made . . . just as Valentino, were he still alive today, would not have believed that he is still a saga.

JK: Did they ever meet, Garbo and Valentino?

DG: I don't know if they met. She's only met a great many people recently. She didn't like to meet people. She likes the way we used to be together. She's a good listener. I never heard her talk very much. How intelligent she is? I don't know . . . but she's a very good listener.

JK: You left Hollywood and America and went to Germany because of a man and sort of gave up your career over here?

DG: I had a contract with Tobis.* The war stopped everything. I made a picture in London once for British-Gaumont. It was a tragedy. [She meant what hap-

---

*Tobis Kangfilm was one of the major film companies in Germany in the '30s before it was taken over by the state.

pened, not the film.] I love London like nothing in the world, and I was so
happy to go there. I was living in Paris, and I was asked to do a picture with
British-Gaumont. We started the film and in the middle of it I didn't get a
permit and so I never finished that picture. It was a talkie.

Oh, dear, I would just love it if they turned my book into a musical. I
went to hear a concert at Lincoln Center three days ago, and the little usher
who took my ticket said: "Miss Godowsky, my mother is in hospital and she
is reading your book, and she's so happy." Isn't that sweet? A little usher . . .
And it came out five years ago. I would love to work. I prefer work to anything.

JK: Do you have to work?

DG: Financially? I have enough to live on *un*comfortably.

Well, her standard of living did continue to include London, Paris, Salzburg,
Hollywood. She was almost eighty when she died, looking exactly as I had first
seen her, and still traveling, still attending first nights, art openings, and following around after the Russian pianist Sviatoslav Richter, whom she claimed as
her . . . well, not discovery exactly, but I think she said that she "introduced him."

1964

LOUISE
BROOKS

T HERE WERE TWO INTERVIEWS as such with Louise. Our first was back in
1965, my first year in New York. Hers was one of a list of phone numbers
I'd been given to call. She was already living in Rochester. I phoned her from
the office of the BBC. If she hung up (and I was told she might), I had other
numbers on the piece of paper before me.

"Hello?" The high, long, fluting voice full of curiosity for everything
soared out from the other end.

"Miss Brooks?" I asked with a note of hesitation that would allow for
rejection.

"Who's this?" the voice asked much more sharply.

"You don't know me . . ."

"Yeah." Curiosity had been replaced by flint-voiced suspicion.

"We have mutual friends."

"Oh, yeah? Who?" But she had thawed again, and when I mentioned one,
she laughed that smoke-cutting nightclub laugh of hers and said, "Ohhhh, are
you a friend of his? How is that cute little bastard?" It was said with bemused
affection; her suspicions were shelved.

Louise was instant and total. As I got to know her better, her moods fluc-
tuated with drink; her patience shortened; she'd snap when things got unneces-
sarily long-winded because uncertainty on my end suggested that I was really
dissembling. We talked a couple of times a week when I was in town, so we
got to know each other, but from the first moment she was honest and straightforward. It was too early in my life to appreciate that fully; my calling her was
not out of friendship or for the woman she was, but I used a friendship to
ingratiate myself with who she had been.

Even then Louise was already legendary in European film circles, a personality who provoked more interest and enthusiasm than many a better-known
survivor of the '20s. Anyone who ever doubted that a picture was worth a
thousand words should have been on the beaches of Cannes or Venice during
the film festivals in the '60s or on the Rue d'Ulm in Paris, outside the Cinémathèque's screening room, crowded with the people who would shape tomorrow's
opinions about movies old and new. When someone showed a photo of this

71

American "lost" star or mentioned having seen her in a film . . ."Ah, Louise Brooks. . . . *sí, oui, Ja,* yes, *bien sûr* . . ." And we'd go skiing on tangents launched by the name, by the collective memory, by the mystery that surrounded her electric screen presence and the unfathomable absence of her name from the history books. It was an excitement surrounding her that only grew deeper as her rediscovery was taking place, film by film, festival by festival.

American film circles were only just beginning to talk about her with some curiosity. But in the States she was still only one of many and not among the top names for revival. In America they still accepted Marion Davies as the lampooned pathetic character in Orson Welles' *Citizen Kane*. In Europe we knew better about that too. And Louise was "hot." That's the way it had been with Louise back in the '20s, when it was still the work she was doing rather than the work she had done that people were talking about.

Didn't you know that the Cyd Charisse character in *Singin' in the Rain* was modeled after her? You didn't? And didn't you know that French New Wave director Jean-Luc Godard's wife (the actress Anna Karina) was given her striking look for *Vivre sa Vie* as an homage to Louise? And Claudia Cardinale in an Italian film . . . And so on and so on. And of course, being very up on those things back when only a few were, I didn't miss the chance to see her in Howard Hawks' *A Girl in Every Port* and William Wellman's *Beggars of Life*. Ironically, although her present American reputation seems to be based solely on her appearance in the two G. W. Pabst films she made in Germany back in 1928, these films, though better known, were not the ones we first saw in England. It was the Hollywood films.

If anything, Louise is probably more striking in her American potboilers than in the German masterpieces, for in those she is Wedekind's Lulu and Pabst's Lulu, but in her Hollywood silents she is "our" Louise: pristine, prickly, fresh as a sudden summer shower, impersonal, riveting, spunky, even a little snarly. And because her parts couldn't contain all these qualities, and all her work was illuminated by her dancer's grace, we got Louise up there: the same Louise whom Pabst saw and knew could be his Lulu, but also a Louise who could have been a whole lot of other things, had it worked out. So okay, that's the Louise I called, and that's how she and I became friends.

We had talked a lot on the phone by the time I decided to record a telephone interview with her. My mistake was forgetting how long she and I usually talked once we got started, and doing the interview at the busiest part of the evening when the telephone circuits were needed for the New York–London link-up. Charles Wheeler's nightly report from the UN had to be rerouted all around my New York–Rochester connection because Louise was reading me a chapter from the story of her life and I couldn't hang up on her in the middle of it. She would never have understood it . . . not then.

We later had a falling out which had nothing to do with this fraught evening, but rather with promises exchanged of visits to be made that finally faltered on an idiotic lie. I said I'd come, this time for sure, to her apartment in

Louise Brooks, photographed by E. R. Richee (Paramount), 1929,
for *The Canary Murder Case*

Rochester. And then I put it off again. She'd stocked up for my arrival. When I knew I wasn't going to make it and couldn't put it off, I called with an excuse. To make it sound good, I told her my mother had broken her leg. Why my mother's broken leg should have prevented my flight to Louise is something I can't explain even now, and certainly it didn't hold with Louise, who unleashed her full bottle of verbal vitriol on me.

Why did I avoid the opportunity to finally meet a woman I'd been in contact with by phone and letters for more than a year? Somehow I was slightly daunted, afraid she might think me a fool when we were face to face; and I'd be up there in God-knows-where Rochester; and New York at that time was a city so full, there was so much, I just didn't want to leave. It was as simple and as selfish as that. After all, I had my interview with Louise on tape. And then, too, she used to drink in those days. I wasn't comfortable with drunks. They saw through you, or they clung too tight.

Ten years later, because of a show I'd mounted in London's Victoria and Albert Museum (about Hollywood's portrait photographers), I'd been asked to do one for a large department store in Rochester. Stores have more money than museums . . . and everything else to make exhibitions ravishing. James Card, a friend ever since he'd read an interview of mine with another of his idols, Eleanor Powell,* told me that I should look up Louise. Between arthritis and worsening emphysema, she was virtually housebound and would enjoy the company. I hesitated and told him why. Jim thought the incident about my mother's "broken leg" was amusing and said she wouldn't hold it against me after all these years.

"Come over," Louise said when I called. That hair, once so black and so short, like something sculpted, was now long and gray, combed back severely from her face, exposing a strong, bony, intelligent forehead; she bound the hair at the nape of her neck with a rubber band so that it fell in a plain "pony tail" down her back. The classic black-banged spirit of the '20s had given way to American Gothic, as striking in its way as that earlier self. We spent a long time talking. How was my mother's leg? She thought that was funny, my being such a dumb liar. Anyway, now here I was. You'd think we'd always known each other. Louise is a keen gossip; she enjoys back-fence tittle-tattle, about stars who were dikes and drunks and fairies and fooled around and fooled everybody else. She gets quite bright-eyed and wet-lipped about it, and laughs a lot.

The conversation turned to the exhibition. It happened that she had kept a little red satin bolero jacket which the great Paramount designer Travis Banton had done for her as a favor back in the '30s, when she couldn't get a job in the movies and had gone back to earning her living as half of a dance team and she needed some new clothes. "He was a genius. Boy, did he drink! That's what ruined him. What a darling." I got Louise to "loan" the jacket for the show, and there it was, decorating one of the mannequins who were posed throughout the

*See page 217.

gallery in different costumes. Sibley's (the sponsoring department store) were so delighted to find that one of the most spectacularly beautiful photos in the show was of a woman who was now a resident of Rochester that they sent her an elaborate food basket and a quilted bed-jacket as well, and got her to attend the opening. Louise made the effort. Nobody recognized her as she took a look around the show, before the pain made it unbearable and I got her into a taxi to take her home.

We remained in touch. Letters when I was in England, phoning when I was in the States. She encouraged me with sharp insights about the Hollywood portrait photographers, and loaned me some of her favorite pictures of herself. Over the years, like everybody else who'd met her, or read her and knew of her fierce love of reading, I tried to get her to write her story. Nothing doing. The book from which she'd read me a chapter (and which I still had on tape) was down the incinerator. Then came the celebrated piece by Kenneth Tynan, published in *The New Yorker,* and the Louise Brooks cult hit the intelligentsia. The emphysema had finally made her give up smoking and drinking to conserve her strength for reading; but now interest was stirring in her, making her think about doing something. The editor of *The New Yorker* collected most of her published articles, including a new piece by Louise about her Kansas City childhood, and they, together with a foreword by him, were published in a book. *Lulu in Hollywood* was a great success. It was in conjunction with the British publication that Louise agreed to an interview. Two decades later, there I was finally doing the interview with her in Rochester. Still for the BBC.

Her renewal of effort and the excitement because of the book had taken its toll: she hardly moved at all now if she could help it, she was frail and in pain, yet she insisted, for the sake of clarity, on getting out of bed to do the taping at her kitchen table. Sitting upright, she felt, would make it easier to think, to talk without coughing. I could see the effort in the lines cutting across her forehead and tightening around the corners of her mouth. But it's impossible to be with her and feel self-conscious or awkward for long, since her mind is so bright and her tongue still so sharp. She's such a fighting force. If she was living alone, it was because she wanted it that way; she had earned the right not to be beholden.

When I'm with Louise, I am reminded of the pioneers and the spirit that enabled them to trek across weeks, months, years of wilderness to find the land on which they built their homes and raised their families and made America what it was. This spirit burned in her when she was beautiful, young, swooned over, coveted, and made her unique. Some of the powerful millionaires who'd been in love with her hadn't forgotten: long before her book, before *The New Yorker,* Ken Tynan, Rochester, articles and revivals in museums and film festivals had brought her name back into currency, before these but all through the hard years when she was living on the edge, small but regular monthly checks from lovers who hadn't forgotten. This was all the money she had to live on when I first knew her. These allowances were not obligations to a discarded "kept" woman, but tributes to her for having been a giving woman. Louise wouldn't mention the names of the senders, that was part of the pact between them. But, quite clearly, what was unique about her on the screen and is unique about her as a writer was there in her relationships.

Her essays about the people she knew have this same fierce independence from cant and nostalgia. This is how it is. This is how it was. This is how she tells it. Her greatest compliment to any of them is not to write about them in a sentimental light. Writing about them is her gift. Her absolute honesty about events and about people as she saw them is her acknowledgment of them and her obligation to herself as a writer.

JK: You're working on a book yourself, aren't you?

LB: I was. You mean "Naked on My Goat?"

JK: John Springer said, "I know why it can't be printed, because she tells the truth and she names names," and I said, "Well, is it dirty or lascivious?" And he said, "No, nothing like that, it's just so honest, you know, it scalds everything off the bones."

LB: Well, as I told the editor, "Look, I know why people call my book dirty, hideous, more vile than any kind of . . . It's simply that I make whoring as ugly as it is, and this is a man's world and they're not going to have it. And that is the truth. I talk about an actress' life. You could finish that sentence any way you like.

JK: It sounds as if you think an actress' life is comparable to whoredom.

LB: Well, it *has* been since as long as I've been able to read about it, going back to ancient Greece! [She laughs.] Men are the publishers, men are publishing books, and anything that kills their sexual pleasure is not going to be allowed. The filth of my book is nothing compared to the filth of perfectly foul books like that Miller *Capricorn,* and that insidious book *The Ginger-bread Man.* [Louise meant J. P. Donleavy's *The Ginger Man.*] It is all right in those books to make up men who beat women and kick them around and get drunk and beat them and screw them and give them syphilis and clap and babies. That is fine because that makes the man a great *hero* in this kind of world's eyes, and I detest all that! And I detest what they do to women. And women are forced into that kind of life, and they are not going to let me tell it. It's desperately hard for me to write. Would you tell the truth, the ugly truth about yourself? Let me tell you, baby, it takes a lot of guts! And I know damn few people who ever did it. Besides Marcel Proust, Dickens was able to face up to himself in his novels. And Shaw wrote himself and his terrible passion for that actress, that silly broad Ellen Terry. But damn few people have been able to. Why should I write all that just to be put in a drawer? I don't have to purge myself. I *have* purged myself. I wrote that book once and threw it down the incinerator. That was a practice run.

JK: I'm just one of many who would want to read this book. Why do you think I'm interested?

LB: You're not that kind of man. I've talked to you enough on the phone to know more about you, my dear boy, than I could tell you in one half-hour, and you don't belong to that world. You are never going to be a rich producer whose sole object is to gain enough power; that is the whole story of *Lulu*! That's why they hate that film, because it shows this rich man, this rich man like Hearst, whose whole life is to build power, to get rich enough and powerful enough to live a life of sex with women. That is every man's ambition. I don't care who they are or how they hide it or whether they are able to achieve it or not, and I write against that from beginning to end.

JK: You are a woman of contradictions. You've been mostly dependent on men all your life, and yet you refused to marry them because that was the one dependency you wouldn't accept. You decided to take a job as a salesgirl at one time in the '40s to prove you could earn your own living. But you said the one thing you always had is that you liked to read, and as long as you had books, you were never unhappy.

LB: Yes, that's right. Saks Fifth Avenue. I was a clerk there. My literary life is astonishing. You know, most people are fakes about books. You know that? They read *The New York Times Book Review,* and since they are all faking with each other, they cast it off very nicely. Now, why it is such a thing to be literary, I don't know, but I'm mad about books like *War and Peace.* My mother read out loud to us when we were very small, from the time we were born. She loved to read, starting off with:

> *There was a man from our town, and he was wondrous wise,*
> *He jumped into a bramble bush and scratched out both his eyes,*
> *And when he found his eyes were out, with all his might and main*
> *He jumped into another bush, and scratched them in again.*

Isn't that marvelous? That's Mother Goose. And I was always mad about reading, even when I didn't understand what I was reading. Well, we were a very reading family. We had a big library, and all of us after dinner we'd go to our rooms and get in bed and read. When my brother wasn't trying to throw me down the stairs [she adds, laughing, as an aside]. And I read logic: John Stuart Mill. I read Proust over and over and over. No one touched Proust . . . everything he felt . . . because isn't that the loveliest line in the world that Proust wrote: "The only paradise is paradise lost"? Isn't that beautiful? It's true. And he says there's no such thing as cause and effect. That's part of logic. He says things don't have a cause and effect. He says things happen, that's all. And another one of his truths is: "You can't project anything." I cannot tell you what is going to happen. Tomorrow or the next day or the next week. Because there are too many variables. You change, I change, the weather changes. Everything changes. What he taught people is that you can't know people. You remember Charlus? He changed, just like all the people in Proust changed.

JK: You seem to have led two lives. And your secret life, the one that kept the other one going, through lovers, through films, through dancing, through starving—reading just kept you going along one continuous line, whereas all the others were the surface things which rocked you this way and that. . . . You were going to write a piece about John Wayne. Did you?

LB: No, I wouldn't write anything about him. My God, what the hell could I write about John Wayne? No, I had a lot of stuff there. I was going to write a piece about Clara Bow. But when you come right down to it, not many people are worth writing about. Lotte Eisner wrote to me, she said, "You are the first natural actress." And I said, "No, no, you're wrong. The first natural actress was Clara Bow." There are only three people I wanted to write about. One was George Gershwin; the other was Martha Graham; and I would like to have done a long piece on Charlie Chaplin. Those three people. They were all geniuses. But ordinary people like Clara Bow, for God's sake, she was a half-witted little girl, her father was a busboy, her mother was in a nuthouse, and she wasn't bright.

JK: But you knew her at Paramount?

LB: Yeah, I liked her.

JK: Because she was extraordinarily bruised. You survived Hollywood, but she really was crushed. [Louise is nodding her agreement.] She *made* Paramount, they needed a star desperately when they got her.

LB: Oh, yeah, yeah. And then Schulberg threw her out because he liked this girl Sylvia Sidney. He'd had an affair with Clara, of course, when she worked for him at FBO, and he brought her to Paramount. That's how he got the job at Paramount.

JK: Clara once said, in an interview that was very moving, "I know I look like I'm having a lot of fun to people. I know that's how I come across and I suppose I am sometimes, but I live like each day is going to be the last. If you grew up the way I did, when you didn't know what was going to happen tomorrow and I'm not trying to blame anybody but you took your happiness as you found it day by day." She was so moving. She didn't punctuate her sentences.

LB: That was the way she talked: nonstop, no punctuation, she just went on. She was a great star. But I could write everything I have to say about her in

1000 words. To learn how to write, I wrote "Naked on My Goat." It's a wonderful title. It's from Goethe; out of the witches' Sabbath, *Faust*. And I did that simply to learn how to write. Because what better way than an auto-biography? And it ran about 400 pages. And I typed and I typed and I typed the 400 pages, and when I was through, I threw it down the incinerator. Then I thought, "Now I've learned how to write well enough to start writing seri-ously." I've led a literary life. My friends were all literary people. And in Hollywood there were no literary people. I went to Hollywood and no one read books. I went to the bookstore there on Hollywood Boulevard—it's still there—and they would say, these Hollywood people would go in and say, "I have a bookshelf, and I want to buy enough books to fill up the shelves." And that was all the reading they did. Don't forget, most people in pictures, they were waitresses, they were very lower-class people, most people in the mov-ies at that time. . . .

JK: But did any of the writers you knew back in the '20s suggest you should write?

LB: No. I didn't know how to write! You see, you can't be a reader of master-pieces, of the greatest literature in the world, and want to write, unless you learn how to do it. You can't learn how to write. You just learn by writing. That's the only way.

JK: What so intrigued you about the Hollywood image that you want to write about it?

LB: Well, I write about the people I know, and they're all in movies.

JK: What about Garbo? I mean, did you know her?

LB: Yeah, yeah. She made a pass at me. I met her at Barney Glazer's; he was a writer at Paramount, and Alice Glazer, his wife, was a friend of Garbo's. I stopped by their house one day and Garbo was there. And also, she would play tennis up at John Gilbert's house. We weren't friends, we just met those few times.

JK: Let's talk about the fact that people often have an image which is quite apart from what you yourself are like. A lot of people kept looking for the Lulu of *Lulu* in you. Then they meet Louise Brooks, who happens to be a dry, spry, very sardonic Kansas City girl. . . .

LB: Well, I learned to stop talking about books to people. They didn't read books and it was embarrassing.

JK: Maybe you should have become a librarian, you know that?

LB (laughs): Did you ever know a librarian who read? They never read.

JK: You describe yourself as a hermit.

LB: A loner. Yes.

JK: Except for your passion for reading. See, this is the one tragedy that people like Monroe, Hayworth . . . they work very hard, but when the spare time comes finally, they don't know what to do with it because they've never been taught, or had any time to discover anything to pursue except their career.

LB: All they do is talk. That was one of my chief objections to movies. You go and sit on the set and you listen to these actors talk, talk, talk, all day long while they're putting up the lights, they're doing this, they're doing that, and you listen to these actors talking about themselves, and you think, "If I hear that story one more time, I'm going to die." So then when you get through with that all day, you go home and you take a bath and you get dressed and you go to dinner parties, and you meet the same actors and they're telling you about themselves through the dinner party, and then you go on to another party and they run movies. The only person I knew out there who didn't do that and who I was really fond of was Paul Bern . . .

JK: Jean Harlow's husband.

LB: . . . who killed himself. No one ever seemed to understand why he killed himself. They've got the silliest idea. His wife turned up, that's why. He was a bigamist. He married Jean while he was married to this other woman, and she turned up. And he was a very sensitive little man, and that's why he left the note and all. They seemed to think it was because he was impotent.

JK: Then the note really had nothing to do with Jean: "To my darling, Last night was a fiasco."

LB: Well, no, I think it was to Jean. He had to tell her that his real wife had turned up. And this would ruin her career at MGM, the fact that he was already married to this woman. I was amazed at Paul doing a thing like that. I was so fond of Paul. He was such a nice man.

JK: Did any of the men you ever loved read?

LB: I don't think I ever loved any man.

JK: Well, George Marshall.

LB: Well, I was crazy about him, yeah. But the word "love" . . . no, I don't think I ever *loved* the men I knew. It's a very strange thing. I've noticed that very often the men who were the best in bed were the men that I cared the least about. The men who were the worst in bed were the men I liked the most. So, for me, that has never worked. It's just never gone together. I don't know why.

JK: I wonder why you never picked the man who might have been a good kind of partner, who had things in common?

LB: Because I always liked the bastards. I mean, before I came up here, when I was so broke in New York, there were three men who wanted to marry me. All of them rich. All of them just as nice as they could be. But I didn't want to get married, and I've always had a passion for some kind of bastard. I don't know why.

JK: Maybe it was because it was the only way you could stay free.

LB: Maybe. I don't know.

JK: I want to know how you felt about Hollywood then and now. And, except for the great big period of mystery and darkness in your life when nobody knew about you, until this terrific reemergence first in Europe and now here too where everybody is talking Louise Brooks and running off to see your films. [Today that question is academic. But back in 1965, when I asked her, it aroused her spirits.]

LB: Well, that's because of the past too. That has nothing to do with the work with Howard Hawks or Mal St. Clair. I was just the same in those pictures. I was almost the same person. As I told you, I was in a cowboy film with Buck Jones with no direction and I was still exactly the same. You see, I just didn't fit into the Hollywood scheme at all. I was never, neither a fluffy heroine, nor a wicked vamp, nor a woman of the world. I just didn't fit into any category.

JK: And yet you were increasingly popular at the time.

LB: That was in spite of the studio. They didn't give a damn about me. They would just as soon put me in a bit. I played nothing more than a small part, for instance, in three or four pictures there. They didn't care. You see, I didn't interest them because I couldn't be typed. It's the very thing I was telling you about the Sternberg picture.* I wasn't Clara Bow, I wasn't Mary Pickford, I wasn't Lillian Gish and I wasn't anybody, and since they didn't know or care to analyze my personality and do something . . . You see, you had to have . . . a Dietrich has to have a Sternberg, and a Brooks has to have a Pabst to establish a personality once and for all, and at the time I made that picture with Pabst, I was just as unpopular in Germany as I was in Hollywood. That picture, *Lulu*, was a huge failure. They expected a *femme fatale*, a siren, a slinking woman with lascivious looks and leers. They expected a man-eater, a sex dynamo with a voracious appetite for men. And lots of people who see that film still insist on looking at it that way, although Lulu does nothing. She just dances through the film; she's a young girl, she leads a life she's always liked. She was a whore when she was twelve, and she dies a whore when she's about eighteen. How can an audience expect a girl at that age to reflect, to suffer?

---

*A reference to her dissection of Von Sternberg's genius with women.

JK: But, Louise, you said that they didn't know how to type you, but yet when I saw *Love 'Em and Leave 'Em* and *A Girl in Every Port* and *Rolled Stockings* . . .

LB: I never saw *A Girl in Every Port*. I have a very small part in that.*

JK: But the moment you come on, it was sheer sexual force. . . .

LB: I use no sex at all. I never had the feeling of sex. I never try to feel sexy, I simply . . . It's true in life that the people who try hardest to be sexy only fool other fools. But Howard Hawks admired me. He was the perfect director. He didn't do anything at all. He would sit, look very, very beautiful, tall and graceful, leaning against anything he could lean against, and watch the scene; and the person who did all the directing was that big ham Victor McLaglen. I mean, when we were shooting, diving into the tank, it was a freezing cold night on the Fox lot, and Howard was walking around in a very smart tweed jacket, and I was shivering with the cold coming out of this damn greasy tank, and he smiled at me and he said, "Is it cold?" [She laughs.] He was just someone who had wandered on the set and being sympathetic, but I liked him very much as a man and as a director. You see, Mal St. Clair was just the opposite and I hated the pictures I did with him, although Mal adored me as an actress and he was always plugging me. At the very end in Hollywood he was still trying to get me to come to the Fox studio when he was only an assistant to Zanuck then, and to make a test for a picture, and I wouldn't. But Mal came from the mugging school of Sennett and he did everything by making faces, and he would mug out a scene for me and then send me into the scene, and I would be so embarrassed. I tried my best to please him and yet not to make all these mugging faces that date so terribly, like Adolphe Menjou. You know, the old type of film acting in those days was because of the titles, to establish the emotions, let's say, a flirting leer at the girl, so Menjou would begin the scene by making this hideous, grim expression #7 of a grinning leer, and then he knew they were going to cut to some title and then his face would drop to nothing at all and he would go into his next emotion, and that was the kind of acting that Mal tried to direct. And I felt Mal was a really terrible director, although I thought he was a charming man, a lovely man. In those days anyone could become a director. As soon as the director got too tough and made too much money, they'd throw him out and give the job to an assistant, a writer, anyone who wandered on the stage and said he'd direct, because their pictures were all presold and it didn't make much difference whether they were good or bad, and so that was the way it was. Mal had become efficient then, he'd worked at Sennett as a carpenter and learned how to mug and make faces, and so they threw him into this

---

*She's the last in a succession of girls encountered by the two womanizing Hawks heroes, though she's the only woman who poses any threat to their male bonding.

picture, I think . . . *Our Children Are People* . . . or no, *Are Parents People* . . . or something. . . . And then he made a success imitating Lubitsch with *The Duchess and the Grand Waiter*.

JK: *The Grand Duchess and the Waiter*.

LB (laughing): That's the one. This is typical Brooks! It's like the time I wrote a girlfriend, and said, "This book is absolutely disgusting. This *Fannie Farmer* is disgusting." And after I sealed and sent the letter away, I said, "My God, Fannie Farmer is a candy manufacturer. I meant *Fanny Hill*!" I often wondered what she thought of that. [Louise laughs with a total girlish abandon.]

JK: Did you read Mae Murray's biography, *The Disenchanted* or *The Self-Enchanted*? . . . [It had just been published when I called Louise.]

LB: No, I must get it. You know, it's so unfair. . . . Wait. [We pause for breath.] . . . It's so unfair the way they treat people. Now, for instance, Von Stroheim has become an idol, you see, and so Mae Murray just stinks all around, all over. Now, she was the most ridiculous woman, and a most ridiculous actress, and let us say insane. In a way. On the other hand, she was a great success, and anyone who made a success in the business has something, believe me. It is the roughest, toughest, most humiliating and degrading job in the world. So they will not allow her to be even barely good, let's say in *The Merry Widow*. It was the best performance she ever gave, and it is cruel, when she was an old woman, not to give her credit for what she had: a lovely body, a certain kind of grace, a kind of silly personality. The fact is, her pictures kept Old Man Mayer [Louis B.] going at Metro for a long time, so she must have had something, for in the end it is the public that matters with films. It was the same with Clara Bow. You know, I talked to Kevin [Brownlow] about her. I was so mad when he didn't go to see her in Hollywood. He said: "Well, I don't think she's so much." And in that year she died. 1965. She was born in 1905. And that was the last chance anyone had to interview her. And he didn't think she was much. And, my God, she was a terrific star! It isn't like great literature which very few people can understand and those few people had to pass it down from century to century. Anyone who goes to a movie can understand it; whether it catches them emotionally or not isn't the answer. All you have to have is an eye and an ear, to have lived, spoken, felt, eaten, drunk and so forth. That's the whole terrible thing about this movie cult, these movie curators [she curdles her voice on the word], these film archives . . . they go from cult to cult. This year they're mad about Japanese films and everything else stinks, and next year it's Ingmar Bergman and everything else stinks; and it's an idiotic, childish way to view . . . The films aren't art; it's like the public library, it's full of books from the beginning of printing, and it doesn't make any difference whether they're old or new. Some are good, some are bad, and to be a cult in reading is as idiotic as—well, to be a cult with film, I think, is equally idiotic.

JK: In a sense, I think it's because people only rediscover one person at a time. It allows them time to explore their films, their directors. . . . Still, I agree, cults are stupid.

LB: Well, that's true about anyone who is inspired and exhilarated and enthralled and enlightened by art. Everyone used to kid me. I remember a blind date, he said, "Don't talk to Brooksie about anything but Tolstoy, Dostoevsky and Turgenev; she's going through her Russian period and won't listen to anything else." And then I went through my Dickens period, and my Thackeray. Now, he was making great fun of me, but as these enthusiasms simmered down, I put them all in their places in my pantheon, and I can love them all. They're all unique. Just as each director is unique . . . Well, I forgot the point, what the hell am I getting at?

JK: How one can appreciate so much more than just one . . .

LB: Oh, yeah. Every picture is worth something to somebody, and there's always a reason for saving it, for not discarding it, for not going . . . I remember in 1943 Iris Barry, who started the Museum of Modern Art film department, had me to lunch with a local wolf and she said she wasn't going to get a copy of *Pandora's Box,* that it had no *lasting* value. That kind of saying, you see; and James Card here at the Eastman House film museum, through me and through Marion Davies' nephew, Charlie Lederer, had an opportunity to get the Marion Davies films. That was back in 1958 before she died, and he was too busy collecting foreign films that he could now get for a dime a dozen, all he wants, and in the meantime they've given the Marion Davies films, which are absolutely fabulous because of Mr. Hearst and his supervision . . . they've given all of her films to the Hollywood Museum. That is what this prejudice and these silly judgments out of left field ruins; that is why they ruin archives, and ruin the curator's work, and ruin for the viewer, for you or me who just go to look at films; that's why these people aren't necessarily instructive. They should grab everything they can get hold of, for sooner or later it's going to be precious.

JK: Isn't it funny? Over in England and France they collect the American films like mad because they realize American films are the most precious gold mine of all cinema history.

LB: And the hardest to get because they used to, after they sent in the copyright negatives, they would collect back all the prints and just ship them off to Eastman Kodak here and have them melted down to get back what money they could get out of the silver in the films. They keep talking now about deterioration and how the films are lost. They always forget that the big way they were lost was because the studios themselves had them burned up and melted down to sell for silver content. They used to make $2 or $3 million a year that way, reclaiming the film.

JK: How did you feel suddenly about 1956–57 when this terrific resurgence in your popularity came about?

LB: Oh, I got an enormous kick out of it. I was killed dead when *Pandora's Box* failed, so from that time on, I just didn't care. I lived for years and years with this terrible sense of failure . . . and to be suddenly reclaimed from the dead was marvelously exciting, and it made me enormously happy. Of course it did! If you lived for years thinking you were a perfect failure and then suddenly you have lived long enough . . . Most people die before things like that happen—to find that you are to a certain extent admired. It's a wonderful blessing. But I was always perfectly willing to face that I'd made my own particular hell. I never tried to push the blame on anybody but myself. I knew I'd done it all myself.

JK: But it didn't provide you with an impetus to go back to films?

LB: You know I never did go out anyplace in my life when I didn't have to do some kind of work. You cannot drag me out. I would still be in Kansas if my mother hadn't sent me off to Ruth St. Denis in New York.

JK: That's right . . . you were with Ruth St. Denis.

LB: And Ted Shawn. That's how I began. I'm a dancer.

JK: Yes, of course, of course. And you danced with the *Ziegfeld Follies* too, right?

LB: Well, yes, after I left St. Denis and Shawn. You know what burns me up? For years, John, my whole career as far as these charming United States of America are concerned has been a blank. Ted Shawn and Ruth St. Denis must have given thousands of lectures, and they've written between them fifteen books, and they have never found me worthy of so much as a *mention* of my name, ever having been with them, and it's the same thing with the *Follies*. Because Ziegfeld was going to star me in the *Follies* when I left, you know. I was supposed to do *Show Girl* and I wouldn't do it, so they gave it to Ruby Keeler. But in all the hundreds of books that have been written about the *Follies* or connected with the *Follies* or pictures of the *Follies* girls, my name, my picture, nothing. And if it hadn't been for the German films I made, and being advertised in Europe, my name would still never be mentioned in movies.

JK: But I didn't discover you in your German films. I first saw you in *A Girl in Every Port*.

LB: Yeah, but don't you see, all that was built up beforehand. By Pabst's *Pandora's Box* and *Prix de Beauté,* made in Paris, because before that no one could remember me. And it's just as . . . For instance, I was looking through [Richard] Griffith's book . . . what is it called? . . . *The Films*. No, *The Movies*. And do you know that there is not one picture of Betty Bronson? I mean, she was incomparable in *Peter Pan*. And not one picture of her. And so it goes, you see.

Well, now you can keep your mouth shut because I'm going into a monologue about Josef von Sternberg. So, quiet. I'm going to tell you about having read *Fun in a Chinese Laundry*. Well, you know the first thing I ask myself when I read a book is "Why that kind of book? Why did he write it?" Because all of us write because we have suffered some terrible humiliation and we've got to set the record straight and get even somehow. And of course I discovered that Sternberg wrote this and, instead of giving us that gag title from one of the first Edison pictures, he really should have called it "Why I Am Greater Than Marlene Dietrich." Because the whole thing is this argument to prove that he was a great director of genius and she was his puppet, manipulated and *created* by him. And it is a long, long argument about direction and acting; and what makes that particularly interesting is that today film writers who write about directors' work are impossible, they never mention actors' names. And they never tell you what's happening on the screen. A person who never saw a film, or never heard of a film, wouldn't know from these books that people came to see those pictures to see certain actors with certain personalities perform. It's amazing, because, as Sternberg shows in his book, the whole problem of a director is how to find out what an actor can do and how to get him or her to *do* it. And I can tell just from experience, because I was married to Eddie Sutherland and I remember he would come home every night after work, throw his feet down on the couch, grab a martini and start talking about Bill [W. C.] Fields: what he did at home, what he did in the scene, what he's going to do tomorrow. He wasn't occupied with the lighting or the camera or the costumes or the scenery, but *with his actors*, which is the whole essence of direction. And of course, in stating his case against Dietrich, Sternberg talks about this over and over, endlessly. Incidentally, his book is very well written. He wrote it himself, and it has wonderful cross-cutting, and movement back and forth in time. It's really an expert job of editing. But to go on—he does a marvelous portrait, of course, of Dietrich. And he does also a grand, illuminating portrait of [Emil] Jannings, because everything he writes about Jannings, his malice and his fights, his jealousy and how he tries to foul up the other actors so he could steal the scene, and his cattiness, you know it's true. You see all this on the screen when you see Jannings' pictures, you know it's true. But to go back to Dietrich, the most marvelous things about Sternberg's direction, whether he knew it or not, but in telling about Dietrich he solves the terrific mystery of her mystery! You know, most directors, or at least all directors whom I've worked for, give the choreography, the action and the words, and leave your inner thoughts alone because on the screen, like in life, a person is doing one thing and thinking another. Just as I'm talking to you now. You can also see that in Garbo, who I think is the greatest actress in the world, you can see that along with her actions is this wonderful mysterious thought line moving below, but it's harmonious, she's at one with her thoughts. But Dietrich always used to mystify me because I wondered what the hell she was thinking about with that long, gorgeous stare. And of course he tells you in one simple line of direction: he said to her, "Count six, and look at that lamp post as if you couldn't live without it." So, giving her these strange thoughts which she was able to concentrate on to fill her mind, he also gave her this strange air of mystery, which of course she never had with any other director. He says that she used to work with other people and say, "Oh, Joe, where are you?" And you can understand why.

He was the greatest director of women that ever, ever was. Most directors, you know, can direct certain women marvelously, and some can't direct them at all. But he could direct every woman he touched, he could make her lovely. He could take the most gauche, awkward, sexless dame and turn her into a dynamo of sex. There are three marvelous examples, and all are full of contrasts; they are Dietrich, Evelyn Brent and Betty Compson. First, you see, he's a very dispassionate man. I can't imagine he ever was very much in love, because most men look at women and they feel either a sexual urge or not, but they never analyze it . . . or they can't analyze it. And, you know, the direction, the terrible things that still go on, and it's gone on from Mary Pickford—when every director says "act like Mary Pickford," and then Lillian Gish, Clara Bow or Garbo . . . then Monroe and Bardot. That's the best most directors can do in trying to form an actress into an attractive shape. But he, that man, Sternberg, with his detachment, could look at a woman and say, this is beautiful about her and I'll leave it, not change it, and this is ugly about her, so I'll eliminate it. Take away the bad and leave what is beautiful so she's complete. As I say, with this Dietrich, if you ever saw her in those pre-Sternberg films, she was just a galloping cow, dynamic, so full of energy and awkward, oh, just dreadful, and the first time he saw her, he saw her leaning against the scenery, very bored, because she was working in a play, *Zwei Kravatten*, and didn't give a damn. And he saw that and it was lovely. But all of her movements were horrible. So he simply cut out the movements and painted her on the screen in beautiful, striking poses staring at a lamp post.

And in direct contrast was Evelyn Brent. I made a picture with her, and Evelyn's idea of acting was to march into a scene, spread her legs and stand flat-footed and read her lines with masculine defiance. Oh, I thought she was dreadful, and then I saw her in *Underworld*, and Sternberg softened her with all these feathers, and he never let her strike attitudes at all. He made her move. I remember the opening of *Underworld* . . . he makes her entrance the loveliest, most feminine thing, like bringing her from standing at the top of these stairs and reaching down, pulling up her dress, fixing her garter, I think.

Anyhow, it's lovely, it established her as lovely and feminine. And the other woman, who was so utterly feminine that she had no more impact than a powder puff, was Betty Compson in *The Docks of New York*. Well, you know, Betty was so soft, so frail, so delicate, so empty-headed that she was just meaningless on the screen, and he gave her emotional depth. He tells himself how he did it. For this one scene he had her sew the torn pocket back onto [George] Bancroft's coat. And of course every woman in the world knows that if she's in a tough situation with a man, that if she can prepare for his angry entrance by being found, you know, with a bit of sewing, stitching under the lamplight, that she's got everything going for her. And this is all I have to say about a really remarkable book.

During this interview Louise began to leaf through a book of film-star portraits of the '40s, and to comment on their rumored private sex lives.

LB: I don't think it matters. Oh, I mean, look at him! He was the boy next door and with her. That's funny. They became the All-American couple: she was a nymphomaniac and he was a homosexual, and there they were on the screen, the ideal couple of the cinema. Oh, yeah, well, they put Billy Haines out when they found out he was a homosexual. And they hate lesbians even more. See, I don't know what goes on in movies . . .

JK (indicating pictures in the book): There's Claire Bloom. And that's Jean Peters, she was married to Howard Hughes. Did you know Claire Bloom has just written her autobiography?

LB: Peters was the one married to Hughes? He's another one they say was a pansy. Did you know that?

JK: Well, if he was, he hid it a lot from himself.

LB: All he did was look at movies and take drugs . . . what was that drug he was on? And he was always surrounded by men. But what were the drugs he was using . . . pills and things? Oh, well. Look, here's Cyd Charisse. She was a marvelous dancer, really wonderful.

JK: Did you see *Singin' in the Rain*? Remember when Cyd did Louise Brooks?

LB: No. I was told about it. I was told she was going to do it. I've forgotten what she does. . . .

JK: Well, she comes on with her hair scalloped the way yours was, with the bangs and black shellac, and she comes into this club and she's a gangster's moll and dances with Gene Kelly.

LB: I heard him in an interview, a very interesting interview, and I thought it was a dead giveaway. He said, "You know, it's a shame that a guy can't dance without being called a homosexual," and then he went into this long routine defending himself—you know, "I'm married and have kids." Now, look at Fred Astaire . . . I don't think he had any sex life! [She bursts out laughing.] But he got married again, didn't he? At eighty-two. Isn't he amazing? No one could dance like that. I didn't care for Ginger Rogers. He didn't care for Ginger Rogers either.

JK: Here's Clark Gable.

LB: Who told me that story about him? When he was out on location someplace where they had a public fountain to drink out of, and he took out both sets of his teeth and then washed them off! Isn't that marvelous? He's so natural.

JK: So wonderful for a man who had such a powerful image. I think it was Carole Lombard who, when somebody asked what it was like being married to the King of Hollywood, said that if his pecker was one inch shorter, he'd be called the Queen of Hollywood.

LB: Oh! Oh, his pecker! You know, a personality is a fascinating thing, isn't it? That's what it comes down to. This may be the most beautiful girl in the world, this the most ugly. In the end, it's personality. Look at Debbie Reynolds . . . Jesus! She ruined *Singin' in the Rain* for me. Oh, look, here's Ava Gardner. I just hate posed sex pictures, I must say. I never meant to look sexy in my pictures.

JK: I don't think she means to look sexy.

LB: Are you kidding?

JK: No, I think her head is somewhere else. It's a job. Like Marilyn Monroe, who knew so well the art of the camera.

LB: Monroe had one great physical fault she overcame, that she had to overcome. Do you know what it was? When she smiled, her upper lip went right up under her nose. She had to learn to control it. Oh, I loved Marilyn in that thing where she lived upstairs. What was that? *The Seven Year Itch.* She was no fool. She was very smart. What did she do? Accidentally take an overdose? You know, I'm taking that Valium, which is a tranquilizer. And you take more and more because they cease to affect you. And more and more and more and more, like Judy Garland and Elvis Presley, no matter who you are. . . .

Another severe case of coughing leaves her physically shaken. I get her something to drink and think about stopping the interview altogether, to let her get back to bed, but after the sip of water she wants to continue.

LB: I hear the Reagans are visiting Claudette Colbert at her home in the Bahamas. Where'd she ever get all that dough?

JK: She never spent a cent. One of the shrewdest women in Hollywood.

LB: Was she? I didn't know. Oh, look, here's my favorite actress, Bette Davis.

JK: Why do you like her so much? A kindred spirit?

LB: Oh, no. No. I don't know. I just like Bette Davis. I liked whatever she did. I think she's a real actress, don't you?

JK: Yes, but why better than another actress? I suppose personality.

LB: Well, yes, it's her personality. For instance, I never liked Joan Crawford at all. Never. I hate fakes. She's one of the girls, incidentally, who went back and forth. And of course she was a terrible drunk. She was an awful fake. A washerwoman's daughter. I'm a terrible snob, you know. Don't forget, in the *Follies* I had to dress alone because I wouldn't dress with the chorus girls. No, they wouldn't dress with me because I was such a snob and didn't approve of the lower classes, my dear, who read the *Police Gazette*. Oh, I was a frightful . . . and still am.

JK: But all those years when you weren't working professionally, weren't on the screen, weren't dancing . . .

LB: I was just starving to death in New York.

JK: But there were different men in your life. . . .

LB: Oh, I could have married a dozen men. That was another thing, you see, I counted on. When I stopped movies, I thought, Well, I'll do what every other girl in movies does, I'll marry any man I like. Any rich man will marry any movie star. But I hated marriage. I tried it twice. I was married to Eddie Sutherland, the director, who was a charming man. I was married to him for a year. And then I married Derring Davies, who was a Chicago socialite; polo, and didn't do anything for about six months. I hated marriage. In the first place, to be called Mrs. Davies or Mrs. Sutherland would simply *inflame* me. My name is Mary Louise Brooks, and don't be calling me Mrs. Davies or Mrs. Sutherland. My ace in the hole, getting married, didn't work out. So I was left alone. And I couldn't get a job. Don't forget, I worked for almost two years as a salesgirl at Saks Fifth Avenue. To prove that I could sell dresses. I must have intimidated more women who left the store without buying anything. "Who was this beauty who looks so gorgeous in these clothes, and she's waiting on me?" I'd do funny things. I'd stand—after they put on the dress, I'd stand and they were waiting for me to zip them up or something, and I didn't do anything. I had a black girl who was my assistant. She taught me how to do things, how to zip people up and unzip them and so on. I was going to prove a point, that I could go out and get a job and work like everybody else. But it didn't really work out at all. I quit. I wasn't fired. Yeah.

Yeah, I never . . . [She breaks off, pauses for the right words, then:] I was never scheming or clever about money. I've never been clever about money.

JK: How does that tie in with your "Dorothy from Kansas–Wizard of Oz" background?

LB: Not at all. Isn't that funny? It's odd. I'm not at all like Kansas. Well, I went to New York when I was fifteen, don't forget. Then I was with Ruth St. Denis for two years, and came back when I was seventeen. Then I went first into George White's *Scandals* and then into the *Follies,* and then into the movies. There was no effort to it. I was in movies, and I made such rotten pictures. I'm speaking about my attitude towards the films I made. The way I felt about myself in movies and how anybody saw me are different things. In the first place, I never went to see my movies. I hated making them. I hated Hollywood. I never stayed there an instant if I could get away. I wanted to be a great dancer like Martha Graham, that was my ambition, and I wasn't a good dancer. I never heard anyone say I was good.

JK: Well, nine out of ten of the greatest stars were dancers. Natural rhythm of movement. I mean, even though Garbo moves a bit like a diesel, there was a kind of powerful rhythm to her, hypnotic.

LB: Tynan said something interesting about Garbo. I was talking to him here. I said, "You've met everyone." He entertains Princess Margaret, you know. She's a drunk. Gin, like me. He said, "Yes, of course, I know Garbo. She didn't do anything for me, but she's got the most interesting walk." I said, "What do you mean?" And the moment he said it, I realized it. "She has a thrust—she thrusts this leg forward with this shoulder." And he's right. I never thought about it. I usually watch movement very carefully. I can remember the railway-station scene in *Anna Karenina.* Looking back, I remember her walking and the thrust of her shoulder.

JK: What was the happiest time in your working life?

LB: The happiest time I ever had, looking back, is when I was making pictures in Paris and didn't speak French. And the reason I was happy was I didn't have to talk to anyone. I didn't have to explain anything. I'd get up in the morning and go to the studio, and didn't have to discuss anything with anyone. [She laughs. Louise may be suffering, but she hasn't lost her ability to laugh.] I didn't have to talk at all. I had a translator. I had this interpreter, but he was such a little devil. He started having an affair with my hairdresser's assistant, the girl who was supposed to assist me. I didn't need anyone to curl my hair, so he was never around. So Rudy Maté, the cameraman, looked down for a parallel one day when the Italian director [Augusto] Genina threw down his American dictionary and he couldn't explain what he wanted me to do. And Rudy, when he started on the picture, couldn't speak a word of English. But he was Hungarian, and he looked down and said, "Miss Brooks,

I can interpret for you." He'd learned to speak English in about two weeks! That's how marvelous Hungarians are about picking up the language. So from that time on, Genina would tell him what he wanted me to do. There was really no directing me anyhow. All I needed was choreography. "You come in this door and you go out that one." Or, "You come in and sit down." They didn't say, "I want one tear right now!" Because if anyone told me what to do or how to do it . . . That was the funniest thing Marilyn Monroe ever said, remember? When that German Jewish director Billy Wilder said to her, "I want two tears, right now!" [Louise is overcome with laughter at the image this story provokes in her] and Marilyn said, "How can I make two tears right now?" And he said, "I want two tears right now." And she thought that was most unfair because it would take her four or five hours to get together two tears right now. [Tears are streaming down Louise's cheeks from laughing so much.] Well, my mother was a natural crier, and I too could cry.

I remember when we were making *Lulu,* we were eating this awful German food for our lunch and Pabst said, "Luuissssse, after lunch you must cry." I said, "Okay, after lunch I will cry." So then we went back on the set and I cried. It was never any problem. But I liked the way he said it while he was tossing in his food, the usual sauerkraut. And that's about all the direction he would give me. In the first place, he directed in German and I didn't speak German. I didn't know what he was talking about. Of course, all the other actors . . . well, Francis Lederer was a Czech, but he spoke German, and Alice Roberts was Belgian and he had to speak to her in French, but as far as I was concerned, I was being directed by a German. *"Die Tür zu,"* he would say as I went off the set. And I'd reply, "Can't you speak English?" I was perfectly natural on the screen. I never did any acting at all.

But you take somebody like Mal St. Clair. He was a great mugger, and he would mug scenes ahead and tell you how to act. I hated working with him. I liked Mal St. Clair, he was very nice. And the last picture I made with him, *The Canary Murder Case,* he was drunk all the time. Plus a broken leg. He was about 6'4" . . . no, he wasn't. Men then seemed taller because there weren't so many tall men as you are now. Remember when actors were so small, like Richard Barthelmess?

JK: Incidentally, before we "leave" Paris, what did René Clair have to do with *Prix de Beauté?*

LB: Well, he was supposed to direct it, and then he said to me one day . . . We were being photographed there at that Studio Lorel. I never knew what happened to the pictures I had taken with him. And as we were driving back on the Champs-Elysées, back to my hotel, René Clair said—and he spoke almost no English and of course I'd never learned to speak French or German, English just barely!—and so he said to me, "I'm not going to make that picture, and if you're smart, you'll quit too." I said, "Why aren't you going to make it?" He said, "Because they cannot get the money together. They still haven't got the money up, they never will get it up and they won't make it. And you're just going to sit around here in Paris waiting to make a picture that will never be made." I said, "Well, I don't see how I can quit, because I have a contract. And if I just get on a ship and go home, I'll never be able to make another picture in Europe. I'll be finished. I have to stay." So I stayed, and they did get the money to make it. And it's a lovely picture—says she, never having seen it.

JK: You are such a bundle of contradictions. You honor your contract in Paris, then come back to America and walk out on Paramount. You could have gone into the '30s as a major star.

LB: That's right. When Tynan was here, he said to me, "That is what is so funny about you. You mess yourself up just as the talkies are coming in, and you have the most beautiful voice, and it would have been so good." It was a lot better then than it is now with this damn emphysema. "And you would have been so marvelous in talkies." And I said, "No one can understand how . . . I cannot think of anything . . . you don't know . . . you never . . ." You see, I don't think anyone can learn to act.

JK: Why? One can learn to dance.

LB: What do you mean, one can learn dancing? That's an entirely different kind of doodad. Movement you can acquire. Elocution, for Christ's sake, you can learn how to speak a line, but I don't understand how you can learn to act. People have asked me time and time again, "What were you thinking about when you did that scene?" And I will sit and say, "What was I thinking about? Well, I was thinking about what I was doing. What the hell would you think I was thinking about? What I was going to eat for breakfast?" Now on the stage . . . I read this little book about Eleonora Duse, and one of the most charming chapters in it—it was written by somebody before she died in Pittsburgh. Isn't that a hell of a place for Duse to die? But she did a very famous play by a German playwright, Wassermann . . . now, what was the name of it? Well, a stock play, like *Ghosts*. Anyway, the point of it was that she does a very famous scene at the side of the stage where she is arranging flowers in a vase in front of a mirror. A very important scene in the play. And they said to her, "Madame Duse, what are you thinking about when you arrange those flowers?" She said, "Oh, I can be thinking about what I am going to have for dinner!" [She laughs.] Now, you see, you can do that in the theater because that's acting.

JK: Louise, since you never liked Hollywood, what tempted you to go?

LB: To make money, to make money. To live, for God's sake.

JK: Couldn't you get money at the *Follies*?

LB: Well, Ziegfeld wanted me to stay in the *Follies* and be a *Follies* star. I guess it was Walter Wanger who talked me into signing a contract. I was young then, and they said, "Oh, you're a fool not to go into movies and sign a contract." So I did it. But it was just for the money, that's the only thing. I could spend a week's salary buying clothes, I was mad about clothes for a time. You know, ermine coats and those things eat up a lot of money. I would go out to a nightclub every night in New York and show off my clothes. I had my literary friends. That's what life was in those days. There was nothing to do in Hollywood. After you'd finish work, you'd go to dinner and then they'd run movies.

JK: So you never really became part of the Hollywood establishment?

LB: Just for the one year when I was married to Eddie Sutherland. We gave marvelous parties. Really marvelous. He was the most wonderful host. We gave that famous, famous party. It was written up everywhere. It was my idea . . . all books. All the place cards at dinner were books. In front of Irving Thalberg's place I put Dreiser's *Genius*. [She chuckles quite wickedly.] That's just before he married Norma Shearer. So in front of Norma's place I put *Serena Blandish: The Difficulty of Getting Married*—she'd been trying and trying, and Irving's mother wanted him to marry a nice Jewish girl. It was so funny because Irving walked right in and saw *Genius* and sat right down. But Norma kept on walking around. She wouldn't sit down in front of *The Difficulty of Getting Married*. Not at all! And there was that writer at MGM who had lost a leg in the war, and I gave him *The Devil on Two Sticks*.

JK: Oh, Louise! Let me jump back a bit to Sternberg. Did you ever know Dietrich?

LB: I don't think I ever met her. Yes, I did, once in her dressing room, in Hollywood. You know, Pabst said an interesting thing. He said, "The trouble with German actresses"—this is when he was looking for someone to play Lulu in *Lulu*—"the trouble is that there aren't any good-looking girls in pictures in Germany." That was true, there weren't. Except maybe Dietrich, and she was too old, too knowing. He wanted a girl who was innocent-looking, and she was too . . . whorish, let's say. But I thought she was absolutely marvelous in *The Blue Angel*.

JK: Did your path ever cross with Sternberg's?

LB: Uhn-uh. I was just put in one lousy picture after the other.

JK: Did you notice the pecking order at Paramount?

LB: I didn't pay any attention to anybody. You see, the clever ones who went around like Richard Arlen wooed all the writers and all the other actors and the producers. And when they weren't working, they were on the lot every day, mooching up and making friends and whatnot. Of course, when *I* wasn't working, I was in New York. This is really funny . . . I didn't even know Schulberg was head of the studio until I was called into his office. I thought Walter Wanger was running the place, but Walter had gone to MGM. I discovered it was Schulberg when he said, "You can stay on at $750 per week or leave." So I went to Berlin. And Paramount put out the thing that my voice didn't record well. They were right: I should have gone back. As I say, I just moved by instinct all my life. It's really true. The only picture I wanted to make, but wasn't the type for, was *Alice in Wonderland*.

JK: Well, maybe you should have played Dorothy in *The Wizard of Oz*! The little girl from Kansas who goes to the big city. [This gets Louise's sense of humor rolling again.]

LB: You know, I saw Brooke Shields on the *Muppet Show* the other day, and she played Alice in Wonderland, and she was adorable. She really is just darling. She's a beautiful girl, there's no doubt about it. But is that all she does, be beautiful?

JK: The comparison of you to Dorothy is just because you're from Kansas. But in a strange way, if you think of going to New York as going to the Emerald City . . . and you come back to Kansas City in the end. Well, not Kansas City, but what is Rochester if not a small town? Yours is an extraordinary life because it's so inspiring.

LB: Inspiring?

JK: People always think that if you don't make it, you're a failure, yet there's so much to draw on just by surviving. It's encouraging.

LB: That's from George Bernard Shaw. If you have an artistic life, if you have music and painting and books and so on . . . See, most actors, when they're through with their careers, there's nothing left. Nothing but the Motion Picture Home. Everyone says I should fight going to the home for as long as possible. It would be terrible for me. Suppose this woman Marge, who lives in the building and she's eighty-two, you know, but suppose she stops coming down and feeding me, what's going to happen to me then?

Even as we sat there talking, Louise coughed a lot, grumbled a lot, cursed her illness, then chuckled at the irony of fate that had brought her to this not very pretty pass. There would be moments when she'd sit there fighting for breath, clawing her cane, gritting her teeth. There was nothing to be done. When the spasm had passed, she'd take a sip of juice to help clear her throat. The strain of sitting at the table for so long was telling on her. But every time I suggested we stop and she go to bed, she brushed it off. Even though her body might show signs of pain, her eyes, sunk back, large, dark, glowed with intelligence and curiosity and life.

LB: No. I'm not. I'm miserable. If I could think of a good way of ending it all, I'd do it. I'm such a coward. I'd like to be out of the whole thing. What can you expect? I lie in bed in there day after day, and this is terrible. Emphysema is just murder. You don't realize it while I'm just sitting here, but the moment I get up and make a move, I can't breathe. It's terrible. And I know that when you go into intensive care in the hospital, you're hooked up with the oxygen tank and with the wheelchair and . . . *God,* it's a rotten way to go. Terrible disease. No, I'm utterly miserable.

We both sit there, quiet for a moment. There's not much to be said after that. My hand reaches out to cover hers. Louise grins. She's gotten her wind back. She doesn't feel sorry for herself for long, and she doesn't like people to feel sorry for her either.

LB: You know, John, Ruskin said, "A great writer is a person who's seen something and tells what he saw in a plain way." And that's the way you can write too, because you're a great "see-er." I've always tried to write like a movie, so that everybody could understand it the same way I saw it. You can't do better than to remember Ruskin! It didn't hurt Proust. Proust couldn't read English, but a friend translated Ruskin for him, and Proust was greatly influenced; he got his way of writing from that.

I could see that Louise had never wanted much. She was a soloist who all her life had to spend time dealing not with what she wanted but with what other people wanted, with what they gave her and with what they expected from her, and with what people thought of her for not showing gratitude for things she had never asked for. She was a woman people learned to resent for not being spoiled by the things that would have spoiled them. When she was young, that attitude, that discipline, that fastidiousness, wherever she was—on a set or in the middle of a party—must have seemed like an implied criticism of the values around her. Louise never was the type to go to bed with someone to get something. Love wasn't a game for her, sex was a biological function. She placed no price on it. It wasn't a reward or a surrender. She could observe it. She'd talk about it like the amusing game it was, but she didn't judge people by it. Her inviolateness must have driven many a person to frenzy, a mad desire to strangle her, to remove her. Why should this Louise be better than anyone else? And now, today, pain was like all these people—it wanted a sign from her, an admission, a surrender, and all it got was a grumble, but it wasn't from her but from pain's own pressure exerted on her as when two things are violently forced together to produce a third: the sound from the collision. And the pain is in a frenzy, all it can produce is weariness. It gives up and Louise falls asleep.

Before her illness can get its strength back for another assault on this indomitable old iconoclast, I walk her back to her bed. Sunk back on her propped-up pillow, she rests. We say goodbye so she won't have to start up again when I am ready to leave.

I thought she was asleep when I was letting myself out. "John? Is that you?" "Yes, I'm just off." "Okay, Sugar Pie. Keep it up. Be a good boy," she calls after me, chuckling, making that last admonition sound like an encouragement to wild and exciting adventure.

1965, 1982

Evelyn Brent, photographed by A. L. "Whitey" Schafer, circa 1936

EVELYN
BRENT

THE GAUNT OLD WOMAN with the wiry gray hair who opened the door to my knock could have been any cautious old woman living in that row of single-story bungalows planted along three sides of a rectangular boxlike shape around a narrow patch of dry grass, the kind of mobile homes without wheels you find all over Los Angeles and Southern California, adapted from the cookie-cutter school of architecture and which should have never been more than a temporary roof and four walls to keep out the sun. She looked like one of the many whose short-term accommodations sort of drifted into becoming their homes. As if to confirm this shift in status, there is a neatly tended border of grass outside the peeling, color-faded walls. The aging, tan-tarred, wrinkle-etched people living there, mostly single and childless, pensioners of the sun, California dreamers far from the beaches for whom time slipped by, like this woman now looking at me, her hand shielding her squinting eyes for a better view before she would allow her face to relax into a less guarded expression, could have come from anywhere in the United States, could have been God knows who in the days before the sun made them all the same. This, after all, is Hollywood, California, and the baked-out faces you see there have a resignation stamped on them as if in their sleep a heavy hand had passed over them and removed their dreams and ambitions in return for lipstick, fluttery eyes and pink hairdos.

This woman, strangely awkward in her stance, like someone who had never been comfortable with her body, as if she were afraid it might give her away, neat but prim in her plain red-checkered dress, would have looked more natural standing in a farmhouse doorway out of Depression photos, checking out a traveling salesman, mildly curious but not about to let herself be sold any frilly things. If it hadn't been for a quick check of the address on the scrap of paper in my hand, I might have thought this was the wrong door, and she the wrong person, a next-door neighbor, a friend looking after the house, anyone but the woman I'd sought out, the Garboesque silent film beauty Evelyn Brent.

Evelyn Brent's career, today almost forgotten but in the late '20s one of the most promising, is a witness to the egalitarian nature that was the source of the Hollywood star system, a lottery anybody might win, and the reason for that

99

system's unmatched attraction to a worldwide audience. Her strong, hard, aggressive stance and her dark, cloudy beauty, like a pre-Raphaelite boy, forecasts such types as Barbara Stanwyck and made her comparable to Joan Crawford, her contemporary. Audiences identified—at first—not with their glamour, wardrobes and the hype surrounding their roles, but with the compelling common streak that had propelled them from the bottom of society's heap to a penthouse view of the world. Both Crawford and Brent had troubled backgrounds driving them out of home and into self-sufficiency at an early age, but there the comparison ends.

If Evelyn Brent had set her sights for one of the lesser peaks, she too could have become one of the major stars of the '30s, instead of drifting with little apparent fuss into supporting roles, down to fifth, ninth, twelfth billing and sometimes even no billing at all. She was still on the casting lists for small roles and extra work when she died. One of her last appearances had been in a Disney TV film. It wasn't much, but it was work. Evelyn lacked Joan's fight; she lacked the Crawford drive; she failed to learn, she didn't bother to look, or else why would she have veered so far off the main road as to never be taken seriously again. In 1930 with sound the rage and her voice a success, she was in all the magazines and in five films. You had to look for articles about her in 1931. By 1932 it was as if she hadn't been there.

She was provocatively beautiful and haunting in the three silent films directed by Josef von Sternberg, yet it was evident from the films she *didn't* make with him—films like *Love 'Em and Leave 'Em,* where she was co-starred with and overwhelmed by Louise Brooks—that it took great skill to photograph her as mysterious instead of bland, svelte instead of thick, haunting instead of obvious. Apparently it wasn't she who had learned to move so intriguingly by the time she entered Von Sternberg's *Underworld,* but rather the things he moved around her to create the enthralling illusion of a woman at the center of powerful forces.

There is a moment in *The Last Command* that rivals Garbo's climactic close-up in *Queen Christina* or Dietrich's in the train compartment aboard the *Shanghai Express.* Evelyn's face in that scene from *The Last Command* was capable of absorbing and returning any emotion the director wanted us to see on screen, as she leaned out of the hurtling train, the white smoke rushing furiously from the stack and lashing out at her broad back before blowing around her as if she were the heart of this white fire; and the wind, also obstructed and caught up in her thick hair, fought its way out by flickering and beating the dark strands around her large white face like thousands of demanding black tongues: at that moment there was everything in her eyes, there was nothing. In this instance our emotions were heightened by the knowledge of the man she loved in the snow back there. She'd saved his life at the sacrifice of her own. But it could just as well have been a baby crying, it could have been a house in flames, it could have been something she was listening to and only she could hear. Her physical gaucheness needn't have undermined her career (it didn't hurt Garbo, who even played a dancer in several films), especially since sound revealed in Evelyn a fascinating voice that was cold, tough and commanding. More often than not, she came across as a hard woman lacking femininity.

Evelyn's career gave the impression of someone who fell into good luck without ever having the good sense to capitalize on her good fortune and to consolidate her position. Instead, she made films—good or bad, major or minor, starring or in support, without regard to how she'd be photographed. Evelyn, clearly, while conveying an optical illusion of self-sufficiency, was the sort of woman who needed a mentor, someone like Von Sternberg, who went on to make Dietrich the legend, or a Lubitsch, or, better still, the David O. Selznick type of Svengali which Jennifer Jones had to guide her career. Was it that she had refused to submit her will to the powerful men she knew who could have helped her? Yet Evelyn, married three times, allowed herself to drift toward men who had only a quick-gain interest in her career, and when it waned, so did they. You can root for someone like this only so long before you give up on her. When audiences found others, like Joan Crawford or Barbara Stanwyck, to take Evelyn's place, she was left where she had begun: a good, competent, working actress like many others who turn up in B thrillers and Western programmers, playing gun molls in trench coats and saloonkeepers in hand-me-down feathers. Evelyn didn't expand, she contracted. She lost her youth, then her beauty, then her money, but it seemed more due to her own uncaring. Confronted with questions about her past, about her successes and her failures, Evelyn simply offered memories like someone who had never realized her own worth and therefore didn't bother to remember anything.

Looking into that lined but still handsomely profiled face, I saw a woman worn by years of work. My feelings were based on magnificent portraits taken at her peak, by photographers like Steichen, Henry Waxman and Arnold Genthe, of the woman Gary Cooper had been desperately in love with and who had turned him down, and of course by what Von Sternberg had revealed of her in *Underworld, The Drag Net* and *The Last Command*. I felt sad thinking of her lost opportunities, and sad that she didn't know why the opportunities had been lost. Evelyn, however, conveyed no such emotions. Her hands were gnarled because they were arthritic and not because she had to take in washing; her face was lined because she was old. And if she was sad, it was because her cat was ill. Only her voice, hardly changed at all, revealed the fact (dotted with the reminiscent "see? . . . it happened this way, see?") that here sat the woman who was Hollywood's prototype for the classic "screen moll." The woman in the chair across from me, struggling gamely to answer questions, was the one who was happier serving tea and cookies when she occasionally attended one of those film-buff gatherings in someone's home, and who could have been the hired help rather than the star whose picture they came from out of town to have signed. "Yeah, I know . . . it's strange, isn't it? . . . But they're good people," Evelyn would say, as if one had anything to do with the other. She would have signed a picture of Norma Shearer if that had been handed to her by mistake, not because she didn't know the difference, but because she didn't think it mattered. She wasn't relating her signature now to her photograph then. She was too like the people who were there, except that they had illusions about stars, but Evelyn had no illusions at all.

The small apartment Evelyn shared with her longtime friend Dorothy and their cats was simple, spotless and sufficient. The shades were down because the sun was shining. Funny, people come from across the world to spend time there in the sun, the major industry grew up there because of the sun, and the natives are forever drawing the shades over their windows in the daytime. "Let's go inside where it's nice and cool" was the phrase I probably heard more often than any other out there. Now, even in the darkened room, Evelyn seemed to be shading her eyes still.

The only way to tell why Evelyn was fascinating on screen is to see her films . . . for, in the end, that is just where she *was* fascinating: on screen. Curtained by the furs, the feathers and the fog machines, Evelyn's edges had been hidden, she had a strength that took on a jewel's glow: there was the mystery of Garbo, the irony of Dietrich, the obsession of Crawford and the humanity of Stanwyck. Or was it just Von Sternberg shouting to her, "Don't move! Don't move! Don't touch your eyes! Leave your hair alone!" And all the time she has been leaning out of a train for hours, her back is killing her, the fog and wind machines are freezing her and she wants out of it. Was it all just the *mise en scène*? So what's wrong with that, you ask yourself, if the result is up there and it works? Nothing. Only . . . where was Evelyn? All these decades later, she had not one picture of herself from any of the films or any of the portrait sittings with the masters. Not one. And she didn't want any.

JK: When you scored your first hit in *Underworld,* you had already been in films for many years.

EB: Oh, long time . . . I was fourteen years old when I started. But I don't remember them. See, another girl and I, who were going to school together in New York—we went to the grammar school at the Hunter College—we were intrigued by the idea of working in pictures. So we went one day, we didn't go to school, and we went up to Fort Lee, New Jersey, where the World Film Company was. It was headed by a man in the film business called Brulatour . . . Jules Brulatour. We found a casting office. We'd never seen one before, and a man came out and he looked over the people waiting: men, women and everything. He looked at me and he said, "There's a pretty little girl, we can get her to do the secretary part." Just like that. And I did it. I didn't know what was happening, I was just a kid. Then, shortly afterwards, things happened in my life that made it necessary for me to work. So they offered me a contract, a guarantee of $5 a day for three days a week, and if I worked a fourth day, I got another $5. Well, that, then, that seemed terrific to me. So I just went on from there. I don't have any recollection of what the people were I worked with. Except Madame [Olga] Petrova, I remember her because she was very sweet to me. She found me crying one day on the set about something, I can't remember what, and she took me into her dressing room and gave me a talking-to . . . and I'll never forget. You know, "You can't let these things upset you this way because they aren't worth it." I had a Christmas card from Madame Petrova, I still get a Christmas card each year, and I always send her one. She's in a sanitorium . . . not that, what d'ya call 'em, a retired place in Florida. She sent a snapshot of herself this time. She looks wonderful, and she must be quite on now. But I met some nice people back then, the Barrymores were very nice to me. . . .

I liked the stage, I'd like to really been able to do the stage, but, as things worked out, I did one play in London. While I was in the play, that darling man C. Aubrey Smith was in it. His daughter was an understudy and I got to know them very well. British Actors Film Company signed him to a picture, so he suggested that they get me for the lead, which they did and that really started things off. You see, I'd gone to London with a friend of mine who had to go there on business, a woman. Lola. She bought things, imported things, and I went with her. My mother had died and I had nobody left. I went first to Paris and she did all her business, and then we went to London, and then I got the offer to do the play through a dancer . . . called Maurice. He was dancing with a very beautiful blond girl called Lenore Hughes or something, and I had met her . . . them in New York, and they were in London. And they invited me to come see them dancing. I think it was at the Savoy, and I met John Cromwell there, who was casting the play, and that's how I got into it. That's when it all started to happen.

I wound up doing *The Spanish Jade* for Paramount, we went to Spain and did that. I did several pictures which I don't remember, except for *The Spanish Jade,* and then Paramount signed me to a contract. I made one in Holland, and then I went to Italy and made one. All before I came out here to LA to work for Paramount here. Paramount bought me—I mean, FBO signed me. See, Paramount didn't want me for *Underworld,* they wanted Estelle Taylor. But Sternberg wanted me. I guess he liked my work and thought I could do it. So he won out in the argument, or it might have been a different story! Of course, I was very fond of Estelle too, 'cause she was a nice girl.

JK: You were always cast in "heavy" roles . . . were you ever an ingenue?

EB: In some of the early pictures I probably was, because I was so young. But not after, 'cause all the things I made, even at FBO, were all, you know, character parts, they weren't leads. They were leads technically, but they were not the regular "love story" type of thing. But I worked in so many. I probably could stand it better then than I could now, 'cause when you're that young you can go on indefinitely. I remember even when we'd go out and dance all night someplace after working all day. Priscilla Dean and I used to do it. All of 'em did it.

JK: How important was your career to you?

EB: Oh, very.

JK: Were you ambitious?

EB: I don't think I was. I think if I had had more urge than I did . . . But involvements came, and, well, it becomes secondary. I don't think it was ever first, you know. I probably could have done more. I only loved it when I was doing something I liked. The rest of the time I didn't like it.

JK: You had nobody to guide you?

EB: No . . . it's pretty difficult to be put in that kind of life when you've had no background for it. The first one I think who really helped me in an advisory way was Frank Joyce, who was my agent for a long time. He and his wife were friends of mine. Frank and Myron Selznick had an agency, and that was my first. Possibly, had I been with him earlier, my career might have gone a little better. I don't know, you can't say. Frank was a very nice man and, like, he would always go with you if you had an interview. Now they don't do this anymore, they just send 'em. And he did all the business talking, *you* didn't do anything. Joyce and Selznick, they were the first important ones, back in the late '20s. And had Frank Joyce not died, I think it also might have gone differently. I liked Myron, but I didn't get along with him. He was a different personality. If things hadn't happened the way they did, I would have probably been able to concentrate on it more, see? I think I was always fairly sensible. I mean, you can't say I didn't make mistakes, because I did, we all do. But I've seen some of these kids, they forget everything else when the social bit comes up. I didn't do that.

And of course these kids made the biggest mistake sleeping around. It's one of the worst things they can do. It's killed more careers. If a girl was lucky enough to find a man important enough . . . but not with this one and then that one and then another one. That's what's so cheap, that's what's ruined so many of them. If they find one, like Norma Shearer found Irving Thalberg . . . there's a perfect example. He was an important man in the industry, he started as a very young boy, grew up with it. He fell in love with her, she fell in love with him, so he concentrated on her career. Now, you take Lupe Velez. She should have been a much bigger star than she was, see, but she frittered too much time away. She was off on a tangent all the time, she was excitable. I think she should have been much bigger than she was, she had great talent, she had excitement about her. Poor soul.

JK: But at this point you were working all the time, you had a name for yourself. In 1924 they were already calling you the Queen of the Underworld because of all the gangster films you'd done.

EB: Yeah. All those pictures I did at FBO were all underworld stories. That's what started that trend, and it climaxed for me by the films I made with Joe [von Sternberg] at Paramount, *Underworld* and *Drag Net* and *The Last Command*. You couldn't get better than that, you couldn't get better parts. But, see, I was working. It wasn't so much a "film career" or a way of life, at least I don't think I ever consciously thought about it. Also, I was never very much, uh, too much like a party girl. I never liked it, going to big parties, unless I had someone with me. They were wild, some of those parties, see? We had a few people out here who liked nice parties at home. Well, that wouldn't have satisfied most of the girls, they wanted excitement, they wanted the Cocoanut Grove, where *we* only went on special occasions.

But, as I said, in those days Hollywood was such a small place and you had so few places to go. There was the Grove, and when I first came out here they had the Biltmore Hotel downtown. They had started a thing in New York called the Mayfair Club, and they started a branch out here. Every second week, on Saturday night, they had a big bash at a private ballroom. They were dinner dances, and people would talk, like Jack Warner would get up and make his usual wisecracks. It was a small industry then too, don't forget. Nothing like it is today. Everybody in the business was at those Mayfair dances, see? If there was an opening at the Grove, say if a big band came in, then everybody, every table would be people you knew. The Montmartre was the luncheon place on Hollywood Boulevard. And the Brown Derby. That was the extent of your Hollywood nightlife, that was it. Except for home parties, and a lot of those got to be pretty bad. Especially for somebody who didn't drink a lot. I mean, I like a drink before dinner, but I don't get smashed. I don't know, it never appealed to me. I always wanted to know what I was doing . . . I didn't want to be someplace and not know what was going to happen.

Now they tell stories about orgies that lasted all weekend and alcohol coming out of faucets; those I never saw, not quite *that* bad. I think a lot of that happened with the set that was out here very early—you know, the William Desmond Taylor crowd, Mabel Normand, Mack Sennett, they were pretty wild. But that was before I got out here. I came out around 1922.

JK: Was fame a hard thing to adjust to? You were so young, a girl. You must have gone to movies, read fan magazines, dreamed those dreams?

EB: I don't think I did, actually, I think it all just happened. See, the first hint I got of it, fame, was my first trip back when I went to New York in 1927. I suddenly realized that everybody knew me wherever I went.

JK: You'd already been making films for twelve years by then! What did you think when you read about Mary Pickford going around the world and thousands and millions of fans following her?

EB: I thought it was pretty wonderful. I was pretty much in awe of people like that. I have never had much business sense. You see, Mary Pickford had a mother who was a wonderful businesswoman. Another one was the Talmadge girls' mother, she was there directing and controlling it. I didn't have anybody like that. When you're a kid and you earn a lot of money, you spend a lot . . . on everything you always wanted to do: travel and everything like that. Suddenly you can do it. The minute I'd finished a picture and they'd have cleared us I'd head right out to New York. I liked it, I knew people, I went out places, to theaters, which I loved. And I could afford to do it. Tickets and all these things are a drain on the pocketbook when you don't have a lot of money! You buy them and you pay for them, but you do too much. You don't do it sensibly. If you have a business manager, if you are lucky enough to get a good one that doesn't cheat you . . .

JK: Were you pursued by "Quick-Buck Charlies"? It happened to Mae Murray, who married Prince Mdivani.

EB: Sure, but she should have known better, because she was no kid by then either. She had a good husband, Bob Leonard, a director. She had worked in a nightclub for many years in New York before she came out to Hollywood. You'd think she'd have known by then. I never thought that Mdivani guy was attractive, the one she married. But he was horrible because I used to meet him at the Embassy Club with her, and he was a most unattractive man, I thought. I couldn't see what she saw in him. No, they never attracted me. Not when you knew a few of them! I think I was always a little suspicious and careful. Because I never got swept away with these mad things that people do. I was married . . . I have to think . . . three times. The last one was the best one, but he died in 1959. That's when it began to be pretty empty. You'd have flings with people when you're young, you don't stop to think if this is what you want to do, I don't think.

JK: When you played with Gary Cooper in one film and Neil Hamilton in another . . .

EB: Not Neil, no. No, I wouldn't do that, I knew Neil's wife too well. But Gary Cooper, yes. When I first met him and we made a picture together [*Beau Sabreur*], it was quite a thing, but it didn't last very long. I don't know why, but I went to New York. The time I broke with him was the time Valentino died, because I was on the way when the news came in that he'd died. I wanted out of it, I liked Gary very much, but you know . . . He was a doll, he really was, a very nice guy. It's very sad about his finish, but it had to happen to him. His mother died not long ago, and he still has a brother living in San Francisco. I knew his mother very well, she lived quite near me. Gary was very nice, but the women were so crazy about him. More than any other man I knew. I think what attracted people was he had a great shyness, he kept pulling back, and it intrigued people. He really was a very quiet, quiet guy.

JK: From all I have read, you were never involved in a scandal other than the time when Fairbanks brought you out—

EB: Oh, that. Now, you see, I made *Spanish Jade* in Spain, and it was released over here, and they saw it, Fairbanks, Pickford and Chaplin saw it. And probably they had some kidding about signing me to a contract, but anyway, when I got to New York, I was staying at the Algonquin Hotel, where everybody stayed. Somebody called me from some office and said that Douglas Fairbanks and Mary Pickford wanted to have me come to lunch with them. So they came to the Algonquin and I had lunch with them, and that's when they asked me to sign the contract, which I did. Then I got married to my first husband before I came out. Then I was supposed to do *The Thief of Bagdad* and *The Black Pirate* . . . but they weren't for me. The one they were originally going to do I could have done, but I knew I could not do the others. I just didn't like the part of the princess in *Thief of Bagdad*. I remember going to Bernie [Fineman, her husband] and saying, "I cannot do that part." After I had been in the studio and talked and done still pictures with Fairbanks holding me up in one hand and all of that silly stuff. I just didn't like the setup.

Anyway, I lived in a house—I rented this little house opposite the Chaplin studios. One morning I went out horseback riding about 6:00 in Griffith Park and I came back and the house was surrounded by reporters. I was living there, they said, because it was near Chaplin's studios and Fairbanks could go to the studio ostensibly to see me. It was absolutely untrue. There was no basis to it at all. As a matter of fact, I didn't even like him! But have you ever tried to deny a story to a bunch of reporters who are looking for a headline? I was *furious,* and that's when I told Bernie, "Look, get me out of this contract." I didn't want to have to deny the fact that I was not living with my husband and that I was a secret date of Douglas Fairbanks . . . it was ridiculous. And what started it I don't know. That thing followed me for ages, and people would not believe me. I had three personal contacts with them—one at the Algonquin, one when I came out here and they asked me to come to some story conference or something, and Mary was not there but he was . . . among the executives and Mary's mother and the whole bit! Then I was told to come and make the still pictures. Those were the only contacts I had with him. I have seen Mary—not lately—out at the Country House when my husband was out there. Mary would come out two or three times a week with Buddy [Rogers, her last husband] to see the director Mickey Neilan, who was very ill and died soon afterwards. She was very nice . . . but we never discussed it.

JK: Did you ever discuss it with Fairbanks?

EB: No! I never saw him again. Bernie did all the arrangements to get me out of the contract. But Mary I saw quite a lot at the hospital during that period. We were very friendly, but she never discussed it. You don't know what starts these things . . . you wonder. I denied it to the newspaper reporters and that's the last I ever did. They even went so far that . . . I had a picture on the mantel of George K. Arthur, he was an actor and I had known him in England. And when he first came out here, I helped him—I don't mean financially, but I helped in getting his wife out here, 'cause she was British. Bernie helped get her into the country. We called him "Kipps" and the reporters insisted that it was a picture of Douglas Fairbanks, Jr., he was a very young man then. It was not true, it was a picture of "Kipps."

JK: Yes, you had become quite popular in England.

EB: I loved it, I met a lot of nice people. I loved it in London, I really did. So I made one film, with Aubrey Smith, after the play. And I did one with the British Actors Film Company and I can't remember the name of it. I met Clive Brook on that first trip, and Joe [Sternberg] was working at the studio. He was like a set designer. And, you know, it was the same over there as it was out here at Paramount: the crew, everybody, it was all one. I have always said that you find your best friends and fans in the crew at the studio, and it's true. I don't know what it's like today. The woman I live with, Dorothy, does things on TV. She was a voice and diction teacher at Goodman in Chicago. I've been on sets with her, and a lot of the crew that are working now I knew from my days. They always remember you. They're nice people. There was warm friendship with the people who worked together, and I don't think it exists so much today. I've been on sets of some of those TV things, and the principals, the regulars, seem not to want to be bothered . . . they're like in a class by themselves. Almost to the point of rudeness. And you know that can hurt people.

During the last few things I did, there was a lack of warmth, a lack of working together. There seems to be a complete isolation of people. The regulars, they're the ones and they don't care less about other people. Now, in those days, when they'd have a scene that called for a lot of people, they would get together all the old-timers who weren't doing so well and get 'em in to work. And you'd knock yourself out being nice to them. I don't think it exists anymore.

JK: If somebody spiraled ahead, as Clara Bow did overnight, to acclaim . . . of course, you had started much earlier. . . .

EB: From the time she was a kid. She was a very nice girl. She was so involved in so many things. I've never known Clara to be mean to anybody. We were very friendly—not bosom buddies or anything, but we'd have a call for stills at the same time and everybody would get together and have fun. But Clara I liked very much. I thought she was good on the screen for the type of thing she did. I thought she was wonderful, and a very warm person, which proved to be true, because she was very ill for many years and never did she fail to send me a birthday card and a Christmas card, up till the last year she lived. She always wrote a message on it.

I think she had been badly hurt many times by the industry and by people. Because I think she was a very trusting little thing, she believed what people told her. You've got to develop a shell, 'cause if you don't, you're going to get hurt. 'Course, she may have hurt some people too, that I don't know. And I don't know what caused the trouble, why she cracked up, which I understand she did. Rex Bell, her husband, he bought a house over in Culver City and he had nurses with her all the time. I'll tell you who used to go to see her all the time was Maxie Rosenbloom, the old-time fighter. He used to go constantly to see her, 'cause he used to tell me how she was each time. He never missed.

JK: What was it like for you, being a star? Did you find that they wanted to remake you, remodel you? They did that to so many people.

EB: Well, with some people, yes. They followed trends. They commenced giving it that look that started with Garbo, the overpainting. Mae Murray made up just the middle of her mouth, that silly little cupid's-bow mouth. I don't think anybody tried to change my makeup, though. The person that affected me most, mainly as far as dressing, was Travis Banton. He was the kind of designer who read the script and would find out who was going to play the part, and work out the clothes that way. When I got to know him, on *Underworld,* he got the thing about feathers and furs, and then the hats were designed to save extra time in the morning. And they ended up being a real fad! The hats were made of coq feathers and velvet leaves edged in rhinestones, and no hair showed. That saved a lot of time. Travis said it would be sensible, knowing how hard you were going to work. It started a vogue. See, Joe called my character "Feathers," and that probably influenced Travis in his designs. Travis was exceptionally good . . . with people like Ruth Chatterton. He had a different flair for each one. So with the hats, I had them made of so many different things, leaves and flowers. They went with the type of clothes I was wearing, long, flowing things, furs, feathers, everything. But he was a damn good designer, Travis.

I'd meet people outside and they would always be surprised that I was so small. They always figured I was tall because I wore four-and-a-half-inch heels all the time. And the clothes had a tendency to have long lines, and that surprised them. A lot of people also have said that they were surprised that I was always so quiet. I don't know what they even expected. At parties I was always a little by myself. That's why some of those stories about people . . . the ghastly stories that came out about Jean Harlow, that she drank herself to death or whatever . . . I don't know what I haven't heard said about her. I met her at twenty parties, and she didn't drink any more than I did. Everybody else would be drunk and we would be sitting in a corner, chatting and having one glass of wine. That's what makes me mad, when they come out and say that the cause of her death was drinking. It absolutely was not. It was sun poisoning, and she had been warned not to go into the sun. These things upset you when you like somebody. That was my only contact with her, at parties, because she was a quiet girl too.

JK: The stories about Clara Bow are pretty extreme too, always the emphasis on the "hotcha" . . .

EB: Yeah, but I think this was based on the parts she played too. I guess she had a lot of love affairs, she was a pretty kid. But I never knew her to be wild. How could she be? She worked too hard. I met her one time in the stills department at 3:00 in the morning having stills taken. She had a lot of personality and she was very pretty. A cute little figure. I could see where people would be attracted to her. Oh, there were other girls, but not with the personality she had. She and Lupe Velez each had a vibrant something. Of the two, I think I liked Clara better.

JK: And you? Men never fell in love with your image and then realized that you were yourself?

EB: No, I don't think so. I don't think it ever happened to me. My first marriage was to a boy I knew at school, I knew his sister. The second one I met out here, and that was a bad one. He was an attractive man and he had good manners. It was a mistake, unfortunately. The last one, Harry Fox, was a vaudevillian. That was good. When he died, I said, "I had a good one, now let it go." Ways of life change. But Harry was the best one. I did personal appearances with Harry, back in Chicago. Only gangsters I ever met were in Chicago.

JK: Were there lots of gangsters in Hollywood then?

EB: I know there were some out here, but their headquarters was not here. They came out on certain business that they had to do, such as when they had to kill somebody . . . like Bugsy Siegel. But no, as I say, I only met 'em in Chicago, and they were *very* nice to me. They liked me because of the parts I played. I saw this man standing in the alley by the . . . I think it was the Oriental Theater or the State-Lake Theater, and he finally came up to me and said something like, "Anything upset you, just let me know and I'll take care of it." And through him I met the man who covered Capone for the newspapers. I can't remember his name, I think it was Reed, but I'm not sure. He was assigned to cover that area. And he took Harry and me to places where gangsters were, and I saw quite a lot, but they were very nice to me always, really were. One of them made a statement that I was the only one who'd ever played a gangster's moll as a gangster's moll should be!

JK: How did you become known as Queen of the Underworld? I mean, did someone bestow the name on you?

EB: I don't know. Tod Browning was the director, and I think he was the first one who set that up at FBO for a series; he directed several of them, the gangster movies. He was with MGM for years, doing all the Lon Chaney things. He's dead a good many years now. He was a very good director. Remember *Freaks*? That was Tod. Anything weird, away from the ordinary, he loved. Regardless. A script was a very loose thing in those days, wasn't like it is today. Tod would read us a sequence that was going to be done, and he'd change the whole thing. There was no dialogue, so it was much easier. He had a great flair.

JK: Would he listen to what you had to say about your part?

EB: I don't think I ever made suggestions. Although many actors did. Lubitsch had the best answer for actors' suggestions. He was a sweet little man with a great sense of humor. An actor would go up to him and Lubitsch would listen very carefully and say, "You think so?" and the actor would say, "Yes," and he would say, "I *don't* think so." I only worked with him on the one thing, with Chevalier, a sequence for *Paramount on Parade,* and Chevalier was a dream. That cute little slapping sequence, about the husband and wife. I don't know how it all came about 'cause all of a sudden I was doing it, and I liked Chevalier so much. I had admired him so, for many years, I thought he was so wonderful. We had fun doing it, and I had never worked music before . . . it was timed to the music of "My Man" like an "Apache" number. Oh, I learned a lot from Lubitsch. He's a great director . . . was. Between Lubitsch and Chevalier, they made it very easy for me to do. I was scared to death when I started it, because I'd never done that type of thing before, but they made it so easy.

But I think it was Tod Browning that started, really, the Queen of the Underworld thing. I probably got the Von Sternberg *Underworld* on the strength of Tod's pictures. I know Von Sternberg had seen them. See, they were silent pictures, you know. But Tod made you use your voice. He was the first one that had ever done that. He gave you lines and you read them emotionally . . . if you were supposed to scream, you screamed. He figured that it came over better; instead of pretending feeling, that it would come over better with what you were doing. If you knew what you were doing, it was interesting. You said something that made sense . . . well, sometimes it didn't make sense. But Tod made you stick to the idea of the script so you said the line that meant what you were supposed to mean. That was unusual.

I had great respect for him as a director. I think he taught me a lot; he taught me to know what I was doing when I was doing a part, and it was the first time it consciously came to me. And you got that with Joe Sternberg too. He had a great feeling for a picture. The actors were not as important as the sweep of the story, the actors moved against it. In *Underworld* and *Drag Net* they all had the bigness and that sweep, see? The actors were incidental, they furthered the story, the action, instead of him concentrating on the actors only. That was why, after he worked with Dietrich, he began a concentration on her, which I can understand, mind you, because she was wonderful. But I think he lost something in the sweep of the picture. *Underworld* is a classic example of a gangster picture, because it's a big picture of gangsterism. And he had people doing what they were supposed to do. I think it was wonderful, I really do. The last time I saw it, I still thought it was good.

JK: Did you mind that you were doing nothing but the same roles so often?

EB: No, I loved them.

JK: I gather one had to be careful about what one said around Sternberg.

EB: No. Well, I was very careful, and a lot of the people were. I remember one very funny episode in *Underworld* with Fred Kohler. I vaguely remember this scene in a nightclub. He came in with a gun and threatened to blow somebody's head off or something. He said, "If you don't do so-and-so, I'll fire this baby and shoot your head off." Joe didn't like the way it was going, and after many, many takes Joe said, "And if you don't say it right this time, *I'll* blow *your* head off!" It was difficult because he had a certain idea of how you should do it. And, by golly, you'd get to it! After all, it was his conception and his story, and he should know.

The only times I ever fought with him were when I was so tired I guess I didn't know what I was doing. And there's one point where you crack. I remember once when there was a dance at the Mayfair, I said, "Are you gonna need me on Saturday night?" and he said, "No, you should be through around 4:00 or 5:00 in the afternoon." So I arranged to go to the dance. He said, "However, on your way home, stop in at the studio just in case I might need one shot." So I stopped by and he said, "Get made up." They were working on the back lot with the fog machines going. And I went out and sat and sat and sat, until it was daylight. I was so mad. I blew my stack. I was so furious, to go in there and sit all night doing nothing. I knew I had finished that street scene.

I think I told you before about the time he made Clive [Clive Brook in *Underworld*] do one entrance thirty times. All he had to do was to come in and put a flower in his buttonhole. They were just cantankerous with each other that day. Clive did it over and over again until I thought he'd blow his stack. And he did finally. It was working too many hours, and under difficult conditions, too fast. It's cold working out in the back lot at night, you have no idea what it could be like. They didn't have portable dressing rooms in those days, they had what they called a stove, that if you stood right up against it you could get a little warm. But you couldn't stay there very long. There weren't the comforts that they've got today. . . . Oh, that back lot at Paramount was miserable, so cold, even on a hot day the nights were cold. And the fog machines going, see? It was beautiful on the screen, but difficult to do.

Now, in the opening shot of *Underworld* I was to come down some stairs into the nightclub and he had feathers down on the stairs before my feet came into the shot. This took a long time camera-wise to get it, but when I saw it I realized why he wanted it. It stamped the whole character. The breeze took a couple of feathers and then my feet came in and the camera panned up. I didn't mind those things. He knew as much about cameras as any cameraman did. That was where a lot of the time was spent. And in those days we didn't have any stand-ins, we had to do the standing in ourselves. He would have it all mapped out. You'd stand under those hot lights while they'd move 'em all around. All this before you get to the scene, and you're exhausted. I never minded it, because Joe was a stickler for making you see rushes every day. It helped you to get an understanding what he was taking the time to try to do. He got very angry if anybody missed seeing the rushes. We used to go in every day. He was tough to work with, but I like working. I could only wish they had more directors like him. Joe had a great mind. When I knew him in England . . . I can barely remember. He was called Joe Stern then. A nice little man. I called him Joe. Joe started a picture with a conception of what he wanted on the screen, and that's why I believed in him and trusted him. In spite of fights, which any normal people have if they have any normal reactions or feelings. And also, see, I was working on a couple of pictures at the same time. Yeah, when you were under contract, you just worked. At Paramount I worked on two pictures at once, many times. I know when we made *Beau Sabreur* they wanted a lot of retakes. So I worked nights on that and days on *Underworld*. You were under contract, you got the same salary; you didn't get paid for doing two pictures, you got paid your regular salary. But 'course you got it when you weren't working too.

JK: Did you feel that *Underworld* was something special?

EB: I don't think I realized it was special until I saw it at the preview. I knew what Joe was aiming for, but I did not know enough then to be able to envision what he was doing, as a whole picture. But, you see, he explained things very well, and he knew just how much he wanted from each person. I think that's why he and Clive had the fights they had, because Clive was not a belligerent guy at all. I'd worked in other pictures, a lot of 'em, with him. It may have been too long hours and too much work. For some reason Clive got, as they say now, "too uptight." But he had some great arguments. And George Bancroft*—George Bancroft was . . . how would I put it? He was like a kid. I don't think he realized what the picture was going to be, and if it hadn't been for Joe, he wouldn't have been good in it. The strength that Joe put into it, he made George put into it. George couldn't have done it himself because he wasn't that kind of person. He had the reactions of a little boy. I don't mean he was retarded. An example of how naïve he was . . . we went to see Priscilla Dean and her husband. He was one of the first round-the-

---

*Bancroft, a silent-film Victor McLaglen type, made four films with Von Sternberg which established him as a big draw.

world fliers, Leslie Arnold. And George went with us down to San Diego to
meet some famous general, I can't remember his name now. We stopped to
have some food and he said, "Do you realize why we were as good as we
were in *Underworld*?" And I said, "Because we had a damn good director."
And he said, "No, it was because in the love scenes I always thought of my
mother." Does that make sense? Priscilla nearly fell out of her chair! That was
George Bancroft. Oh, but Joe, he could be really tough. We remained
friendly. Not too long before he died, I met him over at Sears . . . he liked
gadgets, tools and things. I had no ill-feeling. In fact, I think I'd rather
worked with him than anyone else I know. Except for Lubitsch maybe, and I
only worked with him once because he didn't, as a rule, do the type of things
that I did.

JK: Did your image confine you and prevent you from doing other things?

EB: Yes, people'd say, "She can only play gangsters' molls." And I never tried.

JK: Did you want to escape that image at any time?

EB: Not particularly. But they kept coming and I loved having them, they were
what I was used to doing.

JK: The premiere of *Underworld* . . . was there any excitement about it that
you remember?

EB: I sure do. I remember they had it downtown at I think it was the Million
Dollar Theater. They used to have a prologue, you know, a stage show, and a
little guy named Rube Woolf had the band. And they asked me if I'd go down
and come out onstage and take a bow. I agreed, and I made Gary Cooper go
with me because I was scared to go alone. And Gary went down and that was
when he was first starting, and he was so embarrassed. He didn't know what
he was gonna do, and we didn't have to do anything! Went out and took a
bow and then talked to a lot of people backstage, and that was it.

JK: Did you get a raise in pay?

EB: No. I got it when I signed the contract. It was for so many years at a raise
at the beginning of each year, it just stayed that way. That was before they
did those things, everybody was glad to be working.

JK: But Swanson with her contract, and Pola Negri . . . did you know her?

EB: No, I didn't know her, and I didn't know Swanson. They were always
fighting all the time. It was probably built up by the publicity department,
that I can believe, but I know there was no love lost between them. It was
almost a joke. Another laugh was Ruth Chatterton, who was a very good
actress, but she was rather elegant, you know? She came from the theater and
she sort of felt superior, I guess. Everybody used to gather and say, "She's
coming off the set!" and they'd all hide to watch her because she had a retinue

following her, which none of us had then. She had a long cigarette-holder, and she'd walk like a queen across the lot, trailing a maid and a secretary and a makeup man, all following her. And none of the others were like that.

JK: Do you know why your career went into its decline in the early '30s?

EB: I think it was my personal life . . . I sort of made everything else secondary. And then Harry got ill, he was ill for a good many years. But even before, I think I let everything slide. And it was probably due to the one bad husband . . . that whole episode threw me off very much.

JK: Did the opportunities come to you, though? Could you have taken advantage of them?

EB: Yeah. I was badly advised, see?

JK: Can you remember any specific examples?

EB: No . . . I just didn't do what I should have done . . . to think of "me" . . . as a career . . . to further that. You have to do that. If you are badly advised, you can turn down things you shouldn't turn down and you make money more important than what you're doing . . . which wasn't my way of doing it at all. My last year's contract at Paramount . . . I should have stayed there, you see. But it was one of those economy periods at the studios . . . we were called in and asked would we stay on for the next year at the same salary . . . and I was advised to say no. Which went against what I felt . . . but I listened when I shouldn't have. I think that's been true of a lot of people.

JK: Well, perhaps you could talk about *The Last Command*. Did you consider it special to be in an Emil Jannings film?

EB: Yeah, I'm sure . . . see, anybody would have jumped at the chance. I had already made the two with Joe, and he wanted me, so I was lucky. I think Joe and Jannings got along well, Jannings had a great respect for Joe. And Joe had a way of involving you in a thing. If he was hot on a scene, he'd work with everybody. Jannings was wonderful to work with because he was one of the few big stars who, if an extra woman had one little scene, he would work with her behind the camera—you know, do his part. Most of them slough that and get away from it. But he was always very considerate of the other people. I know . . . before the picture started, Joe had a story conference and said for us all to be there. I didn't know Jannings then. It was his first picture out here, and he had a fantastic contract, I remember it was the talk of the studio. He had all the concessions . . . whoever his business manager was. . . . He had a car at his disposal and all the things that nobody I knew had at that time. Anyway, Jannings came in with an interpreter, and they would say something, and the guy would interpret it into German, then wait for an answer, which he would interpret back into English. I thought that was funny because he spoke English, Jannings did. A few days later I said,

"What's the idea?" and he said, "When I don't speak English, I'm a smart boy." He heard what they said, then he thought it out and gave his answer. It was very smart . . . very cute.

JK: Do you remember the coming of sound?

EB: I sure do, that was *Interference* [1929].

JK: No, I mean in general, when sound hit Hollywood, the Jolson film. . . .

EB: I don't think I was aware of it . . . not till I started *Interference*. See . . . they were stage people, Jolson was a stage person. And I think I knew vaguely that it was on record and it could get out of "synch." I know that I was impressed that *Interference* was going to be the first one with sound directly on the film. Paramount had the first setup. They had the man who had done all the effects shots for years, Roy somebody [Pomeroy]. And they only had the one little studio to shoot talkies in, which had been his studio where he did the trick effects. We shot the picture in that little studio. And if we had a street scene, a lot of people, we had to shoot it silent and then dub it later. They had microphones all over the place . . . everybody would have one. And if you got up to walk toward the other people, you had to remember to stop talking before you left this mike and pick it up when you reached another one. Otherwise, your voice would go out and in. Then they would take you at the finish of the first scene that was shot, you'd go into the other room and they'd play it back. Scared the daylights out of me . . . when I heard my voice. I thought, "This is it." I sounded like this British singer Dame Clara Butt . . . with an enormous voice . . . that's how I sounded to myself. I didn't know at the time that they'd stepped the volume up. I found out . . . I went to Roy and I said, "This is terrible." And he said, "Wait until we've got it adjusted and you'll hear how it really sounds." They had boomed it up because of bad facilities in the studio, because it was experimental then. During that picture practically every star in Hollywood came in to do a test track of themselves—other stars, and they'd take a test.

JK: Did you take voice lessons?

EB: Oh, no. I never had any contact with them. I remember that they started schools and then the police stepped in and then they had to have credits before they could open a school. I didn't know anybody who went in for that. Paramount set up their own sort of school on the lot, and you could go if you wanted to, you know, work with diction teachers, but I never did. I was terrified. I kind of thought it was the end for me. A lot of careers were going downhill . . . poor Jack Gilbert. And it was so wicked, because the fault was they didn't have sound where they could control it yet. Like, if your voice was high, they could lower the register.

JK: Did you see other sound films being made?

EB: Yeah . . . I saw the one with Jolson. But I think only half of that was in sound, wasn't it? Just the numbers. And then I saw one . . . oh, wait, that was one I made at Universal. I was on loan-out. It was called, uhm, *Broadway*. Terrible. The last half was done in sound and the first half was silent.

JK: Were you surprised to see people dropped suddenly . . . like Blanche Sweet?

EB: Yeah, I liked her. I didn't really attribute it to sound. I didn't think about it consciously. I remember thinking about that Norma Shearer and Leslie Howard picture . . . *A Free Soul*. I wondered why he was so good on the stage and not good in the film. I had seen him in plays and was he good! But I think Clara Bow's personal troubles probably drove her out of films as much as anything. It was an upsetting period. And the Depression hit then too. People lost a lot of money because most of the people in pictures were investing on margin in those days. A lot of 'em lost everything they had . . . overnight. It was a very disrupting time for everybody, and that to me was far more important than the other, the sound thing. People were trying to commit suicide, see? Oh, I think it was a very exciting time.

In 1927, the year of *Underworld,* Evelyn Brent had appeared in films for thirteen years; that year she had starred in four films. In 1928 she starred in seven; seven in '29; five in '30. In 1933 she made only one film, and none in 1934. When she returned in '36, she appeared in bit parts. She was born in 1899, and died in 1975 of a heart attack. There was no failure in Evelyn's life—the failure lay in others, those who tried to make her a star. Evelyn didn't want to be a star, she just wanted to work. And at that she was a success, right to the end.

1972

Camilla Horn, photographed for Murnau's *Faust*, 1926

CAMILLA
HORN

C AMILLA HORN was Murnau's Gretchen in *Faust*. She was John Barrymore's leading lady in two films—*Tempest* and the Lubitsch-directed *Eternal Love*. Back in Germany, she was one of the top leading ladies of the '30s, usually cast as the glamorous foil or erotic, worldly other woman, as in *Pantzerkreutzer Sebastopol* and Jacques Feyder's *Gens du Voyage (Das Fahrende Folk)*. Still active in the theater, she lives in Munich. Stimulating, witty, attractive and youthful, despite her nigh on seventy-four years, she lived up to one's expectations of glamorous *femmes fatales*. We met in the garden of the home of an old-time friend living in the fashionable and expensive outskirts of Berlin.

CH: Did you know that I made the first German-speaking film, *The Royal Box* [*Die Kaiserliche Loge*, 1929], with Alexander Moissi, Sig Rumann, Leni Stengel for Warner Brothers in New York? I made it on a stopover during my return trip to Germany, and it was the first German-language film. I don't remember why it should have been made in America by an American firm, or who directed it [it was Bryan Foy], but there it was.

JK: Was your first film appearance in *Madame Wünscht Keine Kinder* [*Madame Doesn't Want Any Children*, 1926—directed by A. Korda]?

CH: No, no. In *Madame Wünscht Keine Kinder* Marlene Dietrich and I were extras. I was an extra for about six months. Not with any intention of becoming a film star—just out of curiosity. By one of those coincidences that occur a lot when you get to my age, my first stage appearance was in the same theater where I'm going to make a personal appearance tonight.

It was called the Rudolf Nelson Theater and Rudolf Nelson ran it. It was an exquisite little revue theater then, and I was a dancer with him. It was very chic and very expensive. Nelson was a popular composer at the time whose songs are still popular today. I sang a little bit as well—I never was a singer, but in most of my films I usually ended up having to sing a little. As long as

I didn't have to listen to it, I didn't mind, and I had a couple of big hits. I wasn't very good, though at least as good as most of the people singing today.

JK: Did you sing like Marlene?

CH: I was more musical than she. Alexander Korda saw me in the show and he thought I would make a good extra because I moved well, and he got me work in a couple of films, or maybe it was the same film. Who remembers? But I remember I was playing a silly cocotte who comes into a restaurant with a tray and sits on a man's lap and flirts. I was so bad, so bad, and I wanted to be good. I tried. Too hard. They kept making me do it again and again, and it was always worse. Then Korda took me aside and said, "My dear girl, I'm going to give you some good advice. Get married. It's better for you." Six months later I was playing Marguerite in *Faust*.

When I met Korda again later on, I reminded him of his advice, but he didn't believe it.

JK: How did you get the role in *Faust*?

CH: I was doing extra work in *Tartuffe*—standing in for Lil Dagover on the side, and they had to do a retake one evening and Lil Dagover wasn't there, but since all it was was a shot of her putting her shoes on and all you'd see in the film was her legs, they told me to do it. But the shoes were one or two sizes too small. I realized this in the wardrobe, but I decided against saying anything because they paid you fifty marks for the work while you only got ten or so marks a day as an extra, and I didn't want to lose it. I was quite poor then, I used to do sewing on the side as well to make extra money. So I went onto the set and sat down. All I had to do was to drop a handkerchief, and as she bent to lift it so, she'd show her legs a bit and tempt Tartuffe. Murnau was sitting over there, and it took over an hour to set up the lights. I was sitting at the table and Murnau came over, looked at my legs, then at me and said, "Miss, are you sure these shoes fit you?" I said, "Of course they fit, very well, thank you." I was very shy then and felt very foolish, and didn't want to let on. So he said, "Okay, then." I felt like a fool because I could feel that he was laughing at me. So he sits down and more time goes by and my feet are killing me. I don't know where to look, and all the while he keeps staring at me. I didn't know where to turn, and every fifteen minutes or so he comes over and asks me, "Are you sure the shoes are all right?" Well, he played with me like that for a couple of hours. My hands were sweating with the pain and with nerves. I wanted to kill him because he kept looking at me in that way of his. And, you know, he was a very strong type. I wouldn't have felt like this with just anyone, but Murnau made you feel that he was looking right through you, into your heart and mind.

Finally, the lights were ready and they could start filming, and Murnau comes over again to look at my feet. Meanwhile the veins had begun to swell up and discolor—it looked a mess, and he said, "This is ridiculous. We can't shoot now—we've wasted two hours for nothing." I went back to my dressing room and started throwing things around because I was so furious. At this point his assistant comes in, stuttering with excitement, and told me, "Murnau wants to test you for Gretchen." I thought he was pulling my leg and told him to get out and leave me alone and he knew what they could do with his Murnau and his film. The whole thing went so fast. Suddenly there was the wardrobe mistress with the costume for Gretchen and a man with a long blond wig—I thought it was all a dream. Things don't happen like this—I had no training. I wasn't an actress. And meanwhile I was being told to hurry up, and that everybody had tested for the role—the biggest stars in the country, Lillian Gish was supposed to come over from America for it. But he wasn't satisfied with any of them.

I came down on the set. He stood there, very serious. This was the first time I was in front of the camera—usually I was way in the background, made up like a tart because I thought that was classy. Murnau, very serious behind the camera, said to me, "You know *Faust*." I said, "Of course. We read it in school." "Gretchen?" "Yes, I know Gretchen." "By heart." "No, I don't remember it by heart." He said, "Okay, I'm going to tell you what to do. You're Gretchen, a brave, good girl. You have never looked at a man. You don't know any. You don't have a boyfriend. You're much too young to think about it. You go to church," and he gave me a prayer book, and he went on. "You're on the way to church, you've said goodbye to your mother; you've kissed her, she blessed you." And so forth, and I did what he said. "You're on the way to church, your mind only on your prayers; suddenly you let your book drop; somebody picks it up. You turn to look at him and thank him, and suddenly you can't turn away from him anymore. You forget everything else." It was wonderful the way he talked to me. It all became so easy. "You are suddenly aware that you've looked at the man too long, and you cast your eyes down and go past him." This test was so wonderful—I can't tell you. In my whole career I never again had a moment in front of the camera as good as this was. Marvelous. I *was* Marguerite and I'd never acted before. He could make you do that.

So I'm signed to a four-year contract by UFA and don't see him again until I was invited along to the story conferences. I remember going home that night in an open carriage and feeling like I was floating. It was all so unreal.

Suddenly here I was, alone with Murnau, the first time I'd seen him since the screen test, and I asked him, "Mr. Murnau—please, you've got to tell me. How did it all happen? Why did you cast me for the part? I've never acted before." And don't forget that when he first saw me, I wasn't even in modern dress but a beautiful rococo court dress and powdered wig. He told me that he'd been looking for somebody for the part for a long time and couldn't find anybody he thought was right, and there was a certain scene he thought was of special importance. That was when Marguerite was lying in bed, with Faust sitting beside her, while her mother slept in a nearby room. And there was a storm, her mother awoke and went into Gretchen's room to make sure the windows are closed, and he said, "In this moment, when Marguerite sees her mother, I wanted to see such an absolute total sense of shame in Marguerite's face, and I've never seen this in a professional actress. I could never believe in her shame. And I had never before in my life met a girl who could look so beautifully ashamed for two hours as you looked."

I later found out that he was very close to casting Lillian Gish and that he'd been in communication with her and she was about to come over. She would have been wonderful.

JK: You were born in Frankfurt. What brought you to Berlin?

CH: Love. Love. I followed the man I loved to Berlin. Mind you, my parents weren't to know. To them Berlin was like a sin trap. It wasn't. It was fabulous. I made such good friends here. He was a famous doctor, much older than I was, and I adored him. We remained good friends till he died, last year.

JK: You sound as if your whole life, or at least your career, was all impromptu.

CH: Yes, nothing planned. Of course I made a lot of mistakes. Especially later on. I should never have left America. That was a mistake. And Reinhardt. Max Reinhardt sees a young girl playing Gretchen in a silent film. Now, he was a fabulous stage director. He says to his righthand man, "She's going to work for me." His assistant says, "But, Professor, you don't even know if she can speak or not. For all we know, she has an accent as thick as my fist." Reinhardt said, "No, I'm sure her voice is good." I have this four-year contract with UFA, but they give me leave to go and see him in Vienna, in the Burg, where he had his headquarters. And I had to do a speech for him, but when I saw him I became so scared—he was only the second man in front of whom I felt so ashamed—that I told him, "Herr Professor, it was foolish of me to come to you, I can't speak. I've never recited before in my life." Reinhardt told me to sit down, relax. "You've played Gretchen, you must know something from it. You've studied it." Well, I always research my work thoroughly, and I did know some of her speeches, and Gretchen has a beautiful prayer when she finds out she's going to have a baby, and I told Reinhardt I thought I remembered that by heart. A very emotional speech. But then I was scared, and he said, "Take your time, go next door, and when you're ready, tell me." Now, Reinhardt wasn't a man who usually had much patience. After all, every actor in the country wanted to work for him, he didn't need a nervous film actress with no previous experience. He kept looking in at me from time to time, very patient. Finally I thought, Well, what have I got to lose? Say it and get it over with and go. I did the speech, all stops out—tears running at the end as if they'd never stop. And then I heard him say, "That was so lovely." That was a triumph for me like nothing else. He took me downstairs, where he was in rehearsal for a play, and he said, "The girl's role in this play is yours." So I went back to Berlin, to UFA, and told them and they refused to release me. I should have put up a fight. But I was new. It could have changed my whole career, working with Reinhardt. Still . . .

JK: Would you, then, rather have been a stage actress than a film star?

CH: No, I wanted to be a film star. But I could have been a better actress, a more serious one.

JK: Going back to *Faust*. Murnau was a difficult man, and Jannings could be very difficult. He had a reputation for being difficult with young actresses. For instance, he was supposed to have been very jealous of Dietrich while they were making *Blue Angel*.

CH: Oh, not with me. He was wonderful to me. But Murnau was very hard with me. Very hard. He really tortured me physically.

In the scene where they pulled Gretchen to the stake, I was being pulled along the ground with my hands manacled to real iron chains; these were very heavy, and it took a great many takes. They tied me to the stake, very tight, and I stayed there for two hours, so that when they untied me I fainted. He really forced me, but I worshiped him.

The extras were crying, seeing me bleeding and in pain, but you don't see that in the film.

And when he set up a scene, he was so methodical, so exact, he really took his time. The smallest detail, whether the camera saw it or not, had to be exactly right. The film took one year to complete. He wasn't like this with the others—Gosta Ekman or Jannings. Just with me. When he went into his dressing room, I'd still be in the jail, with the chains on my arms, till he came back and we resumed shooting. Jannings found me there one time and said, "But you must go and eat," and brought me some grapes, and I said, "Oh, no, I mustn't. I must stay till Murnau comes back." But it was worth it. I learned a lot from him, and it's a film I can always be proud to have been associated with.

After we finished, he said to me, "I'm going to America to make a film there, and I want you to come with me." That would have been for the role in *Sunrise* which Janet Gaynor played. He made her look exactly like Gretchen, did you ever notice that?

There was a very strong feeling between us. I know he cared for me—I was asleep once during a break and I suddenly awoke to see him standing in the doorway, looking at me. And when he saw that I was awake, he became very red in the face, and very awkward, and in a very low voice he said, "Can you come down? We'll start." And he disappeared.

After the film was over, I sent him a large bouquet of red roses and a thank-you letter. He got them while there were some people there, including the cameraman, who told me afterwards that Murnau had been so delighted, showing them to everybody and reading them the letter and saying, "Look, look at these. Camilla sent them to me." But he never showed much affection or kindness to me in person, it was just what others told me when I wasn't around.

After *Faust* was shown, I had offers from the four biggest American companies. United Artists, Metro-Goldwyn, Paramount and Warner Brothers. I didn't go, I couldn't go because of my UFA contract. I made two other films in Germany, nothing very important, because Murnau didn't come back to do *Sunrise* and I had to do something. I was getting paid every week by the studio. But the people at UFA realized that the United States would be very good for me, and they were nice enough to let me out of my contract. That was when Erich Pommer was in charge. It was Pommer who had given me the contract in the first place. They hadn't wanted to, actually, but Murnau insisted they should. They were all very against him casting me, you see— Pommer said, "But we don't know her. She has no name." But Murnau insisted—"She's my Marguerite and nobody else."

JK: Your role in *The Tempest* wasn't exactly without complications. From what I remember, you replaced another actress who had already begun filming opposite Barrymore, and Tourjansky, who directed, was also replaced. John Considine, Jr., took over and Sam Taylor took over from him.

CH: I came to Hollywood under contract to United Artists. There was no film prepared for me. When I arrived, they decided to put me into this film.

JK: What was Barrymore like for a young foreign actress to work with?

CH: Wonderful! Sometimes he was drunk. And when we were dancing together in one scene—a beautiful ballroom scene—he a handsome Russian officer, I was a princess, it was all very romantic and so on, he fell down with me on the floor because he was so drunk. So they had to build a carousel affair for us, he sat on one side, me on the other, it was a sort of criss-cross arrangement, and we put our arms around each other, looked deeply into our eyes and somebody moved the carousel around so it looked in the film as if we were swirling around the ballroom lost in each other's arms. But otherwise he was wonderful to me. He was married to Dolores Costello at the time—a beautiful, soft-featured blonde, exquisite—so he didn't try to make any passes at me. But we got on very well. He wanted to make every film after that with me. Well, we did make another one—*Eternal Love,* which Lubitsch directed.

JK: *Eternal Love* looks like a very unusual project for Lubitsch to be directing, a romantic Alpine drama.

CH: Oh, Lubitsch loved it. You know, it was based on a famous book by a Swiss author, Walter Herr, I think. We shot all the exteriors in the Canadian Rocky Mountains. It was wonderful. It was a very difficult film to shoot, because we had to walk over glaciers in some of the scenes. There were very dangerous things.

Lubitsch himself was easy to work with, but then, all the good directors are, at least I've found them to be that way. Murnau, Tourjansky, Lubitsch, Jacques Feyder—all good people to work with. I mean, Murnau wasn't loud or angry, he always addressed me very quietly and politely. Mind you, they have to be quiet with me—shouting and that sort of thing would just make me dry up. I'd do anything you asked me if you took me aside and explained it quietly and clearly. All the bad directors are hysterical. Especially the bad German ones. Anyway, in *Eternal Love,* Barrymore and I had to cross a glacier because we were fleeing from somebody, or maybe we just wanted to go and die—at any rate, we were supposed to be in trouble. Anyway, in this shot we're both walking, when suddenly there is a call, "Cut," and a voice says, "Oh, Mr. Barrymore, your double can take over here." And Barrymore's double came, but I stayed and we had to keep going on up this glacier. Suddenly I looked down and I couldn't go on. We were on a ledge that was so narrow and there was a drop below that was so deep that I suddenly went weak in the knees. And they were down below filming us. They wanted it to look real, and I didn't realize where we were going till it was too late. I suppose they thought, "She comes from Germany, so she'll be all right on a mountain." Anyway, I said to the double that I couldn't go on. I didn't dare to. He was holding on to me and he said, "Relax. Be very still and put your foot on mine!" And he'd put his foot forward and I would then step on his, and he'd move the other foot and I'd follow that step. I was petrified. Barrymore told me later, "They couldn't care less. As long as they get their shot in the camera, we can go and *drop dead.*" Though, mind you, it wasn't him up there with me, but his double.

Another time Barrymore had to carry me over another narrow bridge in the Rocky Mountains—he did this scene himself. Thank God he wasn't drunk. Really quite harrowing.

But Lubitsch was always in good humor, and he kept us all happy.

JK: What effect did the coming of sound have on your American career and on your decision to return to Europe?

CH: Well, I used that reason as my excuse for going back. I said to myself, you can go home and nobody can say anything since I always say that I couldn't speak English well enough. It wasn't that I wanted to return to Germany, but I missed Europe. You see, three months before I left for America I had gotten married to a merchant in Hamburg. And I wanted to see him. Joe Schenck didn't want to let me go. He didn't even want me to make any sound tests to see what my voice might be like because he thought that sound wouldn't last. It was on my way back to Europe that I stopped off in New York and made my first talking film, *The Royal Box.* My contract had another year to run and Schenck kept paying me even though I was back in Germany because he wanted me to come back. It certainly would have been better for my career. My reviews in New York after *Tempest* opened there said: "Camilla Horn trumps Barrymore." That's not the time to go away. Schenck kept saying, "Camilla, I'm going to make a big star of you." I have only myself to blame for that.

JK: Back in Europe, especially in the first years of sound, you starred in a great many German-language versions of Paramount pictures, like *The Devil's Holiday, Stolen Heaven, Personal Maid*—a lot of the Nancy Carroll films, if I'm not mistaken.

CH: That's right. Those were made in the Joinville studios outside Paris. I was making films all over at that time—one in Berlin, another in Paris, then a film in Vienna, London and so forth. I was always somewhere else. I freelanced a lot at this time—I made films for UFA, for Universal, for Paramount. I made films for Tobis and Terra companies. Lots of co-productions between France and Germany, and Italy and Germany. I was very much in demand at this time, and made a great many banal films; there are very few I like myself—I quite liked *Die Grosse Sehnsucht* [1930], which was kind of my own story—about a little extra girl who accidentally takes over from the star and starts off on a career. It was an all-star film: thirty-five of the then biggest stars appeared in it in guest roles. It was a sweet film, and the first time I sang in a film.

JK: Certainly your career, judging from the number and variety of films you made in Germany and the rest of Europe, didn't suffer from your private life.

CH: We'd be up all night if I told you my tales of woe. I left Germany twice because of the Nazis.

I used to have a lot of confrontations with the Minister Dr. Goebbels. *Weisse Sklaven* [directed by Karl Anton] had been finished without any help or hindrance from Dr. Goebbels. It was a wonderful film, because in the original version even the Communist in the story was a recognizable human being. But Hitler banned the film immediately. It had only had a screening for producers and distributors. Everybody was enthusiastic about it. We were all good in it. Despite Hitler's ban, the producers tried to get it released, everything wasn't state-controlled yet. But nothing helped, so they set me onto Goebbels to go and see him and talk to him, because it was well known that he was very keen on pretty women, especially film stars. Though he liked them all. All! Thick, thin, red, blond—all of them.

JK: Like Lida Baarova?

CH: Yes! Well, at least she was a beautiful woman. He went for all of them. He was a maniac about women. I had to take the script to him and I said, "Herr Doctor, what do we have to change in the script? What do you want us to do?" And he said, "I'll have to see Hitler about it." Because it wasn't he who banned it but Hitler himself. He thought it was pro-Communist because the villain wasn't a stereotype. For instance, he really loved the girl in a decent, human way, and not as a leering fiend. Little moments like when he'd pick up her dog and pet it were cut out. And his dialogue was just crossed out and replaced with lines that were so banal that when I took it back to the director [Karl Anton] he just threw up his hands in horror and said, "It's not possible. I can't shoot this. There is no way to film things like that." He was in a state. I mean, Goebbels had rewritten it so grotesquely that the character was now in a state of frothing at the mouth and shouting "Kill! Murder! Loot! Conquer!" You'd have to read all the changes to believe them, and some of it is in the film. We couldn't get out of it, there was no way we could get a release for the film without making at least some of the ordered changes. Poor Werner Hinz—he played the Communist, Boris—poor Werner, he was at a loss how to play it. So unhappy.

Dr. Goebbels was an intelligent man. He could talk, and loved to talk about movies, but as a producer he would have been hopeless. He would only have made films with a message. They would all have been political. Oh, we had such problems on that film. I got a bouquet of flowers from Tobis for all my running back and forth between the film and Goebbels' office. You can't have any idea of how often Goebbels had me come to him, and on what flimsy pretenses, until we finally finished the film.

He wanted to get me into bed, but I found him repugnant. A man who was with a different woman every day. Not just every day, but one literally handed the doorknob as she was leaving to the one on her way in. He changed women like shirts. But, despite everything, he did exert a certain fascination, even I felt that.

I was remarried at this time, to an architect, and together we decided to pack up and leave. Sell up our homes and farms in Germany and move to Switzerland. I already had money in Switzerland. All the money I had made while working outside Germany—none of my German salaries, though. Anyway, I had this large Mercedes which I brought back from the Riviera, such a wonderful car, but the trouble was it ate up gasoline, and the war suddenly broke out, and the rationing made it impossible to be allowed to drive it. They confiscated it at the border. And my husband was scared now. He was of military age, and he kept worrying, what if they caught him— he'd be tried and shot as a deserter. He kept saying, "Let's go back. Let's go back." I was in love and, like a fool, I went back. The whole war years I was in Germany and that was a terrible time. I could have stayed in Switzerland or gone to England—and as late as '41–'42 I was making a couple of films in Italy.

But I've been away from films for years now. This is the first time in years that I've been out of my retreat. They've been asking me to come to Berlin for years. I finally decided to come this year, but it's the last time. After all, it's over. My time, it's over.

Talking about the past like this to someone like you, I feel the memories rising up again, I get a bit emotional, but in actuality it's all such a long time ago and I'm no longer very interested in the past.

I like the new films—the industry here is becoming interesting again. Fassbinder is very talented. I'm looking forward to his films—I'm curious where he is heading in his work. He's still so young, but he's creating a new form. Funny, most of the actors of my generation don't like that, they don't want to accept what he's doing. It's silly—we can't stand still, after all. We must change to survive.

1974

ANNA STEN

ANNA STEN was not the first huge star to come to Hollywood from Russia. There had been Russian actresses and actors in Hollywood before her— Alla Nazimova in the mid-teens, then Olga Baclanova—but neither of them was brought over or featured as a "sensational discovery." Sten, who'd gone from Russia to Germany, where she had made a great success (most notably as Grushenka in *The Murderer Dmitri Karamazov,* 1931), was seen by Samuel Goldwyn, who thought that he had found nothing less than another Greta Garbo and Marlene Dietrich. With enormous fanfare, she was brought to Hollywood.

Her first film was to be a Hollywood version of *The Brothers Karamazov* opposite Goldwyn's and Hollywood's most prestigious male star, Ronald Colman. But by the time Anna arrived, Colman and Goldwyn's relationship after years of feuding had terminated in Colman leaving the studio. So there was no project ready for her. Besides, after having signed her, Goldwyn discovered or felt that her heavy Russian accent on top of her Germanic one would be too much for American audiences to swallow. And so a rigorous and widely heralded course of training—vocal and physical—was supposedly set in motion, during which time the publicity about her roared that the as-yet-unseen Anna was "The Million Dollar Discovery." This was in 1933, the depth of the Depression, when $1 million was so much money that it created a standard neither Anna nor Goldwyn could live up to. As if realizing that all the way from Russia might not sound as exotic and glamorous as $1 million could justify, Goldwyn's publicity reached for the skies and heralded her (as yet seen only in stills by Ruth Harriet Louise and George Hurrell) as "The Brightest Star from the Northern Skies."

Her first screen appearance, as nothing less than Emile Zola's Nana (UA, 1934), proved to be as bad for Zola as it was for Anna. Several directors had started work on the film, but it was finally made by Hollywood's best-known and at the time only woman director, Dorothy Arzner. Running only a little over sixty minutes, the complex plot still found time for a song written by Rodgers and Hart. (Rodgers reused the song, "That's Love," thirty years later with lyrics by Stephen Sondheim instead of Lorenz Hart's in the musical *Do I Hear a Waltz?* but it still didn't score.) Anna as Nana was lit to death by Gregg Toland, dressed to die by Adrian; but still Zola's book had been reduced to a lifeless synopsis. Her personal reviews weren't all that bad, as if the critics understood that she wasn't to blame, but they had to deal with her as a bejeweled, eyelid-flickering, nostril-curling ikon instead of the arrestingly emotional actress they had been led to expect from her German films.

Anna Sten was probably the first "Method actress" to arrive in Hollywood, for she had studied with Stanislavsky in Russia. But instead of realism she was required to be stylized: it's one thing to think yourself into the heart of a tree, it's another to be turned into a tree. It was a style of acting—volatile, temperamental, outpouring—totally at odds with the high-key glamour personality of that era. The results could have been predicted. But Goldwyn had so much at stake, not only financially but also in terms of his own prestige: the pioneer film producer had set himself up as a star-maker, and Anna Sten was to be his great discovery. Producing films might seem to be a priority in running a studio, but having a stable of stars and, more importantly, to be seen and known for creating stars was as important. Such later Goldwyn imports as Sigrid Gurie and Vera Zorina, before he turned domestic with girls like Cathy O'Donnell and Joan Evans and actors like Farley Granger, only showed that Goldwyn's star-making touch was a poor second to his skill as a producer. And Anna, the pawn in an ego game, was the one to pay for Goldwyn's mistake, becoming known in and out of the industry as his "Million Dollar Folly."

In New York, in the mid-'60s, I sought her out. When she worked in small roles in films produced by her husband, Eugene Frenke, like *Soldier of Fortune* (1955) or the lead in the small-budgeted *The Nun and the Sergeant* (1962) or on the stage (in 1960 she took over the Pirate Jenny part from Lotte Lenya in the famed New York Off-Broadway production of *Threepenny Opera*), few people connected the serious professional actress Anna Sten with that other "Million Dollar" one. She was strictly old news. The '60s were not yet into '30s nostalgia.

Unlike a fellow Slav, Olga Baclanova, she had little of her thick Russian accent left, but she spoke with the slow Slavic delivery that implied windswept and turbulent tundras in every word, and made the simplest thing sound like it was weighted with profound deliberation. On the subject of Goldwyn she was adamant. She refused to talk about him. Wouldn't go into details. Our already heavy conversation slowed to a near-halt. She had not forgotten, she had not forgiven. As so often in the days before people you just met casually confided everything, the intensity of the silence they settle into, the length of it, the darkness of it are more telling replies than any words they eventually use to describe those long-buried emotions. In a very real sense, she owed the destruction of her promising career to this Hollywood adventure. We began by my asking her if she had photographs.

AS: Ohhhh, no, I only have snapshots. I don't know what I've done with them. I really wanted to find some for you.

Anna Sten, photographed by George Hurrell, 1933

JK: Was this a film you enjoyed making? [We looked at pictures from her last Goldwyn film, King Vidor's lushly romantic *Wedding Night,* in which she played a Polish farm girl in America who meets and falls in love with a visiting New York writer, played by Gary Cooper.]

AS: (a long long pause).

JK: Well, you always had good leading men in your films, and good directors, but the story of this one must have been a pill to do.

AS: No. I liked it. Umhmnn.

JK: And did you like working with Rouben Mamoulian? [He'd directed her in the previous film, *We Live Again,* based on Tolstoy's *Resurrection.*]

AS: Oh, very much. Because I felt he was . . . one of the wonderful elements . . . that was around. To this particular story. I don't think I'd seen any of his previous films [*Queen Christina* (Garbo), *Song of Songs* (Dietrich)], but it wouldn't have mattered.

JK: I thought maybe it was because of his work with Garbo and Dietrich that Goldwyn hired him to direct you.

AS: It could be. I have no idea. Actors are given a director, and there you go. Well, nobody asked me to say anything about it. [She laughs ironically, as if to say, Doesn't everybody know that?] I didn't know anything about Hollywood, so . . . what's the sense of saying anything? I'd only been there two years, so, so . . . what do I know?

JK: Well, the first year you were in America you were in hiding.

AS: I *wasn't hiding*. I was *hid*.

JK: Why?

AS: I don't know. Maybe I was ugly. [She is laughing. She is not amused, though.] Really, who wanted to hide? I liked everything around here. I wanted to be with it. I was hid.

JK: That was so the studio could do a buildup campaign.

AS (very petulant): How do I know? It was terrible. I never read those things they printed about me, about Goldwyn's "Million Dollar Discovery." No. I mean, I knew about it, but I never read it. I was told about it. Most of it was done before I came out here. So. While I was still in Europe. I was in France. [She'd made a film there for UFA, *Bomben auf Monte Carlo,* a romantic musical comedy opposite Germany's most popular male star, Hans Albers.]

JK: It's regrettable how an actor's whole career can be tied in to one line of publicity, like you being the "Million Dollar Discovery," or Erich von Stroheim, who was known to his grave as "The Man You Love to Hate" and as an expensive director. Does it bother you?

AS: Not me. I think I'm a Million Dollar Discovery. There is no fault with that. The *fault* is with the material that was given to me. [Sten snorts derisively.] The fault was with . . . how should I say it? . . . not being with it. So what's wrong with being a Million Dollar Discovery? To be a ten-cent-store discovery, that's rather . . . I wouldn't want to be that. There is no glory in that. Except at the very beginning because you don't know any *better*. If you've *done* something that's been appreciated by the whole world, why shouldn't you be worth a million dollars? After all, he did not *discover* me. So I was worth much more than a million dollars then. I was underestimated. That was the only right thing that was done about me. The tag.

I don't think it became a handicap. It didn't prevent me from getting work. It was just my own choosing and refusing. Things I didn't want to do. I made a mistake of it. But that didn't handicap me, except in a serious sort of way. The only thing was . . . when I would say, "Why do you say that about me?" . . . was I'm a foreigner here, let me prove something before the tag is proclaimed. By making good pictures. Like I made abroad. Like *Tempest* and *Brothers Karamazov*. I was right in that. But I wouldn't take less than a million dollars, as far as my talent is concerned.

JK: Well, I felt that when you first arrived in Hollywood, they emphasized your striking visual appearance at the expense of your talent.

AS: Nothing wrong with that.

JK: Didn't this emphasis on appearance prevent you from developing a character?

AS: No. Not at all. I think if a beautiful woman can make herself plain . . . so, God bless her. But if a plain woman wants to make herself beautiful . . . ohohohohoh . . . [It's a shuddery sort of wail.] So there's nothing wrong with that. This is not the point. It's a point of elements. You have to be careful of a talent of any kind. Any creative talent has to be helped to find a certain planet, and a certain given time. You cannot blame it on money, or on beauty, or on talent, or success. It's a combination of elements. If the elements don't combine [she snaps her fingers to make the point], some people do give up, some people don't.

JK: What did you think your planet should have been?

AS: How do I know? I never found it.

JK: Well, where did *Nana* go wrong in its use of you?

AS: It didn't. I think it was a beautiful film. I made three remarkably wonderful films. What went wrong wasn't the work, it was the elements. Maybe being

in Hollywood. I never gave it so much thought. Who cares? Why should I
give it any thought? It's not who I am today. But, actually, I do think that
maybe I was ahead of time, in terms of an image. The talent around me in
America was good, as good as in Germany. It was . . . it was not as . . .
inventive. I had a feeling, a little bit, that I had to squeeze into a preconceived
sort of image, while I expected a totally free environment. Which I was given
the opportunity to have before. That may be. But it's all in the elements.

JK: Well, you see, that's what I meant. You'd proven yourself in Europe, you
were beautiful; you were a great success, and Goldwyn saw that and took
that and wanted this free-spirited talent to fit into the image Hollywood had
for exotic foreign stars. That's why I implied that in Hollywood you were
made a captive of your "beauty."

AS: That may be. Now I'd like to ask you something about that particular time.
Can you mention somebody who was ugly and yet was on top? Because if I
remember correctly, at that time both of them played nothing but ingenues.
[Garbo and Dietrich.] No character at all.

JK: Barbara Stanwyck.

AS: As an ingenue. I watch the Late, Late Show too. And the same goes for
Bette Davis. [Well, in the period she is talking of, 1932–35, that is true, of
course. It was just this sort of restriction Davis fought so hard to get out of.]
But . . . for instance, if you look through the old magazines—well, just because you mention them, but all right, they're symbols, both of them were
fashion models at that time and both of them played ingenues. And both of
them tried their very *very best* to be *beautiful*. So, you see, you still have to
pull up to this particular image. It's only by perseverance and the belief of
somebody in them, the variety of parts they started to get developed a natural
talent, and they didn't have to depend on three sets of eyelashes.

JK: Well, do you think, because your films for Goldwyn were all such lavish,
expensive movies that were so long in production, that you weren't able to
do more in the same period of time?

AS [this is a raw nerve again because she misunderstands my point]: *How would
I know?* I didn't give a damn. I didn't even know about how much they cost.
I'm not a mathematician and I'm not even a producer, I know *nothing* about
it at all. This is a part given to me and it's up to me whether I can portray it
or not. *That's all I'm interested in. Ever was* or *ever will be*. If the film cost
$10,000, and I think I can portray it beautifully, and it appeals to me, and is
a challenge to me, I'll take it in preference to a million-dollar film any time.
So it's still, ohh, . . I don't know . . . there is two sides of the fence in motion
pictures. Either you're the hired help or you're the hirer. You know. That's
why sometimes actors turn producers.

JK: Did you like working with Dorothy Arzner on *Nana*? She's one of the few women directors working in Hollywood at that or any time.

AS: Very much. Very sensitive, very knowledgeable, very talented. Oh, she's marvelous. You see, *Nana* was started with one director, I don't know who it was [the leaden George Fitzmaurice], but it was just horrible. It was not *Nana,* it was not me. I don't know what it was, but it wasn't exciting. And I asked for my release. Then Mr. Goldwyn talked to me, and he changed the whole situation. He changed every actor. I don't know who now, I don't remember their names, don't ask me for names, I don't even remember my own name. But everything was changed . . . the only thing that wasn't changed was Gregg Toland, the cameraman. But it was entirely new actors, Dorothy Arzner became the director, and we started making tests in order to achieve the image, and it became terribly exciting. And Mr. Goldwyn looked at the tests and we went ahead.

Originally, I was supposed to have done *Brothers Karamazov* in the States. That's why I signed, I wouldn't have signed or come to the US for anything else, because at that time I had a choice of anything I wanted, and I signed with Mr. Goldwyn because of *Brothers*. And Ronald Colman was supposed to have played in it and that was at the time that Goldwyn quarreled with Mr. Colman. And as I came here, *boom,* the whole thing fell through. But I did not have in my contract the stipulation that this was supposed to be the film or else, because at that time I had every studio after me. It was only a matter of three or four months after I got here that I started on *Nana* because Goldwyn was looking like mad for something for me to do. The publicity may have started earlier, but I was still in Europe because when I signed the contract I still had commitments in Europe. But once I got to America, there really wasn't long before I started working.

JK: What did that celebrated "grooming" amount to? All those stories about Goldwyn getting you the best voice teachers to teach you English, the best dancing instructors, the riding instructions . . .

AS: *Unhunh*—those are just stories. I was given a teacher because I didn't speak any English at that time at all, and she was a German. I don't know how I ever got out of it without a German accent. I never had any American teachers. My voice was given to me by God, not by Mr. Goldwyn. If he was worried about my accent, why did he give me a German teacher? I don't know what he spent on my grooming. But nothing happened. Listen, if there was a million dollars spent, it wasn't on me. It may have been on publicity, but it was *not spent on me*. All I had was a few weeks with a coach who drove me nuts. As I say, she had a foreign accent to go with my own. That was all. *All!*

I didn't read all that stuff about me being another Dietrich, another Garbo. I didn't read that. I knew Dietrich out here, both before I started working and all through it. She's a magnificent person. She was at my house a lot, we became quite intimate. But they had no influence on me, and nobody else did either. But you can't help what they write about you. What could I do? I thought it was rather beautiful when I got out here. No smog. [She laughs like a coy maiden being tickled behind the stove.]

JK: So what did your fame mean to you?

AS: A good part. Not the money or the rest. I'm not unique in that respect. I think all true actors are like that. They might make a mistake. They might misjudge it, or sometimes they might be pressed into wrong decisions, like, they *have* to make the money. But that's another story altogether. But a true actor, within himself, like any true creator, will tell you that this is what they want. Because they don't want to suffocate. Money is only the final result. As far as fame is concerned, it's nice people admiring you. If idiots admire you, you don't give a damn.

There were very nice people out there then. Like King Vidor. I enjoyed working with him. He was a very poetic director: sincere, creative and receptive. Loving and lovable man. It was very nice working with him. And Goldwyn appreciated what I did.

You don't put your stakes in the director or . . . you just anticipate tomorrow, that it's going to be magnificent. And it does not depend on one element, like it depends only *upon* you, only *upon* the director, or only upon the story. You just anticipate that something magnificent is going to happen. Naturally, if something bothers you . . . that may be something very specific, like a scene doesn't jibe, even the costume will not carry you through, that destroys the mood, or it goes against the gesture. Stuff like that. But it's not one element, like I have twenty lines and one magnificent line and I'm just looking forward to it. It's not like that. You just want to fit in like a link in a chain. A director is the attitude. The story is the thing. It's always been like that, that hasn't changed. The director is the attitude of *how* this particular story is going to be made. But there is no how without what, and what is the story. And I was lucky, the people were very willing to help me. They were wonderful.

JK: So why, if it was all so wonderful and you're not sorry to have left your European career behind you, did you and Goldwyn split up?

AS: I quit him? But I don't want to talk about it. It was just the circumstances, so let's leave it at that.

JK: In Germany you worked, among others, with one of the best-known and most celebrated actors of the day, Emil Jannings.

AS: Right. I made an excellent film with him. As a matter of fact, *Tempest* was my very favorite film, well, after *Brothers Karamazov*. Because it was a great film and Jannings was a very great actor. He helped me tremendously. Before I started, everybody told me Jannings is very difficult, he's always taking the lines away from his leading ladies, and he always has to be Jannings the Magnificent, and the rest of it is all dirt. And that's how the script was written. It was written in the same manner, all about that . . . magnificent so-and-so; and *her* like she was just *eachhhh!* . . . So Erich Pommer was producing it. At that time I was making a film in Paris [*Bomben auf Monte Carlo*?], and I said to him, "I'm not going to make that film. Look how it's written, I can't do a *thing* with that. There's nothing in it. What do you want *me* for? Get a piece of *eachhh!* and do it." He said, "It's true, but you can't get Jannings to do anything unless he's made to believe he's really the one and only, and he's on top of everything, and he's the *only* star. But," he said, "it's not going to be that way. You just look at the part this and that way, and see how wonderful can be this part." And he started playing it for me, and I could see what this part could be, so I said yes. Then, when I started, everybody who knew Jannings told me, "Oh, no, not with him. He's going to crucify you. He's *awful* to work with." So it became a challenge to me. I went to a reading, and he was an angel. He *was* marvelous! He helped me tremendously.

So all right, it's today and there's always tomorrow. There'll be another part. If this doesn't click, so . . . try my best. [She laughs, one of those Russian *Que sera sera* laughs . . . you know the kind. Moscow is frozen over? Thousands dead from the cold? Oh, well, I've known worse winters. Suffering and disappointments are food to the Russian soul.] So it was the premiere. *Huge* big premiere . . . just like every premiere you see. After the film you sit in the coffee house and drink coffee by the gallons. And I sat there and look at all the big men, shaking and shivering and not knowing what the newspapers would be saying in the morning. And all of them come, and they praise the film quite highly, because Jannings was absolutely superb in it . . . and then all of them, but all of them, I think, at least to my knowledge, came out saying, "But *you* stole the film." And it took everybody by surprise. The producers, Jannings . . . and I sat there like a little mouse, because I was quite bewildered by the whole thing. I'd never been to that kind of a premiere, it was quite grand. And yet it was marvelous that it didn't create any jealousy or animosity. [Well, Jannings didn't work with her again either.] But I wasn't a rival to anybody. How could I be a rival to the producer? If I'm good, the film's better. And if I'm good, I'm no rival to Jannings, because he's a . . . man. And because he's a star anyhow . . . And he also sort of understood that I am grateful, because I could never have been what I was in that film without what he's done for me.

JK: Well, at that point he was seeing a succession of his films stolen away by his leading ladies. There was Dietrich getting all the attention for *The Blue Angel,* and when he was still in America, Baclanova in *Street of Sin,* and now you in *Stürme der Leidenschaft* [UFA, 1932].

AS (a merry, joyful laugh of great surprise): Ohhh, I never thought of it that way. But he wasn't that way with me. Maybe he got tired of resenting his leading lady by the time I arrived.

JK: What was it like in Germany at that time, with Hitler about to come into his own? What was the atmosphere like?

AS: I don't know. I was always . . . very sort of . . . I never partook in social life or . . . I don't know. It doesn't matter to me. It never did. You see, I appreciate just the things that rub me the right way. The things that give me pleasure. . . . I don't think there was anything noticeable in the general atmosphere. I had no dealing with the life in Berlin, the nightlife . . . I never saw any moral depravity in the Germans I knew. I didn't know about who came to Berlin, and what they did there when they got there. All I know, get up at 5:00 a.m., go to work, come back tired. Every free moment you study your part. [Well, somewhere in between her studying she had a chance to meet and marry film producer Dr. Eugene Frenke, who later produced a number of American films, including some with her.] Go to bed early, even in your free days. You have to look well. I just don't know the part of Berlin you're talking about. I *really* don't know. As a matter of fact, I have never read about it. Now you tell me, how long have you tried to get a hold of me before today? Well, that's exactly how I am in my social life. No interest at all.

JK: Is that because you are Russian?

AS: I'm not a pure Russian. I'm half Swedish and half Russian.

In her Russian films she was known as Annoushka (little Anna). In the most successful of several silent films, *The Yellow Ticket* (1928), she was directed by Fedor Ozep, who took her with him when he went to Germany later that year to work on a Russo-German co-production. When the film was done, he and Anna stayed behind. It was he who directed her in the most famous of her German films, *Brothers Karamazov;* and he wrote the screenplay for her first post-Goldwyn film, the British-made *A Woman Alone.* Back in America, in the '40s, during the war, he directed Anna in *Three Russian Girls* (1944), a very well-received little film based on a Russian movie.

JK (I am now clearly desperate. So I do what desperate people usually do, I change the subject): How did you get into films?

AS: You see, I had been on the stage since my childhood, actually. I made three films in Russia in one year, and then I went to Berlin, and then to Paris. I started my Russian film career with a very gay comedy; and then all of a sudden they put me in a very tragic film. That was it. And the two of them spread my fame through Europe. So I was engaged to go to Berlin before I knew it. *Karamazov* was my favorite film because it was also my favorite story in literature. I made it in three languages, you see. Two were in film, French and German, and the Russian version was when I did it on the stage, in Hollywood, during the last war. The company was a happy one, not that it matters. I wasn't aware of anything going on around me. There were no politics to worry about. Hitler was already powerful, of course, but I never met him or any of those people. I wasn't aware of politics. It wasn't until after I came over here that I found out that everything I'd left behind me in Germany had been confiscated because I'd left Germany. Then when I went to London to make a film [1936], Hitler sent his emissary there, who was the head of all the industry, lovely manners, who offered me a tremendous job, to go back to Germany. So, and I said to him, "You know very well I'm married to a Jewish man [Dr. Eugene Frenke], why do you ask me?" He said, "Well, you're not Jewish." I said, "Well, I wouldn't know." He said, "You don't know, but *we* know." I said, "How do you know? Maybe my grandmother sinned, for all I know. I couldn't guarantee!" He said, "Ohhh, but we know." The conversation was quite remarkable. I told him to take his offer away. I wouldn't have taken it anyway. But politics have never interested me very much.

I suspect by this time that there is a deeper reason for her repeated denials of politics in her life, since she goes on to tell me that she loves America, everybody knows this, and when Russian delegations of artists come to America and visit Hollywood, she is always asked to translate and entertain, and these are the cream of Russia and they are wonderful but they *never* talk politics.

JK: In the late '20s and '30s you lived in Moscow, Berlin, Paris and Hollywood, fascinating places in a fascinating time. What impact or what impressions did any of these leave on you?

AS: Impact, which impact? I don't know. They had marvelous lobsters in Paris. Every day brings something with it. That's the impact.

By some deep secret logic, Anna is talking about *The Brothers Karamazov,* but I don't know what I could have said that brought it on, since I don't recall mentioning it.

AS: You see, in classics like that you do things in between, in between lines, which is not actually between lines, but it's something like syncopating. It's changing the horses in the middle of the stream, like when Grushenka says, "Yes, I'll kiss your hand" and then she says, snaps fingers, "Umh, maybe I won't kiss your hand." [Fingers are being snapped by Sten, twice, voice rising.] Right then, in the middle of the stream. This is the only time she really smiles, with so much behind. A classic like that is all-embracing. Look what it touches upon: family relationship; religion; *sex;* competition between father and son for the same woman; then, two women fighting for the same man . . . it's endless. If I began to tell you . . . you cannot do it by trimmings only; and the same goes for *Nana* or *Dr. Zhivago.* It's the same with all Russian classics. You have to know *what* you want to say. What part of it is vital to you? What do you want your audience to go for? You want to tell

Alyosha's story? Tell Alyosha's story. All the people are involved, but it's his story. Or you want to tell Dmitri's and father's, that's their story. The other characters come into it, but they are subjugated to that particular line of human weaknesses and human strengths. You've got to know . . . and you've got to trim yourself to it. You see, I'm personal about it because I love this character so much.

Marilyn [Monroe], who was at the Actors Studio, approached me several times when she wanted to play the part. She saw my film several times. She loved it. And she tried to find out what made me *tick* with it. She loved the part very much. I know what she would have made of it. She would have been fascinating in it. Fabulous. I could see that from talking with her. That was a searching soul. You see, the other one was on the surface only. She's Russian because she wears a babushka. So she's Russian! But Marilyn Monroe was probing . . . and searching . . . into why is Grushenka such as she was? What is there to that woman that makes her a classic . . . and far above ever so many fascinating characters? Why? *Why?* What is there? After all, if you put her on half a page, what can you say about her? It's because of the depth of it. You've got to understand such a thing, and *she* did. She sought me out at the Studio. She was that kind of person herself. Oh, yes, she was very deep and very lovely. I only ever saw her do one thing at the Studio, when she did *Anna Christie,* and everybody is still talking about it, how magnificent she was. She was giving and taking at the same time. That's a very rare quality. 'Cause usually it's very one-sided, either you *give* or you *take*. But when you can give both, then you have the audience with you.

JK: Speaking of extraordinary personalities who were also extraordinary performers, what about Garbo's *Anna Karenina*?

AS: Well, to be honest about it, it's about the only thing I like Garbo in. This is the only film in which she was sincere, and innocent. This is why I was always scared of Garbo, looking at her films. She never had innocence. Everything she portrayed, you could give her any quality but that. Now, Monroe had . . . in-no-cence. It's not an ingenuish quality; it's the sincerity of . . . of being able to bare your soul, of which Garbo never had any. I met her . . . that was at . . . well, you know, you mostly met people like that not at the [she gives a knowing laugh] conventional places. Some sort of a gathering, where we have something to say or something to listen to. But I have no impression of her.

After her Goldwyn contract was terminated Anna and her husband tried to go into independent production. They went to England and made one film there.

AS: I just finished one contract and . . . I felt I should be away. And then, you see, there was a beginning of something—I mean, the idea was there.

I was up for fabulous contracts after I left Goldwyn, but I think I was on the run. But I don't regret it. I never regret anything. I didn't sacrifice anything by leaving. You never sacrifice anything if *you* make the choice. It's a sacrifice only if you are pushed and pressed and you're not yourself. But if you got the choice, and you make the choice, you never sacrificed. I had a choice when I left Goldwyn, to stay in Hollywood and sign a big contract with another studio or to go with my husband, to go away. . . . I made that choice.

1965

Lewis Milestone, photographed by Jack Freulich, 1930

L E W I S
M I L E S T O N E

Aftersixty years in America the old director still had an accent that
pushed his voice even further down in his throat, but he spoke the language with an appreciation of the nuances of the English language some foreigners, mostly writers, bring to their work. Born in Odessa, Russia, in 1895—
"on the Black Sea, the home of Chekhov and Kuprin," he said—he was already
in America when the First World War broke out. He'd been stretching out a
sparse living with a series of jobs and enlisted in the Photographic Division of
the Signal Corps. He never got a chance to shoot much more than paper clips
and spitballs at the other men in his division, two future directors—Wesley
Ruggles and Josef von Sternberg. (This was before Joe became a "von.") When
the war ended, Milestone found a job in the fledgling film industry as an assistant cutter, "sweeping the cutting-room floor."

Milestone tends to make a joke of most things, whether they be the troubles
he had with Marlon Brando on the set of *Mutiny on the Bounty* or those of his
early years. He must have been a swift sweeper because he quickly skipped
from one studio to another, from Fox to Mack Sennett. By the time he went to
work for William Seiter, the director-husband of Universal's brightest star, the
comedienne Laura La Plante, he'd become chief cutter and writer. His Sennett
experience came in handy. His ability and clever personality got him a job directing for the hard-up but otherwise ventursome Warner Bros.

His first two films, *Seven Sinners* and *The Cave Man,* established Milestone as one of the brightest new talents working in the industry. Since these
coincided with the influx of foreign stars and directors to Hollywood, his Russian background may have come in handy. Hollywood was so filled with unending streams of jumped-up European exiles that a real Russian must have been
refreshing.

With his third film Milestone consolidated himself in Hollywood's creative
forefront. The "hobo poet" Jim Tully, notorious for lambasting movie-genius
pretensions, even exulted over Milestone's "creative integrity" in print. The film
was Milestone's first for another "boy wonder," Howard Hughes. Titled *Two
Arabian Knights,* it was a World War I comedy, a sort of modern Don Quixote–
Sancho Panza situation, that won him the first and still the only Oscar for

comedy direction. (He won out over Chaplin's *The Circus* and Harold Lloyd's *Speedy.*) His next film, one of the first talkies, was the seminal pacifist war picture, *All Quiet on the Western Front,* based on Erich Maria Remarque's internationally acclaimed best-selling novel. (Though Milestone was to direct three other films based on Remarque novels, none ever repeated this triumph.) *All Quiet* won the Oscar in 1930 for best picture and direction.

Milestone, whose career never again matched those early triumphs, continued for over three decades as one of the industry's most highly regarded members. Other films, as diverse as Cole Porter's *Anything Goes* (with Bing Crosby and Ethel Merman but *without* most of the Porter score); the truly bizarre, melodramatic *The General Died at Dawn* (with Gary Cooper); soap-operatic films like *Arch of Triumph,* and such minor classics as John Steinbeck's *Of Mice and Men;* the World War II antiwar tract *A Walk in the Sun;* the first of the Frank Sinatra–produced "Rat Pack" films, *Ocean's Eleven;* and the troubled multimillion-dollar remake of *Mutiny on the Bounty* all helped keep him in the forefront.

LM: *Ocean's Eleven* was made when I returned from Europe. Bert Ellenberg, who was with the William Morris office, handled my business. He got after me and said that Sinatra wanted me to do a picture with him. I'd never made one with him before, but of course I knew him very well. I asked what the story was and he said, "What difference does it make? He'll hand you some kind of script, and if you don't like it, you can rewrite it. There's plenty of money there." He wanted me to do a picture with him and that was enough. So I met with Frank and he showed me a script. I'd read it before; the story was bought by Peter Lawford.

   We had a lot of fun making it. It was comedy, you know, and nobody was expected to take it seriously. So I let the guys kid around, with all kinds of hell being raised on the set. Once we started the camera, all that frivolity rolled onto the screen.

JK: And after that you started *Mutiny on the Bounty.* [It was his last film on which he got directorial credit. He started work or took over on two other films, including the Kennedy bio film, *PT 109,* but he received or wanted no credit.]

LM: The call came in here about 10:00 at night from a very old friend of mine, Charlie Lederer, a writer. He called up and came over and told me that they were in trouble and he would consider it a personal favor if I would involve myself with this thing. Charlie was an old friend of mine and had helped me out a couple of times, so I didn't feel I could turn him down—it was my turn to reciprocate. So I said, "All right, I'll do it," and then we went over and met with the producer and Marlon Brando, and the first thing I knew, I was in it. I didn't even have a chance to digest the script. They were in the middle of it; see, Sir Carol [Reed] walked out on it—just quit. They were stuck. I did it for Charlie. I wish I hadn't done it.

JK: How much of the film had been done when you walked into it?

LM: That was another thing I fell for; see, they'd been on it a year, so how much of it can be left? I tried to discourage them by the price that I was asking, but nothing could stop them. So I thought, Well, this is one way of getting rich quick—I get the salary and, at most, it couldn't take more than two or three months. After I'd signed the contract, I found out that in that year all they'd had on screen was about seven minutes of film. I spent a year on it. That taught me a lesson for reaching for easy money.

They tried to patch the two books together—and of course it never works. The book ended, as the first film did, with the trial of the mutineers. What they wanted to do was to continue with the second book that Nordhoff whatsisname wrote. Of course there was a big crack in there. But they promised Brando, when he was signing the contract to play Fletcher Christian, that they would do the second book as part of the picture, and that would make him the central character and all—you know, you remember the thing. And that's what seduced *him* into signing it. Well, then, when it came to doing it, they tried everything in the world to get out of it because dramatically it didn't work. But finally they had to give in because he had the upper hand, being the star actor, and he was on film, and the threat hold was that he'd walk out. So they agreed to do it. There was a lot of writing and rewriting going on and arguments and whatnot. I used to walk away and sit in my portable office on the set—I just didn't bother with it. Nobody cared if I was there or not. I just sat on the sidelines because there was nothing I could do. They finally arrived at some kind of an ending and they shot it. But there was no other director. They were afraid, y'see, that if I walked out or they got rid of me, I would be the number-two man after Carol Reed and the whole thing would collapse. So they kept me there as a hostage. [Laughs.]

JK: It's not a film you're proud of, then?

LM: Oh, God, no. I hated it. It didn't represent me at all, and after the first two or three weeks I had nothing to say on it. It all started when . . . Y'see, everything went off fine for the first couple of weeks, and then suddenly we were doing a scene and Marlon spoke to the cameraman . . . right past me. He said, "Look, I'll tell you, when I go like this, it means roll it, and this gesture means you stop the camera. You don't stop the camera until I give you the signal." Well, I was *amazed*, but I didn't say anything about it. I thought, Well, let's see how it goes. He said, "Everybody ready" and the camera started rolling. And as the camera started rolling, I turned my back on it and walked away. I had a magazine stuck in my pocket, and I sat down and started reading it while the scene was going on. The producer came up and said, "Aren't you going to watch it?" I said, "Well, I hate to see movies in pieces, so you let him do this and when it's all finished and cut, for ten cents I can walk into the theater and see the whole thing at once. Why should I bother looking at it now?" He said that after that it would be the end. I said, if that's the way he felt about it, we should call it quits. Because that's what I wanted. He didn't say anything. He just walked away; and from then on that's the way we worked.

JK: You mean Brando directed all his own scenes?

LM: Well, he *tried* to direct; some of them he didn't know how to start. But I concentrated my directorial efforts with Trevor Howard and the English cast. We got on beautifully; they *wanted* to be directed and it was fine. But anything Marlon was in I didn't want any part of.

JK: So what was the matter with Brando? Didn't he know the quality of your work?

LM: Of course he did. Brando is a psychotic man, in my opinion, and there's no accounting for his behavior. He didn't behave like that only with me, but also with the rest of the cast. Since then, with every picture he's done, it's been the same story. I don't think the man's responsible for what he's doing.

JK: Well, it was quite a film when it came out. You could see it was between the devil and the deep blue sea. But your career starts in the '20s.

LM: I started with silent pictures. I started directing in 1925, and my first two pictures were *Seven Sinners* and *The Cave Man*—Gillette Burgess' story. Then sound came in in 1928. So between the end of 1925 and 1928 I did about three or four silent films, *Two Arabian Knights, Garden of Eden. Garden of Eden* was done with Corinne Griffith. *Two Arabian Knights* got me the first Academy Award—it was a war comedy. Then I did a film we handled like a documentary; we had to, there was no script. I did that with Tommy Meighan, who was a very big star in those days. We made the whole thing in Florida. In 1926, towards the end of 1926, Florida had a fantastic real-estate boom; people were making fortunes overnight on paper. When this thing came along, we decided to go to Florida, see what's going on. Actually, I had a writer along with me, Tom Geraghty, acting as a producer-writer. So—he wrote from life, y'know. Whatever he saw there he dramatized. It came out a very successful film, and a very interesting one. It was called *The New Klondike* [Paramount, 1926]. Lila Lee was in it. Then I came back from Florida and cut the film. But we had a disagreement with Warner Brothers.

Y'see, I was on loan-out to Paramount, who produced this picture with Thomas Meighan. Right after that, Gloria Swanson, who was the top star in those days, demanded that the front office [at Paramount] assign me to her because she was doing a film called *Fine Manners* and she wanted me to finish it because Frank Tuttle was directing the film and got ill and she said she didn't want him to come back and that I should take it over. Well, to be assigned to a Gloria Swanson picture at that stage of the game was unbelievable—she was a top, top star. She told me why she wanted me and so on, but I had to say that I wasn't a free agent, I was under contract to Warner Brothers, I was only being loaned out, so her company would have to discuss it with Warners. They started negotiations.

At that time Warners lived from day to day—they had no money—and they thought of holding Paramount up for a lot of dough; with a big star demanding this young director (they were paying me about $400 a week), they saw it as their chance to make a chunk of money, so they asked for $75,000 for my services. Paramount realized what was happening, and that there was a holdup of some kind about that. Suddenly I got called into Warner Brothers' main office in New York, and one of the Warners, Sam, who died shortly after that, said he'd received a telegram from the Coast and they wanted me to return there immediately, that they needed me there. Well, they didn't need me at all. The day before this happened, the same man called me in the office and asked me where I wanted to take my layoff, in New York or on the Coast, and I'd said that since I'd been so busy I hadn't seen any of the shows in New York, I'd take my layoff there and catch some of the theaters. Now suddenly he said that they wanted me to return to the Coast immediately.

I reasoned out for myself what it was all about, because I knew about the demands they'd made of Paramount, so I said I wasn't going. He said, "You're under contract to us and you have to do what you're told." I said, "To a certain limit. But if you think you have more power than that, put me on a train." And I walked out and we started a lawsuit. They were suing me for breach of contract, and the countersuit was that *they* broke the contract. So I engaged a lawyer and we started—as poor as the company was, they still had a lot more than I had—and we went on with it for a little while until I realized that this lawyer was not to be trusted; overnight he changed his whole attitude. One day he said I couldn't possibly lose and the next he said he thought I ought to go back and told me about all the hazards of suing a company. So I opened the door, said, "The conference is over, thank you very much," and threw him out of the room. Then I decided I'd better return to the West Coast and get some lawyer that I *know,* and I'd carry on the fight from there as well as New York.

I returned and sat around here—couldn't go on with anything because the industry knew I was in the fight. Boredom set in and Harold Lloyd got hold of me and started talking to me like a Dutch uncle, saying, "What are you doing? Come on and work." I told him I was in a legal fight and that if I was going to work I'd have to cancel my side of the fight. But he kept after me and wanted me to work with him—I guess he recognized I had a kinda flair for comedy, and he needed somebody. So finally I gave in, because of boredom on the one hand and the desire of working with Harold on the other.

I went to work and I lasted half the picture; I just couldn't look at myself—I hated myself for doing it: the system wins, you know. So halfway through the picture I had to talk to Harold. I explained the whole thing to him and said, "Look, by now you know how I work and you can really get along without me. I'd appreciate it very much if you understood this so I could quit." Well, he was very sympathetic; he understood my story; he believed me and said I could quit any time I wanted. He entered into the conspiracy with me. He said, "I'll tell you what I'll do. We're not gonna let Warner Brothers know that you're going, but they'll send for the check. And when they do, I'll just say that I haven't seen you for a week. I'll say you just walked out and disappeared and then it'll be up to them to find you. The shock will wake them up to something." Harold did that. I quit, but I used to come around nearly every day to the studio because there was a squash court there. And came a day when the check was due. Naturally, Harold didn't pay because he hadn't seen me. The news that I was no longer working came as a shock to Warners, and I could just see Jack [Warner] was so enraged that he'd said, "Sue him, and sue him for everything he's got." The one mistake he made was that he forgot I didn't have anything. So they started the lawsuit.

I picked up a little information from another lawyer that since they only claimed damages of $200,000, not breach of contract, if I paid the $200,000 I'd be a free man—they're not saying I'm under contract and can't work for anybody else. They just want $200,000, so pay them and you'll be free. I said he had to be kidding—where am I gonna get $200,000? I ain't got that many cents. So he said that if I didn't have any money, I was in the perfect spot to take off through bankruptcy. That's a vulgar name for it; in the legal profession they call it "The Law of Mercy," and if you hand over everything you own, you can get discharged and start all over again. Then, when you're in a position, you settle with your creditors for as much as you can—say ten cents on the dollar—depending on your well-being. So I brought it to my lawyer that riding around the block I'd had this idea. 'Course it was obvious to him that the idea had come from a brilliant legal mind—actually, it was from the head of the legal department of Paramount studios. Anyway, he called in about four lawyers and they consulted at a conference and they couldn't find anything wrong with the idea. The only thing that might happen, they said, is that when I came up before the judge and he asks for your signature on your confession of judgment, he might hesitate over the figure—$200,000 is a lot of money. You've walked in and done the equivalent of pleading guilty—he might hesitate. But if you go to Judge So-and-so, he's a creature of habit; come 4:00, at one minute to 4:00 he's already gathering up his papers, at 4:00 he's gone. So if I wait till he's getting up to go and then stick the paper under his nose, he might sign it. So at one minute to 4:00 I do it. He asks what the paper is and I say, "Just a confession of judgment" and he signs it. The next day we filed for bankruptcy. I turned in the few things I had and I was legally free.

But the Producers' Association was another story—so I was blackballed.

I just sat. Probably I was the first man in this town to be blackballed. Later, when the political thing was going, I was blackballed again, but then so were a lot of other people. Eventually, after a little time, Thomas Meighan entered my life again. He met in New York with a lawyer by the name of Neil Mc-Carthy who was representing Howard Hughes [as well as DeMille and Mayer]. Howard Hughes had asked him, since he did a lot of legal work in motion pictures, that if Thomas ever heard of a young director with promise, he'd like to know about it. So the head of Paramount, having lunch with Neil McCarthy, hears this story and talks about me. He said I was nice and legally free, it's just that the Motion Picture Producers' Association have said I'm not allowed to behave like I did and go on working in pictures. Since Howard Hughes is wealthy and independent, and if he wants someone outstanding, let him grab me. So a date was set up and suddenly there were no protesters at all. So I went to work for Howard Hughes and made *Two Arabian Knights*. That's the first one. I did three for him: *Two Arabian Knights, The Racket,* starring Thomas Meighan, and *Front Page*.

JK: You must have known Hughes quite well then; he wasn't as private as he later became.

LM: Oh, no. I liked working with him. He's a different man now. After all, he was about twenty-one years old when I went to work for him and now he's sixty-one. After all the things he lived through and crashes that he suffered, if anybody wanted to sit down and write his story, no matter how superficial, his biography over the last fifteen–twenty years is fantastic. He's a combination of a drawing-room blithering idiot and an engineering-room genius.

He started out by wanting to do the lot himself, which I discouraged very quickly. So he just disappeared. But when I did a picture for him, if ever I needed help in the engineering field, I'd take the problem to him. He had an experimental lab which he supported—cost him about a million bucks a year—and I'd borrow an engineer. This was before he really got interested in aviation. He was trying to marry the steam engine with gasoline, so he had this experimental lab. But unless I went to him, he never came around—he never bothered me.

JK: At that time why didn't you work on *Hell's Angels*—or did he have other directors under contract?

LM: He didn't have anyone under contract; but *Hell's Angels* was his baby because it had to do with airplanes. He became fanatic about it. Anyway, after *Two Arabian Knights* he wasn't going to produce any pictures for a while because he was interested in *Hell's Angels;* it became obvious that that was what he wanted to do. So I went to him and said that since he wasn't going to produce any more pictures, why didn't he let me buy back the balance of my contract? If he didn't let me, all I would have done was sat around, drawing my salary. He said, "Well, I can farm you out." But anyway I bought the balance of my contract, and then I went and did *All Quiet on the Western Front*. I remember the proposition: I told him I'd pay him $250 for every week the contract had to run. If he didn't do that, he'd have to pay me my salary, so I'd be saving him $40,000 to $50,000. I reminded him that he couldn't farm me out because it specified in my contract that I couldn't be farmed out against my consent. So he was stuck. After *All Quiet,* I went back to Hughes to do *Front Page*. Years later he wanted me to remake *Two Arabian Knights,* and I had to explain to him the difference between the First World War and the Second World War . . . one was a romantic thing and you could afford to be funny. And the Second World War was nothing to be funny about. I was in the Photographic Corps in the Army in the First World War, that's how I got into films.

JK: You made a satirical musical during the Depression: *Hallelujah, I'm a Bum.* It must have been poison at the box office.

LM: Sure. First time around, it didn't make any money at all. There's an explanation for some of them why they didn't make any money at all. Like *Hallelujah* . . . it *was* too far ahead of its time, especially in the songs and the lyrics. Larry Hart was a *real* genius, and I was always interested in the political changes happening in the country. So when I got together with Larry, I fed him a couple of ideas. One time I remember we were in Tijuana when I said to Larry, "You know, we ought to have a song for Al Jolson, for the hobo, which should be something like Chaliapin's famous song about the flea who lives in a king's coat." This would be a plea for the rest of the hobos to understand him. Because the accusation was that he accepted a job, which is the worst crime in the world. We were in a car going through the main thoroughfare of Tijuana. He yelled to the chauffeur to stop the car. He rushed out and I went after him into a saloon and came up to the bar and he said, "Gimme a drink." He got a drink and a paper and pencil to write on. He swallowed the drink, and the pencil flew across the paper, and he said, "How would that be?" And he read me the lyrics. This is the plea the hobo makes during the kangaroo court . . . I think I can still remember the lyrics:

> *Look, your honor, please take note*
> *There are two little fleas on your honor's coat.*
> *Two little fleas, and we don't care whether*
> *The fleas are merry, they're just fleaing together.*
> *The way of the world is a he and she*
> *And if it's all right for a flea it's all right for me.*

This was done right there, with a drink, and I had to tell him it was marvelous.

JK: How did *All Quiet on the Western Front* come about? Did you go to Universal or did they come to you?

LM: What happened was I was doing a picture* with Lilyan Tashman, who was a well-known actress married to Edmund Lowe. Between scenes we were talking and she said I must read this new book just out, *All Quiet on the Western Front*, and gave me her copy. I read it and naturally I thought it was fantastic, but I didn't do anything about it. Universal acquired the rights to it and started looking around for a director. They wanted Herbert Brenon, he originally came out of England. He was their first choice, but he was an old-time director and they thought he asked for too much money . . . he asked for $125,000 guaranteed. So they balked at that and they looked to see who else was around. Since I'd made a couple of war comedies, they thought, "This guy must know something about war, what about him?" So they talked to my agent, Myron Selznick, and I said, well, that I knew the book and I'd love to do it. So he told me about this Herbert Brenon situation and said we could make more than $125,000 . . . he'd ask for $5000 a week for ten weeks and then *pro rata*. By the time I finished the film, I'd have more than $125,000. It's the way you present the deal that counts.

JK: If you say "Lewis Milestone" to people, they'll say, "He's the one who makes antiwar movies," because of *All Quiet*. . . .

LM: There was a marvelous review I've got in a top publication in London. They took a span of twenty years of my work, from *All Quiet* to *A Walk in the Sun*. They said, "These two antiwar films are outstanding and . . ." It was a rave notice, I was flattered beyond anything that they ever expected. But then, by the time this piece came out, a picture I did, a potboiler I did for Zanuck, came out called *Halls of Montezuma* [he laughs]. That was a war film done under the supervision of Darryl Zanuck, and I hated most of it. The picture was released in London practically a week or so after that review full of praises, and they wanted to take back everything they said. You can't live down *All Quiet;* all you can say is "Too bad it happened so early in my career."

You see, very early in your career as a director you learn that if you stick to one kind of movie, you develop a reputation. Like Lubitsch created the "Lubitsch touch" . . . but if you review his movies, you see they're all about the same thing. Delightful, wonderful, what he was doing, but one type of movie. Hitchcock developed in another category, suspense, and so on. George Cukor is a woman's director; he's had a reputation from year one . . ."If you need to direct a woman, get George Cukor." That was his reputation. I was always classified as no-woman's director. But my pictures had women in them† and I didn't cripple them. They came in women and they went out as women. [He intersperses his comments with lots of chuckles.]

New York Nights (1929). Norma Talmadge was the star—her first talking picture.
†*Arch of Triumph* with Ingrid Bergman, *The Strange Love of Martha Ivers* with Barbara Stanwyck and Lizabeth Scott.

Most directors find one thing that they like to do and they stick to it—with variations, but basically it's the same idea. And I didn't like to do that; I'd do anything. I'd pick up a book and read it, or I'd hear an idea that had no relation to any work I'd done before, and I'd get involved in the thing and do it. But I never tried to get known for just one thing.

And he really isn't. *All Quiet* may have been his greatest, but he's also remembered for *Arch of Triumph* and his many other films. When I asked Evelyn Brent, "What do you consider the milestones in your work?" she answered, "Oh, I never worked with him." Lewis would have appreciated the tribute.

1969

MAE WEST

MAE WEST was born into an era of America's history when signs of the new nation's success were forests of chimney stacks billowing pollution into the sky to herald the cities mushrooming up beneath. A man's worth then could be measured by his girth; a woman's charms by ample curves that made her look like a scenic railroad. When Mae (the woman who put the giggle into "gigolo") finally struck it big, it wasn't with the plays on contemporary themes that gave her early notoriety (*Sex, The Drag* and such), but by going back to her own roots on the Bowery and to the dreams that had fueled her rise from barroom boards to the heights of the legitimate stage, Broadway.

Mae's earliest theatrical experiences had been as Little Eva in *Uncle Tom's Cabin* and in other such celebrated child roles (Mae was always small for her years), but in between acts she entertained as a "coon-shouter"* from which she got that sassy delivery, that sashaying walk—like a sailor back on dry land after months at sea—and her lifelong love for the black-soul sound that could have made her one of the great white blues-singers, a talent overshadowed by the immortality she gained, drawing on another of her earliest-learned skills as an impressionist of the famous vaudeville stars of her youth. She re-created the two most celebrated symbols of self-made wealth and beauty of her era, the legendary railroad tycoon "Diamond Jim" Brady and the beauty who set the

---

*The term "coon-shouter" came from the Old South, where black slaves used to chase raccoons out of hiding to make them easier targets. The tag stuck, and when in vaudeville black music became acceptable entertainment for white audiences, performed by blacks, not in white- or black-face but as themselves, they became known as "coon-shouters." Down, dirty, funky and blue, they chased white entertainment up the vaudeville tree. Mae even as a child knew a good thing when she heard it, and she took it for herself. By the time, years after, when she had hit her own stride, the term had dropped from the vocabulary, with Mae the sole and soul beneficiary. I'd always had a hunch—nothing sure, just an instinct from watching her perform, trading quips with the black help, not like mistress and servant but like two girls in the dressing room, and from the way she sang—that the oft-hinted-at secret in Mae's past was a touch of color in her blood. I could never get Mae to admit anything like that when I delicately broached the subject, because I felt that she shouldn't be making rock 'n' roll records, but rather the old blues the way they should be sung. The idea really appealed to Mae, but she just explained that her affinity for black music was because it's the best there is. She died with all her secrets intact.

standard for generations of young girls, Lillian Russell, the actress Brady showered with diamonds. Mae took the best parts of both and gave the world *Diamond Lil*, the first white woman with a black soul.

By the time she took the Silver Chief to Hollywood in 1932, Mae wasn't a little girl from a little town trying to make good in the big city, she was a big girl from a big town she'd already conquered. She'd come to save the ailing Paramount studio from going under with the box-office returns from her first starring film, a somewhat cleaned-up version of her nationally known *Diamond Lil*. To appease puritan outrage the film version was retitled *She Done Him Wrong*, and so that Mae's character wouldn't be confused with the notorious theatrical Lil, they renamed her Lou. The guardians of public morality were happy with their silly victory.

She Done Him Wrong rescued Paramount from an MGM takeover by grossing $2 million, a formidable sum considering that film tickets in 1933 cost 10 cents, and lent an additional meaning to the popular song "Brother, Can You Spare a Dime?" In the depths of the Depression, when people lived on nothing and sometimes less, for ten cents Mae gave them back confidence and the notion of a time in America when a man's, or a woman's, get-up-and-go was all that was needed to gain fame, fortune, a bed of roses and a safe full of diamonds. People by the millions, hungry and dispirited, shelled out their precious dimes (enough for a meal) to see her strut her stuff, lick the liars, outwit the politicians at their own game . . . and when she rolled her eyes over a good-looking guy, an audience could feel the goose on their own bottom. Mae's *Diamond Lil* was a raffish, healthy reaffirmation of what an American was capable of achieving in the home of the brave and the free.

Mae's arrival on screen is in a horse-drawn barouche pulling up in front of her Bowery place of work. As she gets out, she greets a poor widow woman and her little girl with a tip and a friendly pat on the kid's head. As Mae née Lil now Lou saunters through the swinging doors into the bar, the widow woman says, "You're a good woman, Miss Lou," to which the nonchalant Mae replies, "Best woman ever walked the streets." In one swift establishing scene Mae had won over mothers (of which there were many) and the poor (of which there were more). Not everyone liked Mae, though. When somebody told her that the jam-packed premiere of *I'm No Angel* at Grauman's Chinese Theater was noticeably lacking Hollywood's elite, Mae put Tinsel Town in its place, saying she liked it that way because "I prefer to play to the best people." Hollywood's churlish attitude lasted no longer than it took to cash in on Mae's success. When MGM's sex star, Jean Harlow, started to sass her way to comedy success (black maids and all), Mae's victory was complete.

By the time I met Mae, in 1970, almost as many years had elapsed since she brought her most famous creation to the screen as had separated that film from the era of Brady and Russell, and by now she had become as much a legend on the American scene as the prototypes for her fame. Once Mae had found Lil, she never really deviated from it—it was the skin that suited her best,

Mae West, photographed by Strand, New York, circa 1918

and subsequent roles, on stage or screen, whether in a contemporary setting or as a historical heroine like the Empress of Russia in *Catherine Was Great,* were really the further adventures and conquests of her Lil. Unlike other performers who made a name by impersonating famous faces and voices of the screen, especially herself (Mae always had a great fondness for male impressionists), neither Brady nor Lillian Russell was much more than a dim name to the people Mae appealed to on Broadway or in movies, and as a result she was never handicapped by comparisons. In the end, she believed in her creation and saw it as an extension of herself in much the same way the paying fans did. Talking to her about Lil was like talking to Mae about herself. It may have been the woman I met, but it was the legend I saw. She was Lil.

I did have an exceptional and unique illustration of Mae's gifts as an impressionist, in a location as bizarre and unexpected as the performer she momentarily re-created. I had no tape recorder to capture the moment for posterity, but I wasn't likely to forget Mae doing Sarah Bernhardt in a Chinese restaurant in downtown Los Angeles one night in 1974. There were four of us, Mae; Paul Novak, her friend, bodyguard, chauffeur, masseur, and, it was said, lover; Paul Morrissey, the Warhol director who'd been wanting to meet her; and I. Dinner was lively even though the subjects under discussion were the well-worn paths of her career and sayings. In the middle of our meal, a semi-drunk black man came over and stood by our table, not threatening, just waving on his feet. He addressed Mae without preamble, as if to continue a conversation they hadn't finished the day before.

"How's Ruby?" he asked. "Ruby," said Mae. "Yeah, she worked for you." "Oh," said Mae, "yeah, she's gone." "When was that?" "Long ago now, deah." "Did she go back to New York?" "Yeah, I think so, deah." "You don't have her address, do you?" he wanted to know. "No, deah, no." "She was a nice girl." "Yeah, very nice. Sweet," Mae added. "Well, you're looking good." "Thanks, deah." "Well, it's been good seeing you." "Yeah, deah." "See you around." He tipped his hand in salutation and ambled off the way he came.

"Who's that?" we asked. "Don't know, deah." "Who's Ruby?" Mae had no idea. "But you sent her off to New York," we persisted. "He sounded as if he knew you." Mae chuckled, "Oh they all do, deah."

So, we were laughing and joking, and in that frame of mind I thought I'd see if Mae really did remember or if she was just parroting a lifetime's performance in the role of Mae West.

What was Lillian Russell like? I wanted to know. Mae wasn't totally sure anymore because in her mind she'd long ago confused Russell with her own mother, probably the single most influential force in her own life. So, then, had she ever seen Sarah Bernhardt, the legendary French tragedienne? I might just as well have said Eva Tanguay or Anna Held, but, well, Bernhardt was a name familiar to all. "Ohhh, sure," Mae drawled and told of the New York actors' benefit one Sunday afternoon before the war. World War I, that is. "1912," said Mae. We were riveted. "What was Sarah like?" I asked. "Well, you know," Mae said, maybe a bit put off by my persistence in wanting to know about anybody except Mae West, "it was so long ago, and she was talkin' in French, you know." But was she good? "Oh, yeah, deah, sure . . . she was a great actress." "What did she do?" Mae, instead of saying how or why she was good, went into an impression. Her little hands with their long, hard, clawlike nails took on the melodramatic gestures of the actors of Bernhardt's era that one can see in the pictures from those days, the hands held out front, one up over her face, the fingers slightly curled as if gripping some invisible force, and her voice became a low, rolling growl, full of long *rrrr*'s and words like "*royame . . . de royame . . . de royame. . . .*" When she had finished, one of the Paul's asked Mae whether this was before or after Bernhardt had lost her leg. "What's that, deah?" "Well," he explained, "Sarah had to have a leg amputated." "Oh, yeah, deah," she answered after a little reflection. "Must have been aftah . . . 'cause she was draggin' things a bit."

So, after that evening I always believed Mae, whether it was a story she told for the first time or so often that everybody had lost count. Sort of her own "To be or not to be," like the story about the cop with the gun in his pocket, or her advice to skinny girls, when she told them, "What the good Lord has forgotten we'll put there with cotton." She never lost her timing for making things sound fresh; and nobody was ever quite as delighted with Mae's success story as Mae herself. Back in England, I told friends about her Bernhardt in the restaurant, and somebody asked me whether or not Mae had been any good. How the hell would I know? I've never heard Sarah Bernhardt, but it sure sounded amazing at the time.

Getting the interview on tape for posterity wasn't as easy as egg foo yung and a pair of chopsticks. Mae hesitated. She hadn't let anyone do a taped interview with her for more than a decade, and she didn't want to spoil the impact of her screen return by letting people hear her . . ."unless," as she said, "the interview is short and the questions are good. They have to be good, you know, whatever they are. You've got to ask the right questions. You know."

Mae had appeared at the Academy screening room, where they'd been having a seminar, showing a film followed by a question-and-answer session. After the screening of *I'm No Angel* they brought in a chaise-longue and placed it center stage beneath a large potted floral growth. George Cukor, who acted as moderator, escorted Mae on. Slowly. She was in her elevator heels, towering over him, her hair piled sky-high, looking like nobody else. She wowed the audience. It was just her and Cukor up there onstage, talking. The standing-room crowd screamed and hollered and made the whole thing into an event that was something of a first of its kind for that time: "camp" was in the air even though it hadn't yet pitched tent in every corner bar in the land. The questions were planted, the answers confident. The result was a triumph: the publicity for *Myra Breckinridge*, still in production, was enormous. Mae felt good. So good, in fact, that she lowered some of her reservations about letting me do the first "taped" interview she'd done in so many years. She promised to consider doing it. She had to approve the questions. I had to have the interview. She was still reluctant to be taped. We'd talk. She'd decide what questions she liked, which answers she liked. We'd tape later. It was a start.

MW: Ohhhhh. Did you see that picture *Dolly*? [*Hello, Dolly!* with Barbra Streisand.] Because I want to look at it. I understand that she's doing an imitation of me. That's a lot of nerve [pronounced "noive"]. Taking your mannerisms and everything, and puttin' it up there like it's hers.

JK: Don't you think it's really a big compliment?

MW: No, no. She's liable to continue doing everything that way, playing all her parts. First thing you know, people will think it's hers. Why should she dare do this? As an imitation, fine, but you can't imitate a person all through a picture. I understand she copies my style all through the picture. She didn't know how she wanted to play it and she thought of me, and it just stuck with her and she couldn't help it. I was never interested in seeing other performers for ideas for my act. I was an individual and I was developing my own personality, you see. I didn't want anything from anybody else that wasn't me. I saw all the shows when I wasn't working, but I never copied them. I mimicked Eddie Foy and George M. Cohan . . . I did these great male impersonations . . . but that was mimicry, which is different from taking tricks from people.

JK: Your mannerisms are classics. It struck me again watching you the other night that, although you don't smoke, you always have these long cigarettes in your films.

MW: Ohhhh. I always have a cigarette for the characterizations. But I didn't like it. I used to have to hold it, but I never puffed. You never saw me inhalin' or anything. I couldn't wait till I got rid of it. But I had to do it, you know, it was for the characters. When I played these, you know, very few women smoked, they didn't smoke in public in the '20s. And they never had sex symbols in films till I came. Or they called it something else, 'cause nobody used the word "sex" till I used it in my play, except to differentiate between the male and female, like he's of the male sex. . . . So now, when the studio sees somebody who looks like a sex symbol, they build it up and stuff it down the public's throat and keep telling the public that this is a sex symbol till after a time people come to believe it. After I was called a sex symbol and the studios saw how much money my films made, they wanted others. But these were "synthetic." When MGM were building up Harlow, they came to me to ask me to write some stories for her, give her some funny dialogue. That was a joke. I was breakin' my neck writing, casting and starring in my own films. If I thought of something funny, I wasn't about to give it to them!

JK: Not only funny, but racy too. Not dirty, but you did make movies that helped bring the Hays Office down on Hollywood.

MW: Deah, when I knew that the censors were after my films and they had to come and okay everything, I wrote scenes for them to cut! These scenes were so rough that I'd never have used them. But they worked as a decoy. They cut them and left the stuff I wanted. I had these scenes in there about a man's fly and all that, and the censors would be sittin' in the projection room laughing themselves silly. Then they'd say "Cut it" and not notice the rest. Then when the film came out and people laughed at it and the bluenoses were outraged, they came and said, "Mae, you didn't show us that." But I'd show them the scripts they had okayed themselves!

JK: Where did you get this feeling for the underworld jargon? The way characters like Chick and Clogg and the others talked?

MW: Well . . . surely, you know . . . I met characters, I met people, you talk and listen to them, they talk that way, you know what I mean, slangy and all. And I knew all that slang. I come from Brooklyn, New York, and a lot of characters are there. I didn't base my characters, like Gus Jordan and those, on real people. They are all characters I made up. Yeah. No, the whole thing just came. Well, you gotta watch all the pictures I made, it's the same way . . . they came to me. I never stopped, you know, I just made one picture after another. You know, *Klondike Annie* and the circus picture you saw the other night, *I'm No Angel,* you know.

JK: There were so many young people there, did you like that?

MW: Oh, God, yeah. Well, I expect this picture *Myra Breckinridge* will get both; the older people will come out to see it, and I've got this young crowd. It can't miss.

At this point, nobody—including Mae—knew yet what the end of the film was going to be. She felt that it should end with a great last line . . . hers. But the film still had a week to shoot. At the moment she was still wondering what she'd do after the film. One of the plans was to do the play *Sextette* in England, but she said:

MW: I'd rather do another picture than do a spectacular for television. Because I think my value is when they've got to pay money to see me. When they start to see me on TV, they just turn you off and on, you know, they get satisfied and then they say, "Oh, she'll be on again," and they just wait. I want to make another picture before I do anything on TV. Somebody's talking to me about doin' *Sextette*. I want to get Christopher Plummer for that. Do you know him? I told Bob Wise after I saw that picture he did with him, you know, *Sound of Music,* I said, "There's your sex person. There's your box office. Him." He carried that picture. She was all right, you know, Julie Andrews, you know what I mean, to play a schoolmarm or a nun, but she hasn't got the sex personality. No, no, no. And unless you put somebody in there with him who has it, it's missin'. That's why I think that picture *Star* didn't do so well. She hasn't got *it*.

JK: I heard once that you rejected George Raft when you were making *Belle of the Nineties,* even though you had worked with him in *Night After Night,* your first film. Didn't he have it?

MW: Sure. Ah, no, I'd 'a had him. But, you see, I would have had to co-star with him again. This way I didn't have to co-star with anyone. I just featured them.

JK: Did you always cast your leading men yourself?

MW: Ohhh, yeah. Like I cast Cary Grant. And I cast Victor McLaglen for *Klondike Annie.* Why I cast Victor was I was up to 142 pounds in that picture, though you'd never know it. And I couldn't get the weight off in time, see, so I figured, well, I'd get McLaglen. He's not only tall but wide, a very thick look in his face, bulky, you know, big. And he'd make me look thin. That's how I put Victor McLaglen in. And then, of course, he was perfect for the part of Bull Brackett. I think he gave a great performance. He got a sex personality. Ohhhhh, yes. He has it. That smile . . . I always cast my leading men in my plays too. Of course, sometimes you can't always get what you want, so you take second best.

JK: It's funny to hear you speak of "second best" . . . you've worked so hard at maintaining your image, your "star."

MW: Deah, I've had an easy, successful and happy life. Show me anyone at my age who can do what I'm doing now and look the way I do and play the parts I play. You know, most women when they're forty [who is going to argue with Mae West?] start having to play character parts. It should give other people hope, deah. If I can do it, they can. It's the body and the mind. Keep your mind youthful-thinking and your insides have to be healthy and young. I have a cold once in ten years.

I never wanted to be anyone else. I was satisfied to be myself. If I wanted to be Florence Nightingale or Madame de Pompadour, I'd play them for a short time till I got tired of the part. Well, I only ever wanted to be a lion tamer. As a child I was always being told that the lion was the king of animals and the most beautiful and ferocious beast, and my father took me to see them and told me how they were the greatest. So years later I wrote myself a part in *I'm No Angel* in which I played a lion tamer. When I went into that cage, I felt at home because I had wanted to do this so much since I was a child. There were about ten lions in the cage, if you remember. That was no fake. They wouldn't let me put my head in the lion's mouth, though. I wanted to, but they said they had to think of the picture, and they got this woman who worked with the lions to do that. I would've done it. Of course, when I think of it now, you couldn't get me into a cage with a lion for anything. So you see, deah, if I want to be something else, I write it as a part and play it, but I never wanted to be anyone else but me for long.

JK: And you've played *that* part since . . . when?

MW: Ohhh, I was in shows and in vaudeville when I was a kid. While I was working, I had an aunt along to chaperone me, and there was a maid who dressed me and all that stuff. I had a very proper family. We never used any swearing or discussed sex at home. It's strange, that, but I never talked about sex with my parents. Even today I don't like to discuss sex with my sister . . . I'd feel dirty. The way I heard about sex first came from a friend of mine when I was nine. Her mother was a doctor, and we were playing in her house one day and there was this book lying there on the table and after I read it I had a funny feeling about my parents. A peculiar feeling—disgust, you might say. It took a long time for me to get over it. They suddenly weren't gods anymore. Ohh, I wish they wouldn't teach sex in the schools. They should teach *health*. Health is what is important.

But I never had much time to mix with other children, but I know I never missed them. You see, I was so carried away with myself, my dancing, my singing, that I didn't need other kids around. Besides, growing up in show business makes you a lot smarter, and it gave me a standing in the neighborhood.

JK: How did you break into show business?

MW: Well, I had a natural singing voice and my mother took me to singing and dancing schools. Nobody else in our family had ever been in show business, but she had wanted to go on the stage when she was a young girl. Her parents wouldn't let her, they were very strict like that. But she loved me being in the theater. I was crazy about my mother. But I never liked my father much when I was small. I don't know why, 'cause he never laid a hand on any of us, you know, and he always provided good for us. The only reason I can think of now why I wasn't crazy about him was that he smoked these big cigars. To this day I haven't been able to stand cigars. He was a prizefighter in the beginning, a very handsome man, and later he had a detective agency and then his own hansom-cab business.

JK: Is he the reason for your partiality to boxing and muscle men?

MW: No, I don't think it's because he was a fighter. I was never much around businessmen because I wasn't in that walk of life. I was in show biz and so I went for that kind of man. I attracted athletes because I don't smoke and I don't drink and I like to keep fit. That gets 'em. Yeah. . . .

Mae was always proud of her body. She maintained it and liked to have it appreciated and was not averse to having you feel her muscles. Back in the '30s

Paramount photographer Bill Walling had done a couple of "at home" sessions with her, and he was present the day Mae came to the gallery for a portrait session soon after she'd signed with Paramount. "She was wearing a slinky low-cut dress that wasn't covering much as it was, and all that flesh was making Gene [the head of Paramount Portrait Gallery, who shot all the big stars like Dietrich, Lombard and, naturally, Mae West] a bit nervous. Gene was a staid sort of guy, not very lively. But he knew his job. Mae was leaning over a round, glass table cupping her head in her hands. The radio was on because she liked music. These sessions could take a long time, and the music helped her to relax. This was during the Depression, and there used to be a lot of these giveaway shows on the air. This guy was forever offering dumb things to his listeners. He was saying how he had these two cute little puppies to be given away. One had a cute little brown nose, and the other had a cute little pink nose. And you were to call in to say which one you wanted. Gene was behind the camera when Mae said, 'Hey, Gene.' She'd taken out one of her big beautiful bazooms and put it on the table. 'Which one do you want? The one with the cute little brown nose or the one with the cute little pink nose?' She was a real exhibitionist. Well, Gene was so shocked he nearly knocked the camera over. She thought that was real funny."

MW: But you asked me about me and show biz. Well, when I was twelve, I had gotten too mature for children's parts, so I went back to living at home in Brooklyn till I was sixteen, when I could get a work permit and go back on the stage. While I was living at home, I used to do Sunday concerts for various organizations like the Knights of Columbus. That sort of thing, you know. And the first boyfriend that I remember was Joe Schenk—he was about seventeen and I was fourteen. He was a pianist and had his own ragtime band, and Saturday nights they'd come up to our house to rehearse. But I had an awful lot of boyfriends in those years at home, Joe was just the first in long pants. I always had maybe one girlfriend at a time, but I wasn't much of a woman's woman. Even then. My sister, Beverly, was a lot younger than I was, so we never had much in common as children. But later we were very close.

JK: So you got your first man when you were fourteen. How old were you when you got married?

MW: I was seventeen. But I had lots of affairs before I married Frank Wallace. But they were just love affairs, not sex-love affairs. We'd neck and hug and kiss and play with each other, but no sex. Not till I got married. Probably one of the reasons I did get married then was because of sex. Frank and I were on the road at the time with our vaudeville act, so my parents didn't know, and before I agreed to marry him, I made him swear not to tell my mother. We never signed into a hotel as a married couple. And I'll say that for him, he never told her and she never knew I was married till the day she died. But

Frank was a problem. Our marriage was a mistake anyhow, even if the judge had tied us with a sailor's knot, and Frank kept on pressing me, making demands, wanting me to live with him instead of at home, but I wanted to be free. So I made up this story that my mother wanted me to do a single act 'cause she thought it would be good for my career. As he'd promised to not tell her, he never went to ask her. I had really gotten this offer to work for the Shuberts in a show,* and I didn't want Frank around. While I was in their office one day, I heard that they were casting a show that was going on the road, and they hadn't a juvenile, so I suggested Frank. I told him to come right over and he got the part and went on the road for a year. We stayed apart after that. And I never got married again because there were enough men to choose from. Besides, I was already married. Even if nobody else knew that, I did.

I suppose I never loved one man enough to settle down to marriage. I was fickle because I had too much temptation. Marriage and one man for life is fine for some people, but for me it wasn't good. Every time I look at myself, I become absorbed in myself, and I didn't want to get involved with another person like that. I saw what it did to other people when they loved another person the way I loved myself, and I didn't want that problem. Because of that, I never wanted children and I never had any. I like other people's children, but I was my own baby. I had myself to do things for. Get my act together, get my material, write my stuff, work. That's what I wanted.†

JK: And you got it. You did write all of your own lines, didn't you, even in your first movie?

MW: Yes, deah. You know, Louis B. Mayer never liked me because I wouldn't go and work for MGM after I'd made this big success in *Night After Night* over at Paramount. That film took sixteen weeks to shoot. When I first came out to the Coast, I sat around for twelve weeks drawing money and I never saw a script. This wasn't for me: either I worked or I wanted to get back on the stage. But they kept begging me and telling me they had a contract with me, so I told them to let me have a script and I would rewrite it. "Hold it," they said, "just your own scenes." Well, it came to shooting my first scene. Everybody was so slow with their delivery. The film was going to sleep on me, I had to come in like a streak of lightning or we'd all go to sleep. So I played my lines very smart, you know, never giving the other actors time to think over their lines, and I'd be always rolling on the axis and breaking into

---

*Mae, still a brunette, played Maymie Dean, the "vamp," in the Rudolf Friml musical *Sometime*, in which she introduced the "Shimmy-Shake" and sang "What Do I Have to Do to Get It?" That was in 1918, and she found the answer.
†In fact, though she didn't want it for her image, Mae was devoted to her sister, Beverly, and her brother, and looked after them, supported them, till her death.

lines with an "Oh yeah" and an "Uh-hummm." You know, to keep the action flowing. And I was mad at Paramount. I'd come from Broadway, where I'd been a top star, and here I was playing this . . . you'd call it a guest part. And it wasn't even ready till I started to rewrite it. The night they screened it, I didn't come along. Then I got these phone calls telling me what a hit it was going to be and I could have anything I wanted. They had no projects for me at Paramount, so they came to me asking if I had anything I wanted to do. I had *Diamond Lil* all ready and I gave it to them. The play department who got hold of a copy wrote something on a foolscap-sized page to tell me why it wouldn't work on film. Well, deah, we shot it in two weeks and they called it *She Done Him Wrong*. It saved the studio. I found out afterwards that MGM were planning to buy Paramount if it went bust, and then my film made money and the studio was okay.

JK: In *Diamond Lil,* how much is the character of Lil—or Lou, as it ended up in the movie—based on you?

MW: Ohhh, well, if I were that character, if I were livin' in that time, I'd do exactly what I write about. That's the way my mind runs.

JK: But is she expressing your own philosophy when she says, "Diamonds have souls"?

MW: Oh, yeah, that's all mine. Well, when she meets up with this good man, he's with the Salvation Army, the one who tells her that "Diamonds have no souls." That's from his standpoint. Then she repeats it, you know what I mean? So she's learnin', you know. She says, "When you're dead, you're dead, that's the end of it." Then he gives her a little of the Bible. See, she's surrounded by all these rough guys. You know, she says, "I've always appreciated good men." I mean, good principle, good character, good in that sense. Because I've met a lot of the other type of man. I wasn't very religious as a child or anything. Every time I went to Sunday School, I used to come home with a headache. But, like I told you, we were brought up strict, and later, when I was on my own, I kept the Ten Commandments and that was enough. And I've always leaned towards . . . for myself, to really be satisfied with a man, I have to feel that he's right, and respect him, you see. And that's why I thought to put this character's line in. Then, as I was goin' through the story and everything, I said, "I need a good punch ending to follow all this great material, all this great stuff." And I didn't know what to do and I didn't want to introduce another character, so then that's when I figured that he was an undercover detective and I made a detective out of him. But I got all that goodness over, and her falling in love with him when she thought he was with the Salvation Army.

JK: Well, you re-created that whole period effectively.

MW: Yeah, and I'll tell you why. My mother was taken many times, when I was a child, for being Lillian Russell. She was the great American beauty for years. Nobody took her place. It wasn't like these, you know, movie stars, these Miss America things they run every year, somebody new. Here was a beauty that nobody could top. For years and years. And then she was in this period, the clothes that she wore and everything. And then I saw pictures of my mother when she was in her twenties or so, with all these kinds of clothes on her and everything, and I was always fascinated with it. That's when I started to write. And my main reason, like I told you, was I used to have 80 percent men in my audience, and I wanted more women. That's how I thought of that period. Then I got the grandmothers and grandfathers, I got three generations. That really made me break everybody's box-office records all over. So *Diamond Lil* did the trick.

JK: But earlier, in the story of the play more than the movie, you have her thinking only about her diamonds when Chick Clark almost kills her.

MW: Well, that character . . . she lived for her diamonds. I was that way when I was about fifteen years old. I saw a great big diamond on Fifth Avenue in one of those jewelry stores, hanging on one of those velvet busts, and it was on a fine chain. It was about twenty-five carats of diamond, and I fell in love with that diamond. And I've always thought of a diamond that size. I've got to have one that big. I've got to have that diamond. And I got lots of diamonds later, but every time I got one, I wasn't thrilled enough with it. I liked it, but I was still thinking thinking thinking of that one. Finally, I got them that size. Know what I mean? Diamonds, ohhhhhh, they just did things for me. I wouldn't wear a rhinestone. I wouldn't wear anything else unless it was the real thing. See, it's only lately that you have duplicates on account of robbery, and on account of jewelry being so high to insure for. So for the stage I wear the imitation, you know. But Lil was a character just like that.

JK: Do you still value diamonds that much? Because one thinks of diamonds and one thinks of Mae West . . . and vice versa.

MW: Well, I've had so many, I've had so much diamonds, and now, because of all these rhinestones they wear, the imitations and all that stuff that almost look as good, I keep the real stuff in a vault. The last time I had my good big diamonds out was when I went over to the college.* Well, I have so many different sets that I wouldn't have room for all of them. I just keep them in a vault. When I took them out one day, it cost me $75 a week just to have one out. This was the $45,000 diamond. So I put it back. It made no sense. It was too expensive. It's sad, but then they've given me the imitations, which look almost as good.

JK: Mae, the public see your connection with diamonds as materialistic, yet you always had some spiritualistic connection with them.

---

*I don't know what occasion she is referring to here, and, short of a fraternity panty-raid party, I can only think that she means one of the dinners in her honor that UCLA or USC gave as a result of the Mae West revival sweeping America at that time.

MW: Yeah?

JK: Well, in *She Done Him Wrong* you sold diamonds to pay for the upkeep of an orphanage, and then sold more diamonds to pay for the lease on the Salvation Army shelter . . . and you did it all anonymously. You are very involved in the spiritual. . . .

MW: Ohhh, yeah. I see, yeah. Sure. And it was the strangest thing. I don't know if I ever told you, but while I was writin' *Diamond Lil*, I had most of my characters but no lead. And I said, "Now I've got to get one man in here that she really falls in love with." I thought, Gee whiz, and I didn't know what I was going to put in, whether it was a young society boy or what, and I hesitated. And I was layin' my whole story out, and I went down to the Bowery just to look the place over because it was nothing like it was in the old days. And that day I just rode down there again, just drove around, you know, just, I don't know, to feel the place. And first thing I know, I saw this door that was open, and I saw an American flag in this dumpy place, this old building, you know. And then I looked, and I was drivin' slowly and, first thing you know, this handsome Salvation Army captain, without his cap on, came out. He walked out of this door, right to the gutter at the end of the sidewalk, and I passed him slowly. He looked into the car, and I said, "Uhmmmm, ahhhh, ohhhh," and I suddenly felt like drivin' around the block again to take another look, 'cause he was so handsome, and I thought, Gee, he should really be an actor. He was so handsome. Then it dawned on me. The forces, even though I didn't know so much about them in those days, I thought, he should be a leading man. Ohhhhh, yeah, a good man. A Salvation Army captain. He's the guy to come in and fall in love with her. He just walked out at the psychological moment, see? I went to see the buildings, and here he was. I had a mirror in my car, and as we were driving past, I looked in it, and I could see him looking after the car and then turning around and goin' back in. I don't know what he came out for; it was just the forces made him come out, now that I understand about the forces, they made him come out for me to see him.

    You know, sometimes I just lie down in a semidark room and I see crowds, individuals coming in like a montage. Now, I'm a very normal, healthy person, I don't imagine things, so when I see things and hear voices, I know there is something that exists around us. Over the years I've developed my psychic powers. Everything was a thought before it was created . . . this table, this vase, they were a thought before we made them. But I really didn't get involved with ESP until I met Thomas Kelly in 1941. The forces for good and evil were coming in, I would hear psychic voices and see people all the time and they kept me awake at night. If you told this to people about hearing voices, they'd think you were mad or something. With Thomas Kelly, you know, he came to my house because I'd heard so much about him from friends who knew I was interested in ESP. He tied a bandage around his eyes while we all were told to ask questions by writing them on a piece of paper and put that paper in a blank envelope so he wouldn't know whose envelope he was feelin'. I wrote five questions: "When will we be in the war? For how long? Who'll win it?" and two other questions of a very personal nature. When we came to my envelope, he said, "In three months we'll be attacked by Mr. Jap when he blows up Pearl Harbor; we'll be in the war for five or six years and President Roosevelt will be up for a fourth term, but he won't outlive it." Then he told me the personal things that I knew nobody else knew. I figured to myself that if he could answer all those questions, there had to be forces guiding him. He passed on, but he introduced me to a wonderful friend, Dr. Richard Ireland.

Now, I know that I must have always had these voices telling me things. One time I got a whole picture, *Every Day's a Holiday,* it came to me in fifty-six seconds, the length of time it took to play a chorus on the piano. It took me fifteen minutes to tell it to my producer and director, who were there at the time, and another forty-five minutes to dictate it to a typist. It was one of my best pictures. When I began to understand more about ESP in 1941, I realized that my having had the idea so quickly, the complete story, had some-thing to do with the forces around us. You see, they helped me several times when I was really in a problem and I didn't know how to get out of it. Like the court case I had. I was bein' sued for $100,000 and I knew I was inno-cent, but I didn't know how to handle the case. I was lyin' in my bed when suddenly this voice comes to me, a very beautiful, deep man's voice speakin' in that old English with "yea, thee and thous" and this was in 1948, and I knew I had heard that voice before . . . back in 1941 and I had always re-membered it because it was very distinguished. And now it told me what to say when I went into court that day, and I won my case, so, you see, it works for you. It does good for you. Ohh, yeah, after it was over, I wanted to know for myself what kind of person the voice belonged to. I asked the dictionary about it and it opened where it said "clergy"—so I knew he was a man from the clergy, you know, back in the 18th or 19th century.

While we were driving back to her apartment after our Chinese meal, Mae was talking about projects she had in mind, plays she was thinking of reviving, other films she was going to do, and an offer from ABC for a television version of the celebrated *Diamond Lil*. She was toying with the idea of the TV production, musing about leading men she had in mind. She ran through a list of television stars who'd caught her eye. She thought Rock Hudson was too old (this was in 1974!). Unable to imagine who could fill her shoes, I blurted out: "But who could possibly play Diamond Lil?"

Mae, who had been lying back, drew herself up and broke the shocked silence: "Why, *Mae West* of course!" and looked at me as if I'd lost my senses.

1970

Anita Loos, photographed by C. S. Bull, 1932

ANITA LOOS

T HERE WAS A TIME, a long time, when Anita Loos (not to be confused with Anita Louise, who was also well known but not like *that*) was probably one of the best-known women in America without ever having been on the covers of fan magazines, nor on stage, screen or radio. Her fame was won as a writer; and there too, not for more than a decade's good work but for a book, written first as a short story, the whim of a moment written to bring a man old enough to know better to his senses. He, with remarkable perspicacity and amusement at his own folly, got it published, though not in his own magazine. The story was entitled *Gentlemen Prefer Blondes*. Anita was a brunette, friend of such blondes as Mary Pickford, Marion Davies and later Jean Harlow . . . she knew whereof she spoke. Before the book became all the rage, blondes were natural, sweet, pre-Raphaelite cherubim and (one hoped) innocent. Until after the wedding. In films they were usually cast as put-upon heroines.

After the publication of the novel *Gentlemen Prefer Blondes* in 1925, natural blondes were out. Dyed blondes were all the rage, and, whatever else men thought they were, innocent wasn't it. If her book and the character of Lorelei Lee seem to rise out of the hoydenish spirit of the Jazz Age, the '20s, Anita had somehow struck a basic chord, found a basic truth which, unlike rolled stockings, hip flasks, the Black Bottom and bootleg gin, survived the decade . . . and the next . . . and the next . . . and the next.

The spinoffs from one book became a flourishing business in themselves, keeping Anita rich, bemused and happy right up to the end; she knew that somewhere in some corner of the globe some blonde would be studying her "textbook," and some stage would be performing it. Long before merchandising of a product had become the big business that it is today, Anita's lark had gone from magazine story to book, to stage as a straight play, to film, to a cartoon series, to the stage as a musical and then back to the films. Should there be any lingering doubts that *Gentlemen* is a classic of American literature, its 1985 reissue publication by the Folio Society should put these to rest.

Of all the small women I've met who made it big—and most of the big silent film stars were physically small women—some would pretend to be fluffy and coy, most would carry themselves as being much taller than they actually were. But Anita, who at seventy looked twenty, with the same black bangs framing her mischievous and merry face that she started out with back in the teens, never pretended to be fluffy, never tried to be coy, but made you notice how small she was. She had taken advantage of it to get into a taller personality's confidence—as back in 1912, when she started out as a title-writer for D. W. Griffith, or when she wrote the film that launched Mary Pickford, *The New York Hat*. Anita Loos—sharp with brains and bright with personality—had no trouble getting work.

With her husband, John Emerson, or alone, she wrote for almost every major star of the silent era. Prior to their marriage, she and John took Broadway star Doug Fairbanks' film career in hand; beginning in 1916, they wrote for him the stories which revealed his personality and made Doug as big as Mary and Charlie. If Anita had never written *Gentlemen* and all the other books that followed, she would still have been sought out for her important place in silent-film history: for her titles, for her connections, for the fact that she bridged the "sound barrier" to become one of the most successful, highly paid screenwriters of the '30s, with such credits as *San Francisco* and *The Women*. Which is why I went to see her. Anita talked and laughed simultaneously throughout our conversation, and started off by asking me about the recent London production of the musical *Gentlemen Prefer Blondes,* starring the British comedienne Dora Bryan.

AL: I adored Dora Bryan, I adored her in my play, I thought she was absolutely superb. But when it got to London, the English critics had never seen Carol Channing in *Gentlemen Prefer Blondes,* and they thought that the role required a tiny blonde. And they immediately started to compare Dora Bryan with Marilyn Monroe, who did it in the film. And it was terribly unjust, because Carol Channing proved that it doesn't have to be played by a beautiful little blonde. And to me Dora Bryan was *so* funny and so completely perfect in the part that I was very, very disappointed when the critics jumped on it. I thought that anybody could be Lorelei! Surely when Carol Channing played Lorelei and was brilliant in it, it proved that it was a part with any number of interpretations. It could be a caricature, as Carol was, or it could be a real personality, as Marilyn Monroe was. They were equally good. But you laughed more *at* Carol than you did at Marilyn. You liked Marilyn enormously. You sympathized with her and she was adorable. But all those things existed with Carol, and in addition you roared at her because she was a clown. I think that both girls were ideal. One as a caricature and the other as a straight character.

JK: Alice White [in the silent Paramount film of the book]?

AL: Alice White never played Lorelei. She played Dorothy. There was a girl named Ruth Taylor and she was the type of Marilyn Monroe, very pretty and very dainty and delectable, and so much the real character that she married a multimillionaire and quit work!

JK: There are so many people who have played this character, and I was just talking to Louise Brooks on the phone and she was saying that she also wanted to play the part. And she said that you said to her that when you write the part of a wooden cigar-store Indian, she can have it because of her wooden face.

AL: Oh, I think she made that up as a joke against herself! I don't think I'd turn down anybody for Lorelei. Alice White was my own choice to play Dorothy. She'd never done anything in Hollywood; that was her first role. And she won it by competition. By tests. And she was fine, and it proved that we were right because she went right on to a very good career.

JK: Also you had a very good comedy director, Mal St. Clair, who now is too much forgotten.

AL: Yes, it's too bad that he is forgotten. Carol does give an illusion of great beauty. She is bigger than life; she's a caricature of beauty. And of course she played the part as if she were five feet tall! And it was her interpretation that made it a great part. Of course, when Dora played it, she just made it an out-and-out spoof, which was perfectly all right with me, because it paid off in laughs. And while we were on tour—I only saw it on tour because I had to come back to New York on business—but the audiences absolutely adored her on tour, the business was tremendous.

JK: Well, she was a sort of comic-strip Lorelei. But that's all right. What's wrong with comic strips? But you've done so many plays; there was one in 1924 . . .

AL: Oh, that was a very early play called *The Whole Town's Talking*. It was a big success; it ran in New York for about eight months. Which in those days was a long run. And *Happy Birthday* was Helen Hayes' *longest* run. She had played Victoria for nine months, but she ran a year and eight months with *Happy Birthday*.

JK: You've been very successful in almost every medium you've tried, but you've never acted in films, though you were extremely pretty.

AL: No. I was a child actress, but the time came when I was beginning to earn more money writing than acting. *New York Hat* [1912] was the first picture I ever wrote. I believe I had other pictures that came out ahead of *The New York Hat,* but that was because it was delayed in the shooting.

JK: That was Griffith, wasn't it?

AL: Yes, D. W. Griffith. Mary Pickford, Lionel Barrymore. And the Gish sisters were among the extras.

JK: For any time, it was one of the biggest casts you could possibly get together.

AL: Yes, but they weren't important, any of them, in those days. Nobody was known.

JK: You worked with Griffith for a long time.

AL: I worked for him until the time came when his pictures with Douglas Fairbanks required too much attention. He couldn't give it to them. So Douglas left. And took me with him. Because by that time I was writing all of his pictures. He created his own image . . . he was the same off screen as he was on, and I just transferred him to celluloid. He had been a very successful juvenile in the New York theater. And Griffith had taken him to California on a contract. But after he got him out there, he found out that Douglas couldn't act. So he allowed Douglas to work out his contract, and then he intended getting rid of him at option time. And while Douglas was fooling around the studio, I had a very good chance of fooling around the studio too! And I realized what enormous vitality he had, and that he was a unique personality. So I begged Griffith to let us make a picture where he wouldn't have to act. And Griffith, reluctantly, did. And I made that picture with John Emerson, whom I later married, and that picture was the start of Doug's career [*His Picture in the Papers,* 1916]. He was an overnight star. Those things can happen very quickly in films. We had the same thing very, very many years later with Audrey Hepburn. I wrote *Gigi* that she did in the New York theater. Not the movie. *But* she went on from that to the movies, and she was a star in her first movie.*

Making movies in Hollywood in the old days was a great deal of fun, because there was a great deal of play (ha ha) along with the work. But those conditions have so changed, and I'm sure movies are no fun today.

JK: Well, you worked with Thalberg, didn't you? During his regime at MGM?

AL: Yes. I wrote the first film that Jean Harlow played, a comedy called *The Red-Headed Woman.* And that was all due to Irving Thalberg, who to me, next to Griffith, is the greatest genius the films in our country ever produced. But Thalberg refused to let his name ever be used on a film; he never allowed any publicity to go out about himself; and to me it's a very sad thing when one considers the power of advertising. Because that man who refused to be advertised has gone into oblivion.

JK: I think his great talent—correct me if I'm wrong—is that he appreciated talent in other people.

AL: Yes. And he would break rules in all directions. For instance, when he hired Jean Harlow to play a comedy, she had only played *femmes fatales.* She

*Her first American movie, that is.

had been a heavy with a long cigarette-holder, and I wrote *The Red-Headed Woman* with and for Thalberg. Because one always wrote *with* him. You would take your material in and go over it with him and his suggestions always became part of the script. And when it was suggested that Jean Harlow was going to be brought into the picture, he gave (ha ha) the script to one of his ace directors, Jack Conway, and said for him to read it. And Conway brought the script back and threw it on Thalberg's desk and said: "I'll shoot this if you insist, but I want to tell you right now, people are going to laugh at it." He thought it was a drama (ha ha)! He couldn't see Jean Harlow in anything but a very heavy drama. And in the end of course it's comedy that made her. And Irving and I roared with laughter because that's exactly what we wanted. And Conway, when he finally took on the job, insisted that I stay on the set all the time. He said: "This woman to me is frightening. I've been involved with too many of those girls . . . it's not funny to me at all." But the success of that picture proved that Thalberg was right, she was a great co-medienne. I wrote any number of her pictures after that. Even some of those I didn't write, I was always being dragged into other people's jobs. I finally became a sort of script doctor. And I was in on everything.

Recently I saw the latest James Bond picture, *Goldfinger,* and, watching it, I was taken back to those old conferences we used to have—Douglas Fairbanks, John Emerson and I—cooking up those same gags they're using today! Nothing has changed, and of course *we* stole the gags! From old mel-odramas. And an early Fairbanks picture is the equivalent of a Belmondo melodrama or a James Bond; the same thing, only the props have changed.

JK: They've gilded the lily, that's all. I want to take you back to Jean Harlow for a moment, because I wondered if you have read that book on her [Irving Schulman's biography].

AL: I have been in a great altercation about that book, as everybody that knew Jean has, and if you want to listen to a very funny episode about it, I can tell you. Recently the University of Southern California wrote to me and asked if they might have the letters that Aldous Huxley had written to me over a period of twenty-five years. And when I wrote back to the university, I said I would take it up with Sir Julian [Huxley] and see what he wanted done with them, but, I said, is it possible that one Irving Schulman, who is supposed to be a writer and wrote the Harlow book, is on the staff of your university? And it seemed to me outrageous that anyone who wrote as badly as that could *possibly* be on the English staff of a university. And they wrote back and said he had been on the staff, but that he had left. I don't know how long before. So about six weeks later I get a hurried call from California. Schulman was going to sue me because he claimed that I had blackmailed the university by saying that unless they got him off the staff, I wouldn't allow my letters from Aldous Huxley to go to the university. Well, of course, the university were dead set against this so-called writer and everything that he's done, and they just made a joke of it. And when I refused to make an answer to it, the matter dropped, because he had hoped the publicity would keep on going, which it didn't. But now he's in trouble with everyone, because Jean Harlow's father is alive, and that he didn't know. So he's being sued for $2 million, and my hope is they collect every penny he's made. But, as a writer, I can say I was just as shocked by the man's pretense of being a writer as I was by the material. And of course it's all lies. We all knew Jean very well; we saw her every day. And we all adored her.

JK: What about Arthur Landau, who professes to be her agent?

AL: Well, he was one of those fringe characters in the early days latching on to people to try and make money, and he'd come on very bad times, was sick and broke, and he was willing to sell out to this man. But even so I understand that he was horrified when he first read the book. He supplied a little information, but he had no idea what the book was going to be.

JK: In a recent interview which he gave, he said that 90 percent of the book was true, and that he had letters to prove she was even worse than that. And I don't know this man, but it's a fact that Jean Harlow kept him on salary even after he stopped being her agent.

AL: That was exactly like Jean, she gave away everything. When she died, her estate was practically nothing. She gave away all her money. And she would have kept any old retainer who was on hard times. But she was an *adorable character*. And another thing that this man didn't take into consideration: she was educated in a very fine girls' school. And he has her talking like the cheapest kind of gangster's moll. Like the characters she played in her earlier films. And she had a tremendous sense of humor. We all called her "The Baby"; that was her name. You don't call a girl by that name if she's hard or tough, or . . .

JK: Oh, I want to go on to another book. I assume you knew Chaplin?

AL: Yes, very well indeed.

JK: You never wrote for him, I suppose?

AL: Oh, no, he never needed anybody! He could do everything. I thought the early chapters of his book were very good. But then it merely became like an engagement book. [Laughter.] His dates with various people. And something that amazed me rather; naturally, I immediately looked in the back of the book for Huxley, because every Sunday afternoon the Huxleys—that was Maria Huxley at the time—and Chaplin and Paulette Goddard and a few others met, for a period, I would think, of five years. And I wanted to know what Charlie would have to say about Aldous. He finishes him off in two sentences. And of course he finishes Paulette Goddard off in two or three paragraphs. Paulette is one of the most complicated, intelligent, fascinating people I've ever met in my life, and she and I have been great, great friends from the time she first came to Hollywood. And she is an absolutely astounding woman. She is the most cultured and the best-read woman I know in show business. Which nobody is aware of, because her looks have always stopped it. And she used always to say to me: "If you tell anybody that I'm taking lessons in political economy, I'll never speak to you again," and I would say: "Why not?" And she'd say: "It makes me seem so dull!" And that a woman of that type could be described in two *paragraphs* is utterly ridiculous. And Sydney [Chaplin] in *his* book gives much more space to Paulette than his father does!

JK: But I want to go back to your films. Writing for talkies and writing for silents. What was the great difference?

AL: Well, it all depends. I think the talkies were more interesting to me because my specialty is writing dialogue, and I had two or three talking pictures I liked very much. One was *San Francisco*—Jeanette MacDonald, Douglas Fairbanks and Spencer Tracy . . .

JK: Doug Fairbanks? Clark Gable!

AL: Yes, Clark Gable! [Laughs.] As a matter of fact, they were a great deal alike—neither of them could act! Terrific personality, though! And I *adored* her [Jeanette MacDonald]. She was of Scotch ancestry, you know. She was very Scotch in nature, as far as I noticed. Her nickname on the lot was "The Iron Butterfly"! Because under all this gossamer she was a very hard-working, hard-headed businesswoman. She had a strange position in Europe that was completely different from her position here in our country. In this country we took her for what she was—a glittering, glamorous film personality. But when I first went to Europe, I found that she had a reputation like Brigitte Bardot! She was supposed to have seduced the Italian crown prince; he was supposed to be leaving his throne on account of her . . . it was like a film! And when I used to tell people that she was just a hard-working prima donna, they used to say: "Oh, don't tell me that . . . I know what she does!" But she had a tremendous position in Europe as a successful star.

I worked with [D. W.] Griffith in the beginning of my career for about three or four years. I was about to do his last film, which was *The Struggle,* and I wrote it for him, but I practically took down dictation—the things that he wanted to put in it. And it had all of Griffith's faults—he was overly sentimental, and this really went overboard. And I knew it was bad, everybody knew it was bad. But Griffith was ill, and he saw it as a chance to come back, and he put it on. And it was a dismal failure. I haven't seen it since those days when he was working on it, but I doubt that it had anything of Griffith in it at all because he was a broken man, and a very sick man, and he'd also taken to drinking too much. I will say this, that there are a few people in Hollywood who do care for those people and look out for them. One of them is George Cukor and the other is Darryl Zanuck. For years

Zanuck kept people on salary when they were no longer capable of working at all. And George Cukor has such a list of people he takes care of that hardly anybody knows about. But Hollywood, as a community, doesn't—except that it runs a very, very fine old-people's home. . . .

JK: But don't you think that hurts the pride of people who were big stars in their time, like Mae Murray? You couldn't get any bigger—and to be put in an old-people's home makes you sound like an out-of-work actress. It seems to have little regard for the feeling of the person involved.

AL: Yes, that's true. They call the home the Hollywood Country Club or the Motion Picture Country Club—but of course that doesn't fool anybody. I don't know what they could do except to supply people with an income and allow them to keep working if they can. But then show business is a cruel business. Because it's based on vanity. And what can one do? That's its basis.

JK: Would you say *Sunset Boulevard* is a true depiction of that type?

AL: Yes, I think it was. And I think that's why it was so successful.

JK: Did you ever write a screenplay for Gloria Swanson?

AL: No, you see, in the old days in Hollywood you worked for one studio. And I was at MGM and Gloria was at Paramount, I believe. I left Hollywood the first time about 1919—no, it was later. . . .

JK: You worked with Harold Lloyd one time. . . .

AL: Yes! I acted with him. But I was a child, actually. I was playing a twelve-year-old child.

JK: You played anything from children to vamps!

AL: Anything! [Lots of laughter.] I had to because I was in a stock company. My father's. I had a better childhood than anyone could have anywhere else! You see, my father was a combination of small-time impresario who ran stock companies, and then he was a newspaperman also. And one time he ran a magazine in San Francisco called the *Dramatic Review,* and he wrote for his own magazines, and naturally there was writing going on around the house all the time. And one day, when I was about twelve, I wrote a little article for a New York newspaper, which was holding a contest for humorous articles. And I won it. And that's what always happened to me—the first thing I did was always a success. Then I could have failures after that! But I always knew I'd done it once! So maybe I could do it again. So, between the ages of twelve and thirteen I was a regular contributor to a New York daily newspaper. And, of all papers, it was a sporting newspaper: The *New York Telegraph,* that specialized in racing news!

JK: What was it like to be such a young child in the early days of the movies?

AL: Well, it was a great big romp, really; nobody had to learn any lines, and the actors didn't have to prepare for anything. My work was doping out plots, sitting around with the producer—D. W. Griffith or Fairbanks or various directors—and doping out plots. And they would be taken down by a secretary, and I would go over them and write them, and write the dialogue. But very often, when the picture was told in subtitles, I didn't write the dialogue until the picture was all finished. And I can say that I invented subtitles, or comic subtitles, or you might call them literary subtitles. I wrote all the subtitles for *Intolerance*. One of them that I remember was a quotation from Voltaire, and I saw *Intolerance* about a year ago here in New York, and the audience roared at that title . . . *today!*

JK: I think if something's good, it holds up. Did you have any favorites of the films you have done?

AL: I think I love *San Francisco* most, because I am a San Franciscan and we're very loyal, and I wrote it out of a feeling for the city which I always have had, and it wasn't ruined in the direction as many things are. It came out just the way I wanted it. In films we generally slanted a story towards some personality or star. For instance, I used to write for Mae Marsh, and naturally I would write things that she did the best. Then I was eighteen years with MGM, and almost always wrote for stars, in fact *always*. Of course, when MGM was going strong, it had practically every English writer in the world. I remember walking into the studio one day with Aldous Huxley, and we looked up at the directory of offices, and Aldous said: "Look at that directory. Every great writer from England and America is on there. How can we make the pictures so bad?" [Laughter.] Actually, the pictures weren't bad. But we thought they were.

JK: Did you have a greater freedom than you think one does now?

AL: Oh, I think that the people in control now—the directors particularly, like John Huston, or the Italians or the English—can do anything they want. I don't think there are any holds barred at all.

Griffith was an absolute inspiration, naturally. He would start with a bare outline, if it was something I had done, and I would sit on the set with him. And he always rehearsed, which later they stopped doing. And as he rehearsed, the sparks would fly. He would think of business, all sorts of things. And you know that every now and then some brilliant scene in a modern picture—for instance, the seduction scene in *Tom Jones* where the man is eating and being seduced by this woman—that is in a film by Griffith. I called up Lillian Gish, because I vaguely remembered the scene, and I said: "Lillian, where did D.W. first do that scene?" And she said: "Oh, Lionel Barrymore, he was eating a big hambone and being seduced at the same time by this woman—"

JK: It's not that anything is new in films, but the way they use it.

AL: Exactly. Nobody is going to quibble about the way something was done in *Tom Jones* because it rose above everything. Oh, I adored it. I go to all films except Hollywood films. I think they're so bad. I think they're so flabby. I sometimes miss a good one because I stay away from them all; they're so self-conscious, and they make such an effort. But I think the English, French and Italians are just superb.

JK: Thinking back to MGM, did you ever write for Garbo?

AL: No, because she just happened to be doing a comedy at that time, and I was busy on other things. I was never called in to do anything for her. In those last days when she did try to do comedy, she needed a comedy writer and she didn't have one.*

I did write one tearjerker once. And I must say, like the first things I've always done, it was a big success. It was called *Blossoms in the Dust*. It was an MGM film with Greer Garson and Walter Pidgeon. And how I came to write it I'll never know, except that they were desperate for a film for Greer on the subject of adoption, and they had dug up this woman who had run an orphanage in Texas. And she had a garbled story to tell, and I had to get together with her and see if I could figure something out. And that was a big success. And that was a real tearjerker.

I'm busy all the time. I wouldn't know what to do with time, because I've never learned to do anything but work. The thing I've enjoyed most has been knowing certain people that I've admired tremendously. And the way I got to know them was through writing *Gentlemen Prefer Blondes,* so . . .

JK: How did that come about?

AL: Well, that's a long story. I was a very great friend of H. L. Mencken—he was our great American philosopher of that period—and, intelligent man that he was, he was always going around with very silly girls! And I wrote the first chapter of *Gentlemen Prefer Blondes* not as a book or even to be printed, but I wrote it to show Mencken what he was going around with at the time! And I had written it on a train going out to Hollywood, and I intended to send it to him just as a spoof. About this girl who I knew he'd recognize instantly and would know I was making fun of her. But I'd forgotten about it; I got to Hollywood and I had a job to do there, I forgot all about it. Until I came back to New York and ran across these few pages, and I put them in an envelope and sent it to Mencken. And Mencken read it, and he wrote back to me and said: "This is very funny, but do you realize that you have committed the great sin of making fun of sex in America? I don't think anybody would publish it." And at that time he was publishing the *American Mercury,* which was a highbrow magazine, and he said: "If I hadn't just started the *Mercury,* I'd publish it. But I'm afraid to, I don't want to besmirch the first issue! But

---

*Loos is speaking of the disastrous *Two-Faced Woman,* Garbo's last film.

if you will send it to someone who has a woman's magazine, they will put it in among the ads and it will be read by anyone that's interested, and it won't shock other people." He actually thought it was shocking. So I sent it to *Harper's Bazaar,* and the editor, who was Henry Sell, called me and said: "This is fine, but why do you stop? You've started the girl going to Europe, why don't you carry her along?" So for six months I wrote a chapter a month. And it was published in the *Bazaar.* But by the time the third issue was out, they had to double the circulation of the magazine; men's products were being advertised for the first time in a woman's magazine, and by the time it had finished in the *Bazaar,* it had created quite a stir. *But* nobody thought of making a book of it, except that I had a beau at that time who was in the publishing business, and he said to me: "Why don't I get out an edition of that book, and you can give it to your friends for Christmas?" So I thought that would be very nice, and he brought out 1500, which was the first edition, and it sold out before noon on the day it went onto the bookstands! And the second edition was 65,000! And from then on it went into forty-five editions and thirteen languages—it just never stopped! But it never started out to be anything at all.

JK: Did Mencken ever get the point?

AL: Oh, indeed he did. He ended up marrying a girl who was a schoolteacher in her forties, just the exact opposite of any of the blondes he'd ever gone with!

JK: *Gentlemen Marry Brunettes!* You wrote that, too [*But Gentlemen Marry Brunettes*]. And Gentlemen Leave Redheads?

AL: No, I didn't write that. Maybe somebody else will. It could be written!

JK: Do you still think American sexual mores need deflating? Do you think it's time for another Lorelei Lee type to come along?

AL: Well, she has disappeared so completely. The dependent woman, the woman who was kept, has gone out of existence. I know more girls who are keeping men today!

JK: Why don't you write one about that? Women Prefer Blondes!

AL: Well, that is really a subject! It's worth going into.

JK: We've discussed Lorelei, but isn't Dorothy you?

AL: Yes, I'm afraid she is. I have always been the brunette who lost out, and I've always gotten the wrong end of everything! I've gone through all my life without a single diamond! But I will say I've been just as satisfied with bangles! And maybe had more fun!

JK: Do you ever have people going around claiming they were the characters you wrote?

AL: Yes, as a matter of fact, fairly recently. Somebody came to interview me and said he had just met the woman who was the original of Dorothy. And it was somebody I'd never even heard about. Well, one always has to base a fictional character on reality, or it doesn't come to life.

1965

J O A N
B L O N D E L L

B LONDELL'S STEPSON, Mike Todd, Jr., writing in his biography of his father (Joan's third and last husband), described Joan as the most maternal woman he ever met. Even when appearing in a play, she'd come home and tidy up, cook the meals and make sure everything was all right. In her film roles, trading wisecracks with the likes of James Cagney, you feel that warmth, that outpouring of generosity. She was selfless and practical. She never abandoned the man even when he had a temporary aberration and ran after another woman. Things didn't always work out that way in life—her second husband, crooner Dick Powell, left her for June Allyson, while Mike Todd, one of the theater's great skirt-chasers, left her for Evelyn Keyes and then left *her* for Elizabeth Taylor—but there was no rancor in Blondell when she spoke of them. Well, not much, and it was said with good humor.

In the more than eighty films made in a career which spanned fifty years, right up to her death, there is no such thing as a Joan Blondell picture, but her image is as strong and enduring as that of any of the great stars of the '30s and the '40s. Even when she played the usual run of cynical blond showgirls, shop assistants, night nurses et al., she came across as a good friend. She may have played gold diggers, but she didn't come across as one. She was sexy in those early musicals without needing to dress up in cut-down pirate outfits for leggy shots. She wasn't vague or stupid, though the men who thought she was were. She gave herself no airs, even when she was one of the top ten box-office stars back in the '30s. Ann Sothern, who played types not unlike Blondell, would hold her nose up in the air when a man whistled after her as she walked by, though you could tell that she really liked it. Joan, in a similar situation, would merely have smiled. "Isn't that what men are like? God love 'em." Joan (who co-starred with Ann in *Cry Havoc*) accepted my comparison of her to Ann Sothern in looks and type, and when I asked what brought her back to the screen after a long absence from films while she was married to Mike Todd, she flashed a broad grin and said, "My friends told me Ann Sothern had forgotten how to do me."

Blondell was a versatile actress and could be anything except unsympathetic. When she played the neurotic mother in the stage production of *The*

Effect of Gamma Rays on Man-in-the-Moon Marigolds, she told interviewers
that it hurt her to play the mother because she loved children and couldn't stand
to mistreat them every night. She was glad when the play folded. On screen and
in life she exuded a longing for domesticity. It's what made an earlier comeback
as Aunt Sissy, the unmarried but much-loved character in *A Tree Grows in
Brooklyn,* so endearing and memorable. The sight of an apron, a kitchen, a
home made her radiant. While Garland sang about being "Born in a Trunk,"
Blondell really was, and for the first nineteen years of her life she saw the world
and played every town in the US, but never had a home to call her own.

When I met her in 1970 at her house in the Valley, she was working more
than ever, in films, in a TV series. She hadn't changed that much from the Joan
you recognized in *Gold Diggers of 1933* and *1937,* in *Footlight Parade* and all
the others—still a blonde, eyes still bright and blue, that generous mouth, that
chesty voice, those apple cheeks, that self-deprecating humor and good feeling.
She knew about sawdust, bare stages, back alleys, hard work and how important it was for show-business families who had nothing except their work to
stick together and look after their own. All the things she talks about are the
hallmarks of a vanished professionalism which is itself astonishing quite apart
from the personal qualities she brings to it.

There is a footnote that perhaps sums up her *esprit de vie* better than anything else. To me she had always looked the picture of robust health. There was
no way I would have guessed that she was in continuous agony, suffering from
a debilitating arthritic condition which made every gesture one of crippling
pain. No one knew; if it had gotten out, she might not have found work because
she wouldn't have been insurable. And, as Joan said, "Without work, what is
life?" Joan accepted the pain. She worked up until her death. Her last film was
John Cassavetes' *Opening Night,* a story of backstage theatrical life. Nothing
about her had diminished. She was a trouper and she died with her boots on.

JB: I don't have any regrets about my career. I really don't have, although I'm
    sane enough to know that if I had taken myself more seriously—and by that
    I don't mean that I didn't work as a professional, just as hard as I could, as
    hard as anyone—I still feel that if I had fought for better roles as, say, Bette
    Davis did or a lot of those gals and guys that walked out and fought for better
    roles or stayed on suspension and all that business, I think maybe I might
    have been a damned good dramatic actress. I know I'm able to be. But I
    didn't get it because I just . . . a peculiar thing with me, I was always con-
    scious of throwing people out of work, which is something kind of silly when
    you're young. But I did feel that way, very conscious of the crew. If they had
    set up a picture for me and I fought against doing it, I'd think of the almost
    forty people who'd be out of work. At least. I couldn't do it. I have no idea
    why I felt that way. Well, there's one thing: I saw vaudeville through to its
    downfall, and we knew what it was to suffer through that, to be stony broke

Joan Blondell, photographed by Elmer Fryer, 1932

and hungry and everything else in our profession, and maybe that had something to do with it. It's funny to think about it now, because people like Davis
or Cagney didn't throw people out of work when they fought roles, because
more people worked when they came back in *better* roles and in their step
higher as a star. But it was just *my* way; I don't think I ever had the security
of feeling confidence in myself, really, ever. I used to think, "I'm just lucky
to be here!" You know, I've been in the business since I was four months old.

When I work, I *look* like I'm secure, don't I? But I'm not particularly,
not inside. And my appearance, while it didn't exactly frighten me, certainly
never thrilled me. I had always watched myself on the screen with a sinking
feeling in the pit of my stomach. I felt I could look and do better if I had had
another chance. Also, I couldn't take myself *seriously* [she says this in a very
grandly serious manner, as though Katharine Cornell were telling a joke during the entr'acte of *Macbeth* and said, "But s-ehrioussly, folks . . ."], you
know, feel the glory of being a star, because I just thought it was luck and
that there were a lot of people a hell of a lot better than I was, that I was in a
nice driver's seat and that I should be grateful. What was foremost in my life,
in every phase of it, has been my home . . . and whoever is in my home, be
it a husband, or children, or whatever. They used to make jokes around
Warner Brothers because the instant they said "Cut" I was whammo out of
that studio and into the car, *zuuuup* out of the gate and *home*. Half the time
I'd forget to put on my shoes, I wouldn't even stop for that. In order to be a
top star and remain a top star and to get all the fantastic roles that you yearned
for, you've got to fight for it and you've got to devote your twenty-four hours
to just that; you've got to think of yourself as a star, operate as a star, do all
the press that is necessary. And yet, from about '32 to '38 Cagney and I were
in the top ten money-makers in the country. But still, what meant most to me
was getting home, and that's the truth.

This has always been the case for Joan. She commented in 1932, on her marriage to her first husband, George Barnes, "I could be happy in a little store or
some business somewhere else if Hollywood wouldn't let us make a go of our
marriage. This town hasn't got into my blood. I like it—it has been good to
me—but I'm my father's child, and if the callboard for happiness ever indicated
any other place, well, a Blondell has never yet been afraid of 'the big hike.'"

JK: Did you never see the image the public saw, the screen's Joan Blondell?
When you went out on the street and people herded around you?

JB: I understand all of that stuff. I've had as much acclaim as anybody, but
when I did show up in public, which was very seldom, well, I . . . Heaven
knows, when Dick Powell and I married, they had us go on a boat through
the Canal and to New York, where they had about eighty tugboats in the
harbor with welcome signs and banners and airplanes going overhead saying
"SWING IT MRS. POWELL, SING IT MR. POWELL." And they had—God!—

parades and crowds jamming, and we made an appearance at the Paramount Theater. I looked out of the sixth floor, and all of Times Square was black with people looking up at us. You know, those kinds of things would make me say "Wow!" But it still didn't stop me from racing home and going out as little as possible. I could kick myself that I didn't think that all that public demand for me could have given me a great negotiating lever with Warners, but I didn't. All I know is that I've had a long career, and that's because I do know my business. I think I made the jump into playing character parts possibly too fast, too, 'cause I started that about fifteen years ago. I made up my mind and did it right quick. Now, looking back, I can see that that was not quite necessary, but I wanted to jump the gun so I would not have to . . . I don't really know how to describe it. I know of a few stars who were around when I was who are now practically in hiding because they've gotten along in years and they can't handle it anymore.

JK: How did you get into films, and why Warner Brothers' studio?

JB: Well, Jimmy Cagney and I were given two great roles in a play written by George Kelly—Grace Kelly's uncle, but he's much more famous than she ever was—who wrote *Craig's Wife* and *Torch Bearers* and *The Show Off*, one Broadway hit after another. I learned from George Kelly. I came to know more about the job and the art and the work of acting under this man's direction than I could have learned in four years at a dramatic school. Cagney had been in musical comedy and I'd been in vaudeville, and vaudeville went to hell, so I started getting jobs outside of New York in little stock companies dotted here and there. Finally, we both auditioned for this same play. I went to Kelly's office, and this red-headed mug was there. I asked him, "Say, what's the name of this show?" He said, "*Maggie the Magnificent*. My name's James Cagney." I said, "Well, I'm Joan Blondell and I got a hunch I'm going to wind up in this cast. See you sometime later."

Maggie the Magnificent opened the night of the Crash in 1929, and it was the first of Kelly's plays that didn't run. But both Cagney and I got tremendous notices, we were really cheered. But that closed, nothing was doing any business at that time 'cause everybody was busy jumping out of windows. Then Marie Baumer wrote a play for us called *Penny Arcade*. Well, while we were doing *Penny Arcade*, Al Jolson saw the show and he bought it, then sold it to Warner Brothers with the stipulation that they take and use two people from the Broadway company, Cagney and Blondell. So they had to take us, and that's how we got into pictures.

We arrived in Hollywood the same day and we were signed the same day, for just that one picture, of course, which ended up being called *Sinners' Holiday*. I think they were kind of annoyed by having the law laid down by Al Jolson about who they were to take, so they gave Jimmy's role to Grant Withers and my role to Evalyn Knapp and they gave us two minor roles. But we were getting paid, and times were tough, so were we happy and grateful! Anyway, the whole bunch of them saw the first day's rushes. We were shooting on the back lot—I'll never forget that day, it was a hot day on the back lot. Cagney and I had done our scene the day before and we were there to do a little more. All the bosses came down: Warner, Zanuck and all of them, with a contract, a long-term, five-year contract, and they signed us on that back lot in the broad daylight. So that's how that started, and from then on, it was one picture after another. I was still in my teens.

JK: You were so young. What had you been doing in vaudeville?

JB: Oh, honey, everything but my laundry. Everything. I worked in an act with my dad. First he did a single, then he married my mother and the two of them worked. Then I was born and at three I went on the stage for the first time in Sydney, Australia. Then I continued with the act on through Europe and everyplace, with zillions of trips back to the States on the Orpheum Circuit and the Pantages Circuit. Then my brother [Eddie] was born and when he grew up he got into the act, and when vaudeville got bad my sister [Gloria] came in and we all struggled in the act. We sang, we danced, we did comedy sketches, we did everything. Always on the stage, always going, a week in each town and then finally a night in each town, then split weeks when it got bad. But we were always together, always together. Finally, we weren't getting any work, so I had to go make the rounds. I got a few punk jobs here and there on a small salary which kept us going.* When the George Kelly break came, then it was uphill from then on. But, you know, I never thought of any other kind of life at any point. When I was a little girl and would, between shows, go into the alleyway to play ball or walk down the street to look into windows, I thought when I went back into that alleyway and into the theater to do the next show, I thought that everybody in the world walked in an alley and went into a theater and did a show. That was what I thought as a little girl, that everybody was in vaudeville. That was my life. That was our life. A few times when we'd lay off, I'd get acquainted with some little kid and play and have the time of my life in some park, and then get hysterical that I had to leave. I learned, as children do, to hold back that love.

There had also been an ill-fated romance during Joan's flush of Broadway success, of which Joan says, "I believe it was the first time in my life I completely lost my sense of humor. He was an actor who was playing in *Coquette*. I was just the girl who was crazy about him. I worshiped the ground he walked on, but he nearly wrecked my life through worry. His main ambition seemed to be to try and drink himself to death. I was the most miserable person in the world during the time I was in love with him. He was so darn good and sweet—but such a drunkard. I still think he is one of the two grandest persons in the world, and somehow I wish you'd skip lightly over this. . . . I just can't seem to talk about some things, the things I felt deeply."

---

*Among other jobs, she worked as a city librarian, a window-dresser and a sales clerk.

JB: So when I came to Warner Brothers and was actually in one spot, it took an awful long time to realize that I'd see those people again, and that I could make friends and not get hurt. We were all living here, my family, by then, and that bond of love was not broken by Hollywood. It could have been difficult for a few people to understand, because families are not that close anymore, at least not all families. But we were completely . . . Unless we held hands walking down a strange street in some town in vaudeville at night after a show, it was like the place was unsafe. We were just tied together. Oh, vaudeville was . . . well, I became educated with no schooling. Once in a while I'd go to a school, but not often. If the authorities were alert in some towns, they'd come backstage and say, "Let's get to school." I must have gone to anywhere from forty to fifty schools in my life. For a week.

When I first got into pictures, there would be something on the marquees saying "Dallas' Own Joan Blondell" or "Battle Creek Michigan's Own Joan Blondell" or "Chicago's Own Joan Blondell," because someone would remember that I'd been to school there for a week. America's own Joan Blondell. Well, that's what they did at Warners unless you fought to be un-typed. What made good and what made a hit, that was it.

You know how they say now "relate to"? Well, I related to shopgirls and chorus girls, just ordinary gals who were hoping. I would get endless fan mail from girls saying "That is exactly what I would have done, if I'd been in your shoes, you did exactly the right thing." So I figured that was my popularity, relating to the girls. They just wanted more of the same thing. All you got were new clothes and new sets, but the stories were pretty much alike and I was the same type. But those early days of talkies were incredible, what with the soundproof camera booth and everything. I think that's why they signed Cagney and me so fast, 'cause we just went through it like we were on a stage and they weren't used to that. We were showing something different, something fast and to the point.

But now someone like Jolson, well, his great magic was singing—down on his knee, bent over an audience, that's how he operated. He was never really an actor, but he was a great personality and the screen didn't encompass enough distance for him. He was a projecter. It didn't do it for him. I remember, as a kid, seeing him on the stage and I think to this very day that there are two great performers that hit this world: one is Jolson and one is Judy Garland. They had some kind of a magic in front of people that nobody could surpass. I don't mean, though, that Jolson couldn't make it, and poor little Judy got fouled up . . . what mark they hit nobody could touch. Nobody. I get chills when I think of the two of them. And I knew them both, thank God.

JK: Once you were in movies, were you tempted to go back to the stage?

JB: Well, you see, what happened was that when I finally got here, I very busily got myself a husband and then had a child, so that my whole life has been the home part of it. So I didn't feel like wrapping up and setting out again. God, my stomach turns when I think of travel now, really, because I've had it. Enough. I've been asked if when I retire am I going to take a trip around the world . . . I can't think of anything worse. I'll take a trip to the bed and read a book. But then, retirement doesn't really come into my way of thinking. I don't think I could do it. I've never stopped working in my life. Even in all the years since Warner Brothers, I have worked somewhere. There was only a period of three years when I didn't; I was married to someone [Mike Todd] who wanted me to quit and that was perfectly all right with me. But aside from that, even if I wasn't in pictures, I started on the road taking shows out, then coming back and starting in again here.

JK: When you weren't the gangster's moll or the comic girlfriend, you would be loaned out. How did that feel?

JB: Well, Warners got a lot of money for me. I got nice fame and a nothing salary, and they got a nice chunk of money for me. I remember when I was loaned out to do *Stand-In* with Bogart, which was an excellent film, that they got more money for me by shelving me out there. But career-wise, I didn't think anything except that United Artists was a little closer to where I was living. I never got away from that little salary, never did. I didn't fight enough. You know, they'd bring in other studio stars for Warner pictures and I'd say, "Oh, you know I could have done that. Doggonit, why didn't they give that to me?" But I just didn't put up a fight career-wise. I didn't even see the stuff I was in at the time, just went home and skipped it all, from the rushes to the premieres. I'm seeing a lot of it now for the first time. Working as hard as I did, you could not get home if you stopped to see rushes or out to premieres. The only few that I did attend, Jack Warner said to me, "Damn it, you *go* tonight!" Every day was filled with work and my only relief was to get home.

Oh, Jack Warner, everybody fought him but me. I just thought he must know something and I like to give people credit for knowing something. But all the others on the lot would tell me to walk. They absolutely did. Cagney was a big fighter with me, he'd say, "Would you just beat it? Get out of there, just walk out, that's all you have to do. Then you'll get what you want and decent money." You know, Cagney and I never worked [together] again although they talked about doing one more for us later on, but we never did. But when we were together . . . I see some of them now and the story always surprises me 'cause I have no recollection of it! We made them so fast and furiously: go in and do it and the next day start a new one. I just did it. During the Depression I was making more than six pictures a year. I made six pictures while carrying my son and eight with my daughter. They'd get me behind desks and behind barrels and throw tables in front of me to hide my growing tummy. And I never had more than two weeks before starting a picture. I mean, just let me have the poor child and get back to work. The only other kind of vacation I had was in the middle of a picture with Pat O'Brien called *Back in Circulation,* and my appendix broke. They took me to the hospital. Well, I was very near the end of that picture and about to start another, so they wanted me out of the hospital and the doctor said, "She can't get out of the hospital." So they made a deal with the doctor to take me by stretcher to my house up on Lookout Mountain, and they had the set designer come and make it look like the bedroom Pat and I had done a scene in, and they got a crew of sixty up there, sound and everything, and changed the end of the story so that I was sick in bed and that I'd marry Pat or something.

They didn't waste any time at all with me. Oh, hell, when I was carrying my daughter, I was doing one picture and they had me squashed into a girdle and I thought I was gonna die. I passed out a couple of times from it. But that was me, I didn't fuss about anything, and I don't know why. I think there were times when I probably should have. But I don't think I was mistreated. I wouldn't have worked all that time *feeling* mistreated. It didn't bother me, it was all part of working . . . no matter what was wrong, broken bones or whatever, you always worked, that's been true all my life. I think only once did I run away and not start a picture on time, and that was one year in the '30s when I did eight pictures, if I'm not mistaken. I was so exhausted that I got in my car and I drove up above, oh, some old inn up above Santa Barbara, and I just got in bed. I took a bath, got in bed and slept about four days. I was starting to stutter and my eyes were blinking so that I couldn't even look at anyone steadily. That's how exhausted I was. But I slept my four days, then came back and they docked me for it. Took part of my salary away, but I had to do it.

JK: Do you remember anything extraordinary about *Gold Diggers,* which was a picture with a great cast?

JB: Oh, Ruby, you had to adore her, she was always *there.* People took all of that love stuff so literally with Dick Powell and Ruby Keeler, who were always playing opposite each other, that several times the fans were actually *furious* that I took him away from Ruby. When we got married, they thought *she* should marry him. It didn't bother them one bit that she was married to Jolson. It was just that *I* had no right to do that.

But just think about it, they turned out about three musicals a year back then. *Gold Diggers, Forty-Second Street* and *Footlight Parade* were all done in 1933. Think of the composers! Al Dubin and Harry Warren—they were darling guys. The way they ground those songs out, wasn't it amazing? I hear those songs even now. And Dick's songs—you know, like "I Only Have Eyes for You" and "Sweetheart, There Must Be Happiness Ahead" and all those songs—he sang those down *my* throat, not Ruby's. Privately, that is. I always think of him and our romance when I hear those songs. He gave me a cigarette case, gold, with the strain written, "Sweetheart, there must be happiness ahead" in diamonds. But written out like music, you know?

Poor Dick. He was juvenile year after year, and he didn't like it. He didn't like singing, in fact, he said it was tough work for him and he did not like it. He didn't like the sound of his voice. It was hard work for him, he had to vocalize endlessly. A lot of singers don't have to, Judy Garland never did, but he had to. You know, he was an emcee in Pittsburgh for many years—he was a tremendous favorite there with, God, such a following—that's how Warners spotted him. He would sing as an emcee. He had a lovely voice at one time, but because he didn't like it, he let it go. He was happiest when he was a businessman, producer.

Oh, those musicals were tough. Much tougher than a straight movie. And the hours were awful because we didn't have unions then. We worked any time they wanted to work. You could come in to work at 6:00 a.m. and work till midnight and then be back at 6:00 next morning. And you might have breakfast at 6:30 and then not break for lunch till 3:00 in the afternoon. You'd be ready to fall over. Then you'd work all day Saturday, and they made it a point to work all night Saturday night. It was awfully tough. And I don't think it was like that at all the studios, I think they specialized in it at Warners. They had something hot going for them: the musicals and the gangster things. And they had a bunch of us who were *hot,* and they were going to wring it dry. And they did. Metro, for instance, took much better care of their people, they were guarded press-wise, they made stars, they forced some people to be stars by treating them with velvet gloves.

JK: Did you all know each other? Did you know, say, Harlow?*

JB: Not terribly. She was a little bit standoffish, and I was very much in awe of just anybody who was around then, the movie stars. I do remember one interesting thing about Harlow. You know, she never wore anything, uh, underneath her clothes—like the kids are doing now . . . they think they've discovered something new, well, we were doing it *long* ago—and she was walking by the guys in *Public Enemy* one day and Cagney says, "How do you hold those things up?" And Harlow said, "I ice them." And she was very serious! Oh, Cagney was a hell of a marvelous guy. It's a shame that he quit. But he loves his life, and he had his reasons. I don't see him much these days, but we exchange letters. He's seldom around here anyway.

JK: Do you have any favorite lines from your movies?

JB: No, it's very difficult to remember dialogue when you work that much. Hell, the series I just finished, I couldn't remember the next day what I'd said the day before. Besides, I've always been a very quick study . . . I can read it once, then do it. Did you know that both Cagney and I wrote an awful lot of our own funny lines? We did. That's *one* thing they didn't stop me from doing. Lots of times you'd trip over a comedy line, and I know it has to be right to the bone. Many times I'd take my pencil and reword the thing to

*Harlow and Blondell were both in *Public Enemy.*

make it pay off. I did that more than anything. But none of the pictures stand out. I can tell you where I lived at the time, who I was in love with, but I can't tell you about a picture. It was more that we were all carried up knowing that we were all in a hit *cycle,* everything that we did was in demand. What we were doing was being eaten up by the screen. So we did it and let it fly.

All those Warner kids were great, that's something I miss quite a good deal now. The people around you, if you run into a number of dead spots, you become bad yourself. But we were all brothers and sisters. Pat O'Brien and I told each other everything, one experience and one joke after another. We'd work together and help each other. There was a camaraderie and professional way of working that's lost now, it seems to me. Everybody's on their own and preparing themselves for this greatness they are going to exude. Now I'm talking about the actors. We were a family, so in front of that camera it was really teamwork. Not for an instant would somebody not feed you a line so that your line would be better. No upstaging or anything like that. You might find that at MGM, where they had four leading lady stars—you know, to each his own—but there the studio itself protected you, so that there, even if you weren't a terrific actress, they saw to it that you *were*. That could be done when they devote that much time to you. It could be done today. But at Warners we were all in it together. Happy, sad, well, ill, we all talked to each other. The crew too. The crew was an important part of our life and they were great. We made them happy, they made us happy. It was like, "Okay, guys, we're all tired and exhausted, but we've got a job to do, we've done it before, let's put up the old fight and do it the best we can." We were never afraid to have guts.

It seems these days that people are all so . . . uptight, that's a nice new word. The actors are so afraid somebody's going to do something not right, and they tell the director how to do it. Back then we all stayed in our own department. If we got a director who wasn't the greatest, we'd go through the bit and make him see what it should look like. Working together. That, to me, is completely lost. You are forever with butterflies in your tummy, no matter how long you've been at it. That isn't what the average man has to suffer with every day at his work. Sometimes, yes. But we had a nervous strain at all times. No matter how cool you look or how happy, or how pleasant the surroundings or how much you belonged, your gut shrunk up when it was time to go on. I know, for instance, Jimmy Cagney made such a big hit in that first show we did together, he had to have a bucket in the wings so he could throw up every night before he went onstage. He was so nervous it was unbelievable, yet look how cool he always looked.

JK: Busby Berkeley. Was he indeed a brilliant tyrant?

JB: There's a story that's told from "By a Waterfall." There were thirty-six girls in the swimming pool when we began filming and only thirty-four came out at the end of the day. It's a big lie. [She giggles.] They were just stuck under one of the pianos. No, well, he was a wild man, he had to be. You know, he'd do *insane* shots. They'd build stages for him three stories up, you could hardly see him up there in a nest with two little birds, then he'd sweep around the set with 500 girls and 2000 pianos, then come right back up again and zoom in on the birds. He was fabulous and strict. He had to be. There had to be such order on the set. And he rehearsed crazily, he was like a general with an army. I always liked Buz very much. But, even so, you'd shoot all day and all night. Those musical numbers were exhausting to do. I remember one number in some picture . . . I don't remember which, but I had fun doing it. I was sooooo pregnant with my second baby. They had me in a little tutu or something and I was squashed to bits and I had to sing "Try to See It My Way, Baby." They had sound trouble first, then something fell down, and I had to do it over and over and over again till I thought it would drive me crazy. Then I slipped and fell and was really frightened for the baby. Actually, there are a *few* outstanding memories, but they are *not* to be told on the air, on television, in print or anywhere.

There was one number that was built around rocking chairs.* Buz was way up near the ceiling and getting ready for the shot. This was going to be *it* after endless rehearsals, and one of the chorus girls got desperately sick in line, in front, dizzy and passing out. They yanked her out, but the assistant director didn't want Buz to know about it, so he grabbed my stand-in, who couldn't dance a step, quick got her into the uniform, pushed her into the line. Well, Buz starts making this long twirl of the camera, and he gets down and he *screams* bloody murder, jumped off the platform, nearly killing himself, stopped the whole massive ninety-piece orchestra and the hundreds of extras and everything in mid-air, and he yells, "That stupid fool down there, she's out of step!" I thought he was going to come down and kill her, 'cause he thought she'd been rehearsing all along. Then they explained who she was and that she was just doing a favor, so he was furious then that the assistant hadn't told him! Oh, there were little goodies like that quite often. There were lots of skinned hips and knees, and people falling. It wasn't easy, but it came out right. Oh, the rehearsals. We would go into rehearsal rooms and listen to the songs and music over and over again until we had become acquainted with them. They'd have the playback playing on the stage set, and the orchestra played it too. So you'd know it! It would become like a part of you. And then, if we weren't in the number, we would be doing the "book" part of it while they were rehearsing on some other set. The numbers were almost perfect when they reached the set for filming. The preparation took a long, long time, but when we were ready to go, sometimes they were done in four days. Superbly rehearsed, those numbers . . . and by everybody: the cameramen, the crew, music, orchestra, the girls, singers . . . fantastic. And it was very seldom that we needed more than one take, it was so well laid out.

---

*"All's Fair in Love and War" in *Gold Diggers of 1937*.

JK: You must have had a tremendous sense of humor. For a long time you were hardly in a picture without taking your clothes off, always spending more time in your slip.

JB: Did you ever see *Convention City* by any chance? I wonder what happened to that picture, because that is the raunchiest thing there has ever been. In fact, it started the League of Decency . . . it got all the women of America together and they formed the League of Decency, which put a big crimp in our work at that time.

We were forever doing things among ourselves with double meanings. I wrote a line having to do with a nail in a log for a scene with Dick, and I can't remember now how it goes. But I remember when it happened, we were doing it and I said to Dick, "You do so-and-so," which we always did anyway. Well, we saw it at rushes at the studio, and not a soul got it, not anyone got it, not even on the set, everybody was deadpan, 'cause we did it fast. But in the theater we said the line, then the next few lines, and the audience got it and the laugh was so tremendous that it ruined the dialogue for the rest of the scene. Well, Jack Warner was hysterical. He had to have it run again and backed up to see what the hell it was we said. Let me try to remember—oh, it's been so long now. Let's see, Dick's feed line to me was something like "I'm sorry to be late, but I have to *go,* and I didn't have any paper," and he handed me this piece of wood with a nail in it which had a note written on it. And I said, "You ought to be careful of *that*." I don't know whether that's the correct line or not. The audience got it, but they finally cut it out of the picture. We did a lot of things like that and then they'd cut it out when they saw it. Finally, they would have people in the front office just watch for what we'd say off-color.

Anyway, to get back to *Convention City,* I don't know what they did with that film because I wish they'd run it now. It was one of the funniest things ever written and the whole lot of us were in it. I played the girl who met all the trains coming into Atlantic City for the conventions and handled every-body's case while they were at the convention, then I'd see them off and wait for the next train to come in. Well, it started the League because we had so many hysterically dirty things in it . . . no dirty words or anything like that, just funny, burlesquy.   .

Making this particular movie must have brought back vivid memories for Joan, who at the age of sixteen had been to an Atlantic City convention . . . only then she was the one arriving on a train. The traveling Blondells had settled in Dallas for an extended stay between vaudeville engagements. While they were there, a contest was announced for the Miss Texas Beauty Pageant, the winner of which would receive $2000 and the chance to represent the state at the International Beauty Contest in Atlantic City. Even though she was no native-born Yellow Rose, Joan donned a pink-and-blue bathing suit and the name "Rosebud Blondell," crossed her fingers and entered. "It was a dirty trick to play on those

Texas girls, the authentic Texans, I mean. But I had used a Southern dialect in our vaudeville act and I'm afraid my bootleg accent was even more real than the Texas brand! There was a judge on the committee from Kentucky, so I proceeded to 'indeedy' and 'suh' him to death. He later told me it was a relief, 'ma'am,' to hear a real Southern accent after all this Texas twang!" Rosebud Blondell won. She got the title, the $2000 and the trip to Atlantic City. She and her mother took off. "If we thought Dallas had been enthusiastic, it was a mild splurge compared to the one staged in Atlantic City. I tried to make it up to Texas, for posing as a native daughter, by being a peppy and popular representative of their state. On the hotel menu they featured a 'Miss Dallas Salad,' a 'Rosebud Blondell Steak' and a 'Texas Ice Cream Pie'! I came back to Dallas bearing the second prize in the Southwest Division. So I hope I made it up to them!"

There is good humor and good fellowship in everything Joan has to say, but none of the blandness that so often accompanies a lack of meanness. Unlike those who lost their innocence when they lost their virginity, she seems to have done one without sacrificing the other. There were three marriages: her first husband, cameraman George Barnes, photographed her in *The Greeks Had a Word for Them* and made her look more beautiful than she had ever dreamed possible; her second was her co-star Dick Powell; and her third husband was the Broadway impresario Mike Todd—he was one of the reasons she gave up her career in the mid-'40s and thus was absent from the screen at an important transitional time in her life, so that when she returned, she did so as a character actress. As Joan put it, "He not only insisted I give up my career, but when his shows were in trouble, he made me give up my money and my jewelry. Or so I thought. Fifteen years later he was married to Liz Taylor and I saw my big ring on her finger!"

JB: You know, Cagney used to say that I was the most naïve sophisticate he'd ever seen in his life, 'cause he knew me very well. He knew I was a shy kind of a gal, and that, playing all these whore-ladies, I didn't know what they did, even. I just played them like mad! I'm certain I admire those gals a lot— I *must* have, to be able to play them, because I was totally unlike that, really. To this day I've played a lot of madams and I don't give them any meaning except juiciness, played from the shoulder.

The naïve sophisticate giving "juiciness" to all those madams had been through a harrowing experience with a man when she was seventeen, one that helped her appreciate a woman's ability to control just who received her attentions. Back in Dallas, an acknowledged beauty queen and one year older but none the less naïve, Joan was invited one night to a party with some of her girlfriends. One man in particular, "an awfully nice old guy" (or so she thought), took a fancy to the "brassy" blonde. Up until now Joan had encountered only men "who tried to get fresh immediately and were squelched, or those who weren't fresh at all." The nice old guy offered her a ride home, which she accepted.

Once in the car and on a lonely street, Jekyll gave way to Mr. Hyde. He demanded a kiss. She refused. "What are you playing me for, a sap?" he yelled. "I gave those girls $200 for fixing this date with you. Now, little girl, don't pretend you weren't in on it. You can't fool me." She tried to escape, only to fall victim to his physical abuse: he tore her dress and began to slap her face. Once he had drawn blood, he started the car and careened down a highway which had steep embankments on either side. Joan seized an opportunity and jumped from the speeding car and slid fourteen feet to the bottom of the gully. She broke one ankle and fractured the other, but managed to crawl to a gas station a mile away. A doctor was summoned; she was returned home, and spent the next three months on crutches. "A Dallas lawyer came to my rescue and offered to befriend me. He said I could send that man to the penitentiary for an attempted assault on a minor. But I couldn't bear to go through with the court action. It would have meant that I had to see him again, and I felt I couldn't stand that."

JK: What do you think of Leslie Howard [her co-star in *Stand-In*]? On screen he was always the sensitive, soft-spoken English gentleman. But off screen he is said to have been a rake.

JB: Oh, he was a darling, a darling flirt, adorable. My dear, he would have your hand while looking into your eyes and be rubbing his leg on somebody else's leg at the same time, while having the gateman phone him before his wife arrived. He was a little devil, he wanted his hands on every female around. He loved the ladies. But I played with most of the fellas over at Warners. E. G. Robinson only once [in *Bullets or Ballots,* 1936] and then again not too long ago, over at MGM, *Cincinnati Kid*. The sad part about that was that they cut our stuff. The pictures now run so long, and they had to cut something, so they cut our *meaning* to each other, which had made the thing interesting. But that's the kind of stuff you can't count on now . . . you can be very easily cut. But I don't see today's movies. Well, if I didn't see those grand old films that we're talking about, that I was in, I sure as hell won't go see these. I don't see anything. In the last four years I've seen *Born Free* at a matinee, and that's it. I'd rather spend that free time with my family.

1970

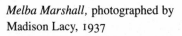

Lois Lindsay, photographed by
Madison Lacy, 1933

Melba Marshall, photographed by
Madison Lacy, 1937

Madison Lacy

MELBA MARSHALL
LOIS LINDSAY
MADISON LACY

NOSTALGIA WAXED PLENTIFUL in the early '70s. It had become big-time business—a lot of books by a lot of people, and a spate of terrible movies made to cash in on the early years, the better times. Some were set in the innocent teens, the frolicking '20s and the hotsy-totsy '30s; and others presumed it was enough just to go through the roster of the surviving stars of yesterday.

In 1969 I'd finished my first attempt at a history of the American musical, *Gotta Sing, Gotta Dance*. I met a lot of the central figures who'd contributed to that genre, but I had never got to the chorus girls, the selfless slavies who were a key ingredient to those pictures. Somebody had given me a list of names and phone numbers of some of the Berkeley Girls, among whom was Lois Lindsay, the third and last wife of Madison Lacy, the Warner Bros. stills photographer, famed for his pinup photos of the girls at the studio. Lois was one of the girls he'd photographed there. It was she who introduced me to her husband and Melba Marshall, a longtime friend—another of the Berkeley Girls.

JK: Why did one want to become a showgirl? Wasn't that limited?

LL: As far as I was concerned, it was a method of eating. It was simply and purely eating, and all I knew how to do was dance, and, after all, this was during the Depression.

ML: At the same time, practically every one of them became leading ladies in Westerns or something of the kind.

LL: Well, we did those things, but at the same time too, when you ask why did I become one, I can remember in 1932 trying to get a job as a salesgirl and you just couldn't. There were lines a mile long applying for every job. I was very fortunate to get a job as a dancer in the studio. I had taken dancing lessons, like every kid does. You know, in those days we had no unions, and if there was a call for a picture, why, 300 would show up. There wasn't such a thing as calling the casting office and saying, "We have a call for a musical number, so send out the dancers who are registered." There wasn't anything like that. In fact, they'd just put the call in the classified ads in the newspapers, and then word would get around that they were casting dancers for a movie and you'd all go, and if you got chosen, you were lucky. It was tremendous because other people were starving and walking the streets. . . .

MM: Thousands would answer the call for a handful of pictures.

JK: How were you selected?

LL: Buz [Busby Berkeley] never made us dance. He never made anyone dance. He never chose a girl on her dancing ability. Chose 'em purely on looks. He would walk down the lines and he would look at each girl.

ML: I don't know about Carole Landis . . . it was on looks and other things in the case of Carole.

LL: Well, honey, looks would cover the body too.

ML: She'd go on the interview, and when Carole started swinging, he said, "Oh, we want her!" Mugsy was on one side and I was on the other, and I says, "Look at that!" She had on a tight sweater, and when Carole started to swing and to dance, why, she was a cinch. She could have become quite a star, but she committed suicide.

LL: Of course Buz was a real tease too, you know. He used to have fun with those interviews. I can remember after we became, you might say, "the old girls" and we'd been with him for a few years, he'd have an interview for girls and then he'd get a bunch of us, oh, maybe five or six, in his office, and he'd say, "Come on up, I'm gonna interview some new girls." And he'd get them in the office, and just for the hell of it, just to be having fun, he would have a girl come in and he'd say, "Raise your skirt." This would be some little kid who'd never been out here before, and she'd raise her skirt just a little. And he'd say, "Oh, I've got to see more than that," and he'd look at us and wink and everybody'd smirk, and he'd keep it up and keep it up until she practically had her skirt over her head and be in tears, you see. But it was a big joke with him. He'd already picked her, he'd already decided she was going to work for him, but this was his way of having fun. This was a gag. But that was it, that was how we were chosen: "Come to work, come for a fitting." It was that easy.

JK: How was it with you, Miss Marshall?

MM: I was later, I didn't come out until '36.

ML: Lois came from New Orleans and Melba came from New York.

MM: I'd already been on the stage when I came out here.

LL: But you . . . She doesn't tell it, *I* tell it.

MM: Yeah, you tell it better than I do.

LL: When she came out here, she thought that in order to get a job she'd have to know someone. So she pulled the standard old gag of telling Buz that she knew Dick Powell and she was a good friend of his, and didn't realize that Buz would have hired her anyway. She pulled this on Buz and then he hired her, and her first day on the set, who shows up but Dick Powell, see?

MM: He was in the picture.

LL: So she pulls the old gag of running up to Dick and throwing her arms around him and whispering in his ear and saying, "Look, you're supposed to know me." And he was a very nice guy and of course went along with the whole thing. And so she was an old friend of Dick Powell's.

ML: Buz had his ten or twelve girls that he called his favorites, his "close-up" girls. You'll see Melba and Lois and Vicky and Judy and Elly, Ethelreda and so on, all always in the foreground. For instance, all the publicity pictures that I would take, or one of the other boys [photographers Scotty Welbourne, Bert Longworth] who happened to be there . . . they would invariably have the same group of eight, ten or twelve girls. They were by far the best-looking girls in the bunch, and in the big numbers they would always be in the foreground, and then the worse-looking they were, the farther back they were. If it was a long number, like that thing with the flags ["All's Fair in Love and War"], what was that in?

LL: *Gold Diggers of '35*.

MM: *'37*, 'cause I was in it.

ML: Anyway, the worse-looking girls were way back. And Buz's favorites were up in the front. They were all beautiful girls . . . no matter how haggard they look now.

LL: But he would keep us under contract, you see. Not all the time, but we would be under contract for the whole picture, and a picture would run three to six months.

ML: *You* were under contract between pictures.

LL: Well, some of the time.

ML: You'd work with Buz, you were always around, I know that.

LL: The point that I'm trying to make is that he would bring in 200 or 300 girls then for the big production numbers which would maybe run a month.

JK: How did you come out to Hollywood? Was it a gamble?

LL: I came with my family, my mother wanted to move out here, and we moved out here as a family. My mother was a Hollywood Mother, she just thought this would be the greatest thing in the world if I could work in movies. It was, to her. She probably had that in the back of her mind when we came out here, but we moved as a family. Melba didn't. She struck out on her own.

MM: I came out here from New York and just came out as a gamble, as you said, just on my own. 'Cause I had worked around in shows in New York and decided I wanted to try Hollywood. And those were the days then of the big musicals.

LL: And a lot of the girls just happened to live here, like Sheilah Ray and quite a few of the other gals.

ML: Where did Ethelreda [Leopold] come from?

LL: Ethelreda came from New York.

MM: Yes. She came *originally* from Chicago, 'cause I remember her from when I was growin' up.

ML: Well, Vicky was born *here*.

MM: So were the Greys.

ML: Yeah, both the Greys.

JK: Were you affected by the Depression out here?

LL: Of course.

ML: Yeah, but later. It took two years to hit here. The first part of the Depression started in New York in '29 and '30, and then hit here in '32.

LL: To have a job paying $50 a week during the Depression, that was pretty good money. I began in the lottery-number picture, what was that? *Footlight Parade*. That was made in '33. I was hired as a dancer. So I went to work every day, and I wore my tap shoes every day. But we never tapped. We swam!

MM (laughing): That was a water number!

LL: And I still wore my tap shoes! I never danced! I can remember going to try on the first fitting that we had for costumes; these water-number costumes were leotards made out of soufflé. And when they fitted us, they fitted us only in these leotards without the diamonds and things. I can remember running out to my mother in tears, saying, "I don't want to work in the picture business." I tried on this leotard with nothing underneath it, I thought that was my costume! But at the same time, do you realize how modest we were? I've always wanted to ask people of this era who go to see these movies if they realize that none of us ever had any navels. Do you understand that the whole group of Berkeley Girls never had navels, because they always covered them up? They covered them up with a little piece of . . .

ML: The feathers kept falling off.

LL: But our navel patches remained on.

ML: And it was hot, it was in the middle of the summer, and they had these feathers on, here and . . . here, and they'd go around with these feathers, and these feathers would drop off.

LL: It was just like a bikini today.

ML: Some of the girls it didn't bother at all. I can remember some of the girls who wouldn't have given a damn if all the feathers had dropped off. But, by the same token, other girls in the group were quite persnickety about it.

LL: And, by the same token, I can also remember that when that number first started to shoot—not when we were rehearsing, but the first two days—Buz had the wardrobe department drag out every smock that they had ever had, and all the girls had a smock on when they were not actually in front of the camera, and this was by Buz' order. We had to wear smocks, and he wouldn't let just anybody in on the stage, he had the doors closed and only those people working on the picture would be there. He wanted it to be just so for the girls. And those were pretty racy costumes, nothing more than bikinis, and we had our navels covered at all times. Even in that "Lullaby of Broadway" number, where we wore those things with our bellies exposed, they covered our navels.

JK: Those numbers must have been awfully hard to work.

MM: I never considered it hard work, did you? I always had a ball.

LL: I had a ball, the only thing I remember is that the hours were hard.

MM: Long hours.

LL: As far as the actual physical work . . .

MM: Some of the actual photographing, when we were really on the job, when he was taking the picture, we'd break for dinner and come back. Sometimes way into the night.

LL: And six hours between calls. This was your job.

MM: Nowadays, if they work over five hours, they're screaming. We had ridiculous hours.

LL: There were no labor laws.

ML: In those days in the motion-picture business, a thirty-two-hour day was nothing.

LL: We did things over and over again. A lot of times Buz didn't depend on us, he had it all worked out in his mind. He'd point to you, and you'd move when he pointed.

MM: That's true. I don't know, that nervous-tension feeling, I never felt that. Never. He was sweet and he also had a sense of humor, tremendous sense of humor. Wonderful. He'd crack a joke and set you at ease immediately, if he could feel the tensions building up.

JK: Were you one of the water-logged girls in the pool in "By a Waterfall"?

LL: Oh, sure. Of course, he'd say little halfway-dirty things like "Okay, girls, now spread your pretty little legs." And it would get a giggle out of everybody. He didn't mean it to be disrespectful, he was doing it to have fun. On the other hand, we could kid with him, and did quite often. He was the butt of jokes quite often on the set. I can't remember anything specific at the moment, but if we felt like it, we would pull gags on him. He would have us, for instance, in a picture like the piano number where we really had nothing to do. We sat at those pianos for days and days and days. We did nothing except that and just look pretty. But he would have us there for maybe two months on salary.

ML: Three months.

LL: And longer. If the front office would call and say, "What are you doing with all these people? Why do you have them there? We're paying them money and don't see any results," he'd say, "Okay, girls, come on now, the front office is coming down and they want to see something." Jack Warner or Hal Wallis would come down and want to see something. He'd say, "Now when they come down, I want you all to get up and do *tour jetés.*" So we'd all get up and do *tour jetés* like crazy. The front office would come down and he'd say, "This is what I've been working on." They'd say, "Well, it looks pretty bad." And he'd say, "Well, I have to have the girls here to work with them in order to know what I'm going to do." In the meantime he's doing the whole thing in his head. And he would have us there and keep us on salary. All these months, and many times we would knit, play poker, tell jokes . . .

MM: And no one else did that.

LL: . . . all day long during rehearsals. Then when it came to shooting time, we really worked the long hours.

JK: Was there any contretemps between the showgirls, the "close-up" girls and the hoofers?

LL: Actually, Buz was a little different in that respect.

MM: Yeah, in that respect he was . . .

LL: Melba and I were dancers, we were not showgirls really. But he used his dancers as "close-up" girls.

MM: He did.

LL: He would keep his dancers, the ones who were also his "close-up" girls, those he would keep on for the longest time because they were the skeleton team. We would work out the routines. He'd say, "Stand here, stand there, I'm trying to get an idea about this and that." So we'd stand and wait for him to get his idea. I think one of the funniest stories about Buz was "Lady in Red" [*In Caliente*, 1935], the thing with Dolores Del Rio.

ML: "The Lady in Red" wasn't Dolores Del Rio.

LL: Yes, it was, honey. *In Caliente* was the name of the picture, but "Lady in Red" was the number. So Buz decided to rib the front office. He said, "I'd really like to get some white horses for this number, but I don't think the front office will let me have them, they'll complain." He said to us girls, "Come here, I want you to hear this," so about ten or twelve of us on the set at the time stood around him while he called and said, "Now, Hal,* for this thing with Dolores Del Rio, I really want to make a barnyard scene out of it. I'd like some pigs, two or three, and I think I'd like a dozen or more white chickens, and I think we ought to have an ox in there too. And some little animals, some dogs or something like that." He named all of these animals, you see, and by this time the front office is screaming, "No! No! You can't have any of this. No!" They'd say that it would make a shambles of the whole studio with all those animals. So then he said, "Well, I'll tell you, if I can't have any of those, how about just a couple of horses?" Of course that was what he wanted to begin with, so he got his horses, just by going round and kidding them. I think he ended up with six.

MM: I don't remember.

LL: Then they got loose one day while we were shooting and ran all over the lot, all the white horses, and we were all running after them, all around the studio.

JK: What went through your mind as you stood on line, in formation, waving flags and looking pretty for days and days?

LL: I was probably thinking about where I was going that night.

ML: She was scared purple 'cause she was scared of heights.

MM: Well, a lot of the girls were scared of the heights because he had us on tall pedestals, very high in the air. A lot of them were scared and used to get up and just shake.

---

*Hal Wallis was the studio production chief, having replaced Darryl Zanuck. According to Madi, this incident happened during the "Shadow Waltz" number in *Gold Diggers of 1933*.

LL: Well, Elly and I tried those things out for him. We were the guinea pigs on
those flag things. In fact, in this picture Elly is here and I'm here, or vice
versa. We were the front girls on those pedestal things. But we cried, both of
us in tears the first day we were up on those things, and Buz came personally
to take us down. I think it was an attention-getting device at that time, got
lots of attention. But I was afraid of heights and so was Elly. But we were
strapped up there with a board up our backs . . .

MM: And you'd be up there for hours. You'd get so tired because the pedestal
was like this, just big enough to stand on.

LL: About a foot square. No glamour. No, it was just a job.

ML: God, no. That's just the half of it. When they'd get in some of these nude
numbers, or seminude with very little clothes on, the executives would all
show up on the stage and get up high. There's one particular number and I
could go on and tell a couple of stories about that that I know about.

JK: Well, tell them anyway.

ML: Well, two or three of the girls . . . in fact, you girls weren't there, it was
before your time . . . well, the girls got up high too, and the executives were
down below, and they, the girls, had had a few drinks. The girl that later
opened the nightclub was one of them . . . and they proceeded to urinate. All
over these people who were down below.

LL: Well, that was one thing, we couldn't get out to go to the bathroom as often
as we'd like, that was for sure. It might be hours before you could get away,
before they'd let you get off of those, like those platforms.

JK: That "By a Waterfall" number must have been quite arduous.

LL: It was, it was. But everything with Buz was more of a, not a physical
activity, it was the standing and the waiting while the cameras and Buz did
the work, really, because his work was more camera angles.

MM: That's right.

ML: One of the things that Buz had that nobody else had, was that on two
stages at Warner Brothers they put camera rails up, hung from the rafters . . .
and they had an elevator that would go up and down, and would also run
along those rails. The camera was mounted on this platform and then they
would motor-drive it, and they could move it all around the stage . . . in
circles, raise it, lower it and everything else. He was the originator of that.

MM: Well, that's when they raised the roof.

ML: You mean on Stage 7?

MM: Yeah.

ML: No. That was Marion Davies for *Cain and Mabel.** William Hearst paid for that. They raised it for *Cain and Mabel,* when the girls were angels and went up into the sky, a full-length shot of the stage, you see. They couldn't raise the girls high enough to get out of the scene going to heaven when they were dressed as angels and flapping their wings. In order to get that number, Willie Hearst paid for the cost of raising that stage's roof thirty feet.

JK: Were you an angel?

LL: I was in *Cain and Mabel,* but I wasn't an angel, thank God.

ML: You were in the canoe, the Venetian number.

LL: Well, I was in the number where the angels were, but I was down on the floor.

JK: Once the camera began turning on a number, could you stop?

LL: Oh, we had white chalk marks on the floor to stand on. And it did stop. It would take days and days to shoot a number. So much of that was done in rehearsal, you know. Remember?

MM: They knew exactly . . .

LL: . . . exactly where, and even then they would shoot it over and over again. But nobody ever cracked up. There wasn't such a thing as temperament. After all, we were making $50 a week.

ML: Weren't you getting $85 or more?

LL: Oh, no! I never made that much as a dancer. I think the highest I ever made was $65. But the classic thing on the "Waterfall" number was day after day after day having to go under that water, and you can imagine with 200-odd girls, why, there were many times when many girls couldn't go in the water!

JK: Do you have a favorite number that you remember?

MM: Well, the only one I remember was something over at Universal, and I can't remember the dance director's name. They brought him in and he was a foreigner. Maybe Lois can remember. I don't know whether she worked on it or not. But we'd been spoiled by Buz, not having to do anything, and this guy was, well, he came in and all of a sudden he was going to set Hollywood on fire, you know, with all these ideas. In one number he had us juggling plates and we had to learn how to juggle plates and dance at the same time, and twirl ropes. I've never worked so hard in all my life as with this guy. I couldn't stand him, none of the kids could stand him. Finally, the producer Buddy De Sylva, he was a great guy. He finally came on the set. He fired the

---

*Cain and Mabel was not a Berkeley production. The musical numbers were staged by Bobby Connolly.

guy right off the set because we all just started to walk out *en masse* because he was so impossible. He expected us all to be geniuses at twirling ropes and juggling plates.

ML: Fox had the same system as Warner Brothers, they had about fifteen or twenty-five girls who they kept all the time . . .

MM: Yeah, but we all worked all over town, Mad. 'Cause I worked with LeRoy Prinz too, over there at Paramount. And if we were shooting, we had to be there at 6:00 in the morning for makeup and stuff, we had to be ready and on the set by 8:30 or something for shooting at 9:00. So we would get there for a 5:30 call, 6:00, unless we were making ourselves up. Did you work over on that picture at Universal with me? On *You're a Sweetheart*? That Alice Faye picture?

LL: I don't recall that.

MM: It was just a madhouse and a mess. What a shambles that thing was. Buddy got someone else. I've forgotten who it was.

LL: I don't remember. But anybody I ever worked for was harder to work for physically than Buz. The hours we worked for Buz were the longest, but the physical work . . .

JK: You were in the "All's Fair in Love and War" number . . . was that difficult?

MM: Well, that's the one with the big pedestals. And the flags and the guns and a lot of cannons, and they also had the two stages moving together, remember that? Dick Powell was on one and Blondell was on the other.

ML: The cannon number.

MM: Yeah. And we came together. That was an interesting thing to shoot, as I remember.

LL: I think one of the most fascinating shots I remember ever working with him on was not on a dance number, but on *Hollywood Hotel*. It was with Louella Parsons and Rosemary Lane, and he did a shot that was the equivalent of a zoom lens today, only there were no zoom lenses in those days. He started . . . we were in a tremendous café in the Hollywood Hotel. Louella Parsons was sitting way, way over there in a far, far corner, and between her and the camera we were all sitting at tables like we were dining and drinking in evening clothes. The camera came in on a dolly and just went. It just went all the way over to her for a close-up, and they did their lines, and then the camera came all the way back out. Now, as it went *in*, we all got up and moved our chairs and tables and everything so the camera could go through. And as it came back out, we put all of our tables and chairs back and sat down like we'd been sitting there the whole time.

ML: You neglect to mention that Louella had on her rubber pants and pot under her table.

LL: Well, I wasn't concerned with Louella, I was concerned with the shot. You're a little on the earthy side of it, huh?

ML: Well, see, she had kidney troubles.

LL: Yeah, she sure did.

JK: Did you get any extra money for being a "close-up" girl?

LL: No.

MM: Not one cent more.

LL: Not a penny more.

MM: No, and it didn't matter. But I don't remember any competition.

LL: Now, there might have been some who did care, who wanted to be "close-up" girls.

ML: Yes, there were some who did care. There was one extra girl . . . you might say they were divided among three classifications. There were the girls of very light morals, putting it politely. Then there was the ambitious group, that was a combination of both. And finally there was the quiet group that were really fine and very sweet and lovely girls. Each group more or less settled in its own clique. One would compare their various affairs, the other would compare their various possibilities in financial gain and the third was just a nice bunch of girls who would knit.

MM: You can imagine which group he's putting *us* in.

ML: And all of us fellows on the set knew which group was which.

MM: And guess who wound up with the little knitters?!

ML: We married the knitters.

MM: Yep. He married a knitter and a friend of his married a knitter too.

ML: But they had uses for those other girls' groups. Harem style, you see.

MM: P.S., they weren't the "close-up" girls. You never saw them in a picture, they were so far behind.

ML: The "close-up" girls were the nicest bunch, they really were. They were also the youngest.

MM: That's true. But I would like to make a point here. As far as the pictures, there was no classification, no difference. We all mixed together, as far as I could see, in any picture I ever worked on. On the stage, no. On stage the dancers and the showgirls were cliquish and the two never mixed. I was a dancer and I know that the dancers resented the fact that the showgirls would do nothing, we thought, but come out and parade the costumes and then get maybe double the amount that we got . . . and we did all the work. But out here I think the equality of the salaries made all the difference.

ML: Now, I'll have to amend that to some extent. It's as you say it was at Warners. But at Metro the showgirls there were either mistresses, or about to be, or had been, to some producer or director. There was a group of about twenty or twenty-five who were kept there purely for that purpose.

MM: Well, that I don't know about. I never ran into that.

JK: But what did the chorus girls think as they were moved from one piano to another, from one pose to another, smiling all the way?

LL: Probably wondering if they dropped a stitch on the last row they were knitting.

ML: I shot all of Buz' pictures at Warners, and two or three of his at other studios. The ones that stand out in my mind are the "Shadow Waltz," the fountain number and the big number in *The Great Ziegfeld,* "A Pretty Girl Is Like a Melody."* Those were the three numbers to me that went over and above everything else. The overall view of the numbers. There was nothing that could compare to the "Waterfall" number of its type, it was supreme. The "Shadow Waltz" was supreme in its line. And the Ziegfeld number was the thing; the staircase, going around, was absolutely supreme in its line.

LL: That was a beautiful number.

ML: Berkeley was a master of making the most of nonmoving girls. He made the camera move so that *we* moved, it was like sitting front row center in a theater.

MM: There's the clue to the whole thing. Just like sitting in the theater watching a stage production.

JK: Were you aware of the inventiveness of the numbers at the time?

LL: Oh, not at all. No. Oh, the tunes, sure. And Dick Powell was great and Blondell was great. But I don't think any of us were really impressed by Buz at that time, and his genius.

MM: I was impressed by his sense of humor.

JK: But these were very expensive numbers. If a girl missed a beat, they had to scratch a fortune.

---

*This number was not staged by Berkeley. The dance director for *The Great Ziegfeld* was Seymour Felix.

LL: They spent money like water. They probably did it twenty times anyway, regardless of the girls. Oh, Buz might scream at you a little, and he did every now and then. But the next time it could be the girl next to you who was out of step, so it could happen to anyone. That was the normal course of events. And you did these things over and over again until 3:00 in the morning, and that was the way every number went.

MM: And, boy, were you tired!

LL: And that's when they did the close-ups. Just before you went home at 2:00 or 3:00 in the morning. So you had to be young and beautiful to come across.

JK: You must have been able to almost choreograph after doing so many.

LL: No. Well, you could choreograph them as far as Buz is concerned, because you knew all you had to do. In fact, this is very cute, we worked in a picture at Warners a year ago. Or was it two years ago, dear?

MM: Two years ago this March.

LL: Yes. It was *The Sphynx.** It hasn't been released. When we were there, they gave us no direction, as far as the story or what they wanted us to do or anything. And suddenly they'd get us all together and say, "Now we'd like you to make an entrance." That was all we were to do, make an entrance. Well, by this time we had all gotten over the initial visiting—you know, who you hadn't seen in twenty or thirty years since the old days in the chorus. And Buz hadn't seen a lot of the people in a long time. They turned to Buz, and they said, "Mr. Berkeley, would you give the girls a step, a dance step for an entrance?" Well, Buz has never danced in his life. Not except for one step he had ever given us way long ago. And so he turned to us and said, very seriously, "Okay, girls, now we'll make our entrance like this." [She does a basic tap step.] That's all he'd ever done and that's all we ever did.

ML: It was incredible on that flag number, "All's Fair in Love and War." They had these flags . . .

MM: You just had to count. The first girl would start "one," then the next "two," "three," "four" and so on, and each girl came up on the count. And you'd just keep going.

ML: You had to stay together.

MM: Yes! Every girl had to count, all the way down, and you had to be together and come up with your flag on count.

---

*A Warners Bros. film made in the wave of the nostalgia boom, a sort of superannuated Ziegfeld Follies, full of old stars like Ruby Keeler, Joan Blondell, Dorothy Lamour, Busby Berkeley and a lot of the girls.

LL: Or else you got screamed at by Buz. But it didn't matter. He'd always then just walk away and look at you and smile.

JK: Were there others who went on to fame, like Lucille Ball or Betty Grable, from being a Berkeley Girl?

ML: No, Betty Grable didn't begin as a Berkeley Girl.

LL: She was singing with a band.

ML: She started in the Collegiates, shorts, they were made at Universal, supposed to be a bunch of high-school kids or college kids. Long time ago. And she was one of the extras on the picture. And the leading lady, the girl playing the lead, was a total flop. Now, they were on location—seems to me it was a beach—anyhow, we were on location somewhere like that, the girls and fellas in bathing suits. And this leading girl was just terrible, whoever she was. The director, whom I've also forgotten, picked Betty Grable to do the lead in this picture. And *she* was terrible. But she was better than the other girl, the results were better-looking. And that's when she got her actual start.

JK: But she did begin as a Berkeley Girl in '29.

LL: Oh, but she had already been around for a long time by then.

JK: How about Veronica Lake? She was in *Forty Little Mothers*.

LL: We couldn't *stand* her.

JK: When you look back, do you look back with fondness?

LL: Yes.

MM: I certainly do. Of those days and the little group, and all of them in it because we were very close, at least I felt that we were. To this day I still feel that, although the years have gone by. You don't see a lot of them very often because life goes down other paths. I don't know any of them in our group who might call me today who I wouldn't be so happy and thrilled to hear from. I feel like a sister to them. There's a closeness that I don't think anyone could ever change.

JK: Have your lives gone the way you thought they were going to go when you first started out?

MM: Has anyone's?

LL: That's a very good question. I must say I never really had a plan for my life, so I'm very happy with my life. Not smug or self-satisfied, but it's been a very happy life, and that's fine with me.

ML: It's me she's talking about.

LL: Well, the best thing is that we've both maintained our sense of humor throughout the years. I think it's still important.

Madison now shows some of his photographs and stills, the first being of Marlene Dietrich.

JK: This is the best series on Dietrich of that time. Beautiful.

ML: I should show him that picture of Dietrich with that makeup on for *Witness*.

JK: You photographed *Witness for the Prosecution*?

LL: Tell him the story of Dietrich on *Witness*.

ML: No.

JK: Here's a picture of Ann Sheridan . . . and one of Audie Murphy. Where is Audie Murphy these days?

ML: He just got out of a problem, and he's living around here someplace.

LL: He shot somebody because of a dog.

ML: No, he didn't shoot him, dear. He knocked 'em out is all.

JK: Here's Joan Leslie . . . though it doesn't look like her screen image.

ML: Doesn't look like Eisenhower, either. How about this picture of Shirley MacLaine? It's my favorite picture. And here's Basil Rathbone without his wig. Now in this one that's his own hair, but in the next shot, that's him at the same piano but with a wig on. This is Cagney. There's Jolson.

LL: Do you remember the *Wonder Bar* movie with Jolson? Remember the night we were out at that movie screening at UCLA? Jolson's movie, with that "Goin' to Heaven on a Mule" number where he went across a bridge? Well, we were little Negroes in that! We were done up in blackface, we were the little Negro girls and what the heck did we do? I think we were sitting at tables or something. I didn't appreciate that number until I saw it at UCLA about two years ago.

JK: Was it harder for you to photograph stars, Madison? Weren't you shooting a known image, while with a starlet you could do something different?

ML: No. It was the same freedom, with the exception of a very few. There's really no difference between the photograph of a star and a starlet. You take Sheridan or Kay Francis or Lombard, they do what you tell them to, no problems. The most attractive ones that I photographed, in a photographic way, were Lois, Ann Sheridan, Kay Francis, Carole Lombard. 'Cause you could shoot from any angle.

JK: Would the studios give you instructions for photo sessions with their stars?

ML: Oh, yeah, it depends entirely on what you're doing and when you're doing it and where you're doing it and what studio you're doing it for. For instance, at Warner Brothers you were left pretty much alone until Alex Everlove came out there as head of the department. He's dead now. But he was head of the publicity department, and he had his own ideas, because he was an amateur photographer. And he would proceed to tell you how you should photograph this, that and the other one, and you of course wouldn't pay any attention to him, you'd go and do it . . .

MM: . . . your own way . . .

ML: . . . and then he'd proceed to crop 'em, which was one of his mistakes. He cropped some of Scotty's [Scotty Welbourne] pictures to heaven, and Scotty quit. Sure. Why should Alex Everlove tell anybody how to shoot a picture? Goodness' sake. But now, there are two pictures of Ann Sheridan over in that frame there, and . . .

MM: Sometimes you can be very sexy in dungarees.

ML: Sure. And in that one she's pulling a pistol out of her pocket, and in another one Scotty's adjusting her dress.

JK: You also shot on the sets, didn't you?

ML: My God, yes. I've got three albums of those. Plus portraits.

JK: These are so beautiful. I've never seen more than five good stills of these color prints. And Constance Talmadge . . .

ML: Oh, Connie. I don't have any negatives of her. A lot of prints, though. They are pretty good because they were shot later, see, they were shot in the remake. They remade two sections of *Intolerance*. One was *The Woman and the Law,* which was the, at that time, modern-day sequence, and the other was *The Fall of Babylon,* which was the Babylonian sequence. D.W. remade them separately. He cut them out of the original print and added a lot of scenes.

LL: They edited and added . . .

ML: . . . and matted it. They took the Mountain Girl, for instance, who was Connie, and they starred her in the remake. That was all just to make some money. See, *Intolerance* didn't make any money, it lost a lot of money.

JK: Here's from *The Wedding March*.

ML: On *The Wedding March,* Erich von Stroheim had two crews, see, so that when one crew got drunk, he'd have another to take their place. And of course he got the actors drunk for the orgy because the result was what he wanted. There was no make-believe about that. That damn pink gin was bitter too, as a matter of fact. It took fifteen hours to shoot that scene 'cause Von wanted Fay Wray to act, and that was a pretty difficult proposition. And as a consequence he kept on it for fifteen solid hours until he got her to do what he wanted her to do. Oh, we used to work forty hours straight on *The Wedding March*. Yeah, they had a hospital there, and I'd go lie down in the hospital, in one of the beds, and get a little rest now and then. Many times we worked thirty, thirty-five hours. Straight. Because he was trying to get the results he wanted to get. He worked too, you know. He worked just as hard, and harder than anybody else. All that business about the legends of Von is a lot of nonsense. He was one of the hardest workers and one of the nicest people, but one of the most exact perfectionists that ever existed. Stroheim was a wonderful person.

You have no idea of the stuff we shot for foreign release! It was probably cut out of the picture, but there were things in that, in the Madame Rosa sequence, that would make things now look mild. Not in nudity, but in the way they were done. They were very subtly done. For instance, there's one scene where two German officers, or Austrian officers, are talking to a girl in Madame Rosa's. Madame Rosa's was a house of ill-fame, politely speaking. They had this one girl talking to two men, she was leaning against a post, and while she's talking to them she takes a banana and peels the banana, then puts the banana in her mouth and shoves it down as far as it goes, then takes it out and then shoves it down again. Then he had another scene on a couch where this girl is lying down on the couch, and he had one officer behind the couch and another officer sitting in front of the couch playing a harmonica. See the subtlety of these things he pulled? Then he had one girl—now, this girl kind of balked at the situation and we later got even with her. Von spread this champagne . . . only it wasn't champagne, it was apple cider, carbonated cider . . . all over her. She had a teddy bear, and was lying down on this chaise-longue. He had sugar in a certain part of her anatomy and then he had three or four Pekinese dogs, and the Pekinese came up and licked the sugar. Now, that was supposedly for foreign release, for France, I suppose. And we were all watching it. There were any number of things like that, that he shot.

JK: Did the studio know what he was doing?

ML: Well, Pat Flowers was the man behind the throne on this thing, and they finally more or less took it away from him and they did the cutting. That's when it became the two pictures, *The Wedding March* and *The Honeymoon*. If they had let it alone, it would have been one of the great pictures of all time along with *Greed*. They did the same to *The Merry Widow*. His *Merry Widow* is superior to anything that's ever been done. He was a definite perfectionist. For instance, I can remember his looking down the cathedral where they had Imperial Guards, men in uniform at the wedding, and one man had his stomach protruding. Now, this man must have been 150 feet from Von. But Von proceeded to stop everything and yell at him, "Pull your belly in! You're supposed to be an Imperial Guard, and they didn't have bellies." Then he had an argument with his wardrobe man as to which side the mail pouch was on. An Austrian cavalryman rides through a scene, and it's merely incidental. It was outside the cathedral when the horse reared and hit Fay Wray and all that stuff. He went through the scene, and they had the pouch on one side, I've forgotten now which side. And he spoke to the wardrobe man and he told him, "That pouch is sitting on the wrong side." The wardrobe man said, "No, sir, it isn't." He said, "Yes it is. Go look it up." Well, the wardrobe man went and looked it up, where he had presumably looked it up before, and Stroheim was right. Stroheim was right from memory, whereas the wardrobe man had just finished reading this book and should have known.

JK: Did he inspire the kind of respect you have for him from . . .

ML: From his entire crew. His actors—now, some of his actors loved him and some of his actors hated him. Because he was brutal with the actors. Not all the actors. If they knew what they were doing, there was no problem at all. But if, on the other hand, there was somebody, you know, he would be deliberately brutal. For instance, I've seen him slap a girl in order to make her do what he wanted her to do: to make her cry, or to get mad. He would haul off and slap or bawl 'em out or whatever was necessary in order to get them to do what he wanted to do. Then, afterwards, he would apologize and kiss them and so on and so forth. But he was a perfectionist. Now, look at *Greed*, the misery they went through with *Greed*. I wasn't on *Greed*, but I wish I had been. I can't say I enjoyed working all those long hours, but with Von you did it.

JK: He seemed to have a tendency for the perverse.

ML: Oh, of course he did. Sure. He did on *Blind Husbands*, he did on *The Devil's Passkey,* he did on *Foolish Wives, The Wedding March* and on *Queen Kelly*.

Madi was old when he died, and until he died he did everything he could to help tell the story of his profession. He was also a historian with a keen sense of the injustice his profession had suffered. The opening night of the show of Hollywood portrait photography, *Dreams for Sale,* at the Municipal Art Gallery, Laszlo Willinger, George Hurrell and Madison were at hand. Lana Turner, whom Madison hadn't seen since he shot her at Warners back in 1937, was the guest of honor. There was a mob of thousands, which delayed things a bit and kept her limousine from arriving on time. She turned up a bit flustered, looking starry in a nice, decorous, lacy black cocktail dress, accompanied by a puffy, dark-haired, youngish man who was there to carry her personally reserved bottles of white wine as she walked around. Everybody was crowding; it was something of a stampede. Edith Head was terrified by one crazy admirer and hightailed it out of there. Lana was more used to it. And then she saw the picture of her that Lacy had taken to get her a job, and she said, "Oh, my God!"

And everybody else said yes, wasn't it beautiful. And then she saw Madi in the background and she screamed his name, and people made room so she could get to him standing there, grinning, as Lana threw her arms around him, never spilling a drop of wine from her glass. It says a lot about these photographers, and what their work meant to the people they photographed, that forty years later Lana hadn't forgotten. After all, the pictures did get her a contract with Warner Bros.

1976

Eleanor Powell, photographed by C. S. Bull (MGM), 1938

E L E A N O R
P O W E L L

THE STORY of Eleanor Powell's life and career is virtually a carbon of all those films she starred in, which might in part account for her success in them. Hers is the story that asks the question: "Can a little girl from a small hick town find happiness as a rich and glamorous movie star?"

She wasn't a great actress or a stunning beauty, and wouldn't claim to be either. But absolutely nobody could dance like Eleanor Powell. *Dance!* She flew. And when she tapped . . . ! She ripped across the huge musical sets conjured up as exotic backgrounds, and for a decade she stunned and exhilarated her public and the critics by an explosion of brilliance in top hat, white tie and tails. An image she shares with the sublime Ariel of the dance, Fred Astaire. While knocking out five taps to the second, her body bent ninety degrees on itself, creating the illusion of huge sweeping arcs that left impressions in the air as she moved on, like a lighted match circling swiftly in a darkened room. And this after only seven tap lessons in her life!

She is transformed when dancing. Astaire and that musical wizard Busby Berkeley have both paid tribute to her. Contemporaries explained that she was so good because she "danced like a man." But there was more to it than that: her drive, her discipline, her total obsession with her work, these were the qualities that made one sit up. What made her distinctive was the expression and fusion of all these into something recognizable and admirable: her dancing.

For a dozen films, from 1935 to 1945, she cut a unique swath across Hollywood's soundstages to tune-filled scores by writers like Kern, Cole Porter and Freed and Brown. Then, still at the top, she got married to a handsome young contract artist at another studio, Glenn Ford, and virtually retired from films. Though other dancers have sprung up—Ann Miller, Vera-Ellen, Leslie Caron, Cyd Charisse, Ann-Margret—none has achieved her fame. In 1961, after her divorce from Ford and, as she says, mostly in response to being goaded to get up and do something by her teenage son, she staged a sensational comeback with a nightclub act that opened in Las Vegas and for the next four years made her a top attraction on the nightclub circuit. She could have gone on—there were offers from TV and Broadway—but, having proved something to herself, she dropped out of sight again.

With such zest and outgoing personality, the lady struck me as an unlikely candidate for mystery. She was elusive, but to find her wasn't as difficult as getting her to see me. The past is not her hang-up, nor is reminiscing her pastime. It was as a favor to a mutual friend that she agreed to see me. So there I was, one Sunday afternoon in Los Angeles, lost in a maze of little streets between Wilshire and Olympic Boulevard, preparing my excuses for arriving late. At last I hit on the right street, drove up, parked, looked about—and saw her waving to me from the top of a flight of stairs leading to her apartment in a small but pretty house on a small but pleasant street. She stood tall, bright, brimming with a contagious warmth.

I would rather dance than eat! Dancing to me is some sort of a god, like a Buddha. It encompasses you, like jealousy. Very possessive. I really didn't know what the outside world was all about when I was making pictures. I couldn't have told you about the newspapers, what the current events were, anything.

I never started dancing because I had any particular talent. As a child, I was extremely shy—so shy that it was pitiful. I'd meet a little girl and she'd want to walk to school with me and I'd hang back behind the door. Or, when people came into our home and I knew them—the next-door neighbor, let's say—I'd be hiding behind the chair or my mother's back and they'd say, "Eleanor, come out, you know Mrs. Smith," but I'd be hanging back. Somebody suggested to my mother, "Why don't you put Eleanor into a dancing school?" Now, if there'd been Girl Scouts about or group therapy, she would have taken me there. But there was a dancing school and my going there had nothing to do with me wanting to go dancing or having big talent or anything.

I was eleven. There was no question of a career—my mother would have thought it ridiculous. 'Cause I come from Springfield, Massachusetts, and anyone who went into show business at that time, way back then, was *"Unhhh! Well!"*—you know what I mean. Everybody thought it was a wicked, bad world.

I went to a Saturday-morning class, 10:00, an interpretative class in a little local dancing school. My grandmother took me because my mother worked. We were very poor. Mother was divorced, which was a disgrace then. I didn't really know about the divorce until I was like thirteen. My grandmother took care of me because I was born three days before my mother was seventeen. Today she lives right around the corner from me. We're more like sisters than mother/daughter. She's a wonderful person.

Anyway, I went into this school and I got out on the floor there with the other children and the music started. The piano was on a little raised platform and they were playing MacDowell's "Water Lily" and all we did was learn the first, the second, third, fourth and fifth positions. We didn't move our feet at all.

My grandmother was sitting there, not really knowing anything, just thinking this would help me, and the lesson's a dollar, which is a lot. This is dancing?
But I just went out of my mind. I wasn't conscious of anybody. I just was gone
with this music. This was where I belonged. From then on, I went every Saturday morning.

My grandmother had a sister in Atlantic City who was ill and we went
down there one summer. I'm twelve now. I was on the beach doing cartwheels
like children do and standing on my hands and stuff like that when this man
walks up to me and says, "You're pretty good. I'd like to have you work in the
Ambassador Hotel." Remember, I don't know from nothing, but I'd been told
never to speak to a strange man. I look at him and say, "I don't know about that.
I'm just here for the summer." He says, "Well, my name is Gus Edwards." That
didn't mean anything to me. Gus Edwards! Anyway, he said he'd like to meet
my mother.

Now, what it was—it wasn't a nightclub but more like the dinner show at
the Ambassador Grove. I went on with my little costume—little burnt-orange
velvet pants with rhinestones—that my grandmother had made for me and I did
a number to "Japanese Sandman." I was brown as a berry and young: I was born
in 1912 and here I was, twelve. Leota and Lola Lane were the star attraction in
this show, and Velone was the emcee. I made $7 and worked two nights a week
in the supper show doing this little acrobatic number that I had learned for the
dancing-school recital at the end of the year. I was good in acrobatics 'cause I
had a limber back and I was good in ballet. The school didn't teach any tap at
all—it was all esthetic dancing. So I did this number—standing on my head,
doing splits, turning round and so forth. Very slow. Big deal!

In the wintertime we went back to Springfield, where I resumed school. I
loved school. I was a very serious little girl, very serious.

The next summer we went down again. I go back to the Ambassador Hotel.
A man comes from the Silver Slipper—now, that's a real nightclub. His leading
lady is ill and he needs to borrow an act from our show. So who can he have?
Well, I was the least important and they said, "Take the kid." The man was
Benny Davies, the songwriter who wrote "Margie," but in those days names
meant nothing to me. Anyway, Mrs. Davies was the first one to put any makeup on me. A little lipstick, a little rouge, no foundation or anything.

Next summer I'm back in Atlantic City and back to the Silver Slipper.
Across the street is a club called Martins. The real super supper club to top
them all, like the Persian Room. That was the club where Stanford White was
shot by Evelyn Nesbitt's husband, Harry Thaw. One of the few things before
my time. They hire me. I'm making $75 a week, working every night, and I've
become mistress of ceremonies as well. This is the club where Jack Benny and
Eddie Cantor and people of that caliber—whom I still didn't know because I
hadn't seen a show, but I'd heard of them—kept saying to me "You're terrific"
and I should go to New York and get in a show.

Now, all this time I'd been doing nothing but classical routines. I had a five-foot purple-and-cerise fan, velvet little panties, and purple chiffon with a band of velvet at the bottom. During this time there have been tap dancers coming to the club and I just thought, well, "Not me, this—loathsome, doing wings and all of that, how awful!"

I'm now fourteen and this is the pattern of my life: Springfield in the winter, Atlantic City and show business in the summer. My mother never had any vocation. She'd been a teller in a bank; in Springfield she worked all through the First World War, the only woman putting the bullets in the belts that would be sent to the boys in the Army. She did everything. Chambermaid! When I was twelve years old, I used to come home from school and I used to help. Seeing her work like that gave me my determination. I had to do something. Whatever it was, I had to be successful so that my mother wouldn't have to do this type of work anymore.

Well, we go to New York. My mother gives me three months and if I don't make it, we go back to Springfield and it'll be college and all that for me—education, education, education. In New York I go to Ben Bernie's Club for three months. Bill Grady, who was then the top agent with the William Morris office, comes and sees me and gets me my first job in a show they were doing on the Ziegfeld Roof—*The Optimists*. Everybody in it was English except for me. I'm also doing auditions for other shows, and everywhere I go, they ask, "Do you tap?" And I say, "No, sir," and they say, "We'll call you," and nothing happens.

Mother and I were living in a hotel on 42nd Street and the three months were almost up and money was scarce. We used to eat all our meals in the dining room of the hotel 'cause they always put a big basket of bread rolls on the tables and we could order soup and eat lots of rolls and fill up that way. Anyway, somebody (I don't remember who) said why don't I go to Jack Donahue's dance school and learn tap. Jack Donahue used to be Marilyn Miller's partner. I went to this school, loathing the whole idea in my heart. I enrolled for the course of ten lessons at $35 for the course because it worked out cheaper than taking individual lessons.

There I was with the beginners. They took me into a room with a parade record and I had to beat out a rhythm on the table, nothing to do with the feet, just sit and accompany the record. Now, Jack Donahue was sitting on the windowsill watching—he wasn't taking the classes any more than Fred Astaire teaches at the Fred Astaire Dance School, he just dropped in now and then. A man called Johnny Boyle was teaching the class.

So he's teaching the first step, then the second step, then the first and second step together, and I still haven't got the first one, I'm all left feet. In the dressing room my mother came and asked me how it went. I told her I didn't get it at all, I hated it, I loathed it. Back at the hotel, she said don't go back, forget it. I said what about the $35 we'd already spent. Forget it, she said. I was angry with myself. It was the first thing that had licked me. The next Tuesday, when I hadn't gone to class the day before, the phone rang and Jack

Donahue said, "Aren't you the little girl who was here last week? Why didn't you come yesterday?"

I said, "It's not your fault, I just don't understand it. They go so fast." He said, "You're not going to give up like that. Come back and I'll see what I can do to help you." So I go back. No change, but he's watching me. "What's the problem?" he says. Well, I was very turned out, you know, very aerial and all. He sat on the floor and took my ankles in his hands and said we'll start from scratch. It was like piano exercises—over and over till you thought you were going crazy. He told me to come back. The next time he had a belt from the war-surplus store and he took two sandbags—the kind they use in theaters for the curtains—and he put one on each side of the belt, which he fastened around my waist. Honey, I was riveted to the ground. That's why I dance so close to the ground. I just couldn't move. That's why I can tap without raising my foot even, because I was taught with this belt and these weights on me.

He must have stayed with me for forty-five minutes and I must have stayed for more than two hours by myself, practicing. It was like an algebra problem you couldn't make out, then suddenly you see the light and it's like you've always done it. From that point on, I was in front of the class with Mr. Donahue, demonstrating the class routine. It was from that routine that I got my first show, *Follow Thru.* Any kid from the class who came to see the show would see me do the class routine on stage because what else did I know? I still remember that routine to this day, every step, and I never went back to a tap class since that time.

I was sixteen years old when I did *Follow Thru,* in which I had a specialty. I worked with Jack Haley in that. In my second play, *Fine and Dandy,* I had the lead. I worked with every renowned big band. I was the first one to do a special at Carnegie Hall with Paul Whiteman's band and Maurice Chevalier making his American "live" debut in 1930.

Once I was identified as a tap dancer, that was it—because nobody had ever seen that kind of thing before. When I hit it, the off-beat was just coming in. This was the big new thing and I used to practice all the time between shows. I used to take a Victrola and those red records—I still have them—were the ones I practiced to when I was sixteen years old. Fats Waller, boogie-woogie . . . oh, honey! You know, there must be some colored blood in me somewhere. I often used to kid my mother, asking her, "Did you have a colored milkman or something?" Because it's a black sound—you see, a tap dancer is nothing but a frustrated drummer. You're a percussion instrument with your feet.

Every dancer in motion pictures owes a debt of gratitude to Fred Astaire because he brought dancing to the screen in the right way. Prior to his and Ginger's films, a dancer would come on in a nightclub scene and would go into a dance and two steps later there'd be Joan Crawford's hand over the screen and a voice saying, "Come and sit down." And then the leading man sits down and looks at her and they talk some more and then suddenly everybody applauds and the dancer is bowing and that was it for him, nothing! This is what the dancer had in films, so I never had an aspiration of coming to motion pictures. My dream as a performer on Broadway was to go to Europe just like they always did in the films. Because there the artists got the *bravo*! Here it was money, money, money. Over here you last so long [snaps her fingers]. You go to sign an autograph and someone else comes out and they leave you flat—"Oh, there's so-and-so" and they're off and running and you haven't even gotten your pen out yet. To be a performer in Europe, that was my aim, not movies. But that's not how things go.

George White said to me (I was in his *Scandals* at the time), "Ellie, come on out to the Coast. I'm going to make a picture and I want you to be in it." It's *George White's Scandals,* directed by George White, written by George White, photographed by George White, acted by George White. Well, I had heard about Hollywood. You've got to remember here was a girl who was dedicated to her work and almost a little prissy, if you want to know the truth. Certainly not the type to go to Lindy's after the show (not that there was anything wrong with that). I was living with my grandparents in Westchester County. The moment the show finished, I'd leap into the shuttle, still with my makeup on, and catch the last train out of Grand Central Station and get home to do my chores there. Made no difference to them who I was or what I was doing and how hard I worked—I had to make my bed and clean my room. And I thanked my grandmother the day she passed away 'cause I would have grown up to be a very overbearing, conceited thing without them. My grandmother used to say, "You can dance very well, I'll grant you that, but what else can you do?" It made me think. I didn't know how to do anything—not even how to make a check out.

Anyway, I came out to do this picture and the rest of the cast—not Alice Faye, but the others, Ned Sparks, James Dunn—were all drinking away. They'd go into this property room and around this big steamer trunk they'd drink. Nobody started shooting until noon. I didn't know that this wasn't the ordinary way movies were being done because it lived right up to my expectations.

Now, I'd got the heavy part in the picture—I'm the soubrette, the one that takes Dunn away from Faye. I'm sitting around and days go by and nobody pays any attention to me. I'd ask George, "When am I going to do something?" James Dunn was so stoned one day that he ate the artificial food that was set out on a table for a nightclub scene we had to play . . . I'm sitting there and I can't believe him eating this make-believe tomato salad and drinking this hot ginger ale that was meant to be champagne.

One day George said to me, "Ellie, go and get made up. You're going to do your number." So I said, "Where do I go for makeup?" "Down the street past the cafeteria and you'll see it." Now my shyness comes into this story. I walk down, looking around, and see a sign outside saying "MAKEUP." I'd never been to makeup in a film studio before. I look in. There are these three barber chairs and a line of people in front of each one and the guys are slapping this stuff on their faces.

Instead of me opening my mouth and saying, "I'm on Stage 24 in *George White's Scandals*—they sent me to get made up," I joined the queue. These are the makeup men who make up extras. They sit me down and this man says to me, "What are you wearing?" Well, George had wanted me to wear the costume I wore in my act—a special pajama costume designed for me by Charles LeMaire with my trademark on it. It was cheaper for George for me to wear my own costume, I guess. So I describe this costume and now he starts slapping stuff over me and I wonder what he's doing. Well, they were making up Egyptians for a film that was shooting there at the time, and when he's finished, all you can see is the whites of my eyes, I'm three shades darker than Pearl Bailey. I get back on the set. Everybody is so stoned by this time, nobody notices. I get in front of the camera and, because I'm doing this low-to-the-ground tap number, they think I'm a Negress. I finish. Nobody notices anything.

Now, Metro wanted to start making musicals and top everything everybody else had done. They hired Roy Del Ruth from Warner Brothers to direct. And now Mr. Mayer is sitting in the projection room looking at every banjo player and harmonica player, you name it—looking for musical stars. And he sees my number because Fox, which has just amalgamated with Twentieth Century, is loaning screen tests of their people around to other studios, a kind of courtesy gesture they don't always do. Now, the two writers who were with Mr. Mayer when he was looking at my test told me about it. He said, "I love that girl, but I can't use her. She's colored." So Sid Silvers, who was one of the writers and who knew me from Broadway, said, "She's not colored. She's as white as I am. That's Eleanor Powell." So Mayer said, "All right, we'll use her for one number."

Johnny Hyde was my agent at the time. I'm with the William Morris agency then and they don't have any clients in Hollywood yet. I brought them out there. Johnny comes to me all excited: "They want you for *Broadway Melody of 1936,* Jack Benny's big picture, and they want you to do a specialty."

I wasn't interested. I wanted Europe and I had had my experience with movies. Well, I said, "I want a thousand dollars"—which was more than Mitzi Mayfair and Hal LeRoy* were getting then—"and I want a part in the film as well, not just a dance or a little bit, but a role." This was deliberate. I might as well have said, "I want a million dollars and my dressing room painted in gold," because I expected them to say, "Go jump in the lake!" Instead, they sent me a script. In the original script they'd wanted me for the part Una Merkel played— which they thought would be funny opposite Sid Silvers (who was also acting as well as writing). Now I raised my fee to $1250 and Johnny was tearing his hair out, but it came back: Okay. It was for one month's work and a very good part. I'd never been offered that much before. I came out on the Super Chief, champagne and all, put up at the Beverly Wilshire Hotel, and my movie career really started.

The very first day at the studio, Roger Edens was the rehearsal piano player, Arthur Freed was the songwriter with Nacio Herb Brown, there was Mr.

---

*They were, with Eleanor Powell, the kid stars of Broadway in a musical together.

Mayer, Roy Del Ruth, the director, and Mr. Katz and Mr. Mannix, but I didn't know who they were. They had heard that I danced other types of dance than the tap and they wanted to see me do other work. I did toe on point and other things. They all got their heads down in a circle and then Mr. Mayer called me over to him and he said, very officious, "We're going to test you for the lead." And instead of being glad about it, I said, "Mr. Mayer, you can't do that." And he said, "Why?" "Because I don't know a thing about the camera. You've got a girl in this picture, June Knight, I've worked with her on the stage—she's glamorous, she's sexy, she sings, she's a good dancer. You've got $3 million, I understand, in this picture (which was a lot in those days) and you can't . . . you can't *do* that." And Mr. Mayer said, "Well, my dear child, you don't seem to realize that I run this studio, and if I want to make a test, I'm going to make a test." I said, "Well, you're just wasting your time." And my agent was sitting there going gray. Being very naïve, not really knowing that this isn't what you do, that you're supposed to flatter him, I was just being honest.

So Mr. Del Ruth told me it was a dual role and to go home and get up on this scene and meet him tomorrow morning at 10:00 in his office. I went down the next morning and he said, "Miss Powell, what do you think?" And I said, "Well, this opening scene, Mr. Del Ruth, is supposed to be about a girl frightened to death and I guarantee you there isn't an experienced actress in Hollywood who could do *that* scene any better! The rest of it, I don't know."

They couldn't have found anything better than that part. It wasn't acting on my part so much as just being myself. Now the shy girl, the Janet Gaynor of Albany, the little Cinderella, was me as Eleanor Powell. When I danced, I became Mademoiselle Arlette, very aggressive!

They got Bob Taylor. I'd never heard of Robert Taylor, and I don't think many people had. He was under contract, he was getting $35-a-week jobs. They figured they'd take this young boy with the widow's peak out of stock, get all the girls excited. Bob Taylor was petrified of me—I'd been in the New York theater and he imagined me like Tallulah Bankhead. But he knew more about the camera than I did!

They wouldn't let me see the rushes. I didn't want to, 'cause Mr. Del Ruth didn't want me to see them. Suddenly one day on the set the lights were all off and Mr. Del Ruth was called upstairs. Mr. Arthur Freed and everyone else were on the set. And I went to my portable room and an hour passed. And another hour passed. A knock came on my door and Arthur Freed came in and he said, "Ellie, look, I want you to promise me that you'll never ever ever let on I told you. Well, they're all upstairs and you're doing beautifully." You know that old gag: "You're doing great, but we just need a different type." So I said, "Okay, fine, I know it." He said, "Wait a minute now. They're just afraid—meaning Mr. Katz and Mr. Mannix—that the marquee is going to read Jack Benny and that's all. Robert Taylor and Eleanor Powell—what's that? They're afraid they ought to put Loretta Young or Joan Crawford in the part and dub the dancing long shots to get the marquee value. But Mr. Del Ruth spoke up and said, 'First of all, if you take this girl off the picture, I will walk off the picture immediately. Secondly, if she isn't a star overnight, I will direct any two pictures on this lot *gratis*. That's how much I believe in this girl.'" And when I heard that, I would have walked through fire for that man!

We did this number on toe points with the Albertina Rasch Ballet and you're not supposed to be on your toes for more than three hours without a rest. Unfortunately, we had to keep on because of the set and everything. D'you know, the blood came right through all our pink ballet slippers? And when we took our slippers off that night, they had big buckets of ice. It was like marching for days or something. I lost four toenails on the right foot on that one picture. They grew a little and I lost them again. Talk about stunts, honey! When I went down in that gun-chute thing, I didn't do it with the glove on—I forgot—and I got a burn all the way down my arm as I'm coming down. It took the skin right off my arm.

Anyway, the picture lasted four months instead of the four weeks it was supposed to. The reason it turned out so well, I believe, is that it was a very good story *per se*. It was a solid, dramatic story, then they embellished it with the songs and dances the way they should do every musical comedy. Set a good solid foundation and then fill in the other things instead of starting off with a song.

I was brought up there to sign a seven-year contract and Mr. Mayer is performing. All the time he's pacing up and down. He starts in by saying, "You're too tall, and you're not *bla bla bla . . .*" and he tears me down. And he says, "I have a proposition to make to you. Nobody, but nobody, gets the money and the opportunity at the same time." Which is true: if you get a big opportunity, you give a little elsewhere if you're starting out. And Mayer said that if I would work for less money on my second picture, *Born to Dance* with Jimmy Stewart, he would use all the Morris Agency clients he could, like Ray Bolger, Sophie Tucker. So I made less on the second picture and the Morris office was set up out here.

I'll never forget when Mr. Mayer came to me and said, "Ellie, how would you like to do a picture with Fred Astaire?" And I said, "You gotta be kidding!" And he said, "No, he likes the script, the money is fine. The only thing is: you may be too tall for him." You know, I'd always had an opportunity to meet Fred Astaire back in New York, but I never wanted to because I'm an idealist. I might meet him and he might do something or say something that I wouldn't like and all my illusions would go. Anyway, I didn't want to meet Fred Astaire at the racetrack back in New York or at a cocktail party. I would have wanted to talk shop. Where could I do that at the racetrack—"What do you use on your shoes? How do you do that? How do you do this?" Fred Astaire was an idol to me, but I had no idea what he thought of me.

Mr. Mayer said, "Mr. Astaire will be in Mervyn LeRoy's office at 11:00 tomorrow morning. You meet him and we'll see if your height is all right." I was there early and I said to Mervyn, "Y'know, I'm so nervous. I took a bath

in Lux last night, hoping I'd shrink or something. I just hope this goes through."
We were chatting a little while, and then the bell rang. Mervyn LeRoy said to
me, "Quick, Ellie, go hide!" and by reflex I ran and hid behind the door. So in
saunters Mr. Astaire and Mr. Hayward—Leland Hayward, who was Fred's
agent at the time—and they sit down and there's a little chitchat about the
weather and the races. And then Mr. Astaire said, "Boy, I'm so nervous. Do
you know how she works? Does she standard record or prerecord? How long
does she rehearse?" And Mr. LeRoy said, "Well, why don't you ask her!
Eleanor, come on out." And I slunk out from behind the door. But the thing is,
I had heard Mr. Astaire say almost the same thing I had said. Mervyn said, "I
had Eleanor hide behind there because she's been a nervous wreck. She hasn't
slept all night." Then the office door opened and, one by one, in walked Mr.
Mayer, Mr. Mannix, all the big ones. And here's the setting: we're just chit-
chatting, polite company talk, y'know, and finally they said, "All right, rise!"
So we stood back to back. Well, believe it or not, Fred is taller than I am—not
a lot, but he's about 5'8"—so I fit in with the part. Now we sit down and
everything's agreed 'cause that was the only thing—if I'd towered over him, it
wouldn't have been any good.

Mr. Cole Porter was there and he handed us both a piece of paper—just a
lead sheet in his own writing—of "Begin the Beguine." He plays it, we listen.
Marvelous. Plays it again and everybody's listening. He hands one sheet to Mr.
Astaire and one sheet to me. This is our first number supposedly—we had nine
numbers in that picture. Mr. Astaire was going on vacation to London to see
Adele, his sister, who was married to Lord Cavendish, and would be back in
three months. I said, "Mr. Astaire, I know how important it is for you to have
your own pianist." (Because your pianist, you see, becomes your everything
when the only thing you have is an empty hall and a piece of music. He's the
man who's going to play this and groove it and probably suggest repeating a bar
or what have you.) So I said to feel free to bring whoever he wanted. And I
said, "Because you're a stranger on the lot, I'll meet you at the East Gate. I
have a little bungalow here which Mr. Mayer has built for me to rehearse in.
Now, what time do you like to rehearse?" And he said, "Any time *you* desire."
So I said, "No, no, no—you select a time." "No, no—whatever . . ." Well, it
was like out of "Mr. Alphonse," you know. So I said, "Well, is 8:00 in the
morning too early for you?" "No, that's fine," he said. I wasn't going to see him
again till he came back, so we shake hands. "*Bon voyage,*" "Have a good trip,"
and off he goes.

The morning comes. In the meantime, he cannot have his pianist, according to the musicians' union—they wouldn't allow another man from another
studio to come over. Naturally, we had to take my man, who was very good. I
have had "Begin the Beguine" played backwards, forwards, inside out, and I
have general ideas about what I would do. So I meet him at the gate and we
saunter down to the bungalow. I introduce him to my pianist, direct him in to
change, and he comes out and there are these two little canvas chairs and we

sit. We know we have all these numbers to get, but here we are, sitting. He says, "Would you like to hear the music?" I say, "Oh, yes, thank you." So we play the music and I'm thinking, we gotta get going, we gotta start, who's going to start? "Would you like to hear it again, Miss Powell?" he says. I say, "Yes, very much." Well, to everyone around the studio it was like a heavyweight boxing match—two champs in the ring, they expect *pow*!—and here we are, sitting an hour and a half listening to a piece of music we know backwards!

We had no choreographer at all. What made it so difficult was that nobody could do what I was doing but me. Up to the time that Fred worked with me, he had always had a young lady that he could teach. And, of course, they would never say that they didn't care to do that, because that was *it*. In fact, Hermes Pan used to take the girl's part. He would work with Fred, two men together, and Hermes would be whoever the girl was—Ginger Rogers, Joan Fontaine or whoever. Then when they'd got it all mapped out, Hermes would go teach the girl her part. When she was all rehearsed, Hermes was Fred Astaire, still teaching her her part so that it wouldn't wear Astaire out. Then they got together for rehearsals. But me being my own choreographer and Fred being his own on *Broadway Melody,* who was going to tell who what to do?

I said, "Mr. Astaire, I have a number and there's something wrong in the middle of it. If I did it for you, would you please help me with the center part of it? It just doesn't feel right." I thought that might be one way we could get on our feet! So I did it, got to the middle and stopped. And he jumped out of his chair real quick and said, "Oh, I see what you mean," and he did a little something and then he stopped and ran right back to the chair. So I said to him, "Mr. Astaire, what are we going to do?" And he said, "Maybe if you go over in that corner and I go over here and we just take a couple of bars and improvise—and if you see something you like, stop me. And the same if I see something." Fine.

You'd be amazed at how many things we did like. Not the same steps, the same syncopation. Finally he stopped and I fooled around and ad-libbed. "What was *that*!" he'd go, and I'd have to define what I was doing, and vice versa. Finally we got it. But it was three or four days before we started melting. Still it was Mr. Astaire and Miss Powell.

One day we did the exact same thing on a difficult piece of music in "Begin the Beguine" and he forgot and he ran over, lifted me in the air, said, "Oh, Ellie!" then put me down and said, "Oh, I beg your pardon." And I said, "Look, basically we are just two hoofers who started off in vaudeville, right? *Please* let's get down to Fred and Ellie." And he said okay. The ice was broken. I don't mean he wasn't perfectly charming after that point—it wasn't "Hi, Ellie!" "Hi, Fred!"—but we got flowing as regards the work we were doing.

If you remember "Begin the Beguine," we did that thing in the circle, counter-rhythm—we went in a circle, he went this way and I went that way. Well, we had more fun working on it! We started at 8:00, remember. My tummy made the worst growling noise—I was so embarrassed—and he said, "What time is it?" But we had no clock. D'you know, it was 4:00 in the afternoon! We had gone from 8:00 right straight through to 4:00, over and over. The poor piano player, he was absolutely dying! He had a cigarette hanging out the corner of his mouth and the two ashtrays were full. So we got a Big Ben alarm clock and we set it at 1:00. And we promised, no matter where we were, we would stop to allow this man to have time. We were crazy, *he* didn't have to be. Anyway, that's what happened and we had one number after another with no choreographer. The little bit of chorus work there was we did together.

Once I got into the studio, I realized I had to learn about the camera if I was going to choreograph my own numbers, so I bugged the gaffers and all the electricians and the camera crew, and they were wonderful to me. "Why do you do that? What's that for?" On days that I was supposed to be over-recording and putting taps in, I'd sneak over to the shooting stage and watch. I spent hours on the set. I slept in the dressing room.

You'd almost design your sets. You would get with the art director and you say, "I'd like a fountain and a staircase." He'd sketch something vaguely to fit with my idea. Because I was going to use that for an effect. You didn't actually design the set, but you gave the idea of what you wanted.

First you would create the number. Then it has to be passed by the producer and the director and so forth—and that's frustrating because they are not looking at the number to see whether it's good or bad, whether they like it or not. If you go to a nightclub and you see an act, you don't think about how many minutes it takes. But in Hollywood they say, "Okay, Ellie, start!" And they look a little while at you, then down at their stopwatch, and they've missed it, you know, and they say, "Honey, it's fine, but it's just two minutes too long." Wow! You create a number so everything blends and jells and melds in and somebody comes and tells you to take two minutes out! You can't just cut in the middle of a thing.

And invariably, unless you sit with the cutter, he would be cutting out the big thing and leaving in the little bits. He didn't know. It was a whole different world from the stage. It was a whole new education I had to learn.

I never had a choreographer, except for the background. I did all my own numbers. For my nightclub act I had a choreographer who would just do the four boys—he'd maybe bring them in for an entrance, and maybe he'd work out how to get them off. On *Born to Dance*, Dave Gould did all the numbers I wasn't in.

I would try to think up something that is still tapping but with something else. After all, you can't just come out and tap. With *Born to Dance* they had me up so high I was way up to the top of the roof of the tallest stage we had at MGM, and they had a big boom camera following me. And, y'know, the excitement of dum-da-da-da-dum coming down the stairs-da-da-da-dum I had to learn from a *fireman*. I had to learn from a fireman that if the pole's too long when you come down, you twirl like firemen do when they come down. But I couldn't go around. I had to be with the camera. And I also had to do it with one leg and one arm held out. Well, this is hard to do: after a while your gravity makes you go around. But they didn't want me to go around, *I* didn't want to go around! I wanted to do it the hard way—one arm, one leg. These were the exciting things.

Now, you're the audience, you know I dance—that's set in your mind. The idea is, how many ways can I dance that? On the floor, on the ceiling, etc. So I have to utilize an art, learn a particular thing—whether it be juggling or roping—so that it's still tapping but it's done with sort of a gimmick. So the three months that one usually had off a year, the studio was very wonderful to me, they handed me the best of everything. When I did the matador number in *I Dood It,* they hired me a real matador. Now, remember, I'm only doing musical license—it's not authentic. But the matador studied with me in the rehearsal room four hours a day prior to going into rehearsal—this is nothing to do with dancing—so in essence I would learn a particular art, the proper feet movements, all the expressions you need as a matador. I got books and read up on it. And usually my teachers got so involved with me that they forgot entirely that I was going to put a number to it. They got interested that I should go into this particular thing.

When I did the roping number with Sam Garrett in *Ship Ahoy,* he said, "You gotta go into rodeos! You're fabulous, terrific, forget all this and go into rodeos!" It was for the lasso thing—oh, if you don't think that was rough! Those iron hondas on those ropes are about *that* thick, like a big pulley. And when you get the rope going up big on your side, it's going about 55 mph. And to jump through that rope, through that big thing over and back, well . . . I started off. You cringe, you know. The inclination as this thing comes toward you is to duck. And then the honda would hit me on the head and knock me right out cold on the floor! So I had to practice in football shoulders and a football helmet in the rehearsal hall. And I had to go gradually, working up. I'm talking about the one trick, jumping through the big loop—there's got to be momentum, but you've got to keep your arm straight, you can't bring your arm down. So I developed such muscle—like fighters or golfers pick up a soft ball and use it to make muscles. Now I got to forget about that and put the tap to it, I have to put difficult steps to it and still keep this going. I perfected it, I could lasso with one finger and pull it back, there wasn't a thing I couldn't lasso. But Adrian, who was doing the clothes, had to take the right seam out of everything I had in wardrobe and make a large sleeve because I had an arm that was mammoth!

When we did the number, they tried to get good-looking chorus boys, but they couldn't do any roping—what I devised was a passing-the-rope—I get a hard thing going with the rope and then pass it one-two-three-four and at four get it to that guy who's gonna spin it while I go over and take another rope and pass it over to someone else, and so on. The chorus boys couldn't do it because they didn't know how. So we had to get real old leathery cowhands: they didn't photograph very good, these old guys, so they had to stay back. The problem they had was they couldn't keep rhythm. You should have seen them being directed through the megaphone, the director yelling to the men to take it on a certain beat.

One of the shots I had was a Western saddle with a pommel, with a line of girls. Without a cut, I did a fast line of turns, I folded up the rope just perfect, gave it to each girl in turn, twenty-four in one take, no cuts. That means I had to get twenty-four bull's-eyes. Well, maybe I got to fifteen and then the rope would slip. They had a cigar box on the set and they were taking bets that this would be the take I would make it in. When I finished that one take, everyone screamed and carried me on high. That was just one little shot in the number.

Or take that innocent little dog number in *Lady Be Good*—I thought of a dog 'cause that was a part of the story. I auditioned dogs, I had dogs of every size and shape. They could bark, they could lie down, stand on their back legs . . . but they didn't have the personality that I wanted. My prop man said, "I have a little fox terrier at home, my little girl's dog. He's very smart, he brings the paper in," and so forth. And I said, "Bring him over, Harold, let me see." That dog had that look, you know, and those human eyes! And so I started working and training that dog. He's smart, but he doesn't know anything. First I took it home with me and it slept in my bedroom and I fed it. I put a rope around its neck and I started in making a figure eight, saying, "Buttons, c'mon, Buttons!" clicking my fingers, and I'd drag him a little bit and then give him some yummy. And this went on until I could take the little leash off and he went with just a snap of the fingers, then next with no command. But he had to get used to my taps going, and that threw his little ears down there. If you don't think that was a job! This dog was just an old house dog. Of course, I fell madly in love with him—and he was so devoted to me. And a ham! When we went through rehearsals, his little body would quiver, you know, he'd want to do his part. He had to go over the sofa and then land on my chest and in the end knock me back on the thing. I had to teach him to stand on his legs, to walk behind me, to sway his little hips with the hula. In three months. Three months to create the thing, whatever it was—roping, matador, dog—during my holidays.

The battleship number in *Ship Ahoy* disappointed me a great deal because it isn't the way I had it planned at all. I had designed a matador number like I did in the nightclub much later on. Then—it was the first time this happened—they decided upstairs that because of the story content they needed a ship number to allow for the comedy scene of Bert Lahr and Red Skelton down on the cases of wine. And I was not prepared for this. They rewrote the story and I had quickly to do this as a fill-in. They said, "Eleanor, there's going to be a gambling boat. We need a number on it, just a café number." All right. You get the idea of just a café floor. So I thought—if it's got to be that, then why don't we have the area where the ship is docked all walled in, sort of like a bull ring? And when you look down into the ship, the ship is all done like a bull ring and the tables are all on platforms and everyone is in matador costumes so that you get the atmosphere of Spain.

Now you have the parade and come off with all the matadors parading and you go over to Red Skelton, who's in the lead, and you bow just like they do and toss your hat up. And out of a little runway comes a spotlight which is the bull. The spot comes out and staggers against the top of this satin thing and you've got your red cape. The spotlight would now become your partner: in fact, you could even have a bull's head with horns in the spotlight. And you do all these legitimate movements—no license, real stuff—until you get your *muleta* and then you kill the bull in pantomime. The lights come up and they carry you on their shoulders, maybe around the tables. Then the number goes on and you're in a café adjacent to this where all the matadors are celebrating. And then I wanted José Greco, who so badly wanted to work with me, to be the other leading matador who gets up and does his flamenco work to "Jealousy." José and I have a real challenge thing with heelwork. Well, this was my idea for the number. Then I find out they've got just this little set. Had I been in this set from the start, I'd have done a pirate's number, come flying down as a pirate on a rope. So there was nothing—it was a throwaway, no story to it—just a girl coming out and doing a tap dance in a costume.

I had to train with real cadets for *Rosalie:* they had about thirty-four West Point cadets. They embellished the rest with the chorus boys. The head man from West Point came down and taught me that drill.

The drum number* was my own idea. We went on the back lot at night to shoot that and it was slippery because the dew had settled on the drumheads. I took one step and I slid from here to there! It was funny 'cause Ray Bolger and Nelson Eddy, as a gag, had an ambulance out there and had Red Cross coats and bandages, so I'm thinking all the time that if I fall they'll be there to pick me up. We had to stop production and put corking on top of each drum because we'd forgotten all about the dampness. Then those hoops that I went through— you had to turn, but your hand would sort of break. Well, in one take I got about a third of the way to the end and a drum bounced me because they had put a thicker layer in. It just bounced me six feet in the air! Well, we just had to go back and shoot that again.

It was very dangerous, they were big drums. They didn't use a double for me. I had to learn how to do a line of turns down those drums—turn and dip a little bit, but not break the flow of the turn. Oh, that was hard! The top drum was about seventy-five feet high and they had to hoist me up there. I could have done that number better, but I was just holding back a little bit because I was afraid of the dew. That number was about two weeks in rehearsal. It took us four nights to film that, starting at 8:00 until about 2:00 in the morning. We were two days in the sound room doing the music—eighteen hours each day. We had to take every one of those drums into the sound room when I recorded

*On a sixty-acre set she taps down sixteen drums, the largest being sixteen feet in height, the smallest ten inches, until she literally flies through the air to land on a platform where she is surrounded by 500 dancers of the ensemble for the finale.

the music because how can you time the leap from drum to drum? There's no possible way I could get the tempo of the thing otherwise. In other words, the conductor used to have to follow *me*. And that wasn't the end of it because I'd have to go back and put the taps in at the end of the whole picture. (Taps are *never* done on the set; they never pick up the taps as you're being photographed.)

I think that was the most difficult as far as the possibility of an accident happening. But you remember the number in *Ship Ahoy* when I went off the top of the diving board and landed in the middle of a swimming pool? There was a great big muscle man. I dive in his arms, I have to keep my body stiff, and he throws me like a bullet. I go from the water and there's a fella who catches me on the poolside. And I'm to be thrown some distance backwards. Of course, I've done adagio and acrobatic stuff before, so it's a regular thing.

We go along in rehearsal and everything's fine. The fellow does it once. We rehearse it again for camera because it was very hard to follow all that. Second rehearsal—wonderful, just perfect. I get in my outfit now and get all fixed up for the camera. Roll 'em, action! What happened was that when the fellow threw me, he hadn't got quite enough *umph* and I can see that I'm not going to reach the concrete. To save my hair and face for makeup, I grabbed the edge of the pool and kept my head up out of the water. Now this other poor guy knows he's got a star and he's been warned by the director and everybody to protect her—he sees I'm hanging, and instead of leaving me alone, he dives in, grabs me by the waist and pulls me down to the bottom. He's panicking, see? But in so doing he pulled all the ligaments in my arm. We couldn't do any more shooting that day because my arm was just torn.

When I came out to Hollywood, I was amazed at the people who came on the set and watched me practice. Mind you, while I was rehearsing I never saw anybody out there, it could have been I don't know who. Garbo used to come and watch me for hours. And Joan Crawford used to come and lay on her tummy and watch me for hours. And I'm thinking to myself these are the people who are *big* movie stars and here they are. Jean Harlow used to come down and watch. It was as though they'd never seen any dancing before. I used to go and watch Jean every once in a while if it was on my way. And I'd see Jeanette MacDonald and Nelson Eddy quite a bit. I think Nelson was over so much visiting the set while I was practicing that seeing us together probably just gave them the idea of teaming us in *Rosalie*. I think he had been complaining to the upper bosses that he wanted to do something away from Jeanette MacDonald, to see what he could do more or less on his own—because in *Rosalie* we didn't infringe on each other's territory.

Mr. Del Ruth—they called him "Laughing Boy," that was his nickname 'cause he never smiled—was such a fanatic about keeping me out of the average Hollywood mold. Like the pencil-thin eyebrows. He said that this girl looks like an American girl in a magazine, she doesn't look Hollywood. Leave her plain and simple.

At that time I did not know that the studio owned you lock, stock and barrel. Stars were like royalty and there was no in between. I remember running into a dear friend of mine who was working in the cutting department, Bob Stringer. I said, "Let's go and have a bowl of soup in the commissary." We sat on stools having a bowl of soup in the lunch hour. And when I got back on the set, I get a call from Mr. Mayer's office. He wants me to come up and see him. He said, "I understand you were in the commissary with Bob Stringer." I said yes. He always called me "my dear child," you know. He said, "My dear child, you are going to be a star. If you were seen with Robert Montgomery or someone like that . . . but I would rather you weren't seen with any of the lower echelon of employees." And I said, "Mr. Mayer, I am terribly sorry, but this is a friend of mine. You can't tell me who I'm going to have lunch with. I'll do anything on the set. I'll work harder than anyone you've ever had in the studio. But as for not speaking to my friends—sorry." So he just got the wrong person—I couldn't be less impressed with somebody big. And, as I say, Mr. Mayer had asked for me—I didn't come asking for this particular job. He said, "Well, if you don't go along with me, you're out." But they needed me more than I needed them in essence, I guess, 'cause I stayed a long time. And I just defied that rule. And I was defiant over other things along that line. I adored the crew I worked with. The crew loved me. I was young and I was very naïve and I was very modest. It was obvious that I wasn't a runaround or anything. And so there were quite a few people who didn't quite take to this, particularly when Clark Gable gave me a car. I used to ride a bicycle, so Clark and a bunch of the chorus kids got together and presented me with this little roadster decorated with ribbon to drive on the lot or anywhere I'd want.

There was a party I went to once. I'm going back now to '36 or '37. It was my first Hollywood party and I think it was my last. Again it was Mr. Mayer, who was charming. I was working on the set with Mr. Del Ruth, trying hard to do what I was supposed to do. One day I was walking to the commissary and Mr. L. B. Mayer beckoned to me and said, "Miss Powell, may I see you for a moment?" I was always trying to tell him that I'm on my lunch hour and I had to be back on the set at a certain time. And he was always reminding me that he pushed all the buttons there and that if he wanted to keep me beyond lunch hour, that was fine. So he said to me, "I'm going to take you to the Mayfair dance this Saturday night." The Mayfair dance used to be held out here once a year at the Beverly Wilshire Hotel. It was a very big shindig. Now, up to this point in my life, believe it or not, I had never been to a dance or out with an evening gown and all that, because I'd just worked. So I said back to Mr. Mayer, "I'm sorry, but I can't go." He said, "My dear child, I want to introduce you to Joan Crawford, to Marlene Dietrich, to Norma Shearer and all the big stars" ('cause I hadn't signed a contract yet). Well, I didn't know what to say, I was so young—I was twenty-two, but I was like thirteen. And I said, "Well, I'll have to ask my mother." Now, can you imagine saying this to Mr. Mayer? I'd heard things about Mr. Mayer and, well, I wasn't about to go out with him.

Married! So he said, "Very well, call your mother." I called my mother and it happened that Johnny Hyde, my agent, was with her at the hotel. And I'm trying to give her the high sign over the phone. "Mother, I'm up in Mr. Mayer's office and he wants to take me to the Mayfair dance." I'm trying to get her to help me give him an answer, and he is just sitting there dying, laughing inside. So Johnny Hyde gets on the phone and says, "Look, Ellie, it's perfectly all right. If you feel out of place or anything happens, you can always excuse yourself to go to the powder room, get in the elevator and leave." So I said to Mr. Mayer, "All right, but I don't have a gown or anything." So he takes me by the hand down to Adrian's and picks out a satin gown with straps. And a beautiful white fox—long, right to the heel. *A la* Jean Harlow type of thing. So I'm all set.

Now, when I first went into the commissary day after day for lunch, Mr. Mayer used to have as his specialty a delicious chicken soup—'cause at one time Mr. Mayer was a butcher and his soups were exquisite. And all I could eat on dance days was a liquid. I used to go in there and a very good-looking fellow would come up to me day after day and say, "Aren't you the new girl?" and "Well, may I take you to lunch?" Finally, I said, "I'm very busy. Don't bother me. Please go away." This is the gentleman that picked me up the night of the party! Mr. Mayer sent some orchids—to the new member of his "family." So I'm a little put out. We go, there's Mr. Mayer, there's everybody cocktailing around. He's no more with me than with the man in the moon. Anyway, we go into the ballroom and there's Norma Shearer, Harlow, Crawford, everybody. I'm sitting in the middle with this man. Across the table from me is a man that I don't know. He kept taking his paper hat, making little spitballs, dunking them in his glass of water and throwing them around the room so they landed on the women's bosoms. It seemed so childish to me. The man was Howard Hughes. You must remember that here was a girl so dedicated and self-disciplined that any kind of playing, of fun-making or silliness like practical jokes—pulling the chair out when somebody sat down—was just too infantile.

So Mr. Mayer suddenly comes down just as I started to eat my food and stands at my chair. He said, "Miss Powell, aren't you going to ask me to dance?" So Miss Powell, in her obvious voice, said, "Mr. Mayer, in my whole life I have never asked a gentleman to dance. And I don't intend to start now." He said, "Do you see Miss Shearer up there and Joan Crawford? They literally begged me to dance with them." I said, "Well, that's fine. But if you want to dance with me, you ask me." So then, in a very sarcastic manner, he bowed. "May I please have this dance?" And I said, "I'm charmed" and got up and danced. Mr. Mayer was very much the exhibitionist on the dance floor. He liked to dance on the outer edge. And at that time the conga was in, and the tango— and the minute the orchestra saw him, they played what he wanted anyway. So we're dipping and going around and I'm getting a great big lecture and sermon on Crawford—Joan and I have often talked about it since—how she came to the studio as Lucille Le Sueur and was so heavy and bound her legs and did this and that. In the meantime they'd been feeding me milkshakes on the set, trying to get some skin on me—I was so thin from working and not eating properly.

Suddenly this gentleman dancing nearby with a young lady stopped very dramatically and said, "L.B., I *must* dance with this fascinating, charming creature!" So Mr. Mayer introduced me—it was Fredric March, who was doing a film at Metro at that time. We exchanged partners, and he is dancing with me, pulling me toward him. I had a dress on that had a low back and he had his hand about there, and it went a little lower and a little lower. He stops very dramatically and says, "Miss Powell, may I ask you a personal question?" I said, "Well, that depends." He said, "Are you wearing a girdle?" Well, I was kinda shocked, I thought he was going to ask me how old I was. I looked right at him and I said, "No, I'm not wearing no girdle." And he said, "You want me just to dance?" And I said, "Just dance." And today, when he and I meet, it's a passing gag with us because he'll say, "Hi, Ellie! Just dance, just dance!"

We got back to the table and, instead of my squab being there, there's a dish with all bones! So I looked over and Mr. Howard Hughes said, "I'm terribly sorry, Miss Powell, I had to play a gag on someone. Allow me to get you another plate." By this time I was thoroughly disgusted. Mr. Hughes disappeared somewhere—like he is now! Mr. Mayer suddenly decides, now that it's thinning out and people are leaving, that he's going to go to the Clover Club, which is on Sunset, *the* place for gambling. I excused myself and went to the powder room to phone my mother. I said, "Mr. Mayer is going to go to the Clover Club. I've only had a parfait and Mr. Mayer's going to get a nice steak. I'm fine and I can take care of myself. Don't worry."

Now, when we all arrive at the Clover Club, it's 1:30 in the morning. Mr. Mayer orders this steak for everybody. He mixes his own very seasoned sauce, spreads it all over everyone's steak. I didn't particularly go for very highly spiced food, so I tried to get it off the steak. Now, this'll show you how dumb I was. Mr. Mayer dances with me a lot and lectures a lot. Finally, he sits down. Now, I didn't eat too much of the steak, but I have a cup of coffee there. Mr. Mayer—or so it appeared to me at the time—sort of glanced around, took something from his pocket, slipped it into my coffee. I'm ashamed to say I thought I was being drugged!

So I don't touch the coffee. And he says, "Drink your coffee, drink your coffee." Well, I had never heard of saccharin in my life. I didn't know it was a derivative of sugar, and I'd have thought it was dope anyway. So I said, "Mr. Mayer, what have you put in my coffee?" As though he's gonna tell me if he did! He said, "My dear child, that's saccharin. Sugar! To keep you thin!" I said, "I've been trying to tell you all evening they've been feeding me milkshakes on the set!"

It gets time to go home and Mr. Mayer starts to pull the chair out. I sat right there and said, "No, Mr. Mayer, I'm very sorry, but where I come from—Springfield, Massachusetts—it's the fella that picks me up that brings me home." Because in my mind I was scared of being in his car because if I thought that was dope, how was I to know what was going to go on later? And Mr. Mayer didn't like that one bit, I knew. And I said to my original escort if he wouldn't mind taking me home. When we got in the car, he starts to sit real close and put the arm around and all. I said, "Now, you just sit over there and I'll sit over here, and when I get out, there's no need to open the door for me. I've had a most enlightening evening, believe me." I got out and went upstairs, where my mother made me scrambled eggs because I was starved. I don't think I went to another big party like that since.

In the long run I gained Mr. Mayer's great respect. Later in life, when I went into the religious show which I did on TV, Mr. Mayer became one of my greatest fans. If I had a choice between a dancing career and religious and spiritual work, it would be kinda hard to choose between the two. The saying that sums up the philosophy of my whole life is: "What we are is God's gift to us. What we become is our gift to God." When I was a dancer at MGM studios, if someone with a little crystal ball had come to me and said, "Miss Powell, I see you on a new invention called television, which will be radio with pictures, and you are going to receive five Emmy awards for religious programs," I would have looked at this person and thought they'd better get the little white man to take him off. But it happened—as much of an accident as getting into pictures.

1971

ARLETTY

A RLETTY IS FRENCH. Arletty is eighty-six. Beautiful Arletty with the large, wide-apart, clear-seeing eyes is blind. Or as good as. Arletty drapes the couch like an elegant odalisque in the small living room of her high-rise apartment in a fashionable arrondissement of Paris. When she moves, to reach for your hand, to touch your face, to raise a glass of champagne in a parting toast, she moves like a cat: feline, purring, able to see in the dark. Arletty is Garance. "You are so beautiful," the love-fevered Deburau tells her. "I am not beautiful. I am alive, that's all." "You are the most alive of all. I will never forget tonight, and the light of your eyes." "Oh, the light of my eyes. Just a little flicker like everyone else." Jacques Prévert, the great French screenwriter and poet, wrote this exchange between her and Jean-Louis Barrault in *Les Enfants du Paradis*. Prévert could write like this because he knew that in Arletty the common became the rare. She is matter-of-fact about miracles.

Arletty of the many loves lives alone. Arletty is an anarchist. "A country with no anarchists is a finished country, and I am an anarchist, but an unconditional one. I have never voted in my life, but I believe that one should contribute by doing whatever one can do as well as possible. I admit I'm chauvinistic about the French mind."

The long, black, lustrous hair is now a short, silky, white cap; the oval of her face, a little blurred; but the nose is as sharp, the lips are as mobile, her smile is as filling, and when she laughs, it's like a shock of cold water. Bracing. This is no little old lady. "Madame, you are beautiful." And though, because I sat away from the window, my back against the wall, she really couldn't see me, she smiled. An accident with eye drops twenty years ago virtually blinded her. A bit of light returned. She husbands every bit of it and sits facing the solid block of sunlight framed by the window. She can see the contours, the shape of things. If you are smiling, she can sense it, but she cannot see details. They are a blur. She cannot read and refuses to go to the theater because that makes her too sad. It's all blurred. She will not do films or be filmed, for she fears the bright electric lights will steal the little that remains of her sight. Now she looks directly at my shadow among the shadows and laughs. The laugh comes from the depths of a woman who has known what it is to hear her own death sentence delivered by her own countrymen, and to have outlived her judges.

"People believe that I am as much a Parisienne as the Eiffel Tower. But, in fact, I was born at Courbevoie. This is the district which Maupassant took for the setting of his story 'Mont-Oriol,' and I was given the name of his heroine—Arlette. So that was how I began life, born Arlette Bathiat, at 33 rue de Paris, Courbevoie."

When she was still a very young woman, she modeled clothes briefly for the legendary French designer Paul Poiret. She became an artist's model and a popular pinup. "I was thin before it was the fashion." As a friend she sat for some of the most famous painters of her age—Braque, Matisse, Modigliani and very often for Van Dongen.

Like all very strong individuals of either sex, she has been linked with women as well as men. Discreetly I alluded to it. She either misunderstood when my question was translated to her or she chose to ignore the implication: she did not enlighten me. All she would say was, "What women do between them, what men do between them, that is their right. That is their business."

It was also said of Arletty, more with affection than with anything else, that her timing was never good when it came to her private life. Her most (in)famous love affair took place during the Occupation when she fell in love with an officer of the occupying German army. As a result, her life was proscribed by the Free French, and when Paris was liberated, she was placed under arrest and kept in prison for three months with a death sentence over her head, guarded by a man who had murdered his wife, before at last she was released without ever having come to a trial. Arletty's comment on that gray episode in her life was to say that "Nobody had informed me that love was a crime." She had loved a German. So what? She shrugs. "Maybe now," she says, smiling enigmatically, "women should worry about falling in love with Americans. Who knows on whose side we'll be in the next war?" Disarming—so final that you can't keep on about it for further details. It should be added that she could have fled Paris before the liberation; that her friend Jacques Prévert, the director Marcel Carné and everybody else she worked with knew of her affair. It had been no secret in Paris. And there were several well-known Jewish artists working in France during that time, such as Les Enfants' composer Joseph Kosma or its brilliant set-designer Alexandre Trauner (though working under assumed names), and there was no problem between them and her, nor between them and the Germans. She was no quisling. She was a scapegoat. Of all the many stories about Paris during the war, the truth would probably be one of the strangest. Arletty's story is one of those truths.

After her release she found it difficult to get work for a number of years. Films begun were never finished. Unlike several other French stars tarred by the same brush, such as the younger Danielle Darrieux, Arletty was too old by the time her career was reactivated to be offered the sort of chances that would help her regain that moment of glory on the screen. They had stolen her momentum. From now on, movies could offer her little more than character roles. One of

Arletty, photographed by G. F. Aldo for *Les Visiteurs du Soir* (France, 1942)

her last screen appearances was in Darryl F. Zanuck's all-star World War II epic, *The Longest Day* (1962).*

Arletty bears no grudges. Her guard, her protection is her truth, her life, her survival. When anything once whispered about her fades back into the void, Arletty through Garance will remain.

A: Prévert saw certain things in me that may not always be there, and he put them into Garance. I was handed a finished screenplay, without ever discussing it. I had made *Les Visiteurs du Soir* before, and Prévert had also tailored my role in it to my personality, a full, complete role.

JK: But no other actress could have played Garance. Could Maria Casares? Or Madeleine Sologne? It was more than a good role, it was almost autobiographical.

A: When I first read the screenplay, I already saw every image in the film. There was nothing left but to shoot it. There's a story Barrault likes to tell everybody: he was shorter than I and had to be on my level for a kissing scene. He had to stand on a box. It took one and a half hours to prepare the shot. I was exhausted. And my line was *"C'est tellement simple l'amour."* [Love is so simple.] Prévert had watched me for ten years on the stage before he wrote for me. I did mostly theater at the time.

JK: And the story was suggested to Prévert by Barrault?

A: There was a real Deburau, a famous mime. Barrault suggested that Prévert write a film about him, and that was it: Prévert was off and running.

JK: Did they realize the film would be as epic as it turned out to be? As extraordinary? As big?

A: Oh, yes, immediately. A big picture.

JK: Did the Occupation pose any problems during the preparation?

A: The American landing interrupted the shooting of *Les Enfants du Paradis*. We were all afraid, and with reason, that the film wouldn't be completed. We didn't know how it would turn out. Robert Le Vigan was playing the Pierre Renoir role, and he escaped to Germany. I encouraged the others. I wasn't scared myself, it's not in my nature. The shooting continued in the South of France.

JK: Did Le Vigan ask you to flee with him?

---

*She plays a patriotic Frenchwoman who helps the Resistance in the days leading up to the Normandy invasion.

A: He had no authority over me. Bad actor. He was a friend of Céline's and he was risking his life. There is a line from Racine: "The friendship of a great man is a misdeed of God . . . *L'amitié d'un grand homme c'est un méfait de Dieu*."*

JK: But were you or Marcel Carné or Prévert aware that the film was a critique of France during the Occupation?

A: Prévert couldn't have said such things to the Paris of the '40s, so he set the story in the 19th century. Same thing with *Les Visiteurs du Soir,* which he set in the Middle Ages. That was very sly, very smart of him. The censors were the last to read the script. They gave permission right away. Not a cut. Nothing.

JK: Did the French public understand?

A: A certain sophisticated sector did. After twenty years on stage, I had very good parts in films. *Le Jour Se Lève, Hôtel du Nord.* I must admit that *Hôtel du Nord,* which really started my major parts in films, is one of my favorite roles of all time. I had gained something of a reputation for undressing in *Hôtel du Nord* by the manipulation of the zip fastener on my dress. I went even further in *Le Jour Se Lève,* where for several seconds I was entirely nude. Then, of course, I had the Prévert films: *Les Visiteurs du Soir* and then *Les Enfants du Paradis.* It was a summit. After the war there was a great deal of jealousy, as in every profession. Success is not easily forgiven. There is a joke about two actors. One says of the other, "He's got talent and I haven't. It's got to change." I was forbidden to work for three years. Before, I did mostly revues and boulevard comedies—light, amusing things. When I returned to work in 1950, I returned as a tragedienne. I played in *A Streetcar Named Desire, Orpheus Descending,* Brendan Behan's *The Hostage.* I was enriched by the experience. I could have never played such parts before. Tennessee Williams came with La Magnani to see *Orpheus Descending.* She played on the screen the part I played on the stage. She had hands of such a beauty! She smoked with such elegance!†

JK: In *Les Enfants du Paradis* you played a Frenchwoman: wise, tolerant, the way the world came to think of the essence of a Frenchwoman.

*Le Vigan fled first to Germany and from there to Argentina, where he made several movies and died without ever returning to France. Céline wrote a famous book about their flight from château to château.

†Even five years later the French were still sensitive about their wartime idols. When Arletty played Blanche Du Bois, there was trouble with Blanche's last-act curtain line: "If I had said, '*J'ai toujours . . .* I have always relied on the kindness of strangers,' people would have thrown tomatoes at me." In translation, the word "stranger" would have become "*étranger,*" which also means "foreigner." "So I asked Cocteau to change the line, which now became 'I have always relied on the kindness of unknown people. . . . *J'ai toujours dépendu de la gentillesse des inconnus.*'" Arletty scored a great personal triumph.

A: . . . The spirit of a woman. Garance is such a complete woman. I think any actress would say the same. There is such poetry in that part, and if I am a symbol today, I owe it entirely to the great poets who asked me to work for them. Prévert never did other than give himself entirely. There is not another like him. All his actors adored him. Jeanson too was a marvelous man. They were poets, not film producers. Today what is missing is the writers.

JK: Your lover was a German. Was that the sole reason for your punishment at the Liberation?

A: Absolutely. Absolutely. If there had been something else, do you think I would have been given those roles?

JK: Did you meet this man when you were making films in Germany in 1932? Was he in the movies?

A: Oh, no. He was a writer who became Germany's Ambassador to the Congo. He drowned in Zaïre in 1960. His name was Hans Sohring. He wrote a book called *Lindbergh* on the Lindbergh baby kidnap case. It wasn't bad. He dedicated it to me. He also dedicated another book to me, *Cordelia*.

JK: Was it not considered dangerous to go with a German during the Occupation? Did Prévert or anyone try to warn you?

A: Prévert wouldn't. If he had disapproved, he wouldn't have given me the roles in both films. No one minded. Everybody, from the biggest actress to the smallest, was seeing Germans.

   Raimu and I were condemned to death on the same day; and when someone asked me how I felt, I replied, "Neither hot nor cold." It was true. I never tried to hide my liaison, never. But it so happens that I could well have known that German before the war and then what would I have been supposed to do? Pretend I'd never seen him before and send him away? They condemned me to death, but they didn't know what to do with me. I didn't give a damn. I was never tried, there never was a decision. I could have smeared a lot of people. I could have said, "You too were there."

JK: And Jewish technicians were working in French films all those years? How was that possible with the Germans?

A: They changed their names, that was all. They were safe, at least inside the studio. Germans were not around the studios. There was Continental, a German company, and every French actor worked for it during the Occupation. I didn't, not because they were Germans but because they never offered me a good script.

JK: Were you shocked that your fellow Frenchmen would do such a thing to you?

A: It could have happened anywhere. I was not shocked. I hate no one. I'm not a complete woman: there is no hate in me. I felt complete indifference toward those people who judged me, and now they are all dead, every one of them has died tragically. And the others who betrayed me? I know them well, I know who they are, but they are the ones who feel uncomfortable, not me. Their behavior was very human, but I don't feel bitter about it, and today they are much unhappier than I am.

JK: Did you know the story of what happened to Harry Baur?

A: He was a very good friend before the war. I was never asked to go to Berlin to work there. Everyone saw them* in the newsreels, going off to meet Hitler.

JK: Irony and hypocrisy. Baur was Jewish, and he had no problems while he made this German film *Symphony Eines Lebens*. It was when he finished it and came back that someone denounced him in Paris.

A: I was not aware of this fact, but everyone knew he was Jewish. He never hid the fact.

JK: Did you ever receive an offer from Hollywood?

A: Before the war, just before the Germans arrived, as did Gabin and others. But I would never leave my country, especially in wartime. When I had my troubles after the war, I could have left and I didn't. I'd rather be killed in France.

JK: Do you remember what studio sent for you?

A: Fox, I would say. No specific role, just a contract.

JK: Like Annabella, Simone Simon . . .

A: Like Gabin.

JK: What G. W. Pabst did for Louise Brooks, or Josef von Sternberg for Marlene Dietrich, Prévert did for you. He wrote a role utilizing everything you did, he wrote lines for your gestures. I can see you arranging your stockings as you say them.

A: He saw me on stage for twenty years. Prévert never paid me compliments about my legs, it was a spiritual sympathy. It wasn't physical love, it was love for the role.

JK: A great collaboration. Did you ever ask for a role?

A: Never. They were brought to me on a silver plate. I never made an effort.

JK: You were born and just like a river you keep on flowing.

*Françoise Rosay, Darrieux, Corinne Luchaire, Pierre Fresnay, etc.

A: And so much the worse if there are storms. The world doesn't get better, it just goes on, like the Seine, which flows into the sea and never returns. I believe that as one is born with fingers, so one is born with a philosophy, and mine has always been to observe and to accept whatever came my way. People behave well, people behave badly, but in the end nothing really matters. There is love, there is great affection, there is tenderness, and it all ebbs away with the river.

JK: Were you friendly with other actresses?

A: I always admired members of my profession, my fellow performers. But I'm a loner. I have always been the cat that walks alone. I became independent at a very young age, and I have always respected the independence of others. I can't say marriage has been one of my temptations, I have always preferred to be independent, even if it has meant facing problems on my own. I am not afraid to be alone. In the business, I had no special preference. In life, since I was three, I've always preferred little boys to little girls. I like humanity in general, not just men and women. Men are simpler, women have all kinds of little weapons, myself included. There's an ambiguity in me, a rather male side.

JK: People came to you because they liked the way you walked.

A: I've met people on the street who stopped me and put me on the stage.

JK: Is that true? Louise Brooks and Lil Dagover told me the same thing: someone saw them on the street and said, "You—you must be on the stage." Did anyone ever try to make you a star before Carné and Prévert?

A: For twenty years playwrights wrote for me, but I never went ringing at people's doors. I would have never done anything against my will. I had an agent to prepare the contracts, but people usually came to me directly when I was playing on stage.

JK: You started your film career rather late [in 1931 she was thirty-three], which is rather unique. Usually at that age, big careers are over. The camera is too close.

A: Yes, women at that age either retire or become grandmothers.

JK: Were you very conscious of your appearance on the screen?

A: Yes, I never let myself go to pot, out of discipline and respect for my profession. I wasn't worried about wrinkles. I grant a great importance to the soul, but I wasn't about to cry because of three or four wrinkles.

JK: Did you see yourself as a great beauty?

A: Not at all. If I had had a choice at birth, I would have chosen another face. Everyone is twenty once, but I never felt the need to boast about being young.

And what are today's twenty-year-olds going to do when they are twenty-five and written off as old and useless by the next generation coming up? They use words, but they don't act. Theories are not good enough. They must show that they have hands and shoulders and muscles and that they can make something. It's too easy to say you don't accept. I want to see another Pasteur or another Blériot.

JK: You admire writers. Did you like actresses as well? Like Mistinguett or Lucienne Boyer? Any idols?

A: Mistinguett was a friend, so was Maurice Chevalier. I admired them, but didn't copy them. I didn't like my face, but I couldn't think of another. I never had a picture of myself at home. I posed for Braque, Matisse and many times for Van Dongen. I didn't like myself on the screen. I saw the rushes every night because it was part of the work. There are actors who watch themselves so much I think they become incapable of change. *That's my opinion* [in English].

JK: You're now speaking English. Do you speak German?

A: I can say *Ja* and *Nein*. I would have been better off if I had only learned to say *Nein*. [She laughs.]

JK: You don't think you were beautiful? Then who was?

A: Garbo was the most beautiful. She had an antique look. As for spirit, that's another story.

JK: Did you go to the movies often? What did you like?

A: I tried to learn from them. I liked certain American and German actors. But I only went to see good pictures, not the silly ones. [She sounds *very* serious saying this.] I liked Joan Crawford's intelligence and acting. And Marie Dressler. Marlene Dietrich was amusing, very sophisticated. I usually watched the acting rather than faces. Same with the theater. I went to see the actors, but also the spirit and quality of the playwrights.

JK: Did anyone help you on the way up?

A: I made myself, all by myself. From *café chantant* to *chansonniers* to the Opéra to the Comédie-Française, I watched everything. Actors always go to see what other actors do. One has to know one's *métier*. I never had a teacher. I learned through the soles of my feet, standing on stage. I will not go into all the details of the parts I played. It went the usual way, sometimes good and sometimes not so good. I sang, I danced; now I played in a farce, now in a tragedy; some of my roles I liked. I especially liked *chansonniers* for fun. I also read a lot. I taught myself, as I wrote in my book.* My father was a

* Her published autobiography, provocatively called *La Défense*. She took the title from the statue of the same name commemorating the struggle of the Paris Communards in 1871. The statue is

miner, my mother was a seamstress. They would never prevent me from going on the stage, but they died young, without ever having seen me perform. I don't think they would have been impressed. My brother saw me in the movies.

JK: Were you play-acting already as a little girl?

A: I didn't stay by myself in a corner when I was a little girl. I already wanted contact with everything. I was inquisitive. I belonged to others. I had the spirit of observation. When I played with dolls, I performed operations on them. I set up my own hospital, laying my dolls in line and covering them with a sheet. Then I made my rounds, looking at the numbered ticket which I had attached to each one, and nursed them through every possible illness.

JK: Did you cut off their arms and legs?

A [she laughs]: My mother would scold me. She said I was a wicked girl and God would punish me. I never believed that, because all the doctors and nurses seemed to get by all right. I let life pass. If someone offered me another chance, I think I would do the same things all over. In any case, I'd do as I like, even if I left my head behind in the bargain. One regret, though: not having loved enough those who loved me. I don't mean physically, but from the heart.

JK: You don't strike me as lonely or sad, as some articles say.

A: I'm not. That's a certain press. Once I was reproached for doing the opposite. Now I see many people, different sorts of people, high and low. It enriches me. Perhaps not so much anymore because of my infirmity.

JK: Was it an accident with some eye drops? You seem very healthy.

A: It would have happened just the same. I come from good stock, peasant stock on one side of the family. Lots of willpower. I used to be a visual person. Now I have learned to listen.

JK: Do you believe people were more unique when you were young?

A: I don't think so. They were a different type.

JK: Did you visit the United States?

A: The first time I went to the States was before the war, for my own pleasure. No one knew me then, I was mainly a stage actress. We were dazzled, my

---

located in her birthplace of Courbevoie. She gives no explanation for a title that conveys a *double-entendre,* other than the fact that it symbolized her working-class roots. Had she intended to refer to her life later on, she says, she would have called it *L'Attaque* because she is a fighter. "I have never needed to defend myself."

friends and I. Later on I returned with René Clair in 1954 or '55. A promotion trip. I went to present *Maxime*. I remember a joke now. What do women say after making love? The Englishwoman says, "You must despise me." The Slav says, "You've had my body, but you'll never have my soul." The American woman says, "May I have your name?" The Frenchwoman says, "Where do we go for lunch?"

JK: How did you find Michèle Morgan, who starred in *Maxime*?

A: She loves herself, no doubt about that. She had the cult of herself. I must admit people liked her in her time.

JK: Was it Prévert or Carné who said you never had a protector, someone to look after you and provide for you?

A: It's true. *No protector* [she says this in English]. The first man I loved was killed in the First War. I never wanted to marry afterwards. I led a free life, but I never wanted to marry. I'm against all wars, especially holy wars. I would never have any children. I didn't want to mourn for them if they died in a war. It's nothing to do with religion, it's a mother's viewpoint. I was raised by an uncle who thought someday I would become a nun, but when I was four I had already stopped believing. I was born an atheist. There are no surprises left. Men walked on the moon and Jules Verne had dreamed of it long before. The one thing left that would surprise me would be if someone discovered a cure for cancer. I don't believe in another life. We're all born without God. Religion is education. You're told that you'll go to heaven. I knew a bishop and he never reproached me for being an atheist. He was later on murdered in Rome. Faith was invented for men who needed a goal, had to be taught a direction.

JK: You must have been an extraordinary child.

A: I was never a marvel at school. The only subjects which I liked were history and arithmetic. It is well known in France that the Auvergnats have good heads for figures, so I could not very well go wrong in math.

I was never beaten. I was free to say what I wanted. My folks were suburban working-class, but they were imaginative. They laughed when I said things, they would say, "What a funny little girl!" I used to say, "Look at that lobster; its eyes are so well made." A sunrise is also quite a feat. When I had my house in Brittany, I used to tell my guests, "Let's get up early and watch the sun rise." Which we did. With adoration.

I put a lock on my heart. As a child I never wept. I could console those who wept, but I used to say, "Look at me, I don't cry." It was an attitude, out of principle. To begin with, I don't like actresses who cry on stage. Emotion should come from the heart, not through some piss coming out of one's eyes. And since I never cried, I was never beaten. I told my parents, "You can beat me, but it won't do a thing." They accepted me as I accepted others. I have women friends who believe in heaven, who go to church. I too had a religious upbringing. To please them, not to please myself. It meant nothing to me.

I used to read a lot. I read the philosophers when I was young. I would look at things. Some people would read mystery novels instead of looking around. I loved La Fontaine, he's the best of the classics, he said it all. I recently read somewhere that Napoleon, at Erfurt, was receiving the Czar, the Khedive of Turkey, bishops, etc., and there was also Goethe among the guests. Napoleon stood before him and said, "Here's a man." Probably the truest thing he ever said.

JK: One of the best presents I ever received was Heinrich Mann's biography of Henry IV.

A: My favorite king. He was in the arms of his mistress, the beautiful Gabrielle d'Estée, when the Paris populace rose to demand that he become a Catholic. "Get up, get up," she said. "Paris is well worth a mass." And as he was getting dressed, she added, "Tomorrow they will credit *you* with the line."

JK: Who are your favorite authors?

A: Poets mostly. I read Baudelaire, Verlaine, Rimbaud among the moderns. I was a very good friend of Céline, because he was born in Courbevoie like me. I didn't know him in Courbevoie. I met him much later, in '42 or '43. To me, *Voyage to the End of Night* is a masterpiece. In fact, I made a recording reading from Céline. I also knew Jouandeau, who died recently. I was onstage around 1930 when we met. He was with the Surrealists. I also knew Breton. Dali and I never liked each other: he was very political and I didn't share his ideas. Otherwise, he was very bright. Always on. I like his drawings, though.

Matisse drew my portrait around 1950. He was near death then. Then Braque chose me as a model for a documentary they made about him, around '49. He painted me through the whole film.

I posed for these painters out of friendship. When I was a professional model, I would get paid: I was very slim at eighteen. There weren't many models then, not like now. Poiret hired me as a mannequin on the advice of some friends, but I didn't stay very long. Later he designed for me onstage.

There were people I admired. I used to question Raimu. We talked shop, that was all. I was a product of spontaneous generation. I didn't look at the bad ones, only at the good ones. I remained curious all my life, about animals even. You can't live without admiring someone or something.

JK: You prefer poets to novelists.

A: Poets first, but I also admire Balzac. Talk of intelligence!

JK: But no contemporary writers?

A: I didn't like Proust. I met him in his *salon* when he was sick. An actress friend of his, I can't tell you her name, brought me to see him. She was then going with Léon-Pierre Quint, who was to become Proust's biographer. Of course I read Proust before I decided I didn't like him.

I adore Colette. She's like God to me: as a woman, as a writer, as a critic. Her theater writings are extraordinary. I was close to her. After her death I was asked to do *Chéri,* but I didn't like the character of Léa: she's too bourgeoise. I liked the role of Chéri better: in real life it was modeled on the son of Colette's husband. I once asked Céline his opinion of Colette, and he replied, "Colette is a gentleman." Oh, she was a *gourmande.* She liked to take care of things. She was hungry for life.

JK: In the '20s your career would have progressed faster . . .

A: It wasn't stationary, if that's what you mean. . . . In Paris, in the '20s, I used to live in hotels. I moved often. I love to live in a hotel. It is so simple, everything is done for you. It's fabulous for someone who plays in the theater. We have to worry about nothing. There are a lot of people who have financial independence and who prefer living in a hotel. Later I had my "palace" period. I was at the Crillon and the Georges V. In 1940 and '41 at the Lancaster, a superb hotel. Then in 1944 I was in a "boarding school" [she so describes her time in prison]. On my departure from the "boarding school," since 1946 I stayed three years at the Plaza Athénée. There weren't many regular women guests like myself staying there, unless they were foreign actresses. But being a Parisienne and living there, in a *"grande palace,"* that's something! And it's wonderful when you come out from the theater; all you had to do was go to bed!

JK: Were revues like burlesque?

A: No. You have nothing like revues. One of them was called *Plus ça change* and it was even political. It dealt with Clemenceau, De Gaulle, etc. Marguerite Moreno also played in Rip's revues. Poiret dressed me for a sketch about Proust: it was in blue taffeta, *très chic,* a *casquette.* I just walked across the stage—I can't do it now, I'm too tired—and said, *"Mais* Proust, *mon Dieu!"*(?) That was the Rip style. And songs too. And a sketch about French queens through history. I played Isabelle de Bavière, Marie Antoinette . . . And courtesans like Du Barry. When Van Dongen painted my picture in '32, which was shown at the Salon . . . [too far from the mike] . . . he called it *La Belle Poule.*

JK: There were no nudes, like at the Tabarin.

A: Never, it was a family audience. I sang, but couldn't dance very well. That's why Mistinguett liked me, because I didn't dance well. I had dancing partners who made me look good.

JK: What was the reason for Mistinguett's success?

A: Talent. Work. She had the voice of a *gavroche,* a street urchin.

JK: Like Piaf? [Arletty didn't like Piaf.]

A: If I didn't dance well, Piaf didn't dance at all. I once did an impression of Piaf onstage—not out of affection.

JK: What made Josephine Baker so successful in France?

A: She was one of the first black women we had seen on stage. A beautiful body, a ravishing voice.

JK: Was your role in Sacha Guitry's film *Pearls of the Crown* a takeoff on Baker?

A: Oh, no, that was the Queen of Abyssinia. I was the Black Pearl.

JK: Why did you write your memoirs?

A: To kill time. I didn't want to explain anything. I worked in movies to make money so that I could afford to work in the theater, which I loved. The stage didn't pay as well; it was a luxury. But from talkies on, actors got paid well in the movies. I never worked in silent movies, and I was asked once or twice. I liked Max Linder: he was marvelous. Chaplin must have studied him.

JK: Buster Keaton had your kind of looks.

A [she laughs]: I went to see him when he was performing at the Médrano Circus. No one recognized his genius: it was near the end of his career, he had no money. I told him how much I admired him. In my opinion, he was a very important actor. It was a long time since people had seen his films here; it must have been around '49 or '50, after the war.

JK: You first came to America in '39. But you never wanted to stay in America?

A: I never felt like staying. If you're not as fluent in another language as you are in your own, you better not play in that language. Look at Chevalier—Americans liked his Parisian accent. You lose your quality. Mistinguett never tried. Of course if there had been someone like Prévert or Rip to write your material, I would have learned American.

JK: Mostly French actresses didn't make it in American films. Morgan, Ketti Gallian, Annabella, Simone Simon, Mireille Balin . . .

A: They didn't cross over in another language, they lost their personality. Only Chevalier . . . and Boyer, who remained *the* French actor.

JK: The image of the world-weary romantic, for Americans. Maybe the reason you didn't like yourself in your early films was because they didn't photograph you well. Roger Hubert* was the first to light and photograph you beautifully.

A: He was the one who best captured my face. And also Carl Hoffmann [the cinematographer] on *La Guerre des Valses,* in Germany. Do you know that film? [She hums Strauss.] Do you know Berger [Ludwig Berger was a German director]? He thought [Fernand] Gravey and I were making fun of him in French; we weren't really. He didn't know French very well, and he kept telling us, "*Ironique, ironique*" [in French].

JK: I liked those multilingual versions with Willy Fritsch and Henri Garat exchanging roles for the different versions.

A: You're right. Berger's strong point was music.

JK: What was Germany like in those days? Very alive? Exciting?

A: Fun. We stayed at the Pension Impériale, on the Kurfürstendam. You could feel the war getting closer. It must have been around 1932 or 1933. The ambiance was incredible. Little kids came to the studio dressed in Nazi uniforms. The Jews were already leaving. Berger only thought of getting out. I loved Berlin. Everything was done with such ease.

JK: How were the various versions made?

A: One after the other, in the same sets. First in German, then in French. There were no arguments, no bother. In the evening we went nightclubbing. There were many Frenchmen dressed as women. One was named Muguette: they all had names like flowers. You could see homosexuals with beards and their boyfriends. It was very amusing, Berlin nightlife. There is an erotic climate in Berlin. Even men who were not homosexual would become somewhat homosexual [*un peu pédéraste*] if they stayed long enough in Berlin.

JK: And women?

A: I don't think so.

JK: Women are more bourgeois.

A: I did another film there besides *La Guerre des Valses,* with Reinhold Schunzel [*La Belle Aventure*] . . .

JK: With Käthe von Nagy?

A: No, not with Käthe de Nagy. Schunzel went to America later. I met Renate Müller in Salzburg at Max Reinhardt's house, which was magnificent.†

---

*He was one of the best cinematographers working in French films of the '30s (*Les Visiteurs du Soir; Fanny; Pension Mimosa; Jenny; Les Enfants du Paradis; La Chienne*).

†Müller was probably one of Germany's most popular stars. At the height of her career she killed herself by leaping from a window, torn apart by official pressure to separate from her Jewish doctor lover.

JK: And did you know Dietrich?

A: I had lunch with Marlene Dietrich in the '30s, with mutual friends, the actress Danièle Parola and her husband, an actor who had been in Valentino films and who then became a producer. He was with Columbia.

JK: What was filmmaking like in the Berlin studios?

A: There were extraordinary dressers working with Berger, very professional and charming. Everything interested me there. Käthe de Nagy was going with Goebbels. They were madly in love. I didn't see them together, I didn't give them away, if that's what you mean.

JK: Goebbels loved Zarah Leander too, and Camilla Horn. He liked women.

A: That's not a defect.

JK: He liked movie stars. That's why he created a Garbo for German audiences, Zarah Leander.

A: I have a snapshot of us together. I met her during the Occupation in Paris at a big party given by Continental. There was Georges Simenon, Danielle Darrieux, Cravenne, the director, all sorts of Japanese. . . . We liked her in France during the war.

JK: You played often with Michel Simon.

A: I was the only actress who scared him. He was a masochist. He would scare everyone on the set but me. He could see that I wasn't afraid. One word from me and he was hidden underground. Producers wanted us to have big quarrels, but I didn't go for it.* He would hide in a cupboard, in *Fric-Frac,* and I would order him to come out. "Will you come out of there?" [Very imperious.] My role allowed me to, and he would come out and make little faces at the audience, as if saying, See how she treats me? And I would tell him, "Stop making faces or you'll pay for it!" I wasn't about to play games all the time.

JK: Men are rather short in France. Weren't you considered too tall?

A: I was right under the line, because Mary Marquet was too tall. The girl who plays with Jean-Pierre Cassel is too tall, but she has talent. What's her name? Anny Duperey . . . If you're too tall, you look like a drag queen. After the First World War, and for twelve years, the fashion favored short women on the stage, like Gaby Morlay. They didn't like my size: I almost didn't make it. Morlay was as small as Piaf. Was Joan Crawford very tall?

---

*Simon had a famous pet orangutan. When it died, he was inconsolable and used to look affectionately at Arletty and tell her that she reminded him of his deceased pet. She didn't know what to make of that and didn't want to find out either.

JK: Five three and a half. Not really. Dietrich was. How tall are you?

A: My passport says one meter seventy, but one shrinks with age. Dietrich and I were of the same height. Dietrich is not a classical beauty. She's intelligent, sophisticated. Garbo doesn't need makeup, she has her eyes, her mouth. When Dietrich sang *"Ich bin von Kopf bis Fuss,"* she was aiming at the crotch. Can you imagine Garbo in the role?

JK: Garbo wasn't much taller than you. Her shoulders were broad.

A: I saw her often. Beauty itself.

JK: Can you explain the secret of her popularity on the screen?

A: Her face, her figure, her shoulders. Not her intelligence, for sure. I couldn't take my eyes off her. The secret is that she was dumb. We were at Gaylord Hauser's house once. He was a friend of hers. Juliette Greco was also there, but she didn't want to stay: she wasn't even curious about Garbo, she said she had an appointment. There was an interpreter, just like now. I had every question ready for her, knew every film title by heart: *Queen Christina, Camille, Street of Sorrow*. . . . She appeared, a great beauty. I praised her. She laughed at every question. [She imitates Garbo's laughter. Arletty's famous gift for mimicry is evident, for as she leans forward, the narrow shoulders broaden out, then fold in and flap with rumbling shakes of laughter.] That wasn't *Queen Christina*. She never knew that I was onstage or in films.

JK: You've worked with some of the master filmmakers. How would you define the "art" of cinema?

A: Every picture, as a work of art . . . and it is worthless if it is not approached as such . . . should be a shaped and complete entity like a jewel, polished and well set. The performance of the artists in full understanding of the author's intention is the pure gold of the jewel's setting. It is complete understanding and sincere interpretation of the role one plays which is most important. One must be natural and sincere and feel what one is portraying. But is not that the most important thing in life as well? When I am no longer sincere, when I no longer say what I think, when I can no longer respond to feeling . . . then I shall surely be dead. Now I am tired.

A bottle of champagne was brought out, glasses were filled. We toast each other. One hates to leave, but other friends arrive to read to her and share her evening. "Call," she says. "Call and see me when you're next in Paris."

1984

George Hurrell, 1930

GEORGE
HURRELL

GEORGE HURRELL was almost seventy when I first met him, working toward his retirement pension and creating no waves shooting stills on films at 20th Century–Fox, like *Star.* I was outside the *Myra Breckinridge* soundstage, standing in the sun, killing time and picking up bits of information from various people outside about the problems within. So few films were being made just then, so few with any sort of potential for excitement and gossip, but *Myra* had Mae West, Raquel Welch, Gore Vidal, sex-change subjects in Technicolor, and everybody apparently hating and distrusting everybody else. (Always excluding Mae. Mae was above it all. Mae didn't waste valuable energy on hating. She'd flick her wrist casual-like to dismiss the gnats of annoyance as of no importance to her.) And below it, thinking it all just a joke, and doing his job, shooting stills, was Hurrell. Hurrell, once the greatest name in the evolution of the Hollywood Image, whose portraits of the stars defined their appeal in images at once splendid and audacious, was now not even doing the "special" pictures for the film, the portraits of the film's stars. Funny that was, since Raquel Welch had studied long and hard the stars of the past, the sort of star she herself wanted to be a modern embodiment of, and the sort of star she was playing in *Myra,* and instead of getting the great Hurrell to take her portraits, she had British photographer Terry O'Neil, who was young and hot. (If you were a photographer and you were British, you were hot. Then, at any rate. *Blow-up* had sold that bill of goods, the way the Carnaby Street, Liverpool-Pop Beatles and *Time* had sold the "swinging London" sort of thing.) O'Neil was good but not in Hurrell's class. But then, I didn't know who George was either. When a man from publicity who knew I was waiting and who was nervous in case I was picking up the wrong stories, said, "Hey, you write all those books about the old Hollywood stars. You'd be interested in this guy we've got shooting stills. He shot all the great stars from your era." My era was the '50s, but I knew what he meant.

George had been standing talking to some technicians and snapping pictures. I thought he was just fooling around, waiting to get back and shoot stars. I didn't realize that every time he clicked his shutter, it was for publicity. The rich old '30s fan magazines were filled with articles that would have been quickly tiring if each had not always been accompanied and illuminated by magnificent portraits of the star featured in the piece. One didn't think of it like that, certainly writers wouldn't have thought of it like that, but it wasn't their prose you cut out and pinned on your wall, it was the photographs. And for a time, in the '30s, when the greatest pictures were being made and the greatest portraits were being taken, Hollywood fan magazines, aping their fashionable up-market betters, would list the name of the photographer at the bottom right-hand side of the photograph in small print. Years of poring over them, years of collecting them, and I don't think that I ever for one moment thought that I had noticed those little names: Bull, Bachrach, Allan, Munn Autry, Coburn, Louise, Willinger . . . HURRELL. But even as we were crossing over to George, pages were turning in the back files of my head. *Photoplay, Picture Play, Modern Screen*—not just covers, but pages: Norma Shearer, something satiny and back-less; Crawford, just Crawford; Robert Montgomery in a white jacket.

"George, this is John Ko . . . Cueball, he's from London, covering the picture. He's a real film buff." "Hi!" "Hi. Did you ever photograph Mae West before?" "Oh, yeah, sure, when she first came out here. I even did some nude shots for her own private use." "So she's not a man?" Hurrell is a great chuckler. If he was surprised by the way our conversation started, he just chuckled. Maybe he even thought, since this movie was Gore Vidal's *Myra Breckinridge*, that the question was quite normal. "God, *no*. She's a small woman, very vo-luptuous, not the way the gals"—he always called them "gals"—"were in those days, you know, they all wanted to be very slim so they would look good in clothes, but Mae had the best figure I'd ever seen for the kind of round, curva-ceous sort she was."

He had a lot of cameras hanging around his neck, and things were moving all around us, but he was calm, unruffled, quite content to stand and chew the fat. With every name he mentioned I grew more eager. "Have you got any old pictures you did?" "A couple." George was modest. "I'd like to see them."

David Chierichetti, a Los Angeles–based film historian, went with me to see George, helping to carry a bundle of '30s magazines in case George needed to be reminded of anything. Not at all, much. In his small valley house, with the noise of kids playing outside in the afternoon sunshine as continuous back-ground noise, we settled in his den. George had brought out the portfolios he'd kept, samples of his work that hadn't been lost during all of his moves over all of the years, some of his *Esquire* stuff, a lot of advertising and a whole boxful of the sort of photos photographers take for themselves when they want to get away from it all—beautiful pictures of Mexican adobes, small children outside small towns south of the border, portraits of natives and of their craft, of pots and such, and plants and trees and shrubs—things that would be likely to catch a photographer's eye. They dated from the '30s, when he was the premier pho-tographer of beautiful, famous men and women, the Hollywood stars.

George had now reached a point in his life when it seemed that his career was over, he saw no chance of its return and didn't think about it or pine for it.

He was just working to make his pension and then he'd enjoy a quiet anonymity with his wife and their children. And everything about "those days" made him laugh a lot, like you might find yourself laughing on awakening and retelling this incredible dream you just had. Even as he did so, his work became clearer, stronger, increasingly hypnotic, and we both came to a discovery about the uniqueness of many of these people he'd photographed so brilliantly for so long, that invariably climaxed with long, absorbed pauses as a Crawford, a Gable, a Shearer, Lamour, Cagney, Del Rio, a Hayworth for *Esquire,* a Jane Russell for the *Outlaw* campaign became a forceful presence in that room; and words like "old" meant a craft now lost. Raquel Welch, on the set of the film where we met, was working, trying to recapture and re-create the past; and here, in Hurrell's photographs, *was* the past, strong, magnificent. Nostalgia was about the only thing absent from these photographs. From that afternoon would come the inspiration for exhibitions that have toured the world's major museums; many books; and the rediscovery of Hurrell and the Hollywood portrait photographers who created one of the most significant bodies of work in 20th-century photography.

GH: This is the first thing I did on Norma Shearer. I did that at my own studio on Lafayette Park Place. And as a result she got her role in *The Divorcee.* [It's true. The session swung opinion around at the studio. But George wasn't boasting. He never boasted, just grinned or chuckled.] She came down there to my studio with her whole entourage in her yellow Rolls-Royce, which she always had in those days. You see, they weren't making her sexy enough at the studio, that was the whole thing. The idea was to get her looking real wicked and siren-like. She felt that I'd done it. Because she was not *that* type, you know, she didn't have any of it. In fact, it was my idea to get her hair bushy—she never wore it that way. First of all, she had such a high forehead, she always looked too intellectual for the kind of role she wanted to play. But by pulling that hair down and getting her head down and, you know, getting some "mood" feeling into her. She always got a kick out of my playing records all the time, and I played—I can't recall just what it was, but it was a record that was popular in those days, and she ribbed me for years about it. She couldn't understand why I was playing it because it had no connection with getting a sexy mood particularly, but we got the pictures.

Shearer came to me because of the pictures I'd done of Ramon Novarro.* He was the first. And I had made some pictures of a gal that he was running around with, Pancho Barnes her name was. And he saw those, and he wanted to become an opera star, a singer, and I made these pictures of him. He came down to my little studio, and I made a few shots. He just

---

* In 1980, with the Hurrell revival in full swing, an original print of his portrait of Ramon Novarro sold to a private collector for $9000.

wanted to see what I was gonna do. He liked them and we went on to make a whole lot of pictures. He was under contract at that time to MGM, and he showed them there and they used them. They had a layout in a roto section, I think it was the *L.A. Times,* but anyway they ran the series of shots of him, and on the strength of those Norma came down. I suddenly got a call from the MGM publicity director, who was Pete Smith, and he wanted to know if I could shoot some pictures of her. I was only too glad to do it. So down she came. It was important, except that I didn't care particularly. I wasn't ambitious. I wanted to be a painter. I didn't want to be a photographer. That's not what I started out as.

JK: Weren't you flattered, though, that the star of one of the major studios that already had photographers under contract should come to you for her "new" look?

GH: Well, the thing that they were concerned about wasn't just these photographers. There were certain photographers who were gallery men, others who were portrait men. Today they don't discriminate. A portrait man is for the birds; they don't care. But in those days a man who did portrait work was a special type of fellow, see, and he had to work in a special way. And through that you were either a portrait man or just a still man. [Looking at photographs of Shearer deshabille, he pointed out technical aspects.] The cleavage wasn't a problem. You could do it with stills easier than in films, with stills you could plan and organize it. But the cleavage—that's lighting; you could give cleavage to gals who didn't have anything. You just get them to do this [he crosses his arms and leans forward] and you cast a shadow and produce it. But then too [he pointed to her left leg sticking out of her chamois-skin robe] her legs weren't too good, you see, and by using her legs, that was something of a sex rendition. By the way you pose them, and you can't do that in motion pictures because they gotta move. With stills you can do that. There are things like that that are being overlooked today.

It started with the stills—the buildup, the exploitation, feeling out the public. I'm not saying this just to make myself more important. They would start with stills, no matter who it was, they would have a stills session when they arrived, and from that they would make up their minds. I used to make 11 × 14 prints. These 8 × 10 stills you see today, they were just for handing out to the editors, for newspapers mostly, because the magazines would get 11 × 14 prints. And then they would go to the producer, whether it was Jack Warner or L. B. Mayer—you know, the top man, not just the intermediary. Then, if they felt there was something there, they'd do the screen test. Most of the time the gallery would take place before the screen test. Sometimes after . . . well, anyway, but through the stills they'd determine so many things.

Because of that session with Shearer I got my contract with MGM. They had Clarence Bull. I think Ruth Harriet [Louise] had just left or was leaving. Maybe her going coincided with my getting there. I don't know.

Somebody coined the word "glamour" back then. That's where it came from. That period. But it was just giving a gal a sexier attitude. Even the "Oomph" gal, Sheridan, she didn't have it either. She had it, let's say, in her physical makeup, in her attitude, but she didn't have it for stills or in her movies. She just didn't think that way. But we got it out of her in the galleries and through negligees; the "bedroom look," that's what I used to call it. Put stuff on that makes you look like you're in the bedroom, that's all. I don't care what it is, you know, black, white, green, yellow, anything.

You can create glamour totally, I think. But a woman in our business generally has some quality of it. Some have it more than others. Joan Crawford, for instance. Well, she projected that quality. Now, maybe it's because she thought in a sexy way; she projected a more emotional thing. Karen Morley, on the other hand, I had to shoot her a lot, but she never somehow, to me anyway, projected an emotional quality. It was always cerebral.* Just like Hayworth. Hayward too, but Rita projected more. She was a very emotional person. Rita was, I would say, not too mentally alert. It was all instinct, and that comes across. It's alive. Harlow was another one like that. They were the products of that period; they *thought* that way and they *felt* that way, they projected that quality. When they'd come through the door—they'd *arrive* somehow. They didn't just walk in the door like Karen Morley might, you know, saying, "Hello, how are you?" They'd *arrive*. They'd develop that thing. You'd see them at parties, for instance, cocktail parties, just idle things, but they'd always *arrive* somehow. I never saw anything like it. When I think of it now, it seems humorous. It was as if they had internal trumpets that blew for them just as the door opens. Lana Turner used to do the same thing. She came out a little later, but . . . they all had it.

JK: Your contribution was to get them to act, like giving a private performance of a film that will never be seen on the screen?

GH: That's one of the reasons for the music and the long hose.

I used a fifteen-foot hose with a bulb on it because the camera had to be stationary. We couldn't run around with it like we do today because the darn thing was on a tripod. But I was mobile. I'd be all over the place; to get them looking over there, I'd go over there, you know . . . bam, bam, bam, bam, bam, like that! And I had an assistant, no matter where I was, whether I was in my own gallery or outside. He'd just keep loading these holders. I'd check the focus once in a while to be sure. There weren't many variations.

It's a different kind of thing from being a first cameraman. I've been one, worked at it, but it's too sedentary. First of all, you sit there and you have to be . . . so . . . immobile. I got accustomed to just moving, lots of activity, lots of physical activity as well as the other. But they just go on for hours.

---

*Karen Morley, best remembered perhaps for her role in *Scarface* and appearances in several Greta Garbo films, was a leading political figure in Hollywood in the '30s and married the director Charles Vidor.

They can take two hours just to make a close-up. We shot 150 shots, a whole sitting, in that length! The cameraman is always at the mercy of the director too. He's motivated by him; he's politically tied to his apron strings. It's a different technique completely. Except when he starts making a close-up: when you consider the time he's allowed to make a close-up, to light it, which we do in two seconds, it's ridiculous. I used to laugh like the devil at that, at how *slow* and prodigious this motion-picture operation was, when there was no reason for it to be so slow.

JK: You didn't start out to become a photographer?

GH: I had been going to art school and came out to California thinking I would become a painter. But I had to make a living. I had a camera, and all the artists down there [Laguna Beach] needed pictures of their paintings. I would take them out in the sun and put a K-3 filter on (we didn't have color in those days) and just shoot these paintings. I'd get so much for them, and was getting my bread and butter out of my photography. I just got to be well known.

Eventually I got bored with Laguna and decided to go to Los Angeles. I shot some society people—the Dockwilers in those days were a very famous social family and I shot them, their weddings, their daughters, their kids and that sort of thing. Then came that Ramon thing, and then Norma Shearer. I dare say it was only after they saw the proofs that I was called out to MGM and asked to go to work.

I had an attitude about lighting that was different from the other photographers out there at the time; and even about the lens quality. They were using Vertone lenses at the time—in fact, that shot of Norma Shearer was done with a Vertone lens. The Vertone lens, if you didn't know, was a diffused lens—diffused all the time, and that's how we worked it, 'cause that was the style. You *had* to work with a diffused lens. But I changed that. When I went to Metro, I used their equipment, and I started shooting sharp—extremely sharp—cut the lens way down and made it sharp. That was one difference. The other was the established way they had then of lighting. I changed everything about lighting, even my own methods, trying to do different things. I started to use backgrounds as well. That came about through my liking to go and shoot on sets, where there were already established backgrounds. I started doing that with Shearer, and then also with Crawford.

I made more photographs of Crawford perhaps than any other. She liked to pose. She was very pliable. She gave so much to the stills camera. She would work at it. She'd spend a whole day, changing maybe into twenty different gowns, different hairdos, changing her makeup, changing everything. She'd spend maybe an hour between changes just getting herself ready for the next attire. In a sense she used this opportunity to try to present a new image that might possibly work for her whole screen personality. I would start out with some kind of different approach before she even arrived. Every time there was a different kind of lighting, to a certain extent, or different background or poses. That's one of the reasons I liked the sets, because you had new things to work with. It was always *fought* by the publicity departments: "Why go onstage and have to have all those electricians and all these people standing around?" You had to have a prop man, you had to have an electrician, you had to have a grip. That was automatic when you went on stage, and that advanced the cost. Whereas in the gallery we worked alone, with just an assistant to help load. So of course they objected to that sort of thing because of money reasons, but I would force it whenever I could because I'd get different kinds of pictures. I was always considering compositions. That came from having studied painting. So I'd compose with light if I didn't have anything else.

JK: How much of the final image was set in the session and how much of it was done in the darkroom?

GH: In this case, this picture of Jane Russell, a single spotlight just covering here; and sometimes I would just manage to shade there, sometimes just with the slide from the holder. I didn't do too much of the work in the darkroom because I wasn't in control of the printing. I would make the original print; then it would go to a studio and they would make the prints, so I had to control it enough in the shooting to be sure that the printing was done the way I'd have wanted. It's another reason for the single light. I used to get questions about the single light on the gal's face. You'd throw fillers on some of those—what we call fillers, when they flood the light to fill the shadows. That too was a part of design and composition. If you saw all the features, you didn't need everything lighted. Like this picture with Hedy Lamarr. This was getting the mood with no particular effort, just having her look away instead of looking at the camera. And then that light—there were just two lights. The one on her head you always had to get at just the right angle to get the design of her features, otherwise they would be lost. Using as little light as possible was mainly so that . . . people aren't too conscious of the lighting. If the light is too strong, they're blinking and being disturbed by the light. If you can keep the light low-key, that's to your advantage in working with people. But the *amount* of light doesn't make too much difference—it's the *balance*. You can take a light 100 candlepower, or you can take one with 1000-watt candle, and do the same thing. Except your subject won't react the same. A low-quality light is better for skin, texture and portrait work. You get more highlights; when the light is hot on your face, the highlights burn out. They just don't show up.

You know, glamour to me was nothing more than just an excuse for saying sexy pictures. In other words, my interpretation was entirely one of saying, "Come on, we're going to take some sexy pictures." The shimmery material they'd wear would always reveal highlights and give the body shape. And I latched on to this big bear rug. I don't know why or how, but I got hold of it and used it for years. One of the things I used to do for a while was get them to lie on that rug. Every once in a while I'd get carried away and say, "Lie down." "What do you mean, lie down?" I'd get a reaction like that. And then, when I had them on the floor, I'd shoot down and automatically it changed the whole business of what they were going to do and the character of it.

JK: What was your reaction to the portraits being taken out in Hollywood when you arrived?

GH: Well, I just felt that they had no . . . they had no special character. And I was trying to get character into my work. That's why I went sharp, because there was no reason for that thing to be fuzzy. And that immediately gave the pictures more character, I think. We had to retouch anyway, because in those days there couldn't be a freckle or a blemish or anything. Even the men. *My God* [he laughs], if they had a little crow's-feet here, it had to be removed. They were loaded with lead, every negative. Sometimes on both sides! It was expected in those days. And then, too, we would get the proofs back. One of the gals we had so much trouble with in the retouching, she was married to . . . Brisson, that's the fella. Oh, yeah, Roz Russell. You'd retouch till you couldn't put any more lead on the thing, because once you got all the lead on the mucilage that was put on the surface, it would just get slick and you couldn't add any more. Then they'd come back and want more put on it! [He laughs.] So you'd have to work on the back! We'd use dyes, use everything. But Roz would retouch and retouch and retouch, and maybe have six different sets of proofs. I mean, you never retouched them to change their features. Not with actresses. If the light or something made the eye look small on one side, or maybe there was too much shadow and they didn't like a certain thing, then we'd work on it.

JK: Were you ever part of the studio's strategy for building up a star?

GH: Sometimes, yes. The outstanding one was Ann Sheridan, of course, when she didn't have it. Norma Shearer too, of course—that was where I assumed the right myself to change her look.

Harry Cohn used Hurrell for Hayworth; Howard Hughes had Hurrell take the portraits and the ad art of Jane Russell that got Hughes limitless publicity mileage; he made Bette Davis feel glamorous, and the "glamorous" Joan Crawford feel dramatic; Dietrich knew everything there was to know about photography and lighting, and so George merely took good but not extraordinary pictures of her; Garbo didn't care either way, and he never got to Clara Bow. George wasn't perfect. But almost. And he shot everybody who was or would become anybody.

Hurrell snaps his bulb and a bit of a man's mortality is now become immortality for at least as long as there is someone to see it, or until the day when that negative dies, disintegrates and releases its stolen life back into the void. Those primitive tribes who refuse to have their pictures taken, fearing that a part of them would be stolen, are right. Yes, George is modest. So, I would discover, were all of them, these photographers who photographed the spirit behind the beautifully printed reality.

There were of course other, more everyday realities to be coped with in their work: things that studios looked for, publicity departments required, advertising departments needed, and what the stars would or would not do. Bathing suits and pinups were popular with publicity because the newspapers would always want them, but . . .

GH: Most of the stars refused to do it. I put them into bathing suits or sexy robes, because most of the stars *did* have an attitude about their clothes. They had their own choice of styles and the type of dress they wanted. Once they'd gained a position for themselves, they wouldn't do certain things. Joan Crawford. You never see bathing-suit pictures of her. She wouldn't do it. Oh, maybe if it was something she wore in a film, but that was wardrobe, not pinup. She wouldn't do it. Well [after a brief reflection, recalling perhaps that he too had to do things if the studio insisted], she must have done it before the first few pictures, because they *had* to do it. Even Garbo had to do it. Garbo did that track-suit thing. [He laughs.] I was only at MGM for three years, from 1930 to '33. Bull wasn't shooting in that gallery when I was— he didn't have a place to shoot, in the first place, now that I recall. There was only one gallery, the one Louise had, on the top of the editing building. Three stories up. And they'd come up three stories too. They would walk up the fire-escape ladder. That's all it was, you know, an outside ladder up to the roof. Everybody'd come up there . . . Garbo . . . Crawford . . . any of them. Carrying their own clothes . . .

The starlets knew the gallery sessions were important for them. Some of them had very decided ideas about it. Of course Anita Page—she never did anything, though. But we used to shoot pictures of her all over the place; whenever we weren't busy, we'd call Nita in. "Let's see, what haven't we done?" God, we did everything with her. It was wide open. In fact, I was always fighting myself to keep from being stereotyped. In other words, I would *try* to interpret *each* sitting as a new approach. I was always trying to *think:* "Let's see; this time you gotta do it differently. Eliminate that top light; or just do cross lights; or maybe do three-quarter figures instead of close-ups; or I won't do any close-ups this time."

Out of that came some classic sessions: Crawford stationed in the swing-door entrance to *Grand Hotel;* Norma Shearer by the Cedric Gibbons penthouse Art Deco fireplace for *Strange Interlude;* Bette Davis in costume for her role as Queen Elizabeth on the set for *Elizabeth and Essex;* and Rita Hayworth on a prop bed for *You Were Never Lovelier.*

GH: My departure from Metro came about because one time when I . . . shot some pictures . . . on a Sunday of a star who wasn't under contract. Who was it I shot? I think it was Joan Bennett—but anyway, somebody I did. And

I was doing an outside job. And while I had no contract with the studio, they *considered* me under contract and I was not allowed to shoot anyone outside the studio. I shot her for Maggie Ettinger, who was one of the old freelance press agents, she was related to Louella Parsons. I saw no reason why I shouldn't do it; and they found out about it and just called me into his— Strickling's [head of MGM's publicity department]—office and laid down the law: that I wasn't allowed to do such a thing; and how *dare* I do it; and I just got upset and told them to shove it.

But in that period you could try almost everything—except for shooting any nudes. The work had to be strictly aboveboard. Any nude work was what I did on my own. You had to get them looking sexy without taking their clothes off. They'd help. First thing, when Harlow came in for a gallery session, she'd come in with something just wrapped around her and then . . . accidentally [he says, spinning it out] dropped it. That was her entrance. That was her way of saying, "Let's do some pictures here, man." [More chuckling as the parade goes by.] But the studios wouldn't allow anything like nude photos of the people under contract. Nothing indicating that she wasn't covered. That was just the rule of operation. You understood that. Because, first of all, there wasn't . . . they couldn't publish it. . . . Even if they got hold of something like that, like that picture of that dancer from South America, Carmen Miranda, who was dancing when her skirt just flew up too much. And the picture sold all over the world in millions, like hotcakes! It was done in the gallery out at Fox. There was an actor dancing with her. The photographer was just shooting, and suddenly *pow!* She didn't have any pants on, that was all. If she'd had pants on, it wouldn't have made any difference, you wouldn't have even noticed it.*

But some of those gals really came into the gallery ready to go—like this gal Maria Montez. She had a great body, she would just come in and lie there naked as a jaybird, she didn't care. I don't know what went on in some of those guys' heads, but I was never asked to do any private shots of the stars for any of the executives in the studios. I was never asked to do anything that I didn't want to do. I've never been asked except once in my life, and that was when I was doing advertising in New York, to make nude photographs of a wife or sweetheart or anyone. But one time—in fact, I did this two or three times—one of the biggest ad-agency men in the business called me into his office and asked me to do some pictures with his wife. He took me to lunch and prepared everything and he sat there while I made pictures of her in the nude. But he paid me $3000, so I couldn't turn it down. Well, the next time, a year later, I got $5000 for the second session. It was done the end of the year, just before Christmas, actually, but the bill would be rendered to him, to the agency, and it would be sent to the client, and I'd always put on it "experimental photographs." [He laughs about it.]

---

*Frank Powolny, the photographer who took that picture, almost lost his job.

I worked with Harlow and Crawford probably *more* frequently than any other big stars. They made themselves available. They liked doing it. They had fun. Toward the end we weren't playing up the sex thing so much. And that's a reason why I didn't do too well with Garbo, perhaps. I was always trying to do things with her. Garbo would come in and she was going to do what she was going to do, and that was that. There was never any give or take. I shot her about three, four times. I did things that I've never got the negatives on, but I do have two or three negatives that I sneaked out of her in this Russian outfit—probably *Ninotchka*. They're pretty straight except for the lighting.

The picture George brought out was of Garbo, but not in *Ninotchka*, which came near the end of her career, when no one except Clarence Sinclair Bull took her portraits; George's negative was from *Romance*, the film she was making in 1930, the year Hurrell first arrived on the MGM lot. In fact, that costume session was George's *only* gallery experience with her. Garbo was set in her ways, not only as to how she would pose but whom she would pose for. She had already decided on Bull after Ruth Harriet Louise left, and her willingness to try Hurrell, or agree to do a session with him, is in itself remarkable. It was the only time between 1929 and 1941 that she sat for any photographer except Bull.

GH: I always liked to work with people who would sort of put themselves in my hands *somewhat*—I don't mean that I would have complete freedom all the time, but where they would be more resilient. She didn't have that. She was pretty much self-styled, you might say. There wasn't any problem with photographing her. You could soften her angularity with lighting. But the thing that I would refer to, which I couldn't break through, was what I would call a stiffness about her. It may have been just because we didn't meet on common ground in some way; because I was wild and yelling, hollering, and she wasn't particularly amused by it; it didn't do anything to her. The session was very private. Most of the time I would insist on it anyway. But with her, of course, she wouldn't allow anybody to be there. Just the assistant, so there'd be just three of us.

Her features were so photogenic. You could light her face in any manner possible; any angle; up, down. Her bone structure and her proportions—her forehead, her nose was just right; the distance between here and here was just right. And her eyes were set in such a way that you couldn't go wrong. Now, Harlow's eyes were deep-set, and you had to get the light under them or her head up, or her eyes would just get too dark. Crawford had the closest face to Garbo's, to perfect proportions. Crawford had strong jawbones, that's about all I'd say, because her cheekbones were good, and her forehead, and her eyes were good—maybe a little on the large side.

Of course, the thing that we haven't mentioned, but the only thing about a subject that interested me, which is why I didn't get too much out of Garbo, because she didn't respond to me, but—if I didn't get kind of a lively reaction out of a person, I didn't get much out of it myself, and I wouldn't get any decent pictures.

JK: Aside from diffusion and soft focus, did you ever try to light in such a way as to not show wrinkles? I mean to fill light under the eyes and so forth . . .

GH: I had to do it on all my society stuff. I had a system for that.

It was just a low, flat . . . a single spotlight, but it was so low, about 250-watt globe and so close to the camera—and that was my whole key light on the face—but I would put it as close to the lens as I could get, and that would be the light on the face. And there wouldn't be any shadow except for the definite line the spotlight would make. I could have used a diffused light completely, but then there wouldn't have been any definition, just too flat. And through that spot, and a little key, I could iron out practically everything. Well, and the makeup guys did so much. That's another thing: I always tried to get them to leave the makeup off. In those days. It wasn't easy. Because the makeup was so caked, and they used such heavy makeup too. They would just iron out everything, and by the time you had retouched some wrinkles out, why, it was completely flat. Some of them would do it. But *even* if they didn't eliminate the makeup, like Roz Russell, she would come in with modified makeup.

But there is no *one* thing you have to have that makes you sexy. They've got to have the face, and the full lips, and their noses must be pretty well balanced on the faces—but a lot of that can be done with makeup, you know, and in the retouching. If the face had the proportions, you could make it look sexy. It's strictly makeup and lighting.

JK: Were the women the world considered sex symbols as sexy when they got into the gallery?

GH: Well, Harlow happened to be. Everything she was trying to be, she was. A lot of them weren't. Marilyn Monroe, for instance. I think it was all just an act with her. It wasn't instinctive, the way it was with Harlow. I shot her later on. In '52 or something like that. She was doing something over at Fox, her early days, but already she was important. I always recall too that she did that same routine that Harlow did—come in wrapped in something and, all of a sudden, let it fall. I didn't know whether she heard of Harlow doing it or whether she just thought it up herself. But she had the same routine. I presume the idea was to get you going—oh, boy, what a good soft tomato, we're going to make some terrific pictures. Well, they were exhibitionists too. It's funny, all those girls that had that quality. Mae West, she had a sexy nature, she'd drop her clothes at the drop of a hat. Garbo was probably the sexiest gal among the whole darned bunch of them, but she didn't project it, because that wasn't her job. Sex to her probably didn't take place until it got dark. When she was working during the day, she was doing a job. She worked in a very logical way. There was no maybe about her for me. It always had a connection with the part. She never played sexy roles while I was there, so maybe that's why she didn't think she had to push the sex in the gallery.

Well, and Adrian dressed them too in a more masculine way than they dress today—all those wide shoulders and all that. And suits, he was a suit maniac. He was a real great artist, that Adrian. I had great admiration for him, a creative genius.

Usually you had them all day for a session. That's the difference between then and now. All the wardrobe changes. You had twenty wardrobes, they'd change them.

Some of the men insisted on coming in with full makeup, and some I insisted that they didn't. Bogart, for instance, he wouldn't put makeup on even in front of the movie camera. Robert Montgomery was stiff. Errol Flynn, now, he would insist on makeup because he wanted to change his eyebrows and do tricks to his eyes. Cagney, he always had makeup because he felt he wasn't good-looking enough. I've almost forgotten what they did; some pencil work with their eyebrows. Because Cagney worked on his eyes a lot. He was conscious of how his eyes looked.

JK: Is that what a lot of people thought was the most important thing about them? I asked you earlier what you think it was.

GH: I think if you had to pick out something, the eyes would come out first.

JK: With Norma Shearer you had a different problem, because her eyes were not exactly her strongest feature.

GH: She knew how to handle the eye thing, because she would always focus— she could never look at anything close. Of course, she worked in front of the mirror so much [he's amused, recalling vanities] that I don't think she was ever in the dark about how she looked in front of that camera. Now, some of them . . . That brings me to Dietrich. For example, she insisted—in the beginning I just refused to have it there, but finally, "Oh, what the hell, let her"—she insisted on a full-length mirror so she could pose in front of it. The first couple of times I'd say I didn't have a mirror in the studio, but finally we got one.

JK: Why were you so against it? Did it interfere with you?

GH: It's not so much that, but they get so set—a foot out here, a foot there, always doing things like this—"All right now, take it." Well, if I didn't like it, I'd say, "Well, I don't like that." So then we were off on rough track. I photographed her a lot over at my studio on the Strip, and I photographed her at Paramount . . . a number of times. Sometimes, if I worked at my own studio with the star, I would make a set of proofs and they would get the negatives and the proofs. That's the way we worked in those days. My original set was stamped 'cause I would send it out that way. But if *they* made the prints, then they weren't stamped. I used to try to get them to do so. Sometimes they did—MGM did. I gave them a stamp, but some of the studios wouldn't bother.

JK: What is the "glamour look"?

GH: You can boil it down to just that "bedroom look." For me, that's it.

  You could do just as much with color—in fact, more, I'd say. [He was referring now to his *Esquire* pinups.] Because you could do more with colors. If you don't see much good "glamour" stuff in color, it's because they don't want that kind of picture today. I could shoot it, but nobody asks for it. And when I do shoot it, anything in a gallery, there's no requirement. I could set it up—you see, you have to prepare for that kind of thing—just like the period in the last couple of years over at Fox, well, a couple of times, like with Edy Williams, for instance, we did all kinds of sexy things, but where do the pictures of Edy Williams wind up? You know. In the wastebasket. You have to do those things with the big stars, otherwise you never see them.

JK: Had you ever done things like that with Mae West?

GH: During the period when I was on the Strip, Paramount hired me to go in their gallery to shoot her. That was the time she insisted on taking her clothes off. I think a lot of the retouching they did on her wasn't because she was heavy, but because she was short, you know, so they gave her a longer waist-line. She's so short. I think maybe five feet.

JK: That's why she wears those built-up shoes.

GH: That's why she can't walk. Her stilts are so high! Oh, sure. She has to *crawl* along, you know. She can't actually achieve that sexy walk of hers anymore because of those stilts. Her face was kind of round and . . . she was just a glamorous-type gal. She was glamorous in personality. *There* is an example of "projecting glamour." That gal *always* projected glamour. I re-member the first time I met her, I was standing in the reception room at Paramount studios, there at the Golden Gate, and she came walking in. Well, she came in like she was *Mae West* . . . it couldn't have been anybody else [and he chuckles].

  I wish to hell I'd stayed with painting, now that photography has gone to hell. I wish I'd stayed with painting because I'd be a better painter today than I am a photographer. Today photography has no place to go. In this business, anyway. Photography anyway is just to snap as many pictures as you can snap. You can't consider it a kind of picture anymore. There's never anything about creating.

JK: When did this whole thing change? When did you stop using the 8×10 sheets and going all out for the 35 mm and $2\frac{1}{4}$?

GH: Well, the transition started with the 4×5. That happened about . . . about 1950. They were still using galleries to some extent, but they were starting to use 4 × 5s in the gallery. And they'd do more work on the set. What started it, I think . . . the magazines were asking for the candid. I remember that word "candid" was being used all the time. Then they decided the gallery work isn't as desirable anymore. You get it on the set, everything is candid. Then too, if they're going to shoot portraits, why not shoot them on 4 × 5? They'd blow up the prints and retouch those.

The original concept was to create a mood. Now the mood is different: they take them out, with grass blowing in the background, under trees in the shadow—under conditions with natural light. In other words, they're trying to achieve the same thing, only with natural light instead of artificial light— with daylight, or getting them into the shadows of trees. It's not the dramatic sex, more the naïve-youth thing. That's the only thing that they do that I see is a little different. They've achieved that innocent quality where it's just there physically without any effort on their part, except they've made that effort somehow, to get that look. I have great admiration for Avedon. I think he was actually the top man out of all the photographers during his period. The late '50s. Still is. Because he *thought* creatively about everything that he did: he approached everything in the same way. I knew him pretty well. I had a studio in New York when he was working there. In fact, he lived across the street from me.

JK: Outside of changes in the people, the makeup, clothes, hair styles, etc., is there much difference between what you did in '30, '37, '49 and now?

GH: Not much, except maybe create more with natural lighting. But I don't think that would *help* dramatize movie stars. I think that natural lighting serves its purpose, but it doesn't dramatize movie stars. There are just so many lighting effects that you can achieve, and there are just so many changes you can make with a certain kind of face. I used to get most fun out of just going out and shooting pictures . . . landscapes or whatever I found. You just saw something that you liked shooting—no limitations, no directions.

I was in fashion photography while I was in New York. I used to work for *Vogue* and *Harper's,* and I used to do regular spreads every month for *Cosmopolitan, Good Housekeeping* . . . I would come back to Hollywood because I'd get bored with New York after a while.

George made as many powerful enemies for what was considered his "high-handed manner" as he made admirers among the stars who realized that nobody else ever made them look so good. As long as those stars lasted, so did George. In the '30s he had it all his way, even after he offended publicity directors at the all-powerful MGM.

GH: Well, that's me; if anything happened that I didn't like, or I got bored or anything, why, I'd just scram out. The same with New York. I got so sick of the . . . the commuting, for one thing. We lived up in Greenwich. *Every day* I'd get that 7:15 down and walk that mile through the station . . . I just got bored with it. I left when I had that studio on Park, I came back here and went into the TV business with Disney.* I set up in the TV business under my own name, Hurrell Productions. I started doing TV commercials, then . . . I set up that *Mark of Zorro* series for him. But then, when I got it all set and made the deal with Mitch Gertz, who was the agent on the stories, and I wanted Gilbert Roland to play the leading role, and I wanted to go to Mexico and shoot all the material down there, and Gilbert, who played a guitar pretty well and had the accent and the whole works, Walt said, "He's too old." Walt's dead and Gilbert's still working, still a star [which strikes George as very funny], and I said, "If that's the way it's going to be, you can have it then, the hell with it." So I moved out of there after two and a half years. Walt wanted to buy Hurrell Productions, but I said, "You can't have my name. My name is mine."

I left Warners in 1940–41 when I came to the end of my contract there. I had two years. When my contract was over, the day after, I was gone. I worked at Columbia for a while too. Taplinger was over there too, you know.

Bob Taplinger, who was head of Warner Bros. publicity, had brought George to the studio in 1938. During his two years there George shot *all* of their stars; made Ann Sheridan the "Oomph Girl"; and did for Bette Davis what he had earlier done for Joan Crawford . . . both ladies swear by him.

GH: After the Warner thing, Taplinger was over there for a year or two and he got me to come over. I think I was only there for a year. But, except for Rita, there was nobody to shoot there. Adele Mara! Marguerite Chapman. She was one you couldn't do anything with. She didn't inspire anything. Just a funny dame, sort of. We always used to try to make Madge Evans sexy, but she would fight it all the time—she would just laugh her way out of it. As soon as I would get serious with her and tell her to get moody, she would laugh like hell.† I used to shoot Carole Lombard a lot. She had a sexy quality, it was just her nature. But she didn't try to project it, to present it in front of a camera. Or even in person. But she was sexy. It's a physical quality first of all. But they have to think it; they have to have it physically, but they have to think it too. It has to be the combination. In other words, just the physical quality without thinking it doesn't work. That's why Mae West comes across. Lana Turner, another one. But you photographed them as they were sent to you. That's the way the job went, and that's the way I reacted to it, I guess. It didn't matter whether it was Wally Beery or Madge Evans. Beery photographed tremendous. Because he projected so much. He never stopped. He was the kind of guy who would be ideal today for the motor drive because

---

*George was married to Walt's daughter at the time.
†Madge Evans later married the playwright Sidney Kingsley. Her brother, Tom Evans, became a successful portrait photographer in his own right, taking superb pictures of many of the great beauties of the '40s.

his face—he kept up this action, he couldn't hold still. He liked me 'cause I
was so fast. I'd shoot a hundred pictures of him in a couple of hours. I shot
pretty much everybody I wanted, except Clara Bow, she came too early.
That's one I missed; too bad, 'cause she was such a lively gal and she had so
much of it. Not like Hedy [Lamarr]. I didn't get too much out of Hedy because she was so *static*. Stunning. But it was the nature of her, she was so
phlegmatic, she didn't project anything. It was just a mood thing. And she
had just one style. It didn't vary particularly. She had a pretty good body. But
she wouldn't dress for it. She was always dressing in black. She liked suits.
You can't do anything—a woman in a suit is a dead duck. Usually, very high-
styled evening gowns or dresses of any kind that are extremely high style are
bad for doing them, because in most cases they are styled for the gown rather
than for the woman's body. Hollywood's designers were ideal. Because their
idea was to sell them—except for the "suit period." The rest of it, their evening gowns were always built for the body. Adrian's always were. But you
couldn't do much more stuff if they were wearing a bathing suit. You're very
limited with a bathing suit. I'd get them in some exotic pose, they'd have to
be a little contrived, like Dorothy Lamour. In a bathing suit, the picture had
to have action and the healthy, outdoor quality to it.

JK: What is your style? How do you create it?

GH: The lighting mostly; and then the posing. But mostly the lighting and then
the print quality. They had retouchers at the studio who would just do it, just
iron it out. Then if they didn't iron it out enough, they went back for another
session and, I tell you, sometimes there were six sessions. Colbert, she used
to like lots of retouching. She'd never let you shoot her except from the side.
Every single shot of her is always from one angle. I fought her many times
on that—I'd even make her look the other way and shoot something, and say,
"Just let me try it." But she had very fixed ideas and nothing could budge her.
She'd tear them up. That goes for Raquel Welch too. She can't be shot in
profile. She just rips up everything that shows the profile. Negatives too. Rips
up everything. But Raquel has some of that old-style glamour—to a degree,
though she's not in a class with a Rita Hayworth, because Raquel's more
manufactured. She makes up her face—God! It takes two hours to make up
her face in the morning. Every morning. She fixes her nose, and she does so
much shading—fills in her cheeks with shading, and even this [he indicates
her cleavage] is also heavily made up. It's practically black there; white over
here and black down there. Mitzi Gaynor is another one of those; she's got
cups too, different sizes; depends upon the dress.

Now, Paul Newman's wife, Joanne Woodward, she's got something
about her that would be fun to photograph. I'd put her in a class with Lombard. Of course she has to see herself that way too. She has to have that
confidence. They've got to make her feel good about being sexy. Stanwyck
was like that, Bette Davis was another. They didn't think they were the glam-

orous type. They were actresses. You had to work with them to give them the confidence so that they'd relax and feel good. You see, they just become that kind of personality some of the time. Like Irene Dunne. Irene Dunne is Irene Dunne, "Here I am, why don't you do something with me?" Nothing you can do.

If somebody wanted to get into that business now—like if my son asked me, let's say—I'd suggest a sound art training if they haven't already got a natural art instinct. Because I think artists are born, that's my theory about it. You've got to have a natural instinct for composition and design, and balance of light and everything else. The rest is training. Making what you can out of it.

I don't think they've scratched the surface with photography yet. That's what's so silly about it all. It's just that the demand for things is so limited today. And you've got to be stereotyped in order to sell it. And anybody who's in it to make a living or make anything out of it has got to do what he's told.

JK: If you had the financial freedom, what sort of pictures would you be doing now?

GH: Are you familiar with Edward Weston's work? He was a landscape man. He would just do that and sell them. Men like that. Ansel Adams might be another. I couldn't go through life just shooting landscapes, except that it would be a lot of fun and I've done a lot of them. I think if one could just do photographs the same way that an artist paints; just to think of something to make it artistic, a work of art. But then, photography is not considered a work of art, or you'd have plenty of them doing it. Even the portrait business has gone too, because the average person has his own Kodak, and goes and shoots his pictures, and takes care of the shooting of the kids, and when Mother is having a birthday, why, she sits by the window and they shoot the picture and that takes care of it.

George kept working, shooting stills, till his pension came due. Then he started. Today, a dozen years after we first met, he is again one of the highest-priced ($5000 for a private sitting) portrait photographers in the business, with every pop, rock, TV and film star going to him for album sleeves and magazine covers. And his old prints, his original work—that too is being printed, lavishly promoted and sold for thousands of dollars. And we might never have met if a careful publicist hadn't worried that I might pick up the wrong sort of gossip on a film that hardly anyone remembers now.

1969

JOAN
CRAWFORD

CRAWFORD'S GREAT CAREER was coming to a sad, fitful close when I met her. Work had been her whole life, but now she was long past the age when the camera would allow her the great romantic roles that had established her, and the American cinema never had a starring place for great talent once looks had faded and youth had gone. Because she was alone, and because without work she was only half alive, she had started playing in a series of increasingly depressing vehicles, horror films whose only saving grace for her was that she retained star billing. She would have been better off without having done films like *Berserk, Trog* or *I Saw What You Did*. When I first met her, she had published her sentimental, starry-eyed (ghosted) autobiography and it repeated what any movie fan already knew about her: that her life had been a grim struggle to make it to the top; a childhood filled with drudgery and neglect, and the glory and reward it was to be one of MGM's greatest stars in the age of the great stars. What we, her fans, didn't yet know was that she had inflicted her own tortured upbringing onto one of her daughters, Christina, the first of her four adopted children, who told the world after her mother had died that the childhood of a Hollywood star's child wasn't a bed of roses. It was the daughter's story from the daughter's point of view and wasn't overly concerned with finding any justifying reason for her mother's behavior. And now we even know one of Crawford's most closely guarded secrets, one which must have cost her studio a small fortune to hush up once they found out: Joan *had* posed for soft-porn photographs when she was still eking out a living working in a New York chorus line.

In the '50s, though she was well into middle age, she was still starring in major releases for the major studios, films like *Harriet Craig, Sudden Fear, Female on the Beach, Queen Bee, Torch Song, Johnny Guitar* and *Autumn Leaves*. They were vehicles built around her, tough films, hard-edged, outrageous. I remember going to see *Female on the Beach* and thinking that this woman was so tough that the person who tried to terrorize her had better watch out once Joan found out who it was. As her leading man, Jeff Chandler looked trapped. It was hardly surprising that few of the secure male stars of that era would want to appear with this woman. Actually, she didn't need a supporting

player, what she needed were stories that could take advantage of this Prome-
thean who'd been spirited out from some giant's valley and dropped into a
chintzy living room.

In *Sudden Fear,* one of her last genuinely popular personal successes, she
was a Broadway playwright who marries and is terrorized by her actor husband.
What was so extraordinary was the Crawford "look" of "fear," a still of which
was shrewdly used in all the posters. This wasn't a picture of a woman afraid,
this was "fear" itself in the raw.

Crawford had become too large for the kind of movie anybody, anywhere,
was making at the time. After *Autumn Leaves* she retired from the screen,
though it was only to get married (and a movie fan knew that a marriage, no
matter what the participants said, was never meant to be more than a temporary
retrenchment in a star's career). She had come back so often that one couldn't
be certain she wouldn't be able to again. What one couldn't imagine was in
which guise.

Her reappearance after a few years' absence was described as a "guest role"
for a friend, Jerry Wald, in *The Best of Everything.* Wald was the producer-
writer whose faith in her at a traumatic low spot in her career back in the '40s,
after she had left MGM, resulted in her spectacular Oscar-winning comeback
as *Mildred Pierce.* It's an irony she must certainly have enjoyed, for she played
a mother who so excessively doted on her spoiled daughter that she even tried
to take the blame for the murder of her faithless husband, shot by her worthless
child. At the same time, so her real daughter said, Mommy came home from a
hard day at the studio to relax by torturing her.

By 1959 Hollywood, not just Joan's but everybody's Hollywood, was at
its shakiest. They weren't making many movies, and certainly none for stars
like her or her contemporaries. Then came the famous exploitation teaming
with her Warner Bros. rival, Bette Davis, for *What Ever Happened to Baby
Jane?* and a low-budget but tautly made Gothic thriller in which these two
Hollywood superstars played two loathsome former stars. It was one of the
great surprise smashes—as if Norma Desmond had made her *Salome* and it
had been a hit.

Baby Jane launched Bette Davis on a renewed starring career, but it proved
to be a clouded dawn for Crawford. Davis was a more flexible, adaptable actress
who played Gothic *guignol* with a relish that let one see that she was laughing.
Crawford was in dead earnest. She *was* Gothic. Out of fashion. The films that
followed, such as those already listed, built a cement box to bury her. Watching
her on the screen, the few people who went to see these pictures may have
laughed. In person, she remained a powerful presence who never doubted her
impact on the people she met. And in 1965, when I called on her at her lavish
suite paid for by Pepsi-Cola, the end may have been in sight, but it wasn't
knocking on the door.

Her apartment? It's been described by others and was featured in a lot of
photo spreads both during and after marriage to her fifth and last husband,

Joan Crawford, photographed by R. H. Louise (MGM), 1929

Pepsi-Cola chairman Alfred Steele. I didn't see much of it. I don't recall if it was covered in plastic, though she did see me between her almost continual promotional tours for the company, so it may have been covered against dust; I don't think I took my shoes off. I'm sure I wouldn't have thought anything of it if I had—the floor was thickly carpeted. Anyway, though she had a German maid, Joan was at the door and led me into her makeup room cum study, after pointing out the spectacular view from the picture windows filling one side of her living-room wall. She was wearing a leotard and a smock, with a kerchief covering part of her hair because she said she was going out that evening and still had much to do before leaving New York, so she'd washed her hair herself and it was drying. She hoped I wouldn't mind. But she wasn't really asking me. She wasn't wearing shoes and looked small but commanding.

Joan had a large head and those mammoth, muscular shoulders from which the rest of her body just sort of plunged neatly down, but what caught my attention and slightly disappointed me about her was not the color of her foundation-smooth, pale pink complexion that seemed to take its tone from a sea of freckles (I hadn't expected those), but the wild color of her hair. I had thought it would be black or brown or some solid dark hue, and instead it was a kind of champagne pink, the color one sees on a lot of California matrons in supermarkets. Only her mouth must have been made up, since it looked even bigger than it did on the screen. Well, Joan had always tried to be a mirror to her fans; this was, after all, the woman who over better than forty years had gone from being the girl F. Scott Fitzgerald described as the perfect flapper of the '20s, switching from daring daughters to modern maidens to blushing brides and hard-working shopgirls in the Depression, to single mother struggling to raise her fatherless brood in the war years, to becoming a successful career woman and distinguished matron in the '50s.

I hadn't come to interview Joan Crawford about a small role in a low-budget quickie. I wanted Joan Crawford, the currently hurried executive who signaled from the outset that she had other plans for the evening and time was going to be limited, to become this thing, this being, this film star with all the time in the world before us. The machine was set up and turned on; the working light flickered, it was her cue to talk about the movie . . . it was an interview for radio, there would be listeners out there, her voice was coated with melting charm. She talked about her part and the subject of the William Castle film *I Saw What You Did* with so much sincerity and concern for the plights of young children, like the teenagers in the film who endanger their lives with silly telephone games, that it would have done justice to an Academy Award acceptance speech. An audience hearing this on the air would have said, "What a lady! What charm! What a star! What a fabulous film!" They would have been right—well, not about the film, of course.

JK: Let's start by talking about your latest film.

JC: It's a movie, John, called *I Saw What You Did*. Mr. William Castle produced and directed it, and it's a story about two teenagers—do you know the current game they're playing now in the States? Well, the minute their parents leave them alone or the minute they're off school, they run over to each other's houses and open the telephone book, close their eyes and point to a name. Whatever the name is, they pick up the phone and dial. And if a man answers and it says Mr. John Reed in the book, they say [Joan acts this]: "Hello, John, this is Suzette; I saw what you did and I know who you are." Well, there are some very amusing instances, but they happen to do this to a man who's just murdered his wife. And he's panicky; he tries to keep the teenagers on the phone to find out where they live, so he can go and perhaps destroy them too. But this voice just says: "I saw what you did, and I know who you are." And the body's lying on the floor. And when he really finds out where they live and who they are, he has to go and kill them. And the chase, with this murderer and these two young girls, is the most horrendous thing—it's not a horror picture, it could happen to any teenager in any city in the world.

JK: The last William Castle film—not the one with Barbara Stanwyck, who I may say when I talked to her spoke so highly and wonderfully of you—

JC: Oh, did you interview her? I'm delighted. She's a wonderful human being.

JK: Oh, she is. But the one before that, *Strait Jacket* [we are interrupted by her toy poodle's bark],was one of the best acting performances on your part . . .

JC: Well, I think it had a lovely premise to it, with the mother and daughter. He had to keep a few gimmicks in because they were in her dream, and it was part of the thing they wanted to make her go insane over. But we did keep a tremendous amount of honesty in it, I think.

JK: You did. But something struck me after I saw it. Do you remember saying in your book that when you were making *Johnny Guitar* your poodle felt very upset about the set you were on at Republic? [Joan gives a modest little laugh, as if to say, Oh, yes, that terrible thing.] And I thought: Well, how does he feel about your working for William Castle?

JC (laughs): Oh, he *adores* William Castle. I have three poodles, you know. Mother, father and daughter. The other two are in the hospital for the moment—they have colds.

JK: But that, with *A Woman's Face* and *Possessed* . . .

JC: Did you like *Possessed* too? Oh, I loved doing that picture. I worked so hard. I was nominated; wasn't I lucky?

JK: I felt that was the film you should have gotten the Oscar for. I was never fortunate enough to see *Mildred Pierce*. But there was no question when I saw *Possessed*—I thought this was it.

JC: I felt I had contributed more to that, performance-wise, than I had in most of my films. You almost had to mesmerize yourself, because playing a schizophrenic isn't easy to do. . . . I went for six weeks to the hospitals in the— what do you call them in England?—rest homes, but these were really mental institutions. And I even went to General Hospital and worked there, and saw these . . . ooh, these poor sick people who go in and out of the world mentally. It was almost like a shell, and a person walking in a dream, and they really believed all these things and they heard these sounds, and the thing that I picked up the most from them was when they talked to the doctor they never quite looked at you, their faces were always a little bit sideways. They didn't trust anyone. They hesitated and they . . . Oh, it was fascinating to do! It was heart-breaking to watch these people, and some of them going through shock treatments, and to see them under the truth serums. The first time I saw it, I went to the first open window and said: "Excuse me." I *really* was violently ill. But, with my compassion, I felt so sorry for these people. And at 5:00 in the morning, and with no breakfast, I just looked at this *poor* soul crying hysterically and sobbing . . . it just tore me apart.

JK: I can believe it; all this came through. One wasn't conscious of the great Crawford image, this fantastic Adrian-gowned woman. Was this the first instance where you really immersed yourself in a part by studying the character?

JC: Oh, no. That's very normal for me. But I never get six weeks to do it in, which is what I had to prepare for this. But I felt it terribly important, while they were finishing the script and while my clothes were being made, I felt it *terribly* important to get as close to these people as I could. Because, after all, there are many doctors in the world who could look at this, and the Medical Association wrote us that it was the most *true* performance that they had ever seen, medically. And we were all pretty proud of that. I think it's good to get away from glamour sometimes. I think at this moment in my career I should get back to glamour now. But they're very difficult to find; they write stories for men only. But I have news for you, women are here to stay. They better do something about it!

JK: But, along with *Possessed,* you had just made *Humoresque* with John Garfield, which was a heavy, lavish . . . That was the one where you walked off into the sea?

JC: Yes. It was wonderful working with Johnnie. Great, *great* talent.

JK: But it was Hal Wallis and Jerry Wald who stepped into your life at that point, wasn't it?

JC: Jerry Wald is the one that found *Mildred Pierce* for me.

JK: Yes. I'm bringing him in because you have worked with people like Wald and like Irving Thalberg and Louis B. Mayer—people who had almost complete power—and I wonder how much artistic intelligence they had as well.

JC: Oh, tremendous. L. B. Mayer, naturally, had all the power at Metro—he was the highest power. Thalberg, he kind of created and built. He had the most artistic knowledge. Jerry Wald, being a writer fundamentally, had *tremendous* artistic taste. And he would like to do the offbeat thing of casting someone whom you'd *never* think of casting. It's too bad those three great talents have left us.

JK: But I've heard so much about Louis B. Mayer, and a lot of it wasn't kind.

JC: Well . . . I don't think you can be a public figure and have everything kind said about you. To me, L. B. Mayer was my father; my father confessor; the *best* friend I ever had.

Miss Crawford lights a cigarette, the striking match, the flame's dramatic whoosh creating mood, adding emphasis; even the trail of smoke from the dead match, and then from the heavily inhaled cigarette, plays a subtle part. She casts a spell. It may be confiding at times, silky, sensitive, tremulous at others, but this is steel talking, fine steel—it may flex, it may bend, but it snaps back, and the point could kill.

JC: And I think most of us growing up at Metro can say the same things. I know Judy would always go to him; Lana Turner would always go to him; every time we had a problem. And he never turned any of us down. Even if he was in a conference.

JK: Did he help you much in getting your stories? Did you have to fight much?

JC: I had to fight *terribly* for good parts, because they thought of me as a dancer, and I wanted to get out of those dancing roles. I wanted to dance in some but not all of them. I was doing the poor little rich girl who married the reporter or . . . I don't know . . . they were all the same stories, it was just awful. It was a pattern I had hit, and they were all making money, so they just kept saying: Put her in the same story, and here we go again. Let me tell you one instance. They gave me a part where it was a young ingenue; now, I never played an ingenue even when I was fifteen. I always played someone who knew what she *wanted* out of life, and not somebody who was shy and seemed reluctant to speak up. And they gave me this part, and the director wanted me to be very shy and cast my eyes down and kind of talk Southern and baby talk, which I can do because I am from the South. But I went in to Mr. Mayer, and I said: "Mr. Thalberg is so busy. We have worked ten days and he hasn't seen any rushes. This picture is *doomed*! It is the worst thing. I am so *embarrassed* when I see the rushes, I am embarrassed with the way this man wants me to do these scenes. Please take a look at these things. Ten days of rushes." And he *knew* how serious I was about my career, and that I never came to him unless I had a serious problem. He looked at the rushes that night. I received a call from his executive secretary, Ida Koverman, and Ida said: "Mr. Mayer says, 'Stay home. The picture is on the shelf.'" It was

$280,000; but *he* saw the rushes, agreed with me, had Thalberg look at them and he overrode him. He said: "It's just dreadful."

JK: Did Thalberg care much about your career? There's a story which says Shearer got the productions, Garbo supplied the art and Joan Crawford made the money to pay for both.

JC: I'm very proud of that. He had larger productions than I was doing. He had a much larger scope; epic productions. And the great big mammoth productions that Miss Shearer used to do. But it's *true* that I did the minor-league bit there for a long time. That's why I asked for my release, because I felt I had something to give, and they gave me a couple of stinkers, so I just said: "Thank you, but no."

JK: You see, your personality was usually so much bigger than the films you were in that suddenly the stories didn't matter. One did wish they'd given you strong, good directors more often. [She agrees.] You did have some good directors like . . .

JC: Clarence Brown, George Cukor . . .

JK: What do you remember about Sam Wood?

JC: Very gentle and very kind; very direct. Clarence Brown was very firm—but he spoke so softly that you had to come out of the scene to hear him, and I've got keen, *keen* ears; and I or Clark Gable would run up and say: "What did you say?" We'd say: "Come and tell us here, we can't get out of the lights." But very gentle and very quiet; no yelling. No screaming. You see, Clarence Brown started out as an engineer, and I always said he could engineer more people together to make a good picture. But he didn't disturb us too much. He let us rehearse, find our way, and gave us a couple of suggestions. He never told us first what he wanted. He knew, like in the picture with Clark [*Chained*], that we had studied what we were doing, we knew our craft, we both still wanted to learn more about our craft; and I never knew of one major suggestion or correction he made. Minor, wonderful things, which gave you a great deal of confidence. Which made you even do *better* once that camera was going, even though you had rehearsed it.

JK: He is a very subtle director, and of course he worked with Garbo a lot. And you worked with Garbo.

JC: No, I didn't.

JK: I was thinking about *Grand Hotel*.

JC: Well, I want to talk to you about that. That's very interesting. My secretary in California has made 120-odd volumes about my career. She saw all my scrapbooks in my basement; and when I adopted four children, I was going to make room for the children and throw all the clippings out, and all the photographs from each picture. And she said: "Oh, *no you don't!*" It's taken her years to do it, but I have them all beautifully stored away; and she's done a magnificent job.

You said I had worked with Garbo. Our dressing rooms were next door to each other, and every morning that I went by when she was working I would just say: "Good morning, Miss Garbo." And *never* a sound from her. Never any sign of recognition, which broke my heart. So one day I was very late for work; my hair wouldn't do (it's very fine), and it was just a mess; they told me the wrong sequence or something, and they gave me the wrong hairdo, but anyway I had to go back and do it again, and I *ran* by her room, and I forgot to say: "Good morning, Miss Garbo," and she missed it, and she came out and she said: "Hullo." Isn't that sweet? We would pass in the corridor, but we were all told by publicity that she was terribly shy and she'd rather go through the bushes than take the path to her dressing room. And she worked until 5:00 every day on the set, and then I started at 6:00. I'd go and rehearse when she'd leave the set, and we'd start at 6:00 or 6:30 and I'd work until—oh—1:00 or 2:00 in the morning. So, anyway, we overlapped, and she was coming up the steps and I was standing there with a friend of mine, Jerry Asher, from the press, and I said: "Oh, here she comes. Stand back, she doesn't like to have anyone on the stairway with her." And we stood back like two kids hiding in the corridor! And she came up, and I thought I'll scoot by her real fast when she turns the corner, and I misjudged it, I mistimed it. I got down two steps too soon, and she just came round and she *grabbed* me, and this *magnificent face* looked into mine, and I looked up at her, and she held my face in her hands and she said [It's Crawford as Garbo talking to Crawford as star-struck youngster. Her voice is Garbo's, but her eyes are a tremulous fan's—which of course would be very effective in close-up. As Garbo's hands take Crawford's face, so Crawford, as she tells it, automatically takes my face in her hands and looks at me as Garbo, I presume, had looked at her]: "I am so sorry we are not working together. It's so sad; in the same film, and no scenes. Wha-at a peety. Perhaps someday soon." My knees got so weak, being so close to this *magnificent* woman . . . oh, golly, it's the only time we ever spoke.

JK: MGM had them. There was not only her face, but your face too. And Constance Bennett was there at the time; and you had worked with her earlier. And this brings me to a point. We were talking about glamour, and that they weren't making the same type of realistic film then as now, but there were those silent films you made, like *Our Dancing Daughters* and *Sally, Irene and Mary*. They look fantastic.

JC: Well, I think *Dancing Daughters* and *Modern Maidens* and *Blushing Brides* dealt with the modern problems of the kids then; and they were tremendously successful. You see, the studio *didn't* make me a star. The public did. On *Dancing Daughters* the theater owners, the exhibitors, *discovered* that I *was* box office. And they put my name up in star billing. The studio didn't first. Wasn't that exciting? The *people* did it.

JK: Because you have been a star made by the public. And you have always given them the full regalia and trappings of a star.

JC: Well, I *owe* them that.

JK: I don't know of any instance when Joan Crawford has appeared where you don't say: "Oh, good Lord, this really is . . ."

JC: Or "Is that *really* . . . ?" [Laughs.] I *owe* everyone on that street, including the doorman, when I walk out, to look like Joan Crawford, *movie star*. As I told you a moment ago, you see me in a pair of beautiful Italian pink silk slacks. This is my day at home working. I have a beautiful silk blouse on, matching. But I am packing to go on a trip to do some work for Columbia, and some television on the West Coast, and with my working week so full, the only time when I can really pack is at nights or Saturdays and Sundays. So you see me in my working clothes; but I know a lot of people who would go out on the street like this. The only time I would be seen on the street like this is in Jamaica, where it's proper, or Barbados.

JK: Your face has such wonderful truth in it. Well, usually when you're made up, you're made up so strongly.

JC: But you don't see any makeup today. I've no makeup on at all except lipstick.

JK: You are exactly what one begins to feel after seeing some of your better films, there must be something very wonderful there. Because your face shows not only great strength, but great sensitivity, which is not always attributed to you.

JC: Yes, I have tremendous sensitivity. And a *tremendous* shyness. Just tremendous.

JK: I think in some sense you could get hurt easily in the machinery of Hollywood.

JC: Well, I think perhaps—excuse this pause, I'm trying to find the right way to word it—I have been hurt, desperately, but you *use* that hurt and hold it inside of yourself, and make it work for you, for scenes. You don't have time to cry out then. You just have to push it all back in and bottle it up. And then let it go when you need it. But it takes its toll on your tummy. Believe me. It churns and churns, and you think: I just can't hold it in another minute. But just let it go easily, in scenes. It also teaches you a great deal about discipline. It teaches you to control your emotions; your temper; and teaches you to have the right kind of temperament. I think people totally without temperament are pretty stupid and dull. Not stupid—just dull. And so many people don't know the real meaning of temperament. For me, I've just described what it is. It's discipline; it's color; it's temperament without temper. That's the best way I can describe it.

JK: I want to go back to discipline, but first I want to ask you this. Bette Davis, I talked to her, and she said: "Joan Crawford, there's nobody else like her. She's got one of the greatest stories to tell when she sits down and finally tells it." Now, what did she mean by that?

JC: I have not the vaguest notion. [I explain that I do not think Davis said this with malice.] Perhaps she doesn't think I was honest enough in my autobiography. You see, Bette wrote her autobiography too. Ahh . . . *hers* was full of . . . unhh . . . I found great bitterness in it. Have you read it? . . . More bitterness than gratitude. And my book is just the opposite. Now, that is her opinion, and certainly she's allowed that, we all are. Perhaps she felt I wasn't honest, but I was as honest as anybody can be in my book. Also, I have no bitterness in me. I have nothing but gratitude for this fine, great industry that I love and worship. It's given me everything that I have in life. And I should be bitter about not getting the parts I want all the time? Never. If it had my name on it, I'd get the part. It's that simple.

You said something so interesting a moment ago about the people you've been interviewing, and the movie stars, that they turn out to be really nice human beings. Why is it that people think that we're not human?

JK: Well, when Joan Crawford appears on this huge screen, ten times larger than life, looking like nobody can ever hope to look, there's a sense of unreality. It's something everybody wishes at some time or other to be, but when you turn somebody into the dream prince or princess you want to be, you automatically establish a distance.

JC: Ah-ha! Is that the parts we play? Or is that *us* as personalities? Do you think?

JK: Well, both. Especially in the great glamour period at MGM. Because you play a part, and the publicity sent out about you that appears in the fan magazines is geared along the same lines. So suddenly you're not just Joan Crawford, who has to eat like everybody else, and takes a bath, and all this, you are this remote, alluring creature who dances on clouds; who goes out with Douglas Fairbanks . . . there is an aura.

JC: You mean they really don't want us to be human?

JK: Well, I don't know if it's that, but there just isn't a chance.

JC: Well, that's where I agree with you. You see, I don't agree with candid cameras; either when you have your mouth open taking a bite of food, or getting you in the sun and showing all your freckles. I think that is the *most* unfortunate thing that has happened in the motion-picture industry. They have deglamorized all of us. They have wanted to make us a part of the mob. And the mob and the people don't want us. If they have us or any of the Garbos—one Garbo only—on a pedestal, as you say, they want to keep them there. They don't want them down with them. It gives them something to look forward to. There's also a phrase that I use: audience identification. Now, when I first became a star, the letters that would come to me from girls of my own age at that time—I was eighteen—they felt "If I could become that, they could." And the confidences that we exchanged, the friendships I've earned through that, and they've earned through their confidences and their questions, and I've kept up a lot of these friendships and correspondences throughout the years. I write about 10,000 to 12,000 letters a month.

JK: Has anybody else ever taken it as seriously as you?

JC: No! I feel that if people take the time to write you, you should take the time to answer. I have seen one star in particular, who shall be nameless [can this be Bette Davis?], walk out of the studio with all her fan mail, drive through the front gate and dump it right in the ash can.

This is a dramatic pause—Joan's delivery, her verbal indentations are superb. Even now, listening twenty years later, I can feel myself being rotated—pulled up and down, ready to swear allegiance, at least while I'm there with her. When you listen to her, it's a one-act drama, and you see every inch of her face: the shift of bones beneath the fine, unlined, freckled skin; the muscles showing shifting signals in her forehead, the jaw line, the cheekbones, it's this Rolls-Royce model of a human body. Nothing is left to chance. Her laugh, mentioned earlier after talking about Davis and her book, was like a gearshift on a Rolls. You hardly noticed, but you had been shifted!

JC: I wanted, when I saw this done, to go and pick them up, answer it and sign her name. I felt so *sad*. I felt sad for her too; not only for the people who wouldn't hear from her. But I felt sad for her that she didn't have the warmth, the desire to make other people happy. I think she's missed a lot. Sure I get a lot of problems in letters; sure I get a lot of crank notes . . . and sure I get a lot of people saying: "May I please borrow $5000? I'm not sure when I can pay it back, but I need it desperately." But those you just answer automatically and just say: "I'm awfully sorry, but I have so many demands on my time and my finances and charities and things, that I cannot help all. Bless you . . . and try somebody else." That's an automatic thing. But the heartwarming things are when you touch someone, maybe in one scene in a picture; it meant something to their life, because they had the same complexities, they needed help and it was solved for them by looking at your performance. Golly, do you know what that *does* to your insides? It makes every heartbreak in the world so worthwhile.

JK: Your greatest love affair is with your public.

JC: Yes [She looks resigned, exposed, the truth is out, it must be admitted], in the end, yes. [She says that "yes" the way Garbo says "I vant to be left alone."]

JK: I can understand this rapport when you're working on the stage and the public is right there in front of you and you can feel it every night when you go there. But in the cinema . . . Do you go a lot when your films open, to premieres? To get that sort of reaction then, which you obviously can't get on a set?

JC: I sit up in the top where nobody can see me, and I sneak out before it's over. I was in the theater the other night, and in intermission they were all applauding the artists on the stage, and I was recognized and they were all saying: "Oh, do you have a pen? I must get her autograph." It was very exciting. And I was rather pushed back against the wall. They were all crowding around, and they were flashing lights and everything to tell us: "Get back in the theater," you know, "the show's going to go on." And one man stood there and looked at me as I was signing autographs and saying, "Thank you so much, thank you," and he said, "Isn't this a bloody bore to you?" And I said, "Are you kidding? You were sitting not far from me, and you applauded loud and clear for those actors on that stage just before we broke for intermission. They get that at each performance. I may get it a year later. Whenever I go out publicly . . . this is my applause. We on the soundstage never see people, except our co-workers. This is *our* applause. And it's so thrilling and exciting, it makes you feel so warm, I get gooseflesh!"

JK: It's important to you to have this public contact?

JC: I *want* to be liked; I want so *desperately* to be liked. [Joan is the little match girl holding out her frozen hands.]

JK: Well, you've been liked longer than nearly anybody else.

JC: Oh, you're going to talk about my *damn* durability! [Laughs.]

JK: No, no. Durability merely means something that lasts. You haven't just lasted, you've transcended it. I don't say: this year Joan Crawford . . . I just say: Joan Crawford!
    I want to go to discipline. Discipline has been a ruling force in your life. Does that mean an attitude towards life as well?

JC: How do you mean that?

JK: Well, has this attitude, this working discipline, begun to affect your life offstage as well?

JC: Oh, no, it has not affected me as far as life is concerned because I accept everything life gives me . . . opportunities to meet new people, to walk in the sun on a brisk day, a lovely clear one like today. But the discipline of

having to get packed would prevent me from going for that walk. Because I
. . . was born with it. I must get each day's work *done* before I can play. And
walking in the sun to me is the greatest thing in the world.

JK: You've given Hollywood so much; Hollywood has given you much. But
have you ever felt that you have lost something in the bargain? Your private
life?

JC: Perhaps. But you spoke a moment ago about four marriages, three with
actors. You see, we're all exposed to a great deal of talent, sex, glamour.
And who knows if we hadn't been in pictures whether the first three marriages might have taken? Who knows? They might not have. Carole Lombard
once made a great statement. She said: "Isn't it sad"—she was married to
Clark Gable at the time—"isn't it sad that all of our co-workers see us at our
glamorous best? From 9:00 to 6:00. When we come home to our beautiful husbands, they see us tired, the makeup off, the hair in curlers ready for
tomorrow's work, exhausted. We eat dinner, study scripts and go to bed."
Now, I think the exposure lends a great deal of excitement not only to the
public, but we stimulate each other. To walk on at 9:00 in a beautiful evening dress, perfectly coiffed, made up to perfection, and the men in dinner
jackets, and we start playing a love scene. That's pretty exciting. And some
of it rubs off, you know.

Suppose your husband is working with a glamorous beauty, it's bound to
rub off on him too. You love the excitement of being with each other and all
of that, but when you get on that set, and you're playing Suzy Smith who's
madly in love with Jimmy Stewart in this picture, and you're married to Clark
Gable, Jimmy is such an enchanter, he would just charm any woman right off
her feet. And you have to—it isn't all pretend in acting. You *have* to feel a
certain amount of emotion. And that really comes through. And when you
break a scene, you say: "My goodness, isn't he a darling!" And if you've
taken hold of his hand and they take a picture, there is a rumor that the
marriage is breaking up and you're going to break up another marriage and
you're going to marry the other actor. You can't help that.

JK: Well, how do you feel about the rumors, the gossip, especially personified
by people like Louella Parsons and Hedda Hopper?

JC: Well, I think Hedda, having been an actress, and she knew the business
backwards, she knew all the producers and directors and actors, she's lived
with us all so long, I think she has a right to criticize us and take us to task.
I'm not talking about the gossip bits; but I don't know of anyone in the
industry who will praise a good picture or a good performance more than
Hedda Hopper. I don't know anyone who will take her whole column and do
that.

JK: But I mean the little items that any gossip writer of that time created about
you, about your private life.

JC: This you resent at times. But I usually pick up the phone and say: "Hedda, you were mistaken yesterday," or "Louella, *dear,* I'm sorry, *but* . . . this is what really happened." And no reporter likes to retract. Once they say it, it's said, and they feel their word is law. But that is part of our problems; they have many problems of their own. They have readers, and I don't think a columnist could exist without a certain amount of gossip. *It* is a necessary part of the trappings of Hollywood.

JK: Miss Crawford, in *Torch Song* you sang, but these songs were never recorded afterwards. Is it your own voice?

JC: Only in one number. India Adams did the whole score. I hadn't danced or opened my mouth to sing—except in the shower—for many years, eleven years as a matter of fact, so when I went back to it, I could either do the dancing or the singing, but certainly not both, because we shot the whole picture in twenty-four days.

JK: Did you record any of your songs? Was there an album?

JC: No, there was never an album. But I studied opera for seven years; I guess I was a better actress than I was a singer, and anyway Mr. Mayer said they had three singers under contract at the time and *they* would give their right arms if they could do the dramatic pictures, so . . . I was so discouraged after seven years. I . . . It was one of the few times I ever gave up on anything.

JK: But have you any records? Can we play some of those?

A sigh. The great lady has put her packing problem to one side, and the old 78 rpm plays, the MGM studio orchestra is on, and there she is, "Ask the Lamp on the Corner."

JK: When did you sing this?

JC: About 1938.

Joan's sitting cross-legged in her silk pants, listening with me to the Joan of 1938. I ask her to sing along, with my tape recorder getting it all. Then she introduces the song *"Du Bist die Ruhe."* Joan used to take private lessons from Rosa Ponselle, and this is heavy *Lieder* time.

JK: Well, Miss Crawford, this has been one of the most thrilling interviews I've ever had. Thank you very much.

JC: I have heard that you are just as enthusiastic about everyone. Anita Loos tells me that you have the most enthusiastic attitude towards pictures and personalities and stars and people, so it isn't just me. It's you—and thank you for your kindness.

1965

Joel McCrea, photographed by Ernest Bachrach (RKO), 1932

JOEL
McCREA

E VELYN F. SCOTT, Adela Rogers St. Johns, Irene Mayer Selznick, Cecilia
    de Mille and her cousin Agnes—when these daughters of famous men
and women reminisced about growing up in Hollywood in the '20s, talking
about their own friends, young people like themselves, the boys they had their
first crushes on but didn't manage to marry, the ones they knew from school
and spent summers with down at the beach at Malibu, they'd name them, describe them, then add, still with the gulp of girlish adoration: "*and* there was
Joel McCrea." His boyish charm, his winning personality, his shining decency,
his dazzling all-American good looks—he was a tall (6'2"), golden, athletic-
looking fellow bursting with health—made him a dream lover for every one of
the girls. They were all brunettes, but blondes felt the same way. He was given
a chance in a film starring Marion Davies, and though his part ended up on the
cutting-room floor, she knew a good thing when she saw him, and he was invited up to San Simeon. Because Joel was such a nice, unassuming, well-
mannered young man, Marion's watchful old lover, W. R. Hearst, liked him
too, called him "the All-American Boy," a tag that stuck to McCrea, and invited
him back as often as he wanted to come. Up there he met Constance Bennett,
who made him her leading man in four films and wanted to marry him. He co-
starred in five films with Miriam Hopkins, and though by now he was already
married to another actress, the beautiful Frances Dee, Hopkins fancied him like
mad. Over a period of twenty years, McCrea made five films with Barbara
Stanwyck, but theirs was the chemistry of bread and butter rather than champagne and breadsticks. Even before he was a full-fledged star and after he'd
made it, several of America's finest, most individual writer-directors, like Gregory La Cava, Preston Sturges and George Stevens, wrote parts for him in memorable films (La Cava, *Private Worlds;* Sturges, *Sullivan's Travels;* Stevens, *The
More the Merrier*). He had everything required for major stardom and he
achieved it, especially after he started to play cowboys, a childhood ambition
he realized in his private life and on the screen.
     Though a California boy, born 1905, raised in Hollywood when movies
were still in their swaddling clothes, as much as acting he loved horses and the
wide open range. He grew up around genuine cowboys, genuine Indians and a

couple of genuine cattle rustlers and outlaws who had migrated to California, the last Western outpost. These men, survivors of the last Indian wars, shoot-outs and cattle trails, found work in the early movies, doing daring stunts for a couple of dollars or playing cowboys like themselves in serials and Westerns; they were straightforward, no-nonsense, hard-drinking, hard-working types who had little in common with the idealized pinup version of themselves and would have laughed the Marlboro Country cowboy out of town. McCrea admired these men, their spirit and their values. Once he reached the point in his career where he could pick and choose his parts, he made only Westerns and played cowboys like those he had known. His biggest drawback, which kept him from just reaching the same heights as his friend Gary Cooper, was an unease with his own desirability.

As his career progressed in the '30s, you could sense him pulling back and clamping down on the attraction created by his good looks, which had made Hollywood's top female stars want him as their leading man. By the time he starred in *Union Pacific* (1939), he'd already squared himself off, buttoned up his lips into a tight and canny smile, hoisted up his breeches and avoided becoming a glamorous romantic star like Tyrone Power or his friend Robert Taylor. American men of McCrea's generation never did feel quite right about being treated as sex symbols. That was for foreigners like Rudolph Valentino or Charles Boyer. As with clowns who want to prove themselves by playing Hamlet, and vice versa, stars popular because of their looks and their sex appeal were always trying to be taken seriously—by removing their makeup and pulling back their hair if they were women, or by getting on a horse and building a log cabin if they were men. In the process, as so often happens, even when they proved their point, it meant becoming one actor among many instead of being a star among the few. Gary Cooper was unique in that his beauty never made anyone think less of him as a man. Of course, though Cooper won two Oscars, critics failed to take him as seriously as more obviously showy dramatic actors. Until it was too late. After he died, everybody started to reevaluate Cooper as one of the great stars *and* actors of the American screen. But throughout his career Cooper accepted the adoration from women as well as men and remained emotionally supple to the end in a way McCrea never could or wanted to. Then too, the attention he gave to his home, his family, his vast property holdings that made him one of the richest movie stars and other interests may have made the pursuing of a film career less and less important. He made Westerns and played decent, God-fearing men because he enjoyed them. But he was good, as a man and as an actor, and his simplicity in films like *Stars in My Crown* was very attractive. When an emotion came, it was always pure, it hadn't been cheapened by overuse.

For forty years—from 1922, when he started out in films as an extra and bit player, to 1962, when he retired from the screen on the crest of that glorious Western *Ride the High Country,* McCrea had known personally or worked professionally with most of the men and women who had been anyone in the movies.

At almost eighty, he was a good-looking man, tall, courteous, kindly, though he hadn't aged as strikingly as his wife, whom I saw hoeing in the garden when I left and who looked like a willowy girl with snow-white hair. What a beauty! But the young Joel from the movies started to emerge as he talked. It wasn't like reminiscing, but as if it all happened yesterday and was all around him, tucked away in different parts of his face to appear when the turn of that moment in his life came. Like a chameleon, he went without effort from being a boy to young manhood to his present status, back, forth, marvelously loquacious, a great raconteur, incredible recall, and when, to make a point while telling me about something that happened to him in 1929, he said, "Now I'll have to jump forward to 1962," the wrinkly-faced rancher went from having been a boy in his early twenties to the man he had been in his late fifties.

We spent the better part of that terrific day in the bunkhouse his wife lets him keep the way he likes it—some old awards, Western paintings, cattle horns and stuffed hunting trophies on the wall, cured skins and woven Indian rugs on the floor. The couch and chair were those big, impressive old leather affairs you see in Westerns but can hardly find anywhere, worn with years of sitting and made slouchingly comfortable from use. It was February, cool but not cold. The room had a stone fireplace, but there was no need for a fire . . . besides, I could imagine one as he talked. The boy who dreamed of becoming a cowboy was the man now telling me about it, of the dreams that came true, of how he enjoyed it all and enjoys it still. A real spellbinder is Joel McCrea.

JK: You grew up with the movies, didn't you?

JM: Yes, and I saw Valentino the first time when he was making *Four Horsemen of the Apocalypse*. Rex Ingram was directing him and Alice Terry [Mrs. Ingram], and I rode my bicycle out to see them. They let you come right along, and I watched and I said, "Gee, I won't ever be able to do it," but I'd see what the good ones were doing, what to do and what not to do. I sat right behind Rex Ingram. Good-looking guy, all the girls liked him. Black Irish. Very attractive guy. He should have been the leading man in a lot of his own films.* Anyway, I did start that way. And then, where I lived on Hollywood Boulevard was Nickolas Canyon Drive, near where Ruth Roland used to make those serials with horses and stuff, and I got a job for $2 a day and lunch to lead six horses; we didn't have trailers in those days, and they'd bring the horses from a stable and lead them up to a location around where UCLA is now. And I watched Charles Ray make *The Girl I Loved* with Patsy Ruth Miller. I was only a kid, maybe twelve. And later, when I was fourteen, I bought a horse . . . first one I ever owned . . . bought it from George Beldam, the guy who became Rex Bell and married Clara Bow. We had gone

---

*After years of casting actors in his mold—besides Valentino, there were Ramon Novarro, Antonio Moreno and Ivan Petrovich—Ingram finally decided to cast himself in *Baroud* (*Love in Morocco*) in 1933, the only one of his films not to feature his wife.

to high school together, and one day he said, "My father has bronchitis and I got to sell my horse. If you buy it, I'll throw in the bridle, saddle, harness and a buggy for $80." So I did. And from then on, I would ride out to these locations on horseback. And Ruth Roland would say, "Could you ride a horse out of the thing here fast? The leading man says he's never ridden a horse; he's a very good actor, but he's scared." And I said, "I'd ride anything," you know, because I was a cowboy. I was delivering papers, and William S. Hart stopped me and said, "That's the first time my dog"—a pit bull—"hasn't chased the paper boy." I've got some books signed "To the Newsboy from William S. Hart." In his handwriting. Anyway, when I was nine years old, we moved to Hollywood from South Pasadena, where I was born, right out to 7755 Hollywood Boulevard. So I was raised in Hollywood. Which was still open territory then, all open territory.

Studios would come out, they'd say they wanted to use the front of a house. They'd pay $25, and then the girl, the leading lady, would stand at the door and say "Goodbye" and the guy would say "Goodbye," and that would be the scene, and then they didn't have to build a set. And I used to watch all of those things going on, and looking, listening, interested, never really *believing* that I could do it, but always thinking that if I was at the right place at the right time, it could happen. But if it didn't, life would go on. I'd still fall in love, I'd still ride a horse, I'd still see the blue sky. But my professor in drama and public speaking at Pomona College told me, "You know, you have a future. With the contacts you have from going to school with all those producers' and directors' children, you ought to give it a crack. Because you could be playing a cowboy and you'd be able to buy yourself a ranch now instead of thirty years from now." And so I did.

And later Bob Arlington Brugh brought me a letter of introduction from my old teacher, who said that as he had advised me, so had he advised this guy. I took Arlington out to MGM, where he made a test for a crime short with Virginia Bruce, and he was made, and he became Robert Taylor. About three years later, when I was playing opposite Stanwyck, we all went to dinner with the president of Union Pacific Railroad, Bill Jeffers, and I said to Taylor, "Now you've done *Camille* with Garbo, and I helped you get started, now you can help *me* because you're doing better than I am!" We ended up best friends. He brought his horse, when he went into the service, out to my ranch. It was a comanche that Barbara had given him, and he's buried up there on top of the hill.

JK: So your idol was William S. Hart when you were a kid?

JM: Yeah, and I didn't want to be just like him, but I wanted to do the type of thing he did. Because he did it with authenticity. He was very meticulous about it, and he wanted the Indians to be right. But unless I'd had this encouragement in college from that professor . . . I did a thing called *Copperhead,* which Lionel Barrymore had done on the stage, and he said, "You don't know it, but you've got something to offer. You better try it." So I've enjoyed the whole thing. It's been great. Rewarding.

JK: Did you say before that your son is taping your story?

JM: Yeah, we just go out on the lawn and I say when I did this and my first test, and I tell him when I did this first thing with DeMille. . . .

JK: What about your wife, is she as well? [Frances Dee has been Mrs. McCrea for over fifty years.]

JM: Frances hasn't taped anything yet. She doesn't get mixed up in things so much. Like I always got mixed up with personalities like Gregory La Cava. He always used me when he could have had Bob Montgomery. Bob was way better. Better actor and better box office. Frances worked by studying her work, it was a different kind of thing she did. She was interested in learning more about her trade. I was interested in the personalities and the people I met. And I got along because I always had people like Greg asking for me, you know.

JK: How did you get to know La Cava? Did you know him from your time at RKO?

JM: That's right. He was at Paramount when he started. Richard Dix was the guy who worked for him there, they were buddies, and Dix was a buddy of mine, a booster of mine; he called me Joey. He got me in *Lost Squadron* [RKO, 1932] with Von Stroheim and all of them. So when La Cava came over to RKO, I was under contract to RKO and I met him, and we got along. He was going to do a picture called *Bed of Roses* with Constance Bennett, she was a huge star then, and he put me in that, with Pert Kelton. La Cava and I hit it off, so when Walter Wanger was going to make *Private Worlds,* he already had Claudette Colbert, Bob Montgomery, Charles Boyer—who'd never been in anything here yet—and Joan Bennett.

I was over at La Cava's house for dinner one night; I used to go home with him, he'd left his wife and lived alone. Gene Fowler dropped in and they began having a few belts, and I ate the wonderful dinner that his wonderful cook had prepared. And afterwards he said, "I want you to do a picture with Claudette Colbert." And I said, "Fine." And he said, "If it's fine, just get on the phone and call your agent." My agent was Frank Vincent, a fine guy. So I called Frank and he said, "Tell Greg I don't know how he can do it, because I also handle Douglas Fairbanks, Jr., and he's supposed to do it. And what's more, I think Wanger would rather have Robert Montgomery than either one of you, and he's going to try and borrow him from Metro." So I told La Cava and he said, "Never mind, you come tomorrow morning and we'll make some photographic tests. Boyer will have to stand on a phone book to be as big as you are." So my agent went in to see Wanger, and Wanger said, "I like Joel a lot and we go to the Hearst ranch at the same time, but I arranged to borrow Bob Montgomery." Anyway, I was down on the set and Wanger came in and said, "What are you doing here?" I said, "We're doing some photographic tests. Didn't Greg say anything to you about it? I came in with him." La Cava had this Pierce-Arrow, with little lights on the fender, you know? And a driver. You couldn't have missed it. And so Wanger said, "Yeah, I spoke to him, and I told him I liked you fine, but I'm going to use Montgomery." I could understand that. La Cava never said a word, and then we went home. And then he said, "I don't care what he says, I'm rewriting the thing and you're going to do it. Just don't worry about it. He can stay up there to justify his shiny-top desk, but we'll make the film. That's what we're going to do, we're only going to *make* the film." So I started the picture, no contract, no nothing. He said, "Don't worry, if they don't pay you, I'll pay you out of my salary." And I did the picture.

JK: Did Wanger pay?

JM: Oh, sure. Not only that, he paid double. I'd been getting $1500 a week, and Greg told me to tell my agent he had asked for $3000. "Because this picture is going to do something for you." And it did. Goldwyn looked at the picture and that's why he signed me for five years. That picture was a big help, it helped everybody: Boyer got started after that film came out. But Wanger was very nice about it, he was justifying himself. It was his own movie, so he had a lot more riding on it.* But that was the only thing that stopped La Cava: he didn't want to show anything.

   He'd have eight or nine pages typewritten and that's what this story was going to be. He would do it as he did it. And in the morning he'd come in and give you two or three pages and say, "This is the thing we're going to do," and he'd go into the trailer there with a writer and write some other stuff. We never had a complete script, and that's what the studio didn't like. They said, "We can't budget it if we don't know what to do," and so finally he made the establishment turn against him. He wrote all his own.

   Before we did *Primrose Path*, I had dinner with La Cava and he said he wanted me to do a picture with Ginger Rogers. I said fine. Doug Fairbanks was up for it too—again! See, my agent, Frank Vincent, was one of the best, he handled Garbo and Gilbert and Rita Hayworth and Rosalind Russell and Eddie Robinson and Cary Grant. Anyway, so Fairbanks went to talk to La Cava and he asked for a script. Greg said, "I said I don't have scripts." And Fairbanks said, "What am I going to do?" So La Cava told him the story, but he told it completely from Ginger's point of view. And Fairbanks said, "I don't see what I motivate." And La Cava said, "To tell you the truth, you don't motivate a damn thing in this part." And they both said, "That's it." But

---

*Wanger had previously worked with La Cava at Metro, and subsequently produced a Hitchcock thriller, *Foreign Correspondent*, starring Joel, so he had an indication of how La Cava worked and he must have been satisfied with McCrea.

you never asked La Cava what you motivated, because if he had wanted you to motivate something, he'd have made it so you would.

I've heard La Cava tell you a story and though you have a secondary role to both me and Ginger, he could tell it so you thought you were really equal. You see, with La Cava, there wasn't any script and he changed it all the time anyway. Well, La Cava said to me, "I'm going up to Monterey and you and Ginger have got to be up there on the day after tomorrow." And I said, "Well, RKO is still arguing about it because they have to pay Fairbanks or give him another commitment." Because he really had a commitment from them. I didn't. I was over at Paramount. But he said, "No, you come." And I said, "Well, I think I'll drive up," and he said, "Fine. I'll meet you up there at the inn." I went up, I never had a contract, I did four weeks up there on location. Wonderful time, dinner with Ginger every night and Greg . . . we all adored each other. Greg adored her even more than I did, but he didn't get anywhere with her. . . .

JK: He gave her three great pictures.*

JM: He sure did. Well, she was smart enough for that. They made her. But she was nice to him. So, when we got back to the studio and started shooting there, this guy came down on the set and said, "You know, we've only got a week to go, and you haven't any contract." Every Wednesday they used to pay in those days. And he said, "Well, I don't know what we're going to do." And I said, "Well, I don't know what you ought to do either, but I want to tell you something. If you don't do something pretty quick, I'm just going to go back to the ranch. And you'll just have to finish the picture without me, because you haven't got a deal with me." La Cava told me to say that. So we got everything we asked for! Paramount didn't get any money, I got it direct from RKO. I only had a two-a-year deal with Paramount, and the rest I could do on my own.

La Cava was a brilliant guy. I think the two most interesting men I worked with were Sturges and La Cava, because they were original guys. They had an idea for a film they wrote with the writer, and they did it according to who they cast for it. If La Cava had gotten Montgomery for *Private Worlds,* he would have done it differently. He always wanted me *not* to be the nice "All-American Boy" that Mr. Hearst called me. And so he made me do things in *Primrose Path,* where I turned Ginger down and called her a tart and everything, and the same thing in *Private Worlds.* That's when Goldwyn said, "Oh, I thought he was just a nice, easy-going boy, but I saw some sparks fly there." I didn't have sense enough to know to do that, but La Cava took it upon himself if he was interested in you. The two people he liked the best among actors were Hepburn and me. And Richard Dix, of course. They got

---

*Stage Door, Fifth Avenue Girl and *Primrose Path.* Her films with Astaire made Ginger a star. The films with La Cava ensured she could survive without Astaire.

drunk together. But I never drank. I would go out to his house, and he never asked me why I didn't drink. I'd eat his dinner, and the cook would say, "Oh, I'm so glad you enjoyed the dinner. I made it for Mr. La Cava, but he never got it until it was cold." And Gene Fowler would be there and write. Well, somebody up there liked me. Oh, the thing I neglected to say is that when he cast either Claudette or me . . . important as she was, and as unimportant as I was . . . he called us in, told us what he wanted us to do, and told us the story and what he expected from us. He said, "You do this and that and the other." So then, the next morning you come in and he would have typed out about three pages, because that's about what we made a day in those days; and we'd rehearse it, and if something didn't fit, he'd change it. He never went to a writer or any executive . . . that's why he never worked for Zanuck. Zanuck had been a writer, he wrote the Rin-Tin-Tin things, you know, and he would tell good writers what to do. La Cava wouldn't put up with that. But actors really loved working with him. Because everything was kind of tailored for you. He wanted *you*. No one forced you on him, it wasn't a commitment, it was what he wanted. And when he wanted it, he saw that he got it. Hepburn hung around his office all the time. Because she needed a La Cava at RKO. The interesting thing about Kate is that she always told me, "You're a cowboy. You really like the cowboy stuff." And I had turned down the role with her in *Spitfire*, I didn't want to do it. Now, she was much more important than I, she'd come out more important in the first place. And she said, "Well, you'll be sorry, because this is going to be a big hit." But when it came out, Ashton Stevens, who was a relative of George Stevens, wrote a column, and all I did was cut out part of it. And it said, "It will be well if all those connected with this one will forget it as quickly as those who see it." Isn't that great? [He chuckles.] So I cut that out and I sent it to her, and she said, "You son of a fox . . ." She was really . . . [He laughs again.]

JK: She had a very attractive Ganymede quality. But you had to balance it very carefully or she'd end up being more masculine than the leading man!

JM: That's right, because she had the broad shoulders and the flat chest. But she had to stay feminine. That's why in *Philadelphia Story* she was so good. Cary and Stewart balanced her well . . . and later Tracy was a great balance for her.

JK: The two of you next to each other would have been very good.

JM: Well, La Cava saw that and that's why he wanted to do a picture with us, but there was some new guy as head of the studio who didn't want to do it, and so I left RKO. But La Cava was a tragedy. Because Hepburn liked him and he liked Hepburn, and we were going to do a thing called *Three Came Unarmed*. He had the property, RKO owned the property, but when they decided on a budget, it was too high. La Cava, Hepburn and me, you know. So . . . I was there at RKO for six years under six different studio presidents.

They were always kind of screwed up. Anyway, they abandoned the idea. And we never got to do it. He sent for me finally when he did the thing with Irene Dunne out at Universal, the last thing he did, *Lady in a Jam*. He sent word to me, didn't send any script, and I said I was committed to do something else and couldn't do it. And he said, "Well, it's too bad because we would have had a lot of fun together." Then he got into a project with Mary Pickford, I don't remember what it was. And finally, he'd been drinking, he'd stopped working, he'd rented a beach house and all those so-called buddies of his would come along and he got too much to drink. And so he just faded out.

JK: Did a lot of friends desert him?

JM: Yes. Except Hepburn. Hepburn didn't. Hepburn was the only one who was at his funeral. I was away, but somebody told me that. They said, "You and Hepburn were the only ones that stuck with him, and you should have been there at the funeral." You know, it seems to me that the enemies that he made when he was at the top, telling producers, "Why should I let you read this script? You probably wouldn't understand it," didn't help an awful lot. He undermined himself with those people. They didn't do anything when he was doing well, making all those hits, because he was too important, but those little things stick with you. Later, when La Cava needed the work and they got the chance on a surefire commercial picture, they'd use Henry Hathaway or something, you know?

JK: Yes, the ones who were most hurt, I think, were the really talented people, like La Cava, Sturges, Borzage . . .

JM: Oh, what a wonderful man. Borzage. I loved him. I made a test for *Liliom*. I didn't get it, but Borzage told me that I could use that test to get myself a lot of exposure. Borzage did a great job. I wish I'd kept the damn thing.

Do you know, I have turned down almost as many pictures as I have accepted because I didn't think I was adequate for them. When Jack Warner wanted me to play Will Rogers, I said, "I'm not qualified to play Will Rogers. I can't play Will Rogers. All I could do would be to get up and ape him, and it wouldn't be any good because he's too great on his own." Now, several other parts came along like that. I remember one for Clarence Brown, *Intruder in the Dust* [1949]. I don't know who the hell did it . . . oh, David Brian. And I turned down *The Howards of Virginia* [1940], and it was with Frank Lloyd, whom I loved. Cary Grant did it, but with the outfits he had to wear, the wigs and stuff, it didn't go. Cary is too glib to play a Quaker, you don't believe it. But when the Will Rogers thing came up, I had a commitment to Warners and Jack Warner said, "You don't have script approval, you have to do the picture." I said, "I want a part I'm qualified to play." And Mike Curtiz said, "Did you hear that, J.L.? That's the first sonofabitch actor who said he *wasn't* good enough. Any sonofabitch who'll be that honest, if he doesn't want it, I don't want *him*!" I was out!

JK: But you were wrong not to do *Devil Is a Woman*.*

JM: Was I? Well, Von Sternberg froze me out of it; and Dietrich afterwards told me, "You just have to put up with that. He calls me a cow, he does this and that." One of the problems was her asking for me in the first place, I think. That's what Frances thought. Joe was jealous. It's interesting how all those powerful men always wanted the women who rejected them . . . La Cava and Ginger, Lubitsch and Miriam Hopkins, Wyler was after her too, Von Sternberg and Marlene. . . . Well, I thought at the time I was asked to do it that it was going to be a plum, that it would be great to do. But I got on the set and all I had to do was snap my fingers; when the waiter came, I say, "Cup of coffee." And it was thirty-nine takes. [Joel shakes his head, imitating Von Sternberg: "No, no . . ."] Then Joe says, "What do you like, Coca-Cola? Seven-Up? Which do you like? You don't like coffee, do you?" I said, "What makes you say that?" He said, "You don't sound *sincere* when you order a cup of coffee." I said, "Joe, you've seen me on the screen. You know I'm no Barrymore, no Bill Powell, you know that. So why do you want me? If I only have one way of saying 'A cup of coffee,' maybe I'm not the actor that you need." "Well," he says, "you should be able to, and so we'll see tomorrow morning." I came in and we're both walking toward the stage, and he said, "We ran the stuff early this morning, and we can't use any of it, it's no good." And I said, "Neither am I, with you." And he said, "But you have a contract. Miss Dietrich wanted you, you have to do it." And I said, "No I don't. You don't know me. I don't have to do any more motion pictures. I can get out of the industry. I'm a cowboy at heart."

I owned 1000 acres, which I paid very little for, and which I sold for $5 million. That was capital gain, and the whole point was that, though I didn't have it back then, I had the same thing inside me. I'd have done the same thing if I just had a newspaper route. Because life goes on. You have a lot of things as a cowboy or a newsboy that a star never gets again. There's a simplicity, there's a meeting of romance and different things that can happen to you if you let them happen. There's just sort of something going all the time. So when I said to him that I could get out of it, and he said, "No you can't, you better go see the head of the studio," I said, "That's who I'm going to see." That was Manny Cohen. I'd never met him, I'd never seen him, he was a little bit of a guy, only there for a short time. I went up there and I said, "Mr. Cohen, he doesn't think I know how to say 'A cup of coffee' in thirty-nine takes, and now he says he can't use any of the takes." And Cohen said, "That sonofabitch, this is the last picture that he's going to make for Para-

*McCrea was originally cast opposite Dietrich in the role taken by Cesar Romero after McCrea left.

mount." And it was. He said, "He's made some good pictures, but he's a phony sonofabitch, and you do just as you please." And he acted as if he were my friend or something, and he was, because he felt the same way. Apparently he'd been talked to badly by Joe, because Joe had a tremendous ego . . . as a lot of small people who are gifted do, and people don't give them credit for it. But anyway, I didn't do the film and never went back, and I never saw it. In his book* Von Sternberg said that there were two big men who were afraid of him . . . John Wayne and I. We weren't afraid of him; we were afraid we didn't want to work for him!

Coop hated him. But Coop was different. Coop was smarter than either Wayne or me. What's it La Cava used to call me? The "cowboy psychiatrist"! [He laughs.] But, you see, Coop was different. Coop didn't like him; they made that one picture, *Morocco,* and he refused to work with him again. Von Sternberg wanted Coop for his next picture, and Coop went to the head of the studio and told him he didn't want to do it. And if he didn't want to do it, why, you'd better just forget it.

Coop never fought, he never got mad, he never told anybody off that I know of; everybody that worked with him liked him, particularly a guy like Vic Fleming; Coop loved him. He did *The Virginian* with him and he was excellent. He liked Henry Hathaway; he liked Lubitsch. He did *Bluebeard's Eighth Wife* with Lubitsch even though he knew he was wrong for it, but he had a commitment, so he did it. And they'd say, "You move over here," and Claudette would say, "No, that's not my good side, you have to move over here, Gary." Lubitsch said, "He [Coop] jorns so much." He meant to say "yawns"—and I said, "I do too." You know, between setups, we both could stay there with the hammers going and the lights and everything, and fall sound asleep. They'd have to come wake us up: "Come on, there's a scene to start now." Sound asleep, both of us!

JK: Maybe it's just the simplicity, the unfussiness in counterpoint to the frantic pace and chaos, but you're very good in all sorts of comedy. Your characters are endowed with the smarts, their instincts are "country," and it takes a lot to ruffle their composure.

JM: Like *The More the Merrier,* with George Stevens: great director and a wonderful guy. When he and Jean Arthur—Jean is the one who wanted me,† and he took me after we met—got me, we just got along great. And he could have used about four other people who were more qualified than I was. But he saw something different in me. And when a guy with the kind of gifts that a Sturges or a La Cava or Stevens and I think Borzage had . . .

The test I did for Borzage, for *Liliom,* took a whole day. It was with Mary Philbin. Her career was kind of over at that time, and Frank had his

---

Fun in a Chinese Laundry.
†Jean Arthur had worked with him previously in *Adventure in Manhattan.*

brother Danny, who played the accordion, play mood music to get us in . . . and this is for a test—a *test*!—for the head of the studio, who didn't know who in the hell I was. But Borzage had seen me a couple of times and had said, "I think we should do something sometime." So when I didn't get *Liliom* (because they then decided not to split up the Janet Gaynor–Charles Farrell team. I was going to be doing it with Janet. In the end Farrell was in it, but Janet wasn't) he said to me, "You take it," and I ran that test for Henry King, and Henry King immediately put me in the juvenile lead in a Will Rogers picture called *Lightnin'* with Louise Dresser and Jason Robards, Sr.

Will and I fell in love immediately, the first day of shooting, when I asked him how to do a certain Texas skip, and he said, "You wait until after shooting." And I said, "That means I miss the last bus," and he said, "You ain't an extra anymore, you ride home with me in the LaSalle." He drove his own LaSalle coupé. And then he said, "Where are you going for dinner?" And I said, "Well, I guess the tavern where we're all staying." He said, "I've got to go over to Caliente with Winnie Sheehan and Henry King and Herb Fleisheicher"—a big philanthropist from San Francisco—"and you come with me." I said, "They haven't invited me." He said, "I just did." We went in and Henry King looked at me as though to say, "How did you happen . . ." I'm a $100-a-week extra here with the president of the studio and all the big shots. I just shut my mouth, I had brains enough not to shoot off. We went through dinner, I listened to them all talk, and then Will said, "Clara Bow and Rex Bell are coming up here later." I went to high school with Rex, his real name was George Beldam. Four other guys and I tested to see who would be Rex Bell, because that was the name Fox chose when they lost Tom Mix and were looking for another Western star. They thought, "Here's an easy name that goes on a marquee, Rex Bell." They tested us all and George Beldam beat us out. So he came up, married to Clara Bow, and Will said to me, "Now you go to the roulette wheel," and I didn't know how to shoot craps or the roulette, and I said, "I don't like to gamble, I don't like to lose money." [McCrea has a reputation for being a man who never spends a penny foolishly. As if he read my mind, McCrea laughs.] No, I don't. I don't understand that part. So I took his $100 bill, he took one, and we all went around and came back again at the end, and he said, "I lost mine, how did you do?" Well, I told him, there was the best-looking Rita Hayworth type with furs and diamonds sitting there, and she bet 36 black, and I bet my full $100, and it paid off! I got $400. And he said, "Give me back my $100!" Then Clara turned up with Rex Bell. I tested for one of her films, but Gilbert Roland beat me out.* It was one of the last things she did, *Call Her Savage,* at Fox. But I never was out with her or anything. Anyway, that was the kind of a way things went.

I was freelancing then, and so I went back to my agent and said, "What

---

* Gilbert Roland later married Constance Bennett after she failed to get Joel.

do you think?" And he said, "Fox already called. Mr. Rogers asked for you to play the juvenile lead in *Business and Pleasure,* the next picture he is going to make . . . the Booth Tarkington story." Then Fox offered me a contract, just on the strength of Will. They hadn't seen my performance in *Lightnin'* yet. Actually, I was good in *Lightnin',* it was one of the better things I did in my life. My wife saw it and said, "That's better than what you did five years later, because you didn't try so hard. You were like Coop, you just let it roll off." Well, I didn't even know I was doing that. I once said to Tracy, "What's the secret of your success, Spence?" He said, "Learn your lines, read your script, read it again, read it again, when you wake up in the morning, read it again, be on time, know your lines . . . the acting takes care of itself." Well, that's what I did. Of course, Spence did a little extra.

JK: Listen, I'm still thinking about you and Joe von Sternberg. Frances had worked with him in *An American Tragedy,* and she looked sensational. Did she say anything about Sternberg or your work with him?

JM: No, she liked him. She said to me, "I don't know what it was that he did, but if he told you that you don't know how to order a cup of coffee, then he doesn't want you." And she knew that it could be because of Dietrich, because Dietrich kind of loved Frances too. She used to send Frances flowers. You know the story about Dietrich and Carole Lombard? Carole said that Dietrich used to slip in and go to Carole's dressing room in the morning before the maid got there and leave flowers there. By this time Lombard was doing well, and she went down to Dietrich's dressing room and said, "If you want something, you come on down when I'm there. I'm not going to chase you."

Dietrich had a reputation for being more sentimental and impressed than her self-assured, impersonal screen image, such as her hard-boiled role in Tay Garnett's *Seven Sinners*. Garnett was another of the feisty, independent-minded directors of memorable movies.

JM: I liked Garnett too. He was trying to get me to do *Postman Always Rings Twice,* but I turned it down. You know why? I've always had a feeling of responsibility towards the image that I'm creating, and if I'm moving in with Lana Turner and going to bump off her husband, then this isn't the image I want. I wanted *The Virginian,* I wanted *Union Pacific,* I wanted to be the guy who rode off into the sunset, "right" over "evil," I always felt that. It wasn't the money, I never turned a thing down because of the money. Like one time Leonard Goldstein [who'd done the *Ma and Pa Kettle* series] called me and said, "I need your help. Arthur Krim at UA will give us the money to make a picture called *Stranger on Horseback.* . . ."

JK: The one with Miroslava? Very strange but very beautiful.

JM: Strange, that's right. God, your memory is great! I had never heard of her until she was in that picture with me. So, anyway, I went over and had lunch with him, and he said, "I've got a thing called *Stranger on Horseback* that I tried to get Cooper for, I'll be honest with you . . . but he's had it for three months and he hasn't called me back, so would you consider it?" I said, "Let me read it." I sat there and read it in his office and I said, "I'll do it." He said, "I can get money from Arthur Krim for everything on the production except the star's salary." I said, "Okay, I'll do it for 25 percent of the profits." My agent said, "You're not going to get anything." We made it. Ray Ranahan, who did a lot of DeMille pictures and was a big man at Technicolor, photographed it. Louis L'Amour wrote it and he's one of the best Western writers, and he called me and said, "You are beautiful, you were just the way I wrote it," and that was enough for me. I never got any money at all for about six or eight months. And then the checks began coming in. My agent said, "You cast bread upon the waters . . . and it's coming back to you."

I enjoyed my contacts with people like Frank Lloyd, even DeMille, though we were never close. He was a little hammy. Well, he'd been an actor, you see. And Preston Sturges. Preston would insist I go to the Players with him. He'd say, "If you'd do just one more shot . . ." It was six o'clock, and Claudette would take off her false eyelashes and say, "That's it, Preston." And he would say to me, "If you'd just stay a few minutes, we can finish this scene because we have these sixty-five extras all ready." I think this was on *Palm Beach Story,* John Seitz was the cinematographer,* a great guy, he did *Four Horsemen of the Apocalypse,* Valentino's first big thing. Anyway, Preston said, "If you do, I'll buy you dinner." 'Cause he owned his own restaurant, the Players. And we'd do it. So we had great times like that. And with La Cava, just the two of us would have dinner and talk about films, and I learned so much from him. I was the kind of guy who was influenced by personality. Like Mary Pickford . . . I loved her. Whenever I'd see her, we'd hug and kiss, and she'd say, "Have you been reading your Bible and being a good boy?" And I'd say, "Yes, I have, Mary." And she said once, "I made a test with you, but they gave the part to Buddy or Johnny Mack Brown."

JK: Was that for *Coquette?*

JM: Yeah, she made a test with me for that. Colleen Moore made tests with me, but I don't remember for what. And Doug Fairbanks, Sr., tried to do things for me. He and Mary and William S. Hart were going to appear at a big livestock show down at the stockyards in LA, which are gone now. So we went there and they introduced them and the people went wild. There must have been about 1000 people, it was a big rodeo. And Doug said, "I have a young man here." Now, I hadn't done *anything* but extra work. Nothing. I

---

*The cinematographer on *The Palm Beach Story* was Victor Milner. John Seitz photographed *Sullivan's Travels,* another Preston Sturges film in which McCrea appeared.

was just a senior at Pomona College. You know, Norma Shearer or somebody would see me on the set and I didn't look bad, and so they'd say, "Who's that fellow?" Colleen's brother, Cleve Moore, came up and said, "My sister wants to know if you'd make a test." I said, "*Will* I make a test? [He chuckles.] I'll sweep out the stage for you if you want."

When I wanted to get out of my contract at RKO—Ben Kahane was president at the time and I was getting $750 a week and playing with Dorothy Mackaill and Bebe Daniels—he called Irene Dunne in. We'd just done *The Silver Cord* with Frances and that's where I fell for her. So he called us in and said they were going to renew our contracts. She [Irene] got like $20,000 a picture, after *Cimarron,* and her next option called for $25,000. And I got $750 a week and it called for $1000. But times were tough, and they said, "We'll renew, but at the same salary. We won't give you the increase." And so I looked at Irene and she said, "Well, we'll think it over." So we went out together. We got along well. No romance at all. She wasn't a sexy girl, you know. Not in the slightest. With Rita Hayworth I'd have been in real trouble. So we went to her dressing room and talked about it, and she said, "What do you think?" And I said, "Gee, I don't know. Times are tough and everything, but I've never let money make my decision. I've hung on to money pretty well, but I've never let money make my decision, whether I got more or not." It wasn't the kind of integrity that I felt was profitable. So she said, "We've got to get an agent." So she got Charlie Feldman. There was Myron Selznick, Charlie Feldman, and Eddington and Vincent. Frank Vincent was the one I chose. She said, "What's the difference, Joel? They get 10 percent . . . they get us 90 percent more than we're getting. So let's do it." So we did. And I *left* RKO. I said I wouldn't accept it, and she didn't either. Anyway, that was the kind of thing that made me realize that you had to think out a thing. You had to decide what route you were going to go, and you had to project beyond today.

JK: She did a film at Columbia called *Theodora Goes Wild,* which made a big hit, and her salary . . .

JM: . . . went right up. And then she had the *Roberta* thing, where she sings "Smoke Gets in Your Eyes," she got into that. And I never saw Ben Kahane for about eight or ten years after that, because he ran out of RKO and he went out and made the deals for Harry Cohn at Columbia. When I went in to make the deal with Columbia, after I'd agreed to make *The More the Merrier* with George Stevens . . . because at first I didn't want to do it, I didn't know what George would be like and I'd been working pretty hard and I was tired. Anyway, I said, "Shall I go see Harry Cohn?" and Cohn said, "I don't want to talk money with you, you sonofabitch, you own more land than anybody but Mr. Hearst." They sent me to Ben Kahane. He had the big eighty-cent cigar, and he said, "So we meet again," and I said, "Yeah, Ben, but it's a little bit different now. Instead of going from $750 to $1000, I've gone to $10,000 a week with a ten-week guarantee." He said, "Yes, I know, I saw it." And he took the cigar out of his mouth and said, "I'm going to be honest with you. I didn't think you'd ever get that kind of money." I said, "Well, didn't you think I was any good?" "No, I thought you were fine. But I didn't think you'd ever get up into that kind of figure, and I was just trying to make a tough deal for RKO."

JK: You've talked several times now about "an image." Did you always have an image in mind of what you wanted to be like?

JM: Yeah! Even at high school. First of all, I wanted to be a frontiersman. I wished I'd been born back in the horse-and-buggy days. I always wanted to be a rancher. I figured the only kind of pictures I wanted to do would be to portray the thing that I understood the most about. That's why directors have often told me that they picked me not for my acting ability but for the way I rode a horse. So when I saw the ones I admired, it was people like Coop. I saw him in *The Virginian,* saw him in those first things he did, and then when I met him, it was up at Pickfair before either one of us was married. We were both bachelors, and he said, "We've got to get together and double date." And he had a crush on Paulette Goddard, but already Chaplin had discovered her.

JK: Wasn't she still just the little blond girl . . .

JM: Yes, she was a little Goldwyn *Whoopee* girl with Eddie Cantor or something. So we got talking at this dinner, and afterwards we were sitting around having coffee and cognac and stuff like that, and he said, "McPhee, you know I got started five years ahead of you, but you're like I am. Decide what you want to be, because our strong point is not our acting . . . like a Barrymore. But we have a personality. We present a figure of a man on a screen. I feel that Cagney can be a hero in one picture and kick his mother in the stomach in the next because of the psychiatric treatment he needed, but we could never do that. Just decide what image you want." And later I saw exactly what he meant, and that's what I wanted to do anyway. I was a heavy with Fairbanks, Jr., in something called *The Jazz Age,* and it was a silent. And then I did a bit as Garbo's brother in *The Single Standard.* And she met me later and we went horseback riding together. And she said, "You're a real cowboy, the way you go with the horse and everything," and she had a lot of guts. That was down at the Riviera stables. And she said, "What do you want to *be?*" And I said, "Well, I want to be an actor in pictures." "Oh," she said, "that's too bad." And that was the end of me for her. She was always riding ahead of me or behind me after that. She didn't want to see any more actors.

She was nice. She was still easy. The only thing she would do—Clarence Brown told me—is she'd read a script and if she didn't think it was right, she'd say, "I think I go home." And she'd go home. She had a Lincoln with a driver, and she'd go home to Brentwood.

JK: Was she sexy to you?

JM: Not that much. I thought she was very attractive, but I knew it was out of my score, out of my reach. If she'd said to me, "We've got to meet and have dinner," I would have sure done my best. But I would never make a move toward anyone like that, and the only ones that I would were the ones that came right out like Dolores [Del Rio]—she said, after we'd worked together for about a week [*Bird of Paradise*] and she had her mother along as a chaperone out there in Honolulu, one night she said, "Oh, my neck is bothering me so, and . . ." I did. And . . . she said, "You're a different kind of a boy." And Evelyn Brent, when I did *The Silver Horde* with her in '29 or '30. I went into Bill Sistrom's office, and while I was there, Evelyn Brent came in. And I took a look at her. I knew Coop had had a crush on her . . . they really had a thing going, but it was over. She would have married him too. But he hung back. So, anyway, Sistrom looked at me and then looked at her and said, "It's going to be incest." I wasn't sure what that meant, but it sounded good! And when we got on the boat to go up to the location in Hotchkotch, Alaska, and I began having dinner with Evelyn, we got to talking about Coop. And we got on pretty good. And when we got back, I would like to have carried it on, but she was married to a guy . . .

JK: . . . who really ruined her.

JM: Yeah, sure he did. She supported him and everything. And I saw her when she was on Motion Picture Relief. I went out to visit, to the Country Home, and I asked the guy who was running it, "Where is Evelyn Brent?" And he said that she was on relief, but she and another actress would rather not come into the home, but they had a little apartment in Westwood. That was around 1936. I was at Goldwyn at that time, doing pictures with Wyler, and so I called her. And she said, "Joey, it's good to hear from you." I said, "When can I see you?" She said, "You can't see me anymore. I don't look like I did when you were crazy about me, Joey." I said, "Well, maybe I don't either." She said, "Oh, yes. I saw you the other night and you were excellent." I said, "Well, it's never changed, I think the world of you. I think both Coop and I blew it when we didn't do better. But have you got everything you need?" And she said, "Well, not quite. The girl I'm with and I would like to get a little puppy dog." And so I sent her some money, and then I sent her some again. So that was the end. Then she started going with a fellow named Harry Fox or something, somebody who'd been an ex-vaudevillian. And she said, "We know that's show business and we've done the tough part and, Joey, I'd rather you remembered me the way we were."

JK: You did a picture with Marion Davies, didn't you?

JM: I was in *The Fair Co-ed* [1927]. I was one of the guys, the USC football players, and we were carried through the entire picture by Sam Wood, the director. It was Johnny Mack Brown's first thing after playing in the Rose Bowl for Alabama. They were whooping it up a little bit at night in a hotel down at Pomona, about four or five miles below Claremont, where the college was. Morley Drury, the greatest sportswriter, said, "Let's start a handball thing at the YMCA." It cost us a dollar each to join the YMCA in Pomona, we got the four-wall court, we got the whole football team. Morley took me because I hadn't played very much, but he was as good with his left hand as he was with his right. He was the greatest athlete I ever knew. And we'd play every night. So, after about a week of this there, Mr. Hearst came on the set to say goodbye to Miss Davies because he was going to New York. He asked Morley who had won the tournament. And Morley said, "Joel and I." And he said, "Joel McCrea?" And he took a good look at me, and he said, "I want you both to come to San Simeon and spend the weekend when we get back, I'd like to show you the ranch." I knew Marion Davies. She noticed me, but she was trying to be nice to Johnny Mack Brown. But now Hearst asked me up because of Morley.

Now, I go up there to the ranch—Morley couldn't go for some reason—and on the way up I ride with Ed Hatrick, vice-president of Cosmopolitan. His daughter was married to someone and had a couple of children and later divorced, she then married Jimmy Stewart. She was Gloria Hatrick. Anyway, Ed Hatrick gets to talking with me, and so when we get up there, he takes me right in with him; we got off the train at San Luis Obispo and there's a car for Mr. Hatrick; so we get up there and there's Mr. Hearst and Marion and some fellow named Paul Bloch and Dick Berlin. Mr. Hearst says, "Oh, this is the boy who was in *Fair Co-ed* with Marion. I'm glad to see you. I didn't know whether you'd come or not." And I said, "Well, Miss Williams called me, and I happened to meet Mr. Hatrick on the train." And that was all. Nothing. Well, now I'm spending a lot of time at the Hearst ranch or the Marion Davies beach house, because that's where the action was, that's where all the big directors were.

JK: One thing about you that Hearst must have liked is that you didn't drink, and another must have been that you didn't succumb to Marion Davies.

JM: That's right. We would hug each other when I first got there, and that was it. There were never any looks, and I didn't know if there was ever any desire. First of all, she didn't appeal to me, but, most important, she was his, and I never saw him take a look at another pretty girl. He never messed with any other girl after he met her, for thirty-six years. He was rugged, he was powerful, he could have had whoever he wanted . . . he was really nuts about her.

One night at dinner Marion said to me, "Can you stay over? We're going to have a barbecue," and I said, "Yes." Raoul Walsh was there too, and he said, "I'll be there too, Marion." And I turned to Walsh and said, "Not only can I stay up next week, I can stay as long as they'll bed and board me.

Because they just didn't exercise my option." Well, Walsh told Marion and Marion told W.R., "They didn't renew Joel's contract." And he said, "Oh, I think they made a mistake." About three days later I got a telegram saying, at my convenience, when I was through up there, would I come to Mr. Mayer's office? So when I got back, I went into Ida Koverman's office and *finally* I get to go into Mr. Mayer's office, and Benny Thau is sitting there and Eddie Mannix, who is studio manager, and Mr. Mayer stands up and says, "Congratulations, you're an All-American Boy." I said, "Thank you very much." Then he said, "While I was gone, Mr. Thalberg failed to exercise your option. I feel it was a mistake, so I'd like to renew it and give you $100 a week more than it called for." I said, "Well, Mr. Mayer, I can't tell you how proud that makes me feel. But I'd like to try and do something on my own. If I can't, I'd surely come back and take you up, but I think the competition at MGM would be tough." I thanked him and I went out. And I went by the Cosmopolitan office, and the secretary said, "Come here, I want to show you something." And she handed me a carbon copy of a letter from Hearst to Mayer, and it said, "Dear Louis, I see where you haven't exercised the option on Joel McCrea. He's never been given anything to do but the one little bit in Marion Davies' picture. In our business, we never hire anyone unless we think they have ability, and we never let them go until we find out they haven't. I don't think that you've done the right thing." And that's how I became the All-American Boy.

L. B. Mayer told me ten years later, when I was doing *Stars in My Crown* . . . and getting $10,000 a week instead of whatever I was getting then. And he had me in his office, where he had a picture of his mother on his desk. "Only God was more important to me than her," he said. "And I never knew why he wrote a letter about you, with all the important things he had on his mind." And I said, "Do you know why, L.B.? Because of Marion Davies. She liked me. She thought I was a good boy, a nice boy." But they hadn't given me any chance after they took my contract over from DeMille.

Now, I may be out of continuity, but I'm up there at the Hearst ranch while I'm still making tests for things. This was before I met Connie Bennett. She had tests of about four guys: MacMurray, Gilbert Roland, Ray Milland and a couple of others I can't remember. Well, I'd been up to Mr. Hearst's ranch a couple of times, I'm up there for the second or third time. And Connie Bennett is up there too. I haven't met her yet, but she's up there. She's a big star. Norma Shearer was there, and Irving Thalberg, and they ran a picture they'd made at Metro with Norma Shearer, this was *before* Gable. And so, at the end of the Norma Shearer picture—Adolphe Menjou was there, and Clarence Brown, Bob Leonard, Sam Wood, King Vidor and all the big MGM people were there, Richard Boleslawski—so they all get up and Mr. Hearst says, "Miss Bennett is here." And she was way back in what would be the loges with a long cigarette-holder. Mr. Hearst always sat way down in front with Miss Davies and a robe over both their laps. I was about five rows behind him. So he said, "Miss Bennett has got tests for her next picture, *Born to*

Love, of some possible leading men and she wants to run them, and any of you who want are welcome to stay." So most of them went out, but there must have been about half a dozen who stayed. So the lights go down and they show each one of them. I thought Gilbert Roland was the best of them. . . .

JK: She married him later.

JM: Yes, she did. And I thought I was about third out of four. So she doesn't say anything. Nobody says anything. I hope they won't hurt my feelings by telling me they want Gilbert Roland because that's what I would have done if I'd been Connie Bennett. But, fortunately, just as we all got up, Marion said, "W.R."—she used to stutter off the screen, never if the camera was on her— "Joel looked very good, didn't he?" And Mr. Hearst said, "Oh, yes, I thought he was fine." "Why can't he be in *Marianne*? Why can't he do a part with me sometime?" And that's all. And he said, "Well, we'll see." And Marion goes out and bows to me, and he smiles with those ice-cold blue eyes. Boy, you never crossed him. So out I go and go to bed in my bungalow . . . with Virginia Valli. Do you remember that name? She married Charles Farrell, and they always put us in the same bungalow because Farrell was never there, he was still in and out with Janet Gaynor: not lovers, but very *close* friends. After *Seventh Heaven,* who wouldn't be?

So I go to bed—say good night to Virginia; Charlie Lederer, a writer who was the son of Marion Davies' sister; Louise Brooks. She wasn't in our bungalow, but she was staying there too. And it's only about 11:00. So I get up the next morning and go up to breakfast at the long table that seats seventy people, and Mr. Hearst sees me and says, "Come in, come in. Now, you get up early like I do, and any time you want to come to breakfast, you come." But I sat away from them, because there were about four or five of them all talking big business. I listened to what I could! And as I got up to go out and leave the castle and went down some steps to go back to my room, I ran into Louella Parsons just coming along. She said, "Well, congratulations." I said, "What do you mean?" She said, "I gave you the banner line in the *Examiner* this morning. That will be in tomorrow morning's paper." I said, "What do you mean, the banner line?" She said, "Connie Bennett told me last night, after they ran those tests, that she had chosen you as her leading man." I said, "My God, how could that be?" "Well," she said, "I don't think it hurt when Marion said to Mr. Hearst, 'Couldn't I have him sometime?' because Connie's a shrewd businesswoman, and if she thinks Mr. Hearst's going to do something for you, that might have had some effect. But why do you care? They did it, they told me, Connie called me herself last night after you'd all gone to bed." And that's the way I got it.

JK: I thought maybe you were going to say you got to your room, you went to sleep and there's a knock on the door, and there's this long cigarette-holder behind the door. . . .

JM: Well, I was hoping for that, John! The next day I met Connie and she was quite businesslike but very nice. . . .

JK: She hadn't yet married the Marquis de la Falaise de la . . .

JM: No, no. The Marquis was between Swanson, and he didn't have anybody right then; he was looking. He found her. But I found her first! So, anyway, I stayed up there about a week, and then I got back and was called in to RKO-Pathé to meet Paul Ludwig Stein, who was the director, and he said, "I make a test. Connie picked you. That's very nice." So now I made a test with Connie, to see how we looked together. Then they told me what wardrobe I had to have, I was an aviator or something. So after the test she said, "We ought to talk this over. Why don't you come with me?" She had a car and a black chauffeur, a big, good-looking guy named Bennett, the same as hers. It was a Cadillac, a V-12. They only made a few of those. So I rode home with her.

I was living at home with my folks in Brentwood, and so she had me for dinner and we talked, and I could tell that we liked each other, we were interested, and so when I left, she said, "Well, goodbye, darling," and she put her arms around me, and, well, it ended in more of a kiss than you'd give to a stranger. She said, "I'll see you tomorrow." She was a big star, *very* sophisticated and, having been married to Phil Plant, used to a lot of money, but she wasn't much older than me. So Bennett took me home in the Cadillac. I felt like a naïve kind of country boy; and I felt that's just what she's interested in! [He laughs.] And I figured that if she isn't, I'm still going to get ahead on the screen. I'm going to get ahead with my career. So I didn't care, I took everything as it came. It put me into the columns. They all said, "Joel McCrea and Constance Bennett were there, and they're going to do this. . . ."

We were an item. They thought there was kind of a steady thing going on. We got along very well together. She was great to me. She was supposed to be a bitch. She was supposed to be tough on the set. She was tough on deals because she was a shrewd businesswoman. And she had this money that Phil Plant left, so she couldn't lose. She was a hit. But she was just doggone nice to me. And we went out together and did different things, and after about six or eight months the Marquis came along, and she said, "I'm going to Europe and I want you to go with me." And the Marquis was hanging in the wings the whole time, and so I said, "I can't do that. You know, my parents . . . I'd have to be married." And she said, "Well, let's get married." And I said, "I don't want to get married, I'm just starting. I'd be Mr. Bennett, that's all I'd be. I'm crazy about you, but I don't think it would be good, and I don't think it would be particularly good for you. I haven't made myself yet." She said, "Well, the Marquis wants to marry me." "Well," I said, "you'll have to see what you want to do." I was very *fond* of her, but I wasn't that kind of in love with her. And, frankly, I don't think she was with me. I think she just thought it would be kind of interesting to take a swing at it.

JK: Well, the two of you did look good together. Your RKO period is very interesting—you did all sorts of strange and interesting films there. How did *The Most Dangerous Game* come about?

JM: Well, it came about this way: David Selznick had come in as head of RKO, and Merian C. Cooper came kind of under David, and he wanted to make this picture. So he got me and Fay Wray, because he loved Fay Wray . . . he loved Fay Wray, but he married Dorothy Jordan, and she [Fay Wray] was married to John Monk Saunders, who wrote *Wings*. And so Merian Cooper put me in that, and before we were finished, he came down to see me and he said, "I've got a great idea." He was a nice little guy, Cooper was. "I want to make a picture called *King Kong;* you and Fay and [director Ernest B.] Schoedsack and I will make *King Kong*." And I said, "Well, doesn't sound like the way I want to go," because *Most Dangerous Game* was enough of that kind of adventure-dream idea, a guy who wanted to hunt men. So I said, "I don't think I want to do it." He said, "Think of somebody who will be good." And so one night David Selznick asked me if I would take Irene to dinner, because she was going to dinner with George Cukor, up to some Montmartre thing on Hollywood Boulevard, and he said, "Would you do it? Would you go with her, because I have to stay here and run a bunch of stuff." So we did, and on the way in I saw the bouncer, the guy on the door, and it was Jacques de Bujac, who later became Bruce Cabot. And I said to him, "Have you ever thought of going into pictures?" And he said, "That's what I came here for. My name is Jacques de Bujac." I said, "Well, we've got to do something about that." But I got him to write out his name and address and phone number, gave it to Irene and she gave it to David Selznick. The next thing I knew, they had made a test of him, and they decided to do it, and he did the thing and became Bruce Cabot. And of course it would do nothing for whoever did it, it was all kind of amateurish except for the great stuff with the animal.

JK: Did you ever feel that, even by today's standards, films like *The Most Dangerous Game* were very erotic? You're stripped down to very little, there's a lot of this sado-maochistic games-playing, and Fay Wray was nearly always half naked back then.

JM: And she was a nice girl too. They started out co-starring her with Cooper doing Westerns . . . five times. She was pretty, but nothing happened. And I could see why. In life it was the same. I could go and spend a week's vacation with Fay Wray and we would just be nice friends when we got back. I wouldn't have a desire to do anything. Now, Merian and John Monk Saunders did. I met him once, when he was with William Wellman. We just said how do you do . . . nothing happened. That's an interesting thing, John; you know, now, when I'd meet a guy like La Cava . . . he was leaning back and he had a cigarette and he was bald and he acted as though he looked down on me, looked down on anybody, and he'd say, "Have you ever read such-and-such?" And right away I said to myself, "I like this silly bastard, I like him. I don't know what it is about him, but I like him." Now, when I found out he liked me, we had something going for us. Because every picture I did with him, the producer wanted somebody better. And they *were* better. Montgomery was one . . . they were more experienced and bigger names. Even Fairbanks. I don't think he's a better actor, because I think he's still aping the old man, but they were more trained, more experienced than I was. But that meant nothing to La Cava, because when Wanger said, "Bob Montgomery's a better actor and better box office than McCrea," La Cava said, "Not when I direct him." And he laid it right on there; he showed his own understanding of what he could do.

JK: Did you like William Wyler as a director? You worked with him four or five times.

JM: Yes, I did, and we were both under contract to Goldwyn. And I remember on *These Three* Wyler wanted Leslie Howard. And Goldwyn said, "No, I've got McCrea on contract and he's on salary, and he ain't working, and you're going to use him." And I didn't know anything about it, and I'd been in it about a week, and Willie came around to my dressing room one night—a funny little guy, he kind of spit between his teeth—and he said, "You didn't know it, but I wanted Leslie Howard." And I said, "Yes, I know." And he said, "How did you know?" I said, "Goldwyn told me." And he said, "I told him not to!" I said, "That doesn't make any difference. I was at his house for dinner." Willie said, "I *haven't* been invited to his house for dinner." But then he said, "I want to tell you something. Now I've worked with you a week, and Merle [Oberon] is crazy about you, and I like what you're doing, and I just want you to know that I'm delighted to have you."

JK: You also got on very well with Miriam Hopkins.

JM: Very well. We'd worked together on *Barbary Coast* with Howard Hawks. Wyler liked her, but he treated her badly. I think he wanted her to do more than she would let him. He used to make her do more takes. . . . With Merle and I, he would say, "Print the thing" after about the third, but he'd work maybe about an hour with Miriam. I think he wanted to get in there, like Lubitsch and King Vidor and a lot of others. She had something going for her, *believe* me, because more guys would ask me about her later, and I never admitted anything. I knew a little bit more than I let on, but she was very nice to me and we got along fine. Eddie Robinson had a hard time with her on *Barbary Coast* and he complained to me a lot. He'd say, "Oh, that son-ofabitch, I'm doing something and she's fixing her dress. Oh, how unprofessional. I'm going to kill her." And I said to him, "I can't do anything about that because she's nice to me." And he said, "Why is she nice to you and not to me? I've spent my *life* doing this business. You've just started." I said, "Yes, but that doesn't matter. You know what it is?" I wanted to make him feel good, so I said, "I'm that much taller than you are. When she plays a scene with me, it's the perfect angle for her. She loves that. The chins go away. I'm not as good an actor as you are, and she doesn't want you stealing scenes from her. I don't steal any scenes from her, I just play the scene. And I'm in it and I get by." "Well," he said, "she does tricks and I think it's chickenshit."

With Wyler I did *These Three, Dead End* and *Come and Get It. These Three* was the first one I did with Wyler, and the first one Wyler did with Goldwyn. I had just done *Barbary Coast* with Hawks. Hawks started *Come and Get It,* but he walked off and Wyler finished it.

JK: Why did he walk off *Come and Get It*?

JM: He said he and Goldwyn had had a meeting the night before, and we'd only been shooting about four or five days. He said, "I had a disagreement with Sam, and he told me, 'Well, I'm the producer,' and so I told him, 'Well you direct it too.'" And he walked off.

JK: But it was Hawks that brought Frances Farmer onto the movie. He left her high and dry.

JM: Sure. He brought her on and then left her high and dry. Well, Hawks didn't care about anybody except himself. But he was a good director. Can't say he wasn't. He never did anything for me like La Cava. He never was personal or anything like that. It would have been the same if I'd been Fred MacMurray or anybody. He never favored anybody except Howard Hawks. Even Wayne, and he worked with him a lot. But he was a nice guy. So Wyler finished that; that was the second picture he'd done with me.

JK: But did he give you much as a director?

JM: He did. It was different from, say, DeMille. Wyler was more personal. With DeMille, the picture was the thing. With Wyler, it was who he was interested in. When he was interested in *Dodsworth,* it was Walter Huston, so he shit on Ruth Chatterton, who was a very fine actress. And he treated Mary Astor better because he liked her better. DeMille never let whoever he was in love with—if he was ever in love with anybody—affect his work. He never favored anybody or things like that. The only guy that he never failed to tell me how much he liked was Coop. But he was a wholly professional man. If I was running a studio, I would like a DeMille to make my pictures. And, of course, another of my favorite directors was Raoul Walsh. I did *Colorado Territory* with him. I did my best to get him again for another picture, when I did *Ramrod,* but Warners wouldn't loan him.

JK: And you got Andre de Toth instead.

JM: Yes, and he'd say to Veronica Lake, "Babee, you gotta do better, Babee, you betta fix you face. . . ." You know? All that shit. And then he called Harry Sherman, who'd hired him, who made the deal, who paid our salaries, who did everything, and who made all the Hopalong Cassidy films, and he'd get up on the boom and make a crossing of a river, with rocks and stuff, and he made them put tracks across it so they could track back. It didn't mean a damn thing. John Ford would have photographed you there, photographed you a long shot, coming, starting the thing, and then bring you into the shot over there. I learned that from John Ford right away. You cut to what you want to see, whether you travel with someone walking along . . . unless there's something going on that has to do with them while they're moving. You're just wasting . . . you're just making film to make it look like you had a beautiful background. Well, anyway, he did that, and when Sherman would say, "Come on, Andre, please let's go. We're running way over the budget, way over the thing, you're tracking every shot. It's going to take four hours for those poor bastards to lay the planks and stuff. . . ." It was ridiculous. But what the hell could we do? We were in it now. So Andre said, "Listen," he'd be up on the boom, looking down, "you're nothing but a poor old Hopalong Cassidy producer. That's all, Hopalong Cassidy with Bill Boyd." That was unfortunate. If I could have had Walsh, that would have been a hell of a picture.

JK: Who got Veronica Lake into that? I always thought that she was so fond of you that she got you into the film.

JM: That was De Toth's wife.

JK: I know. She regretted that!

JM: I'll say she did! At that time Harry Sherman had made the deal borrowing her from Paramount and paying her well, but then he took her husband. He should have known better, but he was used to doing those Hopalong Cassidy films and he really wasn't big enough.

JK: You'd been retired from films for more than ten years when you returned to do *Mustang Country*?

JM: I did that in '76, just to help a guy, and it was just a little program picture. A guy named John Champion. He had it, wrote it, produced it and directed it. He made it for $850,000 up in Canada. And after they ran it, they said they didn't think it would make money because it had no sex or violence. The Universal people said that. But NBC took it for two showings, and it made him the $850,000 back, that was the whole cost of the picture. So they're still making money on it. I have a percentage of the profits . . . I get a little bit, I got $22,000 the other day. But I really don't want to do any more. I shouldn't have done this thing for Champion. I actually feel my career was over with *Ride the High Country* in '62. When they submitted the script to me for that, it was Richard Lyons who was producing, and we had never heard of Sam Peckinpah then. And I read it and said, "I'll do it, Dick, but only if I do Steve Judd. I don't want to do the other part. I want to be the guy with integrity, because that's what I've been working at for forty-seven years, and I might as well just finish it out that way. But Randy [Randolph Scott] is the one who found the story, and so he should have first choice." So he said, "We'll ask him." So he called Randy up and said, "Joel wants to do the picture with you, but he wants you to say which part you want to do." So Randy said, "Well, ordinarily they'd think of me for Steve Judd, the guy with honesty, but I've done it so many times that I'd like to do something different. I'd like to do the sonofabitch that wants to steal and go away. It would give me a little color." So I said, "Okay, you've got a deal." And that's the way we did it. He was the most charming Southern gentleman. Wayne was good, he was fine. But nothing got in his way and he did what would be best for him. Randy was a gentleman. He always called me "Jo-el." He'd say, "Jo-el, it would be an honor if you'd do this picture with me," and I said, "Well, Randy, it's just fortunate that you wanted to do the other role, because I didn't want to play it!" And he said he understood. And we had a helluva lot of fun. We had to cut our salary in half to do it, but they gave the two of us 33⅓ percent of the profits divided between us, and of course it's done real well. It's a classic.

You know, I read a thing the other day either in the *Wall Street Journal* or the *New York Times,* and it said that *Ride the High Country* was among the four or five best Westerns ever made. Didn't say where it fit among *Stagecoach* and *The Covered Wagon,* or whatever, but that's a pretty nice way to go out. I thought it was good, but I didn't know it would be that good. And when we hired Peckinpah, the last time I'd done a picture was on *Wichita,* and he was the dialogue director; he'd rehearse lines with me. And all I remembered is he had a funny name like Peckinpah. He'd done some good Western TV things, and he'd done one picture with Maureen O'Hara. I hadn't seen any of them. I said I'd take a chance on him because I didn't like any of the older ones, like John Farrow . . . he was kind of a phony in life, and so maybe he wouldn't be the one I'd want to work with. He [Peckinpah] brought some things to it. He rewrote the script and directed the picture for $15,000. And I've got a letter from Peckinpah saying really he directed me as though I were his father, because that's the kind of a man he was. He was a judge up at Fresno, and his brother was a District Attorney.

JK: Your grandfather was a stagecoach driver, wasn't he?

JM: Yes, he was. Major John McCrea. He drove a stagecoach from San Bernardino to Los Angeles when San Bernardino was a bigger city than Los Angeles. And then he got into business with the Hellmans . . . with the first bank that was ever in Los Angeles, called the Farmers and Merchants National Bank. And my other grandfather was in the days of '49, he came to San Francisco in '50. Of course, 1849 was the Gold Rush, and he came in 1850 and had a wholesale grocery business and only lived to be forty-nine years of age. Albert Whipple was his name, and he left my mother and one sister. They were all frontier people. No actors. They were ministers, preachers, bankers. James McCrea was president of the Pennsylvania Railroad. There were some big ones and some little farmers.

JK: In your films you played mostly variations on your family.

JM: That's it. That's why my heart was in it. Sure.

1983

Irene Dunne, photographed by Ernest Bachrach (RKO), 1938

IRENE
DUNNE

I RENE DUNNE was brought from Broadway to Hollywood by RKO in 1930. She had been a star on Broadway and played Magnolia in *Show Boat,** touring across America. Her first film, *Leathernecking,* was a disaster, but her second—*Cimarron,* in 1931—became one of the classic Westerns, while *Back Street* the following year was the seminal woman's picture. Because of her deeply skillful underplaying and director John M. Stahl's unclichéd handling of the subject, with a feeling for the mores of the time, *Back Street* proved to be one of the least mawkish, most stylish and deeply moving pictures to come out of that era of Hollywood. Its success, so close on the heels of *Cimarron,* only helped consolidate her rise, which, in those first years of sound, almost over-night put her on a par with that other first lady, Norma Shearer. A steady series of hits over the next twenty years made her one of the richest and most success-ful stars in Hollywood. As she shrewdly alternated between the best of the Fannie Hurst–type soap operas (such as *Back Street* and *Magnificent Obses-sion*), screwball comedies (like *Theodora Goes Wild* and *The Awful Truth*) and musicals by Jerome Kern (*Roberta, Showboat, Sweet Adeline, High, Wide and Handsome* and *Joy of Living*), her popularity increased and lasted far beyond the norm.

Her last film, *It Grows on Trees,* was made in 1952, and after that she worked for the American State Department as unofficial goodwill ambassador, as well as being a representative at the United Nations. Since the death of her husband, Dr. Francis Griffin, she has lived in semiretirement in Hollywood, but still attends functions and premieres and works for charities.

Though she has no difficulty remembering her career, her opinions about the merit of her films seem to be governed more by what was happening in her life at the time than by any esthetic considerations—thus, some of her best films are not her favorites and she still pretends to be displeased at ever having played the "other woman" in *Back Street.* But even when she is least forthcoming, her peculiar but most delightful, unaffected-sounding voice recaptures moments

*The Ferber novel, the silent film, the stage musical and the 1951 MGM film were all titled *Show Boat.* Only the 1936 film, in which Irene Dunne appeared, was titled *Showboat.*

from her films better than some answers do. The way she talked was the single strongest impression I have of this actress—not her poise, nor her charm, her delivery or her warm appeal in a specific role. The tip of her tongue pressed ever so lightly up behind her teeth, which automatically dimpled her cheeks and caused her to arch her eyebrows, not in any exaggerated manner but just enough to transform her whole face into the most beguiling girlish sauciness that endeared her to every member of the audience, men and women alike and children too. One heard it even as one saw it. Laughter was invariable. One would succumb. It was inexpressibly endearing. Her voice was the one thing about her that hadn't aged—it had made it possible and made her believable when, at the height of her career, already a woman in her late thirties, she would still be called on to play characters that required a transition from early teens to ripe maturity, as her Magnolia in *Showboat,* or enabled her most sophisticated characters to retain their common touch, keeping her popular for so long.

She was a grandmother in her seventies when I met her, still very handsome, looking like her old-young self, but not in any forced way. She was lined, she was tetchy as older people can be, especially ones who don't really live in the past but are often called upon to relive it for others, but hers wasn't a preserved beauty in any way. She did have her vanity, or better to call it her magic, like Jimmy Stewart's enduring boyishness, Hedy Lamarr's hair or Liz Taylor's eyes. Her voice, which had made her Jerome Kern's favorite screen interpreter and Cary Grant's most sympathetic partner, still twinkled. It made waiting to get to her worth all the difficulty.

Our conversation was mainly concerned with her musical work because I had written a book on musicals and had just seen *High, Wide and Handsome* the night before.

JK: Tell me why you don't like *High, Wide and Handsome*?

ID: I saw it on television here some weeks ago and I didn't think it was half as bad as I remembered. It wasn't a happy film. It was very costly. Mamoulian was a very artistic director and I'd have to ride back and forth to Chino, California, where in January we'd wait for a cloud formation. The time it took! It couldn't happen today—we were way over budget and there'd be wrangles with the studio. It was an uncomfortable film to make with the location work. Also, I lost my mother in the middle of it, which was a shattering shock to me. I think I had two days off and had to go right back into making the film.

You know, when people ask what's your favorite film, I guess you should say the one that made the most money. But you never do. I remember *Love Affair* was made around Christmastime and we had a huge tree in the studio and everyone exchanged gifts and it was lovely. I guess that was my favorite film. But *High, Wide and Handsome* was physically a difficult film.

JK: Is it typical of you to relate your enjoyment of a film as a finished product to how you felt at the time?

ID: I think I always remember the flavor of working on a film. Because this was a big-budget film, it had the full treatment, a premiere at the Carthay Circle. I went that night and sat *directly* in front of Helen Hayes. I didn't like myself in that film, and all the time I was conscious of Helen Hayes breathing down my neck. This was one of my earlier films and I wasn't used to big premieres.

When I saw it the other night, I thought, if you capsulized it, that it was the story of the opening of the West with an oil pipeline, and it wasn't bad at all—it really wasn't bad. I thought it was a little corny, but it made sense. As a matter of fact, the theme had more significance now than I remember it having—it was lost on me somehow amongst the circus goings-on.

The male lead was supposed to be Gary Cooper. But Randy Scott was so much better than I remember him being.

I also wasn't mad about *Joy of Living*. Jerome Kern wrote a song for me called "You Couldn't Be Cuter." But the thing I'm proudest of is a song he wrote especially for me which became very popular—a thing from *Roberta* called "Lovely to Look At." *Roberta* was a stage play and "Lovely to Look At" wasn't in the original score.

To show how your mind can play tricks, I got so nervous over the song because I knew I'd have to be lovely to look at walking down that staircase singing the song. I got no sleep the night before, and when I went in the next morning, the cameraman told the director, "I'm not going to shoot her today. That's all there is to it. She'll have to go home to sleep." We waited for a day or two, I rested up, and then we shot it. I think that song has been used in more fashion shows than any other song ever written.

JK: As a singer, when did you first cross paths with Kern?

ID: *Show Boat,* I suppose. I don't recall him having come on tour. Oscar Hammerstein was in evidence, but not Kern so much. I became acquainted with Kern after I came to California. He'd built a house and was much more interested in my home than in the music. He used to come up with his measuring stick—he was interested in the kind of flagstone I had on my patio. He wasn't a very great pianist—but better than Irving Berlin, I'd say. I remember when I went to sing for Kern some years ago, I couldn't believe it. You know, a singer with a good accompanist is twice as good, but he was almost one finger. I couldn't have been more surprised.

JK: Was Kern very dependent on his lyricist?

ID: I'd have no way of knowing that. I'm sure they depended on each other. Have you noticed that in all the years Kern was writing he really worked with very few lyricists? Once he found someone compatible, he didn't worry.

Kern wrote a song specifically for me in two films, but of course he didn't come to me about it while he was writing. They didn't work like that, it's a closed corporation.

JK: Did Kern ever say why he liked the way you sang?

ID: I can't remember . . . he wasn't a very loquacious person. He was very down-to-earth and well liked. He had close friends who absolutely adored him. But I didn't feel very close to Jerry. Nor Oscar Hammerstein, really, although you can tell from his lyrics what a warm, wonderful man he was. Had we lived closer together, I would have hoped we would have become closer friends. I never asked Kern how he wanted me to sing a song, but he'd be very free to tell me exactly what he wanted. He didn't look or act like a great composer. They never do. Kern looked like a professor, really.

JK: I suppose movie stars are the only artists who have to look like what they're supposed to be.

ID: Yes, but it's very shattering to a lot of people when they find stars not shaping up to their idea of them. I remember the night I was out in California, I went to a restaurant and saw Hedy Lamarr eating steak tartare—which I've since eaten and liked very much. But here she was sitting in front of this heap of raw meat. It was revolting to me. I couldn't see how such a beautiful human being could eat raw meat.

JK: Was it a conscious effort or accidental that all your musicals were done by Jerome Kern?

ID: I had nothing to do with it. But there were not too many important musicals—like *Show Boat, Roberta* or *Sweet Adeline*—around at the time. And they all happened to be Kern's. It was a sort of sequence of normal events after I'd taken over the lead at the end of *Show Boat*—and there was only one *Show Boat* company then; people don't realize that because since there have been so many road companies. There was only one company and we had over 100 Negroes in the cast, so it was a difficult company to travel with. We went to Chicago, Boston, and played one other place—that's all. I still have the telegram Ziegfeld sent me after I took over the lead. You know, he'd never come backstage and see you, but instead he'd send reams in telegrams. He said he couldn't remember when he'd had a more enjoyable evening at the theater.

But anyway, to get back to Kern, after we'd done the road run of *Show Boat*, RKO had got *Cimarron,* which was written by Edna Ferber, the same person who wrote *Show Boat,* and, having been the heroine in *Show Boat,* it was natural for the head of the studio to offer me a contract to come to RKO and play the heroine in *Cimarron.* In between there was a little film that didn't quite make it: *Leathernecking.* I always like to think that *Cimarron* was released before that, so I can say my first picture to be released was *Cimarron!* I wonder what ever happened to that other film!

JK: Let me ask you about the film of *Showboat*.

ID: James Whale wasn't the right director. I really shouldn't say that, but to me the picture didn't come off as well as the stage play. There were lots of interpolations that we didn't need at all, and I think the ending was stupid. It's so easy to attach blame to a man one feels was miscast as director, so perhaps I shouldn't, but, you see, he was more interested in atmosphere and lighting and he knew so little about that life. I could have put my foot down about it, but there would have been no reason to do so because we had so many of the original people that you could only expect the best. I knew the whole thing backwards. No, you see, I could have put my foot down at the contract stage, but once the camera started turning, I was an angel on the set. No, I never cared for *Showboat* [the film], but I thought the stage production was one of the best things. The score was marvelous, but even the book could have stood up on its own.

You often wonder why a film misses or is a smash. I think *Roberta* turned out most how I envisaged it. I saw it a few weeks ago, and though the soundtrack has deteriorated, and though the story is really inane and silly (I didn't realize it at the time), the *entertainment* value is so good. Astaire danced so beautifully with Rogers, the clothes were magnificent—it was an evening of entertainment and what more could you ask? Today people are getting so involved with problems there's no entertainment anymore, it's all presenting problems. My grandchildren were here and I was looking through the papers at ads for movies and they were all marked R [Restricted]. So, really, forget it! They're not going to those movies, they're better off down the beach.

JK: In those musicals, were the songs recorded after the shooting or consecutively with it?

ID: Most of my numbers were dubbed, and I pride myself on that. First you record the number, then you shoot the scene and sing along to the recording. It's remarkable how you can do it. You can't really do it on the set because the sound engineers aren't happy with the result.

JK: Since your musicals were so successful, why didn't you do more of them? *Irene* for instance?

ID: I'd have loved to have done that. I don't know, I guess I was just busy doing other things. I never searched for them and I never felt they were more successful than my other films or more satisfying. I loved doing them, but I can't say they were more successful than the things I did with Grant. It's mechanical and dubbed and the songs don't weave the same spell on you as they do before a live audience. Lerner and Loewe asked me to do something. But no, I'm afraid I'm not that much of a gambler and I liked the things I was doing.

JK: Had you stayed at one studio, once your image was established by 1935, do you think that studio might have done a Jeanette MacDonald with you and developed one aspect of you?

ID: Well, remember, when I came out here, there were signs up outside cinemas saying, "This is NOT a musical." Warners, I think it was, had done so many cheap musicals that they'd got a bad name. Anyway, it was no time to make a musical! My great love was, of course, music—but after *Cimarron,* which won the Academy Award, I was quite content. After all, *Back Street* was successful too and I began to become known as a dramatic actress as well.

Of course, when I was studying at Chicago Musical College, I wanted to be in opera. Then, when I got to New York and got to know some opera stars, I realized I didn't have quite the equipment to withstand all the rigors of grand opera. But I did work quite a bit in opera: both *Stingaree* and *The Great Lover* have operatic sequences. There was a very pretty song in *Stingaree,* I remember. But the song I'm known for . . . if I walk in someplace that they know me, they play "Smoke Gets in Your Eyes."

JK: You excelled in musicals, were superb in all sorts of comedies and also highly effective in drama. Have you a preference?

ID: I don't think so. I suppose the comedies I made were as successful as anything else, but comedy was always very easy for me—and it's not as satisfying to me as a dramatic role. I think you give more of yourself in a dramatic role. I was talking to Cary Grant the other day and he said of all the people he'd worked with, I had the most perfect timing in comedy. Now, I don't think that's something you acquire. Therefore comedy was easy for me and not as satisfying as a dramatic role. It's something like having a musical ear.

JK: How soon were you aware of what Irene Dunne meant to people going to the box office? When you went independent, you selected your parts very carefully and your career lasted longer than most other people's.

ID: Well, I made a terrible mistake with a film called *It Grows on Trees.* I thought it was a little whimsical sort of fantasy and would be accepted as such. It turned out just a dull thud. Had it been handled by another director— someone with a light hand—it could have been amusing. But as regards getting an idea of my image, I think I was accepted in romance. People expected that of me. *Back Street* was a very, very popular picture with women: the number of letters I got from women who were living on the back street of some man's life and felt that I knew all the answers! Sometimes they'd sign the letters, but more often not. They just wanted to have a chat with me. Then I was fortunate enough to have attractive leading men. Yes, I think it was romance. I still say today that's the greatest thing you can have on the screen.

JK: Were you businesslike in the handling of your career? The roles you se-lected, etc.?

ID: I had an excellent manager, Charles Feldman, and he and I would sit in this room and argue about which pictures to do with what directors. I had only one clause in my contract and I always had it. That was an okay on the director. I always felt that if the director was good, then everything else would fall into proper place. Perhaps that's why my batting average was as good as it was.

They felt I made a mistake playing Queen Victoria in *The Mudlark*. I know it was a screen departure for me, but it's always nice to get away from routine, and every actor likes to play a character role. It's the public that may not like it. The makeup was very difficult for Queen Victoria and I don't think I'd ever go through that again. They had to send a makeup man to England and we had a very thin mask that connected below the eyes and went down on either side of the face—so my eyes, nose and mouth were mine. Then it fastened at the back. But it could only be used once—every day there was a new one. It was hard on the face!

Anyway, though I enjoyed making it, they felt it wasn't a picture that did me any good. Maybe if I'd done it earlier in my career when my image wasn't so fixed, it would have been better received.

JK: I felt that within the range you had selected for yourself—the decent, av-erage person—there was incredible flexibility.

ID: I studied a character very hard. If they gave me dialogue on the set, I'd always ask to be excused for five or ten minutes so's I could find out why I was saying what I had to say, what relation it had to the character, what she was thinking while she said it. As a result, the performance looks natural and easy and nobody realizes the amount of effort you've put in. That can be a disadvantage, and that's why I was so pleased at the Academy Award nomi-nations.

You see, I was never flamboyant in a part, or eccentric, and that's the sort of performance that tends to catch the eye. Not that I'd stay awake nights worrying about it: I was always happy to just get the Academy nominations—which happened five times. But I was running against actresses like Bette Davis, who, as you know, was all over the lot in those days—and tremen-dous, I thought. But, boy, you knew she was an actress! I never went in for that because I was never one for broad gestures—nor great detail either—and I could never have done that. I dare say I was never offered a Jezebel or maniac part because they didn't see me that way.

I'm still offered roles, but I think you tear yourself apart like that. There are other things in life. I think for an old person who's had the success I have to start playing second- or third-rate parts . . . I just wouldn't like that.

1972

Katharine Hepburn, photographed by C. S. Bull (MGM), 1944

KATHARINE
HEPBURN

HEPBURN LIVES A HOP, SKIP AND JUMP away from my publisher. So, when the phone rang in my editor's office just when I happened to be there, and it was Katharine Hepburn, who'd gotten the letter requesting an interview in that morning's mail, and here she was, a block away, calling, as if she'd known I was there, I could have been excused for thinking she was a bit psychic, and had it been anyone but the no-nonsense, feet-on-the-ground, invincible Kate Hepburn, I might have had second thoughts, but there wasn't any time, for she was straight to the point: When did I want to see her? Right now was good for her.

You look at that sparse and lively mien, cheeks apple-shiny and water-chestnut-colored eyes crystal sharp, the hands bony and strong, her mouth, a strong bow, a long bow, full top lip ironically, self-mockingly turned down at the side, the tightly drawn lower lip set, ready for the words to twang and soar forth, rarely missing their mark, and you go careful with your enthusiasm unless you can support it with fact, hold the gush, think before you speak, try not to let your emotions, carried away by her past, trip up your sense. You don't want to be stood in the corner, the interview over before it began because she thought you were silly. Miss Hepburn can do a lot with words like "horse twaddle," and you'd just as soon she didn't have cause to say them to you. She's bound by no constraints and is enthusiastic enough for a roomful like you.

There's a lot of passion there, not like that of her fellow New Englander Bette Davis, whose passion has a broad slice of the Italian to it, but it's a Yankee passion, fueled by common sense, riled by inanities and ignited by willful stupidity. It's not surprising that the character of Jo, which Hepburn played in the 1933 classic version of Louisa May Alcott's *Little Women,* remains one of her favorite roles and fondest film making memories in a career that has passed the half-century mark. (It was the second of the eleven films she made over the next forty years with her friend and director George Cukor.) She is what Jo might have been like in her seventies, a long full life behind her and still filled with the determination and vigor for things to come. If ever an American actress could have taken us by the hand and led us unquestioningly out of the living room into another world, a different land, like trusting grade-school pupils

accompanying their teacher on a nature outing, it would have been this ageless
Alice, who is still having the most marvelous time saying "nonsense" and "fid-
dlesticks" and "horse manure" and letting nothing and nobody get her down.
Not even Sylvia Scarlett.

KH: I remember when we made *Sylvia Scarlett* . . . I owned a piece of it. And
   it *still* has not made $500,000, and it cost a million to make.

Miss Hepburn seems unable to help laughing while recalling that famous disaster, which was her one and only trouser role; well, there was *Iron Petticoat*
with Bob Hope twenty years later, and that was also a bomb. "One of my great
successes," she laughingly calls *Sylvia*.

KH: *Sylvia Scarlett* never stops playing, that's the extraordinary part. I remember Fannie Brice saw it and she said, "What the hell were you all thinking
   about when you made *that* picture?" She was very discouraging about it. In
   its day it was a very daring thing in which I played a boy seven-eighths of the
   way through. When we made it, we felt we had something charming. The
   preview was an absolute disaster. I had a private conviction, because I keep a
   diary, and there was a moment at which I thought, "Something is wrong with
   this," and that was when I was reciting a poem. I had begun to lose confidence
   in the material, and I thought, "Shall I ask George [Cukor] whether *he's* lost
   confidence in the material?" Because I think there was a point at which he
   too began to realize, as I played this poetry-reading scene, that there wasn't
   much there. Anyway, we went down the coast somewhere—San Pedro, I
   think—for a preview, and I took Natasha Paley with me. We went in. There
   was a fully respectable audience. The picture started. I don't know what had
   been on before it, but there was not a laugh. This was supposed to be a
   hilarious comedy, and not one laugh. I was sitting next to Natasha, who was
   Mrs. John C. Wilson,* she was a Russian princess, a charming creature and
   a great beauty, but she had never acted in anything before,† and she leaned
   over to me and said [Hepburn now does a highfalutin thick Russian accent
   befitting a dowager empress], "Kayete, vat is vrong? They don't laff." And I
   said, "Natasha, they don't think it's funny." And so we sat, it was an absolute
   agony. The audience was walking out. They had no idea of what it was about,
   and I thought they were going to lynch me because they saw me when I had
   come in. So I got up to go, and Pandro Berman, who produced the picture,
   and B. P. Kahane, who was the head of the studio and who had gotten up and
   stood in the back halfway through the picture, and George came over and
   said, "Come home with me." So I had to go into the bathroom, and I went

---

*John C. Wilson was a successful Broadway producer-director.
† Hepburn was wrong. The beautiful Paley had appeared in several French and English films before
going to the US, though she made no more films after her Hollywood debut.

down and there was a woman who was lying on the sofa in the ladies' john. Rather in a jovial way, I said, "What's the matter? Did the picture finish you off?" She just rolled her eyes up and never answered me. I went back upstairs, got into my car, stood up too quickly and hit my head on the top of the car door and thought, "Thank God, I've knocked myself out." There was nothing to do but laugh. It was a total disaster. And we came back to George's house, we were going to meet Pandro back there, and when we got there, we rushed in and George and I said, "Pandro, we'll do another picture for you for nothing." And he looked at us and said, perfectly coldly, "I never want to do a picture with either of you again." [If Becky in *Tom Sawyer* had laughed the way Hepburn does while recalling this incident, Tom wouldn't have run off and spent so much time with Huckleberry Finn.] But, curiously, the irony is that the picture, in addition to launching Cary Grant on a triumphal career, did have something gallant and foolhardy about the whole thing. It was very modern. People couldn't understand it at all at the time.

JK: Did you enjoy working at the studios?

KH: Well, then, of course, the enjoyment, the jokes, the fun of being on the set from 9:00 in the morning until 6:00 at night, it has to have a lot of get-up-and-go and a lot of joy. Because it's a longer day than in a factory for actresses, most of whom get there at 6:30 in the morning for makeup. Well, I don't get there at 6:30 anymore, I get there at 8:30. I put on my makeup in five minutes, wash my hair the night before, curl it. . . . I no longer go in for any of that nonsense. I did ninety years ago, but no more. I caught on!

JK: As with all stars, glamour and the publicity surrounding it were part of your work. You certainly did a lot of portraiture work. Did you take much interest in which stills went out?

KH: I'd kill certain ones, but I was lucky. I was very easy photographically, so I suppose that made me confident and made me more amiable than some people. I wouldn't be so amiable now. Time has laid its ugly hand . . . [She laughs.] I'd be much more critical now. I think one probably likes to see oneself in a certain light, but then I was obviously fascinated by myself, for there I am posing away!

JK: How long did those sessions take, since I suppose you had to . . .

KH: I didn't have to do anything. No. But I worked mainly with Ernie Bachrach, and I did it for him just because I liked to do it for him. We usually took two or three hours. I think he had an assistant or someone to light the background, though I can't be accurate now, but I think he did most of the work himself. And I'd arrive with a lot of clothes that I thought were amusing-looking, and then we'd go. He didn't have to do much to get me into a mood. I changed my clothes fast, did my makeup fast, did everything fast. I've always used the same pancake makeup all my life, and that's all

I used for portraits. In *Bill of Divorcement* you'll see a girl with a *lot* of make-up on; they were trying to cover up my freckles. Then, when I'd do a sad scene and tears would roll down my cheeks, they'd make a big track down my face, and it would take about an hour and a half to change my makeup. Then, your eyes get red. If you have my coloring, your eyes get red very easily. So then I said, "Why don't I wear what I used to wear on the stage?" Which was a wash makeup which Max Factor made, makeup that you could apply with water and a sponge, and that's what I used. He created it for me. Other than that, there's a certain amount of eye stuff, eye-lashes, lipstick, but very little pancake. Very little makeup. The lipstick back then was intense, though I use nothing now.

JK: You mentioned *Bill of Divorcement,* which was your first film.

KH: Yes, I remember that when we finally started on it, I remember very accu-rately the first scene I ever did. Jack Barrymore came in with a hat and rain-coat on, and he was fiddling around with some pipes on the mantelpiece, and then he turned around and looked at me. I was standing off-camera, watching him, as George Cukor had told me to do, acting away, full of sincerity. I was watching him do this. And I looked at Jack with the cold eye of youth and thought he was overdoing it. I did. I thought he was overdoing it a bit. I thought, "That's not very good." But while I was thinking all these unkind things, I was acting away, tears streaming down my face, doing a little too much myself, you see, and the take was over. And Jack came over, and he took my chin in his hands and looked at me and said to George, "I'd like to do it again." And he did it again and it was entirely different, he was entirely different to me. Maybe it still looks overdone now, I don't know. But his mental attitude was certainly entirely different. [She puts a world of difference into the word "entirely," stressing the *t* and adding an *h* after the *i* to prolong and intensify the implication of the word.] And I think he just saw a kid to whom it meant a tremendous amount, and he felt, "Well, the poor thing, I'd better do a little better here." It shows what a sensitive actor he was. Spencer always said, "Young actors must show respect." And I would say, "Well, I never showed the *dimmest* respect." When I did *Lion in Winter,* we rehearsed it for three weeks. They said, "This is so unique. We're going to rehearse the picture." And I laughed. "It ain't unique to me," I said. "I rehearsed the *Bill of Divorcement* with Mr. George Cukor for one week, with Jack Barrymore, before we shot, in the restaurant at RKO. And that was the first picture I ever did." Not so unique. They think they've stumbled on something new. I think it's all part of the same thing. The books are too long. Why? Because the people won't cut them, and they won't work over them. The people are all falling apart because they won't bother to have any character, and they won't try that hard. Everybody wants it to come easily. We live in a terribly easy-going society.

    You see, I think the people who survive are the people who are not such insane egomaniacs that they have to put their mark on everything. Now, George is a very generous man. He is a very generous director because he lets the actor put his mark on what he's doing, and he doesn't have to put a big sign on my back saying "George Cukor." Never did have. He was very happy to have somebody else get the credit for it.

When Hepburn praises others, as she does Cukor in speaking of their long collaboration, she does so as a statement of fact, neither asking nor, most likely, accepting contradiction or an attempt by the interviewer to give her her share of the credit on those films.

KH: He was interested in character. Now, character doesn't change. Material changes. He didn't get wedded to material, he got wedded to people. People were his interest. He was totally an artist. He would resent this . . . he thinks he's very practical. I don't think he was terribly practical. I'm much more practical than he is. But I think he was a real, a *real* artist. He was dealing in values of . . . love . . . and hate . . . and sex . . . uhh, villainy, which don't change. He could do that for a thousand years and would never date. The form of the thing might date, and everything else, but he's not easily shocked. He has very high standards. He didn't in the least even notice nudity, any more than I do. I don't give a rap; but I give an enormous rap when people are disillusioned. Now, sex . . . everybody . . . it's the style now to show everybody doing everything. This is a bore. Privacy and the magic of life, and the possible romantic magic between two people, which is what sex should represent, is nonexistent. I don't look at him, and he doesn't look at me, and we've known each other for fifty years, but we don't look at each other with any sense of reality. If he looked at me the way I really am, and I don't spark him, he would never have hired me. And if I didn't feel what he was, and respond to what he had to offer, we would just have been two old things. This is what matters in life.

Now we are living in a totally realistic age. They think sex is what they're showing. I don't think they know what they're talking about. Because I see a woman sacrifice herself totally for a man, I see a man sacrifice himself entirely for a woman; this has nothing to do with reality. It hasn't even to do with character. This has to do with magic. Because character is a bore if you're only doing it because you're worthy or something. But if you love someone, as a woman and some men love a child or a dog, and the dog is run over and you pick up and try to help it or something, *that* is love. That is blind . . . affection. Now, *that* quality goes on forever. Because you can't describe it to me and I can't describe it to you; it's the magic of life. It's the come-on. It's the hope! And that magic can make anything survive.

I was brought up in a hospital, and I talked endlessly to my father, and he would operate on people who were very old, and he would say it was marvelous the way people with an upbeat spirit and a determination, people who couldn't die because they'd be leaving people who couldn't get on with-

out them, and they lived! They *lived*! It's the spark of life, and without it, it's
hopeless. You can take this regard for life too far, to the point of eccentricity
where some won't even kill a mosquito or a moth without feeling guilty; but
apply that to people, but most people are too goddamned lazy to apply that
to people if the people become any trouble.

Now, people in our business go just up and down in their careers, up and
down, up and down. Sometimes you've got to help them, and sometimes
they've got to help you. And it has nothing to do with any sense. I'm in an
up period. Nothing to do with any sense at all. Doesn't mean the snap of your
fingers. And I'm smart enough [she laughs] because I've been up and down
a number of times, so that it makes no impression at all. But there are a
number of people who are your great friends and think you're fascinating and
marvelous when you're up and they don't when you're down. But I do think
that people who stick, regardless of whether you're up or down—now, that
is a rare quality and a wonderful quality.

JK: Did you study lighting or anything like that on the sets of your films?

KH: No. I thought it was too dangerous. I didn't pay any attention to that. I
thought it was too dangerous for actresses to know how they were lit, I
thought it was a poor idea. I mean, the main thing you have is not how you
look, but how you do it, how you come across. And if you're thinking of
how you look, you'll be in a bad way.

JK: You were photographed by most of the great Hollywood photographers.
Did you . . .

KH: I used to pose a lot for Bachrach. I enjoyed it. The results amused me. He
liked me, he liked to photograph me, and I enjoyed it. He was an awfully
good photographer, though I don't think the studio thought anything about it.
Alex Kahle used to photograph me on the set at RKO, and at Metro Jimmy
Mannett took those. He took those lovely Garbo photos of her on the set, and
Clarence Bull did wonderful, wonderful portraits of Garbo. I always enjoyed
photography.

JK: Were you deliberately striving after effects?

KH: I don't think we ever thought of it. You know, a lot of junk is talked today,
and it's all junk. If you're in the business of being photographed, you must
like to have your picture taken, otherwise you wouldn't be doing it. It's part
of your work. You're in the picture business.

JK: Joan Crawford took it very seriously.

KH: Because she took a very good picture. There's a very good reason for it.
It's just sheer vanity. It amused her to have amusing pictures taken of her, and
it must have amused me at that age. I let myself go before the camera. I
mean, you can't photograph a dead cat, so you have to offer something. But

it's just like some faces in movies—no matter how good an actor, they are just not interesting.

JK: You obviously respond to the photographer.

KH: Yes. But then, I respect them a great deal. Especially in the days when everybody was meant to be the most glamorous in the world. These men, my God, these men were responsible for covering up a lot of faults in a lady's face. All the ladies were meant to be absolutely beautiful, beauties, and they sure weren't. I had a very unconventional face, and when they had ugly, spinsterish *African Queen* ladies, I was in the first line for them.

Her lack of vanity is nothing if not consistent. In an interview she gave when she was first in Hollywood (*Picture Play*, February 1933), the interviewer suggested that the camera was cruel to her in her first picture, and wondered if that was to make the unhappy, haunted heroine in *Bill of Divorcement* more believable. "Oh, no," she assured her, "they did everything they could to make me look nice. The cameramen and electricians tried awfully hard. I have a peculiar face."*

JK: Would Bachrach map out little scenarios when you worked with him?

KH: No. No, nothing. I'd go in and do any crazy thing I thought of. And I liked to pose for him. We were compatible. I also liked to pose for George Hoynigen-Huene, a brilliant photographer, and Munkacsi, I enjoyed posing for him.

JK: You were a huge sensation on Broadway before you got to Hollywood and they knew what you looked like. There was a lot of excitement surrounding your arrival in Hollywood.

KH: I'll tell you. You see, when I arrived in Hollywood, I was with my friend Laura Harding, and I had a steel filing in my eye. I had two *bright* red eyes. And nobody paid any attention to the fact that I was really quite ill. I had paid a lot of money for my outfit, and I walked into RKO and met George Cukor. He was very nice oh, yes—"How do you do?" "How do you do?" And he gave me a sort of odd look, and I said, "Mr. Cukor, I have something in my eye. Do you know a doctor?" And he said, "I want you to see the sketches." He *never* answered my question. Well, I walked in petrified. He was probably horrified when he saw me. My eyes were bright red. Jack Barrymore was there. I said, "How do you do?" He came in for one second, and I went out in the hallway, and he told me how to get rid of the red eyes. Because he knew. And he was more interested than George was. So then I went back in and George took out some terrible-looking sketches in order to make conver-

---

*At the same time, while being up front about her working face, she denied that she came from a socially prominent family, and that she had been married. The article was entitled "A Lady Lies."

sation, trying to be very sweet, and said, "What do you think of these?" And
I looked at them, and I thought they were horrible. I said, "Well, I really
don't think that a well-bred English girl would wear anything like that," in a
rather prissy way. [She laughs at her youthful presumptuousness.] And
George said, "What do you think of what you have on?" And I was a bit
taken aback, and I said, "Well, I paid $350 for it," which is like $1500 now.
I must say now that it *was* damned queer-looking. But I said, "I think it's
very smart." And George said, "Well, I think it stinks." [She roars and snorts
with laughter.] He said, "Now we can proceed from there." And we proceeded to the hairdressing department. I had my hair done *à la concierge,* as
I do now, and we went up to the makeup department. And George went off
to dinner. I was left. Alone. And with no doctor.

Hepburn's family background (brothers who didn't take her quick wit lying
down) prepared her for any rebukes or rebuffs from people she met after she left
her family's bosom. Cukor recalled that she was the most self-possessed woman
he'd ever known, and "all my chidings just rolled off her back like a knife."

KH: You see, if I spoke out of turn at the family table, I'd have a glass of milk
poured on my head by my brother, or was told to "shut up" by my dad. So
when George would raise his voice, I'd never listen. I'm sure that's why we
got on. [She snortles.] I remember George hitting people.

Frances Goldwyn's sister, my friend Laura Harding and I came into the
picture business together. We were in this scene together where we come
down a staircase, and we got to the bottom of the stair, and I was standing
there with a sort of dreamlike, angelic dress on, and I waltzed off in David
Manners' arms. Laura came and stood with her hand on the newel post,
waiting for somebody to pick her up, and the ball on the top of the newel post
came off in her hand. And she was a real amateur, terribly funny girl, and she
didn't know what to do with it. She thought, "What am I supposed to do?"
So she handed the ball to the boy who was dancing with her. [Hepburn bursts
into a gagging laugh, like a baseball hitting a sandbar and skidding over it.]
George was in a fury. Because it was a wonderful take and a very, very
complicated shot. The time George hit me, I spilled ice cream during the
dinner scene in *Little Women.* There was only one dress and I ruined it, and
he was in a terrible fury.

JK: *Little Women* was one of those movies that really quite successfully incorporated innocence without being totally innocuous.

KH: Yes, yes. I remember when Tallulah saw the picture. We'd met once before
then, at a dinner with George, and I remember finding her language . . . She
was very free with her speech and I didn't find her use of words very amusing, and Tallulah, so George later told me, said to him, "I think your friend
Miss Hepburn is a New England spinster." And that was just for starters.

JK: She didn't take her film career as seriously. I remember she hated the way she photographed.

Hepburn looked at some pictures of her old friend.

KH: Very few were any good, it's true. Tallulah just didn't photograph all that well. It was something about her nose, too bulbous. They never captured her marvelous personality. But anyway, she was in California on vacation at the time, on her way back to New York, and she saw the first rough cut from *Little Women*, which *no one* had seen. And I was on the set doing another scene at the time, and suddenly there was this frightful scream from the other end of the soundstage. Tallulah came rushing in. She threw herself in George's arms, and then gave me a big hug, and she just burst into tears. She had three black handkerchiefs, which she used. She was absolutely shattered. She fell on her knees to me. She was really darling, and terribly moved. George looked at her with a rather cool eye and said, "Tallulah, you're weeping for your lost innocence." You see, it's true for the enormous hold of any sentimental subject. I mean, they wonder why *The Sound of Music* was such a big success. Well, everybody was weeping for their lost innocence. It's just Cinderella.

Little Women had that extraordinary quality of lost innocence and also of character. It was a child's book, it was always considered like a child's book, but it was like *my* childhood, you see. We were in New England, we had a big family, and everything was always rather exaggerated and I was a *very* dramatic sort, you know, "Chri*s*topher Col*u*mbus! What ri*ch*ness" type. And all that sort. It rather suited my exaggerated sense of things. And they [the *Little Women* family] were a good sort. All of them. They had character and they were funny.

Oh, I remember there was a sound strike in the studios at the time we were shooting, it was during the scene where Beth was dying for the nth time, and although I admired the book enormously, I was getting a little bit unable to play it because I had wept day after day after day, and I had sixteen and twenty takes on these weeping scenes, and they wouldn't get them correctly. We had all of these amateur sound men. Finally, she did die, and I threw up. I cried so many times, I just threw up.

Then we switched and did the scene where I went to New York to seek my fortune and I went to the opera with Professor Bhaer. And I came back home, you know, in the movie, and I said, "Ohhhhhhhh, Ih donh't whahnt to be ah hwritah. Ih whahnt to be ahn ohperah singhah." [Hepburn does an astoundingly good takeoff of Hepburn.] And I came into this room, in this *e*xquisite dress, and I rather fancied myself, full of too much energy, terribly young, all of ten, and I twirled around in this beautiful dress which had been copied from one of my grandmother's dresses and sank to the ground in a curtsy and said, "I want to be an opera singer," and down from the ceiling, on a rope, came a large ham. That was George's idea of a joke. It was terribly funny. And nothing like that ever happened to me until one day when I got stuck on the Milford Turnpike, and a cop came up to me and said, "Well, if it isn't the little girl who sold us those sandwiches all these years." And I asked, "What kind of sandwich?" and he said, "Ham." Isn't that divine? [She burst into laughter.]

JK: But you had an enormous appeal . . . your hair comes down and you are transformed. Or, as in *Alice Adams*, at the moment that Alice is at her gauchest, as the man turns from her, you/Alice are as beautiful as can be . . . Your appeal was in the ability to transform yourself from duckling to swan.

KH: But I was not in any way pretty. I was not pretty. And a lot of the people around then were extremely pretty. But all of them, every one, they were maintaining the illusion. It was a romantic business. The stories were romantic. It was a fascinating never-never land. I mean, look, the theaters were covered with gilt and cupids. I always wanted to be a movie actress. I thought it was very romantic. And it was. It still can be. Granted, there was a dearth of material and I made the great mistake of saying yes to some of it, but there were others.

In a way, the whole business has come full circle, people today are as romantic about the movies we made then as we were making them at the time. They created . . . Louis B. Mayer was romantic about the industry. Today it's all money. Today they have turned that never-never land into . . . They have to offer people something they can't get at home, all these sorts of sexual perversions and weird happenings. That's what they go for now. And that's what they're selling.

I've run into a lot of people who are miserable, and the world is passing [them] by, and I've lived long enough to know why, and that is because a lot of them have just been pigs. They were wildly selfish. They were wildly self-centered, and they don't take anything in. They are giving out, they are not taking in. And the minute you stop taking in, you're dead. I think everybody has about twenty to thirty years' impetus from their childhood, and then look out! Writers especially. Writers go dead. And I've seen directors go dead, and actors go dead. You've got to fill up the well, and the only way to fill up the well is to fill it up with deeds that are generous enough that your imprint isn't on them. Otherwise you're just drinking your own water. It's a terrible state to be in. It's very common today.

For a long time an enormous bulk of the population suffered and were oppressed and badly treated, and now everybody is, oh, so well treated they're beginning to take an awful lot of things for granted. Or if they are badly treated, they do nothing but complain about how badly treated they are, so that they don't recognize the benefits. And *nobody* can build your house for you. You've got to build your own house because you've got to live in it. And if you build a rotten house, it's going to fall down, or dissolve in the rain. When you run out of energy, naturally you become isolated, that is death, and you die. But before you run out of energy, it's terribly important that the doors to your home, yourself, are not closed. And that you keep saying, *"Yes! Yes! Why not?"* And most people say, "No." George Cukor had that gift. Constance Collier was another one who had that great gift . . . she was blind, she could hardly walk, and one would ask, "Constance, will you come to a preview in the middle of the night?" "Yes!"

You see—back to *Little Women*—these kids were brought up in an era where, if you committed a sin, it was your fault and you paid for it. Or if you had a fault or you complained about something, if you tore your dress or you had a rotten emotion about something, or if you behaved very badly and you were sent to your room, it was *your* fault and you had to change.

Now, today, in a rather permissive society . . . I don't say I approve totally of the other, but I've lived long enough to know there's only one person in the world you can change, and that is yourself. So that if you commit an error in your life, or you do something dumb, and repeatedly do something dumb, or if you're caught in a bad act or insult somebody or behave very badly, today you're taught that this isn't your fault. It's your upbringing, or your environment, and it's terribly sad; and you are sick; or you can't study at school; your parents neglected you, broken homes . . . There are eight million excuses, but it is never the fault of the person, therefore there's never anything you can do about it. Now, the tougher you are in life and the more you blame yourself, the better off you'll be. In my estimation. If you want to get on with somebody, and you don't get on with them, change yourself! Now, you change yourself, the relationship will work. But if you have two people, each one waiting for the other person to change, and they get divorced and it isn't any good. And sometimes for something stupid. Something silly. Kids have got to be blamed for something. Now, I don't think you go around blaming people and making people suffer all the time for their sins, but I do think you've got to learn to take your share of the blame and your share of the responsibility. But I was brought up in that era. If there was work to be done, you did it. You earn your thing.

We were also brought up in an era—this is very important—when I can remember walking down the street and thinking, "Here I am, and, boy, I'm full of beans, I'm a human being." And it was a rather individual thing. And you had an opportunity. Today there are five million of you and five million of me, and you walk down the street and you're not walking down the street alone. You're walking down the street with so goddamned many people that if you don't stick your head up or kick someone or trip them up or do something like that, you're afraid you won't be noticed. Now, I dressed like a freak. Uh . . . uh . . . I think I enjoy dressing like a freak. I can understand why they all dress like freaks today. Because, my God, that trip to the big city, and then to go down the drain is very short. And if you don't raise a red flag or . . . or . . . put a wild geranium in your head or do something idiotic, nobody notices you. You feel. It's fascinating to change yourself. I've seen people do it when they had to. And when they didn't have to, they indulged themselves. But the point is, you have to be willing to change yourself, and you must have the sense to change yourself. But a lot of people can't change themselves, and then they go right down the drain.

To Hepburn, the state of the contemporary cinema was par for the course with the current (1981) state of depression or self-indulgence in the arts.

KH: Now, we had a schoolteacher on the set for little Jean Parker. She was a *very* disapproving, rather disagreeable woman with a disagreeable expression. She thought it was all boring and a bit silly. She would sit, always, where we could see her, and she would look as though we were bores. It was a terribly *down* attitude. Instead of the enormous enthusiasm of the average crew, she was just looking at us as much as to say, "Good God." I nearly died. I could hardly play in front of her. And then George came up to me and said, "Have you noticed that schoolteacher? What is the matter with her?" And I said, "Well, she thinks we're a bore. She thinks *some*thing, but it's agonizing." And he said, "She's been absolutely destroying me because I keep wondering what she's thinking." And I laughed to myself that a real disapproving eye, right in the front row, when George was saying, "How lovely," and sort of urging us on, could so disconcert us, and then he said, "I'm going to fire her. I've never fired anybody, but I'm going to fire her." And I said, "Fire her. You're right."

   People are rather insensitive about that. On the screen, when anybody's acting, they're looking out towards the camera, presumably out towards the great nowhere, and people have no hesitation, when they come on a set, standing there in front, so that the actor, instead of looking inward into his or her own imagination, is confronted with this cold eye. I remember on *The Philadelphia Story* when Jimmy Stewart was doing the scene, uh . . ."You've got hearth-fires banked down in you, Tracy, hearth-fires and holocausts." And George said to him, "Now, Jimmy, just do that scene in a romantic way. But *don't* do it as if you were just about to run away to the circus." So poor Jimmy . . . he won the Academy Award for that film . . . and he was struggling with this thing, "You've got hearth-fires banked down in you" . . . it's a bit fancy to say. And just before he did it, Noel Coward stepped onto the set and Jimmy nearly died. So he did the scene, and Noel in one *sec*ond [with a click of her fingers she snaps off the second] could see what was going on, and immediately stepped up to Jimmy and told him how devastating he was. And George said, "Roll 'em," and took advantage of a moment of flattery and Jimmy got a wonderful take. Stewart was terribly funny about that film. There was a scene where he had to go in swimming and he said, "If I appear in a bathing suit, I know it's the end of me. I know that and I'm prepared to end my career, but it will also be the end of the motion-picture industry." And we both appeared in that scene in long white flannel dressing gowns.

JK: How do you sustain the emotion, the dramatic highlight, in the close-up, in all of the many shots needed for one scene?

KH: You act. [She snickers *and* snortles.] You pretend you're somebody else. Discipline and education fixes it so that you must be able to repeat it. God knows, in the theater . . . but I work the same way onstage as I do in films. I've always been a very naturalistic actress, so the two mediums posed no problems. For a lot of very fine stage actors, though, the movie was a different technique to them, and that may have been why they didn't make it in films. It was after World War II that all this naturalistic stuff came in . . . I can remember *Vogue* and *Vanity Fair* and posing for more naturalistic things. Munkacsi brought *movement* to stills. But, you see, there was a whole attitude that went with those old films, and you can't imitate it. Like, for some odd reason, nobody has been able to re-create the Scott Fitzgerald stories. And I think I understand why they can't do them . . . because the madness of that era, the people, were like *noth*ing anybody's ever heard of. They're lethargic today compared to then; they were *vital*. It's all so heavy today by comparison. Then they were light and frivolous and silly and wicked and funny. And it was all done with wit. Today there is no wit.

Now, I've just come back from doing a tour for God knows how long of Enid's play, Enid Bagnold's play. Oh, what the hell was it? Isn't that awful? Oh, dear *God*. I *must* know what I've been just playing in. [She excuses herself and asks her housekeeper the name of the play.] *A Matter of Gravity*. There we are. Now, in Enid's play, for instance, it was enormously witty. And I *love* to make an audience laugh. Some of the play they may not understand, but the wit . . . they adore to laugh. It's strange, the movies and plays that are done today. I don't know who the audience is. It's all so heavy today, ponderous and so full of meaning. I don't think the stories they film today have the charm and intimacy that comes from a knowing, tightly knit relationship. Like the ones in *Adam's Rib* and *Pat and Mike*, where we all knew each other and knew what everybody could do well.

I remember only one thing about working with George and Spencer,* and that was that George never gave Spencer any suggestions *at all*. He gave them *all* to me. And George once said to Spencer, "You know, I think of a lot of things to say to you, and then I don't say them and then I go to see the rushes, and it's all there. And I've never seen you do it." With me, George obviously saw a lot of things he didn't like and he corrected me.

But George was good at making actors feel happy about themselves, creating a climate for them to work well in. And that's what Ernie Bachrach did for us in the gallery as well, which is very important, for most people feel like fools. Everybody does, really, as you start out in the morning. Now, if you're married to a nice creature who tells you how fascinating you are, and thrilling, that's a help. But the great thing about a director is to admire an actor enough, and tell them so enough, so that the actor feels free. Because most of us build a wall of protection around ourselves. And if you think that someone thinks you're a fool, you become a fool. And if you feel that they

*They made three films together: *Keeper of the Flame*, *Adam's Rib* and *Pat and Mike*.

think you're wonderful, you have a tendency to try and be wonderful and live up to what they think of you.

But that time of making *Adam's Rib* and *Pat and Mike* was a very creative and very exciting period. Spencer never used to join those conferences we had, George and Garson Kanin and Ruth Gordon—who wrote the scripts. We'd meet on the weekends, and Spencer would make a general comment on what he'd heard. During the reading of *Pat and Mike*, Spencer sat in a corner of the room when we had a reading of the script one night at George's house. But he didn't join in. They were written and very intimately discussed between us all, which I think was an enormous help to everyone concerned. It was very "ensemble" in spirit. And things we didn't like, or which irritated one, or you didn't understand, you were able to state it, which one doesn't always get an opportunity to do in this business. It was not just friendship, but an artistic collaboration.

You can write about birth till hell freezes over, but there it is. It's magic. And you can write about death, but there it is, we don't know anything about it, where we go or what the hell it's all about. You can analyze love, but they know less about it now than they have ever known, and the whole philosophy in recent years was to say that it wasn't important, but it's still the thing that makes everything tick. You can chew over acting till it goes, and all the spontaneity is gone. And I'll tell you what's really gone out of films: the humor. The lightness of touch. There was a lot of a kind of Irish, idiotic humor in a lot of those old films that made no sense at all but was very funny. It was Irish, because the Irish tradition of humor was still very dominant in the theater at that time, in the '40s. And I don't think it is anymore. It's heavy. It's overserious. They are all just talking a lot of bunk.

Reading about Katharine Hepburn, or an interview with her, cannot give you the full flavor . . . One has to hear her voice, take a rest in her pauses, start up again.The proof of her attitude to life is in her living and in her working, and accounts as well as anything for why she is not merely still with us, but still such an integral starring force in the theater and on film.

1979

BOB

COBURN

B OB COBURN, SR., is one of Hollywood's finest still and portrait photographers. Like his friend Gary Cooper, he came to Hollywood to finish high school; much of his childhood was spent in a saddle and he was good at athletics (he doubled in a pole-vaulting stunt for comedian Ben Turpin, who was grinding out a two-reeler). Coburn's hobby and first love was not acting but photography, and it was in that capacity that in 1916 he entered the business, a high-school kid spending his vacations as film-loader, assistant and all-around stooge to Billy Beckway, and growing up with the industry. Having learned to take pictures in a saddle, the young Coburn was much in demand shooting the unending string of Westerns being filmed around Hollywood all through the '20s.

In 1929 he joined the newly formed RKO photo department to work for one of the most progressive and original photographers in the profession, Ernest Bachrach. In 1936 the opportunity came for him to take over the photo department for Samuel Goldwyn, then still producing films on the UA lot. Coburn was also involved in all the other productions made on the UA lot, like *Algiers* with Hedy Lamarr in her American film debut. In 1941, a year after Goldwyn had split from his UA partners, Coburn left to take over the job of running the stills department at Columbia Pictures for Harry Cohn. By then Coburn had become the highest-paid and one of the most highly regarded professionals in the business.

His pearly portraits of Merle Oberon while with Goldwyn did as much as anything to make him a favorite with female stars. The portraits he took of Gary Cooper, Charles Boyer and Joel McCrea made him admired as much for his photos of men. Coburn had won his peers' admiration long before then; he shot all the stills on *King Kong,* stills which were miniature works every bit as subtle as the film itself; and he could get on with people who were the terror of others in his field: studio chiefs like Harry Cohn; stars like Miriam Hopkins, the bane of many a photographer's existence; and the superstitious, photography-hating director John Ford. Coburn was one of the great all-around talents.

I tracked him down at his retirement home built beside a golf course a little way below Palm Springs. He was as old as the century and looked like a cowboy in a Charles Russell painting, or in a Hawks or John Ford Western. He spoke

339

slowly—not hesitantly, exactly, but like someone pulling things out from the bottom of a chest from time to time; and the second time we met the voice was frailer than I remembered. It took a lot of convincing to get him to bring out any of his photographs. As a matter of fact, he had very few there, only a couple on display in his den, and even those I didn't notice at first. As a boy he may have turned his mother's bathroom into his darkroom, but now, if I hadn't known who he was, admired what he'd done and wanted to know more about how he did it, neither his appearance nor his home, a one-level ranch-style with open rooms, would have given much of a clue. Well, there was that picture of Rita Hayworth, framed, hanging in his den, out of the way. But, whatever initial hesitation and tetchiness there might have been in his voice, it didn't last long; he wasn't a gossip, not really a storyteller, and he was amazingly unassuming about his work, considering the superb quality of so much of it. His portraits might set others to rhapsodizing. From him it produced a matter-of-fact shrug, a smile now and then and a scholarly explanation of the technical difficulties that getting the image might have entailed. He's a man of opinions, and he has his peeves, his idols, and a few out there he'd rather not think about. But if he's the kind of man to harbor grudges, he's not the kind to spill them to a stranger. On the few occasions when he started to talk angrily about this photographer or that, he soon stopped. It was clear that things were not that smooth between Coburn and George Hurrell (Hurrell was working at Columbia for a year in the early '40s), but the facts were not forthcoming, and to pursue the point would only have made him shut down altogether. Photographers are not very good at talking about themselves or even about their work. How many times had I heard them reply, "Well, you just do it" or "I don't know, I just did it." And yet they proved to be some of the most interesting men I've ever met. They revealed not just their own stories but the secrets of the stars they photographed and the industry these stars made possible and powerful.

BC: We all had a sense of glamorizing Hollywood at that time, but each individual had his own sense of working. I'd read a script and I'd get an idea, and that idea would be to sell the picture: what pictures should I concentrate on when I'm on the picture? Or if I'm not on the picture, I always still shot the special stuff after the picture was over. Maybe it wasn't just to get this gal looking like the most beautiful thing. Maybe I had to make an old hag out of her.

For example, Rita [Hayworth] for *Miss Sadie Thompson*. Rita was a completely different girl in that picture than the sweet thing she usually was. Or [Barbara] Stanwyck in *Stella Dallas*. I shot that picture with the fur slung over her shoulders, and she was a slut. And that was the twenty-four sheet. I'd shoot for that sort of result and publicity usually bought it. We'd usually hash things over a bit and they'd give me a list of their ideas, and I'd choose mine too. I brought out some things to give you an idea.

Bob Coburn with *Andrea Leeds*, 1939

He lifted a scrapbook from underneath the tea table. It was the sort of scrapbook I'd kept myself when I was a kid, pictures cut out of fan magazines; stars looking great next to slogans telling you that nine out of ten stars used Lux; ads for films, those pages in the front of the fan magazines; picture spreads. The only difference between mine and his was that this was *his* work. No fine-art prints here, just the results reprinted in the outlets they were intended for.

BC: Now, here [he turns a handful of pages at one time like a man who knows what he wants to get to], one of my old pictures from *King Kong* at RKO. I took the stills on *Kong;* I shot all the stills on the set, and Bachrach taught me how to superimpose [Fay] Wray into Kong's paws for the stills.

Bachrach was an all-round man. He could do *anything* photographic. So it rubbed off on me. I couldn't help but ask him nine million questions a day. He was a *terrific* teacher.

You see, before I joined RKO, I was thinking that maybe I'd want to be a motion-picture cameraman, because when I first started in the business, I started as an assistant to Billy Beckway, your old English cameraman, who was over here at the time, and Billy was another Bachrach, motion-picture-wise, answering all my questions, teaching me. I first got started as his assistant cameraman. He carried around this little, black, locked-up box with all his goodies in it. Those were all the tricks for in front of the lens, gimmicks that he made up personally. He was good at making things; he was a good machinist too. For instance, irises, or stops, all those things which now are done by the trick-photography department, in those days we did it all before the camera. There was no trick-photography department. *We* did the tricks. And Billy was the one who thought them up. Finally, after about three months and I'd asked him nine million questions, he finally said, "The box is yours. Here's the key." From then on, I did all the tricks with him.

I was born on a cattle ranch. They used to say I was born on a horse with a camera around my neck. The first I remember doing photographs, my father came to the ranch—we had one of the biggest cattle ranches in the country then—he came home with an Eastman-Kodak. This fascinated me. I just went completely berserk about this stupid camera. I carried it around on my saddle; I took pictures of everything; I finally had my mother's bathroom looking like a photographic laboratory. I'd send for things mail-order, and they'd send me the photographic chemicals and everything I needed. I developed all my own stuff before I was sixteen. So when Billy Beckway hit the ranch, I wouldn't stay out of his hair (my father put some money into a picture, and they made it on our ranch) and he sensed that this kid had something. I tell you, John, you either have it or you don't. Since then I have had many men work for me who were scared to death to go on a set to take pictures, but I was trigger happy. You couldn't keep me away. I'd go in where angels fear to tread, and *loved* it.

Take John Ford. Now, that man hated photographers around, didn't even like his own cameraman. In fact, John was a pretty hard Irishman to get along with. Well, I'm Irish too. He interviewed me—this was at RKO and I did something special for him. He was just going to make a big picture called *The Informer*. So, asking around, somebody suggested they get Coburn to do the stills because a lot of the fellas were scared to work with him. I went to see him, having heard all about him: "Stay away from him! Don't shoot a picture while he's chewing on his handkerchief! And *never* shoot him on his blind side!" He had a patch over one eye. Well, the very first morning, the very first scene, I went in and sat on a box right next to him, underneath the camera. Here was the camera's lens right here, and I sat right there. I kinda sensed him looking at me, but he never kicked me out. I had a thing cooking with every sound man that I'd never ruin a take with the click of my camera. I got a Leica and shot the whole picture, *The Informer,* with a 35 mm camera. All this time Ford would be looking at me, but never said a word. This went on for about a week, and one day, I don't remember what the action was, but I didn't want to shoot that, so I didn't appear; I wasn't sitting in my usual place that day. And Ford, by God, was looking around and when he didn't see me sitting there, he called the assistant director and said, "Where's Coburn? Get him in here!"

Well [a slight chuckle], I had to sit on that stool next to him for every take from then on. We became very fast friends. I could see his logic in everything that he did. He was such a realist that when we had Victor Mc-Laglen's drunken scene, well, he got him drunk. He took him into his dressing room and gave him a quart of whiskey and told him to drink it. And Ford sat there with him and he drank it, and he came back on the set loop-legged— he couldn't make it from here to there, and he was pawing all over the gal [Margot Grahame] exactly as Ford wanted. This *wasn't* acting. He *was* drunk. That's exactly what Ford wanted. Everything was real with him, but he could control it, which is why he was such a great director.

When I worked for Goldwyn, I not only did the gallery, but I also continued to shoot special stuff on films. Goldwyn wanted me to do that. I was unique in that respect, doing gallery portraits and set stills. As a matter of fact, Goldwyn insisted on that. This gave me a better all-round view of what was wanted to help sell the picture, and when I went to Columbia, that was the only way I'd go: on condition that I took full charge of everything pertaining to still pictures.

At Goldwyn, when we had two pictures at once, I'd get a man on one and I'd do the other. Like Alex Kahle, who shot those stills on Ford's *Hurricane,* and I shot the special stuff, because I was also busy on *Goldwyn Follies.* On *Algiers** I did everything on it: special, portraits, stills. . . .

I got to Goldwyn because Kenny Alexander was a Silver Shirt. It was an anti-Jewish, anti-Semitic group and he was the leader, or a lieutenant, I be-

---

*Walter Wanger's production starring Boyer and introducing Hedy Lamarr, made at the UA studios.

lieve, and they were really a kind of Nazi outfit; and he was working for Goldwyn, and Goldwyn didn't know this. Anyway, the publicity department at Goldwyn found out that Kenny had this stockpile of ammunition and food and everything up in the Hollywood hills and he was going to have a big wingding someday. Goldwyn heard of it and all hell broke loose, and they said let's get rid of him and get somebody else.

Well, the guy at Goldwyn used to be head of publicity at RKO. Anyway, he called me up. I was in the middle of a John Ford picture, *The Plough and the Stars,** and he said, "Can you come over and talk to us?" I did, and he said, "Okay, you're on. But I'm talking about tomorrow morning you start with us, not next week." I wasn't under contract at RKO, but I was Bachrach's righthand man and I'd worked there a long time. I was then making the top wages, which was $85 a week for a six-day week. I was on all the time, I was never let go. My only incentive in staying on with Ernie was that I liked him, and that I learned a lot from him and I was working steady. But anyway, Ernie said you have to see John Ford and see if you can get off the picture. Ford said, "Okay, go ahead, I can't stop you from making more money, but, Bob, *please* get me somebody who can get along with me. You know me."

I went to Ernie and said, "Do you think we could jerk Alex Kahle off the film he's on?" Alex was one of a kind, and I figured he'd get on with Ford if anybody could. So I got a hold of Alex and I told him all about Ford and I said, "This you can't do and this you can't do" and all that stuff. Alex was born in Germany, he had been one of the Royal German Guards back in Berlin, and I'd be telling him these things and he'd be saying, "*Yahhh,* Bob, *yah,* I undastand." And I'd told him, "Above all, Alex, don't shoot him on his blind side." Because we all liked to sneak up and catch as catch can, odd shots of people when they didn't know we were making pictures of them. Well, the first thing Alex did, because he couldn't stand it, there was Ford in the middle of a grinding thought or something, and he's chewing on his handkerchief, and he's got the hat over his one bad eye, and Alex sneaks up on him and shoots a picture. Well, of course the lid flew off and Ford called him over and he said, "Didn't Bob tell you not to take a picture when I'm doing this?" And he said, "*Yah,* Mr. Ford, *yah,* but I yust can't help it." "Well, see to it that you don't do it again." "*Yah,* Mr. Ford." Well, it wasn't ten minutes and he shot another one. This went on for three times and Ford said, "Alex or whatever your name is, get the hell out of here and go down and get your boss to send me somebody else." "*Yah,* Mr. Ford, I do *yust* that." Alex went to the makeup department and he made himself up with a big white beard, white hair, a big mustache. Now Ford is up on a big six-foot catwalk, with

---

*There is likelihood of confusion over dates and titles here. The film Coburn was working on for Ford, if it was in 1935, would have been *The Informer,* since Ford's next film at RKO wasn't made till 1936.

his feet on both sides and his cameras on each side of him, and Alex sneaks up underneath here, aims right up and shoots a picture of him. Well, everybody thought Alex was gonna get killed. And Ford looked down on him: "Go take your goddamn makeup off, you win." Of course he was with him from then on, *Hurricane, Stagecoach.* . . . Anyway, that's how I got off the picture, and the next day I was working at Goldwyn's on a picture—whatever it was.

Only three studios had galleries then. Bachrach had one, and Bull at Metro, and Paramount, and Fox was just setting one up with Powolny and Korman. The photographer on the set would set up his own gallery and shoot the ads for it there, and it was very amateurish really, because it's hard, working under those conditions, to get concentration going the way you could in a gallery under four closed walls, you could sell what's in your mind to the actor and get it done. I set up a gallery when I got to Goldwyn's because there wasn't a real one there before.

We looked at a color spread that had appeared in the Sunday supplement of one of the newspapers. It was a scene from *Goldwyn Follies,* a musical in color, released in January 1938. Its brilliant, lush, classical-art-influenced color schemes remain the most notable aspect of a film that also had choreography by George Balanchine and dancing by Vera Zorina. For Coburn this was another "technical" accomplishment.

BC: Don [Biddle] Keyes and I made the first color pictures in Hollywood, in Don's lab in his home up off Hollywood Boulevard in the Hollywood hills. I'd made this picture of Zorina in the lily pool, and one of Andrea Leeds.* Those were the first color prints and color pictures ever made in Hollywood.

When I joined Bachrach—that was in 1929—Keyes had just come out from New York to take over their photo department. Back in New York, he'd been working for Famous Players–Lasky at the old Astoria studios, shooting Gloria Swanson a lot. Gloria thought he was the only photographer in the world, and when she came back out here to work, he came with her. He'd gone to photographic school in New York. Before then I'd been on independent Westerns, and I'd been working over at Christie comedies, all those crazies. I used to do lots of the independent Westerns with those big-time old cowboy stars like Hoot Gibson, Tom Keene, Tom Mix, a lot of those. I used to do everything on them there was to do to sell a picture, though I didn't know what I was doing. Nobody did! You just *did it*. It was all beginning. It was *new*. We were creating as we went along, only we didn't know that's what we were doing.

---

*Miss Leeds was another highly touted, promising, dark and somewhat melancholic-looking beauty discovered by Goldwyn and oft photographed by Coburn to sell her to the public. She had made a strong impression as the suicide victim in the all-star *Stage Door,* in which she received equal recognition with Hepburn and Ginger Rogers.

FBO [RKO] and Bachrach was my first time working with a major studio. Bachrach believed in *thorough* knowledge of photography. For instance, when I made these montages for *King Kong,* the way to cut—and I had a steady hand and I could do just the same as he could, but you had to cut out a line and not have it show when we made the whole picture so you could print those things with very little retouching, it would look like it just came out of the film. Of course we'd photographed *King Kong,* so that we knew where we were going to put Fay Wray in there, in his hands or someplace, and we had to have a background that would take to this cutting-out technique and also enhance her being in his paw. In the picture they had motion and you can make people not see things when it's all moving. It was very laborious. The picture took them a couple of years to make. I told them, every time they changed to an interesting shot of Kong, they were to call up our department and I'd go down. Sometimes I'd stay all day if it was an interesting setup. Sometimes we'd forget the script and I'd get an idea and ask them to do several different things because I had to shoot Fay Wray the following day in the gallery and I'd like some different angles of him. Of course we were never allowed to touch him.

Many of the most famous, often-published images from *King Kong* are pictures that Coburn dreamed up and do not appear in the film. One such is the classic shot of Kong breaking through a mist shrouding the city he towers over, his arms held out, a girl dangling unconscious in one of the giant paws, his jaw a frightening gape.

BC: Bachrach also taught me and Alex—we were the only three in Hollywood, I think, at the time—to never take a straight shot. We always cocked our cameras. [Immediately one thinks of Kahle's stills for *Citizen Kane* or Coburn's for *The Lost Patrol* and *The Informer.*] We'd either sit on our butts and shoot up or something, or turn the camera. We'd go for the composition of the picture and make something interesting out of it rather than what we call "the company front."

I was already doing gallery work while I was at RKO. It just happened. One day Ernie said, "Would you like to finish this sitting?" I guess he had to do something else, so I finished it, I think it was of Katharine Hepburn [for *Christopher Strong*], and from then on he knew I could do it. Just one of those things. She always insisted on him, but after that she never made anything of it if I shot her too.

The Goldwyn studio portrait gallery was a crumby little old place that was about the oldest room at the studio, just about falling down, but it was the only place I could work and be alone in, so I set it up as a portrait studio, got my big cameras in there and my lights, but it was always precarious.

I photographed Merle Oberon more than anybody except maybe Rita Hayworth. Merle was the type of person that you never got tired of shooting. She was cooperation from the time she walked in the gallery to the time she walked off. She worked hard. She grasped everything I said to her. A lot of 'em never paid any attention. You had to go over and move their hand; they had no grace, no body.

Coburn's voice drops to a whisper, hoping the names I'm asking him for might go away if I can't hear him. Sigrid Gurie? He chuckles and nods. Hedy Lamarr?

BC: Well . . . [he's laughing now] you had to get it out of her. She was such a quiet, unassuming person in those days, maybe it was because she was so young and new out there, and she was afraid to do things. . . . It was a little tough to get her to do things, to relax. But Merle and I, we spoke the same language. She was very enthusiastic every time we had a sitting. It just went like clockwork, so fast it was often over before we knew it. It was like that from the start, from the first time I had to shoot her, when she was making *These Three* [1936].

There are lots of sittings with people who were awkward in front of the camera, afraid of revealing themselves. Like David Niven, he hated going in front of a camera; it was just like going to a dentist's office for him. He told me that just before we had a first sitting. Of course, there are lots of photographers who were never sure of what they wanted, which made it tough for the actors. A good actor can sense right away if the other person knows what they're doing. That's why they were often so wary. Gary Cooper was a good camera subject who was difficult in a way. But never for me. We both came from Montana, and we talked Westerns. He was embarrassed a little bit at constantly being photographed. He preferred to be in movement in front of the camera. I did the stills for most of Cooper's films, like *The Real Glory* and *The Westerner*. I titter sometimes when I watch 'cause you can see when he's embarrassed in front of the camera, because when he's playing being embarrassed, it's because he *is* embarrassed. That's just the way Coop was. But he was a great camera subject.

When he was making *For Whom the Bell Tolls* over at Paramount, he got me over there to shoot the stills. It was the first time I'd been over there since I'd worked there in the '20s when Jimmy Wong Howe was first starting and I was an assistant cameraman. Cooper wanted me on it, so I went over there. At that time I was the highest-paid photographer in the business, getting $750 a week at Columbia, which was more than some of the first cameramen were getting, but I was in charge of the whole shooting match at the time, and my salary was killing them at Paramount, *killing* them.

When I started with Goldwyn, I was in complete charge of my department. Goldwyn wanted it that way. He wanted complete control of everything that was going on and coming out of his studio, so he put me in charge of that section. When I started, I was making $250 a week, and $450 by the time I left him. There wasn't *anybody* that *shot* any of his people except me— *Life, Look* or anybody else. If on occasion *Life* wanted a shot of Gary Cooper when he was making *Marco Polo* (we got a cover on it), I shot the cover.

Goldwyn kept sharp track of *all* publicity coming out of his studio, which is
what still pictures are. And he didn't want anything out that could be cheap
or degrading in any manner . . . pertaining to his studio or his stars or the
type of picture he was making at the time. That was quite unique, that involvement from the top. Harry Cohn was like that later when I went over to
Columbia in '41. It wasn't like it was for the guys over at Metro or at Warners; I wasn't under the publicity department. We worked together. I assigned
the photographers to the different films. I had about five or six guys working
for me for years.

On the subject of recognition, a sore spot with a lot of the photographers I'd
met, Coburn said:

BC: I never felt a lack of recognition. I didn't have that problem. Of course, I
was disgruntled a bit that we weren't known outside the film business. I don't
think that they even knew we existed out there, yet we were a group of very
important people at the time. But these Karshes and those, the big New York
ones, they didn't even know we existed. The work we did, that was theatrical
photography to them, and that was below their thinking. They wouldn't lower
themselves to get into this kind of stuff. But, believe me, ours was the toughest of all. They had nothing but *gravy* compared to us. It was a never-ending
thing with us. I tell you, it was so much a challenge to me that I hated to go
home at nights. That's not true anymore, but it was then. I wanted to keep on
because there was something more I wanted to do, more than I had done.

Except for Hayworth, who liked music once in a while, I hated to have
music on a set; it took away an actor's thinking power, as far as I was concerned. Some would bring their records, and of course we always had a record player in the studio, but I was dead against it.

I didn't like props much either. I did everything I had to do with lights.
I never lit a gal twice the same way. Selling the picture the way I conceived
it should be sold, as with *Stella Dallas*—it was my own conception. This was
my way of working. Nobody told me this. I did it myself. Well, Bachrach
had some of this attitude too, and it rubbed off on me. I only ever used props
when the person was so dull you needed something to liven up the picture, or
when the subject called for it. The first thing I'd always think when starting
on a new film was "What am I going to do for the twenty-four sheet? That's
the one everybody driving down the street is going to see first."

Coburn was pointing to his poster design for Rita Hayworth's *Salome,* the one
that had Rita lying loosely across a couch, one foot dangling on the floor, her
lips smiling—Rita's eyes didn't smile much anymore by then—and a casket of
many-colored jewels open on the floor beside her divan. I remembered that shot
as if it was the first day they pasted it on the billboards outside the Elgin Cinema. The billboard was two blocks from my school, directly on my way to and
from home. I'd stand there and look and yearn. And Coburn had done it. It was

a long time before I finally accepted that the film itself was a dog. Bob chuckles. "Yeah, the film was a dog, all right." How many movies, I thought to myself, had I first seen and never forgotten because of the still man's art. How do you get Rita Hayworth to surrender, Merle Oberon to smile and Cooper to chew a hayseed so that the result seems to promise all things to all who view it?

BC: There are things it's hard to explain, John, how you get people to do things, to respond. You work with them a lot; they become like your second nature sometimes. I'd be talking and telling them things and be focused all the time, having everything ready to shoot, so that when I got what I wanted, I shot like a madman. Film was cheap. I just shot, shot, shot with those 8 × 10s. Some people would horse around and take three shots in an hour; I'd have shot 300. Well, I'm exaggerating. But you had to shoot a lot of film to get a good one; you can't just depend on that *one shot* to be good, to get *that* expression on a Hayworth or an Oberon that would get everybody excited about them.

We talked a bit more, about how he got to Columbia, and worked for Alexander Korda for more than a year when that brilliant Hungarian-born producer was making films in the States, such classics as *The Thief of Bagdad, Jungle Book, Lydia* (with Merle Oberon), *That Hamilton Woman* and Lubitsch's *To Be or Not to Be* (Carole Lombard's last film). Vivien Leigh, Coburn said, "was a memorable subject," not for what happened while he did her portraits as Emma Hamilton, but for what he saw later in the pictures he'd taken. "There was a spark there which I couldn't see while we were shooting. Vivien didn't know she had it, and I didn't either, but it was there in the pictures. Just shooting her was like shooting a statue, an inanimate statue, but she was beautiful and whatever it is she had came across. It's a difficult thing to explain. It's not that I think she didn't like being photographed, but it wasn't the greatest thing to her." Carole Lombard was "fun and games. And she really knew what to do, she knew the techniques, where the lights went. She knew nothing would be wrong if I shot her. And they all knew you wouldn't let their bad points show. They trusted you."

1975

Miriam Hopkins, Paramount publicity photograph, 1931

MIRIAM
HOPKINS

M IRIAM, MIRIAM, LITTLE MISS MIRIAM. The busiest actress ever to cavort
before the cameras; the blond Southern belle who could chase mo-
lasses up a tree. She had an antebellum voice and a cash-and-carry mind. At
her worst, she sounded like a coquettish Helen Hayes, which is often when she
thought she was most cunning. At her best, in an era that has never been equaled
for the spate of dizzy screwball comediennes like Carole Lombard, Constance
Bennett, Katharine Hepburn (who at *her* worst seemed to be doing an angular
takeoff on Miriam Hopkins), Miriam was the dizziest. None of the others was
as busy as Miriam. In *Old Acquaintance* Bette Davis finally had had enough,
hauled off and shook Miriam till her teeth rattled and she stood still. If it proved
effective for the film and also got a lot of Miss Davis' frustrations with her
partner's antics out of her system—both off screen and on—then it was in large
measure due to the fact that it was something members of the audience had been
wanting to do themselves for a long time.

Miriam not only had a hyperactive face, she had a hyperactive body; those
delicate, white, tickling little hands seemed never to be still, her feet forever at
a trot, and her large mouth had so many places to go that it seemed almost like
an extension of her earlobes. She was forever pursing, screwing or generally
contorting her lips, wrinkling her nose, rolling her eyes like a kewpie doll, then
clamping them into slits of shrewish suspicion. Yet, all told, she was not only
curiously pretty but an amazingly good actress who shouldn't have needed
twenty-seven wagonloads of mannerisms. One had only to see her in *The Story
of Temple Drake* or as the pitiful little Ivy in *Dr. Jekyll and Mr. Hyde,* or in any
of her three films with Lubitsch or four with William Wyler to know how good
she was.

She seems to be almost forgotten today. Somehow, her films don't get
shown much on TV, and when buffs recall her, it's for her two films with Bette
Davis, *The Old Maid* and *Old Acquaintance.*

The evening that brought us together was a sixtieth-anniversary retrospective tribute to Paramount Pictures on July 12, 1972, at the Museum of Modern
Art. The film chosen for the opening gala was Paramount's 1933 adaptation
of William Faulkner's brilliant but for those days highly salacious novel *Sanc-*

tuary, which couldn't be brought to the screen under its own name or with all its detail, but became the ever so scandalous *The Story of Temple Drake.* As it was, a lot of states didn't show it. It was, like so many of the films from that era, visually electric, concisely told, and as the sex-crazed society girl of the story, Miss Hopkins couldn't have been bettered. Even in 1933 there was no way she could be raped with corn husks. Instead, she lay on a bed of them and gazed delirious-eyed, a graphic mixture of fright and anticipation, while her captor/lover stood in the doorway picking his teeth, taking his time. After all, she was putting her life in someone else's hands. Lee Remick played the same part in a supposedly freer age. This time they called the film by the author's title, but as for what followed, it couldn't hold a candle to the earlier film or to Hopkins. If you want a case study of sexual enslavement all in one moment in one face, Hopkins provides the standard. But, obviously, 1972 wasn't the right time for it either. The sophisticated, supposedly movie-knowledgeable audience, jammed in for the company of stars and the food-and-wine binge that followed, sat, looked and laughed indiscriminately as the film unrolled.

Steven Roberts, the talented director, had died in 1936. Miss Hopkins, as guest of honor, had no one for support: neither of her co-stars, Florence Eldridge or Jack LaRue, was in the audience. Andy Warhol, Paul Morrissey and I took the opportunity to congratulate her. Miss Hopkins, who clearly felt unsettled by the movie's reception, said things like, "Well, of course it's an old film. I mean, we couldn't do the book the way we wanted to," and "It wasn't easy. You know, Paramount was terrified of the censors." We reassured her that, on the contrary, she had been very good and the film couldn't have been made any better or any more forcefully since. That's when I asked her if she and I could get together.

We set the following Sunday afternoon for the occasion. Her last important role in a major motion picture was in Arthur Penn's brilliant all-star film *The Chase.* Miss Hopkins, old and no longer pretty, played a character role in a small Southern town and held her own with the most exciting new actors of the last two decades: everybody from Marlon Brando to Paris-domiciled Jane Fonda, to the electrifying Robert Redford. She had also had star billing in a European soft-core exploitation film based on the rediscovered 18th-century novel *Fanny Hill,* made in Germany in 1964, that had been the cult sensation of the '60s. It wasn't worthy of her, she shouldn't have done it, but what work— besides horror movies—was there then for old actresses who still had names?

Miss Hopkins, whose husbands had included the director Anatole Litvak, was clearly as financially shrewd as she was gifted; she owned a luxurious apartment in Los Angeles and property in upstate New York. While in the city, where she'd previously sold her Sutton Place house, she had Paramount put her up at the Alrae, a residential hotel prized by its regulars for its quiet elegance and apartments that didn't look like hotel suites. Though she was looking around for a place to buy at the time, Miss Hopkins lived at the hotel until her death a few months later in October of that year. Obviously, only a few people that night at MOMA knew that she was ill.

We spent almost six hours together, during which she educated me to the finer points of Lord Byron amidst a flood of emotion when she finally broke down and reenacted her tiff with Miss Davis—she called her "Bette" with a frosting on her voice that suggested that while centuries of water might have flowed under the bridge, they hadn't washed away *that* sore. She then recited *all* of Byron's "The Prisoner of Chillon." (Obviously, the incident had reached a lot of ears, among whose were those of Joseph L. Mankiewicz when he wrote his acerbic manuscript for *All About Eve*. In it, Gary Merrill makes a quip referring to Bette's legs as a "nylon lemon peel," Miss Davis, as Margot Channing, snaps out in a worthy imitation of Miss Hopkins, "Byyyyyron couldn't have put it better," squelching Merrill the way she had been squelched by Hopkins in *Old Acquaintance*. Movies are wonderful like that.)

In the next few hours Miriam didn't give me so much an interview as a performance. She directed my questions to the shores she wanted to step out on. She breathed theater and drama with every syllable; every so often lighting a cigarette, taking a swig of what she called "tonic water" (though I remember she had said that vodka was "mother's milk" to her), and erupting with bursts of laughter that took the place of intermissions as she fixed her eyes on me to be sure I was following her, and required me to define what it was I wanted. Her voice was like a web slowly spinning around you while she kept you off guard by your own rapt attention. I didn't realize to what degree I was taking my lead from her till, listening to the playback, I heard her saying what a wonderful actor I was and how well we were playing together. In 1934, when Cecil B. DeMille first announced plans to film Samson and Delilah, Miriam was announced for the picture. DeMille liked small women with small feet, but even so, I would have thought Miriam—physically—would not have been everybody's idea of a Philistine temptress blinding a Biblical strongman with her voluptuous sex appeal. But I would be ignoring her skill and her voice: she was an extraordinary actress with a mellifluous voice.

JK: You must have had so many interviews, sometimes when you think of it . . .

MH: Oh, I've done thousands of these! And when I produce a play in summer theater, I used to always say: "Not after the show!"—you know, to other people. But when I did and produced it and financed, you know, and it went very good, it was Noël Coward's *Hay Fever* . . . then I just had all the interviews imaginable afterwards, as many as possible, because I wanted the business in, you know, with the percentage, and to get back what is known as what the dope put into it. [They laugh.]

Yeah, well, don't you want to introduce me? I mean, say: Miss Hopkins,

I've come over to your house this afternoon. You've put me off four times and now . . . [They laugh] . . . finally I've gotten here, and you're charming, John Kobal, and I'm delighted you're here.

JK: Thank you, Miss Hopkins. You look every bit as good as I remembered you the last time I saw you.

MH: What was the last time?

JK: That was last night at three o'clock in the morning.

MH: I know. But that was in a movie that was done years and years ago . . . *Splendor*. Well, that was quite . . . twenty or thirty or something years ago.

JK: Yes, and you look very much the same as the film I saw you in, *Children's Hour*, the remake, which was quite recent.

MH: Yes. Oh, well, I think I look younger than I did in that. They made me look older. But I'm older than I was in *Splendor* [laughs], if you know . . . I'd liked to have been dressed up for you, but I didn't have any help in . . . and being Sunday. I just have on these slacks and pants, so that kind of makes you look like, you know, more on the line of the younger generation. A friend I know, she said when she gets home she immediately takes off her clothes and gets into slacks and a sweater or shirt or something like that—you know, gets comfortable. Today the day of the lace negligee and lying back on the chaise-longue is *past* [chuckles] for practical people. I never did it, though, even in that day. Oh, that was only when I was in a movie doing it! At home, to lie back with all those little satin pillows on the chaise-longue reading a French novel, you know? [They laugh.] Sipping that little glass of sherry, you know? No, no . . . I've had too many things to do.

JK: What ever made you get into *Fanny Hill*?

MH: Well, I don't know. That's kind of a bewildering beginning. The phone rang, it was about, oh, oh, 10:00 in the morning, I guess. And a man said: "Would you like to go to West Berlin and do a movie? Would it be possible? Are you available at this time?" Well, my son, who's in the Air Force, was at a base, Nancy, I think, France, very near the German border. And I hadn't seen him for two years, or his wife and the baby. And I thought, well, nothing would be more wonderful because West Berlin is very near France and that place. And I said: "Well, I'd just love to go, yes, what is the picture?" And he said: "*Fanny Hill*." And I said: "Oh!" because I'd been reading in the paper that the book was banned, but I'd never read it. Had I read the book, I would never have done the movie. Now, the movie, I can't say it hadn't anything to do with the book, it's practically . . . now, let's see how I can sum it up . . . like Fanny Hill arrives from the country in London and she meets, in the movie, Mrs. Brown. I am the madam of the main house with the girls. But she had met three or four other people like that all through the book, you know, as her life developed after she met Charles, the one she loved. But they made Mrs. Brown a composite. In other words, I'm five madams rolled into one and I'm the only one that goes all the way through the film. And Fanny does. It all takes place at my house and I set up these different appointments for her to meet Lord This, and the Mister That, and the So-forth that and the other. It's *suggested* by the book, I would say, and also the whole thing of Charles, and there's something in the book where Charles' father arranged to send him away to get him away from her. I do that, and everything. So I go through, so I have first star billing and "Introducing Leticia Roman as Fanny Hill." Because it's a tremendous part—I handled the whole thing. I make the appointments . . . I talk to the men . . . these different episodes . . . and then she meets with them and I think it's all going to come to pass and I'll get a great deal of money if it does [laughs]. But it's all done . . . with a little Rabelaisian humor, but not vulgar. Fanny always manages to get out of it, and finally Charles is back, and comes back soon enough, so at the end of the picture I say to somebody this is . . . oh, I can't remember the line, but it went something like this is the first time in twenty-two years of brisk trade I ever had a girl come into my house and leave in her initial condition. [Hearty laughter.]

I look at the camera at the end and have a big speech when it's finishing, and go on to the audience and say, "Well, I just can't understand, though . . . you know about how this . . . the fiancé . . . my protégé . . . something . . . could ever have found himself in a house like this . . ." But it's done with a laugh to the audience at the end. I think it's just darling and it's the word . . . or the name, rather, *Fanny Hill,* that has sort of scared certain censors. And I know Mr. Zugsmith, when I talked to him on the phone, he said, "Oh, United Artists or Metro or this one and that would like to release if they changed the title to something like 'A Girl from the Country.'" He said no, he had no intention. I said, "Well, it's up to you, Zug. But let me know if it's ever going to come out." [Laughter.]

JK: I was thinking that *Fanny Hill* has had some censorship problems. And of course you're not unused to film censorship problems because one of your films, *Sanctuary,* had something to do, along with Mae West, in bringing in censorship. And of course there was *Dr. Jekyll and Mr. Hyde* . . .

MH: Oh! Wait a moment! Let's stop right now when you say *Sanctuary* and Mae West. They don't belong in the same conversation or category. *Sanctuary [The Story of Temple Drake]* was written by William Faulkner . . . I don't know whether he wrote the film version, but I know that it was rated as one of the ten best pictures of the year. It was an-y-thing but done in a distasteful way. Also, I don't think *Fanny Hill* was done with bad taste. But *Sanctuary* was done with fabulous style and a fabulous cast by Paramount. Steve Roberts directed it, I think, and he died a few years later of a heart attack, an excellent director. They show it often at the Museum of Modern Art.

And of course there was no rape sequence. That was done all by black-and-white still drawings . . . still pictures, you would say. It wasn't, it was drawings . . . it was a whole notebook. And the first job that Jean Negulesco, who was a wonderful director in California who did most of Marilyn Monroe's things and I've shown you some of his paintings, he's a great painter. And he said: "How I broke into films was being the technical director of the rape scene in *Sanctuary*." [They laugh.] Because he drew how the camera, how the man could advance when the girl was in the barn lying on the corn husks . . . and this beast of a creature came slowly toward her and the light was coming through the shutter sides of this, you know. And the camera was low as he walked and it was photographed on the floor . . . it was just between his legs, walking toward her. And as he got nearer, you know, the black trousers from a triangle level of the camera . . . and the drawings this way . . . just closer . . . and there was a scream. The man was just standing there. There was just the scream. But he [Negulesco] planned all how it could be done in that manner. And it was . . . if you can call a rape artistically done [she chuckles tastefully], it was. As a matter of fact, if anybody would say to me: "What is one of the finest pictures you've made?" I would say: "*Sanctuary*." Oh, by all means! It was done . . . I think it will be remembered that way. There were certain places, like Boston . . . or Philadelphia . . . and then there were problems after it was shown there. But, no, it got all sorts of prizes and everything. And when you mentioned Mae West with that, I had to stop you because Mae West might have to do with something like *Fanny Hill* but not *Sanctuary*.

JK: As a matter of fact, I was going to say, at this point anyway, besides *Sanctuary* and *Dr. Jekyll and Mr. Hyde,* which is Rouben Mamoulian, you made many—

MH (interrupting): Well, don't bring up Rouben Mamoulian because I'd go on about him. So let's don't talk about that. But ask me if you want to talk about any censorable films and we can do that little category, because I would just like to go on about the greatness of Mamoulian and about him afterwards.

JK: I was going to say that you made some of the most sophisticated and daring films, all before the code came strong again, things like *Design for Living, Trouble in Paradise,* which even now—

MH (interrupting): *Trouble in Paradise* wasn't in the least bit censorable. They had that in the Museum of Modern Art; that wasn't censorable. . . . Oh, it was, I guess. . . .Oh, that's right! That's right! I was not married to the man . . . Herbert Marshall. But it was, being Ernst Lubitsch . . . I was living with Herbert Marshall and I wasn't married to him. So that would have been censorable. But not today, *not* today. Kay Francis was the woman that he thought he *might* want to have, you know. No, he wasn't married to either . . . or anything. But he and I had been together all through the film. Oh, I spoke all sorts of languages but quickly in that. We were two crooks that were in Venice and going around the world. The first one I did with Lubitsch was *Smiling Lieutenant* with Chevalier and Claudette Colbert. And I did the French version of that with them, because they both spoke French. I did that, and did two songs in French. Because I thought it would be a disgrace if they had anybody come in, as it was *my* first picture.* And I wasn't paid extra, but I just thought I should do it and I nearly went crazy. I was going around talking these speeches in French to everybody.

JK: It was your first picture! Not *The World and the Flesh* [Paramount, 1932] with George Bancroft?

MH: Oh, no! That was done out in Paramount in Hollywood between something or another—you know, the two years I was with them out there. . . . And, yes, they couldn't show *Design for Living* in the beginning on TV. They do now, because that was with Gary Cooper and Freddie March . . .

JK: It was a play in which you loved both men and you married one . . .

MH: Well, one went away and the other just stayed at the house with me and then he came and said: "What are you doing in your evening clothes [she laughs], you obviously didn't go home all night" or something. But that was Noël Coward, whom I *adore* . . . a great friend of mine. That was his . . . and that was Lubitsch. But with such style and taste, and now they're being shown because there's nothing *vulgar,* there's nothing wrong. But I mean even the *plot,* it was done with humor.

JK: Yes, I know. But I mean you would still accept the fact that a situation of a woman who has two men and can't decide which one she wants and in the end she ends up with both of them again . . . and all three of them live happily, and love happily, ever after.

MH: But you *don't* know what's going to happen when they're in that cab or something at the end, and drive off, and she just reaches and takes both of their hands and says we will go back to Paris, but shakes her fingers in between them . . ."But remember," like she did in the beginning, "no sex!" [They laugh heartily.] So you don't know, you just are left with a laugh and you think: How *are* they going to work this out? Oh, that was extremely sophisticated. *Trouble in Paradise,* I think, yes, that was sophisticated also. But anything that Lubitsch . . . who was really the *master* craftsman that people learned comedy and everything from . . . I learned so much from him that would have been like going to a great dramatic school . . . Of timing, and what to do about everything, very great. . . . And the other one I think I

* Actually, Miriam Hopkins' first film was *Fast and Loose* (Paramount, 1930), made in New York while she was on Broadway in *Lysistrata*.

learned a great deal from was Mamoulian. And you wanted to say something about him. Have you ever met Mamoulian?

JK: No. I want to, though. I've *got* to because I admire that man, the things he did stylistically, and because he is so way ahead of his time. Even today one can still appreciate the fact that the way he used the camera, in the way he cut and tracked along, in his approach to actors and actresses, in his whole style—it is so way out!

MH: But what films did you see that you liked particularly?

JK: Well, there was this fantastic . . . one of his lesser ones . . . *High, Wide and Handsome,* which is beautiful. And also the superb one, *Love Me Tonight* with Jeanette MacDonald and Maurice Chevalier, which is just out of this world. The end shot with . . . Jeanette MacDonald, with her legs spread apart, stands on the railroad track, tall as the Statue of Liberty, and this train . . .

MH: Well, all I can tell you is he's one of the warmest, most intelligent and enchanting people. I did *Jekyll and Hyde* with him, with Freddie March. And, I don't know, it was about the second picture I'd done in California. I'd done the life of Helen Morgan . . . *Twenty-four Hours,* and had to do blues songs; you know, Helen Morgan's thing. And that was the first one at Paramount. And then *Jekyll and Hyde* was the second. That was after, you see . . . what you call *Smiling Lieutenant* was done in Astoria here when Walter Wanger was running the Paramount studios of the East here. Then they closed the studio. And I was in a play called *Lysistrata* and I was crazy about it, it was just marvelous for me. And I didn't want to go to Hollywood. I had *no* desire to go. But I was under contract. And when I signed a two-year contract with Paramount, through Walter Wanger, he said: "You won't have to go because I have the studio, you'll make any films here, you know." *But* they decided to close the Astoria studio. So with the equipment, the cameras, the electrical light bulbs and so forth, I was shipped to California. I had to go.

Well, I got there and I waited around for about three months. Nobody seemed to care anything much about me or any of this. Mr. Schulberg, running the studio, had seen me in *Smiling Lieutenant* and said: She's a character actress playing the little German girl with the buns over her ears, etc. So I had to go in and try out with seven different people . . . I didn't realize that . . . for the Helen Morgan thing in *Twenty-four Hours*. Well, I thought, as long as they don't appreciate me [she laughs] . . . I don't mean that in a corny way . . . but I was being paid by the week, and nobody was giving me a job out there, and so I was asked if I would come in. I didn't know there were going to be seven people and I'd be tested. But I was asked to come in for the *Twenty-four Hours* thing. So I was living on the ocean at Santa Monica and I rushed to a bookseller. I bought the book and I stayed up and read it quickly all night so I'd know exactly what it was about. And then when I got in—I suppose I was sufficiently young that it didn't matter whether I'd had any sleep or not—and they threw me in the beauty parlor and gave me a scene to learn, to do this. And the hairdresser said: "Oh, you are the *fifth* that's being tested." That *insulted* me because I'd just been in *Vogue* and *Vanity Fair* and all of this from the play in New York, full-page pictures and ads. This is absolutely shocking and I don't want to be here anyway, I'm just going to go right back to New York. And I thought: No, as long as they've sent for me, I'm going to do the best I can. And I feel that's the way you always should feel, you know? And I knew she was a singer, and I knew two or three songs that, you know, any of us might sing in a little nightclub thing, fun, late, you know, bar stools and all of this. So I . . . after my hair was done . . . I had half-learned the scene. I went over to the music department and I said: "Who's the head of the music department?" Because I never think you go to a second-rate. With my son I've always said: "Now, if you want a job and you go up, never talk to the switchboard girl, *go* to the boss!" So I went over, and the head of it was Ronald Reagan. No, no, no! Another! Not to do with that. . . . Ron Regan or something.

Well, anyway, I said: "Look, I'm Miriam Hopkins and I've come from New York and I'm supposed to test for this. Now, if I do, instead of just doing this scene, could you get a piano on the set, and would you have somebody there? And I'd like to sit on the piano the way Helen Morgan was famous for. And I'll do a song at the same time. I want my test different than any of the other girls." And he said: "Good for you, let's go in." So we went in. We tried out, you know, and we found a song that would be good and he was over there to supervise it. So I started . . . I did the song first and then I began the scene and I realized I knew what the scene was about . . . with the man . . . but I didn't really know . . . it was a thing that she was in love with him but felt so unhappy of this, you know, and cried a lot. Well, I practically burst into tears halfway through because I got so nervous, I knew I didn't know the words. You know, I was just making up the words and I was ad-libbing and the poor guy didn't have a chance to hardly say anything with this. And the director said: "Cut . . . Stop it . . . Such emotion! . . . She's the one . . . we've got to have her!" I said: "Look, I've got to tell you the truth, it isn't emotions, it's a nervous breakdown." [She laughs.] And that was the beginning at Paramount on the West Coast.

JK: How, from that, did you get into Mamoulian's *Jekyll and Hyde*?

MH: Oh, there wasn't any "getting in." I'd met him then and he said . . . it followed . . . immediately. The Rose Hobart part—I said to Mamoulian: "I'd like to play that, that's such a pretty . . ." He said: "It's three scenes. It's dull! You want to play the little cockney streetwalker of this, it's the greatest." I did, it turned out . . . it was one of . . . I had ten Academy nominations, and that was one of them. But always a bridesmaid, never a bride—I mean, I never got one.

JK: Do you place as much emphasis on the Oscar, especially with the way it's been deteriorating?

MH: Listen, I don't know anything about whether I do or not. It seems like some people that get two or three . . . I don't know—I never think about it. And other people, they sometimes had hired press agents to *plug* them. I don't mean that *every*body does, but I mean some people. I don't know any of that. But it was, I thought, a very fine film—not because of me, Freddie March's performance. And Freddie March's performance because of Mamoulian. And then I had one scene where I had to go into . . . it was a very great part for anybody as young as I was at that time. It was a scene where I had to go to plead with Dr. Jekyll about the horror that I was going through with Hyde. I said: "I know it all very well, Rouben. And I do it good at home in the living room. And I planned, kind of, by the legs at the side of a table, that I might at this moment go down and hold him by the knees, you know, and beg him to do this. And I'd like to do it all *at once* if I could, the whole eight pages, rather than in little pieces . . . I don't think it'd be right." And he said: "Well, now, fine." I said: "Because like in the theater"—and, after all, Mamoulian in the theater with *Carousel* and *Oklahoma!* and all these things that he'd put together. But he had begun in the theater and had a sense of it also. He'd done something in the theater before, I don't remember just quite what. . . .

So I said: "You see, it would be easy for me to do." I was stalling because I dreaded starting this eight-page scene. And I said: "If I only had an audience." He said: "All right, let's get all the crew up here, the lights are set and everything, now you all sit around and make an audience." Well, that made it *worse* even, you know, with embarrassment. And he said: "Now, where do you think you are when he's there?" And I said: "Well, I've come through the door, halfway, and then I'll go right over to him, there." And he said: "If we had three cameras on it to get it all at once, where do you think they'd be?" And I said: "Well, I don't know. Forgive me for saying this, but this is . . . I want it to play itself because it's a *terribly* emotional thing, into deep hysterics at the end, but starting with quiet pleading." And I said: "Maybe if one's [camera] over near his knees there, and one here, one there." So he said: "All right, dear, we've got it all fixed that way. You want it—fine! Now we've got people, you've got the audience." So I started, and about the fifth or sixth line I just blew up and went to pieces and said: "Oh, I'm sorry, Rouben." And he said: "No." I said: "Well, it's like the little child, you know, when Mama says, 'Play the piano now for the company' and they forget. They always should have a second chance." I said: "Well, give me a second chance this way." Then I went through the whole thing that way and they all applauded. And Rouben too. And I was just sobbing like this and a wreck on the floor, holding on to his shoes at the end, and that was the scene printed. And it was done in one take. . . .

And *that's* why Mamoulian is great. The director is the captain of the ship. The director can say: Do this, do that, do the other! But Rouben Mamoulian has a feeling for molding his people and getting the quality and the scenes the way they should be. . . . All right, I was not very experienced, with three pictures, you know, or any of this. But he knew me, and he knew what I meant, that I'd worked this . . . and you couldn't chop it up and do a little piece and then a close-up and another little piece and that . . . to have the whole mood and the thing. I think one of the best scenes that I've ever had to play in my *life,* you know. So it was worth his time to have it done that way, and that's why he's great, because if it hadn't been good in four, five takes or something, then he would have said: "Wait a minute." But he wanted to see first what I wanted to bring to him, without having his ego so great by saying: "Just a minute, what's *she trying* to do?" You see?

You asked me a few minutes ago about people that I'd worked with. And do you know another *doll* was Bing Crosby. Oh, my God! We did *She Loves Me Not.* Now, I thought I was a dramatic actress, you see. And I want to rehearse everything first. And I said: "Bing, can't we rehearse this show?" and I was on his radio show all the time, and he ran through it once and we went out and sat in the car and had a cigarette. And I said: "Can't we do it again?" And he said: "Sweetie, no! We'd get stale. Let's just do it, you know, we've got the line. I'll say something and . . . we used this basically, but you could ad-lib back and forth with me." Well, there was one scene in *She Loves.* I said: "Bing, I'd *like* to rehearse this with you." He says: "Now, anything she wants to do. Now, you know very well, you've been in the theater and New York, and I'm just a guy who dropped a load of pumpkins." I said: "What do you mean, 'dropped a load of pumpkins'?" [Laughter.] And that was his famous line: "I'm just a guy who dropped a load of pumpkins," you know. Oh, but so darling! And that picture, you know, I didn't *sing* the things in it. But there were certain songs that conditioned my life. And in that I was a tap dancer, because I used to dance. And I had one kind of number in a nightclub. I think it was Kitty Carlisle that did the singing in that film, but anyway, in it was the song "Can it be the breeze [she sings] that fills the trees with rare and magic perfume? / Oh, no, it isn't the breeze, it's love in bloom. . . ." Then I'd go back to the first thing, and I was about eighteen, it was a *Music Box Revue.* And I sang this one . . . oh, that was *Little Jessie James.* [She sings again.] "I love you, I love you, / It's all that I can say. / I love you, I love you. . . ." Do you remember that? [JK doesn't. She continues singing.] "In the same old way . . ." It wasn't a *film,* it was a play. [Singing] "I love you, I love you . . . ." Oh, there were so many, all the way through, songs that were connected with my career. I wish I could think of the one at the Music Box because . . ."Love . . ."

JK: Can I cut to something?

MH: Yeah, do.

JK: When I talked to Sylvia Sidney, she was talking about who was working at Paramount at the time you were there.

MH: She was only around there for a couple of years.

JK: Well, until about '35.

MH: Oh, maybe she was there *longer,* because I left, I told you, in two years and went to Goldwyn.

JK: But she arrived there in 1930, so you were there at least for some time together.

MH: I came there in '32 to '34.

JK: But *Smiling Lieutenant* was . . .

MH: '31, in New York. I made that one in New York and then I went . . . and it was early '32 because I adopted Michael in '32. And that was the first year I was out there. And then '35 I was, you know, this way [meaning back in New York]. And then '36 I was in England.

JK: Well, the point is, Sylvia Sidney said that they used you back then—meaning you in general—like a piece of meat, chopping you from one film to another.

MH: I don't agree at all! I think that's utterly wrong! Because after *Twenty-four Hours* and then the Lubitsch things, then I did another with Freddie March. It was something Maggie Sullavan did in New York, *Chrysalis,* but I don't remember what it was called [*All of Me*] and I think George Raft was in it. And then *Dancers in the Dark,* that George Raft was in, and you might say a lot of those were not classics, but I don't think they were . . . chopped up.

JK: No, "chopped up" in the sense of the way that they used you, the performer. They just put you from one film to another and you didn't have much choice, much chance.

MH: No, it wasn't that way at all. Well, it wasn't with me. I didn't feel it was that way. Because I had Mamoulian and Lubitsch, three Lubitsch and one Mamoulian and *Sanctuary* and things of quality in those two years in California. I don't feel that things were done that way. But if you want to go on with what you just said, I think there was a change of the studio head. It was a little man. . . .* Schulberg was a big guy. And Schulberg—I mean big in size physically, I don't mean necessarily in mental stature. But he was back of what is known as the front desk. And you always go in and talk to him about the film, you don't want to do that, and maybe they shift you to another, so forth. . . . But this little man, I don't know—he was from Chicago—and

---

*Emanuel Cohen is the little producer at Paramount she's referring to.

he had run different theaters. But I didn't know who he was and there was one film I didn't like. I thought it was cheap. So I went in to see him. And as I went through the door and came in, I thought: "How rude, he doesn't even stand up to greet." And so I said: "At least you could stand up and be a gentleman." He said: "I *am* standing." And I realized he *was* standing up, but he was so short, you know, I thought he hadn't. I said: "Oh, I beg your pardon." So then we both sat down. And I said: "I don't like this picture, I think it's very cheap, and I don't want to do it. Now I think this: the quality of it, the characterization . . ." and I go on, I guess in a phony-arty way, talking. I wasn't getting to first base with this little cheap man. So I said, in words I never use, I said: "Listen, it *stinks!* It's *lousy!*" He said: "Why didn't you say so?" And that was the only argument I had . . . I didn't have to do it.

JK: Well, the mixture of the money with the artistic sense and the bankers in Hollywood has always been, I think, a great struggle, which is why it's always so wonderful to think that so many fine films really came out of it. And the people like Mamoulian and Von Stroheim and Von Sternberg and Lubitsch thrived just the same. . . . I've got to ask you, since you worked at Paramount and Sternberg and Dietrich were there . . . But first: Nancy Carroll said that she made a film [*The Man I Killed*] with Lubitsch and she was extremely unhappy 'cause he didn't like her and he was always having fits at her and he was being very very Germanic and rude. And yet you seem to have gotten along with him like a house on fire.

MH: Shall I tell you something Lubitsch told me? I remember it was during that. And I would have forgotten this if you hadn't brought it up. The studio put her in the film with him. So he came in my dressing room and I ordered the lunch in. We were great friends and we got on just fine . . .

JK: You and Lubitsch?

MH: Oh, yes! And he said: "No, she doesn't understand what I want her to do. I just say to you, you know, without . . . and you do." And I said: "Don't tell me how to do it, you know, say first and then do thus and so." And he said: "I can't get on with Miss Carroll because she doesn't want direction. I don't know what to do with her. All I said to her is: 'If you would just put yourself in my arms.' And she said: 'That *I* should do that with you German?'" I said: "Ernst, you've said the wrong thing. You should have said: put yourself in my *hands*." [She laughs.] You see; it's so dear! But it's just a question of personalities and whether people connect or don't connect, I'm sure. Practically everybody got on with Lubitsch always.

JK: Well, he directed Garbo and Dietrich. . . . But you worked with two great butcherers of the English language. That was Lubitsch and there was Samuel Goldwyn. Didn't you work with Mike Curtiz as well?

MH: Yes. I said to Goldwyn once: "Sam, I don't want to do *Splendor*. I don't think this is a very good script. After we have done *Barbary Coast* and *These Three*, it's nice but I think it's sort of trite." And but for the grace of God would have . . . And then Audrey Hepburn had it. And I had one that wasn't too good, but nice, you know, when I played the aunt in the same studio years later in the remake of the film. And I said: "Audrey, I had that part once," and so forth.

JK: In your very long, I think very rich career, which of the films do you yourself look back on with the greatest memory?

MH (almost offended): I don't look back on anything.

JK: Well, if you have to, which of the films mean something special to you?

MH: The overall just does. But nothing . . . I don't say [in phony Joan Crawford voice]: Oh, this was so dear to me, this was dear to me, or that dear to me, or *Fanny Hill*. Whatever's coming out will be dear to me, or something I might do next year or the year after, or whether I do anything at all. I mean I don't know.

JK: Well, you do live theater as well?

MH: Well, I did *Look Homeward, Angel* in New York for a year, Thomas Wolfe's thing that I felt was great. And then—I'd never done a long tour—I did for eighty-two cities and I said it was so, so satisfying I could have crossed the country and come back again with that, with a play. . . . No, I don't know. Now everybody says: "Now, Miriam, what are your plans?" I say: "My plans are when the phone rings again." Just the phone rings and something happens, you know? I've had the house in New York for, oh, twenty-six years, and the one in California I sold to David years ago. Because otherwise if you rent one, I had Katharine Hepburn in one and Leland Hayward or somebody in the other. I mean, you're just in the real-estate business, you know, and the plumbing here, or the drapes need doing there, and etc. No, I think you have to be a person within yourself and then you work if you're going to work.

JK: But there's no such thing as a film like *These Three*, meaning something special where you'd say these are the films I liked best?

MH: Oh, there's nothing you can say. I never even think about it. I never talk about them. If I ever see anything that's coming up on something, it's because a friend calls me and says: "Oh, you're on the Late Show or something. You ought to see this." Somebody called me about a year ago and said: "Oh, Miriam, you look so gorgeous, *divine*, I've never seen anything like the way you look as *The Richest Girl in the World*." I said: "Sweetie, that was done twenty-five years ago, and look at it." And then I went and switched it on a

little and I went to Elizabeth Arden and I said: "I'd like a course of facials."
It was the biggest money-seller for RKO for the whole year, I know that.
. . . But anyway, it was just one of those things. We did it in twenty-four
days, having a ball, we all had such a divine time. That was with Joel
[McCrea] too.

JK: Yes, and Fay Wray. . . . You've got a very rich, I would think, life. And I
was struck by something. When we were talking about Bette Davis and that
scene in *Old Acquaintance* when you have the argument, and you went to her
and quoted "Stone walls do not a prison make, nor iron bars a cage" at her.
Poetry means a lot to you, doesn't it?

MH: Well, I think so in a way. When I was in California the first two years, I
got so tired of reading these scripts that would come all the time from Paramount, every script they seemed to send it to me at that time. And I got tired
of plots, so I spent two years reading poetry as sort of a mental balance with
it. At the end, I don't know, you go on and . . . I remember one little thing
of Bryant's, and I'm not sure, you know, you quote better, you could remember, but I would always like to remember and have it for kind of a little theme
song, of Bryant's:

> Live so that when thy summons comes to join
> That innumerable caravan that moves
> To those mysterious realms . . .
> Go thou, not like a quarry-slave at night,
> Scourged with dungeon but, sustained and soothed
> By an everlasting trust, approach thy grave,
> As one who wraps the drapery of his couch
> About him who lies down to pleasant dreams.*

I think it's a nice way to . . . It's nice. . . . And you know there's a love
poem that matters to me. Well, I don't know whether I remember it. And I
pray that I do. It's Christina Georgina Rossetti, and I had to do it being kind
of tight under a table in a bar in a play of Anita Loos' called *Happy Birthday*.
I think I can remember:

> My heart is like a singing bird
> Whose nest is in a watered shoot;
> My heart is like an apple-tree
> Whose limbs are bowed with thick-set fruit;
> My heart is like a rainbow shell
> That paddles in a halcyon sea;

---

*Slightly misquoted, from William Cullen Bryant's "Thanatopsis."

My heart is gladder than all these
Because my love is come to me.

Raise me a dais of silk and down;
Hang it with vair and purple dyes;
Carve it in doves and pomegranates,
And peacocks with a hundred eyes;
Work it in gold and silver grapes,
In leaves, and silver fleur-de-lys;
Because the birthday of my life
Is come, my love is come to me.

That's Christina Georgina Rossetti.

JK: Miss Hopkins, thank you very much.

MH: Good night.

1972

L A S Z L O
W I L L I N G E R

"THE STARS I PHOTOGRAPHED in Hollywood are a complete Who's Who of that period. My portraits were published all over the world. After the war I opened my own studio on Sunset Boulevard and began to specialize in color photography, which was then still in its infancy. I had as many as 150 magazine covers published in one year, and syndicated in Europe and Japan as well as the USA. When television came along, I moved into advertising photography; I am the most published photographer on calendars here and abroad. My work has taken me all over the USA and Canada, and my location work has included trips to Europe and Asia."

Laszlo Willinger was born on April 16, 1909, in Budapest. He was raised and schooled in Berlin, where his photographic career began with his work for *Berliner Illustrierte* and the *Illustrierte* publications in Hamburg and Munich. In 1928 he went to Paris to run the Talbot studios, where he photographed such luminaries as Sacha Guitry, Mistinguett, Josephine Baker, Yvonne Printemps, President Doumer and many others. There was a brief return to Berlin, but the Nazis were gaining power, so Laszlo continued on to Vienna, where he opened his own studio. (This period in Vienna resurfaced some years later when the photographer turned writer and wrote the stories on which the script *The Night They Raided Calais* was based.) From this base he photographed all of Max Reinhardt's plays, contributed pictures to *Pageant* magazine in Chicago, was represented as the European photographer for Colgate soap, and had portrait sittings for Emil Jannings, Sigmund Freud, Carl Jung, Wilhelm Reich, Hedy Kiesler (who was to become Hedy Lamarr), Arturo Toscanini, Lotte Lehmann and Thomas Mann, as well as most of the European *beau monde*. But even in Vienna Laszlo found he was too close to the Nazis for comfort, so he began negotiating with MGM for a contract which would take him to Hollywood. George Hurrell had left, and no one as yet had been found to replace him to the satisfaction of MGM's great star-conscious ladies. At great cost to the studio, whenever Shearer or Crawford needed new sittings, Hurrell was hired. Then Laszlo came, and he was the new sensation. Hurrell had given them allure. Laszlo gave them allure and intelligence.

JK: Tell me about Katharine Hepburn and Dr. Agha and the session you did with them at MGM for *Vogue*. It was a barnyard setting and there were about thirty huge chickens all around her in the picture.

LW: Frankly, I don't remember too much about it, it's been a long time. The thing is worked out long before you shoot. Hepburn had something to say about this shoot, which was that she had to like the dress, it was from *Philadelphia Story*. She didn't mind all the chickens in the setup, she thought it was very funny. See, when people go through a magazine, you have to have something to catch their eye. The average time a person gives to a picture while looking through a magazine is about a quarter of a second . . . if you hold them for two seconds, you're a winner. That was the only time I shot Hepburn, because it was set up by *Vogue* and Mr. Agha [the art director of *Vogue*] had asked for me. The only photographer who ever really took great photos of Hepburn was Bachrach [Hepburn's photographer for the period of her career at RKO].

JK: What about Munkacsi? I have a photograph of him taking pictures of Hollywood starlets at Warner Brothers in the late '30s, around the time you were at MGM.

LW: They hired him simply because he had built up a reputation and there was always the thing that if you had someone who was in with *Vogue* in New York, your chance of getting your pictures printed was much higher. Signing on in Hollywood made him fall down a couple of notches in New York's estimation. Munkacsi brought a new approach to fashion photography; he started out as a sports photographer, he used to shoot football games! I first met him in Budapest, then he went to Berlin and worked as a straight news photographer. We were contemporaries at the *Berliner Illustrierte*. Eisenstaedt was there, and another man by the name of Gerard who was known as Gehr. It was very competitive. It was run very much like *Life* magazine, which was founded by people who had worked there in Berlin. What they did was each section of the magazine had an editor and each editor was given a number of pages. Then came the Monday-morning session when the top editor said, "Your story's out." So naturally there was a lot of competition to get pictures and spreads that would stay in. And once they weren't printed, that was it, they'd never be printed even if they had no topical content.

He chuckles wickedly. To Laszlo, life *is* a wicked chuckle. It's how he kept his balance in a turbulent, not to say competitive, postwar Reichsmark Germany, and how he developed his ironic distance from events to come that would destroy so many of the people and things he knew. Laszlo does not get sentimental. Nor emotional. Nor enthusiastic. This early, self-taught, ironic detachment infuses his work, gives it its style: the stars in his portraits are cool, elegant,

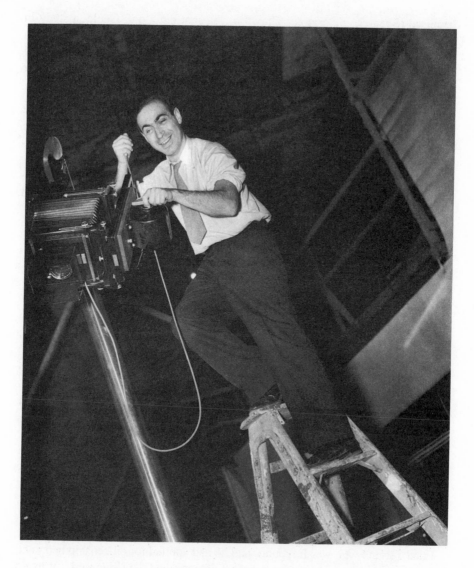

Laszlo Willinger, photographed by Eric Carpenter (MGM), 1939

bemused (Shearer, impervious; Crawford, elegant but aloof; Gable, a study in the mortality that fame can never eradicate, as if this powerful, handsome man on top of the world were saying to anyone who looked long enough to listen, "I was a truck driver. Now I'm a star. Who's to say I won't be a truck driver again?").

LW: So there simply weren't as many pages as they had been allowed. There wasn't just the *Berliner Illustrierte;* there was the *Hamburger Illustrierte,* the *Münchner Illustrierte,* practically all of which were run by Hungarians. Stefan Lorant ran the *Münchner Illustrierte;* later he moved somewhere in Connecticut and started writing books on American history. Very good ones. The magazines had been in existence for a long time, but there came a new breed of editors who were a little more courageous.

JK: Why should so many of these editors and the photographers be Austro-Hungarians?

Laszlo laughs his laugh. His answer is an old joke.

LW: What do you do in Hungary? Naturally, when it got too hot to stay in Germany, most of the people who were working there came here. And *Life* magazine, which started up then, was directly influenced by those magazines, by their style, by this new breed of photo-journalists. It started in Europe. You didn't find this sort of work in France or in England. Nobody went to London or Paris because their publications were years behind Germany. There were two editors, one was Stefan Lorant, the other was Szafranski—I don't recall his first name—who later came to this country and became the editor of that small magazine that *Esquire* published, *Coronet,* and then he wrote a number of successful books on, of all things, Abraham Lincoln . . . one was called *The Glorious Burden.* Well, once you reached Berlin, the only other place to go from there was America. Of course, don't forget, practically all the people involved, from editors right down the ladder, were Jewish. They had to leave.

When you ask, "Why did people leave Hungary?" let me tell you a story. I had a friend who was Egyptian, and he had applied for citizenship here, and I went along because you had to have a witness, and the judge said, "Why do you want to become a US citizen?" and he said, "Your Honor, do you know Egypt?" If you were Polish or Russian, you went to France, because you've got to remember that their second language was French. But, it's true, none of those were photo-journalists. Well, there were a number of editors in Budapest who were adventurous. They gave their photographers and their writers a great deal of leeway. Their only creed was, "Make it interesting." That's really where most of them were trained. Not I. They were very poorly paid, but given an enormous amount of freedom. I can't think of any—well, maybe one or two, but I can't think of any French photographers or English photographers who were in that line of work. Budapest was stimulating in that respect. It gave you the opportunity. And then too, the second language after your own was German, so naturally we'd move there if we could, that's where the best money, the best outlet, the most rewarding work was being done. If you wanted to do fashion, you'd go to Paris. I didn't want to do fashion.

The ideas, the approaches, were tested in Germany long before it became fashionable to work like that here. And evidently Henry Luce knew that, because he hired a lot of the people who had been successful in Germany. When you came to America, it was either to New York or to Hollywood. New York was into fashion; you had to have a feel or a desire to do fashion, which I didn't have.

We were no "*Bund*" of brothers, not at all. We'd cut each other's throats if necessary. It just never occurred to us to sit around discussing our work. I never took work that seriously. I still don't take it that seriously. I didn't do photography for its own sake. You know, I've been asked that question for fifty years: "What do you photograph when you're not working?" Nothing. When you are in the business of photography, the one thought I always had was "Where can I sell it? What's the market?" I've never taken a photograph for its own sake. I think that applied to all of us. It was a good career. You worked for financial security. Don't forget, financial security, especially in those years, was the overriding issue in Germany. It came as a great surprise later on when somebody said, "Those are great photographs." On the other hand, think of the great artists, from Michelangelo to . . . Raphael, they were getting paid for their work. They didn't paint for their own amusement.

When Munkacsi and I met again in America, we didn't discuss photography. He was reading me his poetry. Which I thought was awful. Yes, I was surprised by his success over here. Because there were three dozen others who were just as good. They weren't in Berlin, they were back in Hungary. His ability was selling—himself. The quality of his work was just average. He simply transferred the style of his photography—sports photography, which is what he did—to fashion. It was a clever idea. He was unique when he got here because nobody had done that sort of work here. But he wasn't unique in Hungary. I didn't do his sort of work. Early on I went into setups instead of grab shots. My influence was Eugene Smith. Every one of his pictures was a setup; it looks as though it is a candid picture, but there is more to it. That's the direction I went into. On the other hand, people like Munkacsi said, "This is it, and that's the way I'll show it." One is a reporting approach; the other is a constructive approach where you actually construct your ideas. So there wasn't any competition between his and my work.

Now, with Eisenstaedt he was in *strong* competition. There's very little in Eisenstaedt that I can't think of twenty other photographers who would have done it just as well. He just shot everybody. But Eisenstaedt, first of all, he liked the person he was photographing, and people loved him personally. He's a good average photographer; you send him out on an assignment and he'll come back with something. But you can't compare him with someone like W. Eugene Smith, who is a . . . creator.

In those days the idea of grab shots was brand new. Before that there were no lenses or types of film that allowed for short exposures. The real revolution came with the invention of the 35 mm camera, fast lenses and fast films which suddenly opened up a tremendous amount of possibilities which simply didn't exist before.

There was one man who started this whole thing, his name was Dr. Erich Salomon and he had this new camera, fast lens, called the Ermanox camera, it had an F-2 lens, and he also worked in Germany at the *Berliner Illustrierte;* he went to Geneva to photograph—they wouldn't allow him to photograph with flash powder and he invented a camera that permitted him to shoot pictures without artificial light, just very little light. That was an absolute sensation in those days. Today that's very simple. But it wasn't then. The mechanics of getting candid pictures were very difficult.

I saw what was happening in other parts of the world, in photography, but they weren't impressive. All the good work was being done in Germany. *Vanity Fair,* yes, but there was no outlet for that sort of work in Germany. We had something called *Die Elegante Welt,* but, compared to *Vanity Fair,* it was like toilet paper.

Laszlo's work was regularly featured in many of the leading Photo Annual publications of pre-Hitler Germany. Quite a few of these photos bore the name of his mother, who was also a photographer, but were in fact her son's work.

LW: She had certain permits I didn't have. You had to have a license, and in order to get the license you had to have an established business. It was the same for any business. I could not get a license because I had not gone to a photographic school. You had to have a three-year course in a school that the photographic union had set up to keep new people out. I'd never gone to it. Magazines didn't care if you had it or not. My mother had a photographic business which she received from my father when they divorced. He had the business in Vienna. If it hadn't been for that, she wouldn't have had a business or the license. She hired people to take pictures—it was sort of like Keystone Press. Everybody knew I had taken the photograph even though it had her name underneath it. The magazines in Germany really broke the union's power and this sort of control, because they said, "We don't give a damn if the guild accepts you or not. If you're good, we'll give you work." So those names credited to those photos you're talking about are not always reliable.

Laszlo went from Paris to Vienna, then back to Berlin in 1932. His departure from Vienna was in part due to politics.

LW: The powers in charge in Vienna were an ultra-Catholic operation, supported by Italy. I didn't like them. They didn't like me. My firm had the biggest news agency in Austria, and they wanted to control what went out. They wanted to put a censor into the office. We were connected to, but independent of, Keystone. And this Catholic group was constantly threatening us, "We'll put you in jail!" And we said, "You can't put a censor in here. We don't have that *yet*." And they said, "You wait." Well, they were right! That was the "political" problem I had in Vienna. It was professional and of course I was on the other side. I was in Berlin when the Reichstag was put on fire. That was when I shot my last picture in Berlin. A policeman I knew told me not to go home. I went back to Vienna.

I didn't have much competition when I was shooting portraits in Vienna. I was almost alone there, and it was such a small circle that I'd be photographing everybody who was anybody, whether it was Freud or the Chancellor, or film and theatrical personalities. I mean, there were other photographers, but it had become a badge of "having arrived" to be photographed by me. In Berlin there was Binder, who'd been a very big photographer in the '20s, when he shot all the movie stars. But in Vienna I sort of stood alone. It was from there that I was signed by MGM later on. I mean, my success wasn't just a lucky chance. I worked at it. By having worked as a journalist, with my name in the papers constantly, it sort of grew by itself. But I was never on the payroll of any of the German or Austrian film companies. I worked independently. Of course, I wanted to get to America. That's where you went if you were a photographer. Besides which, things were getting very hot over there.

Prior to being signed by MGM's European representative, Laszlo had an earlier opportunity to go to America. The New York–born and German-raised star Emil Jannings was so pleased with the pictures Laszlo had taken of him while he was making *Les Aventures du Roi Pausole* that he asked him to go to America with him when Jannings planned to return there. But the German government offered Jannings a deal he couldn't refuse: he was to become the leading artistic film personality of the Third Reich. He stayed.

LW: So, I was back in Vienna photographing anything that came into my mind. I met Bob Ritchie, the man who represented MGM in Vienna, and he had orders from Louis B. Mayer to bring in new talent on every level: writers, composers, you name it. He made a wholesale buy of Hedy Lamarr, Luise Rainer, Rose Stradner, Ilona Massey and a lot of other people that came over here who you never heard of, and I was one of them.

I had no technique to speak of. The only thing that was and still is in my mind when I shoot a photograph is that it must stand on its own, regardless of subject, with or without a caption. I picked out the best pictures that I had done of people, from Einstein to Jung and Freud, and sent them to Hollywood. They called me and said, "You're in." So then we talked about money. And we talked and we talked. I wanted this much and they said this much. Anyway, when I signed the contract in Paris, there was a clause in there and

I said, "What the hell does that mean?" It read, "While you are under contract to MGM, everything you do, including television, belongs to the studio." I asked, "What's this 'television'?" And the MGM guy said, "Oh, it's just a word, it'll never be." That was in 1937, and I had never heard the word. Well, I signed it. Later on, I found out something interesting. After we had figured out what I was to be paid and the contract was signed, I said, "Great." [His contract stipulated that he bring his own photographic equipment.] And I came here and was here a week and I checked the contract again and said, "Great." And then it dawned on me that we had been talking about two different things: in Europe you were paid by the month, and here you were paid by the week. So I ended up getting four times as much as I had expected.

When I got to Hollywood [he arrived on July 11, 1937, and started working on the 12th], I was taken to Howard Strickling's office. He was head of the department, and his office was completely plastered with my pictures, covered with them. He said, "You're it! Every star has seen your photographs and they're all excited, they're waiting in line. Here's a calendar—you're lined up for the next three months. One thing I want to tell you," he said, pointing to one of my photos on the wall, "that kind of picture with shadows and things we can't use. We need pictures that can be reproduced in newspapers. Those you did sold you, so shoot two or three like that if you feel like it, to satisfy the star, but for me you shoot flat light with white backing." Well, there was a reason for it. He couldn't print that other stuff in the newspapers. For every magazine picture that was published, they had a hundred newspapers. That was the time when every newspaper had three or four pages of Hollywood every day. Strickling told me one day, "I don't know the difference between a good photograph and a bad one." His yardstick, and I think very justifiably so, was when the clippings came in. And if a picture of mine appeared in 300 newspapers, that was a good picture. I have no argument with that attitude.

I asked Strickling, "What about the unions?" He said, "Don't worry." Well, I did worry. In Austria I was an employer and we had something worse, we had guilds. Austria had a very interesting system. You had a three-year apprenticeship, but you could only take on one apprentice for every five employees. I don't think there were more than three photographers in Vienna who had five employees. So I started working and Strickling kept saying, "Don't worry, we'll take care of everything, unions nil." I said, "I'm only a visitor here." He said, "Don't worry." I worry. I went to Mexico to get a permanent visa, which you could still do then. A year went by and by this time the war was just about to start, the Nazis had already moved into Austria. I was called into the office of the man in charge of personnel and he said, "Your contract is up for renewal and you've got a $150-per-week increase coming. But we not only won't give you the increase, we want you to take a $75-a-week cut." I said, "Don't you like my work?" He said, "Oh, yeah, we just don't want to pay you that much." I said, "I don't see how I'm going to do that." He said, "Well, let me point out to you that you are here on a visitor visa to work at MGM, and if you don't sign the new contract, we will simply notify the State Department that you are no longer working here, which means you will have to leave the country within twenty-four hours. And the only place you can go is back to Austria. Which is now Nazi-occupied." So I said, "Well, since you put it this way, let me show you something." I pulled out my passport and it was stamped "Immigration." And I said, "That won't work anymore." So I got my increase.

Then I went to the union, Local 659, and said I wanted to become a member. They said, "No way. We're going to give you a permit to be a member as long as you work at MGM because we need MGM. To become a full member, you need the following: four sponsors and two-thirds of the membership voting on you. And we don't like foreigners in the first place." Ray Jones, who was the president then, said, "I've seen your work and it's too good. You make 99 percent of the union members look like amateurs and we don't want that." And do you know, the moment I left MGM . . . or was let out . . . it had become too much for me after the war . . . the moment Strickling said, "We're not going to renew your contract," I said, "That suits me." By the time I got home, there was a messenger waiting for me from the union with a notification that my permit had been canceled. Unions are a protection for the incompetent. The result is that now no photographer gets more than union scale, and no one gets less.

It was an archaic system at MGM; if you were there long enough, it was like Japan, you weren't bothered. Of course, the people who made the final selection didn't know the first thing about photographs. They had no idea. Just for my own amusement, I took one negative and made a dozen totally different printings: light, dark, different croppings. I showed them to the man who was in charge and he said, "This one's good! This one's awful. Look at the expression here, that's good." And they were all from the same negative! It was terribly frustrating because you dealt with people who didn't know. And then you had the problem of the actresses, who all—well, at least most of them—had the right to say, "This one yes, but not that one." I remember I shot an awful lot of pictures on *The Women*. I had to do one sequence with all the leads together. It went by hierarchical sequence: first Norma Shearer, second Joan Crawford, then Roz Russell and so on down the line. Shearer would say, "Gee, this is a beautiful picture of me, but I really don't like the way Joan Crawford looks." It was a very funny scene. First I got a note from the publicity department that said they had to be from left to right in sequence of billing. So for one shot I had them on a staircase. I set them up from left to right and turned my back on them to go back to the camera. I looked through the camera and all I saw was legs because each one of them had walked up the steps! There were two who were easy to work with, Paulette Goddard because she was ambitious, and Rosalind Russell because she didn't give a damn. As a result, Paulette got practically 90 percent of the stuff that was published for *The Women,* because she made herself available. This happened all the time.

Oh, it was a delightful scene on *The Women.* I still remember, they took a day off from shooting just for my stills. The call was for 10:00 a.m. Nobody. 10:30, nobody. 11:00, nobody still. Finally, Roz Russell walked in and said, "Sorry I'm late." I said, "You're not late, you're the first one here." She said, "Jesus, where are the others?" I walked outside the stage, and I saw Norma Shearer driving by, looking out of her car window and then driving on; and right behind her was Joan Crawford, also driving by the stage, looking out and then driving on. I said, "What the hell is going on here?" I called Strickling and said, "Hey, there are two stars out here driving around the stage and not coming in." He said, "Don't you know what they're doing?" I said, "I don't have the faintest idea what they're doing. I know only that they're almost two hours late." He said, "Shearer is not going to come in before Crawford comes in, and Crawford is not going to come in before Shearer does." I asked him what he could do and he said, "The only thing I can do is to stand in the middle of the street and stop them." Which he did.

So at last they're here. We had dressing rooms, portable dressing rooms on the stage, and they were lined up and all the ladies disappeared into their dressing rooms. Again nothing happened. Nobody came out. There had been a council of war and it had been decided that they were all to wear street clothes. So everybody is in her dressing room and nobody is coming out. Finally Rosalind Russell comes out in an evening gown. I said, "You said street clothes!" And she said, "That's all right." So I knocked on Shearer's door and said, "Miss Shearer, Miss Russell is ready." Shearer sticks her head out, takes one look at Rosalind Russell, who is standing outside wearing this sort of straight, clinging dress, and Shearer says, "I'll come out when Miss Russell is dressed." I said, "What do you mean? She *is* dressed." Shearer said, "She's not dressed, she's in her slip." So finally I couldn't wait and I called Strickling again. He came onto the set to help. Now, Shearer is about 5'2", Russell is about 5'6" and Crawford about 5'3". Russell comes out with heels about that high and a hat with feathers. "It's not very flattering what you're wearing," I said. She said, "Maybe not, but I sure as hell am going to wear it." So we shot about four pictures, and then Shearer says in a stage whisper you could hear clear across the 300-foot stage, "Don't you think it's about time you started working with the stars and sent Miss Russell home?" Do you know, we ended up with only about three pictures. Not that we didn't shoot more. And Crawford sort of enjoyed this thing between Shearer and Russell.

I remember Crawford. I had my studio on one side of the street, and her dressing room was on the other side of the street. She was supposed to be at my studio at a given time, and she didn't show and didn't show and didn't show, so I finally called her dressing room and talked to her secretary. I said, "We're waiting, we're over an hour late. What's the problem?" She said, "The limousine isn't here. It's in her contract to have a limousine." I said, "I'm only across the street!" She said, "Miss Crawford has in her contract that she have a limousine." That took another half-hour, getting the limousine. It drove up, picked her up, made a U-turn and dropped her off across the street. One day I passed her in the street and I didn't recognize her. It was a totally blank face. If you remember the old Crawford pictures with that little rosebud mouth, and then later, when her mouth went from ear to ear, that was all painted on. Basically, these stars are very introspective people, they're very concerned with themselves. We all have different moods; they're no different, only it's magnified. And they were encouraged to think themselves important.

Now, with Shearer you always had a problem because she used dead-white makeup, which means you can't just light her. And she insisted on everyone else using Pan Number Five, which is the darkest makeup to use. It was known as "Norma Shearer and her Ethiopian cast." When she looked bright on film, the others didn't show up at all. It was a funny thing, working on *Marie Antoinette*. I wasn't trying to do a Watteau, it just sort of came with the costume. I never tried to consciously imitate something else like a painting. I grew up with painting and sculpture, but I never looked to them for influence. I was interested in the end result. Obviously, when you have Marie Antoinette, you use props and backgrounds which add to the overall effect. I liked props. Metro had an immense amount of them, they had about a half-dozen warehouses full of props. After about a year I went to Ed Willis . . . he was the man in charge of these things . . . and I said, "I've used everything you have and I know you go to Europe every year with a million dollars in your pocket to buy all kinds of things; chairs and paintings and you name it. So where the hell is it?" He said, "That never gets into the studio. You go to Mr. Mayer's house and you can see the props there. Everything you turn over at his house says 'Property of MGM' underneath it."

There was a very funny thing that happened. Shearer had a real yen for Tyrone Power, and he didn't reciprocate at all. Somehow they ended the film without any stills of the two of them together for close-ups. She couldn't make it, he couldn't make it. So the picture finished and he had gone back to 20th Century. We went to them and said, "We don't have anything with the two of them. We gotta call Tyrone Power back." Now, Shearer had this headdress which was about this high, and I started shooting with them together, and by the time her heels and headdress were focused with him standing behind her, you didn't see much of him. So I said, "Let's put him on a box." So he had his arms around her standing on the box, and just as I clicked the shutter, at the precise moment the box broke! He fell down, and all you could see in the shot was this arm. That's the only one Shearer permitted to be published.

It was hard on me because, for instance, for about a year I didn't do a goddamn thing at MGM other than photograph Norma Shearer; because Norma Shearer went to Mayer and said, "He is my photographer." I got to be Norma Shearer's pet for something very ridiculous. You know what Panchro-

matic film is, compared to Orthochromatic? Orthochromatic film has a very
low tolerance for red. That means that red comes out almost black. On the
other hand, blue comes out very light. Orthochromatic film balances it better
on the scale, so if you have light blue eyes you will come out fairly dark gray,
as they ought to be. I shot a picture of Shearer and she said, "Gee, I wish
you could make my eyes lighter." She was fussy about her eyes, they were
very small and she was cross-eyed. So I said, "Done." And I had a little
middle light about this size, and I put a blue cell over it which brought just
her eyes back to what she had been used to seeing before Panchromatic film.
She said, "You're a genius!" From that time on, I was *her* genius. And I sat
around for weeks doing nothing because I couldn't photograph anyone else.
It made the other stars hostile, they blamed me and finally I broke the thing.
I was mad, I was bored. She said, "You don't really like me." I said, "I'm
not getting paid to like you, I'm paid to shoot pictures of you." Then the
arrangement was broken because I said I couldn't wait just to shoot her, I'd
die of boredom. You never knew when she would say "Now," and I had to be
there. She had crews waiting for weeks. She wasn't the biggest female star
as far as Oscars were concerned. She just owned the controlling interest in
MGM. She never came close to Crawford. They all had the right to veto.
Loads of photos were taken and the negatives were sitting around, but they
were never used because the stars vetoed them. If Shearer liked 10 percent of
a sitting, you were doing great. With Crawford you could figure 80 percent
would be okay.

I never even tried to do Garbo at MGM. I was told not to even attempt.
I talked to her. You know, it was very difficult to talk to her, 'cause she's not
very bright. She wasn't then and she still isn't. I talked to Salka Viertel, Peter
Viertel's mother, whom I knew very well. Garbo's a lot of trouble. Trouble!
. . . You know, when I first showed the stars their photos, they were already
touched up like mad. And I said, "This is what you look like, now let's see
what we can do to make you look better." And no one, including the men,
ever said, "This isn't me."

I dealt primarily not with the publicity department, but with the advertising department and a man by the name of Frank Whitback, who is dead now.
He was an interesting man. He used to be publicity man for Barnum and
Bailey, and he ran MGM just like a circus. He's the only man I've ever known
who had four elephants for pets. He had a number of artists and they would
make rough sketches of the billboards and the display things, and I had to fit
my pictures into the existing format; not all of them, I shot a lot more, but
this came first. That was a must, the rest *gratis*. I worked very frequently on
a film where the whole thing was planned, how the billboard would look. Of
course, you couldn't always follow it, but at least you did in general terms.

JK: For portraiture, did some people turn you on more than others?

LW: As a matter of fact, Maureen O'Sullivan was the first person I photographed in Hollywood and she was very cooperative. I never forgot that. It

became a little bit difficult, though, when I had to photograph people like Gracie Allen and I'd get a note saying, "Make her look sexy." Well, I mean, you can only go so far. That word "sexy" sort of fooled me when I first came here, because I spoke English but "sexy" wasn't in my vocabulary. There's no such word in any other language that I can think of. So I got one of those notes right at the beginning and I went to Strickling and said, "There's a word here I don't understand." He said, "You don't know what that means?" I said, "No, I don't," and he said, "You know, sort of a suffering look." It wasn't easy. How do you make Hedy Lamarr sexy? She has nothing to give. It wasn't as simple as showing legs or cleavage. She was not very adept at posing. She was just . . . She felt that if she sat there, that was enough. You try to bring it to some life by changing the lighting, moving in closer to the head, whatever, because nothing changed in her face. It never occurred to me that one could wake her up . . . and nobody ever did.

We had problems in those days with the Hays Office. You couldn't show cleavage—there was a whole group of retouchers who did nothing but take the shadow out of the cleave of the breasts. In those days the stars had one breast that stretched from shoulder to shoulder. You could not show the inside of the thigh. Now, have you ever tried to photograph a dancer and not show the inside of the thigh? You could not. And I couldn't just shoot portraits of Eleanor Powell. Unfortunately, she thought of herself as a very beautiful woman, like Esther Williams later did, but they looked best dancing or swimming. Also, the man always had to be higher than the woman because it was not considered nice to do it the other way. The men had to wear tie and coat. Oh, there were lots of rules. In Europe nobody told me what to do. Total freedom. Including the inside of a thigh.

The one I liked best to work with was Vivien Leigh. She was a thorough professional. First, she understood what this was all about; whether she had learned it or just considered it part of her work I don't know, but she was very professional. I would sit with her a week before we started shooting and tell her what ideas I had in mind. Now, for instance, the session for the ballet-sequence photographs from *Waterloo Bridge,* that took a lot of building, and I discussed it with her beforehand. In the photos those are not sets from the stage, those are sets that I had to build.

I remember the stuff I did with Gable and Crawford. They were both interesting. In this particular movie, *Strange Cargo,* they worked well together. Once in a while, of course, you'd run into someone who was a pleasure to work with, like Mickey Rooney. I think he acts when he's asleep . . . you just tell him what you want and he gives you that and more. Now, Lana Turner, when she was first at MGM, was under contract to the studio for at least a year and did nothing but pose for stills. As she came up the ladder, she became less and less available. We had a real problem getting established people to come in to do photographs on their time off. Most of them felt they were not being paid to pose, and to hell with it. They had bought the idea that they were stars and who needs publicity? Tracy, for instance, he would cut down a session to ten minutes . . . moved his head from right to left and said, "Goodbye." If you said you needed more pictures, he'd say, "Tough shit," and walked out. And there were people at MGM or Paramount whose sole purpose in life was to get the stars to come in on their own time once they were established. But this was really a minor part of what I did. The major part was single portraits. Because in a studio like MGM, where at one time they had 250 actors on the payroll, the promotion never ended. As a matter of fact, the actors had in their contract that for every two months or so they had to give one day for promotional purposes without pay, which didn't make them feel any better either. Most actors only got paid forty weeks of the year, twelve weeks you didn't get paid. That's when the publicity department started working. They said, "Now you're free." And the actor had to say, "Yeah, I'm free. . . ."

I remember Marilyn Monroe worked for me as a model long before anyone ever heard of her.* And when she was really going strong, I talked once to Harry Bryant at 20th Century because I needed some more pictures of her. He said, "Let me show you something," and he had a stack of letters three feet high. He said, "Each of these letters is a legitimate request for interviews and photo sessions with Marilyn Monroe. We figure that if she gives three interviews and photo sessions a day, and if she worked every day of the year including holidays and Christmas, it would take over three years to fill these requests with no time for her to make a movie. And that is impossible." But that went for every star: if they were making it, the requests were so overwhelming in number—and I'm not talking about amateurs or con men, I'm talking about legitimate requests—there wasn't time to fill them all.

I always shot enough of flat light to make Strickling happy. I always shot something to satisfy me, and some to satisfy the star. They weren't very impressed by this flat lighting, they're like passport photos. I liked to dramatize, create a little story, that's what I got paid for. There wasn't much in Hollywood at the time that I took as an example, I have my own way of operating. One thing I think I always had in mind was that any photographer, regardless of what his subject is, whether it's a movie star or a box of matches, has a purpose, and that purpose is to sell. I never lose sight of that.

JK: Did you ever work in color?

LW: I think the first color shot I ever did was of Lana Turner. I used an English system called Dufay Color which only had two codes. The third one you had to imagine. It was green and purple, which didn't do much for you! When I was in a studio, I'd never do color. There was a system called a "one-shot" camera which was the same system that Technicolor later used. You shot on three negatives simultaneously through heavy cutting filters, red, yellow and

*Laszlo also photographed her on *How to Marry a Millionaire*.

green. Those were the matrixes for prints. There were no color transparencies, they weren't on the market yet. There were only four of these "one-shot" cameras in the country. Four people had them: Paul Hesse had one, Doolittle was one, one in New York—anyway, only four cameras in the country. If you wanted a color print done, you had to go hire these people 'cause no one else had the camera. It cost an unbelievable amount of money, and if you breathed on it, it went out of register. Also, the outlets were very limited because there were very few magazines which could print color. The biggest outlet was the *Chicago Tribune,* and they sent their own photographers. They were worried about exclusivity, which is why *Life* had their own photographers, *Look* had their own. Not because they were so great, because generally when they came out, they were covered by staff photographers who shot right with them. Very often the staff photographers were better.

There was a thing that *Life* worked six months on. It was MGM's twenty-fifth anniversary and they wanted a picture of everybody under contract. This developed into a logistics problem that was unbelievable—who would sit where. There were about 200 people. Who would sit next to L. B. Mayer, who would sit in the second row, the third, fourth row? That took three months to establish. Then it was presented to the various factions and they all said, "*No!* That's *not* where I belong." Well, anyway, finally it was put together. Some people were on vacation, God knows where, and had to be brought back. All that for a picture. It was an exclusive for *Life* and they sent two photographers out from New York to shoot it. Both of them loused it up. If the staff photographer, Eric Carpenter, hadn't covered it, the whole labor would have been in vain.

It used to take about three or four hours to retouch one negative. We had very good retouchers there, about thirty, and we had anywhere from 300 to 400 sheets a day, which took some time! The average retoucher did three negatives a day. From working in magazines and newspapers, I always leave a lot of space around my subject. Then I put it in the enlarger and make my composition. But, basically, gallery portraits were done on 8×10 for the purpose of being able to make contact prints, which in my case didn't work, so I made a master print that I made myself in the enlarger, and they would follow that. I gave the directions for touching up. I always printed the master print and that was hung up for the printer and he followed it because there's a lot of burning and dodging in them, which you can't do in color. In black-and-white the shooting of the pictures was only half the work. The rest you did in the enlarger, if you know how. I was always being told, "Don't waste all that time on them because nobody knows the difference." But *I* know the difference.

I would very rarely set up more than one session per day. At least I was available. I tried to drag it out as long as possible. The model or the actor, on the other hand, had other things to do, or pretended to have other things to do. So there was always a contest, a tug-of-war: "When do we finish?" So I tried to get as many pictures as possible, because it might be three months before I got him or her again. Strickling had an assistant, Ralph Williard. I'd take the proofs to his office. He'd take the pack of proofs and weigh them. He said, "Not a very good sitting!" I said, "What do you mean?" He said, "Well, normally when I get a set of proofs, they weigh about two or three pounds." There were people like Clarence Bull, who shot as fast as he could, but when you really looked at them, he didn't have more than three pictures even though he had hundreds of proofs. I would say that about 20 percent of the negatives in a session were left after weeding out by myself and the star and Strickling, depending upon the preparation.

Now, if I had the time—for instance, when I was working with Norma Shearer—when I could, I'd take over a stage and build sets side by side, maybe twenty sets, and light them up. That means you have all the lights in position, which takes at least a day, you work with a stand-in, and two or three days to build the sets. It ties up dozens and dozens of lights because they're all set beforehand. So, by the time she came in, all she had to do was go from set to set, and I just flicked a switch and the light's there. It's an expensive proposition, but that didn't make any difference, the profits were so immense. Miss Shearer liked flowers. So the flower man is there to give them to her. He was called the garden man. That meant a two-and-a-half-ton truck, a driver and two helpers, and they waited in case she wanted a flower. The amount of waste was unbelievable. Today you couldn't afford it. You could make a movie for what a session like that cost.

Any movie that didn't make a 100 percent profit for the first three months was considered a failure. And money simply didn't matter. In a gallery session I had an assistant. I also had to have an electrician, a prop man and a grip. I didn't need them, but they were there because of the union. One of my first experiences in Hollywood with the union was I was shooting someone and I said to the electrician—you had to have an electrician for every two lights, which means you had to have a head electrician who told them what to do—I tried to explain to him where I wanted to put the lights, and I just couldn't get through to him. That wasn't the way it was done! So I picked up the light and put it from here to there. Well, I turned around and the stage was empty. Everybody had walked out. I had broken a union rule by touching the light.

When I first came out here, I came by train from New York. On the train I met a man and we started talking. He said, "Where are you going?" and I told him to Hollywood, and he said, "What do you know? So am I. What are you going to do?" I said, "I'm going to start work at MGM," and he said, "So am I. What are you doing?" I told him I was a photographer and he said, "I'm here from the First Boston Corporation"—who at that time were the financiers of the company—"I'm an efficiency expert. They don't know what goes on out here, and I'm supposed to get some order in it." So once in a while I would run into him on the lot and we'd say hello, but nothing much.

But one thing, I noticed he was losing an awful lot of weight and getting sort of stooped. One day he came to my office and said, "I'm going back to Boston." I asked what had happened, why was he going back, and he said, "How can you get efficiency into an operation where the assets take their hats at 6:00 and go home?"

1979

Loretta Young, photographed by C. S. Bull (MGM), 1934

LORETTA
YOUNG

AUTHOR: I shall never understand the weird process by which a body with a voice suddenly fancies itself as a mind! Just when exactly does an actress decide they're her words she's saying and her thoughts she's expressing?
ACTRESS: Usually at the point when she's got to rewrite and rethink them to keep the audience from leaving the theater!

MOST PEOPLE RECOGNIZE THIS EXCHANGE between Lloyd Richards and Margo Channing from *All About Eve*. Because the writing in that film is so good, so eminently quotable, we tend to side with the author. But films are not plays, and, unlike the theater, movies introduced a factor which had no prior recognized standing in the arts. We look at Da Vinci's "Mona Lisa" and think of what Da Vinci did for his model, if we think of her at all. We do not give any credit in that work to the model who may have inspired Da Vinci to achieve it. Who was Shakespeare's "Dark Lady of the Sonnets"? She/he must have been pretty special to inspire him to immortalize her. Onstage, actors are the tools of the playwright. Actors without a script are out of work. Let them read the telephone book, see who comes. But with film the inspiration also becomes in itself an act of creation. There are more films which are memorable because of great stars without great scripts or dialogue than there are great films with great scripts and dialogue but without a star. Of course they help each other. Of course they matter.

When we think of a Bette Davis or a Mae West or a W. C. Fields or a Humphrey Bogart, we not only get an image but we can quote them. But think of Crawford, think of Garbo, of Cooper, of Dietrich, of Cary Grant, of Marilyn or James Dean, and start quoting. Their voices are as memorable as their faces, and they made enough good films for their fame to endure, but their best films were built around them. Take Mankiewicz' great script. Bette Davis was not the only one with choice dialogue and a well-written character. Celeste Holm, superb actress, did not become a great film star as a result, neither did Hugh Marlowe, Gary Merrill or Anne Baxter. They served the writer. Miss Davis transcended him. Eve was the star; her conniving was the subject. Miss Davis as Margo Channing made the film seem like a glorious vehicle. A stalk of celery . . . and *enchanté* to you too.

Among the people I admired and met, a number of them were undoubtedly enormous stars with ten, twenty, thirty years of success behind them and hardly one memorable film or one quotable line to their credit. Their success throws a major wrench into any theory about movies that elevates writer, director, great photography or the power of connections above that of the film star. Probably the most enduring, though by no means the only, example is the career of Loretta Young, Hollywood's fairy-tale beauty. She made her first film, as an extra, aged five. She was one of the children in the desert kingdom of Valentino's *The Sheik*. At thirteen, she was selected to be Lon Chaney's leading lady in *Laugh Clown Laugh*. By 1930, not yet seventeen, she was given star billing. By 1940 she was in the top league of American stars. She was still there in 1950. In 1952 she'd had enough. She was tired of rewriting and rethinking dead lines to bring them alive and keep the audience entertained. She was forty years old in a profession traumatized by the fear of losing one's youth and one's looks.

Loretta Young took a gigantic step, against the well-meaning warnings of friends, co-workers and studio executives who saw nothing but disaster, for her as well as the industry. She was the first of the old established guard to leave movies for TV. The television format she selected allowed her to pick her scripts, her writers, her directors; it gave her control. Her show was a triumph; for the next ten years it was one of the most popular programs on American TV. During that period she was constantly voted as one of the ten most admired women in the country. In the wake of her success came Jane Wyman, Barbara Stanwyck, June Allyson, each with her own anthology format. Loretta Young's career is the unassailable proof that in movies, before the camera, the star is the drawing factor.

Loretta Young looks like the sort of woman a lot of people wanted to let themselves be fooled by. The pretty little lady. The innocent young doll. But "the little woman" wanted more than pretty dresses and handsome leading men, good cameramen, a nice steady raise, the only choices a woman was allowed in the movie industry. And in the end she got what she wanted. She always seemed to get what she wanted—not in a spoiled, petulant way, but in a clear, wide-eyed, trusting way.

She wasn't always right. There's more than a touch of arrogance in some of her opinions, but she enjoys an argument. And, right or wrong, she stands by her decisions once it's too late to change them; she takes the credit and she accepts the flak. Loretta was never defeated. A bit wearier, perhaps a little warier and ever wiser, she regenerated her spirit, rekindled the spark in her eyes. She was not a victim, she is a graceful survivor.

For twenty years now she's been off the screen. Before then, she never read, unless it was a script. Now she started to read; to involve herself in charities; to travel and enjoy friends. Like most of the industry old-timers who saw their business grow and flourish, she's a Republican; she's a prominent Catholic—she and her friends Irene Dunne and the late Rosalind Russell were known as "the Nuns of Hollywood"; still married in the eyes of the Church, though legally divorced from her Catholic husband, Tom Lewis, she's been a leading figure in the Hollywood social world; she keeps her countless awards and trophies underneath dust sheets in the garage, and I've yet to find out where she keeps the Oscar she won for her role in *The Farmer's Daughter*, for which she went blond and learned her Swedish accent from Ruth Roberts, who had previously taught Ingrid Bergman how to lose her Swedish accent for a more mid-Atlantic one. Loretta kept her stills from the films she made, along with many of the superb portraits taken of her over the years, in an old cabinet in her garage. She was an illuminating source when I wrote about the Hollywood portrait photographers. Nowadays it's become fashionable for stars to go on the lecture circuit, telling capsule life histories and answering questions. Loretta should be teaching classes, giving seminars to film students. They might not all agree with what she has to say, but they wouldn't be bored.

LY: Interviews were always a chore to me, a terrible chore. Always. Because I was just free and easy and said what I thought and felt, and I was *always* misquoted. ALWAYS. Not that they intended to, because I have always had a very nice relationship with the press. I've been honest with them and they've been honest with me. But it's difficult. I don't mean talking about somebody else . . . because that's just an opinion of mine. You may ask me a question today, and tomorrow I may feel entirely different. I'm just one of those people. Fundamentally, I stay the same, I believe.

JK: Why did you retire?

LY: First of all, I had always hoped and prayed that I would have sense enough to go before it's too late. Either from a party, or a pleasant interview, or from an acting career. I've seen too many people who wait too long. And they spoil their—I hate to use the word "image," but that's the only word I can think of—that they have spent a lifetime creating.

JK: You were extremely professional. When you finally stopped working, did you miss it all?

LY: No. By this time, I had done everything that I had even thought I might like to do. Nefertiti . . . I was always crazy about that bust of Nefertiti. One day we were sitting in my dressing room and I said, "Ruth [Roberts], I'm just so crazy about that bust." And she said, "I have a marvelous idea for a story about Nefertiti." So we did it three weeks from then, and I played Nefertiti. How many actresses get the chance? For ten years, anything you want to do, do it. In a miniature form, granted. But you did it and you made one point in one half-hour on that television show. And forty million people saw it at the first showing. So there was complete fulfillment of even vague little dreams that I'd had of what I might want to do. Well, when I stopped . . . you get yourself into a pattern of working in a certain way. You take photographs, you have interviews, and though it becomes very hard to do physically, you're still in that pattern. Now, the minute you break that pattern, you don't miss anything at all because you cut off the reason for it. When I quit, I quit. Because I had done what I wanted to do. I knew I didn't even want to do what *they* wanted me to do, meaning the networks or the sponsors, whoever it was. What they want is a nice, sure, dull series. I tried that, and I got twenty-six pictures [episodes] and I just said that I couldn't do one more of the same woman. And I can't. On the other hand, I did eight years of the anthology . . . a different woman each week. This is the mistake that I think Jane Wyman made in her anthology. She always looked the same. That's one of the reasons I chose to be a Japanese one week, Chinese, a Swede, a little old lady one week, or a beautiful, glamorous actress the next. Variety, you see. Anything. Anything to look different. And I loved it.

JK: Well, did it matter to you how many people saw it?

LY: Oh, yes, very much. Because my whole purpose in going into television was to get a good idea into the mainstream of life. Not watered down to the point where it was nothing. You may not have agreed with the point that I made, but it was a valid point. And in motion pictures I found that by the time it gets to the screen, after you have four or five writers with different ideas, and a producer and director with different ideas, and perhaps a star with his ideas, and then the cutter comes in and has *his* ideas, you're really quite lucky if you get anything at all at the end of a six-month job. I think David Selznick is the only man I have seen who was able to capture . . . When he bought a book, he bought a book, and made *the book*. He had a brilliant, brilliant sense of casting and exquisite taste, exquisite. He was a very good writer himself, and a very sensitive man . . . when it came to making pictures. When it came to getting what he wanted, he could be brutal, just a pig. But he was a marvelous producer of motion pictures, I thought. *Rebecca* was brilliantly done. *Gone With the Wind* is a marvelous book, and to be able to get an 1100-page book into a 3½-hour movie is fantastic . . . and not lose all those little delicacies in it. But he was rare too. I don't think there's a producer around today like David. They don't have a studio behind them. You see, if a producer at a studio made one good picture, then that whole studio was behind him and he developed and developed.

JK: Do you miss the studio system?

LY: No, because I left it before it left me. Therefore, I never had a chance to miss it. No, when I see a picture like *To Sir with Love* or *In the Heat of the Night* or *Little Big Man* or *Romeo and Juliet* . . . The reason I'm so crazy about Zeffirelli's work is that he doesn't hedge; it's the only thing of Shakespeare's that I've even *heard,* much less understood and liked. Everything . . . the acting, the sets, the feel of it, the wildness of the gangs that we have today. For me it was marvelous. And I liked . . . it seems a strange choice for *me* . . . *Midnight Cowboy,* which I thought was marvelous because it had what I call a happy ending. A person tries something, and they find it isn't right and they turn on the right road. This is my idea of a beginning and a middle and an end. It satisfies me. So when I see pictures around like this, I guess I can't say there aren't good producers around. There *are.*

JK: Do you believe that the studios could "create" a star?

LY: No. Well, up to a certain point. If there was a spark there. But there had to be that spark. But the producers of those days were somehow able to recognize that little spark which makes a star. No one ever knows what makes a star. But I think it has to do with someone you want to identify with. And the more people that can identify with it . . . Let's say, take the period of Betty Grable. She was the biggest star in the business for ten years. Betty Grable was never an actress, never pretended to be. *Per se.* Like Garbo or Bette Davis or Joan Crawford or any of the big stars. She was still, however, the biggest star in the business. Because more people could identify with Betty Grable and her pretty, beautiful little body, and her cute, pretty, kind little face than they could with Garbo. Garbo was what we call a prestige star. Lana Turner was one of those extraordinary personalities. I think Lana learned to act . . .

JK: Chiefly in *Madame X.*

LY: Well, I've seen her do some pretty good jobs before that. I've seen her do a picture which was almost a straight lead with Clark Gable. She played a nurse and he played a doctor during the war [*Homecoming,* 1948] and you couldn't have asked for a better performance. For what it was. It wasn't *Mourning Becomes Electra.* So if you have enough time and you have any talent at all, and everyone is patient and they keep telling you that you are good, you thrive on it and you open up. And it does develop. It's like a stock company. Only we did it on the screen. With people watching you. And they *did* build their stars. Of course, some people, like Clark Gable, who to me was not so much an actor as he was a star; Spencer Tracy, who was such a magnificent actor that he was also a star, but he was never the star that Clark Gable was, because he didn't have, I guess, the magnitude or the sex appeal or whatever you want to call it that Clark Gable had.

JK: But you couldn't have liked that system much at the time, under Fox, when you literally did everything that was thrown at you.

LY: Well, looking back at it now, I know that it was petulance mostly that made you crab about everything the studio asked you or wanted you to do, or made you do. It was the popular thing to do. When you are in doubt, you crab, you beef, you march, you scream. That seems to go with youth somehow. And since we really didn't have anything to crab about, you just say: I hate you, I hate you. . . . But as for the studio system itself, I have no regrets. I had to go through it. I regret its passing for those working today, because it is virtually impossible to become a lasting star. In what we call the good old days, there were never less than twenty or thirty fabulously important stars in the business at any one time. Well, you can't name that many today. And these stars worked all the time. And they tell me that two-thirds of the theaters are closed all over this country. In those days they were all jammed full. I think television also has had a great deal to do with it because it's so easy to turn it on at home, and it's free. But still to me the caliber of the motion picture . . . when you get a picture that is good, it does make money. Of course, now they say it's just coining money. Yes, it is, at a little theater that holds 300 people. But not in the Music Hall or in the Roxy, where you had to fill it five times a day with 3000 people.

JK: You know, it's been so much a part of your life . . . you were four when you started and fourteen when you started actively in the movies, and then worked nonstop until 1960—

LY: 1964.

JK: Right. Is retirement something you could really settle down to?

LY: Very easily. I know your next question, I think. It is "How?" And the secret is that it was never my whole and entire life. It was my working life. Which I thoroughly enjoyed. But I have an entirely separate and more personal and more important life that I have always lived and enjoyed. It's a very well-regulated, formal, religious life which has always taken precedence over my working life. Always. I come from a very solid family background which I enjoyed. I don't recall ever rebelling against it. My father I didn't know at all. He was gone by the time I was four years old. But my mother reared us, and she was a fascinating woman, still is today. She was never fascinated by the picture industry. In fact, she used to say, "I don't understand how you can be an actress." I said, "Why?" And she would say, "Oh, the people are so rude. The men don't even know enough to stand up from their desks when you walk into the room." She had to go in to sign my contract. It was with Darryl Zanuck, as a matter of fact, and I was seventeen at the time, and she said, "Well, thank Heaven, that's the last time I'll ever have to sign a contract." I said, "Why?" and she said, "Because it's for five years, and next time you'll be old enough to sign it yourself!"

When I started, I was always too young for everything and I not only was too young, but I *looked* too young. So that became an absolute red flag with me, so I always lied about my age. In fact, the studio wanted to talk to Mama six months before I told her they wanted to put me under contract. I had told them I was eighteen. I was fourteen. Finally, when I did get around to saying anything, it was because Mr. Thompson, who was the contract man at the studio, kept saying every day, "Tell your mother to come out here because we want to give you a contract." When I did tell her, she said, "Well, why didn't you tell me?" And I said, "Because I knew you'd be out there and I've told them I'm eighteen years old and you'll tell them I'm not." And she laughed and said, "They won't believe you anyway." So I said, "Well, why not?" and she said, "You don't look eighteen. You look fourteen." I didn't understand that talk, and told her that they did believe me. Of course they didn't. And she finally did get out there. Doug [Fairbanks], Jr., used to kid me all the time because we worked about five or six pictures together and I was always eighteen. I wasn't smart enough as I got a year older to say that I was nineteen. So he caught me one day and he said, "Listen, you've been eighteen for the last four pictures that I've done with you. Are you eighteen or are you thirty-five or are you twelve? What *are* you?" So then I caught on that I had to up it a year. Also, I think that people who saw me when they were twelve years old thought that I was, if I were playing a leading-lady part, eighteen or twenty-five, whatever I was playing. They took it for granted. So that when they are fifty, they think that I am ninety! I showed you that picture taken of me when I was fifteen . . . a profile shot. I could have been thirty.

JK: Because you thought mature, didn't you?

LY: You had to. I was smoking cigarettes when I was thirteen on the set, openly, and they couldn't stop me because I would say that since I was playing an eighteen-year-old it made me feel eighteen, so I was going to smoke. There wasn't anything illegal or immoral about it, so I did. In fact, I started smoking when I was eight, stealing them from my uncle!

JK: So grownup! Were you dating too?

LY: Well, fortunately, they had very attractive people for you to go out with at the studio. I never went out with anyone I didn't want to. I remember one time, one Saturday night at home—and we were a large family and it was a large house—the phone rang, and it was Tyrone Power's stand-in. I've forgotten his name, but he was a darling boy, more than a stand-in, he was Tyrone's right hand, secretary and everything else. He called and said, "Ty's sitting here, and he's embarrassed because it's Saturday night and he's a big movie star and so are you, and he's sure you must have a date. But if you haven't, would you like to go to a movie with him?" Well, I burst out laughing because it was so true. He came and picked me up and we went down to the Village Theater because I lived in Bel-Air at the time, and we went into the movie. We talked about it many times after that. Because I liked him—in fact, I was just crazy about him. Tyrone lived with his mother, a very beautiful woman, but she was also a little star-struck. His father had been an actor too. His grandmother was the Rock of Gibraltar, but his mother had more influence on him. And she wanted him to be a big star. She wanted him to be more than he was. Personally, all he had to do was be Tyrone. I told him, "You *are* a star . . . but you don't have to act like one!"

JK: But did they allow you much choice with your private life?

LY: Oh, yes! I did exactly as I wished, always. First of all, at seventeen I was a star. Before that I was too young, but by this time I could say "no." They had at that time what they called "drape art." It was probably the equivalent of the pullout in *Playboy* magazine now. You couldn't see anything, but it was suggestive . . . drape art. So they called me in for a sitting—I think I was about fourteen, and if you weren't acting, you were in the portrait gallery—and they said, "Today we are going to do drape art. So just get undressed." And I said, "No, I don't want to get undressed." Actually, between you and me, I was embarrassed to get undressed because I didn't have any kind of figure. I was very thin and didn't have much to show anyway! I could cover it up with clothes. So I said, "No, it's not modest." It still isn't modest for me in these days. But they said, "No, you have to." I said that I didn't. They said, "Everybody does." "*I* don't." They said, "We'll take you off salary." I told them I didn't care, and of course at fourteen I *didn't* care. I went home and told my mother that they had taken me off salary, and she said, "Fine. What for?" So I told her and she said, "You are right. No lady does that." So I was off salary for a couple of weeks, and I guess they got bored, so they put me back on. Then they tried it again! Anyway, they never did get any drape art of me. The nearest they got to it was when they wrapped a sheet around me like a mummy! There was one magazine—I think it was *Photoplay,* but I'm not sure—and they had pages displaying first a modern portrait of the star and then her drape art next to it. And, my name being Young, I'm always on the tail end of everything. So at the end of the display there was a modern portrait of me and then a blank space with a caption that read, "We can't find any drape art on Miss Young." It was a very wise thing for me. In the long run, all those things paid off for me. Because when I became an established star, they couldn't say, "Yes, she's a hoity-toity lady now, but look what she used to do." Nowadays that sort of thing makes money at the box office, but in those days it could kill you.

I took many suspensions on contracts because I would not even play something like a divorced woman who marries someone else. The only one that I can recall ever doing was *Born to Be Bad,* which had been written for Jean Harlow. I was under contract to Zanuck at the time. I came back from a trip to Honolulu, and Zanuck said, "Here's your next script, you're going to do it." And I said, "I can't play this. I don't know what to do with it." And he said, "Well, anyway, you're going to play it." So I had to play it. To the best of my ability. We had a marvelous director, and Cary Grant was marvelous in it. But I hated it so, and disapproved of it. And when the picture came out, the review said, "This picture is called *Born to Be Bad*. It is." That's all it said! It never ran in first-run theaters, it went to second-run. So that is the one and only time I tried it, against my better judgment, and it didn't work. So from then on I never played those parts.

JK: What about *Midnight Mary*?

LY: *Midnight Mary*—now, believe it or not, in my mind I didn't know she was living with that man. I know now. To me that little girl started out when she was nine years old and she was just in love with these different people. Now, when I look back at the gangster in it, I remember thinking, "Why does he have to slap me?" And the director said, "Because you're his girl." And I said, "He doesn't have to slap me." And he said, "Yes. He does." Poor Bill Wellman kept saying to me, "Loretta, you're his girl." I kept saying, "Yes, I know." But I didn't know what he was talking about. If I had, I think I would have put it out of my mind. Now, there's quite a difference between a love affair as with, say, Charles Boyer and Irene Dunne, and *Oh, Calcutta!* There's quite a difference—we're talking about sex—between a love affair whose natural—not normal, but natural—culmination is in intimate relations, than in the out-and-out sensationalism of lust. Not sex. Lust, where they're not even involved emotionally. They don't want to be. It's a physical exercise. And maybe that's good for some people, but it doesn't seem to be good for society at large.

JK: People of another, older generation say it's so much worse today. They forget the '30s. The Depression was a very shocking thing.

LY: That's why I say that these pictures do influence . . . because probably those pictures of the '30s are responsible for a lot of this today.

JK: But weren't these pictures just reflecting evil? Because every leading lady played a whore at some point. A whole new breed of star was born because they played gangsters. Is it much worse today, or have you really forgotten that period of the '30s?

LY: No, I haven't really forgotten it. But, yes, I think it's worse today because it's accepted today. We don't even believe in marriage today. I believe it's worse now because it's accepted as not being wrong. We know it's wrong. And we know what's right. I don't care how beautifully you do it. People say it doesn't matter what you do as long as you do it beautifully. Poppycock. And, you know, all these little angry things that go on inside of people all the time, they don't know what it is. *I* know what it is. They all still have a little spark of conscience. We can all brainwash ourselves or rationalize, or whatever you want to call it. I am a past master at that. Because you kind of live in this phony world, and you read all this junk about yourself, and even though you know what you read in the movie magazines was written by somebody in the publicity department, you can, if you're not careful, put everything in that category. You never take it seriously . . . and this is where I had so much trouble in getting down to decide who I was in love with and who I wasn't. But thank God I discovered in time. Because if I could find so many beautiful and reasonable excuses why I should do it, before you knew it I was going down that avenue where I really didn't want to go. Then I got in hot water, and it took me, oh, so long to struggle back upstream. Because in the long run it's uncomfortable. And if I am uncomfortable with myself, I'm going to be uncomfortable with you. And it's going to reflect in every-thing that I do. It will influence either for good or for evil, but there's no in-between. So when they say, "Do you think motion pictures have had any influence?" I say of course! "Do you think television has had any influence?" But of course! This is the big educator of the world. It is one of the reasons I went into television when I did, and thank God I went in when I did.

JK: You started a trend. June Allyson, Jane Wyman . . .

LY: When I went into television, I had two of my very dearest friends, produc-ers, heads of studios, call me in and say, "Please do not go into the enemy court. You will be blackballed out of this business. You will never get another job. We love you, we need you, you're one of our big stars, do not go into this." I said, "Well, I'm going into it for a very good reason. Because I think it's the medium. I think it has great influence." I was one of the first people in Hollywood to have a television. It was heresy. And my two sons were little then, and my daughter was around nine, and we sat down—my husband and I and the children and the cook and the maid and the governess—we were all sitting there looking at our little baby television set. A suspense show came on; it opened up with a woman walking into a dark room. Then she starts to get undressed and the camera goes closer and closer until she's in a head close-up, and you just see her pull off her slip, and she turns around and two hands come in and strangle her, and she falls out of the picture. Well, my children burst out crying. There was murder, right there in my living room. My husband switched off the TV immediately, and the kids were in hysterics. Well, this bothered me for weeks and weeks and weeks. So I decided I wanted to get into it. I would take up one half-hour that didn't shock you out of your skin. That was the purpose behind it. It still took me two years, because my agents at that time didn't want me to do it. I don't think anyone really wanted me to. But I told my two friends that I was going into it for another reason. And, fortunately for me, if you concentrate on your work, the money comes. And indeed it did. While I was doing it, it didn't make any money, because you put it all back into it. And I was used to getting $15,000 a week, and out of the show's budget I took about $500 a week. But then, afterwards, when the thing was all finished and we had sold it—because I owned the shows—then, of course, I did very well. And I remember saying to one of these two men, Dore Schary, head of MGM at the time, I said, "You can't hold back the tide, it's here. So why do you treat it this way? It's another avenue through which you could work if you embraced it and tried to go with it." And he was very reasonable, because Dore was always very reasonable to talk with . . . for me at least.* But they were just frightened of it, I think. Now we know that TV can mold the minds of two, ten or ten million.

JK: But it has all decayed much quicker than movies, hasn't it?

LY: Oh, yes, because it hit more people at once. I believe, because I'm sure there are some very worthwhile people at the head of these networks and the industry itself, but most of them are not really in touch with the fundamentals of life. It's a little cocoon that they seem to live in, interested mostly in sensationalism, primarily in shock value, and the newscasters always say it isn't news if it's good news. Well, fine, but you've got to make up your mind what kind of country you want.

JK: Do you really think it's changed that much, altered that drastically?

LY: Oh, my dear, my dear . . . look around you. After we saw President Kennedy assassinated, and then his assassinator assassinated, and then . . . And you can't just cut that off. To these little eight-, nine- or ten-year-olds a gun isn't something to be careful of, it's something to use, and it looks so easy. You take a picture—I don't know why I went to see it—well, I do know, it's because Bill Holden was in it and I'm crazy about him, it was called *The Wild Bunch.* For the first ten minutes I was so thrilled with the concept of it, I thought how magnificent. But by the time it was finished, there wasn't a child, man or woman in the film who had anything in their entire being but evil. No compassion, no understanding, no *simpático,* no gentleness, no kindness, not one virtue. Now, the world is *not* all evil. It isn't. People tell me that the reason the director did that film was because it's the way things were in those days. How does he know? Did he live in those days? That's a copout. Now, *Bonnie and Clyde* I saw at a private screening with the director, writers and Warren Beatty. Afterwards a few of us went out to dinner, which lasted until about 3:00 in the morning. Maybe I was affected because they were right there and I wanted to like it, because I am that way. But I found the main thing I liked about this motion picture was the fact that it didn't look like a picture made thirty years later about an era thirty years before. I felt as though I was right there. But those are rare, the films that capture that era. Not only historically, but also those that try to re-create the old Hollywood. Today is not then. Actors were more of a stock company in those days. And they were not kowtowed to, contrary to what some people say today. Movies

---

* Schary produced Loretta's Oscar-winning film, *The Farmer's Daughter.*

that are written about movie stars in those days are just ridiculous. Two good movies *only* about Hollywood, and they are *A Star is Born*—the first one—and the Constance Bennett one, *What Price Hollywood?* That was a marvelous picture about Hollywood, an honest and true one.

JK: What sorts of things would you turn down? I know as stars became established, they were able to choose their director, stills man, cameraman sometimes.

LY: When you are freelancing, you can decide on anything you want. And when I was freelancing—that's after I left 20th Century–Fox finally (it took two years to finish that original seven-year contract) because Zanuck I found to be impossible for me to work with. It was just his attitude, and finally I was as unattractive as I could be to Darryl. I used to hold up a whole set while I made him give me permission to carry a handkerchief in a scene in *Suez*. And I'd wait until he got back from playing polo. Because he sent word to me, "These are the costumes she's going to wear and she can't add or subtract anything," so I said, "All right." This was because he didn't like the way I dressed. I said, "Well, I'm a fashion plate. I don't care whether you like it or not. I am known as one of the best-dressed women in motion pictures." "Well," he said, "my wife wouldn't wear a dress like that." I said, "Your wife isn't a movie star. I am." We just never saw eye to eye. We had many meetings about it, and I said to him, "Look, you're great with men, but you don't know what the hell to do with women. You ruin every woman you touch." And he did. Anyway, he tagged two years onto the end of my contract because he'd say, "Well, you're going to do this," and I'd say, "No, I'm not. I'm going to Honolulu instead," and he'd say, "Right. Then you're off salary." When you're off salary, they tag it onto the end of your contract. So he tagged it on and I had two extra years. He started *Alexander Graham Bell*, which was the last picture I did over there under contract. He started that exactly *one day* before my seven-year contract was over. Then he closed the picture for three weeks and finally opened production on it officially. In other words, he hooked me for that one picture. And still at $1500 a week, or whatever it was. So that, I mean, there were all sorts of nasty little things like that.

But when you freelanced . . . by this time I was so burned up that I made sure I had the okay on everything: the story, the leading man, director, everything, right on down the line. But they brought all of that on themselves by misusing people. I remember one picture which I made at Fox years later, *Half Angel*, which they put a director on. I had okay of director because now I was freelancing. The man was called Jules Dassin, and they said that he was going to direct it, and I said that I didn't know his work. Well, this was a comedy, and very light comedy at that, and should be a very sexy little thing. So they said that they would show me something of his work. I told them that I had seen one thing of his, and it was a very heavy spy story. I don't remember what it was [probably *Nazi Agent*, made at MGM in 1942]. Anyway, they showed me another and it was just as heavy. Mr. Dassin was an avowed Communist at the time, and we were naturally diametrically opposed to each other's ideologies. And he didn't like me any better than I liked him, so I said to Darryl, "I don't think this is going to work." And he said, "Well, will you try it?" "Yes, if you think he's good, but I don't think it's going to work." Well, we started off with completely different ideas, and finally after ten days of the picture Mr. Dassin said to me while we were on location, "Miss Young, I don't want to hear one more word out of you. Come in the door, do this." I had said something and he started saying this in front of all these people. I listened all through and then said, "Are you finished, Mr. Dassin?" He said, "Yes." I said, "Goodbye. I am going to my dressing room. Sylvia, would you please call Mr. Blaustein [the producer of the film] and have him come to see me? I would like to talk to him." There was a dead silence and I walked off and went into the dressing room. In about forty-five minutes Julian Blaustein came down from the studio, because we were downtown, and I said, "Julian, you either get yourself another girl or another director. I won't work five minutes more with this man. For ten days we have been doing the old-maid stuff. Now, that's all right, but I couldn't possibly work with this man and play the attractive, sexy girl that the script calls for. I couldn't do it. I don't like him and he doesn't like me." He said, "Oh, Loretta . . ." "No," I said. "It really doesn't make any difference to me. I'll give you back the money. You don't have to bother about it, you can just get another girl." He said that if they were going to get anyone, it would be another director. I said, "Fine. Let me know what you feel when you get home." So he went home and he called at about 9:30 that night and asked if Dick Sayles would be acceptable to me. I said, "Yes, he's very good." Well, Dick came on the set next morning and he was charming. He did a lovely job of it. The next time I did a picture, I forget which one, there were no arguments. Only there weren't any arguments because I was freelancing. I would say, "Darryl, you just can't do that. You may be insensitive, but I'm not, and I have to work. . . ."

JK: You said earlier that you didn't mind how you were photographed, and yet you were also beginning to say that you didn't like your long neck. . . .

LY: All right. I didn't like my long neck and I was trying forever to kind of squish it down. Now, when you get a good cameraman—Horst was a marvelous cameraman, he used to work for *Vogue* and *Harper's*—and there were some beautiful pictures. Every time I'd go to New York, naturally, *Harper's* would photograph me and *Vogue* and *Vanity Fair* and all those. Condé Nast sent me a picture that they had taken years ago. In *Vanity Fair*. He sent me an original print and said, "We've all decided that this is the most beautiful picture of a woman we have ever printed in *Vanity Fair*." It was a picture of me when I must have been about twenty at the most, and I had a hat, a profile shot, and the hat was a Lilly Daché. It was orange and had black lace over it, large black lace that fell over the edge, and I had on a black dress. I remember that the photographer kept saying to me, "Put your chin up further, put your chin up! Make your neck longer!" And all I could think was, "I'm going to kill him, I'm going to kill him . . ." All he was going to see was this long turkey neck sticking up, and finally he said, "Just a minute," and he grabbed this red rose from somewhere and stuck it right here in the bosom of the dress, so you had this marvelous color combination. I've forgotten the color of the background, but this orange hat and the black dress and the black lace and a red rose right there, and all you really saw was this tiny little face, this great big hat and this looooooong neck. But it was a beautiful neck, I mean, if you are twenty years old! But then I thought it was terrible. I was so embarrassed when I saw it in the paper, I thought, "Terrible, awful, all you can see is that long neck." But when they sent it to me all those years later, I thought, "That's quite beautiful," because I was far enough away from it then. I learned to like my neck when we were about two years into the television series. There was a back shot when I had a strapless dress on, and it was on shipboard. I was leaning on the railing and my hair was high. In the rushes I was looking at this, and before I realized it, I said, "Oh, isn't that lovely," and then I realized what the dress did for my neck. I started then to stop wearing high collars and disguises with my clothes trying to cover my neck. Katharine Hepburn does the same thing. She tries to cover it all up as well.

JK: On the subject of your self-image, would you tell me the story about Alice Faye?

LY: Which one?

JK: About when you discovered what she didn't like about herself.

LY: Oh. Yes. Well, now, Alice Faye is one of the most extraordinary girls, she has always fascinated me. Alice Faye, in the parts that she played, had a wonderful talent. She was warm, she was real, she sang beautifully and was beautiful to look at, and she *loathed* working in movies. She hated to walk on the set. One day I went into the wardrobe for a fitting, and a darling man, David Levy, who ran the wardrobe, came out and said, "Would you mind waiting for a minute? Alice Faye is in here and she's upset, so we'll be a little late for your fitting." And after another minute or two he came out again and said, "Loretta, would you mind going in to see Alice, because she's crying." I said, "No, what's the matter?" He said, "Oh, she's always upset at fittings because her bosoms are so large." Well, little flat-chested me, I looked up at him and said, "She's *crying*? Why? Here I am, stuffing Kleenex inside my . . . and this girl with the big . . ." I couldn't believe it. I thought he was kidding me. He said, "No, she's very sensitive." So I went in and after a few minutes I said something about envying her. And she burst out crying all over again. Now, here was a girl, her body was one of the most beautiful things about her. And she hated it. The minute she got married to the man she wanted, she left the business. And I went to a party fifteen years later . . . it was at Ciro's before the Strip went honky-tonk . . . and a lot of big stars were there, and when people were being introduced to take a bow, she got the biggest ovation of all.

JK: One has to be very strong to survive in this business. The term "gutsy broad" certainly is not one that could ever have been applied to you. And yet, to have survived this long, you really must have been a very strong lady.

LY: Well, I would like to think of myself as a gutsy broad, but, in all honesty, I can't think of myself that way. I do have an ambition to do something with this talent that I have been given, and I want to put it to good use. So it does take tenacity, or guts, or fortitude, or stubbornness, or perseverance. You can use all sorts of fancy words for it. Yes, I have survived, and I think without too many scars on my personality. Perhaps on my career . . . I don't know.

JK: Still, growing up at that period, becoming one of the rising top stars, plus all the attractive leading men, plus making a marvelous salary; wasn't it a glamorous time for you?

LY: Oh, very. I loved every new dress I got. But I lived in two worlds. And I could indulge myself in this fantasy world because I had this solid world right behind me. I remember one time I came home and I was crabbing about something, and my sister Sally said, "Oh, you ought to be so glad you have a contract. I'd give anything to have that part in *Suez*. And here you are crabbing about it." So it chopped me right down.

JK: Was there any competition between you and your sisters?

LY: Apparently there was, but I never knew it. Because it was from Sally [Blane]. Polly Ann [Young] was never very ambitious. She didn't kind of understand it or like it or anything. And the minute she got married, she was delighted to get rid of the acting. But Sally, I think, loved the people more than the acting. Sally would be more concerned with the electrician's wife who was ill than she would be about learning her dialogue. Everyone who ever knew her would say, "Oh, Sally . . ." Because she was . . . still is . . . a wonderful, warm, generous mother. But this little incident was the first time I was conscious that Sally had any feeling about my getting parts that she would have given her eyetooth for. And she would say, "How can you sit there and say it isn't right, when it's something I would give my eyetooth for?" And I learned then how to respect privacy.

JK: You lived at home until you got married?

LY: Oh, always, yes. Of course. I mean, such a thing as taking an apartment, I mean, what for?

JK: Didn't this affect your private life a bit?

LY (pause): We wanted it that way. It gave us protection. We could have all the romance without any of the heartache.

JK: Sally didn't call herself Young; she called herself Blane. She had a fairly good career, but nothing approaching the way yours just rolled along.

LY: Sally, I can only repeat, was not primarily interested in the acting itself. I don't think she ever wanted to be a big star. Sally always had more beaux than anyone in our family. She was interested in the people that surrounded her. I was not. I was fascinated by the idea that I could be somebody else. A woman is inclined to play roles all the time anyway, and to make love to a lot of different men, and the moment they say "Cut" . . . no responsibilities. I was always, I think, a little bit in love with every leading man I ever worked with. I hope they felt the same way.

JK: Initially, you had photos taken by whoever was on the set, but later you became so important that you could not only select but also *make* a new stills photographer.

LY: Yes, everybody did that. At MGM there were so many that the stars would just choose one. As I recall, I only did about two or three pictures at MGM, and I don't remember who did the photography. I suppose it was Clarence Bull. But Frank Powolny is the only one that I am conscious of spending any time with. I took him out of that candid stuff on the set and put him into the portrait gallery.

JK: Why? Because you liked the candids he did?

LY: No. Because I liked *him*. And he wanted a chance, and he was very sensitive and he did not barge in. I really didn't think he was going to make it, but I thought, "Well, it's only one afternoon, so what? Big waste." I said to the publicity department that I was going to do some portraits with Frank Powolny in the gallery, and they said fine. But I really did it because he had asked me three or four times and I'd said, "One of these days, all right, Frank?" And finally I said, "Just take a look at all those Hurrell things . . . that's what I like to look like." And so I went in and then he brought me the stills. I don't remember whether I was at the studio or at home or what, but these were marvelous. He was really a good cameraman, but he had never had the opportunity. Everybody would shout out, "Okay, here it is, Frank, grab it!" But I went into the gallery and he had the light on . . . and the main portrait man was off for the day or had gone someplace. But I know, from then on, unless I went outside the studio to someone like Hurrell, Frank Powolny did all my portraits at Fox.

JK: So you preferred Hurrell?

LY: Oh, yes. What I liked about the way he photographed was the way he made you look so glamorous. And your skin looked so shiny. I know the secret with him . . . he was the first man who said that he didn't want any makeup. You used to put a little oil on your face and that was all. You could wear eye makeup if you wanted to, but no greasepaint or no pan stick or no pancake. It looked like you could touch it, it looked like skin. It didn't look like chalk. I remember when I started on the television series, I had the most awful time for the first two or three years, trying to get the makeup off the men. If I ever did a nun or something like that, no makeup at all. And they just died when I would walk on the set and I would say, "I'm sorry, this is the way I'm going to look." And of course it was marvelous because it was real skin, you could look at it, you could see it, it shone.

JK: You have said that the stills sessions were part of the job. But what of the sessions you had to do with leading men?

LY: I had a little crush on every one of them. So those sittings were very pleasurable because you could pretend to be doing a lot of things and still you weren't doing anything, you were just doing your job and you weren't committing yourself to anything. But still you were having a very pleasurable, romantic, glamorous kind of flirtation, I guess you could call it.

JK: But with those more romantic shots, the real close close-ups, did it become a very kind of erotic relationship?

LY: "Erotic" to me is the wrong word. But surely a very sort of romantic, imaginative and mysterious, glamorous feeling. Most actresses, at least in my day, we all thought we were gorgeous because by the time they finished with us we *were* gorgeous. I heard Bette Davis say one time . . . she was on television and she said, "I never could stand my face." And I thought, gosh, she was the most beautiful thing I ever saw in *Jezebel* and in *Dark Victory* and *The Letter*. She was gorgeous. And then she looked at Johnny Carson and said, "However, when I see my movies today, I *was* gorgeous!" And she was, she was. At those times when you were working with a still cameraman, you could almost tell by their pleasure: "Oh, I love it, oh, it's marvelous, oh, it's great, just hold that." But it was not done the way that you see in *Blow-Up*, not done that way at all. There was not one iota of embarrassment or suggestiveness or lewdness or sex. That would have turned us off—turned *me* off, anyway. It was pure romanticism and what I thought was beauty. Oh, they just thought I was too good to be true, and they wouldn't hardly touch me because I might break. And that's the feeling I remember with most of the cameramen I worked with; in fact, I don't remember anyone ever treating me any way differently. As you get more experienced in your work, you're willing to try more things than you were when you weren't quite so sure of yourself. It's all experimental, it's all kind of inventive so that it is really testing yourself all the time.

The most difficult kind of picture for me to take is something looking into the camera. Because in motion pictures you are trained never to look into the camera. Never. And suddenly you are doing something that is actually against all rules. So the only way I got around that was by trying to pretend that the camera was somebody. To look at somebody instead of that black hole. I know that when I first started television, it took me, oh, sometimes fifteen takes when I first started, to walk into the room and close the door and walk down to the camera and look right into it and say "Hello" without looking either silly or stiff or unnatural. Because I knew what I was when I was playing a part because I knew the part, but I didn't know me. And I didn't know really how to behave like me if there was a camera around.

You see a lot of actors who never see their rushes, and I never understood that, because to me that was my homework. You not only learned what *not* to do, but you also learned what *to* do, how to concentrate. I think that is probably why I liked television better than I liked movies, because I could do more, and it was more constant. The most movies I did was seven or eight a year, and in television in the first two years I did thirty-eight half-hour movies each year. Well, you get an awful lot of practice that way. I felt that if I got ten out of thirty that were good, that was good enough. When you give yourself that kind of leeway, you get more than ten because there is a looseness and an ease about it. You're not uptight and tense about everything. You try things that if you only had two chances a year, which was all I ever had in the last high points of my film career, you wouldn't. And you had to be more careful when you are only doing two rather than eight, and so much more careful than if you're doing thirty-eight. Your chances increase as do your productions. Not only that, because what it does is like practicing on a piano . . . the more you practice, the more pieces you learn, the more facile you become with it, and everything is easier. And so it was that by the time I finished the television show, I think I had begun to learn how to act!

I remember when I was four years old: I just loved going to the studios, and the director would say, "All right, now, who can cry?" "I can! I can!" Or "Who can laugh?" "I can! I can!" Whether I could or not. One time I was supposed to be crying in a picture with Fannie Ward,* she was a big star. I was on an operating table, and I was supposed to be crying. That's about all I can remember, I must have been about four. Colleen, my cousin, was supposed to do it, but she suddenly said, "No, I don't wanna." For no reason. So the director, George Melford, said to me, "Well, Gretchen, do you think you can do it?" I said, "Yes, I can do it." He said, "Well, you have to cry." I said, "That's all right." He said, "Right, then, cry for me." And I went, "Uh, uh, huh, huh, unh." And he said, "No. No, no, I mean *cry,* real tears. Can you do that?" And I said, ". . . yes." Well, I knew I could cry. But I couldn't. So my uncle said, "Come here, Gretchen." And he took me by the hand and he

---

*Fannie Ward was a stage actress, remembered today for her appearance in the 1915 DeMille film *The Cheat.* Her great claim to fame then was that she was very old, but photographed young enough to play ingenues. She "made" plastic surgery fashionable.

ran me around and around and around the set, and my legs were just flying, and I got all out of breath, and he put me down and he [she claps her hands together quite loudly] did that, right in front of my face. And he said, "Now cry." And I began sobbing and these big tears came down my face. I have used that technique of working on children. I did a series called *Christine's Children** and I had seven little children, and every time I wanted one of them to cry, I remember I did it to this one little girl, and I'd run her around the set and then smack . . . not hit her, but right in front of her face so that it would scare her. You see, a child . . . well, an actress, anyway, goes with that. They don't resent it. They know what you're doing and it just excites them enough and then they are so thrilled that they can cry that they work right along with you. And, you see, after my uncle did it to me, he bought me an ice-cream soda. Of course, I did the same thing every time I wanted this little kid to cry. After she'd do the scene, I'd rock her for about half an hour, then I'd give her an ice-cream soda or cone or a piece of candy, take her in my dressing room, play her some pretty music and she'd go to sleep. Because any crying scene, whether it's a child or a grownup, is exhausting, and you should always try to have a little rest afterwards or you'll just fall asleep anyway. I spent a lot of time napping on the set, because after you play a scene where you cry hard, you are physically exhausted and if you don't rest or sleep, you're no good for the rest of the day. You've no energy. So that and a little candy and some tea would do a lot to bring me back up again.

JK: And nobody ever gave you any advice? You never went home and said, "How am I going to do this?"

LY: Well, I never wrestled with acting that way. And I know I missed something along the way, because Method actors who are so marvelous . . . I mean, look at Joanne Woodward or Meryl Streep. I really think that woman is f-a-n-t-a-s-t-i-c. I don't know how she does it. Maybe if we'd had that Method and we'd studied it, maybe I could be that way too. But I didn't think it was that involved. Nowadays it is. One of the reasons Bette Davis was so marvelous is because she *was* that involved. And she liked parts that were that involved. When you're playing Berengaria [in *The Crusades*] or Ramona [in *Ramona*], they're kind of straight-line roles. It wasn't until I got into the television stuff that I found the excitement of doing roles that had five, six, seven different facets going at the same time.

JK: But you saw it quite rightly as work. Did you ever see any of it as art?

LY: No. No. I saw it all as romantic and I wanted, I think . . . I was never for what you would call ugly realism. I wanted to make . . . I remember *A Man's Castle* with Spencer. That film was special for me for many reasons: because of [director Frank] Borzage; because of Spencer; because of the kind of

* Actually called *The New Loretta Young Show*.

part. . . . The story was that we lived in a hobo town in this kind of paper house. What my character wanted more than anything else was a stove so she could cook him some decent meals. And it was supposed to be dirty and grubby, but it wasn't. My whole thing was to romanticize everything and make it a little bit more appealing and a little prettier, a little more palatable. Today they want it as revolting as they can get it, and shocking and destructive and ugly. Gosh, I look at some of the men and the women on the screen today, and you can see every pore on their face, every pockmark, every little broken blood vessel in their eye, and I can't look at it. I don't want to be that close to anybody. It's offensive to me. I don't say whether that is right or wrong, I'm just saying how it affects me. But as for art . . . no, I don't know how to say this, but I'm not a connoisseur of art in any form.

There are a lot of things that give me a great deal of pleasure just to look at. Quite often that will be a painting, or a person, or a child or a poem. I think one of the sweetest things is that picture of that little girl, and it says: "Children are people who pass through our lives and disappear into adulthood." To me, that is just beautiful because so many times I have looked at pictures of my kids and said, "Where is that . . . where has he gone?" And, no matter how you look, you can't find him because he's grown into another person. It may be that it's a better person. But where has that child gone? To me, I know it sounds silly, but that is art. When you say an art form, movies must be an art form because they do stimulate a feeling. Good, bad or indifferent, but they do stimulate you. *Gone With the Wind,* for example . . . there are shots in that which are just thrilling. That one still picture of Vivien Leigh when Clark Gable is just leaning down to kiss her is absolutely the most beautiful thing! It's thrilling to me just to look at the outline of her profile and the way he's leaning over her and her neck. But there's a lot of hogwash—actors particularly—"Oooh, this art form. . . ." I just say, "Oh, shut up." It's just a lot of hogwash.

JK: On a film, would you be involved in preproduction?

LY: No. We always made screen tests of all the clothes . . . I always did, anyway. And I was always very glad to. Because it was like a dress rehearsal. But the only preproduction I had was a couple of days on testing. There was no rehearsal time. When you weren't on the set, you rehearsed the next scene, then they shot that scene. And you're supposed to know the dialogue and everything else. But you didn't have two weeks' rehearsal. I did that on one picture called *Cause for Alarm.* And I just loved the idea of knowing just what you were going to do and how you were going to do it before you were pressed to the point of it. And when we did that picture, it came in I don't know how many thousands of dollars under budget. I didn't get any money for it, because I had given them ten weeks for the picture and it didn't take ten weeks. But all the technicians worked on full salary. And I know when I worked on my TV show, we used to rehearse two days and shoot for three days. And everybody got their full salary on that because you had to.

JK: If you look at old movies of yourself, you just see a woman who was doing her job, right?

LY: Yes. That's the only thing the actor sells. It's what effect you have, and the effect that you have is not only acting but it's also your looks. I can give you a perfect example . . . Montgomery Clift. Before his accident when his face was all destroyed, he was considered one of the most attractive, marvelous actors, one of the greats, because his face was so gorgeous and so romantic, and everything he did, if you just looked at him, oh, you just died! Then he had the accident. Now, he was the same actor, saying the same dialogue exactly as before, but now you just thought, What is he doing? So it isn't just the looks and it isn't just acting. It's a combination of your looks and your attitudes and the words and everything about you. You see, I think you have to have an idea of what your character looks like; I always did, even before I saw the sketches. So when they showed me sketches, I'd say, "No, that's not it, that's not it." I knew what I was looking for. I remember one picture we did on the TV show. It was called *Big Jim,* and my character was a prostitute in Chicago, a good-hearted prostitute. It was a true story. She had a baby, and she left town because she didn't want the son to grow up and find out what his mother was. She left him with friends and came back when he was fourteen or fifteen years old, just wanting to take a look at him, not wanting him to know who she was. And I knew what I wanted her to look like, so I went over to 20th Century–Fox and I said I wanted Marilyn Monroe's outfit . . . from any of her pictures. The one I got was a very tight little suit with a little peplum on it. Everything was just a little too tight every place, trying too hard; and instead of gloves, it was net gloves. And the minute I saw that dress, I knew how I wanted to play the part, I knew everything about it. This woman was a great big piece of protoplasm floating around. She wanted everybody to like her, but nobody to know her. So it was all on the outside. Just don't get too near. And very nervous. Couldn't look anybody in the face. So that the look of something, I have always felt, is 80 percent of it. So when you're selling yourself, well, most people thought of me for a long time as a clotheshorse. Period.

JK: And you could get that information from the script?

LY: Yes. And if it isn't in the script, then you had better make up something. There was a schoolteacher that I played one time, and I knew all I needed was a nose that was too big for my face. Not grotesque. I walked onto the set and the director said, "What have you done to yourself?" He didn't know what it was, but it was a nose that wasn't shaped like mine. Mine is kind of cut off here, and this was just sort of elongated and the nostril went down instead of up. I can't tell you what it did to my face . . . put my eyes closer together, made the lip shorter, just threw everything out of proportion. She had to say, "Look at me. Do you think that any man could fall in love with me?" And you had to believe that they couldn't. So when you read a story like that, the look is the important thing.

JK: Well, then, if you got a film script and you wanted to change something, what did you do?

LY: Oh, no, I didn't change anything. There was one thing: I was doing a scene with [Henry] Wilcoxon for *The Crusades* [Paramount, 1935] and he said his line of dialogue, and I was busy looking at him, being in love with him, and I didn't answer right away. And Wilcoxon said, "Forgot your dialogue, huh?" And I looked at him, I was so surprised. I said, "No, I was acting." And he said, "Oh! Oh!" I wasn't acting fast enough for Henry! And I had that once with a new director on the TV show. It was a breakfast scene. The director was Richard Donner, the first show he directed for us. I sat down at the table, my "husband" was there, and I poured a cup of coffee. I went, "Oooh! Oooh!" And he yelled, "Cut! Did you burn your mouth?" And I said, "No, I was acting." He said, "My God. I'll never cut on you again." And he never did. Because he didn't know when I was acting and when I wasn't. I'm not stage-trained, you know. Too much rehearsing and I got stale. We discovered on my show that I shot my bolt on long shots. The first master shot. So very quickly I learned to do the master shot on my close-up. Once you get technically set, marked and lit, then, when the camera rolls, the adrenaline starts and that is when you create. That is when something good happens, or whatever. The reason we liked a close-up on me, because we worked very fast on TV, was because I couldn't remember what I did and couldn't do it again.

   I depended on clothes to help me with the character a lot. I loved clothes. I knew I wasn't a Bette Davis. I wished I had been because I was wild about her. But I wasn't. And I knew I wasn't Lucille Ball or whoever the comedienne was. I wasn't that.

JK: How do you view that industry which you were a part of, which made you a household word?

LY: I have found it heartbreaking and fascinating and tragic and despairing and rotten . . . all of these things. But that's what life is. All of these things. It depends on how we cope with them. I went to a most interesting dinner and it was a tribute to Jack Warner. They ran some film clips of the thousands of pictures that have been made at Warners. If they hadn't shown this film, I don't think most of the 1500 people there would have had any idea of what this man meant to this industry. Because everybody fought with him all the time. I never did, I must say, when I was there, because I wasn't in a fighting mood in those days. But you live and learn in any business. Anyway, this dinner was very thrilling. Ronnie Reagan, who is now [1971] our governor, Bette Davis, Edward G. Robinson, all these big stars were there, but it was also a sad thing in a way, because for the first time I realized, "That was it." I mean the big ones. Like Mayer, Goldwyn, the Warner brothers, Zukor and Harry Cohn. For the motion-picture actor at that time, it was the greatest that ever happened. Because they made stars. If you weren't any good, they put you into enough pictures and brainwashed people into thinking you were.

JK: Why did you leave Jack Warner to go with Zanuck? Did he offer you a better deal?

LY: I left Warners, but I didn't leave to go with Zanuck. In fact, Warners dropped me. They didn't want to pay me my $50-a-week raise, or whatever it was. And they said they would keep me on if I would go on at the same salary for another year. Just on general principles, I said no. So I left. And I did one picture in between. I think it was *A Man's Castle*. It was one of the best pictures I ever made, with Spencer Tracy. I did it for Columbia. Now, in the meantime Zanuck had left and he offered me a contract, and I remember saying to him, "All right, I'll sign with you, but there are two things that must be written into the contract. I do not want to play a lead to George Arliss. I don't want to be a leading lady anymore, I want star parts. And I must have a vacation of three weeks every single solitary year." I mean, by this time they had just beaten me into a pulp. "Oh," he said, "that's marvelous. Anything you like." I said, *"In the contract."* "Well, I can't put it in the contract," he said, "because if I put it in *your* contract, then I'll have to put it in everybody's contract." So, like the dodo that I was, I said, "All right," and he said, "You can believe me." So I signed the contract, and the first thing I did was *House of Rothschild* with George Arliss, and it was two years before I walked out and said, "I'm going on vacation." And do you know he took me off salary? But it doesn't mean anything. He was a hard taskmaster, but he was very good for me. Because, whether they're right or wrong, I have to think that they're right. And it took me seven years to work out my contract. I was very honest about it, and so was he. Mr. [Nicholas] Schenck was head of the studio at the time, and he called us in and said, "Loretta, I just don't understand it. This is a $7 million contract we're offering," and I said, "I know, but I can't work with Darryl because he doesn't know anything about women. Every woman is just a leading lady to someone." You see, a producer like Irving Thalberg was a woman's producer. Zanuck was great in his way, but not in *my* way! After I left the studio, I won an Academy Award and I was very happy.

JK: Was it a deliberate thing to put you into movies like *Ladies in Love,* which had you and Janet Gaynor, Constance Bennett . . .

LY: That was discipline. Oh, he said to me one time, "If you don't behave yourself, I'm going to send you to Western Avenue." Now, Western Avenue was where Sol Wurtzel made his pictures, and I'd just made a most marvelous picture at Western Avenue,* which was *Ramona*. And I said to Darryl before I got halfway out the door, "Let me tell you one thing: I've only done one decent picture on the Fox lot, and that was at the Western Avenue lot." *Ra-*

---

* 20th Century–Fox was making films at two places in Los Angeles, and Western Avenue was one of them.

mona was one of their biggest money-makers back then too. But I had to beg for that. Heavens, how I had to beg for it!

JK: A lot of actresses fought for dramatic roles. Bette Davis and Joan Crawford had to fight to reestablish their careers. For your own satisfaction, have those big dramatic roles never fascinated you?

LY: No, no. Not at all.

JK: You didn't think you were missing the great roles?

LY: Never, never. You see, when I got an Academy Award, it was for a silly thing called *The Farmer's Daughter*. And that year I was up against Susan Hayward for *Smash-up* and Rosalind Russell for *Mourning Becomes Electra*. That's a pretty gutsy role. And I think Joan Crawford was up that year, yes, for *Possessed,* which was also a very gutsy role. Have I counted five of us? All right. I personally voted for Susan Hayward, because I was absolutely stunned by this performance, and when I saw it, I knew I couldn't do it as well. I knew that woman had done that part magnificently. And I voted for her because I think she deserved it. But I got that award playing a straightforward, honest, factual, good girl.

JK: It hadn't even been intended for you. Wasn't it meant for Ingrid Bergman?

LY: Yes. You see, when it was brought to me, I said, "Fine, but I don't have a Swedish accent." And the producer said, "But don't you think you could learn one?" I said, "Well, I could try." And he said great. I asked why he wanted me, and he said, "Because I think you're excellent for the part." I asked if it hadn't been written for Ingrid. He said, "Yes, but Ingrid doesn't want to do it. Why don't you take six weeks, try to learn the accent, and if you still don't want the part, I'll go to someone else." So he sent me to a marvelous woman, Ruth Roberts, who's been with me ever since, as a matter of fact. She took the Swedish accent away from Ingrid and gave it to me. That's the only time I have had a coach of any kind. Oh, no, that isn't true. On *The Devil to Pay* [1931] with Ronald Colman, there was an Englishman there to teach me an English accent. But that was the only other time. I did my next picture without Ruth, but after that I had her on everything. And when I started the television show, she was there right from the beginning. She was my associate producer. Ruth was that important to me. She could stand off and could watch me. But she would never butt in. She would whisper to me. I had that nun's habit on for one show, and she whispered, "You're so kittenish. You're a Mother Superior, but you're a woman too." That was her kind of direction and it always worked.

Well, anyway, I worked on the Swedish accent with Ruth, and for four weeks I didn't get it. But one day I said, "Oh, I've got it!" So I told the producer that I'd love to play the part. I remember in the middle of the picture the director came to me and said, "I've been thinking. This girl has been going to school for about three months and I think we have to drop the accent." I asked why. He said, "I think it might become annoying to the audience. It's not that the accent is bad, but I think the whole picture with that accent . . . it might become annoying." I said, "I don't think I can agree with that. I don't think three months at night school would be enough for her to lose her Swedish accent." And he said, "Well, I think that's a dramatic value we can take advantage of." Well, I couldn't. I told him that if he wanted to start the whole picture over again, I'd do it without an accent, but I would not drop it in the middle. We argued for two days about that. Finally, the producer, Dore Schary, said, "Loretta, couldn't you give in just a little bit?" I said that I couldn't. And off we went arguing for two more days. Finally, we went ahead with it, and I must say that the night of the Academy Awards, Henry Potter, the director, was the first one to throw his arms around me and say, "Oh, my God, how right you were!" How did I get started on that . . . ? Oh, yes, well, now for me that was fighting for a role, only it was for the integrity of a role I had already accepted.

Now, I had a good lesson that I learned. Bette Davis never liked to do her movies as radio plays. She was bored with them. So one time I needed some extra money for some priest friends of mine to do some missionary work. I didn't have it, so I told them that if I could get a radio show which paid $5000, I would give it to them. I told them to get down and pray, and then I called the office. It so happened that Bette Davis had been rehearsing to do *Jezebel* for a radio play, and that afternoon she had walked out, saying she was bored with it. So they asked me if I would like to do it. I said, "Oh, *Jezebel*! Oh, marvelous, marvelous!" And I ran down and did the thing, and I was marvelous in it . . . or so I thought. Six years later they made a record of it, from the tape of the show I did, and they sent me a copy. My kids put it on and I listened to it and thought to myself, Oh, my God, that's just a bad imitation of Bette Davis. Oh, I was a terrible copycat.

JK: Did you have much choice in the movie roles you did, or were you assigned to them?

LY: Most of them I was assigned to. I chose *Man's Castle* and Frank Capra's *Platinum Blonde* with Jean Harlow, and of course I fought to get *Ramona*. But usually they just said, "Go there, do that," and that was it if you were under contract. I remember, one time I was sent on loan-out to MGM for a film I really hated. Actually, it had been written for Jean Harlow. Carole Lombard finally did it—*The Gay Bride* [1934]—and I told Mr. Zanuck that I didn't think I could do it, she was a gal, a dame, a gutsy broad. He said, "I've already loaned you out, it's up to them." At MGM the director, Sam Wood, said, "Oh, Loretta, I think you'll be marvelous in it. Just make a test and we'll see." So I did, and that one isolated scene was very good. So he told me how wonderful I was. So I went to Eddie Mannix and said, "Eddie, I can't play this part. I don't like it. I hate it. I don't want to build my career on it." And he said, "I'm sorry, Loretta, but the only person who can get you out of it is Mr. Mayer." I went right up to Mr. Mayer's office and waited a couple of hours before I finally got in to see him. I said, "Now, Mr. Mayer, if your daughters Edie or Irene were actresses, would you want them to play this part?" I didn't know that I was hitting so close to home. He said, "No, I wouldn't, and you don't have to play the part if you don't want to." And he never held it against me. He said, "Little girl, you know what you're doing. Just keep doing it that same way." So the only time I had to deal with him, he was courteous, considerate . . . Maybe I didn't appeal to him, I don't know. But I didn't play it.

JK: So much for Mayer. What about Harry Cohn?

LY: There was one particular incident where I was wrong and he was right, although we ended up not speaking for four years. I respected him, but he told me that he had a crush on me. For a long time. But he never presumed anything. He never even sent me flowers. But I had been blackballed for nine months when I left Fox. See, the studio heads would get together over a game of poker and say, "Well, you're not interested in Loretta Young, are you?" and the other producer would say, "I guess not if you say not." When you were with a studio, you would get maybe four or five scripts coming in at a time. When you leave, *nothing*. Finally, one of the little leg men for Myron Selznick, who was my agent, said, "Loretta's been blackballed." So we had a meeting and Myron told me that he was going to get me $100,000 because money talks in this town. I told him that I wasn't interested in money, I wanted good parts, I was sick of my being Mrs. Alexander Graham Bell.

He told me that he would cut my salary so that a producer with the right property wouldn't be able to resist, and I just told him, "You do the work and I'll say the prayers." In a couple of weeks he came to me and said, "Read this script. It was written for Cary Grant and Irene Dunne, but they can't do it. A young man called Alexander Hall is directing, and it's called *The Doctor Takes a Wife*." It was a light little comedy which was all right, the woman's part was equal to the man's, so I said, "Okay, I'll do it." Myron said to Harry Cohn, "If you can get Ray Milland, I can deliver Loretta Young." We did it and the blackball was broken. And I just went on from there, very nicely.* But it was always something with the studio heads.

I know with Zanuck they had offered me *Mother Is a Freshman*—that was about nine years after I left him—and I said, "I don't particularly care about that, but you do have a story on the shelf that I would love to do. It's called *Come to the Stable*." They told me that they didn't want to make it because it was a religious story. But I kept on about it, and finally they said, "Okay, we'll do *Come to the Stable* if you'll do *Mother Is a Freshman* first." But I still didn't want to, so Myron said to me, "You silly little thing, they're

---

*Loretta was one of the highest-priced and busiest freelance stars of the 1940s.

offering you two pictures instead of one. And you have okay of the scripts and directors. What more do you want?" I said, "I want roses in my dressing room." Darryl had never sent me any flowers in all the years I'd been with him. So I got my roses and they got their two pictures. Both pictures were most successful. I'm happy to say that *Come to the Stable* was more successful, and it still is. They play it every year on TV.

JK: Did you ever have to test for a picture?

LY: I only made three tests. Two of them I did not get, and the other one I did. They were the only three. The two I didn't get were *Rebecca* . . . the other was *Berkeley Square,* which Heather Angel got . . . it was with Leslie Howard and it didn't turn out too well. I don't know why I didn't get that one, because I was marvelous in the test, and it was for my studio. Instead of that, I did a funny little picture at Metro called *Midnight Mary,* which turned out to be a very good little movie. Well, the one I tested for and *got* was *Laugh Clown Laugh* [with Lon Chaney in 1928], and I think I was one of sixty girls. I got it and I didn't want it. I was scared to death of the director. I was on loan to Metro for that. There I was, loaned out to test for a picture I didn't want to do, and I got it. Oh, goodness, I had a terrible time with that one, but we won't go into that.

JK: Why not?

LY: Well . . .

JK: Was Lon Chaney the problem?

LY: Oh, Lord, no. No. Okay, I'll tell you, it was the director, Herbert Brenon. He was the first director I ever worked with where I had a leading role, and he picked up a chair and threw it at me. If it had hit me, it would have killed me. I was thirteen or fourteen, and at lunch he'd put me up in front of everybody and for half an hour he bawled me out. "What makes you think you're an actress? What makes you think you'll ever be an actress? You are nothing. You are skinny. You have knock knees. You have to wear pads all over you. You have buck teeth. You can't do anything." Why he did this, I don't know. But he did it every single day. I *would not cry.* Somebody had told me that he didn't like crybabies. This went on for at least two weeks, and we were seven months on that picture. I, of course, was getting an ulcer. Each morning I would say, "I don't want to go to work." So Mother would call and say, "Gretchen is not coming to work today." Sure enough, the studio would send the assistant director in a car, and he'd get hold of me and take me in to work. Until Lon Chaney caught on, and he, the director, wouldn't do it if Chaney was on the set. So Chaney wouldn't leave the set while I was there. And when I finished that picture, I remember thinking that I would never, never let anyone do that to me again. I had just been a patsy for this man. Apparently his reputation was that he had a patsy on every picture he did. Before this film he had had a smash success directing Betty Bronson in *Peter Pan,* and afterward he did *Beau Geste.* When we finished *Laugh Clown Laugh,* he said to me, "Well, Gretchen, I know I've given you a hard time, but I wanted a performance out of you." Well, he got a performance out of me . . . in spite of it! Not because of it. And only because of Lon Chaney. I would have cracked up before the picture was finished if it hadn't been for Chaney. And I learned later that the director had himself once been in a sanatorium with a nervous breakdown, so . . .

I didn't wait for the studios to allow me anything. They said we weren't allowed to see rushes, but I made such a nuisance of myself about seeing them that they had to let me. As for the stills, you see, whoever is behind the camera is looking at you constantly. And if they don't like you or you don't like them, it's very difficult to work with them because you get embarrassed. He's looking at you behind a lens and everything is magnified. Ed Cronjager was the cameraman for *Alexander Graham Bell,** and I must say he did a beautiful job on it. But he used the most foul language I had ever heard, and I can't tell you how much it offended me. I didn't like him, and I'd be perfectly fine until he'd stand there and start lighting me, then I'd get miffed. I was playing Bell's wife, a deaf woman, and it was a very sensitive role. It had to be—I mean, she read lips and watched every single little movement. It was difficult because I felt that Cronjager was dissecting me all the time. And I thought his foul language was completely disrespectful to me and every other woman on the set. He probably didn't even think about it. I didn't have the sense to say, "Would you mind not . . ." I think that's where the "swear box" idea started with me, because I finally had to find some way of mentioning it without it sounding cornball. It turned into a gag and it really did stop all of it. But I learned to stand up for myself early on because I learned that if I didn't, nobody else would do it for me. You want something, you do it yourself. Now come on, we've talked enough. Let's eat.

1971

---

* The cameraman for *The Story of Alexander Graham Bell* was Leon Shamroy. Cronjager was the cameraman for Loretta Young's film *Wife, Doctor and Nurse* (1937).

ANN
SHERIDAN

S HE WAS BORN IN DENTON, TEXAS, on February 21, 1915, and her Christian name was Clara Lou Sheridan. The Ann and the "oomph" were to come later. Clara Lou was attending a teachers' college when she went in for a local beauty contest sponsored by the Paramount Picture Corporation. The reason they gave was the making of a film to be entitled *Search for Beauty* (1934) starring Ida Lupino, but their aim was not so much finding new stars in the sticks as in getting free publicity for the company and their product. Thus the contest was being carried out around the world, wherever there were Paramount branches and Paramount pictures. The previous year they had sponsored a similar promotion stunt to find "The Panther Girl" for their version of H. G. Wells' *Island of Lost Souls* (1933). That had proved highly successful and incidentally they found some very nice girls—like Kathleen Burke (who played the part) as well as Grace Bradley, Gertrude Michael and Gail Patrick, popular leading ladies of the decade. But lightning failed to strike with the same force the second time. Of the thirty-three young men and women who went from the local "Search for Beauty" contests and won a trip to Hollywood (where the finals to select six of them for studio contracts would be held), Clara Lou, whose sister Kitty sent her photo in to the *Dallas News* without telling her, was the only one to become a star. But this was not overnight and it was not at Paramount.

I met her in April of 1966 in New York. That year I discovered TV was made for showing old movies, and that these could be seen all day long and all night too. And then there were the popular daytime serials everybody was watching and which we called "soapies," a term of derisory endearment for those tear-stained "to be continued" serials. And everybody was doing them— Dana Andrews was in one, Gary Merrill in another, Joan Bennett too, and an actress one couldn't help but like, Ann Sheridan, in something called *Another World*. It was no different from the other soapies, and no better. What made it a must was Ann Sheridan. The face had edged where once it curved—for "oomph" there was "chic"—but an alertness about her acting made you sit up, an intelligence at work made her role believable, and though she had changed from the glamorous pinup, she looked very handsome. It was the sort of role in the sort of story she had been fighting against when she was young, as she was the first to admit, but she had changed a lot in the years, and one of her attitudes now was that it was better to work than to sit around, that it was up to you to make what you did good. After only a few weeks there came a call from a major TV network to sign her for the lead in a new TV Western comedy series, *Pistols and Petticoats*.

As it happened, having seen her in the series on TV hadn't really prepared me for her in person. Added to that, I had in my mind an image of fur coats, cigarette-holders and stunning glamour. I wasn't wearing my glasses, and some people behind me were trying to get past. When I was about to search for a *maître d'hôtel* for help, a dark, richly resonant voice coming from just below said, "Are you looking for me, dear?" I looked down and there was this woman with gaunt face, unfashionable gray in the red hair, tired eyes, and neither wearing fur nor doused in "oomph." I did a double-take, as ungallant as only someone completely surprised can be, and as if by remote control I said, "Miss Sheridan. What a pleasure. You haven't changed." At that moment she must have wondered whether or not she should tell me to disappear. Then she smiled and looked at me very kindly and said, "I know, darling. I know." I loved her. In that voice was everything my eyes remembered. There was unpretentiousness, and wit and kindness (two things that don't always go together) and an outreaching friendliness that put one at ease.

I kept on and on about Hollywood's glamour. What was it? Who had it? Why was it gone? Did she miss the old days? She was a glamour star of the '40s. She had worked with DeMille, Hawks, Cagney and—to my surprise— Mae West. But these names were like ikons to me. My knowledge of movies was barely above the level of the fan magazines—except that I liked slightly older fan magazines. But she answered, drank her drink, ordered another, smoked, and in our few and always warm meetings tried to tell me not to take everything at face value nor to feel disillusioned as a result of it. Her last appearance in a film had been in Metro's musical remake of *The Women—The Opposite Sex* (1957). Her part hadn't been in the original and she was the best thing in the remake. She filled in the rest:

AS: I will not work in anything that I don't like. Whether it's films, summer stock, road shows. I was in *Kind Sir* in summer stock for quite some time. I did that because Ross [Hunter] wanted me to get some stage experience and then we would do a Broadway musical of a film we'd done together—*Take Me to Town*. Nothing came of it in the end. Ross and I have been trying to work together ever since our Universal days. Then I was in another road show that was dreamed up in New York and was a lot of nonsense because they did nothing about rewriting it. For five months we toured around in this atrocity—a period of tryouts and tribulations. I don't want to do that sort of thing again. I was offered the old Roz Russell role in *Wonderful Town*, but, honey, you don't walk in where Miss Russell has been. You cannot improve on that.

Ann Sheridan, photographed by George Hurrell (Warner Bros.), 1939

Ross Hunter offered me a part in a film he was making, *The Art of Love,* but I didn't feel right for that. [Ethel Merman later played it. It was a madam in a French brothel.] All I want are parts that are right for my age. Something I feel I can play—like the character in this series. But I won't do just anything to have a job. A long time ago I learned not to take what was thrown at me. Mind you, the old days had compensations. Working on TV is just like the old Paramount days. As a stock girl I was doing B pictures, working like a fiend. But it was good.

I was a "Search for Beauty" girl. They're still searching, mind you. But this was 1933, and Paramount conducted this contest. I was one of those kids.

JK: But they discovered you!

AS: Well!

She drawls. I'm reminded that she comes from Texas. And she is looking very wry.

JK: Didn't they?

AS: I don't know. Did they? [She is laughing.] They fired me. I know that. I don't know if they discovered me or not. But they gave me an opportunity to go to Hollywood. I worked from 1933 to about mid-'35 at Paramount. Then I was fired. I didn't suffer—but it can get very dark before things begin to look up. But I'm a Texan, dear, and we Texans are proud. We don't give up without a fight, and I wasn't going to go home and admit I was licked. It's the Indian blood in me—Cherokee! That kept me fighting. But those beauty contests were hideous for kids. Just awful.

Sheridan was also part Scotch and part Irish. I don't recall the Scottish bit, but you heard the Irish bit every time she called you "darling"—dropping the *g* at the end.

AS: They gave a contract to about six of us out of the thirty or so they brought out, and the rest were broken-hearted. You know—they left their home towns—big fanfares, Hollywood, becoming stars—and now here they were, having to go back. I felt hideous when I won—I forget now who the others were, one was a South African, there was a man from Dallas, Texas, another one from Wisconsin and a girl from Scotland—two girls and four boys. Well, we were up till 2:00 a.m. in the studio gallery doing stills, and we walked back to the Roosevelt Hotel, where we were all lodged as part of the prize, and as we walked into the lobby, there were all the other kids. All of them losers. It was an awful feeling. Well, they didn't want to go home, honey, and the agreement the studio signed with the winners in each town was that they would get a trip to Hollywood and if they weren't picked, they were to be sent home. That was the contract. They dragged them to the train stations and put them on the trains, but then the kids would just get off in Podunk or somewhere and take another train back to Los Angeles and be outside the studio gate the next morning. Paramount had a dreadful time trying to get them to go back because it was their responsibility to ensure that they got back, but what could they do if they didn't want to go? Finally they paid a lot of the ones who wouldn't go home to sign a paper releasing the studio of any legal responsibility, and saying they had gone home and had come back on their own initiative.

Well, that put an end to those awful contests, I can tell you. The studios no longer took any responsibility for making sure that losers got home—just a return ticket and you could do what you want. That was such a terrible experience for them. They worked us very hard then—I didn't mind that. All those bits and extra work that I was shoved into taught me something. And of course this was the middle of the Depression and, though I didn't know it at the time, I was damn lucky to be making $50 a week. I was used doubling hands, somebody else's legs in close-ups, their feet—you name it—as long as it wasn't somebody's face, I was used to double everything on the lot. I got a few bit parts, a few lines here and there, not much—mind you, I did have a dreadful Texas accent. It was awful, just like syrup. It took me a long time, but I finally got rid of it. Once in a while it creeps back.

I remember I had a terrible experience with Mr. DeMille because of it.

She throws back her drink and her head and roars with laughter that makes the people at the other tables stop what they're doing, and look, and then return to their own conversation.

AS: Sheer heaven! I adored him! He was a bastard, of course [she adds in a mock-faced aside]. Forgive me. Shouldn't I have said that? A lot of people said after he died, "Oh, but I hated him." Now, *I* absolutely adored him. And I'll tell you why. He was making *The Crusades* [1935]—I was this little Christian, and I had to wear this awful long brown wig—which I thought was going to make me look glamorous, wonderful, like Dietrich. Well, I looked horrible. Like you always do with a wig. And I was a very pudgy kid, and this wig made me look even pudgier. So I felt very self-conscious. I was playing this Christian captured by the Saracens, and I was to be auctioned off wearing one of those dresses, just a lot of chiffon draped so they wouldn't think you were completely naked—and there's J. Carroll Naish playing the auctioneer with a whip in his hand and looking very oily, and he comes and pulls me by the wrist and yanks me to the buyer, and I have this one line to say to this nun, who is also being sold, "The cross, the cross. Let me kiss the cross." Very dramatic. Well! Honey! I had this Texas accent, and I said: "The cwouse, the cwouse. Let me kiss the cwouse." Mr. DeMille turned absolutely red with hysterics. He said, "Cut!" This was a rehearsal. He said to me, "Young lady, where are you from?"

I said, "Denton, Texas."

And he said, "What's your name?"

And I said, "Clara Lou Sheridan, sir."

And he said, and he's trying very hard not to laugh, "How do you say c-r-o-s-s?"

And I said, "Cwouse."

"Do you want to say that again?"

I couldn't hear anything wrong, and felt just terrible. So I said, "Cwouse" again.

He was gurgling. Absolutely gurgling at this. And he said, "Miss Sheridan. We're going to take a little respite now and have lunch, and you go with the drama coach here and she will coach you on this line." He couldn't stop giggling. I worked on that line for half an hour. It really didn't come out right in the end, but finally it was permissible for me to say, "The cross, the cross." Seventeen years later, at a St. Patrick's dinner in Omaha, Nebraska, where Mr. DeMille and I were guests, he stood up and told this story. I had forgotten all about it. I almost fell under the table. I never worked with him again, but he was absolutely dear to me that time.

It was hard work—long hours. I didn't mind the hard work then, I don't mind it now. That's what working and living is. That's the interest. You have to have interest in what you're doing and be willing to work hard. I get up at 4:00 in the morning to get ready and be in Brooklyn at 8:00 a.m. to do the soapies. These things I love. A discipline. It was the same on the coast. The calls at the studio were for 5:30—when you were working—so you had to be up at 4:00 to get there, and have your breakfast.

JK: What were some of the films you did at Paramount?

AS: You wouldn't know them, dear—and I wasn't in them, just my hands were or my feet. What year was *Diamond Lil*?

She meant *Belle of the Nineties,* which uses the same character Mae West had played in *She Done Him Wrong.*

JK: Were you in *Diamond Lil*?

AS: I was not in it at all, darling, I was on the set, sitting on the sidelines. None of us girls were in her films. When they were casting for one of Miss West's films, all of us stock girls were lined up in front of Miss West, and she'd saunter down the line and say, "Yes, dear. You look lovely. Now go over there and sit down." You never worked in a scene with her. She just wouldn't allow it. The directors had very little to do with her films, you know. Miss West said exactly what she wanted done. She got exactly what she wanted.

I remember her very distinctly, being escorted across the lot with her arm being held by this big guy who was her manager. She needed him for support because she was a tiny woman. Oh, very tiny, but she wore these platform shoes built up way high. She knew exactly what she was doing. There was always an entourage around her. After all, she was queen of all she surveyed.

JK: It must have been very difficult for you young girls to get ahead with the big star ladies keeping you down like that.

AS: Oh, Carole [Lombard] didn't have that thing at all. She was really a down-to-earth person. Very special. We all loved her. And Dietrich—I don't know about her. I wasn't on any of her films, but I shouldn't think that Miss Dietrich ever said, "Don't put so-and-so in a scene with me," or, "I don't want her in my film." Dietrich didn't worry about that. She didn't have to. You didn't look at anybody else in a scene she was in anyway. But, you see, Mae West came from the stage, and she knew what she wanted. She wrote her own things. It's not that somebody was going to take a scene away from her, because who notices an extra walking in the background anyway? It's merely that she wanted older women around her. She had a tremendous, tough, wonderful quality. I saw her the last time she was here, doing her act at Ciro's in the mid-'50s. Cary Grant said to go see her. He said everybody must see this woman, because she's the only one of her kind. And he's right. When she quits, there will never be another Mae West, and we'll be the poorer for it. I called together some friends to see her. It was typical Mae. And nobody else can do that. They haven't got it today. She looked like $10 million. And when you realized the age of that woman! It was absolutely incredible.

    Nobody took any interest in me at Paramount—certainly not in the front office. They changed my name to Ann at some stage because they said my name was too long for the marquee. There were some exceptions. Mitch Leisen was a director there and he gave me a bit in *Murder at the Vanities*— I did a sneeze in that and wore nothing, but he must have liked me because I got a small part in a movie he was directing which starred Sylvia Sidney— *Behold My Wife* [1935]. I was the society girl in love with Gene Raymond who commits suicide when he leaves her and marries the Indian girl. Mitch was responsible for going to the front office and saying, "Look, this kid has got something. Give her a chance." Committing suicide was the great thing, you know. Makes everybody look at you and think you're serious about your career. They always wanted you to be seen to be serious at Paramount. When they caught you laughing, the front office would say you weren't serious. Oh, dear! But nothing happened after that, dear. Nothing. As a matter of fact, I got fired.

Miss Sidney had also mentioned this film and her part in getting Ann Sheridan the role, and had said that the best thing about *Behold My Wife* was "a kid named Ann Sheridan."

AS: Those were very glamorous days then. I remember I was so tremendously impressed with these people. Lombard! Cooper! George Raft!

    Marlene Dietrich. The Queen. The Glamour Queen. Unapproachable. I never got to meet her at Paramount. Later on I met her socially, but I was never close to her at all at Paramount. She was a legend. Like Garbo. People had a certain look then. I know that in many instances the people were wrong for the parts they were playing, they weren't cast for acting. But it was accepted by the public. There was a certain kind of fantasy, a certain imagination that is not accepted now. The world is too small. Those were glamorous days. They were trying to build up those legends like Dietrich and Garbo then. And that's what they became. Dietrich still is a legend. To me she is absolutely fascinating.

JK: Even though you yourself were later exposed to this glamour processing?

AS: I guess so. I guess so. I never paid much attention to the glamour bit. You see, Dietrich *is* glamour! Like Garbo was, still is, glamour. There is a mystery to them—and I never had that, dear. I don't think any American personality or, for that matter, any British actress either had the glamour that is Dietrich and was Garbo. *I* certainly didn't have it. That was just a publicity stunt with me.

JK: How about Turner?

AS: No. Never. Never. That was a sweater you're talking about, darling—that's not glamour. None of us girls, Lana, Rita, Dorothy Lamour—we couldn't possibly touch it. We were all well-dressed, well-made-up motion-picture actresses. But we never had the mystery, the touch, these other women had. And never would.

   Bergman had a kind of glamour, I suppose. She's not . . . maybe the accent is part of it, because she's certainly not like the other two. I don't think anybody had quite their touch. The closest we got to it was with somebody like Joan Crawford. She still creates it. She works at it, and she looks like a million bucks when she goes out. She's a star, and don't you ever forget it! And I love her for it. Just love her. But that isn't me, dear. I'd rather be an actress. That's the only thing I ever wanted to be. A good actress. But I suppose I can't get away from that Ann Sheridan Oomph thing. I wish I could. But most people still come up to me and ask about that dumb—ohh, it's horrible.

JK: How'd it come about?

AS: Oh, it was built by the head of the publicity department when I was over at Warner Brothers. That was sometime in 1939. He had picked it up from a squib in Walter Winchell's column. Winchell had seen me in something or other, one of those four-line cleavage jobs—God knows what—and anyway he wrote, "There is this young Ann Sheridan and she's got an 'umphy' quality." He used to make up those words, you know. But there it was in print, and Bob Taplinger, who was head of the publicity department, was looking for something that would get the studio into the papers—to give it a little more publicity. Mr. Warner had probably been sitting in his barbershop chair reading a paper and not finding his name in it, and told the publicity department to get the studio some space. That was how these things worked, darling. So Bob changes the spelling to "Oomph" and organizes this dinner for the "Oomph Girl." They got George Hurrell to take sexy-looking photos of me—he didn't know what "oomph" was either, so he made me sit on a leopard-skin rug—and they had twelve photographs blown up large and hung all around the dining room. I believe Hedy Lamarr was one—the back of her head, of course. I can't remember the others that were in the photographs, but in all of them the girl was standing this way [she covers her face with her hands; pulls her hat over her face; screws it up]. They got photographs of women hiding behind yashmaks. God, you wouldn't believe it—it was all so funny, and there was this photo of me in the middle, sitting on a leopard skin. I was the only one whose face you could see in the photo. It was nothing but a setup. These thirteen hand-picked judges picked me as the most glamorous of all. Bob picked the men who were guests at the Oomph dinner—all Warner contract people like Orry-Kelly, Rudy Vallee, Earl Carroll and Busby Berkeley, who couldn't get out of it, and a free dinner for some journalists. But it snowballed on them. Me too. They didn't realize at the studio what was happening at all, because the next day Jack Kelly, a friend of mine working in the publicity department, caught Jack Warner on his way to lunch and said, "What do you think of this, Mr. Warner?" showing him the paper that said "OOMPH GIRL, OOMPH DINNER" and had used a picture of me and a list of who was there and so forth. Warner looked at it and said, "She'll be dead in six months." He didn't even know I was on the lot. But at least all that silly fuss gave me a chance to fight for better parts like the one in *King's Row* [1941].

Before then I had no parts worth remembering. Molls and nurses: just feminine leads, reactions. I did almost every B picture they made at Warner Brothers. I did some things on loan-out to Universal that were a bit better and where I said something besides "He went that-a-way." *Angels with Dirty Faces* was the first A picture I had on the Warner Brothers lot. You had to fight terribly hard to get a good part there. Even after.

That Oomph thing snowballed—but it gave me a tiny foot in the door. When people asked me what it meant, I told them that it always reminded me of a fat man bending down to tie his shoelaces. The studio hated me saying that. But at least it got me out of playing Sarah Keats in the Mignon Eberhart series. I thought I was going to spend my life in that. Haven't you ever read those, darlin'? They were murder mysteries, and I played this nurse. That's all I'd been doing. Whenever I tried to go for a part, they'd say, "Oh, but you're not an actress." I had to fight for everything at Warners. From the casting director up to Jack Warner. Of course, at Warners everybody seemed to have to fight. Cagney and Davis. That's the only way it was done. A knock-down, drag-out fight. You didn't always win, but it let them know you were alive.

Sheridan walked out of the studio on several occasions. Once refusing the role in *Strawberry Blonde* (1941) because she'd played too many like that already. It went to Rita Hayworth. Another of Sheridan's walkouts was over a salary dispute—she was earning $700 a week and, being one of the studio's top assets, felt she should get $2000. In the war years she was one of the handful of stars who traveled to the faraway corners of the global conflicts to entertain the troops almost on the line of fire. The absence from the screen did not harm her popularity, and she got some of her best dramatic roles—*Nora Prentiss* (1947) and *The Unfaithful* (1947)—as well as her raise in salary after the war.*

AS: I would never have gotten the role of Randy Monaghan in *King's Row* [1941] if I hadn't fought for it, and that was one of the best parts I ever had at the studio. I was very pleased having done that. Actually, it was Bogie who told me about the book in the first place and told me to go and fight for it. We rehearsed three weeks before a shot was made. I was happy with my role in *The Man Who Came to Dinner* [1941], which I did simultaneously with the other film. They couldn't make you do that now. They'd have to pay you for two pictures. But at that time they'd often cast me in two films simultaneously, and I'd be running from one set to the other. Mind you, for every good part I got, they would put me into two turkeys like *Navy Blues* and *Honeymoon for Three*. Then there'd be the scripts I turned down—like *Mildred Pierce*! That's my fault! Nobody else to blame there.

The good thing about working at Warner Brothers was the spirit at the studio. It was a very good group. An absolute family. It was just incredible. I miss that. I was driving in there one day, this was several years after I'd left the studio, and Cary [Grant] and Betsy [Drake] were making a film there, and they asked a group of us over for lunch. I was driving onto the lot, wondering if they'd let me on it even because I hadn't been there in so long I didn't know if the cop still knew me. Well—you could have shot a cannon down the street. There was nobody. No crew. None of the people I knew. They're all in TV now. In the commissary it was incredible. All the waitresses were gone. We sat at this table, the group of us, and the rest of the room, that used to be so packed with people, was almost empty. It was like an old friend dying. I'm terribly, terribly emotional about the old days at Warners and Paramount. The crews then and all the people who were so wonderful to work with.

JK: Did this include the front office?

AS: No. No. It never includes the front office staff; these are the crews we worked with. The actors got along well together then; no dissension, no knock-down, drag-out struggles or feuds like you read about big stars in pictures now, where they say that so-and-so don't get along, and you know it means they hate each other. That never occurred, to my knowledge.

*See the interview with Vincent Sherman.

JK: How about Miriam Hopkins and Bette Davis, or Davis and Crawford?

AS: Ohh! Well, that. They . . . Those were love scenes, darling!

JK: Did you have any troubles with Davis when you worked together in *Man Who Came to Dinner*?

AS: Oh, no. Very, very little. She wasn't happy about a lot of things. I suppose you're referring to that. But this had nothing to do with me. I adored her. Wouldn't dream of fighting her at all—so she got very nice. She was just—temperamental. Who isn't now and then? She probably hated her role.

JK: There was always something about you that came across, a forthright, honest quality which made your work such a joy. How much did the directors like Curtiz or Walsh give you a free rein, or how much were they bound to a studio's idea of projecting the image—like, in your case, "Oomph"?

AS: Well, actually, they just turned you loose to do what you wanted. They were perfectly willing to take an actor who is successful or established and let him do what he wants to do with the part. Now, nobody could tell Cary Grant how to do a scene. No, these directors we had were brain-pickers. They know what they've got on the set—and they're perfectly willing to abide by what the actor more or less decides he's going to do with a scene. I don't think anybody could fault Grant with playing comedy. He'd be the first to know if he did something that was wrong. And no more could you fault Jimmy Cagney in his playing of a scene. A tough guy. Or Bogart. No, dear, these people know what they're doing, and they [directors] knew that we knew ours.

Now only Ross Hunter and Cary Grant are making the sort of movies we made anymore. But it's passé now. They had to find something else, and eventually they will have to find something else again to replace whatever is popular now.

JK: One of the first movies you made after buying your way out of your Warner Brothers contract was a film with Cary Grant directed by Howard Hawks—*I Was a Male War Bride* [1949].

AS: I loved it. Ten months! I got pneumonia in England, where we went to shoot the film. I was the first one to collapse. And then, just after I had gotten back to working six hours a day, Cary came down with jaundice, hepatitis. Lord! The things we went through. We were doing a scene in the haystack—you know, the scene where his motorcycle crashes into it and we have this love scene. It's 4:00 in the afternoon, the fog is coming in under the door and I'm sitting there and praying, "Oh, God, I hope he doesn't get my cold or pneumonia," because I could barely breathe as it was, loaded down with penicillin and all that nonsense, when suddenly Cary, who has just rewritten this scene with Howard, says, "You know, Howard, I don't like this scene."

And Howard said, "But, Cary, you just wrote it." And Cary said, "I don't care, it's bloody awful. I don't like it." And this isn't like him at all, and I looked at him and felt his forehead and it was awfully hot. Very dry. But I thought it was the haystack, you know, because it's in a tunnel, with the cameras, and we couldn't smoke because the hay was treated with some sort of non-inflammable stuff. It was very warm in there, very uncomfortable. Howard sensed that something was wrong. "Well, all right, Cary, the fog is coming in anyway and interfering with the shot. Why don't you go back to the hotel and rest? We'll shoot it tomorrow." At 2:00 that morning we called a doctor for Cary. He took a look and said, "This man has a very bad case of hepatitis. He can't work, he's gotta go to the hospital."

Well, I don't know how long we laid off, but I went to Paris, to Rome, then I came to California. I think it was three months before he could work. And all that time I was on full salary. The insurance company had to pay. Mind you, I cannot get insurance from Lloyds of London now unless there is a special rider on my insurance policy about respiratory ailments. I had it three more times, once while making a film in Africa in 1957—*Woman and the Hunter,* they called it. Ugghhh. Don't see it if you haven't. I'd rather you remembered me for something else, like *Come Next Spring* [1956].

That was a good little picture. It was a sleeper. If it had been sold properly, it could have done well. But, unfortunately, it was part of Steve Cochran's package for Republic, and Herbert Yates [the president of the studio] didn't care whether it sold or not. It was supposed to have A bookings all over the place. Well, it didn't. No point in crying over it, but it could have done well. But they had this personal feud going on between Steve and Yates, and the film paid for it. But I never got better word of mouth and reviews than for that. It was the first time I played a mother. It was a good part, a good picture. It was a sleeper that was never allowed to wake up. Republic was really a cowboy studio, you see.

You know something? All the cowboy actors are far better off financially than any other actors in Hollywood. Randolph Scott is one of the richest actors in the business. Gene Autry, Roy Rogers. They all made fortunes. Dear Bill Boyd—he was absolutely broke when Hopalong Cassidy came out on TV—he had lost his big ranch, magnificent place, and hadn't been working for a long time, but they had bought these Hopalong Cassidy films from Paramount and Bill had had a clever agent when he made them who got a clause in his contract so he would get money if they were ever sold on TV— something like that. This was a stroke of genius because I don't think many people were thinking about TV ever happening back then. This was while I was still at Paramount. All of a sudden the TV network asks Bill to play the role in a new TV series as well, and he made an absolute fortune out of it. More than that, Clarence E. Mulford, who wrote the books and had never seen a cowboy in his life—a dear little man, I had met him when I was in some of them at Paramount—he gave Bill his TV rights. He said, "My needs are very simple. I don't want any more money. If you play this part, that's all I ask." Bill had been one of his favorite actors, as he'd been mine. I first saw him in *The Volga Boatman* [1926]. You never saw that. You're much too young. So, like in a good cowboy story, Bill got his ranch back, and he's retired and rich, and he doesn't have to work anymore. Now, that's a happy ending.

I only realized much later that she must have been in great pain all this time, as she was even then wasting away from an incurable cancer. This was known to her closest friends when she was signed for the TV series. It was a mark of the great and lasting affection she inspired in the people she knew and who had worked with her, who knew she was ill and that she needed work to take her mind off her illness, that they signed her for a TV series when they couldn't be certain she would be able to do more than a couple of shows. But she had completed more than half the series and these episodes were successful when shown.

I read in the paper that she was flying to Los Angeles to Universal studios to begin work. Not having seen her for a couple of weeks, I wanted to phone her to say goodbye. Then I got a message that Miss Sheridan had called, and could I meet her at our usual rendezvous for lunch? It was a quarter to one when I got the message and the lunch was for 1:00 p.m., so I flew out of the building and, for once in my life, arrived on the dot. I waited in the entrance leading into the dining room to catch my breath. On the far side a group of waiters and customers stood around a table. I was wearing my glasses.

At the center sat Ann. What stopped me in my tracks this time was that here was the Ann Sheridan I remembered from her films. Her hair had been done; she was subtly but expertly made up. She radiated vitality and that brand of glamour you don't get anymore, as she signed napkins, checkbooks and the odd slips of paper people dug up for her to autograph. She gave me a conspiratorial wink and pointed to the place beside her for me to sit. I was very pleased to be there and it must have showed. In a throaty aside that felt of laughter, she said, "You prefer it like this, don't you, darlin'?" Our lunch was short because she had her plane to catch and other things to do before. She said how happy she was to be going back to the Coast to work, and that her part was a good one. She must have known she wouldn't be coming back. She looked sensational. Then, before we said goodbye, she added, "You know, darlin' I did this for you."

1966

Joan Fontaine, photographed by A. L. "Whitey" Schafer (Paramount), 1945

JOAN
FONTAINE

S HE WAS ONE of *The Women,* the star of Alfred Hitchcock's *Rebecca* and thrice-nominated Oscar winner, winning once for *Suspicion,* and Olivia de Havilland's ice-blond kid sister. Her film career began with a small part in a 1935 Joan Crawford vehicle entitled *No More Ladies,* but she made her mark as the quintessential blonde, cool and vulnerable English heroine, the Hitchcock prototype.

She had one of the more interesting starring careers of any actress in the '40s. But when we met, work for actresses in her age range had become increasingly sparse. Fontaine had cleverly camouflaged that fact by doing more and more theater—summer-stock revivals and tours—which kept her busy, and she had also gone into the commercials market. At that time the "big names" weren't yet doing TV pitches, they left that lucrative but demeaning field to the extras and character actresses. But Fontaine never was one to give a fig for what others thought, so there she was, hawking products on TV. And then came *What Ever Happened to Baby Jane?* and it suddenly spurred a wave of *guignol* melodramas that featured some of the more famous "older" female stars, haunted by the past, the supernatural or just each other, in films that required all-stops-out self-exploitation. Her sister, Olivia de Havilland, had already gotten her feet wet in *Hush . . . Hush, Sweet Charlotte,* and now it was Joan Fontaine's turn, in *The Devil's Own.*

JF: It's about black magic. You know, it goes on *constantly* in England. Hideous things happened in Saddleworth not long ago; you know, those children's bodies found.

I'm advised to change positions, since it seems I'm sitting on something very fragile, or something is about to spill all over me. Could it be the king-size tumbler of gin? I'd never seen anything so large before in my life, though how was she to know that, since I appeared so self-assured? She conducted herself with great charm, considering I ended up almost slobbering on the floor. *The Devil's Own* was a mystery story written by Norah Lofts.

427

JF: It's been about three years, I presume [she replies to my pointing out her long absence from the screen], but it's the first script I had that I've really liked; I don't see any point in doing films that you don't really like or believe in. So I'm rather keen on this one.

JK: Did you finance this one yourself?

JF: No, *nooooo*. People have made thaaat mistaaake before. I wouldn't do that. *Nehvaiiiih*.

Since she was so selective about her film roles, why, I wondered out loud, had she stooped—she, a great film star—to doing commercials?

JF: Why not? The money is a very good reason. Also, you see, in America you have to keep in front of the public; it's a marvelous way of doing that, reminding them in a dignified way that you *still exist,* without doing a bad film. Everybody does them now; I don't believe anybody would assume that doing them meant one was hard up. That's an old-fashioned way of thinking.

Here I digress a bit. Her voice, it's really quirky and individual and very personable, it skips over pebbles and slides along silk, depending on what she's trying to make a point of at times, even when she goes up into the high Oxford-sounding aaaaa's, or drops to growls to indicate minor irritation or disinterest, it's always attention-getting. The silent days were the era of "great faces," but what one tends to forget is that sound brought in the era of great, distinctive voices. I suppose one wouldn't really think about it unless one had to listen to them as I'm doing now.

Having done my duty, and Fontaine hers with plugging her comeback in *The Devil's Own,* we can now get down to the fun of my being there: her career, how she began—*No More Ladies* (MGM, 1935).

JF: I was in that for *one* second. I don't remember the film, so I can't tell you what I played. The older woman who took the man away from Joan Crawford? I doubt it. Nobody took men away from Miss Crawford. I was eighteen at the time, anyway. But I don't remember it . . . luckily.

Before I went over to RKO, I went on the stage, did a couple of plays. I was found there, doing . . . you know, I've forgotten that. I know that Conway Tearle was in it. And they saw me there and I signed a contract.

I think *The Women* actually started my film career off. I was seen in that and was given *Rebecca* . . . after *many* tests. You know, telling me I didn't get it, and I *had* got it, etc., and I finally did win the marvelous role of Mrs. de Winter . . . in *Rebecca,* and that started everything going. I certainly don't remember telling Selznick he should get Margaret Sullavan for the part! [Her eyebrows show her surprise at that idiotic bit of information I'd picked up.] I know that I sat next to him at dinner, and he said, "What do you do?" and I said, "Well, I'm an actress." So we forgot that; and then we started talking about books and I said, "I just read a fascinating book by Daphne du Maurier, called *Rebecca,* which I think would make a very good film." And he said, "Would you like to test for it?" Well, I was absolutely astonished, but I did. I think I made about nine tests, as did everybody else in Hollywood, and London.

I was also up for Scarlett O'Hara in *Gone With the Wind.* I actually suggested my sister for Melanie, which she got. And I was very happy because that really started her too in Hollywood. She'd done many films by that time, but this is really one of the great films, the immortal films, and started her being taken very seriously as an actress, which she should have been.

Fontaine was nominated for her role in *Rebecca,* but lost out to Ginger Rogers in the soap-operatic saga of a secretary, *Kitty Foyle;* instead she won it the following year for her role in Hitchcock's *Suspicion*—it was said, because she should have won it the year before.

JF: Don't you think that's often the way with people who win Oscars? They get it for the *next* performance, usually. They feel that if you make rather a splash in the first film, they tend to think it might be a flash in the pan, so they wait for the second film to see if you really have talent and it wasn't just luck and the director which made you give the performance you did in the great picture. I think that's almost always the case. It was with Jimmy Stewart, who should have won for *Mr. Smith Goes to Washington;* and it certainly was with Elizabeth Taylor, was it not? And she's a very good actress, I think, but she didn't get it, I think, for the one she deserved to get it for most. But I've seen this kind of thing happen time and time again.

I'm an Academy member, you know, and I take the vote very seriously, I think we all do, and we vote seriously; and I don't think giving the award has anything to do with commercial worth or anything else like that. All our members consider their vote very seriously and vote accordingly. I never found any studio pull, nobody ever told *me* how to vote; and I don't think any of the Serious Members could be told how to vote. Originally, it was Academy members only who could vote [she replies when I suggest that studio power wouldn't be directed on the likes of her, but on the rank and file of studio employees].

The Women? [What it was like, working with such a strong all-star cast as that?] Per-fectly all right. They were all marvelous people, and . . . easy to work with, delicious plot. [But what about the rivalries on the set?] Ohhh, you *do* believe publicity, don't you?

Well, I had already talked to Joan Crawford, who was one of *The Women,* so Miss Fontaine couldn't fob me off there.

JF: The hardest thing about that is that *everybody expects* there to be publicity, and everything you do there can be used against you, let us say. Like the "feud" between my sister and myself. That *began* as sheer publicity. I mean, we had the usual sibling rivalries that most sisters *do* have, but since we lived with my mother in Hollywood, and we didn't go out, and we weren't seen in nightclubs and all that, they had nothing much to *write* about; so they *really* concocted the story, one of the studios, to get some space for us, I think. Principally, Olivia's studio rather than mine; but once that seed is sown, unfortunately, you can't live it down. It's the same thing as "Are you still beating your wife?" Nothing you can do about that. I haven't started to believe it. It doesn't go on.

I'm sitting there wide-eyed in Babylon, impervious to the corkscrew note in her voice, as if she were trying to push this conversation back into the bottle or underneath a pillow, or down my throat. Of course, this was several years before she published her autobiography, *No Bed of Roses* (a book that was no bed of roses for sister Olivia either), which was notable for the way she really let 'er rip with the family skeletons. But this is 1968, and the good stuff is not yet for public consumption. So there's a lot of squirming.

JF: And I don't know *why* it keeps recurring. . . . And we never *had* scandals; and we never fought in nightclubs . . . and we never did any of those things, and we were never flown off by exotic gentlemen to exotic places; we stayed pretty much under my mother's thumb . . . so the studio had to make something up.

Trust me not to let up, but I remind her, "There was this incident with the Oscar, I don't know exactly what that was now. . . ."*

JF (chilling enough to freeze the gin in my glass without the need for ice): *Neither do I,* frankly. I don't know.

Well, there is much more to talk to her about, so we go back up on dry land— her years at RKO and Selznick's guidance of her career once he took it over.

---

*There's an amusing corroboration that suggests a secret conspiracy between the fabled feuding sisters, for feud they did, no doubt about that. Enough people were there the night Olivia received her Oscar for *To Each His Own* and cold-shouldered her sister's attempt at congratulations. The telling moment was captured for posterity by publicity photographer Hymie Fink, showing a smiling Joan moving toward a frowning Olivia turning away as she clutches her Oscar. So naturally I also brought the matter up the time I went to interview Olivia in her New York hotel room where she was staying while in town to promote her appearance in *Hush . . . Hush, Sweet Charlotte.* Nothing could erase De Havilland's catnip smile, but as if on a pre-arranged cue, the sort of signal so rarified only a dog or an alter ego could catch it, the phone rang. Before anyone else might answer, she excused herself, went into the adjoining room, and I sat there listening to a polite exchange about De Havilland's plans for that evening and the shortness of her stay in New York, but that there might be time for a quick visit. She hung up and came back to me, knowing perfectly well I couldn't help overhearing, and smothering me in a big grin. "That was Joan," she said, and I knew she didn't mean Crawford, whom she had replaced in *Hush . . . Hush, Sweet Charlotte.* So naturally in the face of such sisterly affection, and being very young and awed, I accepted her simple protestation of their friendship and that rumors to the contrary were the works of mean-spirited gossips. But later I wanted to go back to that hotel room and look underneath the coffee table to see if there was an alarm button which she pushed whenever the subject of her sister Joan came up.

JF: Well, I'm deeply grateful to him. David Selznick was one of the really fine people in the industry. He had great *taste,* and he was a good friend also. And he had a great imagination, he was very literate, and literary as well. I think eventually he was forced for financial reasons to place us wherever he *could,* and lost his selectivity because of the economic burden of having so many stars under his aegis who had to be paid constantly. I think if he'd had a really free hand, he would have done much better, but I'm *not* complaining, because I was very fortunate, really, that he did discover me, as it were. I mean, he did give me *Rebecca* and *Suspicion,* and permitted me to do *The Constant Nymph.* . . . There were several I didn't want to do, he suspended me for not doing, so that I finally *had* to, which is a shame. Looking back upon it, I wish I had not been forced to do these films, but I was, and there's nothing I could do about it. Such as *Frenchman's Creek.*

I had no choice over roles. And we had contracts at that time which could be suspended, on and on. *All actors* should bless Olivia de Havilland, who fought this in court, at her *own* expense too, and won what was called the De Havilland Decision, whereby a seven-year contract was only for seven years . . . and *she* did that. She fought for all of us. She was magnificent.

It's awfully difficult, for women especially, to fight against the establishment, as it were. We have many strikes against us. First of all, we are far too busy, really; we haven't got any legal training; the businessman knows far more how to trap us, and does. Anyplace. Not just in Hollywood. And we have agents to make our deals. . . . Since we're talking about that, most of the agents aren't far-sighted enough. They could do what Selznick did, if they were really keen about it, and perhaps not be penny wise and pound foolish, that they would look at your career over a longer period than the great money *at this moment.* A few actors have had marvelous agents who have done that for them.

We then went into a long discourse, or rather I did, about the falling off of her roles and the limitations of the parts she did play in films like *Serenade, Beyond a Reasonable Doubt, A Certain Smile, Tender Is the Night,* always as one of those one-dimensional brittle society ladies who mostly looked gastro-enteritic out of terraced windows . . . and Joan laughs and says that she is looking pained right now.

JF: Well there are . . . also, remember that a lot of those great feminine roles died out. I can't really think of one, at this moment, in the last . . . five or six years . . . played by *anybody* who had an enormous emotional range. Most of the films are for men, if you notice today. They have the great roles. Perhaps the war did that—that the woman of thirty, romantic, etc., was a little . . . old-fashioned, a little passé. It's very difficult to find that kind of role, unless, as you say, you go into the horror films. Well, ladies and romance are both terribly old-fashioned, I'm afraid. I don't personally think so, but they seem to be on the screen.

Naturally, this leads us to complimenting her on her looks (except for a slight stoop, she was one of the best-looking women I'd met—she really didn't look her age), and discussing how, if she were in Europe, her career might be going full tilt in the sort of parts Jeanne Moreau was playing; and Fontaine had given one of her most memorable performances in a film directed by the European émigré in Hollywood, Max Ophüls. To end up with him, we somehow managed to skip over several other topics. From talking about the then recent decline of good roles for women like her, we fall back to one of the peaks in her starring career: *Letter from an Unknown Woman*—once seen, always remembered.

JF: That again—we bought that film. Mr. John Houseman was the producer, and together we found the director and put it all together, and a great cameraman, Mr. Planner, who is no longer with us, but he . . . he did the photography, and it was quite a magnificent film. Unfortunately, not very well received in the United States. It had the most brilliant reviews I've ever read, in France, in South America, almost everywhere. But then it was made in 1948, and that sort of sentiment had passed out of the picture, as far as American audiences were concerned. They weren't interested in that sort of thing; they wanted realistic, today problems. I'm not surprised it holds up beautifully. It was costume, after all, and it's a classic.

Ophüls was a very strict director, but most imaginative . . . and . . . gave you . . . knew you had it to give . . . didn't question you for a moment . . . didn't treat you *roughly* . . . and wasn't interested in the clock and making the schedule and all that sort of thing. He was a *creative* man who brought out the *creative* side of one. I think that is one of the great errors that has occurred in contemporary Hollywood, they cease to be *creative* as far—that's your directors now—as far as the actor was concerned. They really, most Hollywood directors, wanted to be the *star* themselves; their hand, their trademark was pushed over the performances. It was a such-and-such film starring . . . and that was rather secondary.

JK: Was Hitchcock like that?

JF: I don't think he ever wanted to outstar the star, though. I have never been aware of *that*. No, he was *more* than generous and eager with me, in the two films I did with him. I also did a TV with him. And his desire to make the film the best it could be was his main desire. His trademark came *before* that, in the creation of it, and the writing of it, and the way it was done. But he left it to the actors to do the rest. One felt oneself a vital segment in his films.

I do think we've reached a time where we're so realistic that if an actor plays in two or three films, let's say, the same type, you don't believe it anymore. You're more inclined—at least in America we are—to find a film with unknowns and find it more credible. But then if it's the same people, they star in it, we say that it's such-and-such a film, and it loses the so-called reality it had when the actors were strange to us.

Which is, of course, partly what I started to suggest had happened to her career. She began to play the same sort of woman in the same sort of film too often to be credible any longer, whereas in her heyday there was so much variety in her films and parts. One of her recent films—and recent, when you speak to stars with long careers behind them, could often mean ten years prior to meeting them—was a beautifully mounted "woman's picture," *Until They Sail.* I had loved it, her and the rest of the cast—Jean Simmons, Piper Laurie, Paul Newman . . . directed by . . .

JF: A man called Mr. Robert Wise. Well, he's the kind of a director that wants you to pick up something on cue; say a line exactly to metronome proportions; and I think *that's* very difficult for instinctive actors. I think it's difficult for *most* actors. But he became the camera, and everything had his tempo constantly. So you could not invent, or do anything original if you wanted to. I never saw it, so I don't know how it came out.

In the '50s I tried to keep making two films a year. You'd be offered six scripts a year to look at, and you'd take whatever you could do the best, you know. I did the films I thought I could fit—well, like *Serenade,* for example . . . but they weren't films made to fit me, however.

Fritz Lang's *Beyond a Reasonable Doubt* was done under contract—that was all what we call a package, and I had to do it.

By now I had some idea of the sort of films and the sort of directors she did not like. "Metronome" directors she most emphatically did not like, so what was it like being directed by George Stevens? He directed her at the outset of her career, in *Quality Street* and then *Gunga Din* at RKO, a period in her life when they were very close, and many years later, after both had won their Oscars, they were reunited as director and star on a follow-up to *Lost Weekend* entitled *Something to Live For* with Milland as a reformed alcoholic helping Joan to dry out.

JF: Let me tell you a little story about that. I did it with Ray Milland, and . . . You know what rushes are. After every day's shooting you go to see yesterday's film. . . . So we had a scene in which I played a drunk, and it went on for *nine* minutes, and I had to be terribly drunk, go and take a shower, come back fully dressed in the scene, go on and finally, after having gone through many emotions, the Alcoholics Anonymous man takes me out to dinner to sober me up. So Ray, whom I adore, and I went to see the rushes, and we stayed in the projection room for two hours, and the camera was still outside the window, filming through a lace curtain [she breaks up]. We never went back to see the rushes again. Stevens was working more like that, may I say, than he had originally back at RKO when we did *Quality Street,* and *Damsel in Distress*—my goodness, yes, I forgot he did that too.

Damsel came about because Ginger Rogers and Fred Astaire had broken up and he wanted to do a film where there wasn't too much dancing. Fred was to play—it was a P. G. Wodehouse story, wasn't it?—and so they wanted an English Lady who could possibly dance a bit—huhmh. I remember going to the dance-recital hall at RKO, and they said, "Well, Miss Fontaine had ballet, do you want to try her out?" And Fred said, "Yes," and we did a waltz around the room. He said, "Ohh, that'll be fine. It's absolutely marvelous." Little did I know that in the public eye I was taking Ginger Rogers' place. . . . Ginger I adore. She's a *very* good friend of mine, a delightful, marvelous person—but then when it came out, the critics said, and probably correctly, that Miss Fontaine can't dance at all and was very little threat to Miss Rogers. . . .

The problem of working at RKO was that it lacked one man continuously at the helm, the way MGM had Louis B. Mayer . . . RKO passed hands continuously, so there was no continuation of plot and plan as there was at Fox or Warners or MGM. I think that that system, the star system, in spite of its many faults, where you were groomed by a studio, is invaluable. I think that's one of the reasons we haven't been having that many new stars in today's crop, because there isn't that head of a studio who sees you through a long span of your career and selects it very carefully, and supervises your publicity and everything else connected with it. Zanuck did it to a great extent when he was running 20th-Fox . . . I worked at Fox on loan-out, so naturally he didn't show me that concern.

In the '40s she had been in the very fine adaptation of Charlotte Brontë's *Jane Eyre,* and in the pre–civil-rights '50s she starred in the highly controversial production (because of the miscegenation angle) of the novel *Island in the Sun,* which was one of Zanuck's personal productions. The notoriety surrounding it concerned two potentially inflammatory pairings: between black actress Dorothy Dandridge and British actor John Justin, and, more explosive still, between Harry Belafonte and the very blond, very patrician, very white Joan Fontaine. In the end, stills showing Joan and Harry clinching on a cliff overlooking a romantic bay inlet were all we ever saw of that scene. The kissing was cut before the film was released, because of dark storm warnings from the South. Casting Joan Fontaine in that part was one of those clever moves, like Hitchcock's use of Janet Leigh in *Psycho*—a calculated play on audience psychology. They were exploited for the familiarity of their names, which had outlasted their actual box-office popularity: they were freelancing actresses taking jobs as they found them, if the roles appealed, but, as good roles were hard to find, they could afford to take these risks, which in their cases were really no risk at all. Basically, they had everything to gain from this fireball of publicity, and little to lose. Yet even to this day people speak of Hitchcock's audacity in casting a "star" who disappears halfway through the picture, while nobody mentions the stars who never got cast anymore at all. That's movies, Hollywood style; it's a lot of publicity and it fools them all the time. Anyway, Fontaine had her experiences with that film . . .

JF: . . . and with that producer, a notorious woman-chaser. I did indeed have a love scene in the film with Mr. Belafonte, and I got the most extraordinary number of letters—mostly signed KKK, and they were really frightful letters—I can't tell you—which didn't make me sorry or anything like that, but I was *shocked* that there was such an *organized* . . . society in the United States, because many of them came from *different* states, but the phrasing was the same, so that I could figure out they were a kind of round-robin that flooded the studio and me. In the film all that was left was [Belafonte] with his hands on my shoulders. He was such a handsome man, so charming and so talented. It was a shame that they cut the scene. I think that once you decide to make a film of that sort, you must go right ahead and do it as it was intended to be. You can't halfway through the film have in mind what will happen in the Bible Belt, or the reaction in the South, and I'm afraid that was what happened. I think the studio should have gone right ahead with the courage of their original conviction, and not halfway got frightened. Which they did.

On her own films, she had no hesitation in naming her favorites.

JF: I adored *The Constant Nymph,* and I adored *Letter from an Unknown Woman,* those are my two favorites. Not to say I'm not grateful for *Rebecca* and *Suspicion,* because the others would not have been possible without the original two. Then I did *This Above All, Jane Eyre.* . . . As somebody said the other day in the *New York Times,* I think it was Hitchcock, indeed it was: No film has ever been made with the perfect cast, as far as he was concerned. He said, if you get 60 percent of your cast right, he finds he must be content. It cannot be perfect, at least in this country. I suppose he was content with 60 percent of the casting of *Rebecca.* [She breaks up.] That may mean I wasn't one of them. Quite frankly, Mr. Olivier wanted Miss Leigh in it. Rather intimated it. I was on *trial* for most of the film. So those tears I shed were quite genuine. In the long run, I can only thank him for his attitude because perhaps it made me a better actress than I would have been otherwise. . . . Of course I knew his work already, he'd been marvelous in *Wuthering Heights.* And speaking of that, lots of people come up to me and say, "Oooohhhhh, Miss Fontaaaine, I have seen you *six times* in one film, the best I have ever seen," and they come up with *Wuthering Heights,* and of course I wasn't in it. They confuse it with *Jane Eyre.*

The gin has loosened my inhibitions, for back I hedge to her role in *The Women,* where she was only one among so many fighting for the top. "Vying for which would wear the crown," she says. "Well, I was very young, and stood on the sidelines and watched it all; naturally, it was a great lesson to me." And in *Gunga Din* she was the only woman in the all-male cast. "Well, again I was so young and only appeared when I had to do my scenes, and then went home to Mother, so I didn't see much of it." And twenty years later she appeared in

Tender Is the Night, based on the Scott Fitzgerald story, but "I haven't seen that either. I haven't seen half the films you're speaking of, so there's not much I can tell you. And I gave up rushes after Stevens, so you know more of some of those films than I do. I was only in that film because of Jennifer [Jones], she asked me to be in it." In *Jane Eyre* one of the little waifs in the beginning of the story was played by the pretty little ten-year-old Elizabeth Taylor. Years later, on a loan-out, Fontaine worked with Taylor again, only this time the starring part was Elizabeth Taylor's in her own studio's production of *Ivanhoe.* "That was the time she was going to marry Michael Wilding, wasn't it?" Liz Taylor, I pointed out, was getting all the lush close-ups, and did Joan have problems getting the same treatment?

JF: I don't know how a star protects herself. There's nothing you can do. You just hope the director will be fair, the company will be fair, and if they're not, that's it. You just go home, take off your makeup and forget it. I love to act, but I'm not going to fight about it; there's no purpose gained. Why get your name in the papers for being unruly or making scenes and being difficult? Life is difficult enough, I don't have to do that. I don't want to. I don't like fighting for a career. I've never fought. I just did many, many films and hoped I'd be recognized, but I never fought for anything. Never.

There were many films, as I look back upon it, that I should have done. That they put somebody even less known in because nobody was looking out for me. The reason I got *The Constant Nymph* was that my husband [Brian Aherne] and I had been flying across the country, and we landed the plane and came into a restaurant in Hollywood in our old clothes before we got home and unpacked, and Edmund Goulding came over to my husband's table and said, "Hello, Brian Aherne, we are having the most awful difficulty, we want a *star* for *Constant Nymph,* but she's got to look awful young, and gangly, flat-chested and freckle-faced, and there's no such thing in Holly-wood." And I said, "How about me?" And he said, "Who are you?" And I said, "Joan Fontaine." He said, "Ohhh, my goodness, absolutely *right.*" The next morning I had it. But nobody ever thought of it. It's one of the parts I liked the best, but then it happened, as *Rebecca* did, by accident.

I played a young girl of *enormous* emotion, and she was a rather bright girl, rather straight-seeing, with a grownup's mind and heart in a child's body. Not the *Lolita* kind of thing *at allll* . . . no, very sensitive, musical girl, not that at all, and it was, I think, quite beautiful. Of course, it's a beautiful role.

Her then husband, Brian Aherne, had played the man's part in the first talking (1933) British film version of the play, which is why Goulding would have approached Aherne with his problems in casting it.

JF: It was a great chance for me, though it didn't do well in the United States either. But I didn't fight to get it. I don't fight.

So then, what must it have been like working with Orson Welles, who played Rochester to her Jane?

JF: I shall never forget the first day. We were called to rehearsal and Orson didn't show up until 5:00 that afternoon, and had all his minions about him, and called for a Bible stand, and put his script down, said to the director [Robert Stevenson], "Now, you sit down there and I'm going to tell you all what we're going to do." [There's a naughty chuckle here.] What do you do? I didn't have my own Bible stand handy, unfortunately. [Lots of mirth from both of us.] He doesn't really like to act, and he always was late and would do anything rather than act, and one day we're going through a door, he was to precede me, and I said, "Orson, stand up, your coat bags if you don't." And he said, "Cut! Cut! Miss Fontaine says my suit isn't made properly. Take it off! Send it to the tailors!" And it was two days later that we started the scene again, so I learned *never* to say anything. . . . They weren't very kind to me that day. I only meant stand up, but there you are. I liked some things about *Jane Eyre* very much; and it only had made more money for Fox than any picture ever had up to that moment.

I also made *This Above All* for Fox with Tyrone Power. He was a very sensitive, gentle person, but he wasn't English, so the balance was thrown a bit, and Eric Knight's marvelous book had to be changed in concept quite a lot. Mr. Olivier would have been marvelous in that. He would have been fine for the role. That's all that matters. I liked many things about *September Affair;* it was almost a beautiful film. Hal Wallis produced that, and Hal Wallis has quite good taste and wants to be known for his sense of fineness in film-making. And it was very adventurous, really, it was one of the very first postwar films made abroad for Hollywood. I was very grateful for that too, because it meant I went to Italy and all around the Continent; and then it had that glorious music by Rachmaninoff; lovely scene like the blue grotto in Capri . . . it was the last of my really good romantic female roles. After that I went back to RKO and films like *Born to Be Bad*.

I hoped it didn't seem that I was trying to push her to give me certain answers, since I found myself going back to the same points again and again, hoping, I suppose, for the answers so far eluding me, but by now we're quite at ease. I asked her about Fritz Lang again. He was, after all, one of the cult giants of movies.

JF: Well, he was very nice. He'd always been known as the bad bully of Hollywood. People were frightened to death of him, and by this time he knew of his own reputation, so really bent over backwards to be nice to work with, gave us absolutely no trouble at all. Knew what he wanted. I don't think the script was worthy of him or the rest of the cast . . . but I don't know why Hollywood keeps insisting on making scripts that aren't the best they can find. I never really enjoyed filmmaking *per se*. I don't like the long hours and the constant interruptions; and I really don't like coming off a set with tears still streaming down my face and having to shake the mayor's hand and be photographed with the studio head's nieces. I think that's awfully difficult and then plunge right back into the scene again. No director can stop that—after all, they employ him also. There's many things about movie-making, unlike the stage, which I found unattractive. On the stage, for a glorious two and a half hours it belongs to you—no autographs, no telephone, no pictures being taken.

I liked to make movies, of course, because I like to act; I like to work; I like to keep busy. I have many . . . various investments that I like to keep control of, which I need to do with that lovely gold that comes from movies. I like the change—the traveling it makes possible.

I don't go to films much anymore, and when I do, they're mostly foreign films—English ones, which I love. They're so adult, they don't belabor the point, they credit you with intelligence. I think Hollywood films used to, at any rate, treat you as if you had a fourteen-year-old mentality, and of course American TV treats you as if you had an eight-year-old mentality.

There's a lot of chatter about this and that: new faces she doesn't rate, can't even think of any names; stars of her own era, like friends, Bergman, who she thought was ever so clever in managing her career to act onstage in France and England, and Vivien Leigh, who "is marvelous, right," and Garbo was the most beautiful woman she'd ever seen, on and off screen—"the marvelous space between the lid and the eyebrow, and that lovely neck . . ." So it's name-dropping: I say Hepburn and she says:

JF: Glorious cheekbones, and such style. I not only worked with her, I *owe my career* to her. I had a small part in *Quality Street* and, unbeknownst to me, she went to one of the producers on the RKO lot and said, "Give that girl a lead in a B picture. I think perhaps you've got something there." And indeed it was through her that I got the first recognition on the lot as an actress. Because I was still a starlet. Oh, she's marvelous. Every day she would bring a picnic lunch for the entire company. That's where I picked it up, bringing the coffee with me for the cast when we're rehearsing. She always does that. She was a real housemother.

We have made a tour of her apartment, looking at fishing awards, golfing awards, critics' awards, and a cup for breaking a house record in a theater she played. Only the Oscar wasn't in the room, which reminded her to say, "I think I should have gotten the Oscar for *Rebecca,* and for *The Constant Nymph.*" (Fontaine was, in fact, nominated three times for the Oscar.) The tape's over. It has run down some time ago . . . and I never did get her to tell the story of how Darryl F. Zanuck used to chase her around his executive office when she first went to Fox, and that he had this big elephant's foot, stuffed, in the middle of the room, so, fighting him off, she also had to keep leaping over it and it wasn't very graceful but it was funny. But obviously she told me that when the tape was off.

1968

JEAN
LOUIS

AS A DESIGNER, he went to Hollywood, signed with Columbia Pictures in the mid-'40s and became linked in the public's mind with the marvelous wardrobe he designed for Rita Hayworth's films, like *Tonight and Every Night, Down to Earth, Affair in Trinidad* and, inevitably as significant to his career as the role was to Rita's, *Gilda*. But how did this small, reserved, extremely soft-spoken man get started, where did he come from, what had he done before his dresses for the likes of Rita, Lana (*Imitation of Life*), Doris Day (*Pillow Talk, Midnight Lace*) and Marlene Dietrich (her Vegas wardrobe) made the headlines and launched trends that are still with us today, especially in the shapes and designs for the bugle-beaded, spangly, glittery, glamorous dresses people take for granted that Bob Mackie invented?

JL: I began in 1943. I was in New York before I came out here; I was with one of the best-known *maisons de couture* in New York, Hattie Carnegie. I was with her for seven years. Hers was one of the first *maisons de couture* in New York. Joan Cohn,* who was the wife of the president of Columbia, had her clothes made at Carnegie's. And one day I got a very mysterious phone call, and somebody asked me if I was interested to go to Hollywood. To make pictures. I said yes. You know, it's very tempting, in a way. So I see that man who was the president of Columbia and he said all right, we make you a contract. And I was at the end of my contract with Hattie Carnegie, and they didn't renew it; I don't know why. So I took the other contract, and when I told that to Hattie, she went *ab*solutely furious. And when I left, and first I went to work as always, I said I'm not going to leave right away, I'm going to finish the collection. So one morning I go to work, and a man says, "Are you Mr. Jean Louis?" and I said, "Yes." He said, "Here's something for you." I said, "What's that?" "Well," he said, "you'll find out." Here it was a summons from Carnegie, suing me and Columbia Pictures. So I arrived in California and Harry Cohn was very happy about the suit because it is making

*Formerly a stock actress, Joan Perry.

big publicity. And I stay about three months doing nothing but watching pictures. I was in the projection watching picture. You know, it was wartime and they were making war picture and there was not anything for me to do until I made a picture with Irene Dunne and Charles Boyer called *Together Again,* it was a remake. That was my first picture.

It's funny because Irene Dunne, if I stay in America, you know, the first time I was in New York, was because of her. I came for my vacation, I stayed a little bit for about two or three weeks and I wanted to stay a little longer, and somebody said, "Oh, if you like it so much, why don't you stay? We'll find you a job. Make some sketches," and so they show it to Hattie Carnegie and she said, "All right, I'll keep him." But six months after, she say, "Well, goodbye," because I was on a visitor visa. During that time Irene Dunne was in the showroom and Hattie Carnegie called to my office and said, "Tell that little Frenchman to bring his clothes down." It was the first few weeks I was there, and Irene Dunne bought three dresses, so she [Carnegie] signed me up to a contract. [He laughs.] So she [Dunne] was responsible for my staying in America and my first picture in Hollywood.

JK: I always thought what the Hollywood designers had to do for the stars had a far greater influence on contemporary fashion than anything the French designers came up with.

JL: Oh, definitely.

JK: What appealed to you about working out here in films?

JL: Well, we had stars, it was fun. We don't have anybody no more. [We are talking in the '70s.] When you design for a film, you have to bear in mind that it has to be in accordance with the script and the character of the star, what she plays, so I couldn't make a sketch till I know who was the star, because they have a different personality. In a film you have to dress the personality, the part, the person they are and what I think is right for them.

JK: How important, in your experience, was the role of the designer in helping to create the image of a star the studio was trying to sell to the public?

JL: Oh, very. Yes. When we develop some talent in those days . . . we develop a few talent, there wasn't very much there. Rita was already a star when I came here, and, well, we had Evelyn Keyes . . .

JK: And Adele Jergens.

JL: *Oh, my God,* you know them all. [He shudders. He dressed Adele.] You could do nothing for her. She was as big, you know, and she don't know how to move, to sit even. [He laughs, his eyes crinkle. He's very quiet.]

Kim Novak . . . Kim Novak was a pretty girl. She had a marvelous . . . here . . . figure and bust was good; and at that time sex was the most important thing; the sexy thing was to wear clothes that reveal, you know; it was

Jean Louis with *Rita Hayworth* at Columbia,
photographed by Irving Lippman, 1954

not what it is now, to be sexy is to be in bed, nude. So the first time I see her, I see that she has a good bust. She doesn't need padding and all that thing we were doing to everybody. Less shoulder and keep her looking very natural, with nothing, just put the clothes on her and show her bosom, it's moving, it's not a stiff thing like all those girls then.

JK: What difference is there, if any, between designing for a star and a starlet?

JL: When she's less important, we don't take so much care; not only that, if the girl don't have it, you know, I can't give it to her in a dress. You know, I made the clothes for Dietrich, the ones she wore in her show in Las Vegas; it's very funny because she can wear those. Loretta [Young] is somebody else who can wear clothes beautifully. They have something. Dietrich wears clothes even though she does not have a good body—this [he points to the midriff] is very short, very short. But you know that and you design for that. But, you know, that dress [the famous Las Vegas bugle-beaded flesh-colored chiffon dress that started it all] when we made it the first time was a big sensation, and somebody from a charity ball asked me if they could borrow the dress from Marlene for someone to wear who will hand out the prizes at the ball. And I said, "Don't ask, she'll say no." And I was surprised when they call me and say that she said yes, on one condition: I select the girl who wear my dress. They had about 200 girls [laughs] from the Moulin Rouge at that time, Earl Carroll's, all over, from the clubs in Vegas, the studios sent over girls, and Marlene picked the most beautiful. You know, we made a foundation to go under that dress, we made Marlene a very young body— oh, and this was a secret. I got the idea from having to do a dress for Rita in *Salome*, where she has to do the dance, and, you know, she has had children and her body was no longer that of a girl, so we made this foundation and covered it with flesh-colored chiffon, and beading to hide the seams so you can't see where the body stocking is, and it makes it look like flesh—and we make this for Marlene. It goes from here [he points to his neck] to there [somewhere around the thighs] and she has this firm, young body under the dress—so she lets them take the dress, but she made a condition that because the dress was very valuable, it would be delivered to the committee just before the girl was to go on and hand out the awards, and she could wear nothing underneath. And the poor girl put on the dress, and all those bugles made it very heavy and it pulled everything down, it just hung on her like this [Jean mimes an ironing board. We should have done this interview in mime].

You know, Betty Grable was a miserable thing to dress. She was doing a musical [*Three for the Show*]. I never suffered so much because that woman was used to Fox studio, she was used to doing period pictures and wearing all those long dresses, and she always wanted long like that and long cuts like this, and we didn't do that. [Throughout this, Maggie's been cooking, people have been arriving. Now the pots, pans and dogs all get in the act. I am going to faint.] Well, she was very disagreeable to me. We put that dress with a fitter on her, and she said, "What is this? That's not for me." I said, "Well, it's exactly like in the sketch," and she had approved it. And she said, "Well, yes, but I'm not like this." She said, "You see, I want to show you something—first you have to put my bust here." I said, "But it does not go there. If you have your bust here, you have no neck." She have no neck anyway. Then she said, "You see, from here down my legs are long. From here [he points to his waist] you see how long my legs are!" So, you see, we have to do all those things and, really, it was just murder.

JK: Did you dress Marilyn Monroe when she made that film at Columbia, *Ladies of the Chorus* [1948], the one where Adele Jergens played her mother and they were supposed to be burlesque stars?

JL: That's a long time ago, but she was not a star yet. Yes, I did them. She was a little baby then.

JK: Well, it was before the Monroe image had even begun to take shape, never mind what she became when you dressed her later.* So what were you designing for back then, the character she played or the girl, the potential she herself had?

JL: Well, it was both ways, but mostly the character because at that time I never even knew that Marilyn Monroe had *it,* that she was cute. But she turned out to be very cute.

JK: Have you ever, in what you designed for a woman, revealed a potential in a personality that neither she nor her producers were aware of before then?

JL: I know what you mean, but that didn't happen to me. At that time she was so different, you know. There was one girl who we made a picture with, it's a picture that was with Rita Hayworth, Janet Blair . . .

JK (interjects): *Tonight and Every Night!*

JL: Yeah! And there was a girl—you know, there were lots of girls in the film, Columbia then had about fifteen, eighteen girls under contract, and one was Shelley Winters, she was playing a chorus girl, who were all supposed to wear the same thing and wear it the same way and all this, and so they had this French can-can costume, and the hat should have been worn this way. All of the girls wore the hat this way, except Shelley Winters. Each time my head was turned around, she pushed the hat back. And I complained to the director, it didn't make any sense, she put it back. . . . Of course I prefer to design for a personality; you don't pay as much attention to the little parts when you have to do all the films at the studio.

Some Like It Hot, the never completed *Something's Got to Give* and *The Misfits* were done by him.

JK: Okay, how long did it take you to come up with the idea for Dietrich's outfit, so that you knew it would do the trick, and she felt that way too?

JL: That took six months. Because we never finished with Dietrich. When we were making those things for Las Vegas, she was constantly complaining every five minutes. Because this bead was too low; to rip this one because this one was exactly the same spot as this one and it should be lower because she don't like symmetry; and it was like this until the last minute, when she went to rehearse at Las Vegas, she take the dress we had been working six months on and put it in her valise like this. [He laughs because he has just mimed the most casual flinging of this expensive, fragile gown into a suitcase as if it were an old linen bathrobe.]

JK: If that took you six months, how long did the clothes Hayworth wore in *Gilda* take you to do?

JL: Oh, that was nothing. The black satin dress was not described in the script. It was just supposed to be an evening dress, with long hair and a sleeveless ermine coat. She never wore the coat, she just drag it on the floor; and I was heartbroken because it was beautiful; and we make the dress, and I say, well, she come home from a party and she's wearing that great ermine coat with that black satin dress under it. It was that simple. I mean, I knew she was going to have to do a number when she's wearing it, but it was a very elegant thing, because Jack Cole describe it to me, "Oh, we are going to take the gloves off, we're going to do this . . ."

But, you know, Columbia didn't have many stars to design for. They had Rita Hayworth. Period. So I tried to make everything for her very special, because it was also my chance to do things, to do special things. She was very easy. She just wore what we gave her. Rita was absolutely the most marvelous girl, but she stand like this, and that's it, you fit her. She hate to fit. "Get me out of it." That's it. That's all she says. But I had great freedom in how I dressed her. She never, never said I don't like one thing—she's really wonderful, no trouble. With Rita you always had to design to show off her body—not her legs, but her body; I mean, you couldn't put her in a business suit. Not because the studio would have objected, but because that was her personality. Rita Hayworth was known for that, for being a beautiful woman, and people didn't want to see Rita Hayworth in a suit.

JK: Well, how would you have dressed Rita Hayworth if you didn't have a public image to consider with her? How would you have dressed her privately?

JL: In a suit, no. Pretty much like on the screen, only softer. Soft clothes, not so flamboyant, but very simply.

JK: Well, how about dressing Lana Turner, whom you did when you joined up with Ross Hunter? She didn't have the best body in the world, but you dressed her very stylishly in *Imitation of Life, Portrait in Black.* . . .

The first time Jean worked with Lana was on *Imitation of Life,* the film that
marked Lana's official screen return after the Johnny Stompanato drama that
had enlivened the news scene and regenerated great interest in Turner on the
screen.

JL (whenever Jean says something even mildly indiscreet or gossipy, he goes all
   Buddha giggly, his eyes get smaller, his face creases with many mirth lines):
   She could be for two hours thin, and an hour after she could blow up. Oh, it
   was the thing with her. We made a picture, it was the last picture with her,
   Madame X, and I suffered on that picture with her. Because Constance Bennett was there, she was playing Lana's mother-in-law, and Constance Bennett
   was like this [he describes a reed in a Chinese lily pond, or any pond with
   reeds in it] and could wear clothes like nobody. First thing, Ross Hunter send
   me to New York to see Constance Bennett and discuss her wardrobe. And I
   came back and said, "Ross, have you seen Constance Bennett?" He said,
   "Yes." I said, "But she looks marvelous." And he said, "Oh, yes, but we are
   going to age her. You are going to age her. She's going to have gray hair!"
   [Lots of merry laughter at the memory of what the appearance of a sylph like
   Constance Bennett playing Lana's mother-in-law would do to a ballooning
   Lana, and of how Ross Hunter had planned to solve that problem in case it
   arose, which of course it did.] So, I say, "Well, I don't think she [CB] want
   it this way. That's not how Constance sees the part." And Ross say, "Oh, I'll
   talk to her, we'll add some gray hair, and at the end she's going to be very
   old and we're going to pad her" and all this. So when Constance Bennett
   came and he tell her, "You know, we are going to put here a wrinkle," she
   said, "You're not going to *touch* me! This is exactly what I want and how I
   want to look." [Now there are hysterics all round.] So we are worried about
   what would happen when they look at each other, Lana and Constance.
       The first time they meet, nothing happens. Now Ross Hunter call me and
   he says, "Now we are going to have a scene when we see them in a newspaper
   [this must be part of the plot]. And Lana will have a fur coat and Constance
   will have a fur coat. So Constance Bennett says, "Sable," and the other one
   said, "Mink." But when she heard what Constance had, she said, "*I* want
   sable. Give her chinchilla, it's more like her, she's an old lady." So we go to
   a furrier's because it was just a montage scene, it was nothing. So we had a
   sable coat, a chinchilla coat, a white mink coat—I don't know what else, but
   we had about ten coats. So Constance Bennett says, "This is my coat, the
   sable." And Lana Turner says, "*I* want the sable coat." So I said, "I think it
   would be younger if you wear the white mink coat." "No, I want the sable
   coat." All the afternoon was like this, spent with the argument between the
   two. In the end I think Lana wore the white mink coat.
       Of course Lana was famous for having worn a sweater and a skirt. Ohh,
   that sweater, I'm so sick of that thing, but we had to have one in every film.
   And then we had this scene, their first big scene together, on a yacht. It was
   a yacht party, and Lana was wearing a sweater and a skirt and Constance was

wearing a sweater and a skirt, and Ross said, "We have trouble now. You know, she's in a sweater and a skirt, and the other one is in a sweater and a skirt!" And I said, "Well, every woman over forty is in a sweater and a skirt," and Lana says, "How can you put two women in a sweater and a skirt?" I said, "What's wrong wiz it? You're not the same color." She said, "You should not put her in a sweater and a skirt. Put her," she said—*her*, not Constance or Miss Bennett, they didn't talk to each other. "You shouldn't have put her in a sweater and a skirt. She's an old woman. I am the one who has sweater and a skirt." So Constance Bennett said, "Does it bother you that much?" She [Lana] turned her head. So Constance said, "All right, I'll put my coat on." And we made her a coat, was a tweed coat lined with lynx. She had a pink lynx coat on, the most beautiful lynx coat I have ever seen. So she brings it down and says, "I'll play the scene with the coat on," and Lana was absolutely livid. So that's what you have to go through. I never made another picture with her. Lana was heavier when the film began, she got thinner at the end. They should have shot it with Lana doing the end scene first when she was heavier.

JK: So who are some of the people you liked to design for?

JL: Rosalind Russell. The way she carries the clothes always made it a pleasure to dress her. You know, it's more important for a woman to know how to carry clothes than to be pretty. Many girl who are pretty can't move. Lana isn't a good clotheshorse, but she has a sexy body and she doesn't move badly. And Marilyn Monroe—but she had so much sex when she was moving. I did her last movie with her [*Something's Got to Give*] and the film with Clark Gable [*The Misfits*], but that wasn't much of a challenge for me, it was a small picture.

    I had a hard time once with Judy Holliday. She was a great actress, but when I saw her the first time in the fitting room, I thought, "Oh, my God, what are we going to do with that?" She was standing with a sloping shoulder, exactly like this [please use your imagination]. I thought, "What are we going to start with?" I said, "Can you raise your shoulder a little bit?" She said, "Oh, yes." She was pretty dreadful. I said, "Do you like this?" You know, when you don't know, when you get no reaction, if nobody reacts to what you do, you get so depressed and you're not sure of yourself. You have to have somebody who reacts. It gives you more inspiration, particularly after fitting and fitting. I was absolutely panicky for the test [this was for *Born Yesterday*]. And suddenly she came on the screen, a different woman. She was a great actress, there's no question.

JK: How important was it to be aware of the fashion trends going on outside the film industry? When doing contemporary clothes for a film, could you make or try to make your own trends, or did you have to go along with what was coming out of Paris, etc.? When Dior dropped the hemlines after the war, could you have ignored it when designing clothes for a woman in a contemporary story?

JL: No, I suppose we had to go along. But, you see, you can't ever do exactly what fashion is doing at that moment because the film sometimes comes out a year after it's been done. We had that experience with Joan Fontaine one time. It was a picture she made with Jimmy Stewart about an aviator, and this was about the time that the new look from Dior came out and she wanted a dress like that, and the picture came out a year later and it was a catastrophe, because the line didn't stay there. So it's a very difficult thing. You see, we speak about a time, the beginning of the '40s . . . '43, '44, '45 . . . and that is the epoch when a woman had to have a bust like this [he describes a Jane Russell]. So you have to deal with that, that was the first constriction on what you did for women in films. The poor girl who was flat-chested, you had to get them like this. And sometime they say they want a décolleté dress and you have to show their bosom, so for that, the poor girl, we had to push her up, underneath, we give her a gay Pierrot, you know, a corset, and push her up like this, put a pad underneath, and that's what they think it was doing, though she only have a little thing like this. So there were all this constrictions. I don't know how they could act. They must have been in agony.

And, you know, I will tell you, think of Joan Crawford. The first time I have seen Joan Crawford when we make some pictures together* and that was the time when the shoulders didn't exist anymore in fashion, it was off, and she came to see me and I said, "Well, she's still wearing those pads." No, it was her shoulders. She had square shoulders, like this. First I was so shocked because I thought she was tall. But she's short. She has a very long torso. Short legs. And then you see those big shoulders and I thought, "My God, those are the Adrian shoulders. I thought Adrian had made them, but they were hers."

JK: Do you recall any studio interference with one of your designs when somebody didn't like what you did to one of their stars?

JL: Yes. When I was at Columbia, some producer wanted flesh, and you can't give flesh when you don't have it. The poor girl was skinny, she had a little arm like this, and you give her a big bosom, it doesn't balance, you know! So you give her long sleeves, and try to cover her up as much, and try, maybe give her a slit and show some leg.

It was frustrating and very hard to work at Columbia because they had so few stars. I don't know how many pictures I made where the woman was playing a secretary! Or a poor girl. That's all they played, and you had to dress them the same way, what else could you do?

JK: How would you describe sex appeal?

---

*Harriet Craig was their first, then came Queen Bee and Autumn Leaves.

JL: It's the way hair falls, it's in the eyes. I mean, it's not because you put ten pound on her bust pad. It's the thing a girl does individually. You know, when they had Rita Hayworth at Columbia, they were training about ten girls to look like Rita. Instead of looking to find somebody different, but it was like you do with a car, you want a series of it. And the poor girls didn't want to look like Rita Hayworth, like Patricia Knight. And then after years of training them, they drop them and somebody else gets them and they become a star. Like Marilyn Monroe—we used to have her, and we didn't do anything with her, except that chorus film, and we dropped her. And Fox picked her up. And she made *All About Eve* and she was a star right after, but when she was at Columbia nobody saw it. Rita Hayworth used to be with Fox and they dropped her and Columbia picked her up and she became a star. I left Columbia because I was at the end of my contract and Harry Cohn had died, and they wanted to cut expenses at the studio after he died. If Harry Cohn was still living, I would be still there. I liked it a lot at Columbia.

There was nobody [no designer] at Columbia when I got there. They would borrow Irene or they would borrow [Howard] Greer or those people. I had nobody else with me when I was there. I usually designed for the star and the principals in the film, the rest would come from wardrobe. The nice thing when I was working at Universal was that we always would meet the people from the other departments involved in the film, we'd be hearing what everybody else did, the color a set was going to be, what the props were. And so you knew what kind of dress would look good. You know, when I first got out there nobody told anybody else anything. The star could come in in a black dress and everything else would be black, and she would sit down on the sofa and you couldn't see her.

1977

INGRID
BERGMAN

P ERSPIRATION BEADS HAD STARTED TO FORM on her forehead at the hairline
and an animated flush was reddening her otherwise healthy, clear, clean
skin. To the people sitting rapt, looking up to her, the effect was only a further
heightening of the glow they got from being in the same room with her. But I
had the same problem, compounded—she was picking up on my nervousness.
We had been talking animatedly and intimately, too intimately. She was staring
intently into my eyes, a signal that our conversation was skirting, if not dangerous (she was too professional for that), at least embarrassing shoals of her life.

How did we get into her private feelings for director Victor Fleming?
Somehow we had reached that stage where we were picking up on the knowledge implied by the tone of voice in answering what were meant to be harmless,
gossipy questions. Instead of a relaxed celebrity-type chat before an audience
of movie buffs at London's National Film Theater, we'd gone off course. I
looked at the table where my prepared notes should have been, but there weren't
any. She wasn't angry, she just wanted us to get back to a more professional and
safer ground. "See if there are any questions from the audience," she whispered
beneath her breath, but I'd been looking desperately for a raised hand in the
packed house. Nary a sign. They were having too good a time seeing Ingrid
Bergman in a setting which had become decidedly *en famille*.

The whole event came about in the first place because a mutual friend in
California told me to get in touch with her back in London (she was currently
performing in Shaw's *Captain Brassbound's Conversion*) because Ingrid had a
trunkful of home movies annotating her life from the time her father, something
of a camera bug, filmed her when she was still a child, to films she and her
husband shot of their life in Sweden and later in Hollywood—of parties, bar-
becues, family picnics, time with friends.

Ingrid, it turned out, was as unlike her celebrated compatriot Greta Garbo
as anyone could be. Ingrid was a regular shutterbug. Maybe that's why she was
always so much at home in front of any sort of camera, whether it was candid
or posed, studio publicity or *paparazzi*. On screen Ingrid Bergman was never
remote—she looked as if she had just stepped into your home. Absolutely without guile. For some time now she'd been thinking about editing all the footage

together for a TV film, or for use in a lecture tour. Her idea wasn't clear, but my friend thought I'd be the person to help her.

In London I called Ingrid. We met. I saw her in the play. I loved all the little bits she did onstage. From the tenth row on down, this was close-up work. Beyond the tenth row, it looked a lot like fiddling and fumbling, though nobody minded. Audiences always went to see her to love her.

The program planner at the National Film Theater asked if she would come to the NFT to do a Celebrity Lecture on one of her Sundays off. "What does it consist of?" she wanted to know. "It's simple. I introduce you. We talk a bit, then we turn the questions over to the audience and they'll ask you about your films, your co-stars. I'll be moderating." So she said, "Fine."

The NFT was delighted with the news. But "John, don't hog the show. Let the audience ask the questions. Okay?" "Okay." "What film clips does she want?" "What clips do you want us to use?" "Clips? Why?" "It helps us if we run out of things to say." She laughed and dismissed the idea. "Just tell them to show *Casablanca,* that'll be all right." Okay. We were making our way into the jam-packed, overflowing theater foyer, people moving aside to let Ingrid pass, without a word, not a hand reaching out to impair her path, just gaping, adoring faces, as if she were each person's most precious possession.

The film is ending—Bergman, Ilsa, has just gone off in the plane with her husband after one last brief but intense, emotion-charged look back at Bogart, and Bogart is going back to Casablanca to fight the Nazis and make the world free for democracy with the help of Claude Rains. The End. House lights. Thunder. (That's applause.) They don't need an introduction to Ingrid Bergman.

A smiling Ingrid in a becoming, brick-red, short-sleeved wool dress, a single gold chain around her neck, looking like she might have gotten off the plane from Casablanca, comes onstage. Everybody is standing, applauding, cheering. To applaud, all you need is love. *But* to carry on an interview you need questions, and, to help out, clips to remind us, clips to refresh us, clips for pauses, clips to see how we're getting on. We had no clips! And I had prepared only a few questions to get us started since I wasn't planning to hog the occasion. But nobody had counted on the audience being in seventh heaven.

Ingrid and I were babbling on about Rossellini, and Vic Fleming, and Cooper, and Tracy.

WHISPER: "What do you want me to ask?"

WHISPER: "*Notorious.*"

Fast thinking. *Notorious:* Hitchcock. Cary Grant. Two films with Grant. He delivered the Oscar to her in Paris after she won for *Anastasia.* He was one of the first people she saw when she came back to America in 1958.

QUESTION: "You had a *very* close relationship with Cary Grant, didn't you?"

INGRID: "Well, not *that* close."

"I mean, I meant . . ." Everything I said implied a very *close* relationship.

The afternoon went on like that. It lasted for two hours. Everybody was happy. When it was over, autographs from Ingrid.

Ingrid Bergman, photographed by Laszlo Willinger (MGM), 1940

Ingrid didn't hold it against me. We should have had clips. I should have prepared questions. Relying on instinct is a surefire way to let things get out of hand.

But it was memorable.

THE CAMERA CUTS PEOPLE UP. Any part of a person's anatomy can reflect the whole person on screen. It's why Charles Boyer could be tall and strong enough to dominate the peasant-built, powerful Bergman. Long shots had to be guarded against, usually done with doubles, or with Bergman walking in a ditch, not to destroy the carefully built-up illusion.

Though Ingrid at 5'10" was much taller than the 5'7" Greta Garbo, she never conveyed the impression of someone towering over her leading men the way we felt Garbo would by the simple expedient of standing upright. Garbo was not merely physically taller, she was emotionally and spiritually taller than anything or anybody surrounding her. When Shubin (Lionel Barrymore, her lover and informant in *Mata Hari*) threatens her, she puts him in his place: "I am Mata Hari, and my own master." We know exactly what she means and we know that he's crushed. And the camera takes its height from the face.

Bergman's appeal was drawn from her face. She was a heroine, not heroic. Certainly not as far as her most memorable roles would have us believe—Maria in *For Whom the Bell Tolls*, Ilsa in *Casablanca*, Paula in *Gaslight*, Ivy in *Dr. Jekyll and Mr. Hyde*, in *Intermezzo*, in *Notorious*, as Anastasia, or as the Welsh charwoman, only five feet tall in real life, who was the heroine of *The Inn of the Sixth Happiness*. Nothing, not even the image-shattering events in Bergman's private life, could dislodge that first, all-powerful impression. To her public, despite three husbands, several lovers, four children (one of whom was born out of wedlock), Bergman was ensconced as heroine. She was the country maid of Victorian literature done wrong by the city slickers. A vast array of classic literary heroines, from the self-sacrificing heroine of Balzac's *Splendeurs et Misères des Courtisanes* to Madame de Renal in Stendhal's *Le Rouge et le Noir;* Maggie Tulliver in George Eliot's *The Mill on the Floss,* Thomas Hardy's *Tess of the d'Urbervilles* and countless lesser boulevard-drama serving maids, discarded mistresses and cowering wives had all prepared the way for Ingrid Bergman's real-life heroine role in our lives. In Ingrid Bergman's uniquely personal success the audience played the leading role. When they turned on her after she left Hollywood—and her husband—to make a film in Italy and embark on her (for those times shattering) affair with the film's director (father of her second child while still married to her first husband), the public played out the role of the *deus ex machina* of the Hardy novels, the turn of the wheel of fate after which society turns its outraged back on Tess, Maggie and Madame X. Whatever it might have looked like from the outside (and probably to Ingrid, locked inside it), in the larger sense her fall was a dramatic conspiracy to enhance her already phenomenal appeal through trial, guilt, remorse and, at last, the celebration of forgiveness.

By the time she left Hollywood in 1949, though physically she was just in her prime, her career was actually in very serious doldrums. Although she was accepted by all as the most beloved woman in the land, her films after *Notorious* had been resounding box-office flops: Lewis Milestone's *Arch of Triumph,* Fleming's *Joan of Arc,* Hitchcock's *Under Capricorn.* She could have filled a Broadway theater as Joan for a year. She could not fill the movie houses in the same celebrated, eagerly awaited screen role for a week. Yet, when she played a far less demanding part such as the (nonsinging) nun in *The Bells of St. Mary's* (by critical consent, a sticky bit of second-rate hokum), audiences had besieged the nation's cinemas to make it one of the box-office triumphs of the decade. By 1949 our heroine was in some danger of fading away from lack of interest. A jolt was needed. Whether we knew it or not, we were all ready for that twist in the story where fate enters to shatter the state of idyllic but stagnating bliss.

The next great chapter in her life was now being played out. Rarely has the old adage "Absence makes the heart grow fonder" gone through such conundrums to affirm its simple truth. Ten years' absence from the American screen (and hearts) had not kept her idle. One read of films she made with her seducer (whether he chose to or not, that's the role Roberto Rossellini was cast in by popular consent) which were avoided by the public, and not just the American public either, *and* dismissed by critics who, when it came to Bergman, showed no more professional discernment than her bitter fans.

Rossellini, whose genius had been praised for films like *Open City* and *Paisan* (made before he met Ingrid), and whose work after they split up was again to be acclaimed, was brutally lambasted for the films he made with her, which have since been recognized as masterpieces. To all intents and purposes, Ingrid Bergman was an outcast, ignored, splattered with mud, insulted in public and in print, and as far as going to see her films was concerned, more forgotten than if she had died.

Ten years in the wilderness is long enough to pay for any crime. After all, even a Byzantine whore needed only seven years of knitting or basket-weaving in the town marketplace to wipe the slate clean and become a respectable member of society. One even married the Emperor, and when Justinian died, Theodora became the powerful ruler of one of the ancient world's most-prized kingdoms. It's an irony, but a choice one, that the ten years Bergman spent away from the limelight kept her from growing older in the public's memory. Loretta Young managed to arrest her own waning popularity by an unexpected and dramatic change of venue. Bette Davis did it by the audacity of her now legendary advertisement in the trade papers to let producers know that she was an actress looking for work. We suddenly saw familiars in a renewed light. We realized in time what we had almost lost by taking them for granted. Bergman's resurrection was more dramatic and effective because she herself hadn't planned it. The wheel had simply taken another revolution and now we had the satisfaction of celebrating the prodigal's return: the last-minute rescue from the gallows. This was D. W. Griffith, pure and simple. Because we hadn't watched her, ten years were shed like nothing. Ingrid returned, unchanged.

In 1958 she came back to American audiences with *Anastasia,* the story of the woman without a country who'd surfaced in Germany, living in near-poverty, claiming to be the lost, only remaining daughter of the last Czar of Russia. Her sad, pathetic life was a tabloid's dream while her fate and the truth of her story (never satisfactorily verified) were being dragged out in the courts. As a character, Anna, whether a czar's daughter or a brilliant deceiver, had attracted enormous public interest and sympathy. The film, based on a play, was enormously popular, and Bergman won her second Oscar. If the judges had seen the film instead of listening to evidence, they would have given Anna the crown.

Ingrid did not go to Hollywood to receive the Oscar herself. Cary Grant collected it on her behalf and, speaking to the nationwide TV audience, said, "Come back home, Ingrid. We miss you." Ingrid was currently scoring a triumph on the stage, playing in the Paris version of *Tea and Sympathy.* "When you talk about this, and you will, be kind." You can just feel the shiver that must have run through the French audience when she spoke that sentimental line at the end of the play. *Anastasia* would have been a triumph for Bergman back in '48. It was exactly the sort of role that would probably have kept her in Hollywood. But then we wouldn't have had the satisfaction of participating in the Rise and Fall and Rise of Ingrid, the greatest popular melodrama of the decade. There's really no other story quite like hers in film history. In a Freudian, electronic, scientific, paranoid age, our most beloved heroine was a Victorian maid, pure and simple.

SHE WAS LIVING in a large elegant impersonal apartment in Grosvenor Square, across the street from the American Embassy. She'd been there for several months, but the only "home touches" were family photographs in stand-up frames on a table. Her husband, the Swedish impresario Lars Schmidt, was in Paris setting up a new show. Her Rossellini children were at school or with their father in Italy. Her oldest daughter, the child from her first husband, Pia Lindstrom, was doing pretty well in New York as a TV anchorwoman. Ingrid was having a great time in the play. There were other plays to be done. She loved the live theater. There were other films to be made. She belonged to the screen. There had of course already been many requests for her to write her autobiography, but not till several years after our talks did she finally decide to do that, and then it was really to do what the home movies had been intended for: to set the facts straight for her children. Now it was just us, and even she was impressed to find how much she remembered.

Talking about *Captain Brassbound's Conversion,* I tell her that I loved the way she covered with gestures when stuck for a line.

IB: We haven't changed a word. It's all Bernard Shaw—the way he wrote it. And that's how we play it. Now, there might be evenings when you get a

blank, so the other actor comes in with his line while you just stand there—
we cover up. The other night James Gibson, who plays the missionary, was
absolutely stuck for a line. I tried to help him. At the end he says, "You can't
do anything more for me now" when he leaves me forever. Instead of saying
"You can't do anything more for me," he said, "I can't do anything more for
you." [Laughs.] Well, that's frightening. And you can see the poor actor's
eyes staring as if to say, "God, help me out of it!" You can't go back and say,
"Excuse me, I mean the other way around."

JK: When actors are very good, like you are, then the mistake is covered up to
look like something very like life. You have the ability to move a thing
around. English actors always love scope for the voice, but really one of the
great qualities you have is the things you *don't* say but yet they come through.
In the play someone says the line to you, "One can see you thinking."

IB: Very often the great close-ups in films are the silent ones. It's something
that I try to get across to Frith Banbury [the director] because I move on a
line when Brassbound is talking, and he said, "You can't move there because
people must look at him while he's speaking. If you move, they'll look at
you." I said that I thought it was better if they look at me because it's *my*
reaction that is important. Not the words, but the reaction. He can't understand that. He thinks that the person who is talking should be looked at so
that you follow the words. But very often in life it's the person who is *not*
talking that is worth watching.

JK: When you played Anastasia, there was a side of that character in which the
real person and the mythical person had almost become one. As an actress,
when you came to it, which aspect did you go for? How did you decide?

IB: My director told me I always played it too sincerely. He said I was playing
it as though I *was* Anastasia. "I want people to leave the theater exactly as
they leave any newspaper when they read about Mrs. Anderson and her trials
fighting for the money she wants and the position. You are giving such a
performance of being the *real* Anastasia that not only will they overlook Mrs.
Anderson but the Bank of England is going to give the money to you!"

JK: Did you meet her when you studied the part?

IB: No, not at all. She was living in Germany someplace. I just looked at it as
a part I had to play: here's this woman who doesn't know and is frightened
and wants to commit suicide, and has been saved and brought to this place
by these men, and they're trying to work on her. She believes that she *is* what
they tell her.

JK: How about St. Joan? She was a real character, yet the image that has grown
up around her has turned her into a saint. What did you go for when you
played her?

IB: The absolute innocence, and the belief she had in her voices, and her courage. She went against her own character. That's what I have against Shaw's *Saint Joan,* because he made her say that she loved to be with men and people at war and the excitement of it. But if you read her answers in the trial, she says just the opposite—that she wanted to stay home and spin and wash sheets, get married and have children. She was a very ordinary peasant girl. She must have been very strong and healthy too, otherwise I don't know how she put on that armor and rode and did all those things. But she did it all against her own character, with a tremendous amount of courage. She went into the battles saying to her troops, "I'm not going to turn around to see if you're following me—I'm going to run ahead." 'Course all the men had to run after her. That I admire. And I admire her sense of humor; in all the things she said and the way she knocked down all those learned men, you know, who came with all their shrewd questions to try and pin her down for having said something wrong against the Church or God. And of course she never did—she always had that enormous common sense.

JK: So you had no trouble deciding between the myth of the woman and her innate saintliness?

IB: Some actresses have played her as a saint, but in her lifetime she wasn't. She became a saint when she was dead. I played her as a very innocent peasant—not at all as a saint. When I did Honegger's *Joan at the Stake*— after Honegger came down from Switzerland, and Paul Claudel was there too, they asked me to read for them. Arthur Honegger sat there smiling in rehearsal and said, "It's so funny to hear you read, for you read it so simply. Everyone who plays this part usually [Ingrid puts on a theatrical voice] goes in for it like that, and follows the music, singing it out. But you don't."

JK: How was it for you coming to Hollywood and seeing Garbo and other stars? Did you feel you were seeing "The Garbo" or "Hello, Miss Garbo"?

IB: Well, of course, I'd read movie magazines and read about their private lives. But what I admired them for was the performances they gave. The first day I was in Hollywood, I stayed at the Selznicks' home and they had a party the following night to introduce me to Hollywood. I remember sitting there in a dress that I'd bought from a Swedish movie—very nervous that perhaps it wasn't good enough. I just sat there and all these personalities that I had seen walked into the room. I couldn't believe it, it was like a dream.

Ann Sheridan walked in and they said, "That's the 'Oomph' Girl." I said, "Excuse me" and went up to my room to look in my dictionary to see what "oomph" meant. [Laughs.] Couldn't find it. But nobody talked to me. They all came up to be presented, and I sat there being in heaven watching all these people. There was Gary Cooper talking to Bette Davis and Cary Grant and Fredric March and Norma Shearer. I couldn't believe it. I didn't realize I looked so lonely until this man came up and said, "We've all come to Hollywood for the first time and had this happen. They're all discussing you over there and saying what they think of you and making bets on your potential." I said I hadn't realized I looked lonely, but he said he'd talk to me anyway. Apparently he'd been invited to look me over too and said that I'd be welcome to come to his pool party the following day. I said how very nice it was of him and asked his name. He said, "Ernst Lubitsch."

The following Sunday I went to his place. My maid drove the car because I couldn't find my way around. There were *lots* of cars outside his house. I went in. There were people all over the living room, but nobody recognizes me and nobody talks to me. I go into the next room, the library, the playroom, the dining room, and everywhere people were having a marvelous time. Then I asked a butler where was Mr. Lubitsch and he said he was out at the pool. Everyone was swimming and diving and again having a marvelous time. I walked around the pool and asked another butler, but he didn't know where Mr. Lubitsch was. So I took the same walk through all the rooms and right out to my car. By that time my maid had just got the car in and parked. I said we were going home! [Laughs.] What can you do when you're alone?

JK: So you remember clearly that all you saw was the images of all these people. So you can understand that even when you personally know people, when you read something about "Bergman" in a paper, what you think of while you're reading is "Bergman" and it's only afterwards that you consider how true or false what was written is.

IB: It is funny. You know, Ruth [Roberts, her voice coach] says that often to me. I say, "This idiot came to talk to me and he kept stumbling and couldn't get anything out." Ruth always says, "You must remember they didn't expect you to open the door or to answer the phone. They are frightened and tongue-tied." I don't forget that I am a walking image. When you meet people, for instance, in an elevator, they talk about you as though you weren't there: "She's much taller than I thought she was." "Doesn't she look nice?" And you're standing right next to them. They must think you're still on the screen.

JK: That's what I mean. They're not really talking about you or to you, but to this other "Ingrid Bergman."

IB: Yes, but I've always considered myself as a kind of circus horse. I'm there and I'm responsible for this horse, but when I see rushes, I always talk about "she": "Why does 'she' walk that way?" "Why didn't 'she' stay put then?" It's not really me I'm seeing—that's the person that earns money for me. I'm responsible for it, but it's not really me.

JK: You're a trained actress, but not all actors become stars and not all stars are actors. How do you feel about it?

IB: I think it means you have talent. I don't think there are any stars truly so-called who aren't talented. It's an acting talent. Lana Turner can act. She may not have been "Lana Turner" if she'd been in the theater, but she *is* a movie actress. She's survived a lot of bad movies, but she still goes on, and that is talent. And she has good looks.

All parts I play are looked at through my eyes, naturally. Be it a suffering mother or a vindictive countess or an innocent child. Whatever the part is, it all goes through me and I suppose becomes alike in that respect. Because it's what *I* feel as a human being that I deliver. There are limits; I can't play anything that I don't understand or can't feel. I am limited by my own character. I've never lost myself playing any character.

JK: You don't think that's a handicap?

IB: Let's consider *The Visit*. I was sitting in my husband's office in Paris, where he has a lot of plays lying around. While I waited for him to finish a meeting, I picked up this play which happened to be *The Visit*. When he was through, I took the play home with me, because it was so amusing. Black comedy, but certainly comedy. I like to laugh, so I look for things that make me laugh, and if I can play something that makes other people laugh, so much the better. My husband said he had seen the play and that it wasn't anything to laugh at at all—it was very dark and very heavy. I said in astonishment, "But it's so amusing. I'm laughing at these things." He said, "Well, she's going to kill him for vengeance." So when 20th Century–Fox came to me—I'd just done *Inn of the Sixth Happiness* and they wanted me to continue with them—they said that they would buy whatever I wanted as a vehicle. So I said I wanted Dürrenmatt's *The Visit* because I thought we could make a hilarious comedy out of it.

Well, three years went by—script after script—they couldn't get anything out of that story. They thought it was awful that the man was killed in the end—they wanted Cary Grant for the part and couldn't have him get killed! So they made the story work the opposite way: *I* was killed in the end! Then they made it a Western with me riding into town! In the end I told them they'd have to stick to Dürrenmatt. Anyway, Cary Grant was never approached.

Then I came to Switzerland to visit friends and I got a telephone call from a film director who said he was a friend of Dürrenmatt's and would like to talk to me. So we met in a hotel and he told me that Dürrenmatt had said if ever *The Visit* were made into a film, then he would be the only man to direct it. So I agreed, though I didn't know who he was—it was Bernhard Wicki. So they started again with the script, and although the man wasn't killed at the end, he was as good as dead because all his friends turned against him and *wanted* to kill him. The picture became a very dark, humorless affair and, from what I saw of it, it didn't seem to come off. That happens very often in my career. But I never regret anything because I always set out to do something I believe in, even though during the process of making it it turns sour on you. Exactly the same thing happened with *A Walk in the Spring Rain*. A marvelous book, but you just couldn't put that quality into the screenplay.

JK: If you'd had complete control over *The Visit,* who would you have chosen as a director?

IB: I don't know. But I also read *Promise at Dawn* [Romain Gary's book] and said, "This is me and I want to do it." Fox again very graciously bought it and again we had script after script. But, having had the experience with *The Visit,* I was even more careful and said the scripts were no good. So finally they sold the rights of the script and I took the money because I really couldn't wait any longer. Vittorio de Sica bought it. I knew him and thought he would be marvelous to direct this sentimental story, but he didn't want me. He wanted Ava Gardner. But *he* went on with the script forever and ever and finally sold it to Jules Dassin, who made it with Melina Mercouri. [Giggles.] I remember then I asked Fred Zinnemann because I thought he would be good for it. But that didn't work out.

JK: To get back to when you first came to Hollywood, what was the big difference between working there or in Sweden?

IB: It was only bigger. It was like buying a perfume bottle that's this big instead of this big. Only more people on set, more clothes, more stand-ins—which we didn't have in Sweden—makeup men and electricians. All those specialized people. In Sweden the same man does the lot. Whereas on the average set in Sweden you'd find twelve people, in America there would be fifty. If I'd stayed in Sweden, I'd have been in movies until I was too old to get the best parts. And then I'd have been on the stage. Exactly as I am now.

JK: If you were ever cast as Ingrid Bergman, could you play her?

IB (giggles): Yes, of course I could. Who could play it better? My life seems fantastic because I've never really had to fight for anything—it's just come my way. I made my own image because I refused to change my name or my hair. They wanted to change me completely when I first came over because that was the standard thing to do. They took stars from Hungary, Germany, France, and then tried to change them—to make them more beautiful to American eyes, I suppose. But then they became just like all the other American stars that were there. Lots of publicity stills in bathing suits and hats and all that. Well, I'd often seen that in the papers and wondered how come they never got anywhere.

Take Michèle Morgan; she failed in Hollywood, but she's still to this day a very big star in her own country. So I was careful. I said I was coming over to do one picture that is good. I want a top director and a top leading man—because I noticed they didn't have that, these other people. So when Selznick came to me, I told him that was what I wanted and after that I would go home. He said it wasn't done that way. So I said okay, then we don't do it. Well, he gave in. He said we'd do one picture and I could go. But if I liked it in Hollywood, I said I'd stay with him. So that was the contract I made—I was very clever.

Then when I came over, they started in on me: "The name's impossible to pronounce," "The name's German and there's a war on," "Your teeth, eyebrows and hair are wrong." But I said I wouldn't change anything. I told them that they'd got me over here because they'd seen a picture called *Intermezzo* and I was here to do a remake, and I was staying how I was because that's the way you liked me in the picture. Then they started on the publicity. But I didn't want any of it—I wanted the public to discover me. I didn't want to be pushed down their throats, because I've seen that: "MARVELOUS STAR FROM HOLLAND, A GREAT ACTRESS" and then out she comes and just does what everyone else is doing. Well, Selznick listened and said it was a great idea. He said he'd work on the idea of a natural girl from whose head not a hair had been removed. He told makeup he'd kill anyone who touched my eyebrows. We did tests in color with no makeup on at all. However, my face was too red in the heat of the lamps, so I had to have a little makeup on. So I became the "natural" star. And it was just at the right time because everything had become very artificial and all hairdos. My hair got blown, my clothes were simple, I looked very simple and I acted like the girl next door. The public didn't hear about me until the picture came out, and that picture has done more for me than anything else because people come to me today, after thirty years, and say that's the picture they like most because *they* discovered me. It's very funny.

The only other difference between Sweden and Hollywood is that here things are a bit glossier and the homes are a little bigger. But with *Intermezzo* they had every scene from the Swedish version there before them on the set, looked at every setup, and made exactly the same movie. It's just that the sets were a little bit more expensive.

Leslie Howard was a charming man and I had no problems there at all. I have a record at home with our voices on it. Ruth did it for me because we didn't have tape in those days. Everyone's talking: Gregory Ratoff, who directed it; Leslie Howard wishing me well. I went home to Sweden because I was so afraid that I'd have the same fate as those other actresses from Europe. I made one film in Sweden that I'd already contracted to do and then went back to Selznick for four years.

JK: The image can limit one, though. Ann Sheridan, who was very sensible about it, couldn't shake that one thing that propelled her from being the nice little girl to the big star. Finally, her career foundered on being "oomph."

IB: Yes, it can't last. But I've never built my career on beauty and youth. It can't last, and that's why I was never tied up in the movies for more than three or four years at a time. After that I would ask permission to go onto the stage again because I knew that there's where I would end up. When your youth's gone, there are some smaller good parts you can do, but if you want to continue living the spoiled life to which you've become used, then you must return to the stage for the work. So I've always been working on the stage and have done things with my voice and sung. I knew it wasn't Hollywood that was going to give me my future career.

JK: What made you want to become an actress?

IB: I never had any hesitation about it in my mind. Alone at home when I was five, six and seven, I was always acting—dressing up in funny clothes and pretending to be someone else. Of course, I didn't know it was "acting" then. I was a lonely child and I think it often happens with "only children," especially when you don't have many friends, that you make up characters to be and be with. My father took me a lot to the opera and one day he took me to the theater—I must have been eleven—and I knew that was it. Acting just grew out of my childhood. It's not that I decided—it was decided for me. Always as a child I play-acted, and then when I got to school and started to go to the theater, I read plays and learned them. I read poetry too. At the Christmas parties for parents and children at the end of term, I would always be appearing—I was a star in school! I've done it all my life.

JK: Is there a difference in the attitude toward stars in Sweden, Germany or Hollywood?

IB: In the silent days, of course, Sweden led the world. Then when sound came in, they were stuck with the language. I had offers from Germany and America at the same time, and I took the German offer because I spoke the language. I thought it would be good to find out how it is to work in a foreign language. People forget that I don't work in my own language; imagine how much simpler it is to say a phrase that you know and feel and which all your life you've said that way. You work in a foreign language and when you get to a violent or emotional scene, the words go; you don't remember the phrase because the words haven't grown into you. So I went to Germany and did a picture—but not with the intention of staying in Germany at all. I had my eyes set on Hollywood, of course, but it was a question of waiting for the right opportunity. They wanted me to stay on in Germany, but I said no because I wanted to work in a totally foreign language. It wasn't that Germany wasn't glamorous enough—it was. The war was looming, of course, but I'd never had any interest in politics, so I didn't know what I was doing. I had no idea World War II was at the door. I just wanted to try my wings in a new language. Knowing I could do it in German, I said, Right, it's time to learn English. But I knew from the beginning that I wouldn't stay in Sweden. It was too far away and too small a country. I wanted to go to big places. There's a very good actor in Sweden whom I always tell to learn English. If he did and went to London or America, he probably would be the biggest star in the world. He says he'd rather be a big fish in small waters than a little fish in big waters. Well . . . I had such a tremendous ego, I suppose, that I prefer to be a big fish in big waters! [Laughs.] His name is Jarl Kulle. But he just doesn't want to leave Sweden. He's like Ingmar Bergman, you see; he feels he has his roots there and he understands the people and recognizes the stones and trees. He knows what he's doing in his own homeland. Ingmar Bergman doesn't move at all. He's been here [England] once, but I think that was the only time he's ever done it . . . for the *Hedda Gabler* that he produced in Sweden and then did the same thing here.* I wanted desperately to travel and get out into the world.

JK: How did you think a character through—in Swedish or in the language you were acting it in?

IB: I'm always asked that. I dunno. Sometimes I speak Swedish to Ruth, and that must mean I'm thinking in Swedish and it doesn't come out in English. Anyway I don't translate: I don't translate a Swedish thought into English words. Many thoughts don't have a language.

JK: But it's where many people have foundered. In a close-up, more is revealed than just the state of your skin—it reveals the way you think. And if you think in a foreign language while you're listening to somebody, it comes across. It slows you up and keeps removing the audience. Ruth was telling me about Ilona Massey [glamorous blond Hungarian who came to Hollywood with Hedy Lamarr in 1937]. I don't know about Hedy Lamarr, but finally it just slowed up everything with Ilona, who was more interested in her social life than in her English lessons, so nothing came across.

IB: But, you see, I had the good fortune of meeting Ruth the first day on the set. She is an excellent teacher for English. Being of Swedish descent, she also understood my character and knew how to show me America—not only by teaching me the language, but coaching me in the feeling and thought too. I was terribly happy in America. I liked it until the very last years, when I just got tired of the big walls that are around Hollywood—it didn't seem to belong to the world. Again, you see, I wanted to get out into the world; I wanted to be where the real people are.

JK: I think you'd agree that *Under Capricorn* suffered at the box office because of your private life. If it had been made in 1945, it would probably have been a very successful film, for you gave a very fine performance in it.

IB: I remember the film being very difficult because of Hitchcock's insistence on shooting whole scenes—you know, he shot those eleven-minute takes which drove all his actors crazy. Usually if you shoot a scene, it takes two or

---

*Events in Sweden changed all that when the Swedish tax man came.

three minutes, a close-up takes another minute, and you've made a whole scene, but it would be intercut. He invented this thing, which he first used in *Rope,* of moving the *camera* into close-up or away—and he could keep a scene going for eleven minutes. All the walls had to be lifted and taken away, and the lights were tied to men who were walking all over the place, tables were moved in by somebody crawling in with the table on their back! Things moved all around you so you could play a scene for eleven minutes without stopping. He wanted to show the industry he could do that—nobody else had thought of it. Of course, the audience watching the movie don't wonder how the cuts were made. It was such a terrible strain. Something would go wrong after five or six minutes and you'd have to go back to the beginning. And the poor person waiting in the doorway just to say "How do you do?" waited and waited and waited, and by the time they finally got to him, he was so broken down and nervous he couldn't remember what he was going to say. It was great hardship to do. In the end he [Hitchcock] had to intercut anyway to bring in certain close-ups.

I remember it was a good story, but I don't think it had much success. But posterity can certainly give new life to a film. *Stromboli* and *Europe '51* and *Trip to Italy* are now classics. They come on television all the time in Italy, and they write the most marvelous things about them—which they certainly didn't do in the beginning. Even if my private life hadn't overlapped, it [*Under Capricorn*] still needn't have been a success when it was made.

JK: After Hollywood you went to Italy even though in Hollywood the exposure was better. . . .

IB: But that became very hollow. I'm very realistic and I didn't think the pictures were realistic enough. But I can't complain. I did marvelously well; I had the best actors and directors. Yet there was something inside me that was just straining for a challenge and the *truth*. In *that* mood I saw *Open City,* which I thought was the most beautiful, magnificent picture ever and which told the truth. I remember going outside the cinema and seeing the director's name and thinking I must remember that name. I also thought, "God, he's even written the music"—but actually it was his brother. Then I waited for the second movie by him [Rossellini] because that might have been a one-shot. When I was in New York, maybe a year after that, in a little theater *Paisan* was on. So I went in to see that and then decided to write a letter. For how was a man in Italy to understand that a person who at the time was number-one box office wanted to come to Italy and make a simple little movie like that, you know, with no fanfare around it? So I had to write the letter and tell him. He sent the synopsis of a story he'd invented and that's how I happened to come to Italy.

JK: After *Casablanca* the roles you were offered may have been varied, but they were on the whole less demanding.

IB: *Casablanca* was early in my career. After that I did *Gaslight, Notorious, Spellbound, Bells of St. Mary's*. I think they all had great variety and were good films. But there came a time when I got fed up. In *Dr. Jekyll and Mr. Hyde* Lana Turner was cast as the little barmaid and I was to play Dr. Jekyll's fiancée. I went to the director and said I was so fed up playing the same part over and over again. I said I'd like to play the barmaid. He said that with my face I couldn't do that. I said, "What do you know about my face? Let's do a little test." He was amazed because I suppose in those days to test meant you weren't sure of yourself. Anyway the test turned out very well and we switched the parts. I'm sure Lana was just as happy as I was because she was always playing barmaids! So that was lucky.

When I played in *Casablanca*—I must have been over at Warner Brothers because I was already signed up to do *Saratoga Trunk*—anyway Mike Curtiz talked to me about it and said I was making a big mistake trying to change all the time and playing the good girl and the bad girl and what have you. He said that in America they like personalities and pay to see what they expect to see. So once they like you, you should never change. Spencer Tracy, Gary Cooper . . . they never changed. They were themselves in whatever they did. A wonderful actor, James Stewart, would horrify an audience if he appeared in a beard or funny nose. I replied that I wasn't that kind of person, I was an actress and I *wanted* to change. I want people to say "Who is that?" He said it wouldn't work in America, but anyway I said I'd try. So I tried it in *Saratoga Trunk* and *Dr. Jekyll and Mr. Hyde*, but you see [Curtiz] was right: Americans *want* the personality they expect. So I wasn't given different parts from the ones you see me in. I had a lot to choose from, I was given wonderful scripts to read and chose the best out of those scripts. But there is the personality, and you don't get away from it. I played *Anna Christie* on the stage and I remember everyone laughing at the idea. I protested that it was marvelous for me—anyway, she's Swedish. I came onto the stage playing the streetwalker and was given a double whiskey and people laughed. They couldn't believe it. If it had been a glass of milk, maybe they'd have accepted it. [Laughs.]

When I came back to Hollywood [after the Swedish film], there were no parts for me at all and he [Selznick] was interested in his work for the government. He said, "You're getting paid, so what are you grumbling about?" Well, I wasn't getting paid very much. I came back and did *Anna Christie* because I had a lot of time off. I went to New York and was offered to do *Liliom* on the stage. And I did a lot of radio work in those days and all those Lux things. I don't know, I never liked Hollywood—all that sunshine all the time. So I used to go to New York, which I thought was wonderful, and could go to the theater a lot. My trips were paid for if I did radio shows. I did *Camille, Anna Karenina* and [gasps], oh, an *awful* lot of things. Pictures that other people made—all kinds of things where I wouldn't have fitted in on the screen but playing over the radio was fine: *A Man's Castle* was another [Loretta Young's part]. Yes, all kinds of old scripts I did through the years. I was always on those Lux programs so I could get out of Hollywood.

JK: By the time you did *Bells of St. Mary's* you were so popular that Selznick could ask for and almost get the moon. Do you realize that you almost lost *Bells of St. Mary's* to Irene Dunne?

IB: No, I didn't know that. But I know he kept raising and raising the price for me, which was awful. He didn't want me to do it. He was very sweet to me in that he never forced me to do anything *I* didn't want to do, but he also said that I didn't have good judgment. He used to say I was too anxious to work and I should wait for the epics. I said to hell with the epics, I want to work.

When the script for *Bells of St. Mary's* came for me, he said it wasn't any good. *Going My Way* had had a big success and he said it was an error to make a repeat performance. And that's true. He said Bing Crosby had played a priest in *Going My Way* and now they were trying to do it again and it wouldn't work. Anyway, what would I do when Bing Crosby was singing? I said that I would be listening to him and anyway the camera wouldn't be on me, it would be on him. Well, we argued this forever and finally he made a very tough deal so that they would refuse: he asked RKO for one year's free use of their studio and three properties—*Animal Kingdom, A Bill of Divorcement* and *Little Women*—and an enormous amount of money of which I only saw my normal contract salary, $50,000 or something like that. Selznick said to Leo McCarey, "Do you still want her that badly?" and McCarey said: "I'm so glad she's for sale." [Gales of laughter.] Well, the picture turned out beautifully, as you know, and it wasn't at all difficult listening to Crosby sing. So he had to eat his words. RKO said I had a marvelous agent—he keeps 90 percent and gives you 10 percent! [Laughs.] It never bothered me at all. I think Selznick handled me marvelously—he was great.

JK: Do you think being an actress in Hollywood has changed now?

IB: There's not the emphasis on their private lives, who they go out with, the clothes and the hairdos. You don't see that anymore. It's come down to being a job—you're an actor or you're a dentist, it's about the same. It's lost the glory. I look on myself as an entertainer. I went in to do a job to entertain people. If, on top of that, you become a star, it doesn't interest me very much. Why would I have gone to Italy if I'd wanted to be a star and on top of everything? I hadn't fallen down at that time—I still got the best scripts. But I didn't *want* it. I wanted to become a serious actress—and I went to Italy to work with Rossellini.

JK: Working with you, Rossellini explored things *he* hadn't done before—less "Italian realism." He began to give a little. Working together, you both broke images.

IB: Having done that, I ought to say that those Italian movies met with no success whatsoever. I then went on the stage in Paris and managed with an awful lot of hard work, because it *is* an awful lot of hard work to learn a foreign language. I did *Tea and Sympathy* there. My husband went to India at that time.* Then *Anastasia* just came up. And why shouldn't I do it? It was an excellent part and I was delighted to do it. It's not a question of being fickle and jumping from one country to another in any kind of neurotic way. It was an excellent part and I was delighted they came and asked me to do it. Also, since everyone said those Italian movies were no good, I thought perhaps it wasn't right for me to stay there. So, especially since my marriage had broken up, there was nothing to stop me going back to do *Anastasia*— but it wouldn't have mattered what country it was being made in. If you give me a marvelous part to play in Australia, I'll go to Australia, I couldn't care less.

JK: There's a scene when Yul Brynner is really torturing you. You've always had a rare mouth. . . .

IB: Ah, a *generous* one. [Peals of laughter.] Yes, I've read about it.

JK: But your mouth controlled that scene, and gave the audience back the dream it had with *Casablanca*. That was a marvelous movie to come back in, you must agree. [Ingrid had no choice. She agreed. Or allowed me to think so.] Let's talk about Carl Froelich, a big director in Germany.

IB: When I got an offer from Germany from Froelich, I knew he was a good director, so I accepted it—merely to see if I could act in a foreign language. I had a teacher who helped me with the dialogue, and I found I was capable of doing it. Froelich took me to see Hitler speaking in a big, open arena with *thousands* of people there. I remember them all going with their Heil Hitler sign and I didn't do it. Now, I had never been interested in politics, but I just felt, "Why should I, a foreigner, do this?" Carl Froelich was very angry with me and said, "You've *got* to do it. We *all* do." I asked why and he said he'd get into trouble if he was seen with someone who refused to do the sign. He said the picture might not get released. Well, I thought that was awful. Then I remember my leading man, Hans Söhnker, took me out in his car and showed me closed places, telling me that behind the wire they were doing military training. They said the men went around with shovels, but Hans believed they were guns. He said it wasn't any peaceful movement—there

---

*While making the documentary *India* (1958), Rossellini, in a repeat of his affair with Ingrid, fell in love with the Indian screenwriter Somali Das Gupta, who became pregnant and whom he married after his divorce from Ingrid. Suddenly it was Ingrid who was the wronged party, and public opinion in America and elsewhere began to turn in her favor. Here was this Italian Lothario who had wrecked her career and now, after all she had sacrificed for him, he was throwing her over for someone new. It paved the way for an American reconciliation and intensified interest and sympathy in her return as the much put-upon and suffering *Anastasia*.

was going to be trouble. He told me about concentration camps—oh, yes, he knew about it, he'd heard rumors, though nobody could really find out about it. He said he was terribly worried and unhappy for his country. Then my teacher in German told me she had a son and she didn't want him to join the Hitler Youth. Because of that, he'd been hit and sent home from school, you know. All kinds of problems. Finally, he'd begged his mother to let him join, but she was firm. But in 1938 the choice was plain: either join the Hitler Youth or that boy would get kicked around at school and fail his exams. Anyway, she refused to buy the flag you were supposed to hang out of your window on days of celebration. The next day she found her windows broken. Every time they were mended, they'd get broken again. And though she didn't earn much working in the studios, she stuck to her guns. Then they came to her door and asked her why she didn't buy it. She said she couldn't afford it, so they broke her windows again. As she said, "What can you do in this country? You just have to do what they say and follow the big movement or you get into trouble."

I remember when I came back to Germany with the American troops to entertain the soldiers, right after the war, I met Hans Söhnker in Berlin. He looked me up and I was with Larry Adler, Martha Tilton and Jack Benny. We went from place to place entertaining the soldiers. I did a sketch with Jack Benny and then did the monologue from *Joan of Arc*. I did all of Maxwell Anderson's monologues and explained the story to them. Anyway, when my American friends heard Hans Söhnker was arriving, they all said, "Watch him come in here and start telling us. . . . You can't find a Nazi anyplace. They're all against it now." So I just had to tell them he really was against Nazism because he'd told me about it in 1938.

So on the set of *Die Vier Gesellen* it was difficult because you could feel there was something brewing, though, as I say, I wasn't interested and just went there to make a movie. Carl Froelich liked me and wanted me to come back to do *Charlotte Corday*. I was delighted because that was a figure I thought was wonderful. Then came a veto—we weren't allowed to do any such story because that would antagonize the authorities. Then the war started. I came back from that picture and sat at home, having done *Intermezzo* in the spring of '39. I sat through the summer in my living room, sewing curtains, and on the radio I heard about the invasion of Poland. By contrast, everything was so gay and free in Hollywood; in Germany everyone had been so frightened. In a restaurant, if you spoke intimately, you gave what was called "the German look": look left and right over your shoulder and *then* say something. I mean, the *fear* was something unbelievable.

JK: Froelich was sort of a mixture of Clarence Brown and George Cukor.

IB: Yes, he was very fine. Very professional. I remember in one scene I didn't speak too well, but I played it well. They said, "Stop, you stumbled on a word, it's not perfect." I said, "Well, does it *really* matter!" because I'd really got the force and feeling and strength that was needed in that last shot and anyway everyone knew I was Swedish. But they said my German had to be the number-one priority. They cared more about how I pronounced the German words than about the acting! [Laughs.] That irritated me.

JK: It's interesting that two of Germany's biggest stars at that time were both Swedish and they epitomized the Aryan look—Christina Söderbaum and Zarah Leander. You look the same, I'm surprised you had any trouble. When you worked there, did you meet any of the German film colony? Was there a welcoming party as in Hollywood?

IB: No, not at all. I was only there for two and a half months at the most. I don't think I met anyone except for the people I worked with. Froelich was a nice, pleasant man, but I don't remember anything exceptionally great about him. I only had experience of Swedish directors, like Molander, and I certainly liked my Swedish directors much more. The UFA studios were much more professional than in Sweden; technically, everything functioned and there were bigger crews. And Hollywood was even bigger. I went from small to medium to large, that was all. I wasn't particularly impressed by their proficiency because I never think of that sort of thing much.

JK: When you were in Germany, was there any propaganda in *Die Vier Gesellen,* made in '37? Nazism was everywhere. Or was it a movie that could have been made anywhere?

IB: There was no propaganda in it, as far as I remember, but, as I say, I was politically very naïve. I mean, actors aren't like that; they talk about their next picture, and the last play, and about other actors. Of course, today they are more aware; look at Vanessa Redgrave or Jane Fonda. They both realize they must contribute towards making the world better in whatever way they think is most effective. So, though I don't remember any propaganda, the picture was nevertheless very controlled, and anything against the regime, against the establishment, would have been absolutely out. It was really an entertainment film, though. I don't remember if there were any pictures of Hitler in it. Wherever you went in Germany, you see, in private homes, banks, studios, there would be photographs of him on the walls. I was so impressed, I said, "In Sweden the King isn't hanging on the walls. And here is Hitler everywhere." I didn't know it wasn't out of love that he was there, but out of fear.

I remember being told that some comedian in his cabaret act had the line "Heil . . . what's his name, what's his name?" I don't know if he went to jail, but he certainly didn't work for a long time. Hitler had no sense of humor. Goebbels was very interested in entertainment, and actresses in particular. It worried me very much because Carl Froelich told me that if Goebbels asks me to go home for a cup of tea, then I was just to go. I'd made up my mind that I wouldn't. I said, "I certainly will *not*. I'm not German, why should I?"

With his reputation for being fond of actresses, I didn't want to, though the story went that if you didn't stay very friendly with Goebbels, he could ruin you. The good thing for me was that he never ever approached me. He wasn't interested in Swedish actresses!

JK: How does a director stick in your mind? How they got a performance out of you? How they behaved on set?

IB: I particularly remember directors who've got a performance out of me that I couldn't have got out by myself. Very often you get a director who tells you to come a little forward to the camera, to watch out for the lamps and keep your eye on the little mark on the floor, and who to look at when you say your line, and that's all. So your own performance is your own interpretation, and they only come through with very small suggestions about intonation or not to use your hands when you speak. Then there are other directors who can really give you marvelous ideas that you've never thought of. Cukor is one of those, so was Victor Fleming, and Hitchcock, and Leo McCarey was wonderful. It's awfully difficult to explain what they did that was so different. So it's a question of whether an actor can show something and then on top of that a director realizes what an actor can do and gives you another push in that direction. That's what makes you open up.

The boxing sequence, for instance, in *Bells of St. Mary's*—that was completely unrehearsed. We didn't know what would happen. So he gave me the words and showed me what to do and then we just shot it several times and new things would keep coming in. Just little touches—doing things with your feet, looking worried about your clothes, a way of pushing your hair back, that sort of thing. Cukor explains everything in such detail that sometimes you feel like saying, "Please don't say any more because my mind is so full of explanations." I used to tease him by saying if it were a little line like "Have a cup of tea," he would say what kind of a cup it was and what kind of tea it was until you got so worried you couldn't say the line.

JK: In *Gaslight* did you study a lot about the Victorian period?

IB: No, not at all. That was just a woman—I couldn't care if she lived in England or America or wherever. If it's a book, then I read the book carefully and read what the author has said about the character: whether she limps, smokes a lot, is deaf, how she moves. Those things I remember and try to put into a characterization and into the script. Like in *For Whom the Bell Tolls* there was so much description of the character in the book that didn't appear in the film script; I used to come along and say, "Look, in the book it says . . ." and "You've lost this beautiful line in the book . . ." So they'd put it in for me. All along in my career they've always told me I read too much [giggles] and that I'm too faithful to the author.

JK: Where did you get your idea of how to play Ilsa [in *Casablanca*], since there was never a finished script?

IB: Well, I played it the way Curtiz wanted it. I saw the film the other day and it's obvious from the start that she loved Bogart very much, in the true sense of love—she respected and admired her husband and went with him because there was a cause and he needed her and so she went with him from a sense of duty. But her love as a woman was certainly for Humphrey Bogart—at least, that's what I got out of the picture, and I'm sure that's how I played it.

JK: Were you in any other films where you didn't know from day to day what would turn up in the script?

IB: In my Italian period, yes. Otherwise the scripts usually were finished, but a lot of rewrites were still done. Even *Intermezzo:* David Selznick was always sending notes down. We'd get these rewrites and say, "We've already shot it, for heaven's sakes." We'd do a scene in the morning and in the afternoon a rewrite would arrive! He was impossible. He never could make up his mind, you know, that that was it—he always wanted something better. We went over and over my entrance because he wanted my arrival in the American film world to be like a shock that would just hit people between the eyes. He wanted people to remember it. Omar Sharif certainly had that in *Lawrence of Arabia*, that you'll never forget—a beautiful entrance. The sun and a camel. Now, *my* entrance was opening a door, hanging my coat up and stopping to watch a father looking at his little girl play the piano—there wasn't much I could do to make a tremendous impression. I can't tell you how many times I did it and redid it. My last day in Hollywood—I'd done so many retakes on different scenes—and he said let's shoot that scene again. I said, "What *can* I do? I mean, there *isn't* anything I can do." We shot until I packed my suitcases to go home. I took them into the studio and I was still doing that scene when my train left. I said I really had to go. I had to run with my makeup and costume on to the station.

JK: It was more Selznick's movie than Gregory Ratoff's.

IB: Yes. To be honest, it wasn't much Ratoff's movie. We had the Swedish version and a moviola on the set which we watched and did very much what the Swedish director had done. Leslie Howard rehearsed the dialogue with me and helped an awful lot. And what with Selznick and all his retakes, I have to say that Ratoff took a back seat there. I don't know how he felt about it. Sometimes he'd shout a lot on the set when he had to wait too long for some lighting or something. Yes, he was temperamental, but he was also a dear, sweet man. And very funny. His accent was very funny to listen to. He used to come up to me and say, "You don't read the line right. Listen to me . . ." And Ruth came up and said, "For God's sake, don't listen to him! Listen to *me*!" Because his accent was worse than mine.

JK: One of the big things about Hollywood, besides the films you made and the people you worked with, was the publicity machine, people like Louella Parsons and Hedda Hopper. Was there anything similar in Germany?

IB: I'm sure I had a publicity person on that picture too. I had interviews, and stories were written about me because I was well known from my Swedish movies that went over to Germany. So I wasn't an unknown face. But it isn't anything that I can particularly remember as I can the Hollywood publicity machine, which was really fantastic—everything they poured out. I don't think there was a German equivalent to the power of Hedda Hopper or Louella Parsons. They were absolutely an American fabrication. And nothing comparable in Sweden or Italy. I was *very* surprised at the power those women had. People were so afraid of them and everyone read their columns—I think it was the first thing they turned to, never mind about the war. It just stunned me that they were so important.

I was doing *Joan of Arc* for Walter Wanger, and this big party was for Louella Parsons in a big locale and *everybody* was going. You had to pay too. You paid $25, I think it was, for the supper. Now, I got my invitation and I threw it in the wastebasket. Then I got a second invitation and I threw *that* in the wastebasket. Then I got a call from my producer, Walter Wanger, saying he'd had a call from Miss Parsons' secretary that she'd sent me two invitations and I hadn't answered. I said, "No, because I'm not going." He said, "You have to go. Everybody *must* go. She has a list of those who refuse to go and we'll be in trouble with the picture." I said I didn't work like that and I didn't see why I should go and honor a woman who has been writing a lot of silly stuff about me and my friends. I didn't want to go to her celebration. He said, "Will you please, then, say that you'll be out of town and can't make it, and send her some flowers?" I said, "No, I will not." I mean, the invitation said are you coming or not, and I wasn't and I didn't see that I had to send her any flowers. Well, there was such an argument about it and I never did do a thing about it. I'm not quite sure if he didn't send her some flowers in my name. I don't know. But she had *that* much power—it's unbelievable.

JK: Did you ever reach an understanding with Hopper, Parsons and what they stood for?

IB: Well, no. I was always against them. I certainly *never* invited them to *my* parties and I knew they were against me because I never sent gifts. They couldn't get into their houses on Christmas Eve for all the gifts they were sent! But I never sent them anything, ever. They were against me, but they couldn't get anything off me. But Hopper was funnier because she was openly nasty and asked direct and nasty questions which made you just laugh. But Louella tried it the other way round; she would be very, very sweet and try to trick you into . . . For instance, she said to me once, "We have so much in common, you and I." I said, "Oh, really? What?" "We're both married to a doctor," she said. "How do you keep *your* doctor?" [Laughs.] But anyway, when I went to Italy and stayed there, they were delighted because for ten years they'd wanted to get something on me. And they certainly did. All hell broke up. Louella Parsons was the first one. She said she cried over her typewriter when she had to write the news [laughs] that I was delivering a son! I think they were tears of joy.

JK: Did Selznick ever say to be more careful how you treat them?

IB: Oh, yes. I was warned all the time that I should be nice to them and so on. But I didn't do anything. Hedda Hopper came to Italy—I invited her to come to a place in the country. And my husband [Rossellini] absolutely refused to say anything. It was very funny because everything she asked him, he said, "I don't know." He knew they were important too. I asked him should we invite her or not. He said, "Well, I don't know. If you really want to see her . . ." I said I thought it might be good if we talked to her because if we refused she might go back and write a horrible story, so maybe it's better she sees how happy we are, how nice everything is, with her own eyes. And then that might stop things they were continually writing about how unhappy I was in Italy and what a terrible mistake I had made, you see. Then, when she came, the first questions she asked were about people in the industry, and was it true that so-and-so did such-and-such. And he hated her gossipy attitude immediately. He said, "I don't know what you're talking about. Those things don't interest me." I was getting terribly nervous because I *had* invited her, so now I had to at least talk and say things. But he was absolutely no fun and walked away. Anyway she wrote a very nasty article saying that I'd had tears in my eyes all the time. You know the sort of thing: "*She* said she was very happy, but I could see through that . . . and as I left she was standing at the window staring after my car, longing for the freedom to go with me and come back to America." I mean, she made the whole thing up! Just the way she wanted. So that's what I got from inviting her to my home. [Laughs.]

When I first came there, I said to Mr. Selznick—when I realized what the publicity machine was like—I said I wished he wouldn't build *any* publicity. Let the audiences discover me with no publicity at all. Well, he said it wasn't done like that in America; when they got stars from Europe, the machine had to go with stories about their temperament and breaking mirrors, screaming and yelling, and their great loves. People have to see their names and photograph them in bathing suits. I said, "I'm terribly sorry, but I'm not going to make one picture in a bathing suit, and I'm *not* going to have my photograph taken in a funny hat. I'm only going to have pictures taken that belong to the movie." He was so stunned by it. He said, "How do you mean, 'let the audience discover you'?" I said to let the picture come out and we'll see what the critics write and what the people say, and then we can go on from there. If they didn't like me, I said, I wouldn't come back to America, because I didn't want my career in Sweden to be ruined for nothing. I said that if they built me up and then the audiences didn't like me, it could ruin me in Sweden. But if we were very humble and I was just presented as someone new from Sweden, then we could go from there.

Well, he was so surprised by this approach that he accepted it. During the *whole* time [shooting the film] I had no interviews—Hopper and everyone was trying to get on the set, but they weren't allowed, except the last day before I left, I was supposed to see Louella Parsons. He [Selznick] kept it up—he was terribly good. And of course he got a lot of publicity from it: that he had an actress from Sweden that he refused to let anyone talk to. That made everyone think, "What is she?" Everyone but Garbo gives interviews, you see. I went to Louella Parsons in her home to talk. She was very sweet to me—there wasn't much she could say or do to me. But I never did see Hedda Hopper that first trip to America. I was very carefully prepared for the Parsons interview: Don't tell them you have a child, because here actresses don't have children—we don't want that image of pregnant women around. You know that most people in Hollywood adopted children to keep their image of the beautiful woman with the beautiful body.

JK: But you were young and unknown and too tall, and here was this man who'd made *Gone With the Wind* and for ten years had been one of the most fêted producers. How come he was so easy with you?

IB: Well, he just was. I gave him good ideas. He was always easy and *wonderful* to talk to. Oh, yes, absolutely. We had a problem when I went away to do Joan of Arc. I'd always wanted to do that and I'd finished my contract with Selznick and wanted to be independent—working for myself, getting the money myself and not giving it to him! But I liked him so much. My husband had arguments with him in those days about contracts, but I wasn't involved in the business part of it. But I remember I was terribly unhappy when I went to New York to do the play [*Joan of Lorraine*] because we weren't on friendly terms since I hadn't re-signed with him. Then I saw him at a party one day, sitting at a table not looking in my direction. I finally sat down beside him and said, "David, I cannot go to New York and do Joan of Arc if you don't wish me good luck. I want us to be friendly again." I think he thought it was a mistake that I was going to be on the stage again. But finally he said very gruffly, "Good luck." Then he started a big campaign that he would do the movie of Joan of Arc with Jennifer Jones. I was then in the play when big ads started appearing all over the place saying, "The next Selznick production will be Joan of Arc with Jennifer Jones." I talked to him on the phone and he said, "You see, I'm going to do the movie." I said, "So am I. When I've finished the play, I'm going to do a movie too." He said, "You can't do that because my movie will come out first." I said, "That's fine because then I can rent all my costumes from you—I'll get them cheaper." He said, "You know very well two movies can't come out together." I said, "Why not? It's interesting. You can compare the performances and the qualities of each." Well, he never did do the movie and I did do mine. But there was just that little period of difference. We got on fine afterwards. I was never unhappy about him selling me for such high prices to other studios and me not seeing a cent of it. People tried to make me angry about it, but I just said that I signed the contract and if he could get $250,000 to my $50,000, it was all right by me because he was clever and I was not.

JK: How many of your films did he personally supervise?

IB: Only two: *Intermezzo* and *Spellbound*. On all the others he sold me to Warner Brothers or whoever. Paramount, RKO.

JK: When you came to Hollywood, you were given really good parts—better than most actresses of the period. You were idealized, worshiped. Why, then, by 1947 couldn't you wait to get out?

IB: I was tired of it because it was the same thing somehow. It was very unrealistic—the pictures—and the censorship was very harsh. So if you wanted to do something a little more risky, it was out. Things were too glossy and everybody talked about box office and more box office. I remember saying, "That picture wasn't very good, was it?" and they said, "Wasn't very good! Why, do you know how much money that picture made?" Well, so you talked about how much money it made and didn't bother about the quality of the picture.

And I wanted to move out of there. I wasn't very happy. It was neither town nor country and you felt as though you were in a factory. Then when I saw *Open City,* it struck me because I had this hunger for something realistic. I saw the picture and it had such humanistic qualities, it was so *true,* and it was shot the way people look—no makeup, no hairdressing, the clothes were right. Maybe there are pictures in America that way. I remember someone saying, "My goodness, those pictures we made twenty years ago when we didn't have good lights and couldn't afford things." Actually, my husband, Rossellini, told me that neo-realism came about through lack of money. They had to go out and get what they could: they couldn't reshoot much, people wore their own clothes and the lighting was very poor. So it was very true to life and I wanted to try that.

I've always wanted to be in places where there was great exchange of thought, where I can learn something. I adore to learn new things and know people's reactions to things. Sweden seemed too small and I felt I had to get to a bigger country. When I got there, I felt I'd learned everything Hollywood had to give.

I'm not ungrateful, you know, for the pictures I made there, because they *were* the best and wonderful people to work with. But there was some kind of longing to make something that was more of an event, more dangerous. I didn't want things to be steady, and there was too much security in Hollywood. I just would like to go out and fly a little higher, you know? I wasn't disappointed when I got to Italy either. I did learn an awful lot and it was as different from Hollywood as night from day. There was not the organization or money to be had, and there was no waste shooting from all different angles. It was shot one way because he had his story already written in his head and he knew what he wanted. It was fast going except for the days when he just didn't feel like work. So there were some days when we did very little because he just didn't have the ideas. He works instinctively on something— he's not a man that can work from 9:00 to 5:00, he works when the spirit moves him.

I certainly *did* find the reality I was looking for in the Italian movies. But I'd then been trained for ten years in America and years in Sweden having a script and dialogue and rehearsal time. I was very upset by having to impro- vise in Italy. You had to just make the dialogue up. Well, I couldn't. There was a cocktail conversation in *Europe '51* and he said to make up the conver- sation just as I do when people come into my home and have drinks. But I didn't know what to say. It was difficult. Another scene in the film was me talking to a man about the housing problems: the poor in the slums and the problems they had and how things should be improved. It was kind of a Communistic way of speaking, and I didn't know what to say . . . just "Yes" and "Really?" They wanted this man's thoughts on film and he wasn't an actor but a real man who lived in that community. They'd built a track and we were supposed to walk along in conversation. It was unrehearsed, and whenever he gave me a chance, my dialogue was "Oh, yes" and "Really?" We finished the track and he went on talking, and finally I see the director and the cameraman standing over in a corner having coffee and there's no one around us. So I stopped and said, "What's going on here?" Roberto said, "You can stop talking to him now because we ran out of film a long time ago." [Laughs.]

He built *Europe '51* around me because he had me and he knew he had a good story and it was for me. He had the idea: What would happen if St. Francis of Assisi, or a man like that, came back today? He'd be called a Communist immediately. He switched the part to a woman to give me the part. So it's a woman who leaves her family and riches to help the poor and lives the humiliation of St. Francis of Assisi. What you would say of such a woman today is that she's insane: she ruins the reputation of her family and she'd be put in an insane asylum. And that's what happens at the end of *Europe '51*.

JK: Having made six films together, did you get more used to the improvisation technique?

IB: No. And I think I realized that I wasn't that kind of an actress. There was Alexander Knox and George Sanders* there as well, but I felt very foreign to the rest of the cast and bewildered by the technique. We also did a German film, in which Mathias Wiemann played my husband. We were all actors in that. But that picture didn't turn out well either.

These pictures were not at all bad pictures, it was just that people didn't

*Knox co-starred in *Europe '51;* Sanders was her leading man in *A Trip to Italy.*

like them. Today they like them better. At the time I thought *Stromboli* was a very touching movie and a very true, believable story. But people were so taken by the private scandal [the Bergman-Rossellini love affair] that they were against it from the beginning. I remember reading in *Variety* when the picture came out in several movie houses at the same time that they would see if the movie were a success, and if it weren't, they'd ban it. I was very fond of *Europe '51* too. The one I didn't particularly like, *Trip to Italy,* is now shown very often on the television and is considered an extremely *avant-garde* picture for its time. But at the time I didn't enjoy it. George Sanders too was very unhappy and couldn't get into the mood of improvisation—he was a problem on the picture and everything was very difficult. I'm surprised that now it is well received. I never thought that would happen.

But I'm surprised at *Casablanca* coming back too and all those old films that get shown on television, cinémathèques and national film theaters. At the time one just thought, That's it, and there was no future for the films. When I was in Hollywood, old films were dead. There were no art houses—that came much later. People would come from Europe and say, "How come Hollywood doesn't have a museum? Shouldn't they have Chaplin's shoes and walking stick, and Chevalier's hat, and Garbo's clothes?" There was absolutely nothing saved. I remember people at Cinémathèque saying, "If we had the money, we'd go over and buy *everything*. The trains, the boats and the clothes. The Americans don't understand that one day these things will be terribly appreciated." People were what they were because of the work they'd done—I mean, you knew that Cary Grant was a great actor and wonderful performer because what he'd done remained in the memory. But I can't remember them bringing back any of those old pictures then. Everything was absolutely for the present. The Museum of Modern Art in New York started the whole thing by collecting old movies—Pickford and Fairbanks. Only in New York could you see Dreyer's *Joan of Arc.*

JK: *Spellbound* brought you into close contact with Selznick and the way he worked. Hitchcock was very much his own man, but Selznick had a reputation for interfering. How was their relationship?

IB: Well, I think Hitchcock was the only director who was independent of Selznick—he wouldn't stand for the notes. On any of Hitchcock's pictures, if a producer or author came onto the set, he'd stop the camera and say there was a mechanical fault. Soon they got the hint that the camera would work when they were *not* present, but not while they were on the set. He was absolutely marvelous doing what *he* wanted, cutting it all himself. I think he handled Selznick the same way and Selznick accepted it. Selznick kept sending the notes, but this didn't perturb Hitchcock, who just said, "That's too bad" if he didn't agree. The movie was his.

JK: How did *Spellbound* come about?

IB: Hitch must have gone to Selznick with the story and he accepted it and asked for me. It was all Hitchcock's story, I don't think Selznick had found it—I don't know. I was offered the part and read the script. I'd met Hitchcock before because he was a friend of Selznick's and I used to tell him that I got so many really *awful* scripts that I got so mad I'd throw them at the wall and say I just couldn't *stand* it. Anyway I got this script from Hitchcock and he said, "Remove your husband and child before you throw it at the wall!" That was *Spellbound*.

JK: How about *Notorious*?

IB: That was made at RKO and was another Hitchcock story. Selznick had nothing to do with that. Hitchcock had said let's work together again and that he'd find another story. Michael Blandford wrote the story* and RKO paid Selznick for me. We worked together again in England on *Under Capricorn*. Then I'd already got fed up working on the back lot. Since the story was set in Australia, I suggested we go there, but they said it was out of the question. Finally, they gave me the satisfaction of getting out of Hollywood to go to England. It was only because I nagged about getting out and seeing new places that it wasn't done on the back lot as usual.

JK: Was there never any attempt to let the character in that be German or Norwegian, or did she have to stay Irish?

IB: Hitchcock wanted her Irish and he said it would be very easy for me to learn the accent. I believed him and I had a teacher to help me.

JK: Outside Rossellini, you had the closest working relationship with Hitchcock: in four years you did three films with him. Did you have a special *simpático* or was it just business?

IB: No, we were just very good friends. I still see him now. He's an extraordinary human being and I like him very much.

JK: He sometimes refers to actors as cattle.

IB: Well, he thought they were stupid, I suppose. He didn't like arguments, you see: "I can't do it this way," "I'm not in the mood," "I don't understand what you mean"—that sort of thing. He had this phrase and I've always been grateful for what it taught me: he had very clear ideas of how he wanted scenes shot and if you started complaining about the difficulties—like "The door's too narrow for me to come through with this big dress, couldn't I possibly just stay in the room?"—he'd sit there as though listening attentively to your problems and then say, "Fake it. Go through the door and fake it."

*Ben Hecht wrote the story.

JK: His complete control must have been the antithesis to Rossellini's "act as you would at a cocktail party."

IB: Yes. And they were both difficult! There are some directors who give out the feeling that they're pleased to be working with you—as Leo McCarey put it, "You are my springboard"—and that naturally makes the actor feel more important. Hitchcock is so sure that what he wants is *it* and that whatever you suggest is something that has to be argued out—which is tiresome for him. But at the same time I'm sure he's liked some of the actors he's worked with and appreciated what they've given to him. But he's cut the picture before he shoots it. He doesn't shoot a lot of angles so that later on he has a lot of footage on the cutting-room floor.

JK: Did Selznick or anyone mind the fact that the character you played in *Notorious* was rather dubious morally?

IB: It was only that she drank so much and drove the car fast, had lots of parties and false hair. That was my idea. Do you remember? You see her waking up in bed and she has a bun. Hitchcock accepted that. I'm always making suggestions like that in a film and many people tell me I'd make a good director. But I think I'm a better prop man! I always push furniture around because the normal set looks so unlived in. I'm always putting my own things in, tossing paper around, mushing up things or doing something. All my directors have said I'm a marvelous prop man: "The room looks splendid, but I wish you'd learn your dialogue." It's important to me that sets look lived in. In *Cactus Flower* I was writing in that book [a prop] all the time—you can't work with an empty book, you have to have all the names written down or it doesn't look right, it doesn't look like an office. Clothes have to look crumpled and worn and the shoes mustn't be new shoes. That's what gave the false quality in so many of these movies: you saw that their hairdresser was always right behind, brushing their hair and making it nicely for the shot. You know, they wake up in the morning after a terrible night and they look absolutely splendid with long eyelashes and their hair tumbling down so nicely. That was the sort of thing I was fighting against.

JK: Did Louis B. Mayer ever come along or have anything to do with *Dr. Jekyll*?

IB: No. I don't think I ever saw him in the studio. But I know him because he's my best friend's father—Irene Selznick, David's first wife, is his daughter. I met him in his home and at parties all the time. Maybe he sat in his office and complained about certain things, but he never came on the set ever.

JK: Did any company ever try to buy your contract from Selznick?

IB: Selznick wanted me to stay on with him after my four-year contract was up. But then the new trend was for actors to be independent. Then they started getting percentages of the movies instead of being on a company salary, and then they made their own companies and worked for themselves.

Tapes get switched, answers get lost, thoughts get changed—somehow a question about producers became an answer about Salvador Dali's contribution to Selznick's *Spellbound*.

IB: The dream sequence in *Spellbound* was originally longer. It was beautiful. We worked on it so much. That statue . . . my death mask was made and then this whole body of a statue. Then the body flew away, revealing the real woman underneath. So much of that was cut out. But I suppose someone didn't like it. Dali was around then—he was already strange! He's stranger now! He enjoyed it very much. There was also a notorious dream sequence in *Jekyll and Hyde*. Lana Turner and I were tethered together like carriage horses and Spencer Tracy was whipping us on with our hair streaming behind us. There was also a drowning sequence. I don't know who designed that— it must have been Fleming. But you know in those days they had a man called Menzies, and he designed every setup. So think what help a director had! First there's the cameraman, who could give suggestions on what a good angle would be, then they had this marvelous artist who drew it. It was all designed—just fabulous. I kept some of those drawings because they were beautifully done. That's a métier that's completely gone now—I'm sure they don't do that anymore.

JK: In some respects, artists like William Cameron Menzies were as important as the directors?

IB: Well, of course the director directed the actors and Menzies only chose the beautiful angle. We had him on *For Whom the Bell Tolls* and I remember his beautiful drawings. They dictated the setup and the director just had to make sure the camera angle was right. So, whereas in Sweden and Europe the director gave the total concept, in Hollywood it was split between the director and the producer and the designer. Then you had a marvelous cameraman who made sure the lighting was just right. So it's the job of many to make a movie, whereas when you're on the stage you're alone—it's up to you.

JK: Hedy Lamarr regretted throwing away the script of *Casablanca*. Did you ever throw away anything you regretted?

IB: No, I never regretted it even when the actress who eventually played the part got the Academy Award for it. I threw away *The Farmer's Daughter* and *The Snake Pit*—Olivia de Havilland finally got the Oscar for that.* I threw it away because I didn't like the idea of playing everything in an insane asylum—it was too depressing. I'm always told I'm an idiot for throwing that away. I admit it was a good part, but I didn't like it, and I can't do anything I don't feel comfortable in.

---

*De Havilland was nominated—she did not win.

JK: Did you react at all to the fact that the great producers—Cohn, Selznick, Mayer—who were not really creative, nevertheless had great power over a movie?

IB: I thought it was unpleasant that producers and directors had battles. But the producers very rarely got in contact with the actors; it was usually through the director. Sometimes, though, you did feel that the producer had interfered terribly with the director's point of view, and that he was under tremendous stress—he knew that if he didn't do what the producer said, he'd be fired. Now, over the producer would be another executive producer and then over all was Mr. Mayer. He was so high up he'd never come down to a set: if you ever saw Mr. Mayer, you were always called up to his office, but there were layers of people he'd call up before he ever called the actors. I don't think I ever put my foot in Mr. Mayer's office—that was God himself up there. Then there were archangels and angels, and then it got to us working people. I met Harry Cohn, but I have no stories to tell of him. I never read his biography and he never interfered with anything I did. But I'm sure the directors who worked for him sometimes were quite unhappy because of his very strong . . . you know, precision. Everyone knew they were very easily fired. There was no lack of putting another man on the job.

JK: Are the numerous books now written about Hollywood by people who were never there accurate?

IB: Well, I haven't read the books. I did read *The Lion's Share* by Bosley Crowther, the New York critic. That was terribly interesting for me because I learned things I hadn't dreamed were going on. I suppose some of it upset Mr. Mayer greatly, I would think. But these were things I was never involved in—it was a completely different group of people. I think if I'd known what was going on, I'd have left Hollywood earlier! [Laughs.] I mean, everyone was walking around with milk bottles because they all had ulcers. If you said, "Who's put that lamp there?" the answer would be this person had told that person, who'd told so-and-so . . . there was never anybody there who'd say, "*I* am responsible"—it was always a long line of giving the blame to someone else, you know. Because of fear of losing their jobs.

Of course, there were so many people on a job, because everyone had to be a specialist: there was only one person allowed to plug in things, and if he'd gone to the men's room, we all had to sit around and wait. Victor Fleming, I remember, would lose patience and plug it in himself—well, that was not good. In *Joan of Arc* I had a girl who was my dresser and she had a whole wagon to put my armor on. She worked like a dog and there'd be lots of people standing around. When I asked them to give her a hand, they refused because they said they'd lose their jobs—they said they could only do their own jobs and nothing else. It was hopeless; the time you spent waiting for the union man was criminal. But the unions became so strong, and if anyone did a job they weren't meant to, somebody else would squeal and the guy would be out. I was told if I wanted shoes, to call the wardrobe girl; if I wanted to rearrange the flowers, call the prop girl; and if you want something else, call the script girl, but for heaven's sake don't do it yourself. I never found that in Italy—everyone does everything there, and in Sweden we were twelve people on the set: the cameraman says he's ready—he doesn't have an assistant to say it for him; the electrician doubled as my stand-in, the hairdresser was the makeup girl and everything was much more simplified.

JK: Does this make for better films?

IB: No, but it makes for *cheaper* films! The cost of American films became tremendous because of the overhead and all the people who had to be engaged. I remember a Christmas celebration when I was on the stage at New York—there was a party for all the cast and crew. There were people I'd never seen before, and when I asked who they were, they said they were the musicians. I said, "But we don't have any music in the show." They said, "No, but you ought to and we're on the payroll." When I bring my own makeup man, he's English, they pay him a salary, but they also have to pay the makeup man who's on the set as well: he has to be on the picture, but he doesn't do anything. It's not that I don't trust anyone else—I just like my makeup man and I like to work with the same people.

JK: Why do you think old movies are so affectionately thought of now, even though they were produced in those union-bound days? Is it just sentimentality?

IB: The movies were better. They had stories and marvelous *performances*. They were very good people making them. In Hollywood there was such a collection of talented people: the best musicians, the best actors, the best directors, and they came from all over the world. There only was Hollywood. The other places to make movies—Paris, for example—were good, but if a French director got the chance to go to Hollywood, he *went*. Hollywood was terribly worried that the Germans, Italians or French would get too good, so they'd literally buy up the talent and bring it over to Hollywood.

JK: You said that when you watch yourself, you see yourself as a circus horse: is that a kind of protective device so that you yourself don't get involved? Do you think other actors did this?

IB: It's just something about being able to see yourself on a screen. When you're onstage, you can't see yourself, you don't know what it looks or sounds like—because, though I can hear my voice, that's not the way *you* hear it. But when you're on the screen, you can hear and see, and I can certainly judge that person as well as the one standing next to it. I can say, "He's not giving a very good performance, and neither is she." You see, it becomes a "*she*" up there—not yourself.

JK: Do you think if you have one major failing, it's that you see everything too clearly, that you can't take things for granted?

IB: I don't take anything for granted.

Bergman, a heroine who gave herself no airs, never stopped growing and learning in her craft, for, more than anything and I think anyone, her passionate love was reserved for her work. Before she died of cancer, she made a film with her Swedish compatriot Ingmar Bergman, *Autumn Sonata,* in which she played a career-obsessed concert pianist who had little time for her daughter. Had this been her last film, it would have been a memorable farewell; but, with only a short time left to live, she tackled probably the most demanding role of her career when she played Israel's first woman prime minister, a woman as formidable and down-to-earth as herself, Golda Meir, in the made-for-TV movie *A Woman Called Golda.* Those who knew that she was dying may have wept secretly as they watched her work.

Ingrid Bergman was a large woman in every sense of the word, with an even larger gift: that of making ordinary people loom large, surviving as they do, rising and stumbling as they do, coping with life as we all must, and always glowing with the joy of living as we all might wish.

1972

HOWARD
HAWKS

I T'S NOT THAT I THINK MEN LIE more than women, or that more men lie than women, or even that men are better liars than women. On the contrary, a woman can lie looking you straight in the eyes, saying she loves you and thinking goodbye. Men, American men in particular, are more likely to be the dreamers, the romantics, and women are the realists: you're more likely to find the boy still pining away inside the body of an old man than a girl inside that of an old woman. Women may not all be smart, but they share a clear reason and pragmatism about themselves to the best of their respective capabilities, while men continue to spin boys' dreams as if they were truths, and few people question them on it because of the depth of the masculine voice, the size, the age. Maybe it's because a man has so few roles which society allows him to play, and a woman has so many to draw on. Perhaps because society expects a boy to behave like a man much sooner than it expects a girl to shoulder the responsibility of adult womanhood. You're told "Be a man, my son," but one doesn't hear "Be a woman, my girl." Before he's finished being a boy, he's already expected to assume the role, if not the responsibility, of a man. This may account for the boy not leaving, merely pulling in, assuming a deeper voice, a more masculine pose repressing a side of himself. But talk to them, listen to their memories, look into their eyes, and what you hear are old stories of a time when life was simpler than life and times could ever have been. They may see themselves as artists; they are embarrassed to see themselves as stars. But they're much more star-struck than the women are. Howard Hawks, the director—tall, craggy, an American bald eagle—struck me like that.

Getting to Hawks turned out to be kind of a Hawksian near thing. He lived in Palm Springs. From LA it takes a couple of hours to get there by car. A sunny day in a convertible with the top down is an invitation to shirtlessness. The radio was on. Peggy Lee was singing "Is That All There Is?"—it was a new song and, whatever station you turned to, that's all there was. Those were still the days of 65 mph, and maybe I was doing 75 mph. A motorcycle cop came out of nowhere, heading toward me, siren blasting, signaling for me to pull over. I had a hunch it was for speeding, but I planned to play it British and dumb about California speed laws; pretending that maybe his stopping me had something to do with driving half-naked, I pulled over. He, a bit behind me, got off his cycle and walked toward me. Now it gets confusing. I knew he'd want to see my driving license, and leaned over the sticky upholstery to get it out of my bag in the back seat. If he said something, I didn't hear him; I reacted instead to his hand gestures. With a friendly smile and a free hand, I waved what I thought was understanding back to him. I came up with my passport and license in my hand . . . and the cold end of his gun poked against my temple. I was so surprised I kept on smiling. "See? Driving license. Passport. See?" He was white as a sheet, perspiration on his face, yelling at me: "You dumb sonofabitch! I coulda shot you! You dumb sonofabitch!" He was upset.

Well, it's nice to be able to write that, contrary to TV shows about killer cops, they don't all shoot first and ask questions later. We straightened things out. Of course it was because I'd been speeding. I'd forgotten to sound British, but he'd seen my British driving license, so I could have been talking Russian and it still would have sounded British to him. He let me off with a warning. I remembered what I'd been told once about what to do if you've been in a near-fatal flying accident: Don't think about it, don't panic, get straight onto the next flight or else you might be too scared to ever fly again. He adjusted his gun back into his holster. I started up the car; the radio was still on; I waved to him and drove off. Not till I arrived at Hawks' house and got out of the car did my legs start to buckle. But there he was, and I had a good excuse for being late. Even he thought so.

I drove down to interview Hawks specifically about one of his films, *Only Angels Have Wings,* and the actress whose career took off as a result of her performance in it: Rita Hayworth. I didn't tell him that when Rita called earlier that same day to find out what I was up to, and I told her I was seeing Hawks, she froze, and suddenly, out of nowhere, she asked in a voice tingling with hostility, "Why?" The film, an important step in her career, had been a humiliating experience because Hawks had treated her as if she were stupid and without feelings. Only Cary Grant's kindness and compassion helped her to get through it. That's how she remembered it, and thirty years hadn't erased that experience. It was something to bring up when I talked to Hawks, but there was so much else as well, for it proved impossible to talk to a man whose active career had spanned half a century without each question and answer leading off on tangents, and these sparking off questions and answers that led to further tangents.

At seventy-five, his long, lean frame looked even leaner, the weather-beaten skin stretched tight across the high bones of his face, the hawklike nose . . . he looked at times startlingly like pictures of D. W. Griffith. You got the feeling that he was looking out at you from inside a cave, or from a nest high above: it was a sharp gaze that made you feel slightly ill at ease at moments, though the look was more studied with time and effect than reality. He saw more than you or I could. Or did he? His speech was dry, the juice baked out of it by the desert sun; his mind was sharp as a rattler's fangs; his memory stretched far

Howard Hawks, circa 1962

back and his temper kept you on your toes. A formidable and imperious man. I wished that I had been photographing him as well as taping him. We talked in the den of his flat-domed ranch-style home, stacked with the trophies of his youngest boy, who had won motorcycle races across the country. Talking of the son, you saw the proud father, and more, for in his son's exploits you saw the shape of the Hawks hero.

JK: You have the most incredible knack—I'm thinking of the types of women you've directed. I mean, if they're normally girlish, you give them steel; and if they're steelish, like Roz Russell, you make them vulnerable, you break the ground beneath them. You have a knack for making the most unlikely women suddenly very sensual and sexual and provocative.

HH: It's pretty easy . . . if you get off to the right start. Roz Russell . . . for instance, Roz had a scene to do with Cary Grant. You should have seen it. She said, "It wasn't much good, was it?" I said, "No." "What's the matter?" "It didn't have any sex in it." "How the hell," she said, "are you going to get sex in this scene?" And I said, "You want Cary and me to show you how?" "Yes, I'd like to see *that*." And I said, "All right, Cary, let me just speak with you for a minute." I said, "I'm going to play her part, and you say a perfectly innocent thing . . . like 'Let's see how long it is.' Don't think about the time since you've seen her, think about . . . your car or something. And I'll answer in the right way . . . so let's see if you can remember." Cary said to me, "'How long is it?'" "How long is *what*?" I said. Then Roz says, "You sons of bitches! Is that what you want?!" And I said, "You're goddamned right that's what we want." "Okay, that's what you'll get!" she said . . . and from that time on we had more fun . . . doing things, and she became sexy out of a funny fighting-cock quality. . . . If you get *off* to something in a picture, then it's good.

JK: You did both *His Girl Friday* and *Only Angels Have Wings* at Columbia. Had you been contracted by Columbia for them?

HH: No . . . I never had any kind of contract. After *Angels* I said I'd do another story, *Front Page* . . . but I didn't want to do it in a routine sort of way. Well, Harry Cohn said, "You could use Cary Grant and that reporter Walter Winchell playing the editor." I said, "You're half right, you can use Grant for the editor instead of the reporter, and get a girl to do the reporter." "Are you nuts?" "Listen," I said, "if you don't want to do it, don't bother about it." Cohn said, "Why do *you* want to do it?" I said that I felt that it was among the best dialogue written. Ever. The idea had come to me one night at dinner at my house . . . six or eight other people. We got into an argument and I gave 'em *Front Page* to read. A girl read the reporter's part and I read the other. I stopped in the middle of it and said, "It's better with a girl doing it," and I called Ben Hecht and I told him. "Christ," he said, "I think it's a great idea. I'll help you if you'll help me with the story I'm doing now." So he came out and I helped him with his story, and he helped me with the . . . the adaptation of that. Hell, I helped him with so many . . . and he helped me. It was a . . . long relationship, you know.* Then I got Roz Russell . . . she really hadn't been a comic at all before. She was just perfect. Of course, Gene Fowler said, "I want no part of this nonsense." I said, "Okay, Gene, but Ben himself came and helped me on the thing." Well, it took practically no time at all to write the script. The only thing that was added after we started was contributed by Charlie Lederer. He said, "How about making these two people having been married before?" So there we were . . . it was easy to do.

JK: Speaking of being married, you also started the famous relationship of Bogey and Bacall in *To Have and Have Not*.

HH: It was . . . Bacall just happened by accident. My wife [Slim Hawks] pointed out a little picture of a girl in *Vanity Fair* or *Vogue,* and I said to my secretary . . . I don't know now what I said then, but she misunderstood me and brought her out here. And here was a girl with the Bacall sweater, a gabardine skirt, just a kid. And I said, "Fix her up with a tour of the studio so she can say she's been here . . . then send her back home." Betty didn't . . . she wanted to go to work. And I had to tell her it was a mistake my secretary made. I said, "What the fuck can I do?" Stories of girls who think differently . . .

Hawks' voice, as so often, trails off with his pipe smoke; he doesn't finish the sentence, but comes back in the middle of another one.

HH: . . . She had a little, thin, reedy voice. I said, "You can't read the lines." "How do I change it?" I said, "I don't know, but I can tell you how Walter Huston got *his* great voice, he told me." I told her. She disappeared for three weeks. My secretary said, "That girl called today, she called quite early to see you." And when she came over, she . . . [he rasps, in imitation of the new Bacall voice] . . . just talked way down, you know. She changed her voice. And . . . what the hell, you have to notice a girl like that.

She came up to a party at the house Saturday night . . . we had one almost every Saturday night . . . and I had to take her home. I said, "Can't you get anybody to take you home?" She mumbled something about a man . . . [Hawks mumbled too!] "So, were you nice to him?" She said yes. I said, "Try *not* being nice to him." Next party she came to, she said, "I got a ride." I said, "What'd you do?" She said, "I asked this man where he got his tie. And he said, 'What do you want to know for?'" And she said, "I'll tell people not to go there." I said, "Who's the man?" She said, "Clark Gable." So I went over to Jules Furthman [the screenwriter] on Monday, and I said, "Jules, how

*Hecht and Hawks go back a long way, to *Scarface* and before.

about a girl that can . . . insult people and make them like it? Be . . . insolent and make them like it?" "It's a hell of a good idea, where'd you steal *that*?" he said. Oh . . . I didn't tell him where I got it, but we started working on it . . . and Bacall was around. And I'd try out almost every scene on her because she had that quality of being able to say something insulting and make you like it. And . . . I made a test with her. I wrote a little scene that had nothing to do with the story. She said, "You know how to whistle?" And Christ Almighty, anybody who saw it said that was such a great scene, how do you get that in the picture?

We had the goddamnedest time working on that picture you ever saw. I didn't put the whole part in the script because . . . I might have been in some trouble, using a brand-new kid like that. So when the picture was finished, they didn't even know how to spell her name . . . the Warners publicity department. What the hell, she just hit like a house on fire. And well . . . Bogart . . . he just fell in love with her. Without *that*, I'd have had a hell of a time taking a girl who was . . . She couldn't act, she was a personality. She learned how to act after three or four pictures in her own particular fashion, but she's . . . What I've always liked is a personality . . . instead of an actor. But that picture . . . now, Jules Furthman . . . Vic Fleming and I liked Jules because everybody else hated him. We worked well together. I remember one thing, he had written the introduction for the girl . . . *Have and Have Not*. She was in this little Martinique town . . . sea-front town. I forget what it was exactly that he wrote, but it was . . . somebody stole her purse, that was the scene. And Jules says, "How do you like it?" And I said, "Jules, that's just a great scene. If there's anything that gives me a rash, it's a poor little girl whose purse has been stolen, though." "You sonofabitch," he says, and the next day, in the scene *she* stole the purse, it wasn't stolen from her. "Now you're talking sense," I said. Of course, that created an entire . . . character for us. And also, I had that idea of making her . . . well, insolent. And Bacall just happened to fall into the part. . . .

But . . . now, you can take people . . . that is . . . if you see something . . . I turned down lots of stories with people that I don't think are funny. For instance, Walter Brennan. The unit manager said, "I heard you telling the kind of character you want in the picture.* There's a guy that just fits that. He hasn't done much, he's really an extra man. But I'd like to have you see him." I said, "Okay, but look—instead of going through a lot of . . . ritual, meeting him and all that, can you give him the lines and I'll tell you how to get him dressed. Bring him up here and just let me hear him read." So he brought in Walter Brennan. Well, I laughed when I looked at him . . . the way he was dressed. I said, "Walter, we haven't got too much time. How about you and I reading that scene?" "Fine. With or without?" I said, "With or without what?" "Teeth," he said. I said, "Without *teeth*?" And he turned

---

*This was when Hawks was making *Barbary Coast* (1935).

around and took his teeth out and put them in his pocket. And he was supposed to do four days' work. I kept him for six weeks, and he got mentioned
for an Academy Award. That was in *Barbary Coast*. The next picture, he
played the strongest man in the north woods—*Come and Get It*—and he got
the Academy Award. And I had him do five pictures, and he got mentioned
for an award or he'd won one every time he did it—*Sergeant York, To Have
and Have Not, Red River*. . . .

   Red River, I called him and said, "I've got a story for you, Walter."
"Okay, fine." When I said, "Let me tell it to you," he said, "Let's get the
contract signed first." I said, "Okay, we'll get the contract signed first. Come
in tomorrow and we'll have the contract ready." He came in. He said, "Now,
tell me the story." And I said, "You sonofabitch, I don't have to tell you the
story, I'll just give it to you to read." He came back the next day and he said,
"Gee, that's a great story." He had one line. The cook's name was Groot. And
I said, "Your name is Groot, Groot Nadine." And he grinned and said, "What
are we going to do?" And I said, "You're going to lose your teeth to an Indian
in a poker game up in the hills." He said, "I read about that." "And every
time you want to have dinner, you're going to have to get them back from
this fellow and he's not going to be too happy about it." "Oh," he said, "Howard, we can't do that!" I said, "Yes, we can." "Oh, God, can we really do it?"
I said, "Yes." . . . Well, he got mentioned for an Academy Award in that
thing. And he didn't even have any part. I just called him to do scenes. He
didn't have any part in *To Have and Have Not*.

   You know . . . it's just like with Wayne. When we started on *Red River*,
he said, "Howard, how am I going to play an old man?" Well, I said, "Let
me squat down on you."

   And Duke comes to me and he says, "Is this one of those scenes?" I
said, "Get up on it as quick as you can." And he did it without a fuss. And I
hear him telling another actor, "For Christ's sake, get it over with! The boss
says this scene . . ." You know. Then he comes around and I said, "Go to
work on this one, this is a good scene." And he's used that as a watchword
since . . . and he became a goddamn fine actor. Well, Ford said, "I never
knew that big sonofabitch could act." And Ford started him. But he didn't do
a goddamn thing for his pictures. And then Ford put him in two or three good
pictures—*She Wore a Yellow Ribbon* and *Fort Apache*—and all of a sudden
he was the biggest thing on two legs. But with Ford or me he never . . .
questions anything that we say . . . not a thing. Some other director who
doesn't quite know what he wants . . .

   Of course, after he got going, we all said that he's a much better actor
than we ever gave him credit for. I mean, Ford and I said that. Because he is.
He'd . . . carry a picture. What the hell? I've only made four films with him
and every one's been successful. Wayne was funny. He said to me one time,
"You know, when I started to work with you, I thought the dialogue was the
same for everybody. I couldn't realize how you were going to get characters.

Then I found out . . . it's because different people say it entirely different. Opposite people talk about it opposite." Well, I said, "Duke, that just happens to be the short, curt dialogue . . . the kind I rewrite after people start eating too many words!"

JK: Being just a naïf, did Rita Hayworth have the same troubles with the dialogue or . . .

HH: Well, Rita . . . worked hard. She had a scene to do . . . one crying scene.

He takes a *long* pause, as if considering each word before letting it out. As you sit and talk, you find yourself beginning to listen to the act of talking and listening, and, while informative, what is actually being said is not complete in itself without adding the pauses, the weights and measures of certain words, totally unimportant in themselves, but important in the rhythm, like a Morse Code that has a separate but complementary message to be added to the first message, and it's not till you put the two together that you get the full flow.

HH: And she worked almost too hard at it. . . . So I moved it out of doors and had the rain put on . . . had rain pouring all over her face . . . and that calmed her down, but it still got the feeling of . . .

JK: Did you have trouble directing her? You said earlier that some have it and some don't have it.

HH: It's hard . . . to give a very good answer to that because it depends on what you're working for. . . . I'm not working on a set scene, never. And I want to do something somebody can do well. She was supposed to get tight in one scene. She was . . . behind the bar with Cary Grant . . . quite a long scene. . . . She hadn't had experience enough to do it. I said to Cary, "What do you think's the matter?" He said, "I don't think she really knows it. Here's what I'm saying, but she doesn't take it in. She doesn't know what I'm talking about." Well, I said, "Okay." And . . . I got the prop man . . . got a big pitcher full of ice water, ice cubes, gave it to Cary, and I said, "Now, when you hear this scene going dead on you, just look at her and say, 'You don't know what I'm talking about, do you?' And she'll react to that . . . and then pour the pitcher of ice water right over her head." . . . And then he took a couple of lines of hers . . . and . . . Well, they finished drying her hair and sent her back, and I said, "Here, blow your nose," something like that. And those things . . . she did well! She did *damn* well because those were in her present capabilities at the time. But . . . she wasn't good, up to being a good drunk at that particular time.

JK: She was young, not even twenty yet.

HH: Oh . . . she was just a kid. And scared . . . and working with . . . Those were a bunch of good actors [says Hawks, with a laugh that serves to emphasize it by understating it]. . . . So we got just as good a scene out of it . . . better . . . without straining things, you see. She could make an entrance. She did her best scenes with Barthelmess . . . by that time she'd gotten to where she could do those things she did . . . she did a beautiful job of it. Rita . . . at her best, was slightly . . . unreal. She belonged in a kind of . . . fairy-tale story. Because she was so beautiful . . . and because that's what people seemed to like to see her as. . . . But then, I couldn't ask for things that were beyond her. That just doesn't happen to be my way. Hell . . . it happens all the time. . . . The worst thing in the world is to ask people . . . to do things they're not capable of.

JK: Rita was the only novice in a film full of stars [*Only Angels Have Wings*], yet she really emerged in the film as a "new find."

HH: Well . . . she was a nice girl. Thank Christ, because if she hadn't been grateful, if she hadn't been receptive . . . Because everybody tried to help her. They're going to help any newcomer. They see how hard a time she's having. . . . And it makes . . . a lot of difference. I've started girls who begin to think that they're . . . pretty good, you know. And suddenly I have to walk around and tell them, "Look . . . you're only going to get by in this picture with the help of these other people . . . and you'd better change your god-damn tune and do it in a hurry . . . because they don't like you . . . because you're assuming that you're as good as they are . . . and you're not." . . . And that usually brings a girl to her senses. And then she comes around and says, "Thanks for telling me, because I learned something by it." . . . Well, to be truthful . . . I don't enjoy working with big stars, girls. They've got ideas . . . as to how they're going to . . . They come over and say, "Will you arrange just to show me on the left side because the left side of my face is better." And they drive you nuts. If you'll notice, I had not worked with . . . big women stars . . . from [he laughs, as though trying to sound shrewd] . . . way back in the beginning.

JK: To get back to the film, though, how did *Angels* get started?

HH: Well . . . I'll tell you a story about that film. Two or three fellers who like my work . . . have written that that's the only phony picture I ever made. Some feller sent me a book . . . on me and said that. Well, every single thing in that picture was true. I'll . . . recount . . . the facts. I was flying in Mexico with a bush pilot who had been burned in the face . . . in an accident. His eyes would smile, but his face . . . He was a hard guy. We went to dinner . . . a party for some pilot and his girl, it was the anniversary, and a guy got up and made a speech . . . said, "A year ago they were married. And they had a lot of fun and went to bed at ten after two, got up at twenty after two, went back to bed again in three minutes and got up twenty minutes later." And the wife broke in, she said, "You sonofabitch, you were peeking on us." "No," said the guy who's telling the story . . . and he drags out a graph . . .

made by a machine they use in flying. And the sharp lines are the takeoff, getting airborne. And the graduations, the curves, are climbing, and like that. Well, they had hung this machine under the married couple's bed their first night. . . . And the girl was . . . delighted. And that was the basis for *Only Angels Have Wings*. And the fellow who jumped out of an airplane and was blackballed . . . so to speak . . . later on I saw him jump and I knew him. I saw the guy he left behind . . . dead. I watched him do horrendous things . . . because nobody would talk to the bastard, you know, nobody would have anything to do with him. So all of that was based on actual fact. Now, the Tommy Mitchell character . . . And all of Jean Arthur's relationship with Cary Grant. And the marriage of the guy and bringing his wife . . . down, you know. Well, it was all true, it all happened.

One day I went over to Columbia to see Frank Capra about something. Harry Cohn knew everybody who came into the studio . . . nobody got in unless he allowed 'em in. And . . . so he asked me to come up to his office and he said, "I'm stuck for a story." "Who for?" "Cary Grant and Jean Arthur." "Well," I said, "here's about ten pages of yellow paper that I scribbled down this morning." And . . . he looked it over and he came down to Capra's office. He said, "When can you start?" "Well, what do you mean?" "We've got to have it going in a couple of weeks." I said that I wouldn't be able to build the set in that time. And I said I'd need a bigger budget. I said, "It's gonna cost you more money." "Well, that's okay, it costs me money if I don't make it." I didn't have anything else going on, so I made the picture. And it was all true.

JK: What about the casting? Obviously, Grant and Arthur were set, but did the studio insist on the others: Barthelmess, John Carroll, Allyn Joslyn, Thomas Mitchell?

HH: No. I just used whoever I wanted to. I mean . . . I had a pretty free hand there. And, see, Barthelmess came about because when talking pictures started, I was out of work for a year and a half . . . and he asked me what I was doing . . . could I handle dialogue. I said I didn't know anything about the stage at all . . . but I knew how people talked. Well, they didn't believe me . . . didn't believe any of us! I think Jack Ford had to go out and make some two-reelers to prove he could use sound. Well . . . I wrote a story. And I paid Johnnie Saunders* $10,000 to put his name on it . . . because he had a reputation for dialogue. I told Barthelmess about it . . . *Dawn Patrol,* of course. He insisted he do it. Hell, it was the biggest-grossing picture of the year. From that time on, I had no trouble at all getting work. And . . . it wasn't only important for Barthelmess . . . it was a shot in the arm for

---

*John Monk Saunders, author of the best of the Gatsbyesque books, *The Last Flight,* was of that post-World War I generation of American writers shaping the image and giving Americans a past. He worked in Hollywood in the '30s.

him. . . . Actually, I was going to put Jack Gilbert in the picture. But Jack was fighting with Louis B. Mayer at the time. And when I asked about Gilbert, Mayer said, "Do you really want him?" "Yes." He got Gilbert to come in and I said I wanted him, and then Mayer said to Gilbert . . . he wouldn't have him if he were the last actor on earth. He hated Gilbert . . . it was terrible. Had me there just listening to it. Well, finally I decided not to make the picture at Metro. . . . Thalberg wanted it. I said, "I won't have anything to do with Mayer." And I told him what happened.

JK: So *Only Angels Have Wings* was an important film for most of the people in it . . . Barthelmess, Rita's first recognizable role, and certainly Jean Arthur *was* Jean Arthur by then, wasn't she?

HH: Well . . . when I got through with the picture, I said to Jean, "You're about the only person that I think is really good that I haven't been able to help at all. I haven't had anything to do with it hardly . . . to tell the truth. . . . But someday you're going to see the girl I wanted you to play . . . and you'll recognize it when you see it." And about a year and a half . . . two years later . . . her chauffeur brought her up to the house and she was waiting outside. She said, "I saw the picture last night . . . and I'll do any story that you ask me to do . . . and in any way that you ask me to do it, from now on." I hope to Christ that I find something else . . . because she's got a great talent. But I didn't think I contributed hardly anything to her performance in that picture. You see . . . Jean's very makeup and . . . style allowed me to go back to old things that I'd done before, where the girl was really . . . the aggressor. But in such a different way than we'd ever done it before. You know what I mean? And it worked out just as well. . . . Jean's own little girl's voice and everything like that. It led us into a lot of things that were good. Like the bit with the two-headed coin in there. In order to keep her from leaving, where she said, "You have to ask me, otherwise I'm going to go." And he flips the coin. . . . Then she realized that he'd asked her . . . that was his way of asking her . . . flipping the two-headed coin. But . . . if we'd done it in another way, you wouldn't like it because it was . . . we'd have lost character. Actually, we had some things that I wanted to do and she'd say, "I've been thinking about it . . . I can't do it . . . that isn't me." But . . . when you get a new girl . . . And I've started a lot of 'em.

You see, with women, I finally figured out that the average girl of my time . . . was brought up as a kid . . . looked at movies and had a favorite star and she'd say, "Isn't she sweet, isn't she lovely, isn't she . . ." Now, I don't want 'em sweet and lovely. I identified with a girl who didn't give a damn . . . whether people liked her or not. And when I did it, it proved successful. If I got mixed up in the other kind, it was no good. . . . Now, Ella Raines was a bit like that kind of girl. And . . . I had a girl in a picture called . . . *Red Line 7000*. Gail Hire. Now, she was a rebel. She was the dark-haired one who thought it was bad luck if she . . . slept with somebody.

She was a rebel in her clothes, her hair . . . everything. Made the most marvelous test you've ever seen. The minute I said, "You're gonna have the lead in this picture," she said, "Christ. I'm a star. I gotta have everybody like me." And she was absolutely . . . no good. Nothing I could do to cure that. . . . But others . . . Carole Lombard. She'd never had more than five lines in a picture before she did the picture with Barrymore . . . *Twentieth Century*. That's the one that started the whole shooting match going for her. She's a second cousin of mine. . . .

You see, Carole was very well educated. She had plenty of money. . . . She was a complete . . . extrovert. And when she came out to Hollywood, she came out to see me. And she used to hang around the house all the time. And she got a job as a sort of . . . clotheshorse at Paramount. Most she ever had was five lines.* I can tell you a story . . . it's been told before . . . people have written about it because . . . I couldn't find anybody to play the part with Barrymore. . . . And I told Harry Cohn that I knew her, Carole. And he said, "Oh, Christ, you can do better than that." I said, "Okay, you find somebody better." And so he came in . . . in a week . . . and said, "I signed Lombard for it." And I talked with Lombard, and the first day's work we did . . . we were working on a scene that had twelve pages of dialogue in it. And I said to Barrymore, "Now, look . . . the girl's new. I don't want to hear one word out of your mouth until 4:00 this afternoon . . . then you can say all you want." "Okay." And so they rehearsed. . . . Barrymore looked at her . . . looked at me . . . he even had his arm around her like this and . . . he held his nose. And I said, "Shut up and wait till 4:00 this afternoon." . . . I told the cameraman to take fifteen minutes so I could talk to Carole. So he made some excuse . . . and I took her for a walk and I said, "Carole, you've been working hard." "I'm glad it shows." I said, "Yes. You know your lines perfectly. How much do you get paid for this picture?" "Five thousand dollars." "That's a lot," I said. "It certainly is," she says. I said, "What do you get paid for?" "Acting, of course." "What if I tell you you've done all the acting, you've earned the $5000, you don't owe me a goddamn nickel. But no more acting." She just stared at me. I said, "When you come in and he says such-and-such a thing, what would *you* have done?" And she said, "I'd have kicked him right in the balls." "Oh," I said, "well, that's what Barrymore said. Now, on the second line, what if a man had said that line to you?" And she said something . . . typical Lombard, you know. I said, "Well, he said that to you. Now we're going to go back in there and we're going to make a scene and you're going to kick him in the balls. You're going to wave your arms. You can do any goddamn thing you feel like doing. . . . Only no more acting." She said, "You're serious, aren't you?" I said, "If you don't, I'm

---

*Lombard had played leading roles in many major films at Paramount prior to *Twentieth Century*—she began in films at the age of twelve (1921). Among her films before 1934: *No Man of Her Own* (Clark Gable), *Bolero* (George Raft), *White Woman* (Charles Laughton).

going to fire you and get another girl . . . this afternoon." "Okay." So . . .
we went back and I said, "Let's try another take." And Barrymore said,
"We're not ready, Howard." And I said, "Jack, who is running this thing?"
He said, "You are." Well . . . So he said the line to her and she made a kick
at him. He jumped back. You can see in the scene, you can see him covering
his balls. And she waved her arms and she bounced onto the seat, kicking
. . . yelling at him . . . doing any goddamn thing. We went through twelve
pages without a break . . . first take. He went out. I said, "Cut. Print." Barrymore came back in and he said, "That was magnificent. Have you been
kidding me all the time?" And . . . she broke into tears and ran off the stage.
And he said, "What the Christ is going on?" "I don't know, Jack, but I think
we've got a star." He said, "My, she's fabulous . . . she's just great." I said,
"She's never played a scene before." Not before that film . . . not more than
five lines. She hadn't done anything . . . four scenes at a tea party or something. And we made that whole picture in ten days. Ten days!

I didn't have much money to work with because Barrymore got $25,000
per week . . . two weeks I paid him . . . ten days' work. What the hell. So
. . . we did twelve pages by 10:30 in the morning. You can't do a page a day
on a usual film. . . . Well, those people just hit it off and just played the hell
out of it. . . . Barrymore would say, "What hijinx have you got for us today?"
And I'd say, "Well, I want you to do Shakespeare when you come down those
stairs, and a coupla scenes of *Othello* and . . ." "Okay, you'll get it." And
. . . he'd do it. He'd figure it all out . . . I'd give him plenty of time before
we started, and down he'd come and he'd see these posters and he'd rant and
rave and get paint and run around gobbing everything. I said, "For Christ's
sake, you've been putting on makeup for fifty years and I've never been
backstage of a theater. You mean to say you can't think of something?"
"Okay, I'll think of something." And out he came as a Kentucky colonel!
They were . . . running around so much I had to put three cameras on
'em. . . . And got it!

JK: Were any other films hatched out of the egg like that?

HH: Oh . . . *His Girl Friday* was pretty much like that . . . *Bringing Up Baby*
took a little time. . . . But, Christ, try working with leopards and dogs. . . .
Hepburn was great.

JK: Let me ask you about Marilyn Monroe. . . . *Monkey Business* and *Gentlemen Prefer Blondes* were the same year, yet one saw the difference between
a girl who was still working to become a star and the girl who now was a star.

HH: Yes, and . . . I made the thing with Monroe for a very simple reason:
Zanuck. . . . I put Monroe in with Cary Grant and she did a damn fine job
. . . not much to do. . . . So the studio got terribly interested. And they made
three pictures with her that lost their shirts. And . . . Zanuck called me and
said, "Howard, we ought to have a great big star here and we're losing

money. What the hell is happening?" I said, "Darryl, you're making realism with a very unreal girl. She's a completely storybook character. And you're trying to make real movies." "What should she do?" "Well, you've got a great story over here, *Gentlemen Prefer Blondes,* that she . . ." "She couldn't do that." "The hell she can't." "She can't sing." I said, "How do you know?" See . . . she used to come to parties down in Palm Springs and she'd come over and say, "Mr. Hawks, would you take me home?" And she's so goddamn dumb that one time I said to her, "Look, if you can't talk . . . the radio's playing . . . sing." And she sang. So I said to Zanuck, "She sings good." "You mean to say you think she could play that part?" "I know goddamn well she could." "Well, you do it, then." I said, "Oh, no." Zanuck said, "You've got to do it." I said, "I'll do it if I can get somebody to back her up, somebody to *hold* her up." "Like who?" "Jane Russell." "You can't get her . . . she's with Hughes." I told him, "Darryl, you're really not too smart. You're just in your own little circle and you don't know anything going on outside it. I found Russell in a dentist's office getting ten bucks a week. And you say I can't get her? Get her on the phone." So . . . I said to her, "Janie, I got a story for you." She said, "Fine, when do we start?" I said, "I want you to know one thing. There's another part in it that probably is just as good or better than yours, depending on how the girl does it." "Well, you want me, don't you?" I said, "Yes." So . . . okay, now the question of her salary. I said, "Start talking." She said, "Can I get $50,000?" And I worked it up . . . with Zanuck listening . . . up to $200,000. I said, "Darryl, she wants $200,000." He said, "Tell her it's okay." And she had only wanted $50,000 to start with. . . . But I just edged her up there. . . .

And . . . it wasn't easy, that film. But it wasn't difficult because I had Jane there. And Jane would do for her. . . . I'd hear them talking, Marilyn would whisper, "What did he tell me?" Jane wouldn't say, "He's told you six times already," she'd just tell her again. . . . We made the movie and I used to laugh, most every scene I made. Here are these two sex queens. . . . Now, nobody would ever take Marilyn out . . . nobody paid any attention to her. She sat with no clothes on the set and everybody just walked right by her. And some pretty little extra'd go by and everybody'd whistle. And she couldn't get anybody to take her out. And Jane Russell had never known anything but one man from . . . the beginning of high school, and she married him and lived there. . . . She was like an old shoe, you know? . . . When Bob [Waterfield, Russell's first husband] was away, Jane used to come over and knock on the door and say, "Can I cook dinner for you?" I'd say, "Come on in." . . . I never thought of either of them as having any sex. I made a test of Jane and cast her for *The Outlaw* . . . and she never worked on a picture or worked on a set before. But, Lord . . . Well, now the whole . . . *thing* . . . was sexy. For God's sake, all I'd do was make a scene of the two of them walking down toward the camera . . . and people'd want to attack them. But that kind of sex isn't my line at all. . . . Hayworth was a

little bit on the romantic thing. I don't think she was . . . terribly sexy. . . .
Sure, she had a sex *quality* that came across . . . on the screen. . . .

JK: You hadn't seen any of Rita's films when you cast her in *Angels*?

HH: No, no. . . . All I can tell you is that . . . I have a theory that the camera
likes certain people . . . and doesn't like other people. And I'm a fairly decent judge of . . . faces . . . that the camera likes. For instance . . . Bogart
would never win any prizes in a beauty contest. . . . But he was a great star.
The camera liked him. . . . Cooper . . . Well, Rita had a face that I knew
would photograph, I didn't have to worry about that. She was very frightened, very . . . nervous. And she got over that during the shooting . . . really
in just a few days. . . . She moved easily . . . she was a dancer. And she'd
listen to every blooming thing that you'd say. When we finished the picture
. . . Cohn saw it . . . and he said, "Just ask for anything you want. I've got
a new star." I said, "I'm going to ask you one thing, don't put her in a picture
for six or eight months. Wait until this one comes out . . . wait until they
start asking who she likes as President. . . . So that she builds up a little . . .
ego. Because right now she hasn't got any. And it was only because the nicest
people were around her . . . that she got through. And . . . if you just build
up her ego . . . you could put her in anything." I said, "It's going to be hard
to hold that girl off the screen, but you've got to do it." And . . . after the
second or third picture with her, Cohn said, "That was the best advice anybody could have given me because she just came right out of her shell . . .
and out of a shyness to having a little ego . . . you know, where she could
just go out and do something." But Rita was quick . . . she tried. Her very
first scene with Cary . . . Grant . . . I said, "We'll rehearse it." He was sitting
at a desk in a little office or something. And she was outside the door. And I
said, "Okay, Rita, come on in." She came in so fast . . . looked at Grant. . . .
I just started to laugh. I said, "Hey, wait a minute. Now let's try it slow. Come
in, lean back against the door and look at him." She did it and I said, "Wait a
minute. Rita, your dress is all molded to fit your figure. Why?" "Oh, I guess
to show my figure." "Okay," I said. "Lean back and show it! And look at
Grant and tell me what you're thinking." She did and she looked awful good
doing it because she had that . . . dancer's quality . . . of assuming a position. I said, "What are you thinking?" She said, "He was looking at me in a
rather peculiar way." "Okay, ask him if he likes your hair that way. . . ."

JK: You made the whole scene up as you went along?

HH: Oh, sure. Out of that, you get started on a sexy part . . . you find out they
can do it. And everything she did after that had a sex connotation to it that
we worked with. . . . They go along with it. For instance . . . I used to . . .
with somebody . . . 'Angie Dickinson in *Rio Bravo*. Did you see that? God,
she's really sexy. Angie. The trouble with her is that she wants to do too
many parts . . . be too many people. And she will not believe me when I say,

"Look. You made good in that, why don't you do that?" . . . Now . . . in *The Big Sleep* I used a little round-eyed girl to play a nymphomaniac . . . Martha Vickers . . . I think she married Mickey Rooney at one time. . . . Lovely. And I made her cut her curls off and gave her . . . a kind of close . . . boyish haircut* and I taught her two or three things. She played a nymphomaniac, and the studio signed her for a long-term contract with more money than she'd ever gotten. . . . Okay, she got her first salary check and went down and bought a lot of girly dresses with a lot of . . . little bows and ruffles and . . . She started playing a nice girl, and they fired her after six months. And she came to me and said, "What happened?" I said, "You're just stupid. Why didn't you keep on playing that part?" "Well, that was a nymphomaniac." "Look, it's only a nymphomaniac because I told you so. They liked you on the screen. And you did such a great job of it because you weren't trying to get sympathy or anything. You were a little bitch. Why didn't you keep doing that?" But you see . . . A strange thing happens. . . .

It happened with that girl . . . the one in *Sergeant York* . . . Joan Leslie.

Hawks squirms in his leather chair, recalling the contrariness of women who will not listen to him and learn from him.

HH: That's what they do . . . they do it all the time, you see. Now, Cooper met her . . . she had bobby socks and carried schoolbooks . . . and she was a cute girl. I said to Cooper, "You better like her, she's going to be your leading lady." He said, "Aw, you're nuts." I said, "No." He said, "How will I play scenes with her?" "Exactly the way you just did when you talked to her. Can you remember what you did?" And we went over and repeated the things that he did, and that's the way he played scenes with her. And she said . . . Well, I said to her, "Tell me, how would you like it if a man got jealous?" Well, she thought that's fine. I said, "Well, that's what we're going to do. You realize there's some jealousy and you're going to try and make it worse. So you're going to . . . prod at him and pinch him, you know what I mean . . . get him going." She said, "Oh, that'll be fun." And she worked that way. So . . . See, I've always pooh-poohed the love scenes made in movies. And made entirely different scenes myself. Okay . . . well, that's just a different way of . . . doing it. They found the women that I made stars . . . sexy too. But I haven't any idea how to do that other kind of stuff. . . . I've never made scenes with people where the moonlight's on the water . . . soft music and all that. I laugh at it. I think it's just kind of . . . It's make-believe, it's once-upon-a-time.

JK: And yet you achieved tremendous romanticism. I'm thinking of the seduction scene in *Ball of Fire* where Stanwyck stands on a stack of books to kiss Cooper. Very sexy stuff. You directed the remake of that, didn't you?

*In fact, she wore her hair long, very sleek, like the girl in a Clairol ad.

HH: Yeah . . . *A Song is Born.* . . . I didn't want to do it. But . . . what the
hell? It's pride . . . you're stuck with being offered $25,000 a week. . . . Oh,
I never saw the picture.

JK: It's actually one of Danny Kaye's better films, though it lacks the "chemistry" of *Ball of Fire.*

HH: Well, you see . . . *Ball of Fire* was a good picture. Written by good writers
[Billy Wilder, Charles Brackett, Thomas Monroe]. . . . The only trouble was
Goldwyn had got himself into a spot . . . he'd hired a writer and paid him
$100,000 . . . then realized the guy had made a fool out of him. He didn't
like anything the guy wrote. Well, the guy really couldn't write, he was trying
to write better than Wilder and Brackett. . . . It all started when Goldwyn
came down to Palm Springs and said, "Howard, I'm stuck for a story. For
Danny Kaye." I said, "Christ, do the one I made, only make it about music
instead of the English language." He said, "Howard, that's a great idea. Will
you do it?" "No." So . . . he phoned me up about three weeks later. He said,
"We've got a great idea, we're gonna lay it in 1922." Well, it seemed like a
Dixieland story and all that stuff. I said, "That's just fine, boss. That's the
greatest idea I ever heard . . . a feller goes off to find new music . . . and
finds Dixieland." Well, Goldwyn kept after me to do the picture, he said,
"There just has to be some way you'll do it." I said, "Well . . . I'd do it for
$25,000 a week." And Goldwyn said, "You just made a deal." I said, "Okay,
I'll sign next week. . . . But there's one thing. I don't want to have to use
Virginia Mayo." He said, "Oh, now, what the hell? . . . Everybody else that
was brought up, you've turned down." It wasn't only Virginia Mayo, but
Goldwyn had her looking at Barbara Stanwyck's scenes in the original. It was
just, oh . . . boy, it was just hell. You couldn't create a scene, what with the
musicians. I used to try and be careful and cover everything with long shots
and separate shots and everything like that. I never went to see the rushes. It
. . . it's not the kind of comedy that Danny Kaye could do best.

JK: You mentioned that that was for Goldwyn. And you've also worked at
RKO, MGM, Fox, Paramount, Warners. . . .

HH: I started directing at Fox, you see. I had a pretty free hand . . . and no
contract. Everything went fine until the talkies came in and, like I said before,
I was out of luck . . . just like most everybody else. Oh . . . I think I had a
fight with Sheehan, too.* He found out that I had made . . . *A Girl in Every
Port* . . . and . . . when he came out of the preview, he said, "That's the
worst picture Fox has made in years." I said, "You're just a bloody idiot."
That's all. God . . . it got its cost back in just one theater. So . . . he didn't
like me. Therefore, I had little . . . compunction about going over to another
studio for *Dawn Patrol.* Almost all the heads of the studios had said, "If

---

*Winfield Sheehan was vice-president and production head at Fox.

you've ever got a story that you want to do, come over here and you can start work." And . . . every once in a while I'd run into them and they'd ask me what I was doing. Most times I'd have stories that I wrote or bought . . . or found. Not in the case of . . . let's say, *Sergeant York.* Jesse Lasky bought that. He had a script that was one of the worst scripts in the world. They gave it to me and said, "We're gonna have to screw a picture out of it." It was a great recommendation, but . . . I rewrote it. It was . . . Jesse gave me my first good job, being story editor in charge of productions.* So I went to him when I got this story and I said, "Jesse, I have a great deal of respect for you as a showman, but why the hell did you buy this story?" He told me a great story . . . which was what he thought was *Sergeant York.* I said it wasn't in the script and he seemed mighty surprised to hear this. He said, "Oh, Christ, I'll give anything if you'll do it." I said, "Look, I'll get Cooper." He said, "We can't get Cooper." "I'll get Cooper if you'll just leave us alone, because you've started wrong on this story." He said, "Oh . . . you'll get any god-damn thing you want." So I went back and saw Cooper and said, "Didn't Lasky give you your first start?" Cooper said, "Yeah." I said, "Well, he gave me mine as well, he's got a story that won't hurt either of us to do . . . he's broke . . . needs a shave. . . ." So . . . well, I said, "Coop, we've got to talk about this thing." "What's there to talk about? You know we're gonna do it." "Okay, let's go and talk to Warner Brothers. We'll do it if they won't bother us." And they offered us . . . 80 percent of the picture, I think it was. And we said, "No, we want your usual thing." We wanted Lasky to have it . . . and he made about $250,000 . . . and Coop got an Academy Award . . . everything worked out. So the good guys won. But, yeah, I was like a free agent before they had free agents. I produced. Ben Hecht worked on *Scarface* and *Underworld,* which he wrote while I was producer. We did that for a friend of ours . . . Arthur Rosson, who got drunk and we had to fire him. That's when . . . whatchacallit . . . Von Sternberg . . . got to do it. The cast was already chosen, story had been written . . . there was a drawing of every single set and costume. Yeah . . . I was a producer at . . . Paramount then.

JK: I had no idea of your involvement with *Underworld* . . . but that might account for the similarity of the women in your films and the women in Von Sternberg's.

HH: Yeah, that's why you might say the girls in our films are alike and . . . Of course, when Joe brought Dietrich over, he asked me to help him. He said, "I'm involved . . . emotionally with this girl, I need some help." So I read his script and I said, "How you gonna introduce the girl?" He said, "I thought I'd show her on this stage with a . . . kind of . . . lovely setting and a shim-mering gown . . . soft light." I said, "That's awful new . . . but what does it do for her? Why not put her in a full-dress suit? Let her sit on a chair on an empty stage with just one spotlight on. Dress her like a man. If you really

*That was at Famous Players–Lasky in 1922.

want to give her a good introduction, let her . . . walk through the audience and let her spot a . . . good-lookin' girl. And let her walk over and . . . kiss the girl. On the lips." And he did.* And . . . then he came to me another time with a scene, and he asked me what about it and I said, "You really want to have her . . . rape Cooper?" "Well . . ." "Well, that's the effect you're gonna get, 'cause this is an awful strong girl. Now . . . instead of what you got there, let him walk around her apartment and say, 'Was this your fur coat? I shouldn't be here. . . .' And then finally let him kiss her and say, 'I'm beginning to like it too much, I'd better go.' And let him start off and have a couple of footpads attack him and have her see it. He walks back and picks her up and carries her off into the house." So . . . I used to help Joe. . . . I don't know why . . . I was the only person that he never got *snotty* with . . . 'cause he was a sonofabitch.

Hawks' films strike few truths, but lots of attractive poses where the men are forever boys and the women have to pretend to be boys if they want to join in. The least successfully integrated women in his films are womanly women, like a Virginia Mayo or Ann Sheridan or Rita Hayworth. The most admired are ones like Lauren Bacall, who looks as much at home in jeans as she does in dresses . . . at least when young. His only way of dealing successfully with a woman is when she plays a masculine role, as Ann Sheridan did opposite Cary Grant, who spent most of the time in drag in *I Was a Male War Bride;* or in an all-out spoof of sex as with *Gentlemen Prefer Blondes.* His men relax around a woman only after she's shown herself to be tougher than John Wayne, like the arrow-pierced Joanne Dru in *Red River,* who barely flinches when it's unceremoniously pulled out of her shoulder, and even slaps the sensitive Montgomery Clift before silently passing out. One of his most successful films, *His Girl Friday,* takes much of its effectiveness from a role reversal that has Rosalind Russell in what was originally written as a man's role and, except for her hats and tailored suits, is played at much the same speed and with even less real sexuality than by the man in the same part. Had Hawks filmed it straight, as Wilder does in the third remake with Hildy Johnson played by Jack Lemmon, whose masculinity is never in doubt, we would have seen what a whiny, basically tiresome old maid lay just beneath the surface. The suggestion of a more complex male-male relationship between the reporter and his boss existing beneath the surface was something Hawks could not have dealt with comfortably; it had no place in Hawks' world. His men would have shied from it; they would have had to stomp it out for fear of contamination. It's their very boys' own form of masculinity that would have become suspect, as, in fact, it is.

1974

*This may be true. But Hawks was not in Germany when Von Sternberg made *The Blue Angel* and had Dietrich sing "Falling in Love Again" wearing a man's top hat, the opening note for future variations on a theme. And same-sex kissing was a familiar pastime in Germany, something Von Sternberg and Dietrich would have been much more familiar with than Hawks.

Barbara Stanwyck, photographed by Scotty Welbourne (Warner Bros.), 1942

BARBARA
STANWYCK

"I HATE COMMON SENSE . . . it's so common."* That line said by someone like
Claudette Colbert would have reeked with pretensions of class. Had Crawford said it, it would have been a challenge, but it would have been sexual,
based on her conviction that all a man wants from a woman are her favors.
Davis would have played on the irony of the statement and made it sound like
the opening line of an aria. Bogart would have filled it with defeat. Barbra
Streisand would have thought that it was a comedy line and would have imitated
Mae West doing it. And Bette Midler would turn the question in on itself, as if
to say, "So what's wrong with being common?" Only Barbara Stanwyck could
say it matter-of-factly and let you know that about the only thing common sense
isn't is common . . . else why would the world be in such a state? Miss
Stanwyck's heroines are not surprised by the state of the world. They may not
like it, but their attitude is: If you're not going to do anything about it, shut up
about it.

I've always considered Davis, Crawford, Hepburn and Stanwyck to be the
great American female screen stars—having said that, and admiring them all
(Garbo and Dietrich belong to other categories that defy nationality), I would
add that the word "natural" belongs only to Stanwyck. Crawford is alluring
(what other actress was born with Adrian shoulder pads?), Hepburn is eccentric
and Davis is tempestuous, but Stanwyck brought an edge of reality to every role
she played—even if it wasn't natural to her, she made it look natural. This may
explain why the greatest natural actress the American talking screen has produced has not generally been recognized as such. She wouldn't allow you to
place her on a pedestal. No one ever questioned whether she was good. She was
simply accepted as a matter of fact, rather than being recognized as the uniquely
gifted actress she has been almost from the first moment she appeared on the
screen back in 1929. After one false start, it was all clear ahead. She wasn't
easy to photograph, so she wasn't considered a great glamour gal, though she
was a glamorous star undoubtedly. She comes on the screen in *Ladies of Leisure*
as a bold new actress, and by the film's end she looks like a star. She could and

---

The Gay Sisters (Warner Bros., 1942).

503

did play everything, so in her heyday she was never put into a niche. Everybody seemed to accept her work, took her on her own merits, never questioned that she would survive, and when the year-end honor roll came about, they invariably passed her over. She never pretended to be what she wasn't. You knew she was regular people, which is to say what you hoped regular people were like. Her attitude toward her career was well summed up when she told a young admirer who praised her for *Night Nurse* (made in 1931, in which she played a crusading young private nurse) and for her performance twenty years later as a sophisticated, rich society matron in *Titanic* (1952), "I enjoyed what I was doing. I had fun. If I hadn't, I wouldn't have done it." Which also sums up her theory on acting. In that reply you can hear two other feisty, upwardly mobile actors, James Cagney and Spencer Tracy. Maybe we're just more used to these traits in men, so that we associate them with masculinity instead of character.

By the '50s, Stanwyck had been a star for twenty years, and while many of her contemporaries were going through traumatic career upheavals, she was as busy as ever; in her career, work took precedence over billing, salary and all the status perks associated with stars while on top but which become ego traps that keep them from working and surviving. Stanwyck seemed never to have bought her own ticket. That was another quality to draw one to her. And whether in hokum like *Escape to Burma* or in cult classics like *Forty Guns,* or opposite Elvis Presley in *Roustabout,* or in *Clash by Night*—knowing, accepting and endorsing the fact that the film's supporting actress, the young Marilyn Monroe, would receive all the attention when the film was released—Stanwyck was never less than the consummate professional. Given the opportunity, as in *All I Desire* (1952), she rose to the occasion as one of the greatest actresses to be seen on the screen.

As early as 1936, years before it became common practice for stars to freelance, Stanwyck freelanced all over Hollywood, and that's why no one studio had a vested long-term interest in building her. Through her work at whatever studio, she sustained her own momentum, giving a continuity to her work. For Goldwyn she made *Stella Dallas* unforgettable. At Paramount her films included *The Lady Eve,* her voice like fingers caressing the nape of Henry Fonda's neck as he bends to slip her high-heeled slipper back on her foot: "Oh, Hopsy, what would I do without a big strong man like you?"; and *Double Indemnity,* playing Phyllis Diedrichsen, an icy, remorseless blond killer who only comes to life seconds before the bullet enters her body. In the '40s, for Warner Bros.—where she had one of the best freelance deals of the decade—she made her own favorite picture, *My Reputation,* a formula woman's picture like those Bette Davis did; and as the eldest of *The Gay Sisters* she had common sense enough for all. She wears a mink slung over one shoulder, not as one born to it or trying to impress anyone, but as one who knows where it belongs. For her, a cloth coat and a mink coat are the same: coats. In one you get a job, in the other you get a man. For Goldwyn she was a *Ball of Fire.* With Frank Capra, who launched her with the five films they made together in the early '30s, she teamed up again to make *Meet John Doe,* the first of her three films with that other American original, Gary Cooper. She worked at Metro, at Columbia, at United Artists, at RKO, at Universal and at 20th Century–Fox. She went where there was work.

Underlying her work you sense a rage that never allows a situation (regardless of histrionics) to become melodramatic . . . but heart-fires are banked as deep and as real as in any Tracy Lord,* though few have made the effort to find or unlock them; she's usually left to fend and seethe. With Stanwyck, hate is a powerful emotion, but her women don't get angry at a person, even the one who has caused the problem. She's a class victim. Her characters unleash their anger at a situation, at society. Rich or poor, they are always fighting a system. While no one could be sexier than Stanwyck when she needs to be (look at *The Lady Eve* and *Ball of Fire*), basically Stanwyck doesn't trade on her femininity. The problem confronted by Stanwyck's women wasn't that they weren't men, but that they lived in a society that didn't give women an equal chance. She refused to renounce her femininity; she liked who—not what—she was, and she would not renounce her rights as an equal. She never questions a man's rights, but treats them as equals. If they lose, that's their problem. They should have looked at the cards in their hands instead of the gleam in her eye.

Brunette or gray, fuzzy or grizzled, in jodhpurs or skirts, the catalogue of American women Barbara Stanwyck brought to greatness on the screen all shared a trait: whatever comforts they were offered, won or inherited, they never forgot the hard times. Even when this insight didn't come with the role, as when Stanwyck might play a screwball heiress, this awareness of shared, fundamental, primal struggles women are heir to as daughters of Eve came with it. Sooner or later, either through an inflection in her voice or a look from her eyes, this underlying knowledge of burden would flash out and sear the spectator. It would not redeem trash, but it kept from ever pulling her to its level. In their heart of hearts, childless or not, liberated or fettered by conventions, Stanwyck's women are sisters; they have an edge and a pride that uplift them. You leave a Stanwyck film with respect and admiration for her sex.

BS: But that's what acting is, it's *re*-acting. When youngsters ask me how to act, I say, "Don't. *Re*-act! *Don't act!*" [She laughs good-naturedly.]

JK: In the last few years there's been a very sad neglect in your film career. . . .

BS: It's not that I don't want to work, it's that nobody asks me. It's a little difficult. They don't write certain things anymore. You bridge a certain thing: you can't play the young love interest anymore, that's impossible. And any actor or actress who thinks that they are what they were twenty years ago is utterly ridiculous. Now you must bridge . . . you must go to another plateau.

*Hepburn's character in *The Philadelphia Story*.

In age and so on. But they are *not writing* that sort of part. So you just sit back and wait until something good comes along. It's as simple as that . . . or as complicated as that.

JK: Which is why you do a great deal of television?

BS: Yes. You see, television doesn't have this problem. Not that you're playing the . . . uhmm . . . young romantic love interest and all that, but they don't seem to be so concerned with age. They write a teleplay, period. If it's good, it's good. If it isn't, it isn't. But they don't particularly . . . uhmmn . . . care about youth and all that sort of thing.

JK: You did a lot of Westerns. What do you particularly like about Westerns?

BS: Oh, I love to do them. I just love to do them. [She sighs happily . . . getting away from questions of age and the big screen.] Well, I'm particularly fond of reading about the early West. I think it was a very romantic era in our country. First of all, I love the outdoors; and, secondly, I love to ride. I love that whole era.

JK: You've worked with some very good directors: Sam Fuller, Allan Dwan twice, William Wellman . . .

BS: Allan Dwan, yes! Oh, gosh, he goes back a long time! He's fascinating to work for, because if you can get him talking about himself and *his* particular era—he goes back to the earliest days in films—it's fascinating to sit and listen to him. He's just one of the top directors.

JK: And people like Hawks and Capra and Ford . . . well, you only did one Ford film.

BS: Just *The Plough and the Stars,* the Sean O'Casey film. Capra, of course, I did five films for. *Ladies of Leisure* and *The Miracle Woman* and *Meet John Doe* . . .

JK: What do you remember of *The Bitter Tea of General Yen*? It's one of the most sophisticated and staggering films.

BS: That was one of the first ones with the color question, the Oriental and the white woman. That was long before its particular theme was acceptable, such as today. But in those days Mr. Capra had quite a bit of trouble, because the women's clubs and things like that just didn't cotton to this fact of this white woman falling in love with this Chinese warlord. They didn't care for that. But I think he did it in great taste. I haven't seen it in I don't know how many years. I remember it now that you mention it.

JK: Someone said that Barbara Stanwyck has taken over the projection of a female who has contempt for the man whom she lures by sexual prowess. Are you aware of this?

BS (laughs): No. . . . Contempt?

JK: Well, I suppose *Double Indemnity* is the key one they pick up. You always seem to be the woman married to the wrong man.

This elicits a marvelous burst of deep Stanwyck laughter from her . . . maybe she's thinking of a lot of films, or maybe it's just the question.

JK: You win him, and then you don't want him anymore.

BS: That's interesting. I never thought about it! Uhmm . . .

JK: In *Double Indemnity* you play a character called Phyllis Diedrichsen, and you wear a blond wig like Dietrich did at that time. Was that deliberate? To make her a sort of American Dietrich, or a small-town *femme fatale*?

BS: I don't know whether it was deliberate on Wilder's part. He wanted me to be a blonde, but I don't know whether it was deliberate or not. He never mentioned it.

JK: What are the key roles in your career, the ones you're especially pleased with?

BS: Well, I would go along with *Double Indemnity,* of course. I liked that very much. I liked *Stella Dallas . . . Sorry, Wrong Number . . .* and I would rather not mention the ones I don't like because [she's laughing] there are more of them than the ones I liked!

JK: *My Reputation*?

BS: *My Reputation* was what we classify as a good woman's picture. It is a problem throughout the world: the widow who is *comparatively* young, who does start to go out with eligible men, and then gossip starts. And, of course, ten or fifteen years ago when we made this film, this was quite a problem.

JK: You mentioned *Stella Dallas,* and in that you worked with King Vidor, one of the greats. And then years later *Fountainhead* was bought because of you, and he directed it. What happened there?

BS: Well, this is what I heard, because I never discussed it with Mr. Vidor at all. I had read the book by Ayn Rand when it first came out; and I talked to Miss Rand about it, and she wrote it, *really,* for Garbo. That was her *ideal,* and that was the actress that she wanted. And who can blame her? But Miss Garbo was unavailable, and I said I would just *love* to do it, because I understand this woman. Well, Warner Brothers bought it. Henry Blanke at that time was one of their top producers over there, and I brought it to his attention . . . because I had done *My Reputation* for Mr. Blanke. He liked the book, and they bought it. And they assigned King Vidor.

Now, originally, it was supposed to be Humphrey Bogart and myself.

That was the original casting. But when they assigned King Vidor to it, naturally his idea of casting was completely different. So it wound up with Gary Cooper and Patricia Neal, who is certainly one of the finest actresses in our industry . . . at least, I think so. And Mr. Vidor just didn't think that I was sexy enough to play the part. And he certainly is entitled to his opinion. So that's that. And these are the things that happen in the business. You take them in stride; they are disappointing, of course, but it isn't the end of the world. You *have* to take it in stride . . . not only professionally but personally. Otherwise, we'd all cut our throats.

JK: Now, how about Bette Davis, who had an ad in *Variety* saying, "I'm out of work and it's a crying shame"? You had just as much right to say that when the parts stopped coming your way after all the money you'd made for the studios over the years.

BS: *Well,* each and every one of us to his own. We're all different personalities. I think this was quite right for Miss Davis, it worked exceptionally well for her, and she is entirely right as far as she is concerned. This is a great . . . *great* . . . talent. And it's ridiculous to let it go by the boards.

JK: So is yours.

BS: Well, that's why I say, "To each his own." She could do that; I couldn't do it.

JK: You fought for salary once. Was there a time when you said, "This is stupid, I won't do it"?

BS: Well, I turned down several things. When I was under contract, for a couple of years I was known as "the suspension queen" purely because if I didn't like a part, and didn't want to play it because the script was entirely inferior, they would suspend me. Well, that's their prerogative. I was suspended for quite some time in there! In the '30s and early '40s. But then, around, oh, '37—'38—'39, I started to freelance. When the contract was over with, I thought freelancing was better for me.

JK: How much choice and artistic control did you have over the roles that you played when you became one of the biggest money-making stars in Hollywood?*

BS: Well, not . . . not very much. You have a certain amount. They're fair; they listen to you. If you're under contract, you say, "I don't like this script, I don't like so-and-so," well, by and large, most of them will listen to you. And if they think your ideas are valid, they will call in the writer and you sit and discuss it as adults and professional people should. Now, if they don't agree with you, they say, "No!" Well, all right, if you are under contract and

---

*In 1944 she was the highest-paid woman in America.

you say, "This I can't do, I just don't believe in it," then you're put on suspension and somebody else does it. It's as simple as that. You have a little more say in the last eight or ten years, because, after all, we're not all idiots. They used to think actors were nuts!

JK: You were originally a stage actress. Did you ever want to return to the stage?

BS: Not really. I loved making motion pictures because you play such different, varied roles. Now, nobody wants a failure in the theater, you want it to be a success. But if you have a success, you are honor-bound and contractually bound to stay with it. If it runs a year, oh, dear *Lord,* you are *bored* with that. No matter how great the part is. You get tired of doing and saying the same thing. And I *like* the variety of film roles, so I just sort of stuck with the motion-picture field. Now I've been away from the theater for so long, to be perfectly honest with you, I would be frightened to death to return to the stage in front of a live audience.

JK: The last thing you did was *Tittle Tattle*?

BS: Yes . . . *Tattle Tales.* A musical revue.* It wasn't very good. I lost quite a bit of money on that. Nobody likes to lose a lot of money, but from then on I decided to stay out there in California.

JK: Have you ever financed any of your own films? Have you any interest in that?

BS: No. No! Leave that to the powers that be. They know. I don't know that end of it.

JK: Since you've worked in every medium, which one did you enjoy most?

BS: Well, I believe the motion-picture field is the most fascinating. Television is very interesting, and it's great, great hard work. Still and all, you get better quality from motion pictures. Because you can take your time. In TV they want everything yesterday.

JK: But, career-wise, in the parts you play . . . because you played comedy with great success . . .

BS: Oh, only when they were beautifully written. I am not really a comedienne *per se*. I'm not very good. But when they are written as well as *The Lady Eve* or *You Belong to Me* . . . both of those films I did with Henry Fonda, who *is* a wonderful comedian . . . or if it is a situation comedy, I'm all right. But—just for me to be funny—I'm not a funny person.

JK: Well, I would also include *Ball of Fire*.

---

*She financed it to star her then husband, Frank Fay, at the low ebb of his career, before his return in *Harvey*.

BS: Ah . . . but that is the writing.

JK: But I've seen a lot of well-written parts just tossed to the winds. They remade *Lady Eve* as *Birds and the Bees* and it was abysmal; now, the writing was still there. So I think it has a lot more to do with it than just the writing.

BS: I did not see the remake. With George Gobel? Did they rewrite the entire thing?*

JK: It was pretty much like *Lady Eve*. The plot structure is there, but the ability to toss lines about and everybody catching them, this was gone. But you're talking about approaching every role from an acting viewpoint, where you see every role—comedy or otherwise—as a human relation?

BS: Yes, that it *could* happen. That maybe it *has* happened. You have to believe that, I think.

JK: Have you cared very much about how you *looked* in a film? Gregg Toland photographed you beautifully in *This Is My Affair*.†

BS: Well, now, if the part calls for a glamour appearance, then I want to look the very best that the cameraman can make me look; if I'm not supposed to look like that, I couldn't care less. I'm the type that cracks up all of a sudden. I'll wake up some morning, take a look at myself in the mirror, phone the studio and say, "Well, boys, you'd better get yourselves another girl . . . unless you want me to play the grandmother part!" It depends on *what* I am playing. If I'm supposed to be an old bag . . . then fine, let's go. I'll do anything at all to make it real.

JK: What do you demand?

BS: A good story. First of all comes the story. It's like building a house. That's your foundation; the basement, the steel and the cement. That's solid. That's the important thing. *Then* your interior decorator is the second thing . . . that's the director. *That* I want. The third thing is all your decorations. That's my actors. But without the story, goodbye. I think the little things will take care of themselves. If the big things are good, you won't pay any attention to the little things. If your story is good, and your direction is good, and the other actors . . . The little things? No, I don't think so.

JK: May I ask you why you turned down the role of *Hush . . . Hush, Sweet Charlotte*?

BS: Oh, now this is a misinterpretation. You mean after Miss Crawford? I was never offered that part. Now, that was printed and it was *not* true. That Robert

---

*Mitzi Gaynor took Stanwyck's role.

†*This Is My Affair* was the second of her two co-starring roles with Robert Taylor at the height of their affair.

Aldrich offered me the part opposite Bette when Crawford became ill? That is not true, he did not offer the role to me. I didn't turn it down. That came out of Hollywood. What happened was that *originally*, with Bette Davis and Joan Crawford, Bob Aldrich wanted me to play a little vignette in there, about three or four days' work. Mary Astor subsequently played it. I read it and I didn't care to play it; it's as simple as that. Now, when Joan became ill, this story suddenly came up. They said he offered me her part, which is not true. But *had* he offered me the part, I *certainly* would have checked with Joan first, because Joan is a friend of mine, as to whether or not she was able to carry on or what.

JK: This kind of integrity is very rare, especially today, when it is catch-as-catch-can.

BS: Well, I most certainly would have done it. I would have called Joan and said, "Are you available? Are you going to be well enough? Or what? What shall I do?"

JK: Now, this horror film . . .

BS: You mean *The Night Walker*? It is *not* a *horror* film. It's a shocker. A suspense movie. There's a difference! *Horror* is with the heads rolling and the blood and gore and all that sort of thing. This is a shocker-suspense film.

JK: Well, what's coming up next?

BS: I don't know. William Castle, who produced and directed *The Night Walker*, just bought a book. It's an English book called *The Possessors*. And he's been talking to me about *it*. But it's right in its infancy now. It's an interesting character, and I would be very much interested in playing it. But we'll see what comes out.*

JK: This is sort of an embarrassing question, but this is the first picture you've done in a long time with Robert Taylor.†

BS: No, it's not embarrassing at all. We've been divorced fourteen years. Actually, the last picture we did was *This Is My Affair*. So that was long before we were married. It was Mr. Castle's idea. He sent me the script, and I rather enjoyed it. And when I went in to discuss it with him, he said, "I have an idea, and I don't know *how* you will feel about it, but how would you feel about Robert Taylor playing the other . . ." I said, "I think it would be a wonderful idea, you'd better ask him. And Mrs. Taylor!" So he did, and Bob said, "I'd be delighted." It was as simple as that. Naturally, it makes people very curious, of course. But I hope that they see two professional people giving good performances.

---

*It didn't. *The Night Walker* was Stanwyck's last big-screen feature.
†He was her husband for sixteen years.

JK: The last thing you did before was with Elvis Presley. *Roustabout.* This was a Hal Wallis film. I must say, you looked terribly good in that.

BS: I didn't see it. I enjoyed making it very much. When Hal Wallis called me and said, "I'd like you to read this script. It's an Elvis Presley," I thought, My goodness, what on earth would I do in an Elvis Presley film? It sort of set me back a bit. But I've worked for Hal Wallis several times, and he's a wonderful producer and a fine gentleman, and I thought, Well, if he's calling me, there must be something to it. So I rather liked the whole idea. I didn't know Elvis Presley at the time; as a matter of fact, I had never seen one of his movies.

JK: You had heard of him?

BS: Oh, yes, I had heard of him! But I thought this might be very interesting, this would give me an entirely different audience, a very young audience. And I liked the part, I liked everything about it. And he's a very fine young gentleman, this man, this Elvis.

JK: Do you find much loyalty from the old fans? Do they stay very close?

BS: Yes, they have. But what surprises me is this young group following me around. I just didn't expect it. And I kept saying, "How old are you? Why aren't you in school? Go back to school!" I was quite surprised. It was very nice.

JK: What is your relation to fans?

BS: Well, I don't have very much contact with them unless I come to New York. You see, at home they don't bother you . . . unless it's tourist season! But out there you can walk around and shop. I do all my own shopping, and nobody pays any attention to you. They're so used to you it doesn't matter to them. They couldn't care less. But when you travel around, that's a different story. Then you do come in contact with them. I must say, by and large, they've been terribly nice to me. I've been very pleased by them, very grateful.

They're always so curious about "How do you live?" and that sort of thing. You make a statement and then everybody says, "Oh, my goodness, the poor soul lives all alone." Well, it isn't intended that way. I live very simply. I have a nice home and a few friends. I don't go to many big parties or premieres or anything like that, mainly because I don't care for them. And I have a few good friends, and I enjoy them as I hope they enjoy me. And apart from my housekeeper, I live alone. Well, of course, I'm a bachelor woman! But so many people take it out of context, then they dramatize it and it's like, "Here's Madame X walking down the street, poor old soul." Well, that's not true at all. Hundreds of thousands of people live alone, and it wasn't intended to sound any other way. But I have been questioned about this several times, and they pull it *out* of a paragraph and make it look very sad and poignant. Not at all. *Not at all!*

JK: I'm glad! And what do you want now?

BS: Oh, I don't know, to tell you the truth. Good health, and an occasional good part. I do love to work. I enjoy it. I really *do*.

JK: One last thing. The reason I found out you were in town is that somebody said, "Barbara Stanwyck went to *Golden Boy;** and when she walked in, the audience gave her a standing ovation."

BS: *Not* when I walked in. There was this group of young fans who were following me around, and I made a deal with them. They had been at the hotel asking me for my autograph, and I said I would come down half an hour early before the theater. I would come down to the lobby and do whatever they wanted, but please to stop following me around. Well, I made the deal with them, so I went down a half-hour before dinner, and I stayed there. And I took the pictures, and did the autographs, and they were very sweet. And then my friends and I went in to see *Golden Boy,* and at the end of the show we got up to go backstage and congratulate the performers . . . and here comes this little group of fans with a dozen red roses, which touched me very deeply. It meant they had been going up and down the street trying to find a dozen roses for me. They were so grateful that I had come down and given them a half-hour that they waited until 11:00 p.m. to give me this little bouquet of roses. Well, naturally, the balcony people saw that. The orchestra people had practically left, but the balcony hadn't. Nobody had noticed me until then. Anyhow, this was their way of reciprocating. And when the balcony saw this, they said, "Who is it?" and all that, and the balcony started to applaud and . . . I was deeply touched. . . . And that was that.

In 1981 the Lincoln Center Film Society honored her with a gala retrospective of her film career. When she agreed to attend, she quipped, "I thought they'd made a mistake. I thought they wanted Barbra Streisand." In 1982 she won an Emmy for her portrayal of a rich matriarch with a passion for a man of the cloth in *The Thorn Birds,* a made-for-TV movie. In accepting the award, she devoted most of her speech to complimenting a fellow-nominee, Ann-Margret, on *her* portrayal.

To ease their guilt, the Academy awarded Stanwyck a Special Oscar for Lifetime Achievement in 1978. In accepting the statuette, Stanwyck commented that her lifelong friend William Holden—who had died just months before—had always wanted her to win an Oscar. "Tonight, my golden boy, you got your wish." Always thinking of someone else, not herself. She leaves that to us.

1964

*The stage musical based on the Clifford Odets play which Stanwyck had done on film.

John Engstead with *Carole Lombard* (Paramount), 1935

JOHN
ENGSTEAD

E NGSTEAD WAS THE MOST SUCCESSFUL Hollywood portrait photographer of
beautiful women and handsome men in the years between 1940 and
1960. There wasn't a beautiful star he didn't photograph; his work appeared on
the cover of every woman's magazine, fan magazine and *TV Guide*. His subjects
are a Who's Who: Loretta Young, Rosalind Russell, Barbara Stanwyck, Cary
Grant, the last pictures of Joan Crawford and the first Hollywood portraits of
Lauren Bacall; all the Gabor sisters, almost monthly; Lana Turner, Ava Gardner,
Rita Hayworth, Marilyn Monroe, Mae West, Clint Eastwood, Jane Wyman,
Ann Sheridan, Gable, Cooper, Stewart and, for almost ten years, the tireless
Marlene Dietrich. The moment these stars were no longer under contract and
had to look after their own publicity, they went to John's studio. His photos
were to Hollywood's supreme egos what in a later age Andy Warhol's Polaroids
are to the sated rich. Both men share one trait: the subjects are often unrecog-
nizable.

From the day John opened his own studio in Hollywood back in 1939 and
for the next forty years, stars, on becoming forty, reached for their mirrors with
one hand and for a reassuring photo session with Engstead with the other. Thus
fortified, they gave out interviews, illustrated with their latest portrait, saying
how being over forty is the best time in a woman's life, after which they were
only seen out in the evenings. Engstead's best work made regular patrons of
such shrewd, no-nonsense professionals as Loretta Young and Marlene Dietrich, women who knew that the picture has to make you look like what you
can deliver. His latter portraits—soft, diluted, diffused, sugary—kept a lot of
other actresses happy, but these portraits get a bit hard to take if you're not
wearing the subject's own rose-colored glasses.

Engstead had few illusions about his own work—he felt he could be as
good as the best of them, whether Willinger, Hurrell, Avedon, Coburn, but he
was perfectly content to give the customers what they wanted, though the Doris
Day school of lighting a star can be rather frightening when not seen from afar.
He was seriously ill for the last few years of his life, which accounted for his
more than usual degree of acerbity, but he still kept up a grueling work schedule. He first called me because of the increasing interest in and critical apprecia-

515

tion of the work of the Hollywood portrait photographers, men he knew from having worked with them in his years in the Paramount publicity department, and whose ranks he later joined when he started to take photographs. When he talked about the people he had really loved—not just photographed, but loved—he laughed: Clara Bow, Carole Lombard, Gail Patrick . . . Those were the good years, the Paramount years, when he was a kid, just starting out, and everybody was full of life and had great ideas.

JK: Why don't we start with how you got into Paramount, and how you ended up becoming a photographer in your own right?

JE: I was seventeen. Clara Bow had just made *Wings,* and I thought she was absolutely sensational. First thing she did, she dashed into the office one day, and the publicity department—all the writers were round in a circle—and you came down the hall and there was an opening in the middle facing those offices, and when she came down, of course everybody just stopped dead. And Clara came in with her little socks and her little high-heeled shoes and her short, short dress, silk dress, tied-around sort of thing, and she was wild, just flying around—she was just happiness personified. She was so natural. I've never taken dope, but it was like a shot of dope when you looked at this girl. I was an office boy, you see—a messenger is what I was hired for.

I was born in Los Angeles. I was really stage-struck. I thought actors were something marvelous, and I was going to high school and wanted to meet them, and the only way I could figure how to meet them was to go and interview them. And Gilda Gray had been here—she was a great, *sensational* Ziegfeld shimmy dancer—she was always in the Sunday supplements. She was married to a guy who was supposed to be a gangster in Chicago, and of course this whole thing had a great aura of fascination for me. And so she came and made a personal appearance at the Metropolitan Theater in LA. They had these great big enormous billboards all over the city that said "GILDA GRAY"; didn't say the theater, didn't say anything. Well, this was pretty exciting because this sort of shocked LA at that time. This was 1925. It was just a small town; we only had a million people here then. Beverly Hills wasn't developed, nothing. They had a racetrack in Beverly Hills where the Beverly Hills Hotel is. But, anyway, I thought, Oh, my God, I've got to go and see this woman.

So my mother and my sister and I went down and there were just lines getting into the theater. We had to stand in line, and we could only get into the balcony, way upstairs. But, anyway, you looked down and suddenly this sensational music comes . . . jungle rhythm, you see. And all of a sudden this woman comes out on the stage and she has nothing but this leotard with silver spangles on it. And her hair has two-inch bits of silver all over, so everything moved when she shimmied! You've never seen anything like this.

She wasn't pretty, but she had great glamour. And I thought: Oh, my gosh, isn't this woman wonderful!

I didn't interview her, but the next one who came to town was Ann Pennington, who had also been in the *Follies*. And she came down to the Kinema Theater, which wasn't quite so good, it was on Grand. So I thought, Well, I'll go and interview this one. And so I called up the theater and said I was from the LA High School and I wanted to interview Ann Pennington for our paper, the *Blue and White*. It was a daily paper . . . you know, about twelve inches tall, but it came out every day.

I had to see her before her first performance. One o'clock or 11:30 or something. My mother said I could stay out of school, gave me the car, so I drove down, and, gosh, it was a dirty little dressing room . . . and she was sort of a little crummy herself! I was amazed by this woman, and she wasn't enthusiastic about me at all! To be interviewed by some stinking little fifteen-year-old kid! So anyway I got a story from her. For a high school, the only thing you can ask them is: "How is the best way to start being a dancer?" or "What is the best way to success?" You couldn't say anything about her sex life; I didn't know anything about her sex life anyway. So she gave me a little 5 × 7 autographed picture and I did my little interview, and I took it back to LA High, and I took it to this Katherine Carr—the kids used to call her Kitty Carr—she was the journalism teacher. Head of the paper. I wasn't taking journalism, but the next day in the paper the headline says: "L.A. BOY INTER-VIEWS ANN PENNINGTON." That was the headline of the paper. And my story was in. Well, that's how it started!

I was very enchanted with Adela Rogers St. Johns. She and her husband were in *Photoplay* magazine. I wanted to meet her, and I found out where she lived. About 6:00 one night I went up to her house on Hollywood Boulevard. I said I was from LA High School, and I asked her if she would write a story about success for the paper. She was a graduate of the school. So she wrote the story, and I picked it up the next day or the following day. It was a sheet and a half or something, you know. Double-spaced. It wasn't a big story. But I took it out to Kitty Carr, and I said: "I have got this story from Adela Rogers St. Johns that she wrote for our paper." And KC looked at me as though to say: "What do you *mean* asking her to write a story for our paper? We can't print a thing like this in our paper. We have a small daily paper and how can we print all this stuff! Where is it?" And she took it, and I'll never forget the story, it said: "If anyone asks you 'What is success?' it's hard work. That's all there is. There are only two words. There is no such thing as luck. It's just HARD WORK. I spent sixteen hours a day when I began, just smelling news-papers, and this is the whole story." And Kitty Carr said: "This is marvelous. Take it down, we'll have it printed, we'll run it tomorrow." So we did, and then I took it back to Adela and gave it to her, and Adela said: "How would you like to interview Colleen Moore?" "Well," I said, "that's fine." So she arranged for me to go to First National studios to see her. Colleen was making

Irene, and I got on the set when they were making this big production number of her coming down in the Irene dress ["Alice Blue Gown" number] and, my God, it looked marvelous! Anyway . . . I interviewed John Barrymore. He was making *Don Juan.* I got him about 8:00 in the morning, before he went on the set, and, God, his breath! All I can remember is this man with these *red* eyes . . . he had been drunk the night before, obviously, and he had this terrible hangover, and he didn't say much.

And then there was another one . . . Michael Arlen. He was out here in Hollywood, and he was a tough little character and he had said: absolutely no interviews. And Adela Rogers St. Johns had said to me: "If you ever want anything at Paramount, you call Harold Hurley." So I wanted to see Michael Arlen, and he wasn't seeing *anybody.* Finally, I saw that he was staying in a hotel only three blocks from my house, the Ambassador. One morning about 9:00—I got my mother to let me stay out of school again—I went down there and they told me his number, and it was one of the bungalows, out near the front. And I went there and knocked on the door, and a Chinese servant came to the door, and I said I was from the LA High School and I wanted to interview Michael Arlen. And he said, "He asleep, but you come back in an hour."

JK: Why? Because he just liked your face?

JE: Well, I guess because nobody else had asked him, you see. So I left and I came back in exactly one hour. And this Chinese guy was all excited and said: "Where you been? He said he see you and now it too late. Go to New York this morning." And I said: "Oh, God." And he said: "Wait. I see what I can do." So he went in to see Arlen, and Arlen came out. He said: "I'm leaving *now*. But I'll tell you what I'll do. You can walk over to the desk with me and back to this bungalow, and I'll answer all the questions you want, and that's *it*." It wasn't a very good interview, but I had interviewed him. And then of course the paper said: "JOHN ENGSTEAD INTERVIEWS MICHAEL ARLEN."

Once I was interviewing Louise Fazenda, who was very nice, and her boyfriend at the time was Hal Wallis, and he was head of publicity at Warner Brothers over there on Sunset. And I took her the interview and she said: "This is very good. Would you ever like to work in the studio?" Well, I never dreamed . . . this was like heaven! "I'll make an appointment for you to see Hal Wallis." So I went to see him and took him my little interviews, and Wallis said: "Well, you'll have to be a messenger boy, you'll have to start as an office boy in publicity." But he said he had to get an allotment from New York. He wrote to New York, and New York wouldn't let him spend the $18 or $20. But Louise Fazenda had given me the idea, and so I went over to Paramount to see Harold Hurley. I had my little interviews. He said: "What do you want to do?" I said: "I want to be a writer." Well, he looked at me and said: "What have you got?" He thumbed through the things and they didn't impress him, of course, but then he got to Michael Arlen. And he said: "Did you interview Michael Arlen?" And I said: "Yes." "How did you do it?" I said: "I went over to see him at the Ambassador." He said: "Come here." He took my hand and he took me into Arch Reeve's office, this oak-paneled office, and he said: "Arch, this is the only guy in the whole of Southern California who's interviewed Michael Arlen. You got to hire him. That's all I can tell you, you got to hire this kid." So they said: "Can you type?" And I said yes, but of course I couldn't. So I started . . . $18 a week, as a messenger and office boy. Richee was there, and Otto Dyar. George Hurrell came in later.

JK: How soon after you joined were you in the situation where you started styling?

JE: Well, I didn't do styling, I produced the things. God, I got everything. The backgrounds, everything. They had a meeting one day in the publicity department and all these guys were sitting around Arch Reeve's office. And he said: "We have a squawk from the New York office. They don't have enough art . . . enough photographs. We have to do more. And if anybody gets a good idea for a sitting, get a photographer and get the star and do it yourselves. Just get it done." So I thought, well, I could do this. And I'd always seen pictures outdoors, but they didn't have any pictures in gardens or on boats. So I went to Barney Hutchison, who was the publicity man on *Wings* and was Clara Bow's publicity man. And I said: "I want to do a sitting of Clara Bow in a garden, and what about it?" And he said: "I think it's a good idea." So he gave me her telephone number. I was only about eighteen. I'd never met her. So I thought, Well, I'll get some clothes for the wardrobe, and I'll find a place to photograph her. And I said: "Who shall I get to photograph her?" "Otto Dyar." But first I called up Clara Bow and I said I was from the publicity department, and she didn't know whether I was twelve or fifty-five, and I said I wanted to do a sitting of her in a garden, would she do it? And she said yes, she would. She said 1:00 in front of her house. And Barney told me how to get a Cadillac limousine. And then I had to have a grip, of course, and then I had to get Otto Dyar, and he helped me with the grip. I went up to the wardrobe department and Travis Banton went through the wardrobe and got me dresses and some bathing suits and shorts and things for her to wear around the garden.

The day I was going to do this, I rushed down to the newspapers early to make all the rounds and get back to the studio by noon. Then I picked up the car and I got Otto and I got the wardrobe and went out to Clara Bow's house . . . she lived at 512 North Bedford Drive. Before that I had found a house that I liked very much, and it belonged to the head of Bullock's Wilshire at the time. And he had beautiful gardens and ponds and all this stuff, and I asked if I could bring Clara Bow out there and take some photographs. "Well," he said, "I guess you can do that. Sure." So that was all set. And I took her out and of course she was marvelous. You gave her a tree and she'd just hang from the limbs, and she'd come through garden gates.

Lombard was marvelous, but more calculating. She thought about what she was going to do ahead of time. With Clara, it never even entered her head what she was going to do, it just came to her. It was just like a spring that came out of her. And Otto—it was 8×10 film then, you see, and as fast as he could change his film . . . and after we'd done all this, we went back to the studio and it was about 6:30 at night. And one of the secretaries in the department said: "Were you out making pictures with Clara Bow this afternoon?" I said: "Yes." She said: "Oh, my God. There's been hell to pay around here. Nobody knew where you were, and Arch Reeve found out about it, and he said: 'Who the *hell* gave permission to the office boy in our publicity department to take pictures of the highest-priced box-office star on the screen today?'" And Harold Hurley had hired me, and so he said: "Well, wait until tomorrow and see the pictures." The next morning I had to go down to the papers again and so I had to be out of the place, and when I got back at noon there was a little memo on my desk—they were always on orange paper—and it said: "In case you high-powered publicity men want to know it, the best sitting that Clara Bow has had in years was done yesterday by John Engstead and Otto Dyar." So he called me into his office, he used to always take his cigarettes and roll them around the ends, and he said: "Now, John, you can do some sittings. But you've got to do all your other work too. You've got to do all your own clippings from all the newspapers and all the other stuff, but if you do that, you can do another sitting once in a while." He wasn't going to say all of a sudden I'm a whatever, after one sitting. So anyway that's how I got into it.

Richee resented it. There's no doubt about it. I mean, Gracie Allen and George Burns came in one day to do a sitting, and Gracie said: "John, those last pictures you did with me I just think were marvelous." You could feel Richee just D-I-E! And I said: "But I didn't shoot those pictures. Richee did." But, you see, I *did* it. I told him what I wanted, and I showed her the poses. I said: "Pose like this . . . let's do this," you know. Sylvia Sidney would come in with the most beautiful Travis Banton evening gown on and sit down with her feet spread like this and say: "Now, what'll I do?" So you have to direct the whole thing, you see. Richee would get them to do a couple of poses— one with hand on hip and one with hands clasped—and that was all he knew. He didn't *care*. He thought the Hurrell stuff and all that other stuff that I'd shown him was *terrible*. The first time Cecil Beaton *ever* shot in Hollywood was at Paramount. We gave him a camera. I *knew* this was for *Vanity Fair,* and I loved *Vanity Fair;* I knew these were going to be good pictures, and so I got everybody on our lot to pose for him. You know, Kay Francis, Bill Powell, Cooper . . . everybody. In half an hour. He only took ten minutes. And we would also develop the negatives, and so we'd see them. And they would look at these things and say: "Oh, my God, that's nothing." They didn't realize what he was doing, you see. And then Arch Reeve let me ride on a couple of pictures. *The Case of Lena Smith* with Von Sternberg—that was my production, I did the publicity on that. I did *Stairs of Sand* with Wallace Berry . . . all the publicity.

I was much too young to do this thing for Sternberg. He didn't help much. And it was a lousy picture anyway. James Hall and Esther Ralston. Esther Ralston was never anything. They tried to make her a star, but they couldn't do it . . . she didn't have it.

JK: I want you to tell me about that session with Clara on the beach, because for years, whenever a magazine wanted a new Clara Bow, they went back to that series with her on the boat with her hair flying in the wind.

JE: That was another thing. She did a whole lot of pictures on a yacht, and another time we were at her house. I did the bathing-suit sitting at her house; she lived at Malibu. I went down, she was going to be there at 1:00 so we could get started by 2:00 p.m.; and it was a nice sunny day and we waited, and she was late. She got there about 4:00 in the afternoon; and a lot of days at Malibu the wind comes up in the afternoon, and, boy, that wind was coming up! She knew she was late, she knew it was her fault, and she was such a good sport, so she put on her bathing suit and went right out. Well, we had our coats on, and she was running around in the sand with all this wind and sand hitting her. 8×10 pictures, these were; you can imagine how much trouble Otto had trying to pose her. She knew how to pose, she knew how to hold still. She just knew what to do. She stayed there and she worked for half or three-quarters of an hour. It was just so damn cold, but we took about twenty-five pictures in that time. We worked fast. And then after I did these couple of pictures, I started doing photographs and I met all the editors of the magazines.

And then I got all these requests from New York for foreign publicity: how they [the stars] live at home, how they eat, how they dress, their pets and their boats and their cars. You're always getting stills, you see. So this went on, and finally I was doing so many stills Arch said: "Look, we're going to take you off the fan magazines and you're going to be Art Supervisor. You're going to handle all the stills of the studio."

I was twenty. I had to decide, you know—this picture's good for newspapers, it hasn't got too many shadows. This has more shadows, it'll be good for magazines. This with all the background, like Loretta coming through the door—that's for a magazine. It's exclusive to New York for a magazine. You decide where they go and you send them around: twelve prints on this, two prints on this, retouch this, then check on the retouching . . . and then I had to make all the sittings for the whole studio. All the portrait sittings, all the fashion sittings, everything. And I had to take care of the still photographers on the set and get them to take more pictures. They could be lazy.

JK: And also there could be problems with directors like Sternberg—did he ever object to the stills photographer?

JE: Oh, no, no. He helped him. He and DeMille were really marvelous. He would pose it and tell them: "Let's do this. This is the way to do it." And get the guy and do it. He came in the gallery all the time with Dietrich at Paramount. He did everything; he lit them, he posed her . . . He would get her to lean over a chair for five minutes. It was a God-awful pose, and he would tell her in German: "Raise your head," and he would try to get these expressions on her face, you see, and he would work this out of her, and then he would push Gene Richee when he was supposed to shoot the pictures. . . .

JK: All the photographer did was press a bulb. Listen, about Clara. I mean, the feeling you had for her. People seemed to have liked her a lot. What happened to her career? Why was she someone that the studio clamped on so badly?

JE: She did the same picture for five years. It was practically the same picture. I mean, this is a cute girl . . . maybe she's in a store, maybe she's in Hawaii, and there's some little problem, and then she gets the boy and that's the end. There's nobody to look after her. You see, B. P. Schulberg was head of Paramount and he brought Clara over there with him. They took him because they wanted her. But now he was interested in Sylvia Sidney, and she was his protégée, you see, so he kicked Clara out of *City Streets* with Gary Cooper and put Sylvia in it the minute she got there from New York. She was eighteen or nineteen years old.

JK: It wasn't because Clara was ill and had to withdraw?

JE: *No.* Not at all. They [Schulberg and Sidney] were shacked up and everyone knows that. She [Sylvia Sidney] got dressing room number one; she got Clara's dressing room. After that, she [Clara] started to go down.

JK: But why would they dump on her . . . a big box-office star? Her private life?

JE: Well, her private life . . . nobody could control Clara, really. And it was sad. . . . I mean, I loved Clara. But she put on weight. And she said to me once: "John, you know I used to just love to come to work. I just couldn't wait to get here. But now I hate to come." And so she was late. She needed help. She needed what Norma Shearer got from Irving Thalberg; what John McCormick gave to Colleen Moore. You have to have someone—either your mother or your father or your husband, somebody to help you. She had nobody. Daisy DeVoe had stolen money from her—you know, the secretary. Harry Richman [the nightclub singer who went out to Hollywood] and all these people she was going around with . . . nuts, nuts. A dentist from Texas! Nobody *helped* Clara. And in some book I read, Victor Fleming said that she would have been one of the great dramatic actresses of the screen. She had a marvelous voice. Charming, light, lovely. As you said, Clara's voice was a happy voice; it was almost singing.

JK: Did you have that marvelous kind of instant rapport with anybody else besides Clara? Pola Negri was still around.

JE: But you couldn't talk to Pola Negri. She had all these things around the sets; nobody ever spoke to her; you never even looked at Pola Negri. When she walked out of the studio at night, her Rolls-Royce would come up in front of the studio and there was a whole procession . . . I don't know who went first. They all went single file out of the studio (you couldn't drive a car on the lot in those days) . . . there was Pola Negri, and there was Mdivani, who was her husband . . . and there was the maid, and there was the chauffeur, and they were carrying boxes and her lunch basket and her robes . . . nobody spoke, they just went in single file and got in the car and they were off. She never went into the restaurant; she always ate in her room, and they said she had a glass of bourbon for lunch; and you couldn't even see her work.

JK: You were young, Cooper was just beginning, everybody was just beginning.

JE: Oh, Cooper! The first time I ever saw Cooper, I'd read about him in the paper. I don't think *The Winning of Barbara Worth* had been out yet, but Paramount signed him, they were fortunate to get him, and he was playing a bit in a Clara Bow picture, he was a reporter—

JK: *Children of Divorce—*

JE: No, no. *It*. He was only a reporter. All he did was ask her a question. Nothing. Some people say now he was in *It,* but it was nothing. Then he was in *Children of Divorce*. And that was for Frank Lloyd. You know, with Esther Ralston and Clara Bow. But at that time they had all these marvelous suits made for him and everything, and of course he was just nonplussed, he didn't know what to do with all this. And one time he left and went down to the bus station—he was going to take a bus and go back to Montana! And somebody caught him and brought him back. He was really going to leave. He'd had too much of this stuff, see? Oh, he was wonderful, wonderful! Now, in books I read, I gather that he was quite a stud. But this I never knew about.

JK: Clara was in love with him, Evelyn Brent was in love with him; he almost wanted to marry Evelyn.

JE: Evelyn Brent, yes. She was a snazzy woman. But she was stupid. In a way. Evelyn Brent was married to B. F. Fineman, who was Schulberg's assistant, and she was a *big* star. I remember her coming in to the publicity department one day. Julie Lang was handling the magazines at the time, and she was handling the sittings. So she came up to Evelyn and said: "Evelyn, we'd like to make a portrait sitting of you." And Evelyn said: "Oh, fine, that's all right. We'll do it Friday at 2:00 . . . what'll I wear?" And Julie said: "Can't you bring something that you wear?" And Evelyn said: "I wouldn't *dream* of wearing my clothes in *front* of the camera. I buy these at I. Magnin's. These are $500, $600, $1000 apiece. If you want to *buy* one, you can buy it and I'll pose in it, but I'm not going to use my own for the thing." Well, she'd only been doing *The Last Command* and that sort of thing, which didn't have much wardrobe changes, so she didn't have any clothes from the studio. So Julie said: "Well, I'll see what I can get from the wardrobe," and Evelyn said: "Look, I'm not going to wear anything cast off by Louise Brooks or Clara Bow or any of these other women. I can't do it. So you'll have to figure out something I can wear." Julie said: "Well, what if I get some furs?" So they just got furs and they did her in furs, and then they sent the furs back. And that's the way they did the sitting. But this was stupid of this woman. Nobody else ever said this. And B. F. Fineman was standing right beside her, and you'd think he'd say: "Well, why don't you do it?" I'll never forget this. And then, of course, she went downhill two or three years after that to *nothing*. Later on she came back to the lot and she did a little tiny bit in a picture, and Travis Banton called me up, because he loved Evelyn, you see . . . she was very chic, you know . . . and he said: "Look, Evelyn's in this, and she needs a couple of pictures. Could you have Gene make a couple pictures of Evelyn?" I said: "Why, sure." And she came down . . . and this time she used her own clothes.

On *A Farewell to Arms* they had Gary Cooper's costume ready, and they had Helen Hayes' nurse costumes, and she was marvelous, and Cooper was awed by Helen Hayes because she was this great star from New York, so I wanted to get these stills from them, and I did. They got them in before the picture. This was ideal for me. I read the script and think: Well, this is a big love story; I'll take these love pictures of them together. So I got them in the gallery, and the first thing I said was: "Would you please lie down on the floor." So Helen Hayes got right down on the floor and Cooper sort of looked at me, then got down with her. And they lay down on the floor and we took these marvelous love pictures. It was wonderful. And it was really great of me to think of it because it broke the ice.

JK: Do you remember other sessions that were as important as that, where the director would even take an idea from it?

JE: Well, remember all that stuff I did with Katharine Hepburn on *Dragon Seed*. I gave her a set of these little proofs, so she said: "I'm going to show these to the director because I think these are wonderful. I think we should try and get some of this on the screen."

Well, you know, some people . . . Madeleine Carroll was just a lazy blonde. And it was just hell to get pictures of her. She had a boyfriend in Paris and she would go there, and we had a portrait sitting arranged beforehand and she would only come in for about an hour. I said: "What do you go to Paris so often for? Do you buy clothes?" "Oh, no," she says, "I don't need clothes. All I need is a nightgown!" But then she'd come back just in time to make the picture and not in time to do the sitting. And she'd stop in New York and she'd have dinner or cocktails with Bob Gilliam, who was head of publicity in New York, and during dinner he'd say: "Now, I want to do this kind of a picture with you. We have to have a lot of pictures of you, Madeleine, a portrait sitting, and an 'at home' sitting, and you doing this and that," and he would outline all these things which she'd agreed to do, and then they'd send it to me. I'd call her up, and she'd say: "Oh, John, don't be a fool. I'm not going to do that. Don't be silly." She lived down at Palos Verdes and she'd come in in her Rolls-Royce, and she wouldn't be in till 2:00 in the afternoon, and then she'd have her makeup and her hair done, so she'd be in at 4:30 or 5:00. But I had a whole list of pictures I wanted to do for various magazines, and she'd do 'bout four pictures, and then she'd say: "Oh, I'm sorry, I have to go for cocktails," and she'd leave. You know, this is unbelievable.

We had to do a session once with Fred MacMurray, and he had finished the picture, *Virginia* or whatever, and he had it in his contract that he had to have two weeks off between pictures. Well, he was on his two-week layoff and the assistant director called me up and said I could do these stills for the film this afternoon. He said: "But you've got to get Fred, and you can have Madeleine at 3:30 or 4:00." And so I called Fred's house, and Lily said he's out at Lake Sherwood and he's fishing with Zeppo Marx, who was his agent. So I called Lake Sherwood and told him: "Fred, I got to have these stills of you and Madeleine," and he said: "Oh, well, I guess I can do that." But I said, "Fred, you can't add it to your layoff, because you can't break your layoff with these pictures," so, because he was really a friend and helping me out, he said, "Well, okay, but call Lily and tell her to bring a dark suit to the studio, because we're going to go right to dinner from the studio." So he came in, and I went to the set about 3:30 to get Madeleine, and Madeleine said: "Nobody told me about this. I'm not going to do this today, I couldn't possibly." I said: "Madeleine, Fred's coming in especially," and she said: "That doesn't matter. I'm not going to do it." And this poor guy had come in specially on his off time to do this, while she was working anyway and her filming had finished early. And, you know, this is just being a *bitch*. I was just *disgusted* with her, I want to tell you. I had a lot of them. Jeanette MacDonald, she was a shit too, at times. I want to tell you. Oohooh . . .

Well, you see, Chevalier didn't want her in his last two pictures. They had let her go. She was through with Paramount. She went over to Paris and she sang at this Olympia [variety theater], and she sang her songs in French with an American accent and she was a great success. She was with Bob Ritchie, who was her manager. That was her boyfriend. So Jesse Lasky said: "We've made a mistake." And they signed her for two more pictures and brought her back. And Chevalier didn't really want her. But they did the first one, and she was going to be paid $5000 a week right straight through. There was no stopping in between the pictures—they had to do one right after the other. So I forget which one it was, but they had pushed up the release date of one of the movies. So they sent a note from New York saying: "We have to have new pictures of MacDonald and Chevalier by New Year's."

I went out to the set and this was New Year's Eve. The assistant director said Mr. Chevalier is through at noon and Miss MacDonald will be free at about 4:00. So I talked to Chevalier, and he was then quite close to Dietrich, and I went to his room and they were there talking and he said: "Yes, I'll do it. I'll wait. Okay." You know, he was a businessman. And about 3:00 I went out to the set to get Jeanette—and you must remember I had done pictures of her sister, the one who was later the witch in *The Munsters,* and we did pictures of Jeanette's sheepdog for *nothing:* anything to make her happy— and I told her what I wanted, and she said: "That's fine for Maurice, but I'm going to a party tonight and I'm going home. I'm not going to do any stills." Well, I never ever asked anybody at the studio to do anything personally for me because it wasn't for me, but I finally said to her: "Would you do it as a favor to the publicity department, because we really have to have these stills?" And as I opened the door and she walked through—she had these little tiny feet, about size two—she stamped her foot and said: "If Adolph Zukor came out here and got on his knees on the ground, I wouldn't make these stills." And off she went.

She never really had a lot of talent. She was as cute as she could be around directors, she would be practically kissing their asses. So coy. She and Miriam Hopkins—that was another old bitch—you should have seen how cute she was with Ernst Lubitsch. And Lubitsch never saw through Miriam Hopkins. You see, B. P. Schulberg never knew what Jeanette MacDonald could do; look what she did when she went to MGM. She made up on all this phony-baloney shit. She was a terrible actress. Absolutely awful. She talked every line as if she was going to sing.

She was an absolute manufactured product. She took a singing lesson every single day of her life. *Every* day. To get that poor little voice where it was! And it wasn't very good.

JK: When do you start getting an inkling that you're going to become a photographer yourself?

JE: Oh, I didn't think of this at all. I never thought of this. If I did, I would have taken this offer in 1934, when I did the sittings for a month, right away. I had never shot a picture. I had a Brownie camera. But I knew how to light. And I knew the mechanics; but I didn't know anything about f-stop 11 or 16 or any of that stuff. So when all the guys walked [this was during a union strike], I was just told: "You're going to photograph." Tom Bailey was head of publicity then, and he said: "You're going to go in and do photographs." And I said: "Oh, my God. Well . . . I can." And he said: "Well, get someone in tomorrow morning. Get your sister; I don't care who you get—but practice." So I thought, I may do a good sitting, so why do it with someone who can't use it? So I called up Cary Grant, and I said: "Cary, would you like to come in and make some pictures with me? I have to try and take some pictures in the gallery, and I've got to learn how to do it. Would you come in and just pose for me?" And he said: "Sure." So he came in, and we worked for two or three hours, and I did all this back lighting with cigarettes through the fill—all that kind of stuff—and he came in at 9:00 the next morning to see the proofs and he was so excited. And by this time Tom Bailey had wired New York and said: "We have a new portrait photographer at Paramount. It's going to be John Engstead from now on. Either Walling or Richee will go." And, well, I didn't want to get in the gallery, I didn't want to sit there as they do, and besides that, I would have kicked them out of a job, these two guys. They never knew this; Walling was always a little antagonistic to me, and Richee sort of hated me a little bit, because I had to tell them what to do.

JK: Well, Walling was telling me once that he had great trouble with people like Miriam Hopkins, and you arrived and you were able to deal with her, and that obviously only made him feel worse.

JE: I couldn't deal with her either. I had terrible times with her. But I could usually get people to do things, what I wanted them to do. And I would do things *for* them. It's a feeling you get with people. You know, Joel McCrea and Gary Cooper. Gary Cooper was lazy, too. You hardly ever got him in, but he would come in finally. You know, even after he left, I did the last sitting he ever did. I did three or four sittings with him, and he paid for them.

JK: Do you remember Louise Brooks? Do you remember her well?

JE: Well, Louise always seemed to me to be a little lazy. I don't think she ever thought of being a really big star, I don't think this was in her schedule. Because she was very arrogant. She never sort of worked with them; if it pleased her, she would do it. She just knew what she wanted to do. And of course when you're in that position and you're earning $750 a week—like with Thelma Todd or with Evelyn Brent, they put Evelyn with Moran and Mack once, they had an act as the Two Black Crows! Well, this was the worst thing they could possibly do. They killed Evelyn Brent with that one movie [*Why Bring That Up?*, 1929].

JK: Did they do it to punish her?

JE: No. Schulberg *didn't know* what the *hell* to do with these people. I told you he *didn't know* Claudette Colbert could play comedy. He *didn't know* Carole Lombard could play comedy. I mean, this was beyond him. He got a set image of these people and tried to push them into that image. Nancy Carroll was a little bit of a bitch. She was a very talented woman, very talented. But she always went around with a chip on her shoulder like someone was going to do her in, they were hanging around the corner; and she approached *every-thing* that way.

JK: Wouldn't Clara have played the same roles? They were the same type.

JE: She [Clara] couldn't have played *Abie's Irish Rose* . . . no. Though she could have played a lot of things, like *The Shopworn Angel* with Gary Cooper, sure. But this was Paramount, they didn't know what the hell to do with her. Clara was making money doing the hula, why not keep on making millions with her just doing the same thing?

JK: And Louise . . . what did people think about her on the lot?

JE: I don't know. I thought she was marvelous. She was as smart as they come. Very few people had her . . . I hate the word "chic"; she was just *elegant*. Elegant. Her legs, her ankles, her hands, her body, the way she held her body, the way she walked, the way she dressed, furs over her shoulder, off her shoulder, her hats—she was like Lombard. Lombard could do the same thing; put anything on her and it was right. Dietrich can do that too if she wants to.

JK: How exciting did it seem to you being inside a studio when suddenly . . . this was the time of Garbo at MGM, the whole sound revolution . . .

JE: She came over to our place once, Garbo. Not to make a movie. But Mauritz Stiller—they had kicked him out over there, and he came over and I think he did *Hotel Imperial* with Pola Negri. And he was—ugh!—he was the ugliest man in the world. Great big gross features, you know? Sweet man, nice face, but God made him like out of putty, you know? But the girls in wardrobe said: "Garbo was here today, Garbo came over to see him," but she had only just begun. She hadn't really become the great . . .

JK: The great myth. In *Flesh and the Devil* she wasn't yet the Garbo Garbo.

JE: No, no. I remember that first movie, I went down to Sunset Boulevard to track it down. *The Tempest* or *The Torrent,* whatever it was . . . she was absolutely marvelous. The reviews were just great. She was a completely new thing on the screen. She changed everything. She just changed everything from . . .

JK: From Pickford to Garbo.

JE: Well, there were the flappers. Crawford was a flapper, Shearer was a flapper, Colleen Moore was a flapper. That was the day of the flappers. And all of a sudden the flappers were gone, and she's in. Everybody wanted to copy her. It was Constance Bennett from then on, and that kind of stuff. . . .

JK: Do you remember when Dietrich arrived? Was that a big thing?

JE: Oh, yeah. Well, Von Sternberg saw to that, that she was a big star. She really was something. She wasn't a little stock girl that you bring over from somewhere or other; she'd done *The Blue Angel* and they'd seen it, see? And it was like "this big new star is coming," see? We had a lot of them. We thought Isa Miranda was the same, and of course nothing ever happened to her. Franciska Gaal . . .

JK: But when Dietrich arrived, you would have to work a lot with her anyway.

JE: No, I didn't. Because Von Sternberg controlled everything. I would ask them to do a sitting, and they would say yes, and then they would come in the gallery . . . and I don't know if I was doing stills when she first came; she came in 1930, I think it was. I think somebody else did it. I wasn't in on the first sitting.

JK: Richee.

JE: Oh, Richee did them. I'll never forget, I was handling the fan magazines. And I went to the preview of *Morocco,* and I didn't think *Morocco* was this great, great movie. I thought she was marvelous, and I liked Cooper, but I don't know . . . But when I came in the next day, she was at the mail desk, and you had to pass by the mail desk to get to our office, so I said: "Hi. I saw your picture last night." "Vot did you tink of it?" And I said: "Well, I didn't think the picture was great, but I really enjoyed you very, very much, and Coop too. I thought he was very good." So about ten minutes later my office phone rang, and it was Von Sternberg's secretary, and she said: "Would you please call and see Mr. von Sternberg." So I went over to see him, and he said: "I believe you're handling all the fan magazines. Now, I don't want you ever to tell them that you didn't like my picture last night." I said: "Mr. von Sternberg, I'm working for Paramount the same as you, and I wouldn't dream of telling anybody about this. Why would I say this? But if you're ever running *The Blue Angel* sometime, I'd love to see it." And he said: "You're not interested in my work, and I don't care if you see it or not."

JK: Was Dietrich really upset having to work on *Song of Songs* without Sternberg? Was she really that dependent on him?

JE: I don't think so. I think she wanted a change too. On *Seven Sinners,* I'd never photographed her before, and Von Sternberg came over and helped me on that sitting too. It was on Sunset Boulevard. A little studio we had—half a studio. He brought her over there. He helped me with lighting, suggesting things, talking to her, to me. The pictures are marvelous.

JK: On the first session with Dietrich that you did—which was from *Seven Sinners*—she called you in for that, because she was working for Universal, so these photographs were primarily for her.

JE: I don't know how that came about, to tell you the truth. Oh, sure. You know, in Hurrell's book he says that when he went to Warner Brothers, they arranged for him to do the Lux ads at Warner Brothers. Well, that's an absolute falsehood. Because when he went to Warner Brothers, they wouldn't allow him to do it. I was at a party at the Brown Derby with Gail Patrick and

Bob Cobb and Danny Dank, who were the heads of J. Walter Thompson on the Coast, and Danny came up to me and said: "George is going over to Warner Brothers and can't do these stills anymore, so can you do them?" And I said: "Well, I'm not a photographer, I don't photograph at all." Danny said: "Look, all the stars around town know you, and if I say John Engstead is going to handle these stills, they'll come in to you. I've got to have somebody that they know. You get a photographer, and it'll be just what you did at Paramount. That's the way we'll do it." And so I did. We did them up at J. Walter Thompson's offices on Vine Street. That's the only reason I got them, because George couldn't do them.

JK: Is that why he might be resentful of you years later? You know, people remember certain things in their lives.

JE: Well, he remembers a lot of things. He remembers that I worked for every single magazine in the business and he didn't. I couldn't turn them out fast enough. I mean, all the time for *Ladies' Home Journal* for twenty years. They'd fly me to New York for two or three days to do a sitting. They'd fly me to Washington, to Dallas, to London. . . . I went to Paris for *McCall's* for five years. Every single magazine . . . *Mademoiselle, Charm* . . . I worked for everybody except *Vogue* and *Harper's*. And *Vogue* wanted me to go to New York—that's when I'd just begun, and I'd done one sitting for *Vogue* here. And they asked me to come to New York and see them. And when I was next in New York, I had lunch with Jessica Daves and Alexander Lieberman, and they said they'd like me to come and work for them in New York. But I had a house, the war was on, I had two cars—a station wagon and a Cadillac—I had a dog, I couldn't drop all this. So I stayed here and worked; and that's the time that Selznick wanted me to be a motion-picture cameraman, see?*

I was influenced by Steichen, by Beaton, by Munkacsi, all the others. The only thing I never did was photograph with a small, little camera. And I should have done that earlier in life. See, Avedon started off in New York at the same time I did, and I was always pissed off because they'd send me clothes to photograph out here and I would have to photograph them on some actress who didn't know how to pose; and in New York he would have Suzy Parker—this was later—but the best models. And he had gone to school with Brodovich, who was the art director of *Harper's*.

JK: At Paramount you had to set up the sessions, and even then *Vanity Fair* and the others preferred their own photographers.

JE: They didn't like what the studios designed for clothes, they never used those, nothing that came from Hollywood was good enough for *Vanity Fair* or *Harper's*. Now you see *W,* all the things that are in *W* are all Adrian. I

---

*Engstead took the first portraits of Ingrid Bergman when she arrived in Hollywood in 1939.

threw away a lot of the crazy things that I should never have thrown away, that I thought were too fantastic, but Adrian did them and I photographed them. They were *crazy* things . . .

JK: Let me go to Dietrich now. During that session on *Seven Sinners,* those portraits must have been strictly private because I never saw them.

JE: They were. They got the prints and that's it. I photographed her then, and I think I did something for her in the war effort for the boys, and I never photographed her again until she went to Las Vegas.

Nellie Manning, the hairdresser, called me and said: "Marlene has just opened," and I'd seen her picture in the paper in the morning. "She's just opened in Las Vegas and she wants you to come up and make some pictures. Immediately." So I said: "Sure. I will." So we did it right away. And we rushed them back. I remember Van Johnson was there, and there was a place in Vegas where we could develop them. We couldn't shoot until after she got through at night, and that was at 12:30 or 1:00. At 3:00 or 3:30 we took the negatives into Las Vegas, developed them and made proofs, and then I came back at 8:30 or 9:00 in the morning, and she was there with Van Johnson and they were talking. They were lovely pictures, and we rode back to Hollywood and sent them out.

The sitting wasn't hurried, because you don't hurry Dietrich. She's slow. She knows what she's doing. She knows the tempo of an 8×10 camera. This is what she wanted.

JK: What is the tempo? What is that?

JE: It's slow. You can't shoot it with a flash and all that going on. You light her. You go up on the stage and you light her. And sometimes I'd be up on the stage and sometimes out in the audience. We had big tables. A table for the 8×10 camera and a table for me to stand on, and stairs to get up. And you have to arrange the lights, and then he had to hand me the holders and then we had to shoot. It takes time.

I won't say I'm great; I'm capable. I work hard, and I work as hard as I possibly can on a sitting, whenever I work. There's none of this trying to get through faster, and she knows that. I'm a professional, and I hate people who are late. I learned this from Barbara Stanwyck. Gene and I were waiting for her one day for a sitting, and we had everything ready . . . no, I don't think we *did* have everything ready. And she walked in the gallery right on time and she was all ready . . . and we weren't. If she says she'll be there at 2:00, I'm ready at 1:30. And at twenty minutes to 2:00, she's there. Stanwyck was professional. She doesn't have the inspiration that Clara Bow had, or Lombard. But she's very nice and a good subject, and she's on time.

Dietrich did a thing for *The Monte Carlo Story* or whatever it was; I had the stairs made and all that. That she did here. She always had two dresses; she always had duplicates made, and Otto had to take one to Las Vegas once because it wasn't ready when she left. Four or five days of fittings, from 8:00 in the morning until 8:00 at night. She's absolutely unique. She and Claudette; but Claudette wouldn't do it for as long as that. I'd say: "Well, Marlene, can't they make this second dress from the first? They've got *it*." "No, I've tried that. It doesn't work. They have to fit the second one." She had a German Teutonic thing: nothing is unimportant.

You see, I always felt the Marlene up at Las Vegas had nothing to do with the daytime Marlene. I mean, she'd go to sleep at 4:00 in the morning and she'd get up at 3:00 in the afternoon or something. So she'd take these pictures and work on them for hours; there wasn't much else for her to do. She loved Marlene Dietrich's face. She had made a great thing out of this. This was her creation. She was going to be sure that I helped her as much as I could. She worked harder than anybody else I ever knew.

JK: Loretta?

JE: Oh, Loretta. I don't think Loretta ever thought she had to have much retouching done. She didn't. She really didn't.

Claudette said to me once, when I was in Paris, to call up Madame Spanier,* who said: "Oh, come for cocktails." So I went over and there was Richard Avedon and Marlene Dietrich and Madame Spanier and Estelle Brent, who was the fashion editor of *McCall's,* and Marlene came in and sat down with her legs so perfectly posed; I mean, they were the most beautiful, and her shoes and her hose were all perfect. You know, she loves beige, this sandy, warm, orangy beige, and, as Spanier said: "I don't know how she did it for half an hour!" She sat in this one pose for half an hour. And everything was right. This was Marlene Dietrich.

JK: I'm just going through these pictures of yours here—and I suppose at the time the look of Dietrich must have affected a lot of people. I know Carole Lombard began to pose like her.

JE: No, she *didn't*. She *never* copied her.

JK: Well, the lighting in those shots is very Dietrichesque.

JE: She never tried to copy anybody. She's too smart for that. But who really did was Nancy Carroll. Nancy went back to New York and then she came back to Hollywood. She had made *Laughter* in New York, with Freddie March, and some other things, and she came back out here and I said to her: "While you're out here, why don't you do a sitting?" She said: "Fine." So she went up to the wardrobe by herself and to the makeup department [he laughs] and they shaved her forehead high and they got all her hair back and they plucked her eyebrows and made her look like Marlene, and she just tried to look like Marlene Dietrich. Oohhh. We did a sitting that way. And she

---

*Ginette Spanier was *directrice* of the Balmain *maison de couture*.

went back to New York and did the picture almost made up like that. Of course, she had a round face and no cheeks; she couldn't do it. They tell me people like Faye Dunaway have taken out their back teeth so . . .

JK: Well, you know the stories. One heard that Dietrich had ribs removed.

JE: Oh, no. Dietrich just was fat in Germany. She was *fat* when she got here.

JK: Quite different in the way she appeared in *Morocco* from the way she appeared in *Blonde Venus*.

JE: Oh, yeah. Well, I tell you. Travis Banton had a problem with her. They had a cocktail party for her to introduce her to the press when she first arrived, at the Cocoanut Grove. Marlene came in, she didn't know how to dress at all, and she must have weighed 150 pounds. She was wearing a printed chiffon dress with those little things hanging off the dress, and a great big sort of horsehair hat. She couldn't have looked worse. Everybody died when she came in. This was introducing her to the press. And they were all there.

JK: Didn't somebody like Travis Banton try to advise . . .

JE: After. He hadn't gotten hold of her yet. She hadn't made a picture.

JK: But she certainly did start to learn fast, didn't she? She must have taken advice from everybody.

JE: No, she didn't. She took it from Sternberg and Travis Banton. She's not stupid at all. She looked at photographs to see what's happening. She had that face when she came; she had those cheekbones.

JK: How big a part do you think Travis Banton had in the evolution of the Dietrich image?

JE: Well, he dressed her.

JK: How many sittings do you think you did over that seven-year period? Every Las Vegas show . . . and those were the pictures she would also use in Europe, right?

JE: About seven, I'd say.

JK: Over seven years. Plus for the movies. You also shot for *Witness for the Prosecution* and *Monte Carlo Story*. When you were doing these sessions, was there much talk through it?

JE: No, she knows her angles. She has a mirror. She photographs with a mirror at all times. Even in Las Vegas she had Nellie Manning get her mirror out of her room and hold it right next to where I'm shooting with the camera, angled right at her so she can see it.

JK: Have you ever had this kind of working relationship with anybody else?

JE: Oh, sure. I was much closer to Claudette Colbert and Carole Lombard—
oh, yes, and Gail Patrick.

JK: Did you have to worry a lot about people's sides and angles? I mean, Claudette with her right side. She always tore up pictures that were from the
wrong side. What was wrong with that side? Because at the very beginning,
before she became a big star, they shot her from both sides.

JE: Of course. But, you see, when she was fifteen, Claudette was run over by
a truck coming home from school, and it broke her nose and broke her back.
And that's why her back is a little funny, see. And she said that when they
fixed up her nose, one side looked swollen. So that when you light her from
this way, the nose goes all over the face. But from *this* side it's okay, because
you get the shadow down the side. That's her story. But I did it once the other
way. She was in the gallery and I said: "Oh, Claudette, you look so good that
way." "Shoot it," she said. So we did it the other way. She said okay and
marked it for retouching and they used it even for a fan-mail picture at Paramount.

JK: In the end, why did you and Dietrich stop working?

JE: She was all through, baby. Another thing was she wanted me to come back
and reshoot her because she said she looked like a female impersonator in a
session we did, and I wouldn't go back. I said: "I can't do it, Marlene." You
know, in 1959 I was busy every single day.

　　She didn't care about the retouching. She cared about the type of photographs we were making. See, we did only one type of photograph with
Dietrich, but with Carole Lombard we did her in bathing suits by pools, we
did her in tweed coats, she would buy her own clothes for photographs . . .
nobody ever worked like this. I tried to get Lana Turner to come in and talk
to me once before we started so we knew what we were doing, but it was no
good. But with Lombard, everything was set beforehand. She had this beautiful white dress that Irene had done for her; made with tiers of organdy ruffles
and things. This was for a film she was making at RKO. She said: "RKO will
do anything you want to do, John." And I said: "Let's get a whole bunch of
geranium blossoms and line them up." They had to go out and buy these fake
geraniums in pots, because she wanted them all behind her. I read later that
she was at a party and she jumped in the pool with this dress on!

1982

I D A
L U P I N O

I DA LUPINO never seemed to be a movie star who gave herself airs. Take her name. Ida. What an incongruous name for a glamorous film star! A secretary maybe—Louis B. Mayer's secretary was called Ida, so was Eddie Cantor's homely wife—but for a platinum-blond ingenue it didn't sound right. In England, where she began her film career, they wouldn't have minded things like that. But when she reached Hollywood, where it was common to change everything about you once they had you, first of which was your name, one would have thought that somebody in publicity or up front would have said, "Movie stars are not called Ida." She's such a resolute character that while she may have allowed Paramount to bleach her hair platinum, to pencil-pluck her eyebrows, to miscast her for years in a succession of unsuitable ingenue roles, a sort of a cut-down Joan Bennett (who was then just edging out of the Bing Crosby leading-lady look-alike chorus, with Ida taking over and no one noticing the difference or noticing her when she made *Anything Goes*), but she wasn't about to let them tamper with her name. If Lupino, a celebrated theatrical name dating back to the 17th century, was good enough, so was Ida.

She had her sixteenth birthday in Hollywood (she was born in 1918—her father was the British music-hall and revue star Stanley Lupino; her uncle was the equally famous comedian Lupino Lane; her godfather was the idol of England, Ivor Novello) and she'd been brought over by Paramount to play *Alice in Wonderland*. She lost out when they found her too mature on arrival for the role. Since they had her and they were making more than sixty films a year, they started her as the female lead in a Paramount potboiler, *Search for Beauty* (1934), something dreamed up by the publicity department to promote free press for the studio by launching a worldwide contest. The only thing of any note to come out of that was a girl from Texas, Clara Lou Sheridan, but Ann's story of that contest was a grim one of trial and error, and error, and error.

When it came to discovering and grooming new stars, it is clear from talking to many of those involved that the people in control of their fates had little idea of who had what and how to bring it out. Had they done their job, they would have seen that Ida was a mature professional long before they brought her to Hollywood and that she looked too old for Alice, since she was fourteen when she made her film debut opposite her godfather, Ivor Novello, playing a seductress in a British trifle called *Her First Affair*. Her actress mother (Connie Emerald) had gone up for the role, and Ida only came along to keep her mother company. Ida got the job.

In her first year in British films she worked so hard and made so many movies that Hollywood beckoned. Uncle Lupino Lane had already appeared in several films in America, most notably in Paramount's *The Love Parade*. It was up to Ida to make the family name as famous in America as it was in Europe, but only after a long, dispiriting slog, during which time Paramount had dropped her, another budding dramatic actress, Frances Farmer, took her place opposite Crosby, and Ida freelanced around town, finding no niche until, having meanwhile returned to her brunette roots, she went to Warner Bros. in 1939 and made *They Drive by Night*.

After that, Ida was there and anybody who went to the movies in the '40s knew it. She was unmistakable. She was dramatic. She was more American than the hash she slung, the waterfronts she prowled, the barstools she warmed and the cigarettes she worried to the bitter end. She was a young girl who had a curious hard edge that peeked out from behind her eyes. On screen she dealt with trouble. Anything set her soft mouth into a firm line, and there were lots of reasons for firmness at Warner Bros. She was high up on the list of powerful dramatic actresses dominating films in the '40s except that all of them seemed to be working at the same studio at the same time. Let's not even talk about Bette Davis. Miss Davis not only had the pick of all the best roles, she smoked the best cigarettes . . . only with Davis cigarettes were an affectation; with Ida they were a vice. When Ida smoked, you saw the streets, kids huddling in back alleys, passing a fag around. Geraldine Fitzgerald, who was also at Warner Bros., also smoked, but she held her cigarettes close to her face and delicately picked bits of tobacco from her tongue; Ann Sheridan smoked like a man, her cigarette clamped between her lips, casual-like, both hands at the ready; Crawford never inhaled, hers was movie-star smoke, her cigarettes came in engraved silver cases and were there to give men something to do for her, lighting them, fetching them. Bette Davis made smoking her trademark, waving cigarettes about like a baton conducting invisible emotions. It was a challenge and an assertion . . . one recalls *The Great Lie* and Davis' thoughtless treatment of the nicotine-starved Mary Astor, whom Davis had forced to give up smoking when Astor became pregnant; and to Mary Astor's frustrated cry, "But *you* smoke your head off!" Bette, while nearly suffocating poor Mary with the exhaust from her own lungs, blithely replied, "But that's me. I'm not special."

With so many great actresses and only so many good roles to go around, is it any wonder that Ida smoked, habitually, down to the last puff, nearly burning her fingers? Waste-not, want-not Ida. She had a lot of reasons. With her you understood it.

Her most memorable roles seem to have been supporting parts to which she brought star quality, whether as the little cockney in *Peter Ibbetson,* or the

Ida Lupino, photographed by Scotty Welbourne (Warner Bros.), 1940

girl off the streets driven to hysterics in *The Light That Failed,* or the murderous wife going insane in the witness chair in *They Drive by Night* (a role that had once done wonders for a blond Bette Davis in *Bordertown*); and what bitter irony that Ida should star in a film, *High Sierra,* for which her co-star became so famous that when the film was reissued, the posters proclaimed Humphrey Bogart in capitals above the title, with Ida Lupino in smaller print below the title. And if there is one image of her, it comes from what was probably one of Warners' artiest messes, *Devotion,* with Ida as Emily Brontë. Was it a scene or was it a still shot for the film? She stands on a fog-seething hill above the Warner moors, her hair hanging long, flat, dead; the dress, from an age of ruffles, was, like her hair, long, flat and muted; and on her hand a black leather gauntlet, where perched a falcon. She looked as if she'd trained it. It's not how one pictures Emily, but it's how one pictures Ida: a woman out of time, waiting for her moment.

Ida's moment on screen seemed to come near the end of the decade, after she had left Warners and scored a great personal hit in *Road House* (1950). She smoked, she spent time on barstools, she was waiting for the right man to come along, and in her own husky voice introduced "Again." Ida was still young; young enough for the great dramatic parts to come. Bette Davis had retired . . . for the moment. Geraldine Fitzgerald had moved to New York; and nobody was doing the sort of thing Ida was doing at Fox. She could have stayed. She *should* have stayed. Zanuck wanted her. Instead, the '50s are a footnote to her Warner years on screen. She was still making a lot of films, but the roles were once again supporting ones, at RKO, Columbia and UA. And, worse, she seemed mannered for one so good, as if she were determined to send up her roles, her own innate sense of humor taking the upper hand over prison matron, gossip columnist and similar types she played.

Ida had started writing scripts with her second husband, producer Collier Young. And she revealed unexpected though perhaps not really surprising facets of her talents as one of the few commercially successful women directors in Hollywood. Her films were justly praised—small, black-and-white, shot on tight budgets, but with feeling. As with many of the smart great stars of the '30s and '40s—Loretta Young, Charles Boyer, Jane Wyman, Dick Powell, Barbara Stanwyck—TV had given her the opportunity the movies no longer could. For drama she had the *Four Star Playhouse;* and in the series *Mr. Adams and Eve* she and her third husband, actor Howard Duff (her first husband had been the actor Louis Hayward), played a couple of married movie stars. A lot of the amusing incidents were based on things that supposedly had happened to them for real. By now Ida had done drama so long and so well, it came as a surprise that she was such a good comedienne—she had dipped into the family tradition. And if Eve Drake wasn't a "real" movie star, she certainly was funny, running the gamut of affectations, funny mannerisms, flying mink coats, and the dazzling swivel turn to punctuate everything.

With all these achievements, one would have expected Ida to be a forceful and dynamic woman, full of articulateness, strong opinions and a sharp tongue. Surprisingly, the woman I met was subdued. Perhaps it was the divorce—she and Howard Duff had only recently split up. Yet she's made a number of films since, like Steve McQueen's *Junior Bonner,* and *Deadhead Miles,* which reunited her with her *Drive by Night* co-star, George Raft. She's better at remembering her mistakes than her successes. Like certain creative but shy people, she can tell you about what she's doing now, and what other people did then; and she remembers personal family things, though she may not necessarily talk about them. Yet she agreed to see me. It may have had something to do with the fact that William Wellman, whom she adored, gave me her number. It may have been because I had come to talk about Ronald Colman and *The Light That Failed,* the film that really put her on the map as an actress. But for the rest, well, she's not unlike Fred Astaire or Vincente Minnelli—they remember, but it's not served up on a plate.

JK: One really doesn't think of you as an English actress.

IL: I don't. I don't know.

JK: I mean, you sound very English now, very much like a BBC interviewer.

IL: Yes, well, I'm with you, it's taking, it's rubbing off! I wasn't part of the British colony. I had more American friends until after *The Light That Failed,* and then Ronald Colman and his wife, Benita, would have me over to dinner, and I grew to know David Niven very well, he became almost like my brother, also Bob Coote. I'd met Benita Hume in England just to say, "How do you do?" to her, you know, when she wasn't on the stage. I was making movies over there then. I think I made about six or seven. Quota pictures. Yes, as a matter of fact, the most important one I made was opposite my own godfather, Ivor Novello. I played a streetwalker at the age of fourteen . . . seduced my own godfather. And Jack Hawkins was my boyfriend in the picture. Isn't that marvelous? Here I was, you know, terrible thing, this terrible cockney girl—and I *was* a cockney, I *am* a cockney—terrible character seducing him. He said, "This is absolutely ridiculous, Idah. I held you in my arms the night you were born during the Zeppelin raids." He said, "I paid a taxicab man a lot of money to get Stanley back to Herne Hill to see you." He had his [Stanley Lupino's] understudy go on for him in the last act of *Arlette.*

Anyway, I came to America very early on; in fact, I had my sixteenth birthday shortly after I came here. I had done a picture in which I played a dual role: a bad girl and then the twin, the sister, who was very sweet and innocent. That's the only reel they saw when they brought me over here for *Alice in Wonderland.* I had no desire to play Alice in *Wonderland* at all, absolutely no desire. Of course, I was tested for it and I wasn't right. There was something that was wrong, quite wrong, and they said, "No, no, no, she has to get rid of the British accent." So they took me to the drama coach. I found myself dancing on top of tables and doing things like *Come On Marines* and lying in lifeboats with Bing Crosby singing to me. And *Artists and Models,* which Raoul Walsh directed, with Jack Benny. *Gay Desperado* and *One Rainy Afternoon* for Jesse Lasky and Mary Pickford.

Of course, they didn't think of me in serious terms because they were comedies, you see, musicals. They were very successful pictures, but again I was only playing the little round-faced blonde, you know, singing and dancing and carrying on. They really didn't think of me in very serious terms. There was no variety to it at all, and boredom sets in, which is a bad thing.

I played a little cameo in *Peter Ibbetson* with Gary Cooper, directed by Henry Hathaway. I just went and asked for it: "The little role." They said, "Well, you don't make any sense. Here you are, you turn down one thing, and then you want to do a little role like this." I said, "Yes, but it's a *good* little role, it's a standout, and it's in a big picture with a big star and a big director, and that is important." Not that Raoul Walsh wasn't a big director, he was, but the roles were so awful and namby-pamby and nothing, you know. Hedda Hopper said to me, "Which way are you going, Ida? I don't care what you do, but don't run around with all this bleached hair and penciled-on eyebrows. I have a feeling about you that you really have tremendous talent." And I said, "Oh, Hedda," and she said, "I really mean it, either you be a terrific comedienne or be a dramatic actress."

JK: Which do you consider yourself?

IL: Well, I enjoy doing comedy. I love it.

JK: Your comic timing was always very sharp and to the point.

IL: Well, thank you very much. I suppose, in a way, what I did at Paramount was rather helpful when my husband and I came to do our comedy series, *Mr. Adams and Eve.* Plus the fact that I inherited, I suppose, a little from my father, who was a great comedian. I . . . really, I was happiest at that period of my life, when I was doing the series.

JK: At Paramount you were, well, what amounted to a glorified starlet, wouldn't you say?

IL: I wasn't a Wampas Baby Star, thank God. No, but, as you say, a glorified starlet. They told me it was a great honor to be in a DeMille picture. And I said, "Well, I'm sure it is, but not doing this." I don't know when it was, but it was something to do with Claudette Colbert and I had to wave a fan behind her . . . you know, playing one of Cleopatra's handmaidens. Mr. DeMille was very miffed with me. Later on we became very friendly on Lux Radio Theater, because I used to do a lot of them. He was the host. One day he said to me, "You were a spunky little devil!" And I said, "Well, did you blame me, Mr. DeMille?" "No," he said, "you were right." I said, "Well, I really have to thank you, in a way, because I left the studio." Then, of course, came *The Light That Failed*. There weren't too many British actresses over here at that time and I was out trying to get it. It did seem an impossibility for me because of having left the studio, you know, having been dropped. But, as I say, it was completely Bill Wellman who gave me a boost.

JK: Did you know that Ronald Colman wanted Vivien Leigh for that part?

IL: No, I didn't really, to be honest with you. I must say, Ronnie was marvelous to work with. Oh, marvelous! He was . . . If he didn't want me, he never let on. But of course Bill was a tower of strength, just a tower of strength. I was really scared when I had to do the mad, hysterical scene. Oh, I was in such a state, I was so nervous and frightened. Bill walked me around the set and I was shaking from head to foot. I hadn't done anything really, you know, the grand dramatic stuff.

Ronnie was very gentle and very quiet and nice, and he waited for quite some time while Bill took me off and talked to me and walked me around. I wasn't being difficult, I was just absolutely scared, you know, stiff. Ronnie just grabbed hold of my hand before I did the scene and he said, "Now, you're going to be marvelous, do you understand? Good luck. Go on. Do it." And of course we had to do the master shot together, and then came the close-ups. I thought, "I've got to go through it all over again, and I can't bear it." You know, Colman and Wellman were just temperamentally complete opposites. I remember that Bill and Ronnie did go off and have a few words, to put it frankly, and, you see, I didn't quite know what it was all about. They were cool, quite cool, with each other for several days. Bill was protecting me in this role he'd stuck his neck out to get me.

I used to have a little tiny dressing room on the third floor that was hot and the plumbing was very bad, and he brought me back [to Paramount] and he said, "This girl's going to have a decent dressing room downstairs." I was so grateful, you know, to come back to my own studio under these conditions. He took such a chance with me. I can't blame Ronnie, you know, for wanting Vivien Leigh for the role as opposed to me, whom he didn't know anything about at all. Obviously, he must have thought I was the daughter of a comedian, a well-known comedian. But Bill took a tremendous chance. He wouldn't even test me. I never made a test for the role. I just walked into his office and he said, "Read it." Bless his heart, oh, I love him! But do you know, after *The Light That Failed*, I didn't work for, oh, close to fifteen months. I've had strange ups and downs.

The next big break came when Mark Hellinger saw *The Light That Failed* and said, "I'm going to take a chance, I'm going to make a test." And Raoul Walsh, the director, who was along the same lines as Bill Wellman, marvelous, rough, tough, down-to-earth man, said, "I've worked with her. I worked with her twice. You're quite right, Mark, let's make a test." And they made a very elaborate test for *They Drive by Night*. I had to play a down-to-earth American gal. I made the test with Bogey, Humphrey Bogart. He made it with me, which was wonderful. I didn't understand him really, at first. You see, I had very little to do with him in *They Drive by Night,* but I didn't understand this wry, strange, almost . . . it seemed as if it was sarcasm at first, and it wasn't. That was Bogey. I didn't dig that right away. But then, as the picture progressed, I'd keep my ears open and I'd listen to him, and he was doing it only with people he admired or liked. We became great, great friends. He was quite a guy.

Bogey, you know, had made a big success with *The Petrified Forest.* They were only punishing him with the role in *Drive by Night.* He'd been a naughty boy, and he'd done a succession of rather nothing pictures, do you remember? Well, that was because he was naughty. He wouldn't do what he was told, so he was given a succession of rather mediocre pictures. But I had nothing to do with getting him the part in *High Sierra.* I knew that their first choice had been Paul Muni; well, he turned it down. He said it didn't have a message. So that's where the famous line, which Arthur Lyons is supposed to have said, came from: "For a few bucks you can have Western Union deliver you one." But I wasn't part of the casting decisions on that. Hellinger cast me right from the start. But I knew that the film was going to be something special, because I'd read it. I just loved it. I thought this was it. I knew Bogart was going to be sensational in it.

JK: The big change in your career came when you went to Warners. Was it Warners who loaned you out to Fox?

IL: No, I had a picture deal with Fox. Two pictures a year with Fox was the contract, but Warners had the right to preempt—in other words, they had first call on my services. It was after *They Drive by Night.* Actually, Darryl F. Zanuck—or the studio, we'll say—would ask in advance. If they didn't have anything lined up at Warners, then I would go to Fox.

JK: Davis, Stanwyck, Crawford and Lupino. They all worked at Warner Brothers at the same time. That must have been very tough at times.

IL: Yes, yes, it was.

JK: The moment a good part came along, they must have all wanted it.

IL: Well, I suppose so. Actually, Bette was *the* top star of the Warner lot. You see, Joan didn't come there until later, and Barbara Stanwyck was sort of split up, she only had picture deals, you know. But then there was Olivia de Havilland too on the lot, and Ann Sheridan. Well, you see, the type of thing that Ann did was not the type of thing that Bette would do, or Olivia, or me. Actually, I don't think of it as competitive in that way. I don't really think *they* did. Because Bette fought like mad to get me to play in *The Corn Is Green* with her, playing the marvelous role of the young girl. I was committed to another picture, I'd already done wardrobe fittings and things. It would have been very exciting to do a picture with her. I didn't know her very well. I met up a couple of times with her and some people. Tremendous wit, this woman has. Great sense of humor, and about herself too. I found her to be a charming woman, you know, not a frightening dragon lady or the queen. She was very friendly with a good friend of mine, Geraldine Fitzgerald. They were great friends. They were always casting Geraldine in goody-goody roles, suffering goody-goody roles. She had so much more to her than that, you know. She had a marvelous sense of humor. But I don't know—you kind of get in a rut and that's it.

The worst of all for me was *The Hard Way*. I didn't want to do that. I was terribly worried. You see, I knew my father was ill and I couldn't tell my mother. I was in a terrible state keeping it to myself, and, as a matter of fact, I had a breakdown right in the middle of the picture when my father passed on. I had been keeping it in for a long time. And that was the only award I ever won. I won the Critics' Award for *The Hard Way,* and I hated myself in it. I went to the preview with my mother and I said, "Connie, excuse me, dear, you stay and see the rest of this. It's making me terribly nervous, my performance." She said, "I'll never speak to you again if you walk out. Don't you dare walk out." And I said, "No, I've got to, I have to, I can't stand it." I walked. I couldn't stand myself in it, and I won the Critics' Award. The only award ever.

I would really like to have been nominated for *Ladies in Retirement*. That's the one. I've only seen myself a very few times on the screen, because I'm allergic to me. I don't go to see rushes. When we were doing our television show, it took my husband [Howard Duff] all his time to get me to go to the rough cuts with him, because he used to handle a lot of that with the editor. But I did see *Ladies in Retirement,* and I knew I was giving a pretty good performance for a twenty-one-year-old girl. I was twenty-one and playing a very difficult age, about forty-six or forty-seven. That was the age of the woman in it, you see.

There again was a man who took a great chance on casting me. After all, Flora Robson had made a great success of it on Broadway. I had never seen her in the play, but Lester Cowan, who produced it, chose me for the movie role. The only switch he made in the film was that the sisters were older sisters and I was the younger sister, which actually lent a lot of sympathy to the terrible woman murdering her employer. It gave the sisters much more sympathy, being older and yet childlike.

When Harry Cohn heard that Lester wanted me to play the role, he said, "You're out of your mind. For what unearthly reason would you want her for the role?" And Lester said, "Well, I do, I just know she can do it." And we did extensive tests, you know, with the hair and not overlining the face or anything, but to give the face more maturity. And of course I was very thin at that time, which helped. There were three men in my life who really took great chances with me: Bill Wellman, Mark Hellinger and Lester Cowan.

JK: Well, their chances paid off. You obviously gave people their money's worth.

IL: Yes. I would like to have some of the money they made! If I had to do it all over again, I would have listened to Darryl Zanuck. He was a brilliant head of the studio. That man could, *had* read every script on the lot; he watched every wardrobe test of every male star, every female star; he could remember—with all the people under contract!—that he didn't like a spotted tie on a man in test number three, or he didn't like the cut of a skirt on me in test number four. The man truly deserved to be called a brilliant man. After *Road House* he wanted me to stay with Fox for three pictures a year. Today I would be a very rich woman if I'd done that. But the great solace I have out of it is that I did give some newcomers a chance by going into independent production. But please don't remind me. I say, if I had to do it all over again, I'm the one person who would do it differently.

JK: Did the studios control your life?

IL: Well, yes. I mean, you did what they told you to, otherwise they suspended you, which means that you went for weeks without any money coming in. And I used to get suspended. At Warners too. One would have a call from a very nice man called Steve Trilling, who has since passed on.

Ida becomes quiet, subdued in her recollection. There's a melancholy tinge as she speaks of people gone, "passing on." One is reminded that in movies nobody spoke the word "dead" or "killed" with quite the same vehemence as did Ida when confronted by the incredible fact that man could kill his fellow man. When Ida herself played a killer in *They Drive by Night,* she went mad. Killing was not comprehensible to her. It's what gave her performances almost classic Greek overtones. That is why, when on the screen Ida said "dead" or "killed," you felt a chill down your spine. Off screen, in life, for Ida there was just melancholy. .

IL: Steve would say, "Come up to the office, dear. Now, are you going to do this? Now, don't be difficult. And don't make me suspend you." And of course he had been ordered, I don't know by whom, to suspend you. He had to. Thank goodness I had radio work still. Nobody else at Warners had a radio clause. I had a—he's passed on—marvelously cunning agent called Arthur Lyons, and how he got that radio clause in there . . . well, the test for *They Drive by Night* was so good that the studio said, "We want her." And Arthur said, "Not unless we have radio." So I could do radio on the weekend whenever I wasn't working. I'd call up madly and say, "I've got to pay the bills. Quick! Get me on *Silver Theater.* I worked with Charles Boyer and Tyrone Power, and did a lot of *Lux Radio.* There was one period there when the suspension went on and on.

My mum and I had this great barn of a house in Beverly Hills which today would be worth a fortune, but then we got it for a song. We were down on our hands and knees, scrubbing the floors, because we couldn't afford to pay anyone. And here goes a tourist bus by and I can hear the conductor saying, "On the left is the home, the gorgeous, sumptuous home of that glamorous movie actress Ida Lupino."

Oh, yes, I had a rough time. But then, to me, of course, in the days when I was at Warners and Fox, it was a marvelous time, because there were so many tremendous personalities on the lots. And I really used to enjoy, I grew to enjoy, going to work. Everything's changed now, everything is panic button, you know, and they press the panic button and it's all false. There doesn't seem to be any laughter or spirit left. Gone. But then there was a wonderful warmth and camaraderie between us all on the lot. We'd meet in the makeup department in the morning and say, "Oh, how do you feel this morning?" "Terrible, it's too early. . . ." And we'd go and visit each other on the set, and it was just a marvelous feeling, you know, that existed in those days. And you were able to drive somewhere then, and you could go walking at night. I don't know. They call it progress, but I don't. For my money, I wouldn't call it progress. We've lost heart. And laughter. And I'm awfully bored with the films today. The working conditions are such that, I don't know, there doesn't seem to be any of the spirit.

JK: Did you direct *Women's Prison* as well as act in it?

IL: No, no. There was only one that I ever directed that I acted in. That was *The Bigamist,* because Joan Fontaine insisted I play "the other woman." [Collier Young, Ida's second husband, was Joan's ex-husband.] It was kind of interesting. She'd already okayed me as director, but she said, "Look, Ida, it'll give us more help at the box office if you play . . . Please play the other . . ." And I said, "Well, you'd better watch me. I don't know when to cut and print *or* when I'm good or bad, you know." People assume that I began directing because I was an actress who wanted more control. Not at all. That's not so. I'd co-written a screenplay and was co-producing it with Collier Young. The director, Elmer Clifton, was taken sick—Elmer did the original *Down to the Sea in Ships.* Our company was too poor to hire another director, so I took over for him. And the picture got rather good critical acclaim. The money people, a little outfit called Film Classics, insisted that I direct the second picture.* It was my original story and I had co-written the screenplay with Collier. We made this at the height of the depression in motion pictures, and, strangely enough, without even knowing him or what his subject matter was, Stanley Kramer, who was the only other independent at the time, had made *The Men.* I believe Kramer was the first one to do a basketball game in wheelchairs, and we were the first ones to ever do a square

Not Wanted is credited to Elmer Clifton as director, with Lupino serving as producer and co-scenarist.

dance in wheelchairs, with real polio patients. The movie was called
Young Lovers with Sally Forrest, Keefe Brasselle and Hugh O'Brian.*

As far as women not having the right stamina to be directors, I don't
know. I think it depends on the subject matter. For instance, I couldn't under-
take a [John] Frankenheimer kind of picture. It is physically very, very demanding, and you're on your feet, and you just may as well make up your
mind that you're not going to eat properly, sleep properly, that you just . . .
that you're on a turntable, morning to night. You get home, and no sooner
home than you have to get up again. But I like it when I get something I'm
interested in.

For instance, I used to enjoy directing *Mr. Novak,* or *The Untouchables,*
or *The Fugitive.*† I enjoyed it because I liked the company, you know, the
group. Like a family thing. I'll tell you, I enjoyed directing motion pictures
when I was doing it for our own company. It was a family thing, everybody
put something in the pot. If the gateman had a good idea, we'd say, "Fine,"
and write it down. Everybody was doing it together, you know. The attitude
towards a woman directing back then wasn't too bad because it was our own
company, and when Howard Hughes took over RKO, he insisted that I direct
The Hitchhiker. So I didn't find any problems there. There have been occasionally some moments in television which I wouldn't say were the happiest
moments of my life. But I haven't had trouble telling men, crews, to do
things. I don't do it that way anyway. I say a man is a man and a woman is a
woman. I say, "Honey, could you help old Mother here, just to do this for
me, or that," or "Eddy, Mum's in a bad spot, I want to get the camera over
here and I think I may have painted myself into a corner," or something. I
don't believe in giving orders. I don't like it. A man, when a woman asks for
help, usually likes to help her.

JK: Speaking of men and giving orders, did you ever fight with Jack Warner?

IL: No. When my contract was up, coming to an end, he told me to come up to
his office. He wanted me to sign for seven years straight. I said, "No, I don't
want to do that. I want a personal life. I don't want to be looking at my old
press notices seven years from now and that's all." He said, "Seven years and
no options, Ida, fifty-two weeks in the year." And I said, "No." He said, "All
right, I'm going to tell you something. You'll never act at this studio again."
And I never did and I never have. I met him in the dentist's office one morning, very early. He said, "Hello, Ida, sweet as apple cider," and broke into a
time step, which he is wont to do every once in a while. He said, "See? I
kept my word." And I said, "Yes, but I came back and did two *77 Sunset
Strip*'s." And he said, "That's directing, that's not acting." His memory!

---

*Lupino directed *Hard, Fast and Beautiful* (1951), her second *officially noted* directorial work,
with Sally Forrest and Keefe Brasselle, hence the confusion. *Young Lovers* was a working title for
Not Wanted.
†Television series for which Lupino directed some episodes.

But of course, while I was there, I did things. Remember *Escape Me Never*? I enjoyed that very much. I loved Errol Flynn, who was one of my dear, dear, dear friends. I mean, if you had Errol Flynn for a friend, you were doing fine. I'm not talking about romantically. He was just marvelous. Fun and, well, a very kind person, very sensitive. He used to call me "Mad Idsy" and I used to call him "The Baron." And Raoul Walsh, who directed Errol and me so often, was "Uncle." So it was "Uncle" and "The Baron" and "Mad Idsy." The three of us were great friends, great buddies.

Then there was *Devotion*. Oh, Olivia—de Havilland—and I worked very hard on research on that when we were cast in it. Strangely enough, she was cast as Charlotte and I was cast as Emily. I think Olivia was top-billed, no, we were co-starred, and then, well, I can't remember. I don't care who gets first billing. But we did a lot of work on it and Olivia said, "It's strange we've been cast in these roles. Let's really go for the way they were." Charlotte was blond and near-sighted, wore glasses, and Emily was very dark and she had a falcon she used to have chained to her arm, and a mastiff dog. So we did our tests, you know, and I went for the dark wig parted in the center, and Olivia wanted to go blond. The next thing we knew, Mr. Warner said, "I will have no such thing! Olivia will play with the hair and curls, and Ida will play with the long red hair. And she's going to have a sheepdog." And our producer saw, when he had to break the news to us, that the two of us were just destroyed. Mr. Warner said, "I'm not going to have the two of you wandering around looking like that!" And we said, "Well, we can just see the notices now, and all the Brontë Societies, you know."

Sure enough, they tore *Devotion* to pieces. You see, it altered the performances so much. And performances are, can be, so—well, I don't know how to explain it. I try to understand the role I'm playing. I try to dig into it as much as I can. I don't have any method. I just don't know how to explain it other than to say "Try to make it as real and as sincere as you possibly can." You know?

1973

Vincent Sherman, photographed by Irving Lippman (Columbia), 1952

VINCENT
SHERMAN

I N HIS TEENS, Vincent Sherman worked in the theater as an actor, writer and director before he went into movies. His first film work, in 1933, was as an actor, re-creating his stage role in Elmer Rice's *Counsellor-at-Law*. Though it was neither as actor nor writer that he would establish himself as one of the linchpin directors at Warner Bros.—*Mr. Skeffington, Nora Prentiss, The Hard Way, The Adventures of Don Juan, Old Acquaintance, Harriet Craig, Affair in Trinidad*—in the '40s his background and expertise came in handy with the studios' talented but often frustrated roster of great stars, a frustration due to lack of good scripts, front-office exploitation of their box-office appeal, and misuse of their talents that served to uncover and inflame personal problems and result in flare-ups on the set. He worked successfully with Ida Lupino, Bette Davis, Ann Sheridan, Joan Crawford, Humphrey Bogart, John Garfield and Errol Flynn, directing them as they wished to be seen, as well as the way the public wished to see them, which is not always the same thing. Unlike other directors whose rapport with actors found them shunted into the lucrative but snidely dismissed realm of melodrama and women's pictures, Sherman worked with them rather than treating them as pampered pets. Bette Davis once said about working with Miriam Hopkins in *Old Acquaintance*, "Miriam and I were always old this, or old that; everything in fact except old friends." Miriam had her own say. Here is Vincent Sherman's view of it—and more.

VS: The setup at Warners at that time was like this: they had an A department run by Hal Wallis and a B department run by Bryan Foy. Wallis would make about twenty pictures a year and Foy about thirty-five. When a picture got to be, say, seven or eight years old, Foy would turn around and take that A picture and make it into a B picture. The first picture I worked on out there was a picture called *Crime School* [1938] with the Dead End Kids and Humphrey Bogart.

   Mervyn LeRoy had signed up the Dead End Kids and Robert Rossen was working on a script for them, but it did not work out and so after six months Jack Warner said that he was damn tired of paying these kids salaries for sitting around on their asses doing nothing, and told Foy, "See what you

549

can do with them. You've got them." I had just been signed by the studio and Foy called me up, as I had worked with the Dead End Kids in the play *Dead End,* from which they got their names. "Well, we're going to put together a show for them, we're going to do half of *The Mayor of Hell,* which was an old Cagney film, and half of a picture called *San Quentin,* a picture Pat O'Brien and Annie Sheridan had made. Now, use the first half of *The Mayor of Hell* and the second half of *San Quentin.*" I went off to my office with the script. By the time I got to my office Foy called and said, "Look, you've just started here and it's a little unfair to throw this at you, because I've got to have this script next week. I've got to start this picture in ten days' time. I've got an old hand here who knows how to do this switch very quickly, he'll do the first draft and you follow up and you do the polishing and the rewriting." So he gave it to a man named Crane Wilbur, who had been working for him for some time. So Wilbur would do like forty, fifty pages in two days, he just changed a few names and a little word here and there. Then I got the script and started to read it, and the first half was fine, but it didn't begin to jell with the second half, so I had to go back and establish things in the first part to make it tie up with things in the second part. Then I started really fixing the script, working with the characters to make it all blend together, and the result was I was dialogue director on the picture and had the screenplay credit.*

I was getting $200 from Warners, having just started. But on this picture, when we started shooting, I realized that things were not right, because *The Mayor of Hell* went in a different direction from what we were going in, so the characters had to be changed to make it work. I found myself sitting up every night after shooting, rewriting for the next day's work. I would call the director around 10:00 or 11:00 at night and tell him what I was working on and he would say "good" or "not good" or "I'll stall in the morning, get it ready," so I'd be there in the studio at 7:00 at the typewriter and he'd be on the set about 8:30, read it over, then we'd give the kids the pages 'cause they could pick up stuff very easily. And that's the way that picture was done.

We were about two-thirds of the way through the picture, with it getting better and better. The more I rewrote, the better it was. The director, an old-timer called Lewis Seiler, was happy with it. Anyway, about this stage in the picture we wanted to put some humor into the piece, but it was not until 10:00 at night that I got an idea. I called the director on the phone. "Gee, that's great," he said, but I said, "Lew, I'm exhausted. I'll try to finish it up in the morning. Have you got anything you can do?" "I don't have anything to do. I'll stall, you get in the dressing room early." Well, I was in the dressing room writing at 9:00 when the production man came down and said, "What the hell are you doing?" "I'm trying to get this scene together," I replied. "Goddamn it! You've been rewriting every page and this production is six days behind.

---

*In fact, the adaptation was by Crane Wilbur and Vincent Sherman.

I'm going to tell Mr. Warner that it's your fault, you're causing these delays." Well, I turned to him and said, "You ——!" I wasn't making that much money. I didn't do that sort of thing later, but at this point it didn't mean so much to me. "Listen to me, I don't sleep at night. I've been working until 11:00 every night, and if you guys don't like it, to hell with it." He never forgave me for that. During my thirty years there he never forgave me for that, because I'd told him off, told him where to go.

So they blamed me for the delay in the production, but when it comes out good, you also get the credit! And that's what happened. I was like the white-haired boy.

It was stupid, but I was a success overnight because that picture cost $186,000 and it grossed over $2 million. It was one of the biggest hits of 1938. That and *Robin Hood* were the two biggest money-makers for the studio, and *Crime School* was an even bigger money-maker because it cost less. It was the first time I met Bogey and we got along very well. The kids were marvelous as well, for often I did not have time to write all the scenes, so I'd get them together and tell them the situation: "Here's the scene, now let's improvise." So when we improvised, I'd jot down some of the best lines and incorporate them into the script!

JK: How did you become a director at Warners?

VS: I began as an actor. Around 1930 I met Moss Hart, he had just written his first play, *Once in a Lifetime*. My wife was working in a playbroker's office in New York that was handling Moss Hart, so I went up there with a play of mine and they introduced me to Moss. He asked me what I did during the summer. I said I went into stock or something like that. "Do you think you could direct?" he asked. "Well," I said, "I could try." Then he told me how he had spent the nine years previously as a social director in these big Jewish summer camps just outside of New York. He had a job in a camp that summer and he was going to get $2000 for putting on the plays there, but he could not take it because he had to stay in town to rewrite *Once in a Lifetime* with George Kaufman. So he said, "Do you think you could put some shows on?" I went over to see this man who ran the camp, and he said, "You don't have any experience for this kind of thing, you should perhaps start at a smaller place. My audience is a pretty tough crowd, but I've got a friend who has a camp, he has only about 400–500 people for a weekend. I have 1000 and these are tough New York Jews and they sit on their hands and you'd have to give them really first-rate stuff." So I went over and I got a job with this other camp, I don't remember the name of it.

I started doing shows that summer. It was the first taste I'd really had of directing. And the thing that was marvelous about it was that you had to put a show on in four or five days. You had to create entertainment, and I have never been under such pressure in my life. That's why even doing B pictures never bothered me. The pressure was great, but it was nothing to that. And in addition to that I had to do other shows too in the week. That was the most marvelous experience; you had to do everything, trick things, and yet make it look presentable. *And* to a sophisticated crowd! I did that that year, and before I had finished the season, a guy came to me and said, "These are good shows, what are you doing next season?" And he took me over to another camp. I followed a man named Don Hartman there, who later became a producer, wrote the *Road* pictures, and at one time was in charge of production at Paramount. The man who followed me was Max Liebman, who did the Sid Caesar [television] shows. I did this for about three years, after which I was exhausted.

I came back to New York, where I had worked for Elmer Rice in *Counsellor-at-Law,* and he got me into the Federal [Theater]. So I had experience at directing and trying to do some writing. And I had been out in Hollywood to play in William Wyler's first important picture, *Counsellor-at-Law* [1933]. This was with John Barrymore and Bebe Daniels. I played the young Communist. He only had one scene, but it got quite a bit of notoriety at the time. It took us four days to make that one scene because Barrymore could not remember his lines. So anyway, when Elmer Rice became head of the Federal Theater, he called me and said, "Look, you've done some directing, why don't you come and join me?"

I did one of the early productions, a play about John Brown, and then the Sinclair Lewis play *It Can't Happen Here,* which was not terribly good although I got to know Lewis very well out of that. Anyway, I was working on a play at home when Marty Gabel, an actor I knew from the play *Dead End,* called me and said, "Vincent, how would you like to go on the road with *Dead End*?" "Doing what?" I asked. "Playing Baby Face Martin." I had originally tried for this part and lost out, and so this came as a surprise. I went down and read and got the part and went on the road with it, and now I was playing in Hollywood and the girl that used to be Wyler's girlfriend when he was doing *Counsellor* was now going with Foy and they came to see the show. Foy came backstage and he said, "Hey, I hear you do some writing and directing, why don't you come out to the studio and talk to me tomorrow? If you've got anything you've written, bring it." So I went out the next day and he said, "How would you like to spend some time writing some movies out here?" I had mentioned that I did not want to go on with acting. "I'll give you $100 a week for ten weeks." "Well," I said, "I make more than that as an actor." I had quite a bit of money in the bank and I was feeling pretty independent.

So he told me to go to lunch while he talked to Warner, and after lunch Foy came back and on the back of a piece of spearmint chewing-gum paper Warner had written out a three-way contract, a seven-year deal, $200 the first year, $250 the second year, $300 for the third year and so on. "If you'll sign this three-way contract—" "What's a three-way contract?" I asked. "Well, if you don't work out as a writer, we can use you either as a director or an actor.

If you don't work out as a director, we'll put you into acting." "Well," I said to my wife, "let's take it. We'll take the dough for six months and then be off, 'cause they won't take up the option." I had been at the studio almost six months and nothing had happened. I'd worked on one script, and when I got through with it, they said: "Charming, if we had Cary Grant or some big star, but we can't get anybody for this kind of thing." I thought that that was the end of it. That is when *Crime School* happened.

In the next year and a half I had my name on about five or six of the scripts I was doctoring up. After *Crime School,* I wrote another for Bogey, *King of the Underworld* [1939], with Kay Francis. Now, Warners were trying to get rid of her at that time, they were paying her $5000 a week. To Warner, actors were commodities, and with Kay Francis it was fine while her pictures were making money, he kept increasing her salary. Then she made a few pictures that went downhill, the exhibitors said, "We can't sell Kay Francis anymore." That was it. Warner had two years more to go on her contract, so he thought, I'll give her to Foy, she'll get angry and walk out. That was his usual method of getting the actor to break the contract. But she didn't walk out. Foy called me one day and said, "Listen, I got Kay Francis. Warner's trying to get her to break her contract." And to be given to Foy in those days was like the kiss of death, but Francis said, "As long as they pay my salary, I'll sweep the stage, to hell with it." The first picture I did with her, Foy called me, it was on a Friday: "I got to have a script by Wednesday." Johnny Farrow was going to direct. "There's an old play around here called *Courage* done by Janet Beecher in New York, get me a script out of this." He just handed me this little play and said he wanted the script on Monday. I got about two hours' sleep for the next three nights, but I got the script to him. Farrow started the film the next Friday, and I was with him on the set, it was called *My Bill* [1938]. Terrible picture, with Ian Hunter* and Bobby Jordan, but, listen, I had four days to do it in. Throughout it Kay was real professional on the set; a very attractive woman as well.

Then Foy said we've got to make another picture with her. And what they did was to take the first part of an old picture called *Dr. Socrates,* a Paul Muni vehicle. It was the story of a doctor whose wife had died and he became unhappy and he went to a small town, but he didn't get along there until some gangsters tried to take over the town and he found a way to get rid of them and became the town hero. Ann Dvorak played the girl the gangsters picked up. Foy said we're going to switch *Dr. Socrates* and make it a vehicle for Kay Francis, she'll play the Paul Muni part. I said, "How the hell is that going to work?" They had a good English actor, James Stephenson, who was going to play the Ann Dvorak part, and Bogart was going to play a part that had originally been played by Barton MacLane. It worked, and it was called *King of the Underworld.* There was only one problem on the script—in the

*Ian Hunter was not in *My Bill*. The leading man was John Litel.

original the doctor gave the gangsters some kind of shot because he told them they were catching some kind of disease. I did not want to do exactly the same thing, so I had it that they could not see properly, they saw triple images. It was more filmic as well.

After some more doctored scripts Foy came to me and said that Warner wants to make some new directors, "and I told him I would make you into a director." Well, I'd worked with the actors on the set and I'd been on these pictures and they turned out all right, and besides I wasn't getting that much money, so I could afford to take a chance, and they seemed to have some respect for the fact that I had been in the theater for ten years or so. "I don't know much about the camera or cutting," I said. "Oh, you'll soon learn that." And they gave me the cameraman I worked with on *King of the Underworld,* Sid Hickox. Foy said he had two stories; one was a very charming little story . . . Well, the minute he said the word "charm," I ran, because I knew I wasn't going to get the actors for the charm. Then he told me about this horror mystery, *The Return of Dr. X* [1939], that sounded more like me, because I can do the theatrical. Besides I felt safer with this as a B picture. And I got Wayne Morris, who had started off like a house on fire at Warners but got nowhere; and Dennis Morgan had just been put under contract, so I had Dennis. Dennis was playing the doctor. Wayne was playing the newspaperman and then there was Bogey. I talked to Bogey, saying how this was my chance to direct a picture, and he was very cooperative and besides we were good friends. We met on *Crime School,* which had helped his career, for with Warner Brothers, when a picture was successful, everybody associated with it was helped as far as the attitude of Warner was concerned.

We did the picture very inexpensively, and since it turned out quite successful, it led to the second picture. I used to sit at the writers' table at lunch, and also there were Philip and Julius Epstein, who had done a rewrite of *Saturday's Children* [1943]. This was a Maxwell Anderson piece which Warners had done years before. Anatole Litvak was supposed to have done the picture with Jimmy Stewart and Olivia de Havilland, but neither of them liked the script. They all felt, and rightly, that it was a sweet picture but it did not have enough to be a big hit.

The Epsteins got annoyed when it was turned down, and, as I subsequently learned, they went up to Hal Wallis and said, "Why don't you let this kid Vincent Sherman make it?" And all of a sudden I get a call from Hal Wallis and he said, "We want you to do *Saturday's Children.*" Henry Blanke was the producer. I read it and I thought the script was charming. They said, "We're going to give you Johnny Garfield." Now, Johnny and I were old friends. We had been in *Counsellor-at-Law* together. And I had another personal friend in the cast, Claude Rains, with whom I'd been in the Theatre Guild, where we had done three or four plays together.

Anyway *Saturday's Children* was not a big commercial success, although it did get marvelous reviews, especially in New York.

After my third film, an anti-Nazi picture called *Underground* [1941], Warner called me up to his home. I had not even met him prior to this time, although he did come to the premiere of *Dr. X*. Warner got quite excited about the picture, as it got fine reviews, was a big success everywhere, while it only cost about $280,000 and they got back a couple of million. It was an invitation to breakfast with the boss, and he took me for a walk and said that if I would let him guide me, he would make me one of the big directors of the town. I just listened and was very polite, but I was still only getting that lousy $250 a week, having made three or four pictures already. Then, before I made my next film for Wallis, there was a little disagreement.

I had to make another film for Foy, *The Man Who Talked Too Much* [1940], with George Brent. Brent, who was one of Wallis' top leading men opposite all the great women stars, didn't want to do it because it was a B picture, and I didn't want to do it because it had been a bad picture when Zanuck made it back in 1932 [*The Mouthpiece*]. I didn't like the script. But I did find out what Zanuck's formula was: Grab 'em at the opening, don't worry about the second act, but make sure you have a fast finish. Well, *The Mouthpiece* opened with a lawyer (Brent) in court defending a client on a murder rap and he's saying, "How could my client be guilty of poisoning? This is what he gave that person to drink. He could not have died of that," and at that he drinks it himself. And while there's a big hullaballoo in the courtroom, he walks out fast and gets into a car where they got a stomach pump waiting for him, because it was poison. Well, it hooked the audience right away 'cause they thought he was a real slick lawyer. Then you went into the story, which was a bunch of crap. And now I had to remake it.

Well, there was this little rivalry between Wallis and Foy, 'cause I'm sure Foy felt that it was easy for Wallis to make pictures with all that money while *he* only had a couple of hundred thousand at most, even though Foy sometimes came to the studio's rescue with a film like *Crime School*. So when he asked Warner for Brent, to give his film a bit of class, Brent, who wasn't doing anything at the time, was sent down to do it even though he objected and got Wallis to object. I got friendly with George during shooting and one night after a really grueling day, 'cause when you work on small budgets you really work your ass off, not like on the A pictures, he told me, "Jeez, man, I've never worked this hard since I've been in the studio." He must have been nice about me because one day while I was in the dining room having lunch, Bette Davis, who was very buddy with George, came over and said, "Hi, I've been hearing some wonderful things about you. George says he's very happy and you're doing a great job. I hope we work together sometime." It was all very nice and unexpected and I didn't see her again for some time.

When it was over, Wallis called me back and told me Jerry Wald was going to produce *All Through the Night* [1942]. I think this was Bogart's first starring role in an A picture. This was just before he became a really big Warner star. They gave me this Damon Runyonesque little story about Fifth

Columnists in America and these New York crooks doing right for Uncle Sam and exposing them. When I first got it, it was a little too charming, a little fey, and Bogart got a bit irritated, saying, "What kind of dialogue is this!" and wanted it toughened up. I was, as I always do, working very closely with the writers, and we completely rewrote the script, and I helped put a lot of intrigue and fireworks into it.

Basically I stole most of it from the Hitchcock films I'd seen. The auction was a typical Hitchcock scene. I think I got the idea from *The 39 Steps,* where Donat accidentally walks into a political meeting, but I twisted it around. Of course I had this marvelous cast to work with. Apart from Bogart and Judith Anderson, there was Conrad Veidt and Peter Lorre, and in the opening scene of the film, which takes place in a restaurant like Lindy's, you'll see Phil Silvers and Jackie Gleason playing two bits. They were under contract to Warners, getting like $200 a week, and Warner said to me to put those two comics in there too. I said, "I've got nothing for them." "I don't care." "But I've already got five comics in the film!" I was up to my neck in Warner contract people—I had William Demarest, Frank McHugh, Allen Jenkins, Wally Ford . . . you know. Warner said, "So you'll have two more. What the hell, give them something to do, find something for them." So I said to them, "Look, fellas, I don't have time to write anything for you. Write some gags, do a few ad-libs, bring them in and I'll work some into the script." Being comics, they came back with pages of stuff. I used what I could, but I could have gone and played the whole picture in that first sequence! The picture was done. I think it cost $600,000. My wife saw it and thought it was awful. But it went to New York and started to do big business. Now I get a call from Jerry Wald to do a picture called *The Hard Way* [1942], and that was really the beginning of the good years.

I was getting $300 a week and I said to Jerry, "Damn it to hell, I'm directing people who are making five times, ten times what I'm making. Damn it, I'm tired. That isn't fair. I've got three more years to go, then, damn it to hell, I'm going to blow this joint." I was really annoyed. Well, Jerry must have passed the message on, 'cause Warner called me into his office: "Hi, Sherman! Hi, boy! How are you? Good to see you. Glad to hear you're doing a good job." He said, "Listen, Vince, I didn't realize you were working for so little money. Tell you what, we'll rewrite your contract for another seven years, and I'm going to raise you to $750 a week. How's that?" I said, "Well, let me think about it." In the meantime I'd gotten myself an agent who was supposed to be a big agent and change things and he didn't do a damn thing. But I went over to talk to him about it and he pretended he'd been doing things behind the scenes, but I knew he hadn't and that it was Jerry's doing. And Warner, well, when you're making money for him, he was ready to share a little of it, *but* very little.

The agent's idea of a deal was really dumb, and for that I had to pay him 10 percent, but I was dumb too, because I took it, because my real concern was making pictures. I wanted money, but I wasn't money crazy, or power crazy. I was happy making films. And there was the promise of bigger and better films and I was about to start on *The Hard Way*. There was a great crowd at the studio. The hierarchy was so-so, but the studio was great. There was a great spirit of camaraderie. The crews were great, everybody was doing their job, the pictures were successful and making money. When things are going well, everybody feels well.

You did not have too much interference in the Warner studios. Nobody ever called you up to tell you how to shoot the picture. That was up to you. But you knew, having been there for some time, that there were certain classic rules to observe. Audiences like to know where they were in a scene—I went to see *The Last Tango,* I didn't know where the people were in that picture, in the hotel, in the apartment or where. We had to have a straight story line, not go off on unnecessary tangents, and we were pretty efficient at our job. Also the studio liked to have a certain amount of coverage; I learned that anyone who says that this is the way it's going to be in the finished film is just foolish, he's an amateur. The values that you see in an individual scene, in the context of the whole, may decrease in value *or* increase. The things that you say to yourself, like "I want to play that in a close-up," you may want to play in a long shot later when you see that whole thing put together.

Sometimes values come through that you don't expect. Sometimes an actor or actress brings something to a film that you could not anticipate, which in turn expands and illuminates other things. Otherwise it would be just like cutting cloth and making shoes.

Nobody at the studio wanted to make *The Hard Way* [1942] because they thought it was very depressing. It first came my way when Jerry Wald came on the set of *All Through the Night* and said, "I got a great script. Greatest script ever in the studio, written by Irwin Shaw. I gave Irwin the idea for the story." According to Wald, it was the true story of one of the most famous stars of the time and her mother, but Irwin switched it around and made it about two sisters. Wald had interviewed the ex-husband of this star after he'd tried to kill himself, and then gave the story to Irwin to turn it into a script. I said, "Well, can I direct it, since I'm doing this bit of crap for you?"

"I'd like to let you have it," said Wald, "but there are a dozen big directors wanting to do it: Leo McCarey, William Wyler, Hawks . . ." Well, I figured I didn't have a chance, so I forgot about it and finished *All Through the Night*. About a week later I got a call from Paul Nathan, who worked for Wallis, and he said that they were sending me a script and Mr. Wallis would like me to make a report on it, telling him what I thought of it. I asked what it was and, sure enough, *The Hard Way*. So I said, "But what about McCarey, Wyler, Hawks and the others?" Paul said he didn't know, but that Wallis wanted my report. So I read it and saw marvelous possibilities and wrote a four- or five-page memo suggesting changes, etc., and sent it back, and got a call to see Hal. So I asked why for, since I'd heard from Jerry that all these big people wanted to do it. And Wallis replied, "Because I like you." "Well, now we got the crap out of the way, tell me the truth." "Well," he says, "everybody read it and liked it, but you sent in four pages of changes after you read it." "That's the way I feel about it, Hal." "All right," he says, "let's talk about your changes. Why don't you get Irwin Shaw to do them?" So Jerry Wald gets Irwin along to the office at about 6:00—possibly we were going to have dinner—anyway, I'll never forget that evening. Jerry introduced me to Shaw: "Irwin, I want you to meet Vincent Sherman. He's going to do *The Hard Way*." And Irwin says, "What happened to McCarey and Wyler?" I felt an idiot sitting there, wanting to say, "Screw you too," but you learn to take those things and forget about them.

I wanted to make this a realistic story, a backstage story that told things as they really were. The story started in a coal-mining town and I wanted to go to Pennsylvania and shoot some of the towns on location, but they wouldn't let me. Instead we dug up an old film that Pare Lorentz had made and we took some scenes out of that of coal-mining villages and I blended that into the opening scene of *The Hard Way*, where Ida Lupino and Joan Leslie were looking out of the window. And I got Jimmy Wong Howe as my cameraman, he'd been on *Saturday's Children* with me, and asked him if he could get the same dirty, smoky quality into the picture. So he got smoke pots on the set and we had smoke drifting in at the side of the set. The first week on that film I'd asked Ida Lupino not to wear any makeup. Ida was under contract and Jack Carson and Dennis Morgan were around and Joan Leslie was a youngster on the lot.

I knew that Leslie would be fine as the young, starry-eyed girl at the beginning, but I was concerned as to whether she could play the girl who had been corrupted at the end and would give you that necessary feeling of disillusionment and bitterness. As I suspected, she could not give me that, because she did not have that in her as a human being. She was too young, only about sixteen, and came from a very simple, religious family and had not experienced disillusionment in her own life.

Anyway, to come back to *The Hard Way*, we got Ida to drop the makeup, although she did not particularly like doing it. I wanted her grimy because I wanted to contrast the background from which these people came in the early scenes with that to which they would be going later on. As we went along I was getting Lupino to do things she did not want to do, and after a few weeks she said to me, "This picture's going to stink and I'm going to stink in it." I said, "Miss Lupino, if you do as I ask, this picture is going to win you some kind of award." By the end we were not even speaking because she was objecting to playing what she thought was a bitch. And although that was the way the part was written, I thought I had developed it enough to explain why she was this way. I thought it was a fresh approach to let her play this kind of thing—she wasn't *just* a heavy.

Warner saw the picture at his house and said, "Holy God, I think we've got a flop on our hands." I asked him why, and he replied, "Ah, Vince, who cares about these dirty people in the coal mines?" Ironically enough, when the picture opened in New York, those first two or three reels got the reviews. *The Hard Way* was a tough film mainly because of Ida. She was a very attractive girl in those days, and I was trying to get the kind of performance I wanted from her, and I suppose there were times when she felt I was pushing her a little too hard and she felt she was becoming a little too bitchy. It was really a Davis role and Ida was fighting it. I've discovered one thing over the years which I think is axiomatic, and that is that people do not like to play things that are close to themselves. Ida would rather play a very sweet, innocent little girl than to play a bitch. Because Ida could be very sharp and vitriolic if she wanted to be; she was a ballsy lady.

At the end of the picture I was saying to the dialogue director, "You tell Miss Lupino I want so and so," and Ida would reply through him. But she won the New York critics' award for the performance; I was told about it by Mark Hellinger. I called her on the telephone and I said, "Miss Lupino?" "Yes, who's calling?" I said, "Vincent Sherman." She said, "Darling!" From that moment on we were very close friends and made a couple more pictures together. She wasn't always easy, but she was worth it.

There's a funny postscript that sort of ties it all up. Wald originally sent the script to the actress whom it was based on. I suppose he wanted her for the part of the younger sister. Anyway, she read it and told Jerry, "This could be my story." Jerry had to control himself from blurting out, "It is."

But she didn't know.

Anyway, this film took me out of the rut of thrillers and melos and horror films, and my next was *Old Acquaintance*.

Old Acquaintance was a new thing started for me. What happened was I was at the house when Wallis called and said, "I am sending you a script." He said, "[Edmund] Goulding was supposed to do this, but he has had a heart attack and he can't do it." Well, I was told later that Goulding had gone through *The Old Maid* with these two ladies [Bette Davis and Miriam Hopkins], you see, and somebody said he just felt he wasn't up to it. So I read the script. It was lightweight, what I call women's-magazine stuff, didn't think it was my cup of tea although I felt it was nicely done, and Wallis said, "You don't want to do it?" I said, "Well, I'd like to work with Davis, but I don't think this is my dish." Well, I heard later they'd given it to Irving Rapper. Irving heard that I didn't want to do it and he said *he* didn't want to do it.

JK: Because of the difficulties between the two women?

VS: Yes. He'd heard stories too, and he was about to go into the Navy and he didn't know whether he would be able to do it or not. Anyway, they called me back and Wallis said, "Look, I want you to do this picture." Okay, so I got into the studio and met Hopkins. It was the second time I'd worked with

Henry Blanke, we got along marvelously, I liked him very much as a producer, a wonderful guy. And we started work and I started with Miriam. Well, it turns out we're both Southerners—she's from Bainbridge, Georgia. I was born in a little town called Vienna, Georgia, and we went to work and worked for about four days. Davis was in Palm Springs, I think on a vacation—then she came back to the studio at the end of the fifth day and she came round the set. She said, "Hello, how's it going?" I said, "Why don't you go down and look at some of the rushes?" She said, "Oh, may I?" And I said, "Well, of course, I'd be happy." So about an hour later I got a call from Davis, she was in the projection room: "I just think it's marvelous," she said, "I don't know how you got Miriam to do all those things, they were wonderful; when do you want me to report for work?" I said, "Tomorrow morning at nine." She came in and we went through the picture, there was no problem except the two ladies.

Now, what happened with them was this: I found that as we were working—and I hadn't been in the business long enough to realize that there were so many tricks that could be played—I began to notice that Miriam would do little things that I wondered why she was doing them. Let's say, for instance, the two of them were sitting on the sofa in the living room. Davis would be there and Miriam would be here, and I'd make an over-the-shoulder scene. Well, Miriam came to me once and said, "Do you mind if I use this long cigarette-holder for this character?" I said no, I think that's right for her. Well, the camera's back of her and I'm shooting across her shoulder on Davis, and Miriam would take a puff of the cigarette and hold the cigarette right across Davis' face. And I said, "Oh, Miriam, please, honey." She said, "Oh, I was just trying to match up what I did before." Well, if she did it, then she did it deliberately, you see. Little things that she was always doing that I finally caught on to.

And Davis knew, of course, and would burn, you know. Well, it got so bad the last three weeks of doing that picture that Miriam would say to me, "Well, I know Bette doesn't like me, Vincent, etc., but I must do this and she must do so forth," and I said yes, yes. I'd then go to Davis, and Davis would say, "Now, she's going to do so-and-so, but, God darn it, this is my job and so forth." Anyway—they wouldn't speak to each other, you know.

I'd go to one dressing room and then the other dressing room, you see. Well, one day there was a scene which was around about five pages of dialogue between the two of them. Miriam said, "Vincent dear, couldn't we just sort of walk and feel around the thing ourselves without you telling us where to go and what to do?" I said, "Ladies, I would be happy if you staged the scene for me. It's five pages of dialogue, I've got them moving around and so forth, let's see how it feels, you know, fine." So Miriam opens the door, Bette comes into the room, they stand in the center of the room and they're each watching the other to see who's going to move first, and where, like two people onstage, so that they don't get upstaged. They stood right in the center of the room, didn't move for five pages.

The cameraman, Sol, looked at me and began to laugh. So I said, "Thank you, ladies, that's just right, you stood right in the center of the room and didn't move for five pages." Bette laughed. Then I began to stage the scene. As we progressed toward the big fight that the women had, one of the things that apparently Bette got annoyed about was that as they got older Miriam got younger. Bette said to me, "That bitch," she said, "you look at *Old Maid*. I get older and she gets younger. And she's doing the same damn thing here. I'm going to be looking old, she's going to be looking younger than she looked at the beginning." And Bette wanted to get older, you see, because she planned putting gray in her hair and so forth. Anyway, when we approached the scene of the fight, word got around the studio about this, that there had to be this scene where Bette came in and shook Miriam and threw her on the floor.

JK: And there had been no big blow-ups before that?

VS: Well, little bits here and there, you know, little bitchery. But I would say that Miriam was more guilty of that than Davis was. Miriam told me later something that was interesting: she said to me, "Vincent, I know this is Bette's home lot and I felt that you were going to protect her more than you would protect me." And I said, "Miriam, if my own mother was playing in it, I wouldn't protect one against the other. I'm protecting the picture, I'm protecting me. I'm not protecting you or Bette, I'm doing the best I can for both of you, and I have no personal feelings about it."

Warner called me up and I said, "Listen, *Life* magazine have heard about this fight with Davis and Miriam, and they want to come down and photograph that scene." He said, "I don't want any of that stuff, I don't think it's good for the picture, two dames hating each other. What they feel about each other is one thing, but I don't figure that's good publicity, you know, I'd rather not have it." I said, "It's up to you, Mr. Warner." He said, "Okay, just forget about it. I'm going to close the set when you get ready to do that."

Well, that morning as we were getting ready to do the scene, Bette said to me, "Now, Vincent, I'm going to shake Miriam, just as I have to do it, there's no way I can fake that." I said, "I expect you to do that, Bette, I want you to do what this calls for." And she said, "I hope she doesn't try to pull anything and start complaining about it, so just warn her that I'm going to do it." Then I got a call from Miriam: "Vincent, I know that she has to shake me, but I got up this morning with this terrible thing in my neck, and I hope that she won't overdo it because I know she doesn't like me, but she doesn't have to overdo it." And now comes the time to do this scene, and I staged it very carefully, and I said, "Ladies, let's rehearse it carefully so we know what we're doing, so we only have to do it once, because Miriam's neck is not right." So we got ready to do this scene, everybody is a little bit tense about it, and Bette starts shaking Miriam. Well, normally if somebody starts to shake you, you resist a little bit, you see, which makes you work harder with the shaking and looks better. Miriam went limp and her head went that way—

and when Bette got through, she turned to me and she said, "She just went limp," you know—which was unnatural-looking. Her head was wobbling around a bit and it just was not right.

Miriam didn't hear this because Bette went off the stage in a fury, slammed the set door. She really was burning. I went back to Miriam and I said, "I'm afraid it—it might look funny because your head was wobbling around like that." Well, she said, "I didn't want to fight her, I just wanted to let her do it." We did it once more and that time it was done well enough to be all right, and that's all there was to it.

So we got through the film all right and finished up and it really was fine so far as I was concerned. When I got through with the picture, Warner was very happy about it and proud of it and showed it up in his house to his friends and everything. And Blanke, he came to me and he said, "You know, Vince," he said, "you are really a woman's director. From now on you do the women's pictures." And I got stuck with it, I couldn't get away from it. I did that one with her, then I did another one with Ida [*Pillow to Post*], then I did *Mr. Skeffington* with Davis, and it went on like that.

JK: The two pictures you did with Bette Davis are sort of legendary. I've heard it said that on other films, not yours, she was so strong she directed them herself.

VS: Well, she is a very strong gal. We did not get along too well in *Skeffington*. I thought she went overboard.

Let me just say it was a very difficult time in her life. Now, when we finished *Old Acquaintance,* she and I had got along beautifully on the picture and everything was lovely. And I came to her and told her I'd read a script that I thought would be great for her, and this was *Mr. Skeffington*. She read it and subsequently she thought it marvelous and she said she'd love to do it. And we'd do it together. She went away for a vacation to Mexico, and when she came back, that's when her husband dropped dead on the street. Finally she was anxious to get back to work. She thought it would be good therapy for her. She just didn't feel like sitting at home. And Claude [Rains] was going to be marvelous in this picture, and he was. Anyway, we started the film and I don't know what it was, but Davis began to challenge things that I would say to her. Anyway, we came to the elderly part after Fanny Skeffington had had the illness.

That morning when she came down, she looked so hideous I said to her, "Bette, I'm very upset. I think that the woman should be affected, but I don't think she should become so hideous that it's hard to look at her." She said, "Don't worry about it, my audience likes to see me do this kind of thing." I said, "Well, I think it's hideous, it's too much."

Then came the aftermath of the illness and these lines on her face got heavier and heavier. So one morning I got hold of Perc Westmore, who was doing this makeup—the other thing is she would come in very early, like

5:00 in the morning, because it took her three hours to put this stuff on. Then by the time she got to the set at 9:00, she was jumping, like she was tight as a drum, for God's sake, because she would itch under all this rubber, you see, and it was very difficult. It was difficult for her, it was difficult for me to work with her.

JK: And Claude Rains?

VS: He was marvelous to her all the way through. Never had a moment of trouble with him. In fact, Claude was surprised at her behavior doing the thing. They admired each other. They were very good friends. But anyway it was difficult. So one day I went to Perc Westmore and I told him, I said, "Perc, she's getting to look like a mummy, for God's sake, and it's wrong. I have to stay away from the close-up stuff and I shouldn't be away from it. Please ease up on it. Don't say anything to her." Well, next morning I hear click click click, her heels coming onto the stage the way she walks, you know, and I can feel her standing on the edge of the set behind me. I looked round, she said, "How dare you speak to Perc Westmore behind my back and tell him to change my makeup? Why did you do it? Why didn't you speak to me about it?" I said, "For the same reason that you're acting this way now. It's gotten so difficult to talk to you," I said. "You seem to resent anything that I tell you. You challenge me and I don't want to go through the arguments, so I went to Perc and I told him that I think it's getting too heavy and I want him to go easy on the makeup, and Mr. Warner agrees with me." Well, she got angry and she walked away.

The problem with Bette was always holding her down. The problem with every great star is holding them down. Anyway, we got through the thing. After the picture was over, I met her on the lot one day and she said, "Mr. Warner called me last night and he was very happy about the picture." And I said, "Well, I'm glad he was, but I'm not." And she says, "Why not?" I said well, this is wrong, and that's wrong, and so forth. And she said, "Well, Mr. Warner's very happy with it." I said, "Well, that's good. He wants us to do another." They were talking about *Stolen Life*. And I said, "Well, Bette, I love working with you, and so forth, but I feel that *Skeffington* is not my picture completely, it's not yours completely, it's not anybody's picture. We'll have to have some kind of understanding, let's talk about it." She said something about, do you want me to be like one of these little girls who's just starting and you tell them everything to do? I said no, no, I've never been that kind of director, I don't have that kind of ego, and if an actor or an actress gives me an argument and it's a valid argument, I'll change it, for God's sake, I'll rewrite the whole script if they give me a valid argument and I find out I'm wrong. I learned a long time ago that the man who doesn't listen is a fool. If his ego is so big that he won't let anybody tell him anything, he's just an idiot. You become wiser the more you listen. You take what's good and you discard what you don't think is good. Well, she got very upset, and I said

I wouldn't work that way, and we just never did anything together after that. I'm sorry about it.

I remember when I was doing *The Unfaithful,* which was in fact a switch on the Somerset Maugham piece *The Letter*—anyway, let me tell you about this, although it's out of context. Jerry Wald came to me and said, "Vince, I've got a great property for you. I've bought James Cain's *Serenade.*" "*Serenade,*" I said, "isn't that the story of the young man who is a singer who gets involved with the older man who is a homosexual? Then things go wrong, according to Cain, the boy's voice changes because he's having an affair with a man." I was a bit skeptical of that, but Cain told me he based it on a true story. "So the boy runs away to Mexico and meets a Mexican whore and he regains his 'manhood' and then he comes back and he meets the older man again, but the Mexican girl kills the homosexual. How the hell are we going to do this?" Wald said, "Very simple, we'll just change the man to a woman." But I said, "What does one girl do for him that gives him his manhood that the other does for him which takes it away?" "Well, we'll figure it out. You go to Mexico and pick the location."

I came back and got the script and it was the same damn thing and you get to the obligatory scene and it makes no sense. "Jerry," I said, "I can't do this. I would not know what to tell the actors." "But it's already cast." He had Annie Sheridan as the whore and Dennis Morgan as the singer. "We'd better talk to Warner."

We go to Warner and he said, "Now, Vince, what's the problem?" I tell him the story, how the young singer loses his "timbre" when he falls for the man, etc., etc., and Warner looks at me and says, "What the fuck kind of story is that?" He had never read the book! He had no idea what the story was. So Warner said, "What are we going to do? We already have a cast." I said, "Jerry's got another property that he's titled *The Unfaithful,* a remake of *The Letter,* but it's about a divorce and a postwar marriage and so forth." Warner asked if we had a script, and I replied that we had a script that was not good but could be made good. "I believe if we get to work on it, in three or four weeks I can have something ready." Warner said he could not wait four weeks; shooting had to begin in a week or two, these people were all on salary, Zachary Scott and Lew Ayres had commitments.

I said I'd see what I could do and perhaps I could get them to start it without a full script. "No chance," said Warner. I said, "Let me talk to them." I get them all to the office and I told them the story and they agreed to do it, and I said I would have twenty pages by the following week. And this was how we started the picture, with twenty pages. I also gave them an outline of what the story was going to be from that point on, the basic concept of each scene, and I had their confidence and we began to shoot.

Two-thirds of the way through the picture Warner called me up and asked, "How are you feeling?" I said, "Fine." "Well, for God's sake, don't get sick 'cause nobody knows the hell what's going on but you. Is it going to come out all right, is it going to make any sense? It's the first and last time I go to the post without a script, nobody knows the hell what's going on." I said, "There'll be no problem, Mr. Warner, it'll be fine." We finished the picture and cut it and ran it at his house, and he said, "Goddamn, come up to the office, I want to talk to you." And he said, "Any sonofabitch that can make a picture without a script and make it come out like that can stay here as long as he likes." (I had two years of my contract to go.) He said I could have what I wanted, so I told him I wanted five years straight deal, no options, the money I wanted, and he said "You got it." Well, everything was fine, most of my pictures made money and he knew I had pulled him out of a hole several times.

JK: Both *Nora Prentiss* and *The Unfaithful* starred Ann Sheridan and belong to the category of films you made that might be classified as "women's pictures." Between *All Through the Night,* an early Bogart starring film, and *Adventures of Don Juan,* one of the last of Flynn's starring films, your films emphasized the female star. Do you prefer directing women?

VS: No, but after *Old Acquaintance* I just seemed to get a preponderance of the female stars at the studio. And then Goulding had left. I didn't mind, I was always going from one thing to another. I would love to have worked with Cagney and with Robinson, but I just never got a chance.

JK: It didn't become a case, as it did with Cukor, where a male star would say he didn't want to work with you because you favored the women?

VS: Not that I'm aware of. The way I got to do *Don Juan,* I didn't know at the time but I found out since. I was going to do *Johnny Belinda,* and Jean Negulesco was supposed to do *Don Juan.* All of a sudden I got a call from Warner saying come up to the office, I have to talk to you. He said, "You're going to do *Don Juan.*" I said, "Well, I thought Negulesco was doing that." He said, "Well, no, for some reason or other Flynn doesn't want him, he wants you." I said, "Why me? I've only met Errol." He said, "I don't know, he just decided, he felt you'd be good for him." I didn't know until later, oh, months later, when the picture was finished, that Annie Sheridan had called Flynn (they were very good friends) and said get Vince to do it because he'll play straight with you. She told me this herself.

JK: What did she mean by play straight?

VS: Well, that I would be on his side and not double-cross him with the front office.

JK: Was there a lot of that going on?

VS: Well, Flynn told me subsequently that he left [Raoul] Walsh because he said Walsh double-crossed him with the front office. I don't know whether that's true or not. Let me say, insofar as Flynn is concerned, he started out with Mike Curtiz, Mike made every one of his early pictures and did a hell of a job with him. Then he got sore with Mike and said, "I will not work with Curtiz again." Then he went to Walsh, then Walsh did every one of his pictures, about five in a row, did a hell of a good job with him too. Then he got sore with Walsh, you see. Walsh—when I finally got the picture, Walsh said, "Be careful, that sonofabitch will drive you out of your mind. He's dirty and he'll trick you." Oh, he was bitter about Errol—and Errol was bitter about Walsh. Errol wouldn't work now with Walsh and he wouldn't work with Curtiz.

JK: Two men who'd done so much to create the Errol Flynn image.

VS: That's right—you're damn right. Anyway, we went to work on it, and the first script that I read was a very charming little script. George Oppenheimer had written it and he said to me it's like a piece of Venetian glass. So I told Warner, "Oppenheimer says it's like a piece of Venetian glass." Warner says, "Oh, to hell with that. You know Flynn, he's either got to be fighting or fucking." They used to say, with Flynn it's got to be nuts or feathers, or something like that, see? He's either got to be in the saddle, or he's got to be wearing the costume. I found him a delightful guy—although he drove me out of my mind. He'd come in—on time, but only just. He said to me when we started, "Vince, I promise you I'm not going to drink. I don't want to be any trouble, I'll do what you tell me, don't worry about me, I know you've heard stories about me," and so forth. And I said, "Errol, I'm not worried."

My first job was getting the script fixed. A lot of the sets had already been built when I got on the picture. It was my first film in color. I didn't want to touch it because I knew it was going to be too expensive. But—when I went down to look at the sets, like that big staircase thing, oh, my God, that had already been built. Apropos of that, when I was shooting that sequence, I had 110 electricians on that set, and Trilling came down one morning, he looked at it and he says, "Good God! Where did this come from?" I said, "The set was built, Steve, before I was ever on it." But it was a pain in the neck to work with.

One significant thing happened on the picture, relating to Flynn, that I must tell you. At the end of about the fifth or sixth day of working he came over to me one day and he put his arm around me and he said, "You little sonofabitch, I really love to work with you, I really love you." And I said "Well, I love you too, Errol." Everything was going fine. At the end of the first week I was in his dressing room one morning and he had just opened in a film in New York, *Escape Me Never*. And he got very bad notices in that, and he said, "Oh, did you see the reviews from New York?" I said no. He said, "Oh, boy, they really love me." I read them and they said some very nasty things—they said in essence that without a horse or a gun in his hand or something, he was a bum. And that hurt him very much. Everybody used to think that he didn't give a damn about being an actor, or he kidded the whole thing: I think just the contrary was true. The next day, that's when he started drinking. He'd come in at 9:00, but he wouldn't come out of his dressing room until 11:00. He had some phony doctor who was always coming in and giving him shots, you see. And he was also having trouble at home with his wife. Little things happened that led me to believe that.

I always felt that Errol was like the Don Juan character himself, trying to prove himself constantly, and, so far as I know, he may have been an incipient homosexual. He certainly never practiced it, but in his treatment, in his attitude toward women, I felt that to some extent. He liked to debase a woman—I could tell in the way he talked about his mother—he's the first man I ever heard talk about his mother in a scurrilous manner. Loved his father, detested his mother. Then he would do . . . well, all kinds of things that would be . . . that would surprise me. And I know that once a girl came out of his dressing room, a youngster that he had, and she said: "He stinks." And then he designed his own costumes in that movie, and the cameraman said to me once, "I can't photograph that thing." The character didn't have a codpiece—this thing was sticking out to here, you know, in profile. It was all right straight on, but in a profile shot it was awful. So Nora, his wife, was in the dressing room that day and he showed her these pictures, and asked what do you think? And she said to him in front of me, "What did you do? Stuff a towel in it?" And he turned red in the face. I don't know what went on there, I don't know whether he was having some problems in life. But anyway he was a delightful guy to be with, just charming.

JK: It's a very stylish period film, though, visually beautiful, the costumes are. The fencing scenes are fabulous, some of the best ever, especially the climactic duel on the staircase.

VS: That took a long time to shoot. When I got the story, I started doing research in the whole Don Juan legend, and of course you know it goes way, way back. It was a serious play, the old Spanish play, and there had been half a dozen different versions of the damn thing. I felt that we couldn't do any of those very heavy, serious versions, this was supposed to be a little light piece of entertainment. But I had to put enough action in it to make it move along. Originally, it was a very lightweight piece—as George Oppenheimer said to me, it's like a piece of Venetian glass. Well, you can't do Venetian glass with Flynn—it was too delicate when I first got it. We had to goose it up in every place we possibly could. And I did some research and then I thought, well, what have I got to get to sell in this story? I can sell beauty, I can sell production values, pageantry and so forth, and I saw a chance to appeal to kids with the sword-drill stuff—I got a marvelous man in, Freddie Cavens, who was an instructor, I laid it all out with him, told him what I wanted to accomplish, and together we worked this out. He would be working while I was shooting another scene. Flynn got sick twice on the picture— we stopped once for two weeks, we stopped again for four weeks. In fact, between the first sequence and the second sequence, some of the kids in the school had grown two inches! I felt the thing to do was to put as much humor in it as possible. And to make it as beautiful to look at, as graceful as possible.

What happened on the film was that costs ran up. Warner would call me half a dozen times and say, "You tell that sonofabitch, you tell that so-and-so . . ." I was getting annoyed about it because I had to work with Flynn and he and I got along beautifully—and my wife loved to go to his house with the kids and everything. Personally, he was the most charming guy you could possibly meet. And I tell you he was very good. Very few people can wear a costume like he could; even though he was no great fencer, when he took that thing out, you thought that he was the greatest. Even if it was just one or two passes or something, but he did it with such style and such grace. Incidentally, if you see the film, you will notice that most of it is on one side of his face, because one side was good and the other was his bad side, and my sets were built so that he'd always come in like that. You'd never see round the other side.

JK: You worked with Joan Crawford three times? *The Damned Don't Cry, Harriet Craig* and *Goodbye, My Fancy*.

VS: Yes. She was a real pro, she was marvelous to work with—for any director. She knows her job. You don't have to tell her where to look to hit the light, and if you give her reasons why you're doing a thing, that's all right. You explain to her what you want done, why you want it done, that's it. She will sometimes make a suggestion—what you have to watch with her is also what you do with Davis, that it doesn't get too much. But apart from that . . . Very rarely you have to say to Joan it's not enough. Mostly what you have to say is it's a little too much, play it down a bit.

JK: I wonder what the situation at Warners was with Davis still top lady and Joan Crawford having this incredible peak in her career suddenly at the same time that Davis was just slipping. This was round the time of *Humoresque, Possessed, The Damned Don't Cry*.

VS: I don't know, I never discussed it with either one of them, but—I know that there was a great rivalry between them.

JK: Because Crawford suddenly got all the good films.

VS: That's right. I think Crawford always looked up to Davis, I think Crawford always felt that Davis was superior to her. And I understand Davis made some scurrilous remarks about Crawford, she said something—well, she says, "I wouldn't mind her personality if she could just act." And I was told that Davis once said that about her when they were working together on *What Ever Happened to Baby Jane?* I didn't hear it, but somebody told me that.

JK: How was she in comedy? Because she did very few comedies.

VS: I don't think either one of the ladies is what I would call a good comedienne. Davis just can't touch comedy at all, that's my opinion.

JK: Why? Because they're so heavy emotionally? They analyze everything too much? Overemphasize?

VS: I think so. Annie Sheridan was a good comedienne, Annie could throw things away. Whereas I don't think you could put Davis in *I Was a Male War Bride* and have her do it the way Sheridan handled it.

JK: How did you feel when you went back to Warners so many years later, especially after the way you left, when you came back to do *Ice Palace* and *The Young Philadelphians*? Was Jack Warner still there?

VS: Yes, Warner was still there. What happened was that I was a little bit bitter about Warner because I felt that in that time when I couldn't work he could have helped me, but he didn't; even after I was supposed to have been cleared, nothing happened. I went to Cohn and got involved in redoing *Garment Jungle* for him. Then I was in Europe, in London making a picture, *Naked Earth,* with Richard Todd and Juliette Greco. And the head of the studio there, Robert Clark, he said to me, "Jack Warner's in town." I said, "Oh?" He said, "He's coming out to the studio tomorrow. He asked about you." I said, "Oh, is that so?" "Yes, he probably will be round to see you." And I said, "Fine." So, sure enough, the next day Warner came down to the set. "Vince, how are you? Good to see you," so forth and so on. And then he said to me, "Listen, why don't you come back to Warners? It's your old home." Well, I was quite surprised to hear this. I wondered when this change of heart had taken place. And then he started telling me that he had some great scripts and that he had one script that he had given to Cukor, but Cukor was trying to get Olivier and somebody to do it, and Jack said to hell with it, I'm not going to bother about him or Olivier or whoever the hell it is, and says you do it. It was a script that Mervyn LeRoy did later with Jean Simmons, not a very good script.

JK: *Home Before Dark*?

VS: That's right. I read it and I didn't want to do . . . He said, "When you get back, come on out to the studio and have lunch and let's talk." So I came back to the studio, and we talked, everything was very pleasant and so forth. And he said, "Go up and talk to Steve Trilling and work out a deal." Well, they offered me one-third of what my salary had been when I last worked for them, and I said, "Why, that's ridiculous! If you want me, you want me; if you don't want me, you don't want me, that's all." "But it's been a few years since you made a film—" (I'd just finished two). And he said, "You don't know whether you're going to make one while you're here or not, if you come back, whether it will work out or not. I'll tell you what to do," he said, "if you make a film in the first year that you're here, we'll give you a bonus to make up for the lack of the salary. So consider this like a drawing account." I said, "Okay, that's a different thing." . . . I did *The Young Philadelphians* for them. I was there about nine months and they were very happy with me.

1975

JUNE
DUPREZ

S HE WAS THE PRINCESS in Korda's *The Thief of Bagdad,* a film I've never forgotten. I first spoke with her—June Duprez—some ten years ago in the showroom of one of London's leading fashion designers, Bill Gibb. It was really Bill's partner, who knew of my enthusiasm for *The Thief of Bagdad,* who called me and said, "Guess who's here?" and put me on the phone to June, who listened, eyes growing large with astonishment, as I quoted to June from the film:

"Where have you come from?" "From the other end of time."
"Why have you come?" "To find you."
"Now that you have found me, how long will you stay?" "Until the end of time."

It's the first exchange in the film between the Princess and the King, whom she mistakes for a genie in the pool of her garden, and now it was the first exchange (though one-sided) between June and myself and all she could do was laugh.

After that, we met, and over the years she would be a guest at my house, and vice versa, but June never showed a desire to talk about her film career, and this film even less so. I'd show her the film and quote more lines of dialogue to her. She said it was so long ago, and claimed a bad memory. If she didn't remember the film . . . well, I did.

I was eight. My sister was four. Mom was ill. Dad was out of town. It was winter, very cold; the torn-up ground hedging the borough at the edge of the city was slippery with ice. It was a Wednesday, there was no school Wednesday afternoons; and with the money to buy a ticket for a movie that Saturday, I didn't care about the cold air. I ran to get that ticket, just to possess it, hold it in my hand even though I couldn't go till Saturday. Mom needed me today and our deal was that in exchange for the money I'd return straight home. But movies were the opium and I was hooked and hungry. As I stood in the slow-winding queue waiting my turn, my resolve crumbled. When the woman behind the glass said, "When?" I said, "Now." I couldn't resist the world of Technicolor poster adjectives, the death of a thousand stings, the blue rose of forgetfulness, the pink elephant. The aroma of chocolate from the confectionery counter added its arguments; you could taste the movie. What if I did get home a *bit* later? I figured out that if I walked home slowly *with* the ticket, I would get back only a little bit earlier than if I saw the film now and ran home. A half-hour difference at most. I was in my seat.

The music, the color: *The Thief of Bagdad*. The giant red sails drove that ship into the harbor of Basra with me on board. And then it was over. Achmed, the King, had his Princess; the villainous Jaffar was dead; and Sabu, the little Thief, was flying off on his magic carpet to new adventures.

But, outside, it was suddenly dark. My half-hour's difference had tricked me. To make up for the stolen afternoon, guilt—not cold—shot me home. At eight your legs are as strong as your ability to delude yourself and who knew? Flushed cheeks and heavy panting might be an exonerating touch when I had to explain.

Even as I saw the house, the first one in the square, I had a queasy sensation. The door to our apartment on the second floor was open. People were inside. From the doorway I saw Mom lying on the living-room couch, eyes red, sobbing, terribly upset. I looked for my sister. I couldn't see her. Only my mother, she raised her hand, but was too weak to do more than shake it and cry, "You . . . you . . ." which made me feel worse than when she'd been strong enough to hit me. From the way everybody looked, I knew somehow it was my fault. "That kid, always at the movies." "You shouldn't give in to him so much, Paula." "All he does is go to movies." Something was terribly wrong and it was because I had gone to the movie. While I'd been away, Mom needed some milk for our supper and had sent my sister to fetch it. The route kids took to the store was through a rundown park in which the heavy snows had covered the slippery rocks and the holes left unfilled from old bomb explosions. Postwar reconstruction hadn't gotten round to suburban playgrounds. The holes made great hiding places. But Monica, my sister, carrying the cold milk bottle in her little hands, had slipped and fallen; the bottle had smashed and cut open her face. Crying, the skin hanging loose, blood pouring down, she had somehow stumbled home. They had rushed her to the hospital. She never cried when they sewed up her face. She was so brave. Now, more than thirty years later, you only see the scars if you know where to look.

That drama became woven into my memories of *The Thief of Bagdad*, giving it a special significance. Not all my movie-going memories are that traumatic, but for a long time the exiled young King was I, the raven-haired Princess for whom he risked his life was my sister, and the dangers he faced were like those in the world in which they lived.

Years later, in London, standing in line at my bank one day, I spotted the actress Mary Morris, who'd played Halima, the sinuous-voiced agent of the demoniac Wazir. Miss Morris, small, her hair cropped short, bicycle clips fastened to her baggy-trousered legs, her pinched face turned severely toward me, was a bit annoyed when I recognized her . . . not from a recent performance on

June Duprez, photographed for *The Thief of Bagdad* (United Artists), 1939

TV, but from a film she'd made thirty-five years earlier. "You were marvelous in that great film." "I've done better things since," she replied in a reprimanding tone. "Nothing better than that," I told her.

Later the film's designer, Vincent Korda, brother of the producer Alexander Korda, was bemused by my passion for the film. He possessed no sketches, though his studio was covered with paintings and samples from some of the other projects he'd worked on. He did think that maybe he'd better look at the film again. There I left things until finally I decided to pinpoint June, the Princess of the story.

In one of the most ravishing buildups to an actress, the magician who first saw her in his magic crystal praises her beauty: "Her eyes are Babylonian eyes, and her eyebrows like the crescent moon of Ramadan." When you first saw June on top of her pink elephant, you knew what Conrad Veidt, as Jaffar, meant. Her role in one of the great works of cinematic fantasy, Alexander Korda's dream project, which has found few equals, should have launched June on a brilliant starring career. For the Princess, as much as Vivien Leigh's Scarlett, Arletty's Garance (in *Les Enfants du Paradis*) or Louise Brooks' Lulu (in *Die Büchse der Pandora*), was a pivotal character, a woman who, though always true to herself, becomes the obsession of many different people.

But now in her garden flat the Princess was still reluctant to remember. Rather naïvely, I put her reticence down to vanity, to not wanting to be reminded that she'd made the film forty-five years ago. (June didn't look that much older even then.) But that wasn't the reason. Her reluctance traced back to what happened to her career after the film premiered in America and she became the outsider at her own party.

June was just twenty years old when she made it, Korda's latest discovery, following on the heels of his earlier star-spotting successes, Vivien Leigh and Merle Oberon. June would appear to have been on the brink of international stardom. By the time the film launched in Los Angeles, war had broken out in Europe and she had to pursue her career in America. And nobody wanted her.

The sardonic twist in June's life forged a fascinating link with the fortunes of those other actresses, Louise Brooks and Arletty. After *Pandora,* Louise returned to America and a rapid descent into oblivion as far as her film career was concerned. After *Les Enfants,* Paris was liberated and glorious Arletty found herself a prisoner under sentence of death, and her career in ruins. *The Thief of Bagdad* found June in Hollywood, stranded, deserted.

Forty-five years, three husbands, two grown daughters and a grandson later, she was back in London. Her story is a cliché of the tales one hears of what happens to young girls in Hollywood.

JD: I've always gotten along frightfully well with other women. I like to think it's because I'm not bitchy myself and other women recognize it. And in all my life I've only met two bitches: Wendy Barrie and Merle Oberon. They were both ex-Korda girls. Maybe that's the reason.

Korda, Oberon, *The Thief of Bagdad* . . . now we are remembering. One moment at Korda's Denham studio near London, sitting on top of a pink elephant, clearly a potentially enormous new British star. And the next moment, in Hollywood . . .

JD: The night of the Hollywood premiere of *The Thief of Bagdad,* I wasn't invited to anything afterward. Nothing happened. My mother had come over to America to join me and be with me for a while. I didn't want her to go back to England because of all the bombs, so I sent her on to Australia, where she was born and where she had two spinster sisters. But she was in Hollywood for the opening of *The Thief of Bagdad*.

In those days everyone went to Ciro's after a premiere. So we went . . . and quite near us was this enormous table with Korda and Merle Oberon and everyone. Myron Selznick, who was at that table, came over and said, "June, why aren't you here with us?" And I said, "I was never invited."

JK: Why wouldn't Merle Oberon have invited you? You were the star of the movie, after all.

JD: I heard something. Some things came back to me. There was some sort of skulduggery going on. I seemed to be sort of blackballed from practically every studio. This wasn't because of my not re-signing with Korda.* He wasn't that type of man. There's something to do with Merle Oberon. It all sort of came to me in funny ways. The composer Miklos Rozsa,† who was a great friend of mine, was also handled by Selznick, and he heard various things . . . though I really can't remember now what they were. Anyway, Merle did behave very, very badly. Myron made her phone me and apologize . . . say something to me about why I hadn't been invited to the party. It must have looked terrible. She was the hostess, after all, the hostess of the party for the film in which I was the star!‡

So she phoned me. Mind you, she'd known me in England, very slightly; then I was financially secure, had a very well-known husband, had a lovely home. But now I was all alone in California, and she'd never contacted me or done anything at all. Nothing, not a phone call even, until this time when she said, "Ohhh, Myron said that I behaved very badly and that I'm to apologize." And that was exactly how she put it. I never heard another word from her. Not a word. I was so upset that night that I really don't

---

*June had told me about signing on with the agent Myron Selznick, who was renegotiating her contract with Korda. The deal fell through when Selznick, feeling he could do better for his new client, asked for too much.

†He wrote the music for many of Korda's films—*Knight Without Armour, Four Feathers, Jungle Book*—and went on to become one of Hollywood's foremost film composers.

‡Merle was by then married to the film's producer, Alexander Korda.

remember if anybody except Myron came over to me. You see, I was so young . . . what was I? Twenty-two? A twenty-two-year-old girl then was very different from a twenty-two-year-old girl today. I just couldn't handle that sort of situation. And at the premiere they had a statue of me, wearing one of the original costumes, standing out front of the cinema, looking into the pool, as in the film.

I suggest to June that the fact that Merle, who had taken over from Norma Shearer as one of Hollywood's leading hostesses, did not invite June to the opening-night party was like telling Hollywood that June was *persona non grata.*

JD: Yes. Of course, I'm sure that's what happened. I don't know why she would have done this. We only met once on screen for that little scene we did together in *The Lion Has Wings.** An hour and a half our scene took to shoot, that was all. I was working on *Thief* at the time, and they didn't even bother to change my makeup. I still had the slanted eyebrows to make me look exotic in that scene I did with Merle. I was meant to be British, of course, but all they did was to take off my wig. I never understood it [Merle Oberon's behavior in Hollywood]. Never. Certainly she had no reason to be jealous of Korda and me. I always called him Mr. Korda. He certainly didn't appeal to me one little bit. And I obviously didn't appeal to him in that way. . . .

Ohhh, wait! This is like psychoanalysis. You're bringing back all sorts of things I'd completely forgotten. We *had* met before. At the opening night of *Four Feathers* in London.† That's it! It was televised in color, because I remember I had to have color makeup on for the cameras. After or before the film, there was a dinner, and Merle and I were seated on either side of Alexander Korda, and . . . oh, this is really very petty, I can't believe this would explain it, but . . . we were dressed almost identically. I had a magnificent white lace dress on, a magnificent dress with a low neckline, and Guy [Beauchamp, June's husband] had borrowed a magnificent diamond necklace from Gerrard's of Regent Street for me to wear. They were very famous jewelers, and Guy had bought me some jewelry from there before, and they were quite pleased to loan it for the occasion. Well, Merle was wearing a white dress and a diamond necklace as well. It was probably her own necklace. It could have been borrowed . . . but we were so alike, sitting on either side of Korda. And was there some comment? People said I was a young Merle Oberon. Oh, well, it's unbelievable. I was in Hollywood and there was no work offer.

If there was some other reason, June didn't remember. But one can speculate on it, and on the socially very ambitious Tasmania-born Queenie O'Brien

---

The Lion Has Wings was a British propaganda film which went into production four days after the outbreak of war in 1939. Korda used all of his available stars, some of them, like June, in what were really just "guest roles."
† June had the female lead in that classic adventure story.

Thompson, the half-caste girl whose roots were in India but who rose to the top of the Hollywood tree by gathering her haitches as to the British manner born and impressing all the H-Hollywood crowds with them. But in England Merle's background was no secret, and there she was, dividing her spotlight with the new, up-and-coming and socially prominent young star in Korda's stable. If she wanted to get her own back for that one-upmanship at the premiere, London wouldn't be the place for her to do so. But in Hollywood Merle was in her element. The result was like one of those Grimms' fairy tales, the one about the princess and her maid traveling to another city . . . but the maid gets there first, pretends to be the princess and marries the prince. When the real princess arrives, no one knows her and she finds work in the stables.

JD: And then, finally . . . I don't know how I got those little jobs; I suppose I must have found myself some little agent somewhere. I was no longer with Myron Selznick's agency. I suppose he dropped me because he couldn't do anything for me. He never talked to me about it. And they all thought I was Oriental! It was absurd. I'm not. Merle was.* Oh, well, that was a known fact. My mother was Scottish, my father was American of French and German parentage. So the Scottish-French-German-American made me look like this.

JK: Your father [the actor-producer Fred Duprez] was well established in the British entertainment business?

JD: Yes, he was. He produced plays, he directed, he performed in some of his own comedies. He was sort of a Will Rogers, where he did monologues, sitting up onstage. I didn't see him very much, I was never even allowed to see him onstage. Hardly ever. But I have a brother, who is fourteen months older, and our father was totally against either one of us having anything whatsoever to do with the theater. The German side of him made him very strict. My mother was very gentle, always had tremendous theatrical longings herself back in Australia. I was sent to boarding school at the age of seven, which in those days was pretty young to go to boarding school. He wanted me so far away from any theatrical atmosphere or people, or anything else. He just didn't think it was, well . . . in those days it wasn't quite . . . *He* was in it, yes, but for a woman, for a girl, it was never quite respectable for a girl in England until Sarah Churchill started.†

It was always a little bit dizzy for a girl to be connected with the theater or anything like that. And I think he thought it would be a very unhappy sort of experience for me. But I didn't find his attitude strange, no. No. I remember the first . . . funny, this came to me only yesterday . . . the first knowl-

---

*Oberon was the daughter of a British father and an Indian mother, a fact Oberon played down in Hollywood, introducing her mother as her maid.

†Sarah, the daughter of England's wartime Prime Minister, Winston Churchill, appeared onstage and in films, including *Royal Wedding* opposite Fred Astaire.

edge that I knew I wanted to be an actress, or that I knew that there was something there.

I suppose my father knew somebody who wanted a little girl for—well, they weren't called commercials then, they were advertisements that were screened in cinemas. And I remember I was just home from my first term at boarding school, I think I was seven, and this advertisement was for Ovaltine. They came to the house and it was summertime; we were out in the garden, and the scene was supposed to be that I was riding in the garden on my cycle with my dog. I fell off my cycle, ran to Mommy, she took me up on her knees and then I burst into tears, I had the Ovaltine, and felt so much better. They were wondering, "How ever is this child going to ever burst into tears?" And I did it. I just did it on cue. I made myself do it by thinking of something that made me cry, like having to go back to boarding school. I wept and wept and wept. And it was so marvelous, being able to turn it on. I think *that* was the moment I knew I wanted to be an actress.

And then, of course, I wanted to be a ballerina. That was allowed. I could have ballet lessons for deportment and all that sort of thing. But the sad thing was, as a little girl, I was very plain and thin, and I had this straight, dark hair with a fringe, the way children wear it, and I was always cast as the boy. If there was a pantomime, I was always the principal boy . . . and I wanted to be the principal girl. I was brought up to think that I was very plain. Nobody wanted me to grow up conceited. I never liked my looks, not till a long time afterward, after I'd been on the screen for quite some time. Finally, I convinced my father to let me go on the stage. Actually, my mother convinced him because she saw this urge in me, and she wanted it for me.

Well, by the time I was seventeen, I was allowed to go with Ann Casson [Sybil Thorndike's daughter], we were both sort of chaperoned, to the Coventry Repertory Company, as a student. My father realized that I was set and he really thought this would kill my ambition. I had to paint the scenery and sit in the "prompt" corner. Never a darn thing to do, or perhaps a bit as the maid with one line. There were two performances nightly; you worked all day and sat in the prompt corner all night. And then I got my big chance, because I had rather exotic looks even then . . . to play Tondelayo in *White Cargo*. I went to a chemist and got some permanganated potash and stained myself all over. I was so young, so innocent. I remember I was supposed to sidle up to the man and get very close to him with my body. My bottom stuck out because I was too shy, and I sort of put my face next to him, but couldn't get myself to bring my bottom or my body next to him. Anyway, it was a great success . . . except that I couldn't play another role for three weeks until the stain had worn off.

Well, by that point I met Guy Beauchamp, who then had a house and was practicing gynecology in Warwickshire. It was terribly embarrassing because, as I mentioned, there were two performances every night and after every single performance I was handed the most enormous bouquet of flow-

ers. That often happens that some of the fans or admirers would bring bou-
quets on the second Saturday-night performance. But every single performance I had this *enormous* bouquet . . . because by then Guy was very much
in love with me, you see. When I was working at Coventry, I wasn't earning
a living. My mother actually yanked me out when she discovered that I was
smoking; she saw nicotine on my fingers. But it was coming to the end of the
season anyway, and Guy wanted to move to London. And we became engaged after that. And once I was married, I could do as I damn well pleased.

Ida Lupino and I became friends when we made that film [*Forever and
a Day*, RKO, 1943], both being English and both of us being interested in
music. We wrote a couple of songs together. At that time I was still living in
a lovely apartment with a grand piano . . . that was the time when Harry
Cohn tried to break in . . . and Selznick too . . . but there was a grand piano,
and I thought I'd try to write some songs. I'd had all of this classical education. I wrote something and later, at a party, Hoagy Carmichael was there. I
gave him the lead sheet and he wanted to buy it and put his name on it. Just
the melody. I thought if it was good enough for him to buy, it was good
enough for me. I said, "No." I wrote lyrics too, and somehow I got some
publisher. This was at the time of the rhumba, all the Mexican, South American music was becoming very popular in America. They offered me a job
writing lyrics for all this new South American music. I didn't want to do that
particularly, I was much more interested in the music side of it. I did write
one that eventually was performed on the air, on Johnny Mercer's program in
New York. And Jo Stafford and Paul Weston recorded it. I wish I had a copy
of that . . . it got lost. But, ohhh, I hated my voice. How funny you should
like it. I hate my voice now, can't bear it. Well, that's beside the point.

The Coventry Rep experience didn't lead to anything because I got married. And then, I don't know how it happened, but I was asked to do some
sort of a second female role in a tryout play at Richmond Theater. I loved
doing that. I was pretty terrible really, but I certainly had self-confidence.
You see, when I became engaged to Guy, I just wanted to get married and
have children. He never wanted to feel that because I was so young and he so
much older, he was stopping me from a budding career. So he urged me, he
urged me, urged me on. It was very sad because he was hoisted on his own
petard, because he became so insanely jealous and I became so frightened of
him, which was why, when Korda asked me to go to America, I went . . .
not saying that I wouldn't come back. Guy had become insanely jealous of
me, and it later turned out that he used to have me followed.

So then how *did* she first meet Korda and sign with London Films? There was
a long pause. For a long time now June had been better at forgetting about her
old career, her early days, than she was at remembering any of them. When her
films were on TV, she didn't watch them and certainly never told anyone else
about them. She had hardly a single photo of herself other than those that show

her as mother or as granny or with friends on lawns or in houses, and these are
the sort of snapshots that tell you absolutely nothing about a person's other life
outside of family and friends. What was more, June had never even expressed
a desire to see pictures of herself from any of her films. So now, asking about
Korda, there's the usual long pause, and . . .

JD: Ohhh, yes. I remember, yes, I know what it was. It was only one week, this
play at Richmond, but an agent saw me there and thought that perhaps I
should make some sort of film test. I suppose we, Guy, paid for the film test
because he really was encouraging me. But the agent was very clever, he
must have seen something in me, I suppose. He chose a scene—*Winterset*?—
where I could just stand in front of the camera and do it by myself. And I
remember he put me in a black raincoat. I think he thought I had a look like
Margo at that time, and that's why he picked that scene for me to do. And he
took that, I think, to Korda.

Now I remember. I thought I'd met Korda socially somewhere, but I'd
forgotten that screen test. And Korda saw something in that, and at the time
he was looking for somebody for *Four Feathers* [UA, 1939]. And it was a
perfect vehicle for someone new. The part was too small for someone established and too important to cast with just anyone. He wanted someone new. I
mean, it was a brief role, but the only girl, and a wonderful showcase. I met
Korda, and he had a test made of me. It was nerve-racking because they were
testing every young actress in England at the time; I can remember Dorothy
Hyson, Dorothy Dickson's daughter, because she was there the same day. I
did want to act. And I wanted to act well. I've *always* been a perfectionist.
Remember those little canvas chairs that have your name on them? "MISS
DUPREZ" and so forth? Mine was "WORRIER" because I worried and worried,
and I worked and worked and *cared* so desperately. As far as I was concerned, I was never torn between my social life and my career, not in England
where Guy encouraged me to go ahead, nor in Hollywood. So long as I was
acting, I was going to be the "best." Until "Mr. Right" came along and I
could have my babies! I never sort of split myself in that sense. They were
absolutely separate, those two desires.

JK: What was Alexander Korda like?

JD: *Terribly* impressive. I was *terrified*. This *enormous* room in this beautiful
house in Denham; and he was behind this *gigantic* desk, and I practically
trembled, and for years I always used to call him Mr. Korda. He used to put
the fear of God into me. Oh, he was sweet, and nice, and kind, but he was
miles away. I was always rather frightened of him. He said very little to me.
I went through agony waiting to know if I were doing *Four Feathers* or not. I
think I first read about having gotten it before I was told. It was a long time
before I knew, and by then I wanted it desperately, having made the test.

JK: So it wasn't a pleasant experience?

JD: Ohhh, now I do remember something rather nice in there that happened during the making of *Four Feathers*. That's when I started to hate my voice, because Soli [the film's director, Korda's brother Zoltan] used to make me say a word over and over again because of this drawing out of the vowels I did. And I know I do it now and I hate it and I can't stop it or control it; never have been able to. But anyway, for that scene we were all at the dinner table where the card is handed around, and he's been given the card and she realizes that he—the hero of the tale, who's been given the white feather and who has gone off into the Sudan to redeem himself in the eyes of his friends—is still alive, and looks at the card and starts to cry. And it was so nice because the whole crew applauded after it. That was exciting. Lovely. I felt so terribly insecure with that cast: Ralph Richardson, C. Aubrey Smith, John Clements . . . Clements wasn't so nice to work . . . well, he was all right . . . he's just absolutely . . . as a performer he thinks only of himself. He doesn't really *give* anything of himself, or help one. Richardson was lovely, but I was rather in awe of him.

We broke off to have dinner; she'd cooked a superb wine-sauced breast of chicken. We had cigarettes, an after-dinner drink. And now, laid out on the coffee table were my stills from *The Thief of Bagdad*. The silver-rich photographic paper gave the burnished images an even richer, subdued, magical sheen. June noticed the production stills, the off-set shots, with Michael Powell (one of the directors of the film) standing beside a ship docked—I thought in a seaport somewhere on the English coast—talking to Korda, hat on head and cigar never out of his mouth, pointing to some work going on at the side; Conrad Veidt, always in turban, listening intently to director Ludwig Berger (the first director on the film, but taken off it when partway into the production because his view of the film differed from Korda's); and a shot of Mary Morris, who played Halima and the eight-armed dancing silver doll in whose arms the toy-crazed Sultan finds the embrace none of his wives could give him: death.

Picture after picture: the stars' stand-ins, June's, Conrad Veidt's, John Justin's and Sabu's, sitting in a corner of the set around a little card table, concentrating on the cards in hand; and the magnificent costumes . . .

JD: They had real gold thread in them. Oliver Messel did the costumes. Ohhh, at the time it was the most expensive movie ever made in Britain. But you know what's so amazing? You know when you're young and someone aged forty looks awfully old to you? I never realized how young Korda was. He looks young to me now, and I've always remembered him as being old. Ohhh, but I love all these pictures to do with the production. I've never seen any of them. And here I am climbing up a ladder to get on top of the pink elephant! Ohhh, good Lord! Mary Morris! Doesn't she look marvelous here? Beautiful. Oh and, heavens, Rex Ingram. And there's me bicycling on the set. That's my bicycle, the one I rode to and from location on every day, with the lights out. But it didn't look that beautiful on the screen, did it? The sets? There's something about these black-and-white pictures that is beautiful. Well, and Georges Perinal's camera work.

Then we come across a photograph of June looking not so much Oriental as Babylonian.

JD: That was Ludwig Berger's idea. He had my hair all curled into ringlets, and he had me do funny things in the test, he made me sort of use my hands like this . . . [Her fingers curled inward to match the curls of her hair; the look was something akin to paintings on shards of old Mesopotamian pots or fragments of old temple walls.] Whenever I spoke, my hands sort of going around. And Alex didn't like it and fired him. The whole thing was changed and I got this straight wig.

JK: Did you like what Berger was trying to do?

JD: He was very difficult to understand, because he gave you no *reasons*. He was just sort of technical, technical in the sense that René Clair was technical. But I remember this scene, and it was all close-up, and my hair was all closely sculptured. This was his whole vision of the way this girl should look. It's unusual, more interesting. I think he shot very little. Well, I only know about my scenes, and he didn't shoot many of those for the actual finished film. I was frightened and overawed by him; remember, I was very inexperienced. Mind you, his version of the film might have been much more wonderful than Korda's . . . I don't know. Michael Powell did a lot of the second-unit work, and he shot some of my scenes. I don't recall Korda directing any scenes, not any with me in them. He was involved with every aspect of the film, I know that; but he wasn't much on the set when I was there. And Zoltan directed a lot. The long black wig, that was the Korda look. Of course, the film had a wonderful unity, no matter who directed . . . it was all kept of a piece. And then William Cameron Menzies did all of the design of the film. How strange that I don't remember any water there.

The water was in a picture of the boats in the busy, bustling port of Basra, which must have been shot in a tank or on the coast, I thought.

JD: Ohhh, yes. We got on the boat from the fields. It was built out there in the fields outside Denham. There was no water. They must have spliced that in later. Yes. Menzies did the major part of the design. Vincent Korda did the actual sets, but Menzies designed the *entire* film, and directed all the miniature work. All of this would be his design, frame by frame. I was never in any of the things he worked on, but I met him; he was a charming man. And he was very sweet to me when I arrived in Hollywood. He gave me quite a few words of warning, oh, yes, about the men in Hollywood, and how they all talk and how ghastly they all are. He was so sweet.

JK: Did Menzies work well with Korda?

JD: You see it was shot over such a *long* period of time and there were so many different directors on the film. Well . . . I've never seen Selznick work, but, from what I've heard, he worked pretty much like Korda. One got used to having different people working with one on different scenes. It was a little bit of a shock when Ludwig Berger left, of course, because one began with him. But the whole thing was done over two years. Also, there was so much done when I wasn't there, when I wasn't on the set. There were weeks and weeks and weeks when different units were directing. Michael Powell was the actual official second-unit director.

I wasn't aware of Berger being fired. I wasn't aware of these things. Or the way things worked. It wasn't a shock for me the way it was for Vivien Leigh and the cast [of *Gone With the Wind*] when George Cukor was let go. I've got a funny feeling that I had a sense of relief when he left. Yes . . . I think I felt very uncomfortable working with him. Had he explained, or had he been an Odets and said, "Look, you are this and you feel that . . . ," then you'd know what you're doing, you wouldn't just be doing it because you were told to move your hands left here and right there. I think . . . I think it was a slight sense of relief.

JK: These sort of goings-on weren't things you'd discuss with your co-stars like Conrad Veidt or anyone?

JD: Veidt would never discuss anything with me anyway. I was like a little child beside him. He was simply playing his role. There was *no* rapport between us. Well, I *was* the same age as his daughter. We . . . well, I never got a whole script all at once. It just came along in sections. First of all, there were little scenes that they were going to try. And one of my first scenes was when I was lying on the bed and the Prince comes to see her and she's in the enchanted sleep. It all segued in, it all took so long, all the preparation. It was a lovely thing to be in, but it wasn't all of one piece; it was all over the place, and I was never on location anywhere. The scene where I'm on board the ship preparing to throw myself into the ocean was shot on the grounds of Denham. I was standing on grass with a lot of wind machines blowing at me.

I used to have to get up at five, five-thirty to be in the studio by quarter to seven for makeup and hair; and very often then they worked till after midnight. Ohhh, those were long hours, hours in which you did nothing, just sat around and waited. There was no union control. Then there were weeks when you didn't work at all. It was so massive that there was no feeling of being a company, as it were. Everything took *days* to shoot. I had a caravan on the grounds when we were shooting out of doors. I used to play with Conrad Veidt's daughter, she was the only one I had to talk to.

The war hadn't begun yet; one didn't think it would. And there was no shortage of materials. No, you see, war was declared in '39, but the production had begun in late '38 or early '39. It was so near completion before war started. We hadn't done various sorts of location shots that we would have gone abroad to do. It was only because of the war that Korda decided to move the whole thing to America and use the Grand Canyon. There was no thought before of ever going to America and using the Painted Desert and the Grand Canyon. But none of those scenes actually concerned me.

June is referring to the scenes when Abu, played by Sabu, is washed ashore on a deserted beach, finds the bottle, uncorks it, and out of it, in a mushrooming swirl of smoke, comes the long-imprisoned, revenge-seeking Genie; their subsequent flight (special effects) to the temple of the all-seeing-eyed Goddess; his reunion with Achmed, the King, in the mountain pass, and the subsequent destruction of the magical eye before Abu finds the flying carpet and the arrows of justice, with which the little Thief manages to save the day just before the lovers are sentenced to the death of a thousand stings. None of these scenes, nor the special effects accompanying them, included June.

JD: I never did any location shots. The furthest away I went were the grounds of Denham studios, where they had the ships [supposedly anchored in the seaport of Basra]. The scenes that had me on the rocks with John Justin [the romantic King] were also shot here in England.

Korda just went on spending and spending and spending, because this was his personal project, and time and money were no object. I remember, during one of the periods when I wasn't doing anything, I got terribly *fat*, and Irving Asher, who worked for Korda, came and gave me a lecture. I used to eat chocolate bars and things. I had to go on a diet. It was very serious. I'm frightfully fat in some parts of the film because I went up and down. Well, there were these *hours* with nothing to do except eat chocolate bars. And ohhh, there must have been a million changes in the script. The whole thing to me is utter confusion and an enormous amount of time. And for a time I was staying in an inn near Denham, on those lovely grounds near the studio. I remember I used to go riding every evening with an Army colonel. Just as something to do. But . . . the first time I saw the completed movie was the night at the premiere in Los Angeles. And then, as you know, I was so unhappy, I blotted most of my reactions and thoughts about it *out!*

There I was, stuck in America. You see, when I came to America with Korda, I stayed in America—not because of the war, but because I was married at the time to Guy and I wanted to be free of him. That's why I stayed behind in the States. It *killed* me not to be in my own country during the war. I remained simply so that Guy would divorce me for desertion. There was nothing else to keep me there. Nobody . . . no film company was after me or anything like that. I was still signed to Korda, of course, and in the meantime I had been taken on by the Myron Selznick agency. He was a good agent, *but* . . . My contract was due, and I was getting something like $200 a week. You see, when I signed with Korda, I didn't have to work for a living. I was in England, I was married, I didn't *have* to work to earn a living. But then, when I came to America, things were very difficult. Because I couldn't get any funds from England, because of the war. Nothing at all. And I still wanted this separation from Guy.

JK: And Myron couldn't get you work?

JD: Well, I had signed a seven-year contract with options; it was an option that came up in Hollywood. Myron was handling it and, being very high-powered, said, "We won't accept this option unless the salary is increased" to some outrageous, ridiculous amount, oh, I don't know, thousands and thousands. Now, Korda was back in England at this time, so he [Selznick] had to negotiate with his legal man, who turned it down. I mean, he called Myron's bluff and said, "Very well, we won't renew the contract." Which they didn't do. And here I was, Myron Selznick asking enormous sums of money for me and having let me go from Korda. So Myron . . . he kept me out . . . *he* kept me *out* as much as anyone by the price he was putting on my head. *He* could *afford* to ask it, all his clients were huge stars; *I* was the one who would be out of work and starving. [Merle Oberon, Mrs. Korda, was one of Myron's clients.]

And now I was typed as some sort of Oriental princess, and nothing happened. Not a single offer. I was desperate. In the end, I had to do serials, like *Tiger Fangs*. I had sold all of my jewelry, I was desperate. I tried to get work in an aircraft factory so I could be sort of on the lookout during the day and earning money at night, but I couldn't get a job because I wasn't all American. I was half English.

JK: You were *that* desperate? But didn't you know anyone who might . . .

JD: I knew a few people in Hollywood because I had introductions from a very, very old friend of mine, Barcley Ormrod. But those were social introductions only, Pasadena and that crowd, nobody to do with the film world at all. I didn't know how to fight this. And it *wasn't* as if this was my first film. I'd already done *Four Feathers* and that had been a great success. But now I had to start from scratch.

Oh, but the loneliness was awful. And there were all the nasty agents who made passes and all that sort of thing. Word even got around that I must be a lesbian. I mean, "There must be something wrong with her, you know, because . . ." You know, "What's wrong with her?" Just as they used to say, "She's putting on this English accent. She's been here nine months and she still sounds English, so she's affected. She ought to be talking like us now." It was all very different in those days. People were very cruel. Hedda Hopper had a nasty thing . . . ohh, and Jimmie Fidler first, he came first; something he said on the air, "June Duprez was heard to say that she hates America and Americans. Did she say this?" Of course, I was in an absolute *state,* and,

being English, I said I'd sue for libel. But he was protected because he had
said, "*Did* she say this?"

JK: But you stayed . . . because of the divorce?

JD: Yes, after *The Thief of Bagdad* premiere and all this nonsense, I went to
work for the British War Relief. It was there that I met the Ronald Colmans
and the Charles Boyers, who were very, very nice to me. And that's when I
appeared in this film, *Forever and a Day,* which had the whole British colony
of Los Angeles doing a bit in it. Then, onstage, to raise money, they did one
of those Noël Coward plays, and I was in one opposite Nigel Bruce, playing
his young wife. It was very funny. I was absolutely broke by then, and in
order to do this play, I was given a certain amount of money . . . because of
union rules, you had to be paid basic salary, which was then handed over to
British War Relief. So all that money went . . . ohhh, and because I had to
join the actors' union in order to do it. The money I got for the job barely
paid for the membership. I was *so* desperately poor at that time. But there
were some people who were frightfully good to me, like the Colmans and the
Boyers, and Basil Rathbone and his wife, Ouida. Actually, I was dropped
pretty quickly by the Boyers and the Colmans. But not the Rathbones, because my friendship went on with their niece. I wasn't that interesting as
company for them, their friends were all older people, so that was under-
standable. But Ouida really had what you'd call a salon, and every Sunday
Artur Rubinstein would be up there, playing the piano.

JK: So at least you got to go to parties.

JD: Ohhh, but, you see, I could only go out at night because I still had some
beautiful, beautiful evening clothes . . . but all my shoes were worn out.
They didn't show under long evening dresses. And I used to *stuff* myself at
these cocktail parties and dinner parties and things. I *know* it sounds just like
a movie . . . unbelievable. If you write this, it will sound like it was invented!
But, being around these British actors was one of the reasons people began
to realize I was available for work, available to be hired. It was fortunate that
I was still so young at the time. I wasn't worried about starting off on another
great career, I was worried about eating . . . and *surviving*!

Before I'd gone to see June, I'd spent the better part of an afternoon browsing
through old British film magazines for any articles or interviews that might
unearth some little tidbits I could confront her with; but British film magazines
were more concerned with Hollywood stars, and June's career was just taking
off when she left the country. But I did come across an item critical of Merle
Oberon, who had returned to Hollywood after her bit in *The Lion Has Wings*
and was telling everyone in Los Angeles that she would like to be a spy for the
British government as her contribution to the British war effort. The editor of
PictureGoer Weekly found her offer to be in embarrassingly poor taste. I found

it amusing for another reason . . . for June, desperate, as she tells it, went a step further and applied for a job with the FBI.

JD: Ohhh, but that was much later. Yes, I was desperate. How did I get to the FBI? I don't know. I didn't know anybody else who was doing anything like that. It was just . . . a romantic turn of mind. I suppose I must have found out who to go to. Ohhh, I know what gave me the idea. There was a German girl who was going around socially a great deal, nothing to do with films, and perhaps I had a funny idea about her. *Must* have been something to trigger it. *That's* it. So I went to the FBI in Los Angeles. What a riot! And I'm on their files now . . . how *funny!* Yes, I had begun to wonder about this girl. She was going around all that semisocial thing and of course I knew everyone there . . . Thelma Furness and Gloria Vanderbilt and Lance Reventlow, all of those people. I don't know how that came about that I should know them. Well, to put it frankly, the time that I was there, there were not so many young English ladies there, so I was rather *grabbed* socially, they needed me to fill out a party. And these were part of the social connections I had from England.

Now, here I must admit to some skepticism, because one of the first people I ever met at her house was a distinguished elderly gentleman who painted in his spare time but had previously been with the British Intelligence Corps, and who told us that incidents in his former work had served as the role model for the character in *The Spy Who Came In from the Cold.* June could easily have met a number of people like that purely socially, without having been an undercover agent. But it did make me think, just a bit, that June could be one of those "still-water" beauties that run very, very deep. And you'd never guess it just to look at her.

JD: But then, I always sort of knew people, and my mother knew people. And I was married to Guy, who *was* a very, very famous Harley Street specialist, so there was a lot of social life there. And then, British Information Services, that was Major Ormrod, he was the head of it, and a great, great friend of Guy's and mine. Still is; now he's *Sir* Barcley Ormrod. And he sent introductions to various people in Southern California, so those were social introductions, you see. That's what gave me the idea, this German woman at all the parties. And also my sort of "super imagination" . . . I still have that. I thought, "Hah, I might do something here." So . . . they did ask me to try and find out something. I made one definite luncheon appointment with the German girl. And I tried to sort of prod her a little bit. I don't think I got anything very much, though. And . . . that was the last of it.

JK: Was there any *other* intrigue in your high-society circles?

JD: Ohhh, I remember I was at a party at Barbara Hutton's before she married Cary Grant. She was still married to Lance Reventlow, whom I used to know years before when I used to go skiing. David O. Selznick was at the party. I was then staying in this bungalow, around the swimming pool. I went home alone, got ready for bed; I was in a nightgown, and there was a crash through the windows which led out to the pool, crashing through the Venetian blinds. And here in my little bungalow, in my sitting room, was David O. Selznick . . . *very* drunk, very big, very strong man. And do you know, I had to fight him physically until it was daylight? Until he finally passed out. And then later he went home. And I was terrified to phone anyone for fear of scandal. *And* I was due to make a test for him for something Gene Tierney finally did. She played an Indian girl; I think it was *Sundown*. I know that Selznick had something to do with it. Or perhaps he was thinking of signing me and thought I would do this film for him. Anyway, I made the test, but I knew that it was dead before I made it because I had turned him down, I had thrown him out. Well, nobody did that in those days. *Nobody* did. I had the same sort of thing with Harry Cohn of Columbia Pictures. He lived in the same building and he tried to get at me, tried to get into the apartment.

There was only one thing for me to do, try and find some work, try and find a film. I had nobody in America I could ask for money. Finally I thought, "Ah-ha, I will enlist in the Canadian Air Force" as a WAC or a RAF or whatever they were called, because I thought, being British, perhaps they'd take me and I would get three square meals a day. And I knew that one of Nigel Bruce's two daughters, Pauline, was in the Canadian Air Force. So I telephoned them [the Bruces] and they told me later that I sounded so desperate that they realized something was very wrong, and they suggested I come over and stay a couple of days, be with Jennifer, their other daughter, and we'd talk about it. Of course, when I got there, they realized just what a terrible state I was in. I was living in a tiny little shack that had been loaned to me. And I had a tiny little Ford car, like the ones you see in the Mack Sennett comedies. I was living in the Valley, off Ventura Boulevard, and had to go chug-chug-chug over the hills to get into Beverly Hills to them. Well, I lived with the Bruces for a year. And it was somehow, during that time, that I got that test for *None But the Lonely Heart*. They tested everyone. They were desperate. And I don't know why . . . why they tested me. Did I meet Clifford Odets before? Because I did nothing until *None But the Lonely Heart* except for those ghastly little serials.

June had spied a shot of herself in her last Hollywood film, leaning on some carved Chinese lions in a nightclub, singing, while Alan Ladd, William Bendix and Gail Russell were sitting at a table looking at her.

JD: Well, you know, it was such a joke, really, casting me with him, with Alan Ladd. Because he's *so* little, and he had lifts on his shoes and I had to be in a little trench for most of our scenes! You know, he would suddenly, during this speech of mine, pull out this gold cigarette case that would flash in the lights. He had these marvelous ways of stealing the camera.

And after that movie I left. There was nothing to keep me there. Nothing there I wanted to stay for. I had made a marriage there which was annulled. I always forget it because it never counted . . . though it did to me, emotionally. He was head of the radio department at RKO. I met him when I was doing *None But the Lonely Heart*. He was unusual, a Southerner, from an old Southern family. Rather nice. And of course in those days, instead of having an affair with somebody and getting it out of your system . . . I'd had nobody, but nobody; I hadn't even been out with anyone that I liked. It was so long that, like an idiot, I married him. But then I discovered that he had been married before and didn't have a final decree. It was another year before his divorce was technically final. So technically, happily, I was not married. Which was good, as far as I was concerned. Because I was a proper little English girl and he was a charming cad.

June brings out the bound, worn-down copy of the script of *None But the Lonely Heart* that Clifford Odets had given her, with a letter from him asking after her, speaking of his disenchantment with the Motion Picture Academy for a number of reasons, one of which was that June hadn't even been nominated for Best Supporting Actress; and he concluded with a request that, when in town, she should come up to visit him, "just to talk . . . to let me look at you."

JD: It was the first *real* role I had to play. Ohhh, what I learned from Clifford. I learned my craft from him. I mean, I learned how to act. Just by the way he directed. I suppose the "Method" thing . . . after all my technical background in England, to suddenly be shown this whole other way of doing things. It was just the way he directed. There was a scene in the film . . . I just saw it the other day. [June drops her voice to a whisper.] To give you an illustration of what Clifford did as a director, we [Cary Grant and June] had just come home and we were standing outside the front door, and there was a sort of "good night" scene; and Odets said, "You're there and you're very relaxed. I just want you to feel that you've almost been to bed together, or you're expecting to be." It was all that sort of yawny, very relaxed sort of thing. He didn't tell you how to read a line, he just very simply gave you the feeling that he wanted. And you often played right against the actual lines. It was extraordinary, it made it all very real.

We then got into discussing the finer points of Odets as a writer, his sensitivity and his sexual hold over women such as actress Frances Farmer. Had Odets held a similar magnetism for June? Single, lonely and alone at the time? The Odets who apparently could charm women out of their Beverly Hills mansions only to later—having led them on—break their hearts . . . had she known this side of the playwright?

JD: I didn't know anything about that. I never felt or sensed that sort of quality about him. Nooo . . . ohhh, I had a terrific sort of crush on him while we were making the film. I mean it never . . .

JK: Odets more than Cary Grant?

JD: Ohhh, I *never* thought *anything* about Cary Grant at all. Nothing. But there was something about Clifford. He had this extraordinary sort of intensity. It was very flattering to feel that somebody could get so *inside* you and bring that out. George Kaufman was somewhat like that. Mind you, I never even had dinner with Clifford alone, never had five minutes alone with him. Except, I mean, to talk. I met him because of making the film. Not before. No, I made the test . . . how did that happen? Well, it wasn't through Cary Grant. No. No, because at the time I was *dead*. I was *absolutely* dead. I'd done all those *ghastly* little things.

I was living absolutely down and out at that time. Well, I was having quite an affair at the time, a love affair with a very high-powered New York attorney. No. No, I'm mad, that was before . . . it was George Moffat. It was during, right after, or just before the play I was doing with Kaufman opened in Boston for the tryout. I became engaged to George Moffat. The play was called *Town House,* George Kaufman directed it . . . it was based on a series of stories that had appeared in *The New Yorker* magazine by John Cheever. It was terribly funny, terribly funny.*

Ohh, I was mad about George Moffat . . . but I adored George Kaufman. He was so brilliant, he was so wonderful. He was the ugliest man I'd ever seen, which of course attracts me anyway. I'm not mad about pretty, pretty, beautiful men, never have been. But he was *really* ugly. Tall, lean, just a wonderful sort of way of speaking. Wonderful personality, and a wonderful way of drawing one out and making one feel at ease. A magnificent director. You felt that you could do anything for him, the way you felt you could do anything for Clifford. Whereas René Clair I *loathed*! Everybody did!†

That was the most unhappy production you have ever known; he was such a technician. I can see now that he was right, because the picture was very good. I enjoyed it when I saw it on TV the other day. I hadn't seen it for years. I just looked at it as if it were someone else, I didn't even know it was *me;* didn't feel like me, look like me or anything else. And he had a fine acting cast: Judith Anderson, Barry Fitzgerald, Walter Huston . . . but he would say, "Now, I want you to walk in, count two, then look up." And he gave you the reading of the line. That was my recollection of that film: everyone was very unhappy. He treated everyone like that, it was just his way of directing . . . he didn't treat me any different from anyone else. I didn't give *any* sort of performance in *Ten Little Indians.*

JK: But back to Kaufman, who had quite a reputation . . .

Town House ran twelve performances.
† Clair directed June in Agatha Christie's *And Then There Were None.*

JD: Was he supposed to have been a great "swordsman"? Really? Ohhh, yes, I remember hearing about his affair with Mary Astor. I could see that he could have a power over women. He was so nice, I liked him so much. I'm sure I never would have been attracted to him. But he was fabulous. Ohh, what I learned from him. The only theater I'd really done before that play was with the American Repertory Theater, a sort of attempt to start an Old Vic in New York. I did J. M. Barrie's *What Every Woman Knows,* Anne Boleyn in *Henry VIII* and Lavinia in *Androcles and the Lion.* That was after I left Hollywood . . . after *Calcutta.* I know it was after *None But the Lonely Heart* because Clifford Odets was talking to all his theater friends about me, and my name came to the attention of Margaret Webster and Eva Le Gallienne, who founded this thing with Cheryl Crawford, who was a great producer at that time. Eva Le Gallienne came to California to see me, to interview me. And I was *dying* to get away from Hollywood, I just hated it. I was *so* miserable, so I was only too happy to leave. But it was all a bluff because I'd done practically no theater at all. They must have presumed that, being English, I would be able to act on the stage. And also Clifford had told them that he thought I was a very fine actress.

Every now and then I long, *long,* to do something. Because *now* I know I could do it and do it well. All those years since and I've learned so much. Well, all that goes into one's acting. All I regret is not so much the career part of my life, but that I had to spend all those miserable years in America, in Hollywood. Much more than what I did or didn't do, I regret that I wasn't in my own country during the war. But I don't regret *much,* because I don't think back on things. You've made me remember all this. Ohhh, I can't remember another thing, John.

It was the following day; I had a plane to catch, but other questions were stirring in my mind, raised by some of June's amazing stories. I also wanted to get her age right, and my own memory had been jogged back to my youth and the drama involved in the first time I saw *The Thief of Bagdad.* It seemed simpler to ask June about them while I was still in London than to call her from New York. It was then that the wheel turned and a twist surfaced, one that would link the past—hers and mine. I told June what I planned to write in the intro, and why, and she found the story about my sister amazing. So it seemed natural to casually check her birthdate. No problem. No secret. She also added the month and day. "I'm a Taurean," she said. "May 14th." There was a little click. My sister's birthday was on the same day. "Oh, John!" exclaimed June. "I don't believe it. What does it mean?" Nothing, I suspect, but it does make a good ending to the story.

1984

Jack Cole, photographed by Will Rappard for *Alive and Kicking*, 1950

JACK
COLE

J ACK COLE was the razor-sharp, high-powered, dynamic, workaholic choreographer who went from Broadway to movies, who choreographed many
of the Rita Hayworth movies in the 1940s (*Tonight and Every Night, Gilda,
Down to Earth*), all the movies at Columbia, for that matter. In the early 1950s
he worked at 20th Century–Fox and was a vital support to Monroe there. He
was very influential on Broadway, in the theater (*Kismet, Man of La Mancha*),
with his fusion of American jazz with Eastern rhythms.

I first met Jack Cole because of Rita Hayworth.

JC: Rita Hayworth is just a Spanish teenager, really, she's never grown up.
Unless Rita's got somebody around her to say "Don't," she acts just like a
teenage girl . . . you know: eat, you're bored; go to bed, you're bored; get
plastered. I like Rita Hayworth, she's a very nice lady, one of the nicest ones
in the movies to work with. She wasn't really as dependent on men as one
might suspect. Curiously enough, she's not really a sexual lady. I've worked
with all of them: Grable, Lana Turner . . . the whole bloody bit, and what's
very curious, well, Lana Turner's a little bit different because she really liked
men, she liked to fuck a lot. But most of the others, it's the idea of it. Like
Rita liked a sort of father, really. That was why she liked Orson Welles. She
was very much like Monroe with Miller. It was the same kind of bit, the same
kind of daddy. And it was somebody who had great stature in the area in
which they had always been put down. You know, Rita Hayworth was always
told by people like Harry Cohn that she was a dumb Latin cunt: don't talk,
don't think. And so Orson had a great calm . . . he had a great mind for
adoring her, which was perfect. Even though in the end he used her like the
others. I remember the first thing I did with her, I did something on *Cover
Girl*. Val Rassett was really first doing the picture. He's a very dear, old-
fashioned ballet man who was not adjusted to doing that kind of film at all.
Seymour Felix was a very old-fashioned "girl" dance director from the old
days; and Gene Kelly was doing his own thing. And finally they had to do
something with Rita, and Harry Cohn asked Gene who they could get, and

they got me, but I didn't know that I was doing somebody out of a job or I wouldn't have done it. That was the first thing I did with Rita. The first time we really worked together, when I did the whole thing, was her next film, the one Victor Saville directed. Victor Saville was absolutely a horror, a very nice man, very unlikely man to be doing what we were doing.

Well, I usually am very careful in doing a certain kind of research, and for some reason *Tonight and Every Night* came up very fast, and Harry Cohn was always a bad boy. He was marvelous to work for, I always had a marvelous time with Harry Cohn because I had a very *sharp* tongue and would use absolutely foul, colorful language, more than he did. *Only* when you were alone; he never could be humiliated in front of people, that was the absolute no-no. You could make *certain* kinds of jokes in front of other people; but if you were alone, you could say anything to him. He was a very good executive. And when he'd get into an argument with you, when you thought you were having a really bad time, he would suddenly say, "I just want to see if you're going to like what you do. Go ahead." He'd just start giving you a bad time, you'd scream and holler to sort of let him know that was what it was about. Part of what he used to do was to divide and stay in control. He would tell me, "Don't pay attention to Victor Saville, he's a dumb British dumbo, dumb, dumb. Just do what you want." Then he would tell all the various people something else. Now, most of my background is theater, where the director is the director. The one thing that I thought was very funny was that I thought Victor Saville, being British and so forth, would know about what things were like in London, which is where this story was set . . . so I didn't do any kind of research which I do, usually, very carefully. *Nobody* told me that the stage was the Windmill Theater, which I had never been to, and which I went to about a year later like I held on to the wall. It was so small. The stage is about as big as one of my bedrooms. Nobody could do anything. I mean, six girls could stand this way. It was a lower-middle-class burlesque house. The broads stood there, with tits and ass out, and didn't move. This was nothing like the huge set we used in the movie. And I went, "Phew, why would Victor Saville let me do that?" Well, it was "license." But I could have done another kind of number just as well. You see, the whole point was that Harry Cohn said, "Don't do it like the dumb picture." So the numbers actually look more like Metro than they do like Columbia.

I had a very strong contract, which Harry Cohn took over from Metro. I had absolute control over sets and costumes in pictures on which I worked. It made kind of trouble after a while, but it was also a very good thing. My thing was to not do those old-fashioned bits where they'd color the air. Most of the very funny movies at that time were all about ten years behind the theater in a kind of a way. I used to tease Harry about another part of my contract where I also didn't have to work on pictures unless the budget was $1.5 million, which was a lot of money, especially to Harry Cohn. So that reduced me to practically only doing Hayworth pictures. But I did, oh, a

million Z musicals, only because Harry was quite willing, if he *liked* you—
and I was sort of his little white-haired boy—that if you wanted to learn about
how to make movies, he'd let you . . . he'd let you design the sets, costumes,
then cut, shoot, clean up the john, everything . . . he'd let you do it, as long
as you didn't goof. You know, people always make fun of Harry Cohn, but
he was an extraordinarily bright man. A very vulgar tongue and nasty to
actors. He just didn't like actors; it didn't have to be Glenn Ford or Rita, he
just hated actors, thought they were all tough as shit and he could replace one
in a minute. Anyway, in I came and Victor Saville didn't tell me one dumb
thing about the Windmill Theater. Rita was kind of a hard one to get *with* in
the beginning. She was like the perfect object for a movie studio of the period, doing anything you told her, if she trusted you, and she got to trust me
very quickly because she knew that I knew about what she could do. Later
on she had Valerie Bettis, and Valerie was a dancer, and a good one, who
wanted to be an actress, and that always makes problems.

Already they were competing ladies: Valerie was a little younger, very
expert in her own right, but Valerie always did numbers for her like Valerie
Bettis would do. Valerie was a *very* fine modern dancer of the Hanya Holm
crew in New York, but Rita Hayworth wasn't a dancer in that way, nor did
she pretend to be. She was a beautiful lady and you always had to treat her
like the *most* beautiful showgirl who could move. You couldn't treat her like
a dancer, because you couldn't put that burden on her . . . she didn't go to
class every day. She was trained as a dancer, but as a Spanish dancer. A
Spanish dancer always has his girlfriend or wife who is absolutely beautiful
and dances all right, doesn't knock anybody's eyes out. They're not supposed
to be marvelous. . . . The men are supposed to be marvelous dancers, and
then you have the marvelously beautiful lady with ass and the tits and pie-
plate castanets so that you shouldn't miss them. And Rita Hayworth was
more or less brought up in that kind of tradition. She was the young girl
in the family, and very beautiful, even with her hairline way down. And
the main object in life with a star in movies at that period, which is why I
always objected to someone like Valerie Bettis, was not to prove your
point but to make them look marvelous; don't prove anything about dancing
or anything.

Rita would just come in; she was absolutely always on time, you know:
ten o'clock rehearsal, she was there at ten minutes of ten, dressed and ready
to do it. I can see her sitting there smoking a cigarette and drinking coffee,
just like she was one of the dancers. It wasn't Rita Hayworth, Star; she was
always very pleasant when she came in, always very nice to the kids; it wasn't
a star bit at all. If you just wanted to work from 10:00 a.m. to 6:00 p.m., she
just did it. She had *no comment,* no feeling about it at all. None. We liked
each other and she knew I was very understanding about what she could do
and what she couldn't do. *Once* in a while I would make a boo-boo in my
efforts to make her look marvelous. She would never say no. She'd rehearse

for about a week, then when it would get close to shooting, we'd do this one thing and she'd sit down and a big tear would come, and I'd say, "Oh, God what's the matter?" and she'd say, "I'll never be any good." And I'd say, "It's not important. Why didn't you tell me long ago? There are a *thousand* other things you can do. I don't want you to do something you're going to be sad about," naturally. I just had to push her. If it was within her nature to do what you were asking, she would do it and she would do it well, with energy.

I did have some side problems. Jean Louis was marvelous. . . . Rita did not have a good figure. She had beautiful breasts, *beautiful* arms, the most beautiful hands in the world and shoulders . . . if you wanted to do a portrait of the Spanish Lady, she was it. The close-up would be extraordinarily beautiful, and she was always this young woman who was much more beautiful than she photographed. They really did icky makeup for star Columbia ladies, you know, that too-hard glossy mouth. She was a very beautiful woman in life, but rather difficult to photograph in terms of lighting because her face was not a dish face, low bones, and it took a long time to light her for close-ups. And the hair was always a problem because it was real Spanish-growing hair, baby, and it had to be done practically every other day. The day it was done, it was red. The day after, it had just the slight mark of black which photographed marvelously, made it very strong. By the third day the black was *there* and it was a real Spanish lady. She had to get to the studio at 5:00 in the morning to get the hair done before the makeup. It grew that fast and it showed.

There were problems in dressing her. No ass and no waist: her legs went right into her rib cage. The legs were perfectly good legs, but not extraordinary. It was just the top of her that was very beautiful. It was just a problem to get the clothes proportionately right. It seems like it was a very simple problem. Oh, and then there was one picture, I think it was *Tonight and Every Night,* yes it was, she was pregnant. We had a problem at one point, but she was so good-humored about being pregnant. They couldn't paint the set because she was pregnant and couldn't inhale the paint fumes. So we always had to paint when she wasn't around and then air out the set.

I began to develop with Hayworth a kind of technique I did to an extreme degree later with Marilyn Monroe. When we'd do close-ups of certain kinds of things, like singing or lying in the sand in close-up, I would just get within three feet of her and she would mimic me. I'd wet my mouth, open it like I couldn't breathe, and she'd look at me and we would just have each other. She'd just do it, she didn't have any feeling about it at all. She didn't have any compunction about somebody showing Rita Hayworth how to do her fucking eyelashes. With Rita you could always just say, "Baby, you're dragging your feet, come on." She had no vanity that way, about being Sarah Bernhardt. The only thing she'd get her feelings up about was Harry Cohn when he'd been particularly nasty.

She got very angry one time where she wanted to kill Hedda Hopper, who was riding Orson Welles. One day at the studio Hopper was walking around and we were rehearsing and she said, "Would you excuse me for just a minute?" She was trying to find out what set Hedda was visiting 'cause she wanted to go up and call her a dirty cunt and let her have one right in the nose. She was out to get Hedda for what she was writing about Orson, and she really wanted to punch her. I called up the public relations and said, "She's on the warpath." That's what used to be so funny, they took that stuff seriously, it used to be a big deal if Rita Hayworth punched Hedda Hopper in the nose. I thought it would be fun if she caught up with Hedda and let her have it. But they kept them separated and they got Hedda out of the studio before Rita could find her, and with Rita's nature, by that night and one drink she'd forgotten.

Oh, it was very funny when we were doing one of the numbers, "What Does an English Girl Think of a Yank?"—as a matter of fact, I did that number with her, as a sailor. Now, I was a very well-known dancer who had come out to do choreography in the pictures. I had picked somebody who was absolutely correct to do a sailor part—you know, American sailor jazz bit, not my type of thing at all, it was a real jolly, windy kind of a bit. The boy I picked had black, curly hair and the cap down with the hair up over the top of the hat, he was chunky, laughing with lots of white teeth and the dimples of death, and just as we were about to shoot it, he sprained his ankle. It was always a big deal—particularly at Columbia with Jack Fier, who was the production man—to have any kind of a hold-up. So Saville said, "*You* do it. You dance, you know it. *You* do it." Well, the first thing is that I am not, by nature, a jolly, laughing performer. So Victor Saville would hold up a dollar on the sidelines and every time I smiled he would give me a dollar. That's how I rehearsed. A couple of times around and I knew the dumb thing, I danced, and rehearsed with Rita, and all was fine.

Well, baby, I didn't know what hit me when they turned the camera on, 'cause Rita was just like Monroe. When it was for *real,* look out! So for the first shot I just went up six ways from Sunday because suddenly this mass of red hair, and it looked like ninety-four more teeth than I'd ever seen in a woman's mouth before, and more eye-rolling, and more shoulder—I mean, the most animated object known to man. The minute *film* was rolling, it was for real, it was gonna be on a large screen, it was like, *Stand back, man, this is how it goes.* And I was not able to deal with it. I'd never seen so much animation and giving out.

Rita always did it for real, whereas somebody like Betty Grable, who was a very talented lady but she was sort of fucked, having been a child performer with her mother, she just *had* show business, she was just the most old, tired gypsy as a young girl. And her problem was that she could do all those pictures forward and backward, which she did. She never looked at a script, she'd just come in, put on her makeup, look at the three pages they were going to do that day and then go, ready. She could do it all in a haze, you know, while thinking about what horse was going to win that day.

There was one number [in *Tonight and Every Night*] with a marvelous

man, Professor Lamberti. He'd always lean forward and say, "You like another piece? You really like that piece?" He was a dirty old man who had
been doing that act for one thousand years, we just hired him to do it for the
movie. Then Rita did what the showgirl used to do; he always had a showgirl
in the act. I was familiar with the act, so I just did the act for him. In his act,
for real, at the end the showgirl was stark naked, and when he became aware
that it was the naked showgirl the audience was applauding, he'd pick up a
seltzer bottle and let her have it right in the ass. But we couldn't do that
because it was Rita Hayworth and because of the period.

I was constantly being called up to Harry Cohn's office and he'd say,
"No." And I'd say, "For God's sake, Harry, come on." And he'd say, "What
are you trying to do?" I'd say, "Look at my contract. The first line says 'For
your peculiar and unique talent.' I'm trying to exercise my peculiar and
unique talent." They always used to hire you because you were peculiar and
everybody said you were marvelous, and they thought some magical way that
you'd come out and do the same thing that they'd been doing except it would
come out differently. That's why I used to tell Harry that those backstage
musicals were . . . As a matter of fact, one time Ann Miller asked me about
something and I said, "Darling, let's don't talk about this script, it's a piece
of shit." So the next day Harry Cohn called me in and said, "I'm going to tell
you one more time, keep your *big mouth shut*." When I asked what was the
matter, he said, "Ann Miller is at home and won't come to work because you
said the script is a piece of shit." I said, "Well, I did and it is." He said, "I
know that. What the fuck does it matter to her? She's just a dumb broad with
large thighs and I'm paying her so much money, so what's she give a damn
whether it's a piece of shit or not? I want her to do it. You go to the phone
and you get her back here." So I told him I couldn't do it in his office because
it was too embarrassing. I called Ann on the phone and she said, "Who's
this?" 'cause she had taken it very big that she'd gone on suspension. And I
had to say, "Pussycat," because that's what she called me.

But Ann never had what Rita had on the screen. Rita always was instinctively, marvelously erotic. She instinctively knew it, though she wasn't that
kind of person herself, really. She knew that that was what it was about first.
She knew that what Harry Cohn was buying from her was eroticism. I got to
know what she could do and I was always trying to make her feel confident
and not do those numbers in that way that everybody used to do them, like
they were getting it by radar with a shortwave set. It looked like she really
could do it, but I'd stand back and make her move.

You know, Virginia Van Upp really used to write for her, that was why
Virginia was at the studio, really. She could write scenes that Rita Hayworth
could act with a dumb director. Built in. Because Rita was always just as
good as her director, and she had very few good directors, in the beginning
particularly.

You had to be very careful with Rita. Harry or somebody in the production office would say something to her and she'd start to cry. When she was angry, she'd cry and really get worked up to the point like she was going to go in, no matter what Harry Cohn said, and let him have one good "Shove it up your Jewish ass." There was animosity between Rita and Harry. They say he proposed to her at one point and she turned him down. At that point, more or less all the studios' executives were like that, they'd make a pass at somebody. Anyway, I think that's around when we got Kim Novak.* She was the thing to get Rita Hayworth, that's why she was there. She was Harry Cohn's bid so if Rita Hayworth made trouble, there was always Kim.

What was very peculiar was every once in a while, if we didn't want to see people from the studio, we'd eat up the street on Gower across Sunset in a little Italian restaurant. I used to see Kim Novak in there. Later she turned into this sort of ethereal, "Where-am-I-what-are-you-saying-to-me" girl. When I first saw her, she was this tough Polish broad from Chicago, *really* tough lady, really *tough*. I never worked with her, but later on I saw this new kind of girl and I thought it very strange.

The only time we ever had trouble with Rita and another woman was *Tonight and Every Night,* and it was with Janet Blair, her first big chance. Janet was very bright and not a very amusing lady, her whole career has been based upon aggression. She might learn something quicker than Rita, but it never looked the same. She was very pulled together and a little grand, as opposed to Rita. Harry was very good to me with my dancers, he let me keep a lot of them like Gwen Verdon, Carol Haney and others on salary while I was training them. When we weren't working on a picture they'd still be on salary taking classes. Eventually, Metro wanted to hire them, everybody knew about them and Harry was very proud that his experiment had paid off, that we had developed a lot of very fine people.

Anyway, Janet Blair came down and asked if she could have some ballet classes and I said, "Yes, darling, 9:00." And she said, "Oh, you mean with the dancers?" And I said, "Yes, madam, that's the way we have class here." She said, "Oh, I wanted personal." I told her that I didn't do private lessons, that we were all professionals and we all took class together, and it didn't matter if she was Janet Blair and couldn't dance as well and all the kids were fine dancers. "They're professionals and we expect that." Rita never cared, she'd just go to the kids and ask for help.

Well, Rita likes men, and she doesn't really like women. She just liked to be around men. It isn't that she wanted to fuck everybody, she was just not amused by women at all. She never did anything overt with Janet, she just didn't pay attention to her. Oh, they'd talk, but they never had lunch together or like that. So we had a number that, as a matter of fact, Shelley Winters was in, "The Boy I Left Behind," and they did a "boy" going into the Army and all the examinations are by women, and it was a funny number. Shelley

* Novak didn't appear till 1954.

was one of the examiners, and Jean Negulesco's wife, Dusty Anderson, was also in that number. Well, they had to strip for the heart test, and they put the thing on and pumped it up. Rita and Janet came out and did the strip, side by side, the same thing. Well, sir, that was really competition day, the day Janet Blair was going to show that Rita Hayworth wasn't really so much and that Janet Blair was marvelous. And what was funny was that they had to wear men's long underwear with the banjo seats. And, like all very female people, though Rita didn't have a marvelous figure, she was terribly secure of herself as a woman. So she just felt marvelous in men's underwear with the crotch hanging and the banjo seat, her boobs looked marvelous. Janet Blair was unfortunately a little thing with no ass and no boobs in particular, real Nellie Forbush [in *South Pacific*], which she played later—she just looked like a girl who didn't look too attractive in men's underwear. But when she started doing the number, I thought she was going to give herself a hernia. They made no reference to it except they both came down the middle, bumping and grinding, and Rita looked *big,* she could do all that jazz; and Janet was like her teeth were almost falling out of her mouth with the effort of trying to show up Rita. I didn't know what we could do. I'd say "Cut" and look at Victor Saville and he'd look like we were building up to a girl fight here. The second I'd say cut, Rita would go and do her hair, primp and act like nothing was happening. Everybody on the set knew what was happening. We finally had to print it before it got worse.

Now, *Gilda* was difficult. For one thing, Rita had had her baby. Well, first the picture started without a script, really. The script pages would arrive practically the morning that we were going to shoot, they were making the picture up as we went along. If you really look, you can tell that was the way the picture was done because it doesn't really make any sense if you try to follow the story. The only thing that made it interesting was that Rita and Glenn Ford look like they want to fuck each other's brains out. It was all sick, sick, sick. Marvelous! One of the things I did was at the beginning when she came up with her hair—you see her for the first time and all the hair goes up. I did a lot of things on the picture that were like that.

I remember one thing, I don't know whether I should tell you or not because it was the only time that we had sort of a funny thing between us. She was in a very difficult situation all during the filming: she was breaking up with Orson Welles. She was very nervous, but very good. And Anita Ellis was the one who sang "Put the Blame on Mame," and then the really good one, the close-up of "Mame" Rita sang herself, in the shot where she sits on the table with the guitar. But Anita did the big one. Of course, I must say, of all the things I've done with Rita, "Mame" is the one that pleases me most, that I can really look at on the screen. If you really want to see a beautiful, erotic woman, that still remains absolutely first-rate, it could be done right *this* minute [1973] and still be fantastic.

Jean Louis wanted to know how to dress her, and I told him to use Sargent's painting of "Madame X" as a model. That black dress! She was just so wildly suited to do what she was doing. She didn't have any pretensions.

But this one time they were doing a *Life* magazine cover and they were doing an interview with her and she got very nervous and uptight, and I just happened to be in the room with her—we had broken for a little while from rehearsing. They were asking "Was it your voice in *Gilda*?" and she said, "Yes," and made no reference to Anita Ellis. Well, afterwards we were having lunch and it's the first time I felt peculiar with her. She didn't say, "Oh, fuck 'em" or "I shouldn't have done that, should I?" or whatever. That just wasn't like her. I never read the interview, but I imagine she was always like that, embarrassed about herself. She doesn't like to talk about herself and doesn't evaluate what's happening to her except whether she's having a good time or not.

She liked to dance, and she liked to dance socially. She liked to rhumba. Well, I'd finally say that we had to go home because we'd have to be up early in the morning. But sometimes I'd go out with her to watch Orson shoot. I remember one time he was doing *The Stranger* over at Goldwyn, where the guy dives off the roof. There was an enormous crowd the night they were doing the church-steeple scene. And she said, "Come on," because I had never met Orson Welles. And I thought, Right, just what the fellow needs. It was bloody cold, as I remember, and she was still playing adoring wife watching Daddy work. All that kissy-kissy crap. He was very considerate of her then. After we'd stood around for some time and Orson had come over, we went over to the Beachcomber, you could eat late there, and just drank. She wasn't a bad drinker then, but she liked to unwind if she felt safe, with friends.

JK: Tell me about *Down to Earth,* which I have never seen.

JC: Oh, Rita danced marvelously in it, and she was very beautiful. It was one of her best-looking periods, the peak of her looks. Sort of a *Gilda* in color. It was with Larry Parks, who is not quite the same thing as Glenn Ford. Larry was always a little bit angry and never looked like a big fuck. Glenn always looked like he was fucking the whole time or he was playing with himself or whatever, that was his whole bit. I mean they really pushed that with Glenn and Rita, they just stared at each other like they were saying, "I'm going to eat your ass from here to kingdom come."

So Larry was one of the things that was not too good about *Down to Earth,* but Rita was fabulous. We had a great big problem with one of the numbers, though. Terpsichore, Rita's character, had to do this number in the movie that ruined the show they're putting on when she arrives. It was very difficult for Rita to do what was supposed to be a boring number and still not be boring. And I must say the song itself was very beautiful, and the shot of her as Terpsichore and she has gold sand falling through her hands with the wind blowing, and she was so beautiful, not to believe. You must see it. Some of the numbers are the best she ever did. She does some great serious dancing with Marc Platt in that number. Virginia Hunter was in it, did one of the numbers with Rita. She came from Metro, and she now is chief buyer for Bullock's. But she was a very pretty girl, and they worked *together* in that number, "People Have More Fun Than Anyone," in the fairground, with all the skyscrapers leaning to one side.

Down to Earth took a long time, it was very hard work. Rita worked for me, like always, like a Trojan. The things I wanted her to do she liked because she trusted me for the fact that I knew all of her capabilities and what not to get her to do. Once in a while Harry Cohn would look at the rushes and say, "What's that she's doing?" Or he'd use one of his Jewish expressions, *mishegoss,* which means madness: "What's that *mishegoss* of yours?" Especially when I'd do a good cut of her going out with her hair, because she had such beautiful hair. . . . God, they were at that hair that whole time, it's a wonder she's got a hair left on her head. But she used it, she knew how to use it very well, and I was always using it for cuts and Harry would say "What's that?" but he tried to understand.

But working with Rita, intensively for four years from '44 to '48 was a very happy experience for me because along with that I had all these kids. Harry Cohn was treating me marvelously; that kind of dance-training situation was never done before or since at a studio. And they all developed into a first-rate group of people—Rod Alexander, Bob Hamilton, Bambi Linn, Matt Mattox, Gwen [Verdon] . . . they all got very good training, and Harry Cohn paid for it, *and* they were paid very well. But about that time I finally wanted out of my contract—I still had about a year to go. It was very acrid at the studio at the time—union problems—because the dance part was so powerful. They were doing several musicals at the time, and these kids were now so expert that I could supply numbers for two or three pictures at once because they could do it so fast. I was really paying off Harry Cohn. I remember I said to them, "We must do something all together. We must not cross the picket line all together." They were very bright, liberal kids. Harry got very angry at me. He called me up and said to come to the studio. I said I wouldn't come because I had no work to do. He said, "I want every department head here, business as usual." I said, "I don't have any work and I'm not coming to the studio today." And he said, "Goddamn you, you're suspended." So then, when the strike was suspended, we came back and I remember Max Arno, head of casting, who may still be down there. The kids came in and they all had to meet with a labor representative for the studio. Max Arno walked in and started whistling the "Internationale," and the kids all got up and left. I said, "You just blew it, Max, they're not those kind of kids. They're very bright, I've worked with these kids, they're not amused by that kind of joke. They know exactly who they are, and life has been a very happy situation here." I went to the kids, who said that if Max Arno would apologize to them, they'd come back.

They had a very closed little group in the movies, Mr. Warner, Mr. Cohn,

Mr. Mayer, Mr. Zanuck. And one of the rotten things that I used to see was if anybody *really* gave them a lot of trouble, they'd pick up a phone and say, "Baby, you're not going to work." And you didn't. That's where it was. You were finished in movies. At that time they really would do that with each other, they'd say, "This prick did this, tried to hold me up," and they could do that.

Anyway, these kids were very involved with me, and I told them that this wasn't good. I was free, because I had worked in the theater and could go and work there if I had to, and I could say, "Fuck you, Harry Cohn." I told them to get free of the studio, to get something on their own so they wouldn't be completely dependent on the studios. So we didn't have much to do, it was going to be a long time until the next Hayworth picture because we had just finished one, so I said to Harry, "Do you mind if I take the kids out and we take suspensions on our contracts?" It was going to save the studio an enormous amount of money, so he said, "Sure." I got them all together and called up the Chez Paris in Chicago and asked if they'd like us to dance in about five weeks, and they said yes. So I took all the kids—it cost me a fortune—and we just went. It was wildly successful. Everybody came to see this group of absolutely beautiful dancers.

Then we came back to California and we were going to open Circus Maximus with Lena Horne. It was a big deal, and they were now paying us a monumental amount of money, and Metro was trying to hire us. Then Harry Cohn's legal department called me and said, "You're not opening." They wanted me to sign a new contract, a five-year contract for one Hayworth picture a year, and I said, "I don't want it. I want my contract over with." The opening was three days away and they were going to stop it. Now realize that I still had a year to go on my old contract. I was really up shit creek because I had spent so much money on the kids—wardrobe, orchestrations. Harry said, "Come and see me, talk," and I said, "Baby, if I come see you, I want to leave free." So I finally made a deal with him where I paid him a lot of money to get out of it altogether. And the next year Rita got out of her contract and left.

They treated her rough, they didn't treat her the way other studios treated stars. Harry was always like, "Aw, what the fuck does she need chintz in her dressing room?" They didn't do all those dumb things. Fox was the same way with Monroe . . . if they'd just done a bit more. A couple of hundred dollars' worth—get her a car; take her from the hotel to her dressing room, it costs the studio nothing. And they'd say, "Why should we?" And I'd say, "Baby, just because it shows you adore her and it's a different attitude. And she likes the studio." All the bright ones knew to wait two weeks into shooting a picture and then make their demands. I mean, what are they gonna do? There's all that footage and it could be about $750,000 down the old draino.

Marilyn was very different [from Hayworth]. She was totally unknowing in terms of dancing. She wanted to be a mother. She could sing . . . she had a beautiful voice, and she had a good ear. She worked very hard. She was neurotic, you know, a nice little girl, and they were all rather evil to her, not ever anybody ever bothering . . . I never had any trouble with her. Once she came late, and I said, "Marilyn, don't ever come late for me." She'd been drinking wine, and she arrived at about 11:00 a.m. for a 10:00 a.m. rehearsal, slightly jolly from the wine. But after that she was fine.

But that was it. In terms of my career as a choreographer, I was wasting a lot of time doing things for people who were not really talented. And somehow my own curious neurotic way, coupled with being close buddies with very important movie stars, they adored me and trusted me and I became the brother/mother, trying to make them look good without much talent, being wildly protective and saying, "Oh, it's a very interesting problem." It was possible to make somebody very beautiful, especially in film—you can't do it in theater—to take people who are the right type and who have a kind of a cinematic quality and make quite a lot of things happen. A lot of those people you see who get marvelous reviews for things, *baby*, it's the director who did it.

But with Monroe we finally did the test for *Gentlemen Prefer Blondes*. Jane Russell is a very likable, easygoing California lady, no vanities at all. I had done the most extraordinary beautiful pastel for "Diamonds Are a Girl's Best Friend" . . . with Monroe, all pink and reds, Empire style, with a great enormous Empire bed, pale pink chiffon sheets, black satin cover with the Napoleonic emblems, a big blackamoor maid with an 18th-century turban, a great mahogany tub. She was in bed, this lady with diamonds, just brushing them, it was beautiful. Anyway, we didn't shoot the number until last. By that time there had been a lot of trouble with public relations because the studio was getting letters from women's clubs who were asking members not to see Monroe's pictures because she was too flagrantly sexual. So Zanuck called me up and said, "No way, baby, you can't do that test for real." And it was so beautiful because she was to be wearing nothing but diamonds with a little horse's tail coming out of her ass with a little diamond horsefly on the tail. Well, all that's left is the test, I guess Fox has got it somewhere. Oh, it was so extraordinarily beautiful. Artie Arlen, like all very famous cameramen, could smell a new star and would knock himself out so that when you did the test, the lady star would say that nobody could shoot her but Artie Arlen. It was true in this case, because he did her so beautifully.

Marilyn almost had to go into the hospital when she heard we were not going to do this number this way and would have to do another one. Then when we did the wardrobe tests for the picture, I said, "Darling, the cameraman is Jane Russell's cameraman." It was a big deal to get Jane Russell from Howard Hughes for this film, she was so in demand for the role and she had the say-so on everything. We did the double test for clothes, just walking, the two of them. Monroe was *never* bitchy in that way. She wasn't amused with women particularly, but she wasn't a woman-hater. She was very sure of herself. Well, Jane was being Jane—you know, like an iceman in drag—and as soon as the camera would go on, Marilyn would . . . well, I said to her, "Darling, Jane Russell is Jane Russell, so don't walk in front of her." She just unconsciously would cross in front of her. We looked at the rushes, and it was disaster for Jane. Mr. Zanuck requested that the film be destroyed and that Jane never see it. Then Jane got a whole new wardrobe because, next to Monroe, Jane looked like what I said she looked like . . . a very good-looking, sexy iceman, but an iceman. And Monroe just looked so screamingly beautiful. It was very funny, her look on screen was very different from in person. She was a most attractive lady and she never wore makeup. On the screen she did, but off screen she looked like the *most* attractive sex-maniac girl-next-door. She looked like the kind of person who would say, "Can I use your pool to take a sunning?" and then get your pants off in about six minutes.

JK: Zanuck was the man who fired both Hayworth and Monroe. He really didn't have a great eye for women as a star, did he?

JC: They both had the same thing, Zanuck and Cohn, they thought they could *make* a star . . . the right makeup, the right coach, the right treatment, the right writer. Harry used to say of his stars, "I can get a broad off the street. Fuck her." But one never can, even though they tried it a million times. Monroe did have a very peculiar cinematic thing, and so did Rita Hayworth, who could turn into a total pussycat, very different in life. She was just absolutely like the housewife next door. You know, people would look at Monroe and worry, she looked so inept, and I'd say, "Don't worry." And you'd photograph her and it would happen.

Well, Joan Crawford was like that in her early, *early* ones. Baby, she may be a big, unpleasant, aggressive broad, but, my God, she was in there working. She wanted it and she deserves it. She made a lot of very good actors look like they were standing still. *Dancing Lady,* she was absolutely marvelous, she acted dancing. She knew what she was doing, she had learned to do it.

Monroe was a very realistic girl who *knew* that she didn't have any technique, that she was just a terribly pretty girl whom all this had happened to, and all of a sudden she was a star, she was going to have to go out and do it and everybody was going to look at her. And she was just terrified! She knew that she was not equal. What made her not show up at the studio was that she couldn't sleep, she had a great deal of problems with that. She'd come to the studio with the line that she was sick, because the one thing she counted on was the way she looked. If she had a line in her face, she would not be photographed. But she'd get into makeup and always comb her hair "just one more time," because she was frightened of coming out; and she was such a little girl that she didn't know how to apologize. If it was Clark Gable who was waiting, she would be beside herself with fear and remorse.

When we did *Let's Make Love,* we had a terrible time because she was on pills, it was awful. Paula Strasberg was around and would give me trouble occasionally, although I could handle it pretty well. We were doing one scene where she [Monroe] was just watching Yves Montand do something, she was just being photographed. She looked uncomfortable and I said, "What's the matter, darling?" She said, "I don't have anything to do," but she said it in a rather disagreeable way. That particular phrase is a very unfortunate one with a Method actor, you never give actors "things" to do. So I was getting righteous, because George Cukor, the director, used to use me to get things done because of my effect on Monroe. They were paying me some monumental amount of money, and Fox was complaining, even Zanuck was saying, "Baby, how can you justify all that money?" I would just say right, nothing I could do was worth all that money, but I was getting it because I didn't want to be doing it! And I was doing everything else on the set except what was my skill. So I got angry.

I had been through this thing for about six months. The script was a mess. I was making up numbers as we went along, on the set. So I said in an angry voice, "Do you want me to give you something to do?" She said, "Yes." So I said, "Then stick a finger up your ass, I think that's quite within the realm of your technical facilities," and walked away. Monroe went white and started with the tears, and Paula glowered at me, and Cukor looked at me as if to say, "Could you please hold on, we only have one month to go." Then I felt, naturally, awful. She started saying, "He was my last friend," she was at the point where she didn't think she had a friend in the world: Arthur Miller hated her and everything. I remember Louella Parsons was there that day, she was a crazy nut, fisting down the sherry. And, drunk as she was, she always knew when something was going on . . . baby, any time she looked like she was fumbling, *forget* it! She had a mind like a steel trap. So I went over and said to Monroe, "Darling, I'm terribly sorry, it was quite unforgivable and, no matter what anybody does, we are friends, this has nothing to do with that." I got her back together, and that was that.

We finished the picture, and it was really a terrible ordeal for everybody. Cukor was not crazy about Marilyn for a number of reasons, he was not good for her. Josh Logan was good for her, he was like me in a way. He'd get everybody onto the set, lock the doors, get everybody crazy and then start photographing. Just keep everybody crazy. That's the way Monroe worked best, just turn it on and keep people away. Josh is very verbal, you know, he never stops. His teeth get to going and sometimes you think it's castanets. But he'd talk her out of her thing. Well, anyway. The picture finished and she was going to New York and she called and said, "Can I stop by, darling? I want to see you for a minute," and I said, "Yes, of course." She drove up on her way to the airport, got out of her car and gave me a big kiss. She gave me a little card and we said goodbye, and I said, "See you in New York when I get there, we'll have dinner and go to the ballet." When she left, I opened the card, and there was a check for $1500, and a note that said, "I really was awful, it must have been a very difficult experience, please go someplace nice for a couple of weeks and act like it all never happened." It was very dear. Then two days later I got another card with another check for $500, and the card said, "Stay three more days." And that was her only way, she was such a little girl, she didn't know how to say she was sorry, that was her only way to say she loved you and didn't want you to feel mad. But she was right, *Let's Make Love* was a terrible ordeal.

I had to make the numbers up on the set, and Monroe was just not that kind. I'd look at Arthur Miller like, "Baby, next time she goes to the dressing room, you send back notice that she's sick and has to go home." Because she'd be out of her nut on the pills, we were shooting things with no film. Now, I've had trouble with some stars where they'd get grand, but I'd just tell them to get away from me. I'm not very passive. But with Rita, sometimes like four days before she was going to do something, she would suddenly feel that it was not her "thing" and that she was going to be awful doing it. She'd cry. She'd never say, "Can we do something else?" She kept trusting you like eventually you'd see she couldn't do it, but it would be something you'd really want her to do because it would make her look so marvelous. But she'd just cry, and you'd say, "Darling, don't cry, we won't do that, we'll do something else. Just forget it. Blow your nose and don't worry. I wouldn't let you do something you feel that way about."

1973

Henry Hathaway, 1966

HENRY
HATHAWAY

RIGHT OFF, even at the distance across the long room that looked still larger because it was virtually bare, you got the feeling that the snow-haired man sunk back into the massive leather desk chair with his arms and head resting forward on the table, a cigar chomped in his powerful teeth, was a large man in every way. Henry had a pencil in his hand, he was doodling; he looked across to me, then down to the paper on the table; he turned it over, smiled sheepishly, surprising, so boyish a smile in that crinkly-lined, broad face, Huck Finn as Executive, an impression emphasized by the cut of his hair, neat, short, parting on the side, a style that must have been standard for boys like Henry when Mark Twain first characterized that type. All that was missing were the "cowlicks," the bits of hair that would never stay down and made the boy look more mischievous than he probably was. He'd probably played the best game of marbles, worked on a rig, got involved in memorable brawls, told his troubles to women he'd never see again, made friendships that lasted a lifetime even if work parted them and they'd never see each other again, listened to a lot of bull and could spot a liar a mile away. This description sounds like it might be a character in one of his films, but there was something of all of them in Hathaway's face. There was also a liquor cabinet to which he swiveled his seat, asking what I'd like, and it seemed right to say "Scotch." He was bent over, looking at the bottles, the cigar never shifting, funneling his voice: "How'd you like it, John?" which allowed me to say, "Tea," and he said, "Oh, sure," and made use of the phone on his table to get the secretary to bring us some, and add, "Listen, if there are any calls, hold them." Looking at me: "How long is this gonna take, John? Half an hour? Hour?" "It's up to you, Mr. Hathaway," and we both established escape hatches in case either one of us got bored or whatever. He might be needed, his time was valuable, there were films to be discussed; I would have had all my questions answered.

Henry Hathaway was still toying with projects for future films after more than fifty years in the business, forty of which were spent as a top director of gutsy, action-packed films, ranging from the rousing *Lives of a Bengal Lancer* (1935) to John Wayne's Oscar-winning *True Grit* (1969) and across a host of films, commercial entertainment in their day, trend-setters in retrospect, like the

609

location-shot crime-in-the-street films *The House on 92nd Street, Call North-side 777, The Dark Corner;* psychological war dramas—*The Desert Fox;* historical adventure—*The Black Rose;* and wildly romantic, delirious-with-sexual-longing melodramas like *Peter Ibbetson* and *Niagara*: Marilyn Monroe in her greatest close-up, her wild-red lips like the heart of the rose, in a face where longing was just a step away from killing. You don't usually think of a man like Hathaway when you think of images of women like that.

But more than anything Hathaway made Westerns: Starting as a director on Paramount's popular quickie Zane Grey Westerns (seven in 1933); pastoral Westerns—*The Trail of the Lonesome Pine; The Shepherd of the Hills;* epic Westerns—*Brigham Young* . . . Westerns, whether made in black-and-white or in color, that had the bluest skies, the greenest range and the whitest hills. It was the West where a man could ride a horse all day and see nothing but beautiful country; where a man was always a man.

What the list of his films may lack in "classic" stature, they never lacked in entertainment. Hathaway was a classic Hollywood director. His stamp may not be as obvious as Hawks' or Mann's or Ford's, but he drives the best team the studios could muster. In Hathaway's films the stars shone—Susan Hayward, Tyrone Power, Cooper, Monroe, Linda Darnell, McQueen—they got noticed for their acting; the men didn't have to be ashamed to be stars, and they wanted to work for him. He also seemed to have something of a reputation for bullying women. Those were just the stories I heard; you wouldn't know it from the films in which a newcomer like Kim Darby, who made her debut in *True Grit,* shone forth with a singular promise she never again revealed.

Hathaway's parents had been actors in San Francisco stock companies during the Barbary Coast era; he started in films when they weren't much older than he was, doing everything and doing it well, so that by the '20s he was the assistant the best directors wanted as backup. He never forgot working with Victor Fleming, another man's man but one who always treated a woman right; with Von Sternberg, who knew everything there was to know about lighting, and the little that was all a camera needed to see; and Lubitsch, who influenced him the least but taught Henry how to work with actors. Lubitsch was head of all Paramount production in 1935, the year Hathaway's career as a major director got under way with a bang.

If one can tell anything about a director by his actors, then it's good to know that Hathaway made more films with John Wayne than anybody else except John Ford; and while Ford won his Oscar for directing Wayne, Wayne won his for being directed by Hathaway. He worked more often with Gary Cooper than with any other star. You meet stars, you've seen them on the screen, so you think you know something about them. You meet a director, you've never seen him before, yet even before you really get going, you get the sense that you know the man, that you've always liked him . . . the way I liked Cooper in *Lives of a Bengal Lancer;* Cooper, leaning back in the wicker chair in the military quarters he shared with Franchot Tone and Richard Cromwell up by the

Khyber Pass; and the way Coop listened to his younger comrade. There was a sensitivity and a trust between the men that allowed feelings of affection and camaraderie to flow back and forth. Hathaway understood that, and his films have that quality.

HH: My folks were on the stage before we got into pictures. I went to work in the first motion-picture companies in California. The American Film Company, "Flying A," was the first, and at that time—about 1910—we made one-reel pictures.*

Allan Dwan was the director, and he's still around today. Gee, I'd like to see Allan. I worked for him later when he was directing Gloria Swanson in *The Great Moment,*† the Elinor Glyn story where Gloria got bitten by a snake on the tit and Milton Sills sucks out the poison! Anyway, that was the great moment in the picture. I was an assistant director then. I got my directorial debut at Paramount. I worked there for eighteen years, and left on account of Frank Freeman when he took over at Paramount, and went over to work for Darryl F. Zanuck at Fox and stayed for twenty years, so I've never worked at Warner Brothers or Columbia, and I only made one picture—*How the West Was Won*—at MGM.

Being so long in the business, I got to see through my own family and other people in the movies being destroyed by alcohol, so I've never touched a drop of liquor in my life. And it's only because I've seen so many people absolutely destroy themselves. It must be a failing in the people themselves; they can't handle it, or don't know when to stop, or they need it for strength. Some people are not comfortable with other people, especially when they're expected to be sort of super—so getting a couple of shots inside helps them speak out a little more and strengthen their egos. I can understand, especially in the case of female stars, how they get to hit the alcohol. They're glamorous, sought after and chased and fawned over. Then one day they find they're fifty years old, because I know our life here goes so fast. Because it's one picture after another and, the first thing you know, it's the next year. And all of a sudden, without realizing what's gone through, you're there and you're fifty, you lift up your head and the time's gone.

Hayworth is a really nice lady and it's a shame she drinks now. She wasn't that old when we did *Circus World,* so it wasn't a big problem at that time. Men have taken all her money. Aly Khan blew his own fortune of $2 million in a year—he was popular that year—and then she supported him. He had an allowance that wasn't even enough to gamble on, let alone live on

---

*Henry was born in 1898 in Sacramento, California, and entered films at the age of ten as a child actor in Westerns.

†Dwan directed Swanson in seven films between 1923 and 1925, but *The Great Moment* (1920) was directed by Sam Wood.

and have horses, etc., etc. He was always in trouble money-wise. 'Cause I knew him during that period too, when he had all this inheritance from his grandmother, and then his father just cut him off. He used to come here to LA to see Rita and we used to go up to Darryl's place quite a lot, in Palm Springs, on weekends. And I knew Aly in Switzerland, and in Paris, and different times. With him, nobody could have done anything except sit and watch. Rita too. Well, Rita loves to do that anyway. Rita loved it. Just loved it. She was in seventh heaven. Rita should have been Madame du Barry. She's got a lot of vitality. You noticed her when she was in a room. She was so lovely and nice . . . affable. The sadness of her after she broke up with him, the sadness of the films she made after, is the sadness of her life ending up without a man and without any money. That's automatic, that you finally sit alone one night.

JK: But she was still young when they split, she still had a long career ahead of her.

HH: I don't care if you're twelve and it happens to you. You marry a dream prince and find he's conning you for all you're worth and leaves you. Rita was no wallflower. She only seemed self-effacing because she was always surrounded by strong men who monopolized attention. Rita was constantly being used because she sort of chose the wrong men—but what the hell! I mean, domineering women have never been accepted in this town, because this town was always run by a strong set of men.

   You never heard of Bette Davis being anyplace because Bette Davis took over all the time; *she* was the man. But she was never in that social circle because they said: "Fuck her, let her stay home." [He gives a matter-of-fact though not very nice chortle after saying that.] The kind of women they had around were the sort of women that listened. My God, I mean, you'd have Darryl and Preminger and Gregory Ratoff, and when men like that get to-gether, they didn't want no dominating-type woman. As soon as someone became too strong . . . Not that they didn't want to accept it, but they were a bunch of men, this town has always been a bunch of men. There's never been a fraternity of women that invited the men out.

The kind of women Hathaway was talking about, the women that the men liked around them, were women like Marilyn Monroe, who may have been used along the way, or let themselves be used, but they weren't dumb, they knew what they wanted and, in the end, got it. You hear from a lot of the Hollywood men who knew her that Marilyn was a really good listener. Obviously, that flattered their egos. Few of them thought she was stupid. Hathaway was at 20th when Marilyn was there and he directed her in *Niagara,* which looked less like her official launch than her coronation in color by Technicolor, and when he talked about her, I got the feeling—it's really no more than a hunch—that he'd been in love with her. He just stopped more often . . . and thought about it . . . and his voice would rise in anger at the injustice, and soften with concern.

HH: She was very special. Marilyn was scared to death, and never sure she was a good actress. The tragedy was that she was never *allowed* to be. I saw her one time over at Paramount, this was the time she was married to Miller. She was walking up and down outside the stage. I thought, "Jesus, that's Marilyn out there." I went out to her and she was crying. I walked up and down with her and said: "What's the matter?" She said: "All my life I've played Marilyn Monroe, Marilyn Monroe, Marilyn Monroe . . . I've tried to do a little better and find myself doing an imitation of Edie Adams doing an imitation of me. I try to do a little better, but then I do an exaggeration of myself doing the same thing. I want to do something different. That was one of the things that attracted me to Miller when he said he was attracted by me. When I married Miller, one of the fantasies I had in my mind was that I could get out of Marilyn Monroe through him. . . . And here I find myself back here on the stage, and I just couldn't take it, I had to get out of there. I just couldn't face having to do another scene of trying to do something with Marilyn Monroe."

Hathaway was old-guard Hollywood, the kind of man they generally accuse of ruining Marilyn when she was out there but, to my mind, the only kind of man to really understand her, and respect her, and take her dreams of stardom seriously, and try to help her.

HH: I think her whole life might have changed if Darryl Zanuck would have let her do . . . I wanted to do *Of Human Bondage* with Marilyn and Jimmy Dean way back then, because after I did that picture with her I found her marvelous to work with, very easy to direct and marvelously, terrifically ambitious to do better. And *bright,* really bright learning. She may not have had an education, but she was just naturally bright. But always being trampled on. You talk of Rita being trampled on by men. This little thing was trampled on by bums! I don't think anyone ever treated her on her own level. To most men she was, I won't say a bum, but something that they were a little bit ashamed of, to put it bluntly—even Joe DiMaggio. If she had been allowed to do this picture, it would have put her in another category. I think she would have been absolutely marvelous doing it. But Darryl said: "Jesus Christ, how can you think of it! How can I say I'm putting Marilyn in a very sensitive Bette Davis–style play? We'd get lampooned before we started. There would be a problem with her work, and meantime I'd lose $3 to $4 million on the films I could be making with her being Marilyn Monroe."

JK: Well, Zanuck was never that smart about women. Look what he did—while he had people like Marilyn, he signed up people like Bella Darvi.*

---

*Darvi was one of Zanuck's string of European mistresses he tried to turn into film stars. Others included Simone Simon, Juliette Greco, Irina Demick and the last one, Geneviève Giles. None except Simon ever established themselves with the American public, although a lot of money was spent, and even Hathaway took turns directing some of them, like Bella Darvi in *The Racers.*

HH: You can't judge Zanuck from Bella Darvi onward. You can't judge his career from then because he was berserk then—he was senile. But he made his own particular type of picture. Let's think of the plus side: he started Cagney, Edward G. Robinson, Clark Gable, he started Bogey. . . .

JK: But those are all men.

HH: Is that a crime? Every man has his own thing. You gotta understand that. He always believed that action pictures were what movies were all about, and women didn't fit that category. He said women had to be in pictures, but they weren't what made pictures successful commercial movies.

JK: I know he's a major influence on good writing in screenplays, and when he ran Warners, he created lots of trends. I just meant that he was never much good when it came to women stars and used Monroe as an example.

HH: He did one brave thing that has hung on in this industry for a long time and he created it himself. In early days we always had as a leading man sort of Tyrone Power and Wally Reid types, and the sort of elegant, fashionable men who had good speaking voices. And Darryl said: "Fuck! Women love bums!" He took all the heavies, Bogey was a heavy; when he picked Clark Gable, Gable was playing a heavy in a play, *The Last Mile,* here in LA in which he was the killer. Zanuck said that women *want* that quality in men. So he took all the heavies and made leading men out of them. Richard Widmark, after I made *Kiss of Death* with him—he was the worst fuckin' heavy in the world. And Darryl makes a leading man out of him! [The table vibrates from the heavy pounding Henry is giving it to emphasize his point.] He said: "Women want that quality in a man. That's a *he-man* and most of them are goddamn heavies, they kick them in the ass once in a while and push them around and dominate 'em." And it's still true. Look at the Burt Reynolds and the Clint Eastwoods and all of that crap coming up. They're all abusive to women.

There was another guy a long time ago who definitely changed the whole style of acting; that was the guy who played in *Lightnin';* that play ran for nine years. He was down-to-earth, a natural actor who scratched his ass, picked his nose, all the things Brando does. In those days it was a kinda brave thing to do to come out onstage with mussed hair and old clothes. He started a whole vogue on the stage. He was accused one day of not projecting, and he answered that he thought a good voice had ruined more actors than whiskey. And it's true—that voice they used to have is now gone. Motion pictures—good ones—are made to carry an emotion, and if that doesn't show, if they don't have that quality, then it's no good. But the actors of *that* day, and now, used their voices. If they wanted to be happy, they were *so happy* or whatever. But it never penetrated on the screen. They were the two great changes in styles. One was made by this guy, Frank Bacon his name was (his son Lloyd Bacon became a fine director), back on the stage in *Lightnin',* and the other was made by Zanuck, who said no one wants these fucking pretty boys anymore. That was back in the late '20s and the '30s and he brought in a whole era of that kind of picture with *Public Enemy* and things like that. Darryl made a great contribution to pictures.

Since Hathaway directed any number of extremely romantic-looking 20th Century–Fox male stars in the '40s—Tyrone Power, George Montgomery, John Payne and such—he was conscious that Zanuck was willing to stretch a point, but he was talking about a transition in the screen image of male stars, and not the *finis* of the matinee idol.

HH: But you're right, he never created a woman star except for Betty Grable and Alice Faye. But his women were severely limited because he made men's pictures—action pictures in which the women were just window dressing. To put it in simple arithmetic, he always made a picture with two men and a woman, and never, if he could help it, the other way around.

JK: Well, what about all those '40s musicals with two women and one man?

HH (chuckles): Well, that was the war and Darryl couldn't help that. The trouble with Marilyn was she never had any confidence. Rita always had it because she was one of the great dancers. She always knew she could do that. Some people like to use a lack of self-confidence as a kind of prop—"Protect me, I'm just a poor girl and you'll have to help me." Rita did a bit of that, but it wasn't really necessary because she was always goddamned sure of herself. Rita also invited tremendous camaraderie from the camera crews and technicians on the set. They'd shout: "Hey, Rita, another take coming up!" If you'd said that to Norma Shearer or somebody, you'd be out of a job.

    I knew Norma when she first came down from Canada and I worked on the first movie she made here, *Empty Hands,** directed by Victor Fleming. And I lived through that love affair she had with Victor.

What repercussions their passion must have had for Henry to speak of *his* living through *their* romance. Or is it that, as with so much in memory, things were just better then, they were *more* of a thing, and the thing itself was at once simpler, less inverted, there was "more" because there was "less"? The codes were stricter and people believed in them; men could be shamed, women still blushed. You think that's funny, or unrealistic for 1921? By 1940 those simple virtues were apparently so rare that when a big blond girl came along with a scrub-faced look and blushed, really blushed, and so gave her feelings away in such a direct, honest and appealing manner, the country, the world, fell in love with her. That was Ingrid Bergman, and Vic Fleming fell in love with her too.

Empty Hands was made in 1924. Shearer began as an extra on the East Coast in 1920 and had appeared in many films before she was directed by Fleming in 1924.

HH: Every dame he ever worked with fell on her ass for him. Norma Shearer. Clara Bow. Bergman. I made every picture Fleming did for eight years at Paramount. Did you ever see *Mantrap* with Clara Bow and Ernest Torrence? Clara Bow was a personality. Strictly a sexpot. It. That's all they wanted her for, like Betty Grable. She had great warmth because she was timid. You'll find that someone who's timid has more warmth than someone who's bold. Rita was a much better actress than Clara, and I worked with both of them. Clara was always "on," all day long—and alone at night. Marilyn Monroe lived in a life all by herself and was always mixed up with one thing. One day I said to her: "Marilyn, you gotta move out of that fucking one room that you're in at that little hotel, and you gotta start to get some clothes and do something for yourself. After all, you're making $500 a week and you're living alone, so get a better room, because when you go home, you're *so* alone. I'm not talking about living big, I'm just talking about hiring a maid for $50 or $75 who'll press your clothes, wash your blouse and have a cup of coffee ready." She said: "Henry . . ." and she went through a list with me of what she did with her money: she was taking singing lessons, dancing lessons, elocution lessons. She said: "I pay $375 a week worth of lessons." I said: "I don't believe it. What about the school here on the lot?" She said: "They ignore me." So I went in to Zanuck and said: "Jesus Christ, this girl's got great talent, why the hell don't you treat her like a human being? Not somebody you put under the desk to suck your cock while you're having your story conferences and having fun out of it. Treat her like a goddamn human being! Here's this girl living like a bum because she's honest enough to want to make herself better. She's paying out $375 for her lessons. *You* pay for her lessons and give her the $500 she's supposed to have." He said, "Don't tell me how to run the fucking studio," that he knew how to handle people and, Jesus Christ, he didn't need my advice.

Hathaway broke off there, pausing for a minute before going back to his original track before he blew up at Zanuck. In *Niagara* he gave Marilyn a film to remember—it was wild, it was over the top, it was Marilyn the way Von Sternberg had revealed Dietrich to the world. Years later he was finally going to do *Of Human Bondage* with her, and when it fell through and Marilyn was replaced by Kim Novak, Hathaway withdrew from the project.

HH: She had a voice teacher, she had this goddamned Russian woman called Natasha with her all the time. She took walking lessons and all the rest, trying to do something with herself. When I did *Niagara,* I said: "Look, I want you to wear your own clothes," and I'd take her and buy her a whole new wardrobe after.* She said she hadn't got anything. I didn't believe her, so she said to come on over to her apartment and look. It was one goddamn room and a

---

*See the interview with Loretta Young, in which Loretta talks about getting a Monroe-type dress from wardrobe to help her get into character.

bath and a little stove thing over it. She opened up the closet and there were some slacks and sweaters and in the back was one black suit. I said: "What's that?" She said she'd bought it when Johnny Hyde died, for the funeral. She said: "That's why I have to borrow clothes from the studio when I have to go out. I don't have any of my own."

JK: Well, she sure made the studio pay for the way they treated her on the way up.

HH: When they did *Seven Year Itch,* her contract was just about up with the studio. Now they were trying to talk her around. I'd got her to take on Charlie Feldman as her agent after Johnny died. Now, Charlie was a friend of Darryl's, but that didn't affect it. Anyway, after the preview of the picture—and it was a big hit, you know—he got her a deal that gave her just about the whole studio.

Henry sat there, chomping on his cigar, having made his point.

HH: I had a very mixed school of learning because I've worked a great deal with three completely different directors. Vic Fleming first, who I adored, and liked his work better than any; and Von Sternberg, with whom I made *Underworld, Last Command*—Evelyn Brent, Bill Powell. I used her in one of my pictures years later when she was around. I worked on Jannings' first American picture with Fleming, *The Way of All Flesh.* And Lubitsch was the other director. They were all good friends of mine, because I worked so goddamn hard for them, and they are strong men.

JK: Well, I adore Sternberg. I always thought when Hawks made *Scarface,* it was really a talkie version of *Underworld,* camera setups and all, and Sternberg created or he projected the woman as the equal of a man in any of the ways we think a man being, well, in ways we think only men are, like chivalrous.

HH: He always felt, if you watch his pictures, that a woman, deep down, dominated the man; it comes out in *Blue Angel.* Underneath, the woman was the one who was pulling the strings; that reflected in a man's behavior. He felt that very strongly, that the male-female relationship was what made the world go round. I worked on *Morocco* with him and Dietrich and Cooper.

JK: Howard Hawks told me that he had cast *Underworld* and that the whole thing was written and the set built before Sternberg came on the scene.

HH: Oh, bullshit! Listen. I was on the whole thing. Ben Hecht was the writer and Arthur Rosson was going to direct it . . . and Von Sternberg had made just that little picture *The Salvation Hunters.* They were working on the story of *Underworld* and Schulberg sent Sternberg up to make contributions to the picture's style—because B. P. Schulberg was fascinated with style and he felt if they got some style in the picture, it wouldn't be just an underworld movie, and maybe 'cause he figured Joe was German or Austrian or something, he'd know all about giving it style, and he sat Joe in on the conferences, and Joe was brilliant. Each time, he dominated the thing. He'd sit back quietly while they were talking till they said: "What do you think, Joe?" And he'd say: "Jeez, I wouldn't do it that way, I'd do x, y and z."

As I understand it, he developed the character of George Bancroft to show power. He always said that if you want to see that a man's a heavy, then have him come in and kick a dog, you know, or throw a fucking cat out of a chair. He was the one that suggested having Bancroft enter and throw a dollar in the spittoon for the other guy to pick up. Which Howard Hawks later put in *Rio Bravo* with Dean Martin. Well, Howard of course doesn't need anyone to help him remember anything. One time we previewed a picture that Von Sternberg did that Jules Furthman worked on,* and Jules had got the longest memory of anyone in the world, and when they previewed the picture, the credits said: "Story Remembered by Jules and Charles Furthman." Listen, Howard Hawks is brilliant, he's a good friend of mine and I think he's brilliant, but he's got the biggest imagination of anyone in the world and the most gall. He'd steal any goddamn thing and change it around a little. He even steals from himself.

JK: Well, Hawks did acknowledge a certain influence Sternberg had on him, but, on the other hand, he claimed to have originated all those ideas and bits of business which seem so Sternbergian, like putting Dietrich in trousers and having her kiss the girl in the nightclub.

HH: Well, I don't know. I didn't think Sternberg and Hawks were that close. But my opinion of Von Sternberg is that when he left the business, he'd forgotten more about movies than most directors knew. He was brilliant in ways of making movies, absolutely brilliant. When I worked on *Morocco*— remember that street they come down to get to the town at night? Well, I said: "Jesus, I got to get this street ready for you because it's getting close to shooting," and I asked him which part of it he wanted to use. It got to two days before and he said just to use a lot of eucalyptus poles and palm leaves. That's all. He didn't want any more dressing. We went out in the morning and laid the eucalyptus poles across the street with the palm leaves hanging off them. All you saw were the shadows and stuff. We never dressed the fucker—nothing.

---

*Jules and his brother Charles Furthman were screenwriters who worked on a number of films with both Von Sternberg and Hawks, and lots of the situations in a Von Sternberg film would resurface years later in Hawks' films. Dietrich's insolence hosted a whole generation of women and the way they summed a man up, and when she found the man she liked, as in *Morocco*, she went after him the way, years later, Bacall went after Bogart in *To Have and Have Not*. Before Sternberg, that was the way the man used to go after a woman.

Von Sternberg's masterful, evocative use of light and shade to create more than a beautiful picture, led to insight, to mood, to the life behind those walls. Hathaway put a lot of that feeling into his great film *Lives of a Bengal Lancer,* a lusty adventure but one that resonated powerfully over the years long in advance of those '70s male-bonding films like *Butch Cassidy.*

HH: That was brand new. That was the first time we had a love story between two men instead of a man and a woman. Because there is no woman in that picture.* It came out of a cycle of things that Louis D. Lighton did.† He was of the opinion that a man entered into someone else's story, solved their problem, and then went out. Whether he died or lived, it didn't make any difference. That was *Captains Courageous* that he did, which had the kid falling off the boat—this kid had this mixed-up relationship with his father, and the man comes in and clears up their lives and gives the boy back to his father. In *Bengal Lancer* he put in that story between the father and the son. He was a brilliant producer; he always had an underlying theme that was never spoken but nevertheless existed. The point about *Lancer* was that in India 400 million people were controlled by 40,000. They were kept in line by discipline. The discipline wasn't in beating down the natives, but in being very disciplined among themselves so that the natives watching it thought: "Holy Jesus! If they punish themselves so harshly, what will they do to us!" So I could always find solutions to scenes by referring back to the thesis. When the man punishes his own son so severely that it breaks down his son and estranges them, Cooper is brought in to fix that up, brings the son back and makes the son understand, and then Cooper dies. All of Buddy's pictures were around that theme. That's the trouble when people try to make "improvised" pictures. How can you improvise if you haven't got a basic thought? I also made *Peter Ibbetson* for Buddy Lighton, and *Now and Forever* with that little Shirley Temple. Cooper was in all of them.

The first picture that I ever made in which I really felt my strength—I never felt any strength in making the Westerns—was *The Witching Hour* [1934] with Sir Guy Standing,‡ but that picture, because it was in a realm that I really didn't know, made me feel quite differently from how I felt in Westerns. I made so goddamn many Westerns when I was still an assistant that I didn't feel any different directing them than I did when I was doing so many second units and directed big parts of them all. The guys working today mostly come from television and they get used to working within a proscenium arch: there's a door, a bar, a chair, a sofa and a set way to bring people in and take them out. But when you're not in a proscenium situation, they

---

*Kathleen Burke appeared in it, but her role was minimal and had no influence on the relationship or the story. She was just a woman in the emir's palace whom the publicity department could build up in the poster campaign.

†Lighton was an associate producer at Paramount.

‡Also Judith Allen, Olive Tell, Jack Holliday, William Frawley.

don't know how to direct people's entrances and exits. You'll find even when
they work in cities they'll go to corners, they'll go to alleys or cars for people
to come in and out of. They just don't know how to bring people together
without having a chair or a couch or a bar. So even outside they confine
themselves to a lot of rocks, or around a wagon, and they constrict themselves
unconsciously with these crutches. In the early days we always laughed about
it. Some directors, even when working in a room, would end up in a corner.
They weren't comfortable even in the middle of a room. Sternberg once in a
while would be caught like this. I'd say: "Joe, you've got the whole fuckin'
set behind you out here." Over and over again you find an entrance shot,
come in, and *boom*! Right in the corner. It may be a natural human instinct
to surround yourself with walls, but it's not good movies.

Hathaway's last movie, *Hangup*, wasn't very good, but his other films will keep
on. They'll run on television and in revival houses. They will look after his
reputation.

1975

HERMES
PAN

NOBODY IN THE WORLD, including Hermes Pan, would think of Hermes Pan without thinking of Fred Astaire (including Fred Astaire), Ginger Rogers, Ann Miller, Betty Grable, Bob Fosse, Jack Cole or Eleanor Powell. When any of them mentioned Hermes, they would add, as if it were the middle part of his name, "You know, he did all those wonderful things with Fred Astaire." Only Rita Hayworth, who knew Hermes for most of her years in Hollywood, would say: "Oh, Hermes, he's so good. Isn't he sweet?" Rita responded to his nature before praising his reputation.

Hermes, who started in the chorus in the late '20s, began in films in the early '30s, and his last choreographic credit to date was for a 1983 Italian romantic wartime musical comedy. He works well with a high-kicking chorus, and their memories of him are only pleasant, but he's at his best with the stars in close-up, sweeping, stretching, serenely independent and content because he makes them all look so graceful—Cyd stroking the hose across her thighs as she yields to the pleasures of capitalistic undergarments and bourgeois blandishments in *Silk Stockings;* Rita rising up out of bed, tousled and yawny, showing you what it feels like to be "Bewitched, Bothered and Bewildered"; Audrey Hepburn, with a facecloth for a partner and a two-step for a dance as the steam fills up the little bathroom and she recalls the wonderful evening she spent and how she "Could Have Danced All Night."

Hermes is a quiet man, modest, self-effacing to the point of almost vanishing. He has been a highly successful choreographer almost since he first arrived in Hollywood back in the '30s, when he became one of only three dance directors to win an Oscar for his work. He received it for his contribution to Fred Astaire's first solo outing in *A Damsel in Distress*. After that the Screen Directors' Guild brought pressure to bear on the Academy to eliminate the dance director as a credit for Academy consideration, presumably since it made it only too apparent that the success of those early film musicals owed more to the man who made the movie move than to the man who directed it, and the award was dropped.

621

HP: I arrived out here during the Busby Berkeley era, when choreography in films was more or less the geometrical designs of Berkeley, the top shots and the typical huge numbers where the curtains would open in a small theater and you'd go into a football field. Of course it was something new and imaginative, but actually you didn't see much dancing on the screen! I began with *Flying Down to Rio* in the fall of 1933. And *Flying Down to Rio* was the first time that dancing as such had ever been seen on the screen: a routine set to music, an intimate dance number especially. Before that, it had been mostly scenes, but I think that Astaire and Rogers were the first ones who did a dance routine. Before that, everyone was still in the Berkeley school . . . Sammy Lee and Bobby Connolly and Dave Gould. . . .

This was before they called them choreographers. They used to be called dance directors. And the word "choreographer" was practically unknown. I think the first time it was used was by Agnes de Mille when she did *Oklahoma!** That was the first time I had ever been conscious of the word. I was always called a dance director, and as time went on, I became a choreographer! My credit changed on screen: "Choreography by" instead of "Dances by" or "Ensembles by." But that was not until after I left Fox, maybe when I was at MGM. At Fox I was a dance director. At one time the Directors' Guild refused to let anyone have that name who was not a director, so many times it was "Dances by." But I had more control over the camera there than, say, at RKO. And so you'll notice that even in *Flying Down to Rio* there was less of the big production type of number with twenty girls and twenty boys, even though they were still doing geometrical designs like the Berkeley thing.

I love dancing as such, and I really like to see a few people rather than huge productions where dancing was lost. To me, it wasn't really dancing. I don't think I would have ever gotten into it anyway. It was just a fortunate situation that I did meet Astaire and that he was of the same outlook, feeling and mentality as I was. It sort of blended into a beautiful thing, it worked out very fortunately.

JK: Was it a jealously guarded field? Did Dave Gould and all those people worry about your coming in?

HP: No, not really. And the competition was minute because there were not all that many choreographers . . . dance directors. When you think of all the musicals that were done, the competition wasn't very big. But Dave Gould, he was a very quiet man. He was in charge of dance at RKO when I joined them. He wasn't a dancer, strangely enough. I don't think he could even do a time step. I guess you would call him more of a promoter type . . . he promoted ideas. But he couldn't begin to do anything, to carry out anything

---

*Actually, the first use of the credit "Choreography by . . ." in a show was for George Balanchine in *On Your Toes* (1936).

Hermes Pan, 1954

in dancing. And also that was fortunate for me, because, being in a dancing film for the first time with Astaire, I was the only one of his staff that danced. He was concerned with production and getting the big number together, and ideas and things, but my work was mainly with Astaire.

JK: And most of the big numbers in *Flying Down to Rio* were your idea, like the big airplane sequence?

HP: Yes. As a matter of fact, I had to write that out when I got the job. And also "The Carioca." I got together with my sister and made up a routine to show Gould of a dance called Carioca with only people's heads together. He was very pleasant about it. I think he could see that I was getting more attention than he was at the time, but I must say he was always very big about the whole thing.

JK: In terms of creating dance for the screen, you and Astaire were unique for quite a long time, until about the end of the '30s.

HP: That's true. Astaire and I introduced a new era in film dancing, some years before other people got into it. There was Jack Whiting, and then later on Eleanore Whitney, Tommy Wonder, Dorothy Lee; there was quite a rash of dancers that came afterwards, but very few of them clicked until Eleanor Powell and people of that caliber. Oh, and I almost forgot about Charles Collins. They brought him over in '35 to do two movies in Technicolor . . . *Dancing Pirate* and *The Cucaracha.** I don't know what ever happened to him. Then Ray Bolger came along in the '30s, but he was what you would call an eccentric dancer, "leg-mania." Buddy Ebsen was also an eccentric dancer. There were very few Astaire-Rogers ballroom type of dancers. Well, there was Velez and Yolanda, they were very good, but they never did anything else outside of appearing in one film.†

But just to dance in a film, unless you have some relation to the story, doesn't mean an awful lot. If someone just comes in and dances, you say, "Oh, they're good," but forget about them. But when the person who's part of the plot suddenly goes into a beautiful dance, you are captivated by that situation more. For instance, when Fred and Ginger would have a fight, they would make up in a dance. He would woo her and win her back, and that was part of the story. The dances were usually indicated in the script, you know: We'll have a dance number in this section, such as in *Top Hat* they will go to the park and have a dance. That was "A Lovely Day to Be Caught in the Rain." I would work with Astaire and we would figure out how to get into the number without it jarring, because people then were beginning to be hor-

---

*While Charles Collins, a Broadway dancer married to Dorothy Stone, was brought to the Coast for *Dancing Pirate,* he did not appear in *La Cucaracha.* His co-star, Steffi Duna, was in the short, *La Cucaracha,* which launched 35-strip Technicolor.
† Popular '30s ballroom dancers, they appeared in film and as a specialty act.

rified by the idea of a person bursting into song or dance without a reason.* So the main trick was to get into a dance before you realized they were into a dance, to get in so gradually and unobtrusively that suddenly you were transported from the spoken word to the visual, and still keeping that idea going of what you had last seen.

In the park number Irving Berlin had the idea of the song, he had played the score, and we knew that when they went into the park, it would take place there and it would be raining. Our problem was how to get into it. We had to start with thunder: Ginger is furious. But the thunder makes her jump into his arms. Then she's embarrassed about being so frightened, but he's loving it. It thunders again and then he starts to sing, "The thunder and lightning, de-dah, de-dah dah dah." And it was so beautifully blended from the scene into the dance that you were just transfixed.

See, at that time they had been established as such a tremendously popular pair on the basis of the first three films that people were dying to see them again in something. So for *Top Hat* they had several exceptional people creating their material, from Pandro Berman [producer] to Mark Sandrich [director], score by Berlin, Allan Scott, who wrote the dialogue; they all created an original movie with Astaire and Rogers in mind. "The Piccolino" was going to be a big production number, because everything then had the big production number, so we knew that as a finale we had that. And Astaire and I wanted to make it a dance. We wanted it to say "*Do* the Piccolino"— about a dance—rather than have it saying "*Hear* the Piccolino"—about a song. But we didn't get our way because Berlin wouldn't change it. So then the other numbers were written and through meetings we decided where to work them into the script. Astaire had quite a bit of influence about where he would like to place these things. And sometimes he would cut a line of dialogue and say, "I can't say this." He would always be adding or subtracting to the script, especially the dialogue.

JK: Did Ginger exert any ideas of her own?

HP: No.

JK: She just came in and did her job?

HP: Yes.

JK: That didn't affect the attitude of one to the other?

HP: No.

JK: He would have danced equally happily with somebody else?

HP: Yes.

---

*A reaction to the unrealistic grandiose or operetta-style musicals of a few years before.

JK: The chemistry was just an accident?

HP: I think so. See, I think that Ginger realized it more than Fred that they had created a . . . uh . . . a chemistry together.

JK: Were you about to say "a monster"?

HP: Well, Fred was getting a little tired of being known as a team, and for a long time he was the one who wanted to break away. But the public demanded them. It was like divorcing your wife! It was a crisis for Fred when she left. I mean, she just moved into another range and the public accepted her as a "single," but there was a lull before he found his second wind. It used to make him furious. But then, let's see, the first time he tried to break with Ginger was, I think, *Damsel in Distress*. That's the one I got the Oscar for. And of course Joan Fontaine was no dancer at all. And I could never understand why they would cast Fred with Joan Fontaine. The poor girl couldn't even walk. Naturally, she was terrified, and they didn't really do much dancing, but there was one number ["Things Are Looking Up"] where I had to work with her. I had her walking, doing little turns. But I think Fred was so delighted to be on his own that he couldn't have cared less who he danced with.

JK: Everybody had noticed that the RKO thing was a team, but just how important was, say, Mark Sandrich's contribution as director? Was he very musically oriented?

HP: I think he had a great appreciation for the musical *feeling* of the film. He had wonderful taste of story and style. But, as a matter of fact, we never used to show any numbers—until they were half finished—to Sandrich or Berman or Berlin or anybody, because we didn't want any suggestions or interference. Like Berlin might object to the tempo of a song, or Sandrich might feel he would like the story to do something! So we would rehearse on a guarded stage for weeks, and when it was fairly finished, we would let them come in and see it. That was Fred's idea; he would say, "Sorry, I'm not ready to show it." By then he could pretty much say what he wanted.

JK: And when Ginger left and Fred branched out, that was also a major trauma in your movie career?

HP: Oh, certainly. Because when they broke up, for about a year there I didn't do anything, until I went to Fox. The Betty Grable era. And that was a whole new era for me with the *Coney Island* pictures, although the first film I did at Fox was *That Night in Rio* with Carmen Miranda and Cesar Romero. They had had Seymour Felix doing the Shirley Temple and Alice Faye numbers before I arrived. Seymour was of the Sammy Lee school, New York stage. You'd never think he was a dance director to look at him. He looked like a shoe salesman. He was a very pleasant little fellow, but he was anything but what you would expect of a dance director, who I think you'd expect to be a little more esthetic. As a matter of fact, most of the dance directors of that era were sort of the hard-boiled, slangy types with the cigar, who would shout at the girls, "Get your fannies on . . . get the lead out! Come on, get the lead out!" They were always sort of the nasty type. And even Fred would kid me, he'd say, "You know, you're the first dance director I wouldn't call a shit." Oh, but they'd shove 'em around . . . LeRoy Prinz would make some girls hysterical. He would just love to have them in tears. And that seemed to be the thing, to swear at the girls and be nasty. Fred and I used to kid, he'd do an impersonation of that type and say, "Go out and get me a cup of coffee, and come right back so we can do the shit-heel dance number. All right, kids, come on, let's get with it!" But I worked out the dancing for the boys and girls. I would also work with him and Ginger to find out where they would come into the number, and Fred would say, "Now, when we dance, I don't want people jumping up and down and doing 5000 things." And he was right, because it would detract. He'd say, "Just remember, when we dance, have the background as unobtrusive as possible." Which was right. He would have an awful lot to say even about the sets, the floors, or if the background was too busy.

JK: How do you differ from Astaire?

HP: I don't really know, you know. I've often wondered, because I'm sure that I absorbed an awful lot from him, subconsciously even, and from his style. On the other hand, I'm certain that he has gotten certain things from me. In *Silk Stockings* I got him to do some slides, which he would never have done, or catch Cyd Charisse as she fell off a box. He's never been the physical type, he's not very strong. But to lift, there are little tricks always, so there are many things that I've gotten him to do where he said, "Oh, I can't do that. I will not. Oh, forget it." And I'd say, "Just try," and I'd sort of sneak up on him. There was a thing in the "Yam" number in *Carefree* where I wanted a finale of him throwing Ginger over his leg over six different tables. . . . I was always conscious of the camera. And we would try to work things so they went across the screen, because if you see a dancer coming towards you, you don't see anything except him getting larger.

JK: Did you have a camera in rehearsal?

HP: No, just a mirror. The mirror was the camera.

JK: Did you choreograph on paper?

HP: No, never. Just remembered it. I've never been able to write anything down. I wouldn't know how. I'd just tell the director where the camera should go, like "This has to be designed from this angle, otherwise it doesn't mean anything." But sometimes you'd get a stubborn director and he would say, "Well, I think this and that," and then you'd have to sometimes let him have his way. A lot of film was wasted that way. Many directors have wanted to see something a certain way, and when they see it on the screen, they realize it doesn't work, because they're not dancers. Now, George Stevens [*A Damsel in Distress*], I must say, had a lot of good suggestions for me in the funhouse number. This is a number I got the idea for . . . there was nothing written for it. It, the song, was called "Stiff Upper Lip," which has nothing to do with a funhouse, but I was down at the beach one day, at the funhouse at Ocean Park, and I thought, "Wouldn't it be great to have a number with these crazy turning tables and barrels and distorted mirrors?" The next day I couldn't wait to tell Fred about it, and Stevens and the producer liked it right away. But they said, "How'll we do it? There's nothing in the script." So they wrote a sequence where they just went to an amusement park, and they used "Stiff Upper Lip" although it had nothing to do with the scene. If we hadn't been so far into the film, I think Gershwin would have written a special number for it.

JK: Speaking of Gershwin, why was "They Can't Take That Away from Me" done to perfection in *Barkleys of Broadway* when it was originally written for *Shall We Dance* and then literally thrown away?

HP: I suppose because they didn't realize what a hit it was going to be. See, there's a long thing with Harriet Hoctor doing this incredibly ungraceful dance with back bends all over the place and splitting her legs. I don't know whether they thought of her as a future partner for Fred, but he was very much opposed to it because she was too big for him, she was too balletic, and he didn't like the idea of dancing ballet or classical stuff. And Harriet was always on her toes . . . and when she wasn't on her toes, her head was in between her legs.

JK: How often did you work out a number and choreograph it before you really had a song for it?

HP: Well, I remember one thing, and that was the waltz in *Swing Time*. We wanted to do a jazz waltz, and we'd be on the rehearsal stage and the pianist would play a waltz beat and we'd do things to the rhythm. We were very excited about the idea of doing a swing waltz. So we told [Jerome] Kern about it, and he wrote a swing waltz. But I think it was very difficult for him because he didn't really understand what we meant. I must say that Hal Borne, our rehearsal pianist all that time, had a great deal to do with it, and with adapting Kern's music into a waltz. We used part of "Never Gonna Dance" and paraphrases of other songs, and put them into the thing, so Hal was a tremendous influence. We really couldn't get Kern to write what we wanted. I don't think he really knew what we were talking about.

JK: So the numbers were already written when you started the choreography, on the whole?

HP: Yes. But we'd take them and maybe go into different rhythms, and we'd paraphrase them in a way to suit the dance, because you just can't go from verse to chorus, verse to chorus. Maybe you put in an interlude, or a start, to get into the number, and that has to be done right on the set.

JK: And Ginger simply went along with that?

HP: Yeah. I don't think she minded that. She'd just come into rehearsal and seem to enjoy every minute of it. She was agreeable, she worked hard and was wonderful about doing anything you'd tell her.

JK: Until it came time to put on a dress . . .

HP: Oh, with feathers! She wore a dress full of bugle beads once, in *Follow the Fleet,* that slapped Fred in the face. It was "Let's Face the Music and Dance," and the dress weighed forty-eight pounds. The sleeves were long beads, and one time she turned and knocked Fred clear across the room!

JK: Why did you go to Fox? Because of Grable? Did she ask for you?

HP: No, it's funny because after I got my Oscar I didn't work for fifteen months. You know, there's an old superstition that an Oscar brings bad luck. I just finished up my contract, which was *Irene and Vernon Castle* [the last film Fred and Ginger made together at RKO], but of course that was done before the Academy Awards came out, as I remember. But, I don't know, just bad luck, I guess. Then suddenly I got a call from Darryl Zanuck and he wanted me to do *That Night in Rio.* Just like that. I don't know who thought of it or what. So I was just signed for the one picture, and it turned out quite well . . . the "Chica, Chica, Boom, Chic" number was quite a success. That was Carmen Miranda's second film. Her first was *Down Argentine Way.* I think Seymour Felix choreographed that.*

JK: Did you have a lot to do with Betty Grable's development as a dancer? Because she was primarily a hoofer. Are you the creator of Betty Grable?

HP: Well, I worked with her an awful lot, on *Coney Island* and practically every picture she made outside of *Down Argentine Way.* I started with her on "Let's K-nock K-nees" in *The Gay Divorcee,* when she did a thing with Edward Everett Horton. She was cute and she moved well, but she was never a great dancer.

JK: Was she ever considered a partner for Astaire?

HP: I think she was, but I don't think that Fred wanted it. He just felt that she wasn't the right type.

JK: He seems to prefer being a solo artist, doesn't he?

*Nick Castle and Geneva Sawyer are credited for *Down Argentine Way.*

HP: I think so. Yet he enjoyed working on the romantic type of number like "Night and Day" and "Cheek to Cheek." He loved working with Barrie Chase, and he liked working with Cyd Charisse and Rita. He always felt that Cyd was a little too big for him. But he's been put with some awful partners. Think of Paulette Goddard and Joan Leslie . . . and who's Arthur Freed's girlfriend? . . . Lucille Bremer. Fred's ashamed that he had been subjected to some of these . . . Marjorie Reynolds, Jane Powell, Olga San Juan, Sarah Churchill, can you believe some of those!

JK: But back to Betty . . . how adventurous, how creative could you be with her?

HP: You couldn't do much with Betty outside of letting her be Betty Grable. I really don't think she could be other than Betty Grable. Pinup girl, cute blonde who sang and danced. I can't imagine her doing any serious number like the mountaintop number that Cyd Charisse did in *Sombrero*. You know what I'm talking about? Where she goes to offer her life to the old Inca gods if they'll spare her boyfriend.

JK: Jack Cole once said that Betty Grable was really very underrated and that she could do a lot of things that she wasn't allowed to do.

HP: I don't really agree, because I worked with Betty on so many films, and I can't imagine her doing something lyrical . . . even . . . flowing, like the "Silk Stockings" number. No, as I say, she was so . . . Betty Grable. And I'm not knocking it because she was number one at the box office; but the way I work is to make them do what *they* do best, because if you try to change them, I think that you're fighting a lost cause. It can't come out right. The films she got were all in one mold.

JK: Was there no desire on Zanuck's part to get a male partner for her? To do a sort of Astaire-Rogers thing?

HP: Not that I know of. I never even heard it discussed. I think that probably she was such a big draw on her own that they wanted her to be Betty Grable *with* different people. And sometimes the director would come up and say to me, "Look, we need someone to dance with her. Why don't *you* do it?" And, you know, I don't think I got paid for that extra something. No, I didn't.

JK: What was Grable good at?

HP: She really was not a great tap dancer. And she couldn't do great ballet. But she could move, and she had beautiful legs, and she had a certain magnetism when she was on screen. Her color was beautiful and she was pleasant to watch.

JK: Well, you must have felt when you and Astaire split up after RKO that it was the end of your relationship together.

HP: I felt that a chapter had finished, I really did. But I felt that we would work together again sometime. But for that next fifteen months of unemployment I didn't know. I felt that I was at the end of that period, and I'd have to see what happened next. I really thought very seriously of retiring altogether and going into a completely different and more spiritual sort of world. It had always been in the back of my mind, so now I thought, Oh, well, it doesn't matter. I've had my little fling.

In that one statement about a crisis period in his life, Pan suggests something of the strength of his character that made it possible for him to work in the shadow and yet retain a personality strong, assured, his own.

JK: What was it like for you then?

HP: Well, I thought it was sort of a nice era, because they had nice glamorous sets like those for *Coney Island,* and wonderful color, which we didn't have on the Astaire-Rogers. And also the music had become easier, the way of recording it became so much better. At first, when we started Astaire and Rogers, we had to dance to a piano track, then they'd put in the music later, which was just horrible. And then sometimes they'd try and record the taps at the same time as we were shooting it. Then they finally overcame that and we had playbacks. But for most of those Astaire-Rogers things we didn't have playbacks. We danced to a piano track for quite a few of them. I think we ended that after *Follow the Fleet* or the picture after that; then they started to put in the taps later. And then we'd do them with earphones. We'd watch the film on the screen, and I would do Ginger's taps. You couldn't turn around, you had to watch closely to get the synch right.

JK: When you were dancing up there on the screen with Grable in *Coney Island* and things, did you have any offers to become a dancer?

HP: Never in the '30s. Only at Fox, when I danced with Hayworth and Grable. I think I danced with Grable about three times—*Footlight Serenade, Coney Island* and *Rosie O'Grady*. And *Pin Up Girl*. But nobody offered me a career as a dancer in films!

JK: Why were there no male dancers for Betty?

HP: Well, Cesar Romero passed as a male dancer for a time, and Gene Nelson. I don't know why, but there were so few performers who were dancers. For instance, George Chakiris, who was a good actor and a good dancer . . . Marc Platt was a wonderful dancer, but why they didn't come off I don't know. He never meant anything as a screen personality. I think it was probably his looks.

JK: How did the studios differ?

HP: I had more freedom at Fox because I was more independent. And outside of the Astaire-Rogers pictures, the RKO pictures didn't have big budgets and they were very tight. But because of the team, they would give them almost anything they wanted. They were such sure money-makers. But the other films I worked on at RKO were terrible. You know, like *I Dream Too Much,* with Lily Pons, and those pictures with Ann Miller, Wheeler and Woolsey . . . they were very tight on budget. Terrible.

JK: You also did some of the Sonja Henie skating numbers?

HP: Yeah, I did *Sun Valley Serenade.* Zanuck told me that they had decided not to spend much money on her pictures because she was giving everybody such a hard time. This was particularly the case in the "Black Ice Ballet" in *Sun Valley Serenade.* That was a number that I created, an idea I said I wanted . . . the reflection of black and white. I got together with the set man and he said, "Well, we'll flood it with nicozine dye." Anyway, Henie was very difficult to work with, extremely difficult. She wouldn't listen to you, she wanted to do everything *she* wanted to do. She would get into a sit spin and she wouldn't get out of it even if her life depended on it. Every time she got into it, she would stay in it for about 5000 years. And I'd say, "When I count to eight, Henie, *leave* the spin. Because there are about sixteen boys coming down to you and they'll run into you." And so I was on the microphone and she got into a beautiful sit spin, and these sixteen boys came down on her . . . and you can't stop them when they're on skates . . . and they hit Henie and she flew over there, down into the nicozine dye. And when she got up, she was *black.* Her face and her costume were covered in it, and she went into her room with her mother, snarling and screaming, and she refused to work for the rest of the day. So Zanuck called me into his office and said, "Tell Sonja Henie that if she doesn't finish the number tonight, there will be no finish to the number at all." She was trying to hold out because after so many days she'd go onto overtime . . . and she was getting a fortune anyway. But in the afternoon I came back and told her what Zanuck had said, and she went into a storm. She and her mother used to swear in Swedish . . . or Norwegian, rather . . . and scream and holler. She said, "I'll work some more this afternoon, but I won't come back tomorrow." So we did a few more shots and the next day the picture was closed down. Anyway, there was enough film to get the number together, because with that sort of thing there's not much continuity . . . you can have a wipe and then another wipe, and you can always cut it and make a finish. Whereas with the Astaire-Rogers numbers we did one take, large pieces. But with Henie you'd have a large circle or a formation, and then you'd have a dissolve or something, or some girl fly up in the camera, and then we go into another thing, and you cut and make different designs. So it turned out well. You had to be very versatile with Henie. I mean, how much choreography can you do on ice? So I got a pair of skates, and I used to go down to the rink on Stage Fifteen, and I'd see what you could do and how easy it was to turn with music, and at least I'd see what a skater would be able to do. Apart from that, it was almost like dancing.

JK: During this '40s period when so much that was new and exciting was happening over at Metro, did you feel that you were being left out?

HP: Well, I liked what I saw happening over there, and I was very glad when I did go to MGM. The first film I did there was *Three Little Words* with Fred. And that time I was no longer the country cousin I had been at RKO. I had much more to say, even to Astaire. And I would discuss with Jack Cummings [the producer] about the dances. Remember that number "At Home," where Vera-Ellen comes in and they dance through the room and go out through the wall, read the paper, and the toaster and all sorts of things? That was a thing I had the idea for, and I think Saul Chaplin wrote the music. Then I went to Paramount for *Let's Dance*.

JK: Were you loaned out?

HP: No, never. I couldn't even get away for a vacation. Oh, wait, I was borrowed from Fox for *Blue Skies*. That's right.

JK: What did you think of some of those people like Bob Alton, Michael Kidd . . . were you worried at all?

HP: I loved it. Anything I see that is good gives me a lift. If I see something bad, it depresses me so much that I don't want any part of the business anymore. But I loved Michael Kidd. He was so talented. And I loved Jack Cole's work because he had a new look. And he would inspire *me*. So I would always love to see anything by Jack, or Jerome Robbins. To me they were inspirations, and I would think dancing really can be good. Sometimes you would lose the sense of what you were doing and think that everything was more or less the same, so I like to be inspired. I never felt threatened by new people or things, it was always an elation.

JK: I remember Eleanor Powell telling me that if you are disciplined, dancing is like a religion. It's your temple, your service, the whole thing.

HP: In a way, it is. It *is* like a rite. Dancing is a liturgy, using your body as an offering, and at the same time as a means of communication. That's true. I never thought of it, but it's true.

1972

Arthur Freed, 1934

ARTHUR
FREED

ARTHUR FREED was the Ziegfeld of MGM, the single most creative and controlling brain in the shaping of the American film musical as we now know it. He had the power and the opportunity, both of which he exercised, to surround himself with a continuous stream of the freshest, most exciting new talents on the American musical scene, in Hollywood and from Broadway. From his first producing credit on *Babes in Arms* (MGM, 1939) to his last as producer, a sensitive nonmusical about teenage romance, *Light in the Piazza* (1962), whether they were box-office hits or misses, his films were among the highlights of Metro's yearly output and set the standard for other musicals.

Freed had worked in vaudeville as a boy, and later turned to writing lyrics with a number of people, including part-time composer Nacio Herb Brown. He joined MGM in 1928 to write the songs for what would turn out to be the first original score for a film musical, *The Broadway Melody* (1929). The film won an Oscar. The songs "You Were Meant for Me," "The Wedding of the Painted Doll" and, of course, "The Broadway Melody" were the first in a list of standards he and Brown wrote for MGM musicals over the next decade. Jukebox and orchestral evergreens like "You came, I was alone, I should have known you were Temptation"; "The Pagan Love Song" for Ramon Novarro to sing in his first sound film, *The Pagan;* "I've Got a Feeling You're Fooling," "Sing Before Breakfast," "After Sundown" and perhaps the most celebrated of them all—"Singin' in the Rain." Though Freed stopped concentrating on his lyric-writing after becoming a producer, he still managed to come up with two time-stoppers, "This Heart of Mine is looking very well . . ." with Harry Warren's music for *Ziegfeld Follies*, and "Make 'Em Laugh, make 'em laugh," which reteamed him with Herb Brown for *Singin' in the Rain*, the film whose score was a catalogue of their hits.

He took a break in the early '60s after two less than memorable but by no means embarrassing nonmusicals, but with plans for future projects to keep him going. L. B. Mayer was gone; so was Mayer's successor, Dore Schary; the studio had been winding down productions for some time and had started to sell off its premises and its props and to concentrate more on TV series like *Dr. Kildare*. It was no longer Freed's MGM and he preferred to rest on his laurels and raise orchids rather than sit in an office where he no longer felt at home. He lived quietly, mulling over possible comeback projects, of which the best known was to have been built around the music of his friend Irving Berlin. *Say It with Music* at one time or another was to have had an all-star cast headed by Judy Garland or Julie Andrews and be directed by Vincente Minnelli. First musicals died; then Judy died; interest waxed and waned; then Freed died.

An old producing friend of Freed's from his first days at the studio, Lawrence Weingarten, was the basis of an introduction. I went to see Freed with Weingarten's daughter, screenwriter and novelist Norma Pisar. Never tall, Freed (born Arthur Grossman, September 9, 1894) at almost eighty was white-haired and crinkly-faced, a quizzical Jewish leprechaun more interested at first in asking about Norma's father and his possible projects, in serving tea, talking about the weather, showing us his orchids—everything interested him more than musicals. As with a lot of very old people I've met, his concentration wandered in and out, like the sun behind a cloud bank. Mention Fred Astaire and he'd tell you that he called him the other day, only that day was a year ago; Irving Berlin, almost twenty years older than he, made him feel like a kid, and they phoned back and forth, arguing over *Say It with Music*—Berlin was for it and then against it, wanted it autobiographical, then didn't, but didn't want it to be a story about some mythical composer because he was afraid that modern audiences might think the character in the story had written the songs and not Berlin.

He spoke slowly, often coming to a halt while chewing over emerging memories. He did not pat himself on the back or look for praise; rather, he was a man who stood on top of his accomplishment and saw the world below it. He didn't claim to have always made the right choice, but you got the feeling that he regretted few of his decisions. They [his films] were precious jewels he was talking about, and he didn't need to bite them to reassure himself of their worth, or be upset because time had somewhat tarnished their settings. He was a man of his time, but the core was always true. Of yesterday he spoke with undiminished authority, and the further back you went, the more matter-of-factly current his voice became.

AF: When I was a kid in vaudeville, Fred was with his sister and his mother; we were traveling on the Orpheum Circuit together.* I sang with Gus Edwards.

As a shy little twelve-year-old spending her summers in Atlantic City, Eleanor Powell, to become one of Metro's greatest musical assets in the '30s, had also worked with Gus Edwards. At Metro, Freed wrote songs for her musicals, but at the time he and I met I didn't know enough about it to bring the subject up.

---

*Freed had been a song-plugger in Chicago when Minnie, mother of the Marx Brothers, put him into their act.

AF: I tried to write with Gus, but I never did. But I wrote with Lou Silvers, his musical conductor.*

One of Irving's [Thalberg] chief writers at the time was Ralph Spence, and he was a friend of mine, and sound had just come in and he said Irving was talking about doing a musical, and he said Irving would like to meet you and Herb Brown. We were already out there. The others hadn't come yet. So we went over there and had a talk and went to work on a picture called *Whoopee,* but we couldn't use the title, it belonged to Ziegfeld, who had an Eddie Cantor musical with that title. I had the title *Broadway Melody.* And, funny thing, Irving said since we, none of us, knew much about making a movie musical, we'd just experiment with this and not spend too much money. That's why it had no big names in it. So *Broadway Melody* played fifty-three weeks at the Astor [in New York] and won the Academy Award. We didn't even know how to get the sound in, we were on stepladders holding the microphones over their heads while they talked.

The tough thing was that we had cameras that were not quiet. So they were put into a box. And you couldn't pan or move the camera. So we got the idea of prerecording. Because otherwise you'd have the sound coming from the camera, which was noisy, and the music playing at the same time. We were ad-libbing. The script was ad-libbed.

Oh, sure. Yeah. Well, Eddie Goulding was in there, and he had written a script, and a couple of other people monkeyed with it, etc. We had the basic idea of two sisters like the Duncan Sisters,† and I got Charlie King from New York because I'd known him from vaudeville and he could at least sing. The trouble with him was he couldn't remember the lyrics, and we had to put them up on a board like cue cards. I got them to use Bessie Love 'cause I knew what she could do.‡ But a funny thing about "The Wedding of the Painted Doll"—Irving Thalberg had gone to New York and we'd shot it, and when he came back he didn't like it. So he said: "Let's do it over again in color." He'd seen some color footage while he was in New York and he could

---

*Lou and Arthur subsequently worked at Metro on the backstage musical *Stage Mother* (1933) before Lou moved on to Columbia and from there to 20th Century–Fox as musical director.

†Originally signed for it, the Duncans, vaudeville and Broadway headliners, turned it down and made their movie debuts subsequently in the similar but nowhere nearly as successful *It's a Great Life* (MGM, 1929).

‡Freed had said that he'd been Love's boyfriend, and his writing partner fell for the charm of actress Anita Page, who played the younger sister and was Mrs. Brown for a time. Producers' and songwriters' infatuation with starlets and the people who sang their songs was not uncommon, though it nearly always led to their more fallible decisions, such as Mayer's with vocalist Ginny Simms: all the king's horses and all the king's men couldn't convince the public that she was a star. Freed's own infatuation with dancer Lucille Bremer accounted for that sulky-faced redhead's short-lived starring career, including twice as Fred Astaire's partner in films whose failure at the box office, especially the costly *Yolanda and the Thief,* brought Astaire to the brink of retirement. Four years later Freed offered Astaire the male lead opposite the box-office powerful Judy Garland in *Easter Parade* and made up for his earlier mistake.

see that this would be a plus for musicals. So that was the only color number in *Broadway Melody,* all the rest was in black-and-white.

The film had other pluses going for it: the authentic-sounding, slangy show-biz dialogue in a year of marble-mouthed clichés (the hard-boiled dance director exhorts the chorus girls to "Cut 'em deep and let 'em bleed"); a startling dramatic performance by Bessie Love as the self-sacrificing older sister; and the songs, originals for the film, lending punch and lifting it above the competition.

AF: We wrote the songs especially for the film . . . that's where the title came from. We wrote that and "You Were Meant for Me" and a couple of other songs.

With a bushel of hits first time off the mark, Freed could afford to be casual about songs that were all hits and a film that launched a trend to original-to-films backstage stories.

AF: Doug Shearer worked on the sound for it. Norma's brother [and Irving Thalberg's brother-in-law]. Irving saw the dailies all the time, and even when he wasn't there, Larry [Weingarten, at the time married to Thalberg's sister, Sylvia] was Irving's assistant, and he was very close to it, right through the picture.

Freed's role model for his future producing career was MGM's twenty-nine-year-old boy genius, Irving Thalberg.

AF: Whenever you could get to watch him, I would. He was the hardest man to see. He'd sit in his office for two or three hours at a crack. If he made a date with you for 2:00, you were lucky to see him at 5:30. Or 7:00. Because he was doing so much. But he was wonderful. He supervised the picture pretty strongly. Because it was important to them, sure . . . it was the first all-talking musical made. See, in the Jolson picture before, Al sang the songs, but the rest was silent. And, as Irving said, we should treat what we were doing as an experiment. And if we get through this one, we'll make a good one. Won the Academy Award.

Freed was in. For the studio's next all-star super-duper vaudeville show, *Hollywood Revue of 1929,* for which dramatic stars turned up doing comedy and song, Freed's old boss Gus Edwards wrote the score, "but we interpolated one number, which was the hit. We wrote one song for that," he repeats with an impish grin, "and that was the big hit of that film. That was nominated for an Oscar. 'Singin' in the Rain.'"*

---

*Considering its immortality was assured when over two decades later Gene Kelly splashed his way through a downpour singing it, it's worth noting that it was initially introduced in the film's two-tone Technicolor finale with virtually the whole MGM roster of stars singing in chorus: Joan Crawford, Marion Davies, John Gilbert, Buster Keaton, Marie Dressler, Bessie Love . . .

AF: Well, Irving and I got pretty close. He said to me: "You can be here as long as I'm here." When I started out at Metro, I had a lot of talks with Thalberg. Thalberg had two or three great qualities. First of all, he had great taste. Second of all, he had a great sense of women. Most of the stars on the lot at that time were women, and Thalberg was mainly responsible. The other thing was, even in those days of hack writing in most cases, he had a sense of reality in writing. Of honesty in writing. He didn't like trick things. We did *A Night at the Opera,* we wrote a big hit for that, "Alone," and there were a lot of meetings with the Marx Brothers and Irving, and that film is still a classic. And that's Irving. He was my ideal for what I wanted to become. There are certain fundamental things that all producers got from Irving. An honesty in writing. Character more than plot. Irving always said, "To hell with the plot." *Meet Me in St. Louis* was built on characters. The only story there was "There's No Place Like Home" when the family wanted to move to New York from St. Louis. But when it came to musicals, Irving was basically for the operetta; he never did understand what we call musical comedy.

We made so much money then [Freed recounted, returning to when it all began in a big way and he and Brown were writing songs for one film after another]. We made more than anybody else in the studio out of royalties because we had five big hits. I went away to Europe and took time off for about eight or nine months. That was when everything had to have a song. They wanted a song for a picture which Ramon Novarro could sing, and the picture was called *The Pagan,* so we just called it "The Pagan Love Song." And my publisher said, "What the hell is a pagan?" Well, "Pagan Love Song" sold 1,600,000 copies of sheet music in the country.

For Joan Crawford's talkie debut Freed and Brown wrote her the title tune to sing. "Untamed" wasn't one of their best, but later they wrote another standard, "All I Do Is Dream of You," which Crawford introduced in the weepie-but-good *Sadie McKee* (1934).

AF: Sometimes we wrote the song ahead of time and then we'd use it in a picture. Like we had written "Temptation" before we knew it was going to be used in *Going Hollywood* [1933]. That's why I wanted to get Bing Crosby, because I knew Marion Davies couldn't sing it. So I got the studio to borrow Bing, who was under contract to Paramount, through Louella Parsons,* because the picture was a Cosmopolitan Picture in which Hearst was a partner. And Hearst didn't like Bing.† And I had a tough time selling Hearst on letting me use Bing opposite Marion. But Marion was fine. Hearst was so in love with Marion. He even bought a pair of tap shoes, and he did Marion's tap number better than she did!

In the early pictures our job finished when we wrote the songs. We had

---

*Parsons was the semiliterate but hugely influential Hollywood columnist for the Hearst papers.
†This was in part due to Crosby's reputation as a womanizer and drinker.

no specific amount to complete a year. We just had a contract to write, the same way a writer did. Except that our contract was different from a writer's, as we owned our royalties. There was a lot of competition, but it was never song for song on the same assignment, it would be more for a film. But we didn't write that operetta stuff, and we had some of the big titles, you know, *Dancing Lady,* three of the *Broadway Melody*s [1929, 1936, 1938]. . . .

Like Harry Warren and Al Dubin, that memorable composing duo of Warner Bros. musicals, Freed and Brown stayed and thrived in the studio system while many of the Tin Pan Alley and Broadway giants never could.

AF: Well, George [Gershwin] was a good friend of mine, and the funny thing was that Ira liked to live out here, but George liked to live in New York. But they wrote some wonderful numbers for pictures, like "A Foggy Day," that was for *Damsel in Distress,* and they were still pretty active on the New York stage when George died. I wanted to write a show for the Broadway stage, but Herb never wanted it. After I started producing, he did go and do one show with Buddy De Sylva.*

   Louis Mayer was very interested in musicals, and that's why there was so much backing for MGM musicals—even MacDonald and Eddy.

Arthur adds the duo dismissively, since he liked to keep a clear distance between his sort of musical and theirs. When, as with *Kismet,* he strayed into their pasture, it was a deadly dull work. But in that aside one has a whole chapter on why, with Freed's rise, so many of Metro's established musical stars were slowly but surely eased out.

AF: And Mayer said to me: "Arthur, I want you to be a producer, and to make musicals." And I brought in all those people . . . Judy Garland, Vincente Minnelli, all that. Well, I had already shown Mayer what I wanted to do on

---

*There's a confusion here with three different people and projects rolled up in the two names. Nacio Herb Brown did write the music for a Broadway musical, the 1932 *Take a Chance,* where Ethel Merman introduced "Eadie Was a Lady," but that show's producer was not songwriter-turned-theatrical-and-film-producer Buddy De Sylva, whose songwriting collaborators included lyricist Ray Henderson and Lew Brown, no relation to Freed's composing partner, Herb Brown. De Sylva's Broadway producing credits included the 1939 Cole Porter musical *DuBarry Was a Lady,* which MGM bought. Freed produced it as a movie, as he did with *Good News,* which was a De Sylva-Brown-Henderson musical written in the '20s. It's easy to see why Freed might have gotten things a little confused. Buddy De Sylva was the only one in his group, and one of the few songwriters who, like Freed, had a major film-producing career. Among others, he wrote Gloria Swanson's *Indiscreet,* and for a time in the '40s he was Paramount's head of production. Unlike Freed, who has yet to be impersonated on screen by anyone other than himself, De Sylva was played by Walter Abel in *Star Spangled Rhythm,* and by Gordon MacRae in the biographical musical *The Best Things In Life Are Free.* But trying to unravel Hollywood connections would require Charlie Chan. Clearly, old school ties are not so strong and nowhere near as complex as old vaudeville ties. Add to these the strong family ties that made Hollywood the capital of nepotism, and the mind starts to reel.

The Wizard of Oz. I not only brought the property into the studio. I cast it; I . . . Mervyn LeRoy [credited on the film as producer] has got the biggest false credit on that that was ever given.

I brought Arlen and Harburg here; in fact, I even gave them titles of songs. I gave them "Over the Rainbow"—not the title, but I told them what kind of song we wanted. And "Follow the Yellow Brick Road" and all those things. . . . Arlen wrote in his book what I did, and so did Bert Lahr's son. *The Wizard of Oz* was a very shaky proposition then because Nick Schenck in New York didn't like it at all. Sam Goldwyn had owned the rights for years and he wouldn't or couldn't make it. And I sent Franklin [could this have been Sidney Franklin?] over to Goldwyn to make the deal, because they got on. We bought it because he didn't even know what the property was. He said to Franklin: "What is it?" And Franklin said: "A fantasy." Goldwyn said: "Let 'em buy it."

I was responsible for getting Vic Fleming to direct it. We had another director on it first. Dick Thorpe. Originally Mervyn had put him on and he no more belonged to that project than . . . So I got Victor. That man was a poet. Probably one of the great unsung men of this business. I mean, apart from *Gone With the Wind,* his pictures have really stood up. I used to have bread and coffee every morning with him at the studio. Except for *Reckless* [1935, which starred Jean Harlow in a backstage musical drama], no one had ever thought of using Fleming for a musical before. But I knew he was the right man, from having coffee in the morning and feeling out his mind and the kind of things that he liked. He was this strange fellow who started out as a cameraman and was part Indian and had this feeling. Gable owes everything he was, his personality, to Vic. He modeled himself on him. And if you go back to *Captains Courageous* and all those things, the way he handled kids . . . I think he's even greater than John Ford, who was one of the masters. Someday someone's going to bring up what Fleming meant to this business.

The others, like Arlen, Minnelli, and Bob Alton, Chuck Walters, Roger Edens, Gene Kelly, Irene Sharaff, I brought out from New York as self-protection. You take the old-time directors like Jack Conway and Bob Leonard and those fellows, they didn't have the same kind of feeling for things. Mayer gave me the freedom to sign anybody. I waited a year after he told me to produce until I found a property, because there are too many people around who are ready to shoot you if you don't click. Good friends of mine, like Eddie Mannix, who had *no* feeling for my kind of thing. So I was taking a chance on Judy Garland and Mickey with *Babes in Arms* [based on the 1937 Rodgers and Hart show]. Well, that became the biggest picture Metro had that year. So I was in good shape. Now, the toughest one to put over, though, was *Meet Me in St. Louis,* which nobody at the studio liked. Finally we had a meeting and Mayer said: "Arthur's record has been so good, either he'll learn a lesson or we'll learn a lesson. So go make the picture." And it was the biggest-grossing picture they had for five years.

Even before Freed became a full-fledged producer at the studio, he'd taken an increasingly active part in '30s musicals far beyond his duties as a lyricist.

AF: Yes. I revived the *Broadway Melody*s of '36 and '38. I instigated them. That's how come Mayer said to go ahead and produce. I brought Eleanor Powell over. Talent. That's what she had. That's what Streisand has got today, because she sings so great. You can take Rin-Tin-Tin and write a drama around him, and he can bite a rattlesnake and save the baby, and he's a hero and that's your story. But in a musical you've got to be Fred Astaire; you've got to be Gene Kelly; you've got to be Judy Garland. You've got to be able to deliver. You just can't fake it. Even Cyd Charisse, who we dubbed, was a wonderful dancer. You couldn't cheat that. So Eleanor represented a show-stopper to me. Which she was.

She was ideal for the kind of film they were doing then, but she didn't last beyond the period. She was not a good actress like Judy was. Finding these people was part of my work at the studio. For instance, if I hadn't brought Bing Crosby into *Going Hollywood,* we wouldn't have had "Temptation." So these are all extras you do to protect your own work. And later, when I brought Alan Lerner out for the first time, we worked closely together, because they were brilliant people . . . Betty Comden, Adolph Green.

But most of the things they were doing in the '30s weren't for me. Being a songwriter myself, I had no feeling for operetta. It's the difference between Victor Herbert and Jerome Kern. Both were great, but Kern revolutionized popular show music. He was the daddy of Dick Rodgers and Burton Lane and all that group. Even Gershwin. They liked living out here. Really, they looked more forward to doing pictures than they did shows. Especially Kern. I did his story, *Till the Clouds Roll By.* Romberg had the house next door to George Gershwin's on Roxbury Drive. Irving Berlin came out here. He did many pictures. I did two with Irving, *Easter Parade* and *Annie Get Your Gun.*

Chronology wasn't the strong point in his reminiscence; his past was all one long, glorious moment out of which he picked and to which he added a song that played in his head and might have been written for and about him, Lerner and Loewe's "I Remember It Well" (for *Gigi*). Keeping him on one subject at a time wasn't easy, yet into the middle of a sentence he would drop an aside that tingled with a chapter of unspoken but fascinating details. When he worked on a film for which he also wrote the songs, I wondered which came first, the story or the songs?

AF: Well, that's like asking which comes first, the words or the music. It kind of comes together. We'd written some songs for *Broadway Melody of 1936* and we wrote the script up to it; but certain things like "Sing Before Breakfast," which they did up on top of the roof, we wrote because we knew Vilma and Buddy Ebsen were in the picture and we needed a scene for them. So you wrote for the talents to a degree. You don't know when you're doing them which are going to be the show-stoppers and which won't. For instance, in *Going Hollywood*, "Temptation" has been one of our big standards, but we had another song Crosby sang, called "After Sundown," which we thought was the hit. It was a lovely song, but it was never a big hit.

Since Freed would keep turning the answers to his work as producer rather than that of lyricist, it was time to go the way he wanted to go. His fame, after all, rests on his gift for creating the great musical unit. At about the same time, the studio launched two other units for making musicals, one headed by former Universal whiz kid Joe Pasternak, who was sort of specialist in an up-tempo contemporary equivalent of the MacDonald-Eddy films, and the other by Jack Cummings.

AF: Because they wanted more musicals. Musicals were selling. They weren't units really, in the sense that mine was. I didn't do the sort of things Pasternak did at all, and Jack didn't just do musicals, he made other pictures. He did a couple of very good things. One of them I gave him: *Seven Brides for Seven Brothers*. Sure. I bought that and gave it to Jack. He had nothing to do. He had my whole group on it. Michael Kidd, Stanley Donen, [Walter] Plunkett and everybody. Every producer is different, as every director is different. A creative producer like Irving Thalberg or David Selznick *made* the picture. It wasn't a question of hiring the writer and the director, they made the picture. I can show you wires from Alan Lerner and those kinds of people after they saw a preview. I even gave Alan the title for *My Fair Lady*—he inscribed the script to me after that.

As a producer I was primarily concerned with the end product. Then, who's going to write it? Who's going to do the songs? Who's going to do the choreography? To get the top talents. In these things I did a lot of research myself. For example, in *The Wizard of Oz*, how do you do the Munchkins? I said: "Get Singer midgets." Who's going to do the lion? I said: "Bert Lahr is the lion." I was supposed to have screen credit on it and Mervyn stopped it. I don't care. All the papers on it, all my work, is down at USC.

You want to know how I worked? I'll give you a for-instance. Take *An American in Paris*. I've got a poolroom in my house, and Ira and I used to play a lot. Now, for years I'd been wanting to make a picture about Paris in the Lautrec period. Minnelli and I used to talk about it many times, but then [John] Huston made the picture about Lautrec [*Moulin Rouge*]. So then, this night Ira was at my house and we sat down after we quit playing, and I got a flash and said to Ira: "How about selling me the title *An American in Paris*?" He said: "If you use all Gershwin music, yes." I said: "I wouldn't use anything else." So we started talking about it, and I said: "What I want to do is take George's composition of 'An American in Paris' and use it *in toto* for the finish of the picture as a ballet." Irving Berlin was here at the time, as I was doing *Easter Parade,* and he said: "Kid, I hope you know what you're doing. To do a twenty-minute ballet in a picture!"

Now then, I didn't know whether it would be a Fred Astaire or a Gene Kelly. So I told the idea to Vincente. And he was crazy about it. And we decided that in doing a ballet Gene was more of a ballet dancer than Fred. Now, Gene was on a vacation in New York and we looked over some French girls. The studio tried to get me to put Cyd Charisse in—she was under contract, but she wasn't right. There was a girl in Paris called Odile Versois. So I called Gene in New York and asked him if he'd fly to Paris and make a test of this Versois girl, and I said: "Incidentally, there's this other little girl we saw pictures of, who we called 'the cat girl.'" It was Leslie Caron. I said: "Make a test of her." So we made the two tests and brought them back here and ran them, and I asked Gene which one he liked and he said: "I won't tell you. You go down and see who *you* like." So we ran the two tests and I said to Vince: "Which one do you like?" He said: "I won't tell you. Let's run them again and we'll write it down on a piece of paper." Versois' test was pretty good. She was an experienced actress. But we both wrote down Leslie Caron. We brought her over here and it was the only time she'd spoken a line. She was always in the ballet over there. She was a kid. She came over with her mother. I think we paid her $500 a week, which was more money than she ever saw, but she's still got $400 of that $500.

Now came the question of who's going to write it. Ira was stuck on Alan Lerner, but I was afraid to approach Alan on it because he likes to write the songs and we had all Gershwin songs. So I told Alan the idea anyway and he said: "I'd like to write it." I said: "You're kidding." He said: "No, I'll write it." And he won the Academy Award for it.

There was a copy of *Life* magazine lying around with an article about the fellows over there studying on the GI Bill. So I said: "Let's make the character a painter." Because George Gershwin had been in Paris studying painting and it gives you a little feeling for character. Alan liked it. The Oscar Levant character was based on David Diamond, who was always broke and lived on scholarships but never had enough money to come back to America. But the rest of it was Alan, of course. Then our original idea was to shoot the ballet on the streets of Paris. So, about the middle of the picture, I got the idea that since the man was a painter, in his imagination he would see the paintings of Renoir, Rouault, all of them. I called Vincente and Gene up after shooting one day, around 6:00, and we already had the passports to go to Paris to shoot the ballet there, and I told them the idea of doing it in a dream on the set here. And they loved it and canceled our trip, and we brought Irene Sharaff out to do the costumes for it.

I remember one trick in *Easter Parade* when the fellow sends the Easter bonnet. I said: "For once let the *girl* send the Easter bonnet!" So she sends him the silk top hat with the flowers around it. But there are many producers work that way. . . . When I first told Mayer I wanted to make a picture called *An American in Paris,* he said: "Where did you get a title like that?" I said: "It's Gershwin." He said: "Make it." He didn't say: "Who's going to be in it? What's in it?" He always supported me. See, when I started, I felt a lot of stuff in the musical field was stale. It had become a cliché. And I was trying to find new talent. Mayer supported me.

Like when I first brought Minnelli out. I couldn't get him an assignment because they said: "Who the hell is Minnelli?" So I bought *Cabin in the Sky,* it was an all-colored picture. There were no Metro stars in it, so Mannix and the others couldn't scream if it didn't work. Then after that picture everybody wanted Minnelli. I'd seen things he did in New York for the Shuberts, *At Home Abroad* [which starred Eleanor Powell, fresh from her first MGM musical] and all those revues he did. I didn't know him, but I said I'd like to meet this fellow Minnelli. So Howard Dietz, who was running the publicity department out of New York, he took me up to Minnelli's apartment one evening, and I said I was a great admirer of what he'd done and how about coming out to Hollywood? He said: "I've been there." It turned out he'd been out at Paramount for $2000 a week and they'd never given him an assignment.* They finally settled his contract. I said: "Well, they just didn't understand you. I'll tell you what to do. Come on out for no salary. We'll pay your hotel bills and whatever your expenses are for six months. And if you want to leave after two months, you've got no obligation. And if you want to stay, we'll do something." So he says: "I'll let you know." I went back to the Coast and about a week later I got a phone call from him and he said: "Do you still want me to come out?" So I made arrangements with the New York office and they brought him out and gave him $300 a week and his hotel bill, and he sat in the unit there for a couple of months, just watching, learning, and then he did a couple of numbers for me and I started him on *Cabin in the Sky.*

Or take Comden and Green: I'd seen the show they'd written with Leonard Bernstein called *On the Town,* which I bought. It was based on the Jerry Robbins ballet *Fancy Free.* I don't remember what their first picture for me was [*Good News*], but they did several. But I felt a great fresh talent there. Nobody had asked them to come out because Hollywood didn't like stage people. I had a feeling that if you could write for the theater, you could write for pictures. Or if you were great on the stage, well, Fred Astaire was a big star when he first came to Hollywood.† I had a helluva time bringing him over to Metro because Eddie Mannix said: "How can you photograph him?" He said he was so ugly. Then later Jack Cummings made a picture with [Tommy] Dorsey's band with Frank Sinatra in it [*Ship Ahoy*] and Frank sang two songs and Mannix wanted to cut them both out after the preview because he said: "You can't photograph him." Sinatra did *On the Town* and *Take Me Out to the Ball Game* for me.

Being a songwriter, you had to admire certain people like Cole Porter and Irving Berlin. I think I did about four pictures with Cole Porter—

---

* Actually, Minnelli staged a number, "Public Melody #1," for Martha Raye and Louis Armstrong in *Artists and Models* (1937).

† Astaire, whom Freed knew from vaudeville, made his film debut playing himself in the MGM musical *Dancing Lady.*

DuBarry Was a Lady, Panama Hattie, The Pirate and *Silk Stockings*. Irving Berlin is a kind of a snob about writing. And he knows who the good writers are. When Cole was sick, Irving called me every day from New York to find out how he was. The same admiration Cole had for Irving. Well, I've got to give a lot of the credit for that to Mayer because he completely backed me. Absolutely. He gave me the authority, when I was in New York and saw somebody I liked, like Bob Alton or Chuck Walters, I could just go ahead and bring them out.

Walters was brought out as a choreographer on *DuBarry Was a Lady,* and then he did the choreography on *Meet Me in St. Louis* and *Summer Holiday* and a lot of others. He turned into a good director. I only made two pictures that were not musicals. No, three. There was *The Clock* with Judy, one with Gable [*Any Number Can Play*] and one later with Grant [*Crisis*].* Of course, Judy I got out here. She came to give an audition with her two sisters, and her mother played the piano. The worst piano player you've ever heard. Then I said: "Let me hear the little girl sing alone," and she sang, "Zing Went the Strings of My Heart." So I signed her for $150 a week or something like that. Just her.

Garland was undoubtedly the brightest star in MGM's musical crown, the undisputed Queen of the Freed Lot, but after her initial signing she languished till *Broadway Melody of 1938*. Freed dug up an old song by Joe McCarthy and James V. Monaco, "You Made Me Love You," and got Roger Edens to write an introduction to the old song; she sat mooning over a portrait of Clark Gable and sang "Dear Mr. Gable . . ." before segueing into the sentimental melody. After that everything fell into place. She was the symbol of the best of Freed musicals concentrated into one small, very human, contemporary figure. As he spoke about her, a complex variety of emotions resurfaced—pride, thrill, guilt, confusion and just plain blotting out of certain uncomfortable realities.

AF: I made fourteen pictures with Judy. When she was on, there wasn't anything she couldn't do. Do you know why? She was real. Unless you gave her something false to do, she would do it. This girl was real. She was not a stunt. She was not a great dancer, but she could come in with Gene Kelly or Fred Astaire and after about an hour's rehearsal, do it and give the appearance of a great dancer. Whereas Liza [Minnelli] is a wonderful dancer—a better dancer than she is a singer. Every songwriter there ever was, whether it was Kern or Berlin or Cole Porter or Harold Arlen, wanted to write for Judy. Now, with my early pictures, *Babes in Arms, Babes on Broadway, Strike Up the Band, Little Nellie Kelly,* Judy Garland was a great big musical talent besides being a damn good little actress. So you believed it. I just looked at part of

---

*Freed preferred to forget his last two films, which were also nonmusicals.

Meet Me in St. Louis the other night and watched Judy sing "Have Yourself a Merry Little Christmas" and there was nobody like her. She was one of the greatest musical talents ever. She was every songwriter's favorite. The reason I got Irving Berlin to do *Easter Parade* was on account of Judy. Roger Edens helped a lot. Kay Thompson did. They were on the set. They did an awful lot in laying out her music and her recordings. Up to *Meet Me in St. Louis* she was easy to work with. Even in *The Clock*. There was never an evil bone in Judy's body. There was never a mean thing in Judy. All this talk about the oppression . . .

   First of all, all the time she was sick or in hospital, Metro paid the bills. Louis Mayer took care of everything. I had to take her out of *Annie Get Your Gun*. The girl just couldn't function. She couldn't get out of bed. What went wrong was something within her. I'm not a psychiatrist. I don't know what it was. Even in *The Pirate* we had some problems. And I wasn't able to shoot the finish—"Be a Clown"—until after a couple of weeks and she got well enough. She came in and with a rehearsal she did it. I always thought that Judy would come back. I thought she was made out of iron. She came back so many times. And in the interview I gave Bosley Crowther before Judy had passed away, I said: "Judy will come back."

JK: Once you started producing, you hardly ever wrote another song, yet two that you did work on were as good as anything. Didn't you miss it?

AF: To a certain extent. But then, I had so much admiration for Lerner and Loewe, and for Cole Porter, that I wanted to bring their music to the screen. "Make 'Em Laugh" was really only written because we needed a piece of business for Donald O'Connor in *Singin' in the Rain*. I was trying to find something for Donald to do. And I never thought anybody else would ever do it. It was just right for Donald as a piece of material. And the way I got to write "This Heart of Mine," which Fred Astaire did in the *Ziegfeld Follies*, Harry Warren came up to my office one day and played me this tune. I said: "That's wonderful." He said: "How about writing the lyric to it?" I said: "Okay." I think we did it in one evening. At that point there was no thought of it being used as a number for Fred and Lucille. We knew we needed something and we thought we'd be getting a Kern song, but he was using it in another show.* Then Fred heard it and said: "I'd like to do it." And Vincente did a great job on that number. The whole story outline of the jewel thief and the girl wearing them† was an idea that Vincente had had for years,

---

*Jerome Kern at the time was doing the score for *Cover Girl* and he was holding out one of his best numbers unless he was assured of its getting a great treatment. Producer and songwriter Arthur Schwartz (later to work with Freed on *The Band Wagon*) promised Kern it would, so "Long Ago and Far Away" stayed in *Cover Girl,* and Astaire and Bremer danced to "This Heart of Mine."
†George Balanchine had choreographed "Raffles" to music by Vernon Duke, danced by Ray Bolger and Betty Bruce in the Broadway revue *Keep Off the Grass* (1940).

he wanted to do it as a dance number. And this just fitted it. We did several big dance numbers in that film, and that one was easy. It just came together.

But "The Babbitt and the Bromide," this was a tough thing. First of all, I wanted to get Fred Astaire and Gene Kelly together. This was a tough job. And then it became a question of what number will they do. Well, each one had a different idea. Finally I remembered this piece of material, a number of George and Ira Gershwin's, and I finally got them to agree on it. And when I'd talk to Fred alone, he'd say: "Gene is wonderful, but why does he want everything his own way?" And when I'd see Gene alone, he'd say: "I admire Fred so much, but why does he want everything his way?" They did a lot of rehearsal on it. It wasn't that they were being competitive. It's a funny thing. Fred Astaire, with all his success, is a very shy person. Fred would never look at a number we'd shot until a week or two later. He wanted to hear the word of mouth on it . . . he was afraid to look at it. Now, in my mind, the problem here was that Fred didn't want people to say: "Which one is the best?" Fred had no inferiority complex, but it was a form of protection. Finally, they got on just fine.

Fred is so sensitive about everything. You know, it took me three years to get Fred to kiss a girl on the screen. On the lips. I think Cyd Charisse was the first girl he kissed. He might have been afraid of his wife, I don't know. Fred always hated the front part of *The Band Wagon* when they had to auction off all of his stuff, which was a wonderful scene, you know!* He liked to dance with Cyd. He thought she was a great dancer. I don't think he ever danced with a better dancer. She was a bit tall, but not too tall . . . well, he started out with Ginger, who was not that tall at first, but she got taller. See, Judy was small, so that was no problem. They got on so well on *Easter Parade,* that's why I was going to do *The Barkleys of Broadway* with him and Judy. Then she got sick, and I brought Ginger over and we reunited them for that one picture. But he loved to dance with Cyd. That's why we reunited them with *Silk Stockings*.

The only time we had a problem in *Silk Stockings* was when Cole [Porter] jumped on me a little and that was because of the lyrics for "All of You": "I love the north of you, the south of you . . ."—you know. You couldn't be as suggestive in a film the way you could on the stage. No, Cole understood pretty well what you didn't put in a picture.

The Band Wagon is basically another idea I had. There was this producer in New York who was going to revolutionize the whole business.

To my question on whom he based that character, which in the film was played by Jack Buchanan, Freed only grinned. His outburst over the *Wizard* contretemps was unusual, he didn't like to tattle-tale. My guess was that he was thinking of Jose Ferrer.

---

*Fred played a great song-and-dance star of films, whose career was on the skids and whose belongings were being auctioned off prior to his setting out for New York to visit old theatrical friends, and ending up in a Broadway musical.

AF: And finally he revolutionized himself out of the business. And Fred, who had gone from Hollywood to Broadway, got in the hands of this director and everything went wrong. So they finally went back to the old-fashioned stuff and they had a hit. That was another Betty-and-Adolph script. I liked working with them, very much. They didn't get hurt if you didn't like something, or wanted to do something a little different. It was a good collaboration. Well, *Band Wagon* started because I'd always wanted to do something with Howard Dietz—he was head of our publicity in New York and he'd been so good on things I'd done in New York, and was a great lyric-writer and had written all these great songs with Arthur Schwartz. So I told Howard I'd like to do a picture with him and with Arthur Schwartz' music. Now, years ago they'd done a show called *The Band Wagon** and they'd sold it to Fox, so I got the title from Fox. They said: "We'll give you two if you take it." They didn't like it. They never used the title. Then Dietz and Schwartz wrote one new song to put in there which has become quite a standard, "That's Entertainment," because I told them we needed a number like "There's No Business Like Show Business." And then "Dancing in the Dark" was one of the greatest dances that Fred did with Cyd. See, I brought Fred back for *Easter Parade*. He didn't want to do it. He wanted to retire. Gene Kelly was going to do *Easter Parade* and he broke his leg skiing and he couldn't work for eight months. So I called Fred down at his ranch and said: "Come up and talk to me about it."

As Louis Mayer said, "Business is not an exact science." It's a collaborative affair. Take *An American in Paris*. It was Lerner. It was Minnelli. All of them. Now, I had a helluva fight with Mannix about putting Chevalier in *Gigi*. He said: "That old son of a gun—nobody will go to see the picture." Chevalier had been out for ten years. And Louis Jourdan had done nothing. It was just cast on who would be right for the picture—there were no big shots. Take today. Streisand is a big star. But *Hello, Dolly!* was a bust. So it isn't just the star. *Funny Girl* was a hit. Because that was right. Streisand was the biggest piece of miscasting in *Hello, Dolly!* in the world.

Easter Parade, made when everything Freed touched turned to gold, not only brought back Fred Astaire but also established choreographer-dancer Chuck Walters as another of the major musical directorial talents to come out of the Freed unit.

AF: I knew Chuck Walters wanted to become a director, and I called him when I was doing *Easter Parade* because by then Judy and Vincente were on the complete outs, they could hardly finish *The Pirate* together; I couldn't put Vincente on it. So I said: "Chuck, I'm going to give you *Easter Parade*." He'd done one picture before then, a little film I gave him, *Good News*, which

---

The Band Wagon (1931) was a Broadway revue starring the brother-and-sister team of Fred and Adele Astaire, with sketches by Dietz and George S. Kaufman and songs by Dietz and Schwartz. 20th Century–Fox had used some of the songs in a musical called *Dancing in the Dark* (1949).

had a script by Comden and Green. That was their first for me. And Chuck said: "Do you think I can do it?" I said: "Of course you can." Then Irving Berlin came to me and said: "I don't like the idea of Walters doing this." Because he knew Walters from New York as a dancer. And he said: "I'm going to discuss it with Mr. Mayer." I said: "Irving, go ahead." So the next day he comes to see me and I started: "You're making the picture . . ." And he said: "Forget it." He went back to New York, and when he came back about four or five weeks later and we ran the stuff for him, he said: "You were right."

When I brought Gene Kelly out here, nobody liked him. So I put him opposite Judy in his first picture [*For Me and My Gal*] and Judy was crazy about him. Judy never picked a cast at all. She liked to know, when she became a big star, who her leading man was, but that was about all. So that made it possible, because before then Mannix and all of them had been saying: "What are you going to do with this fellow?" I'd seen Kelly in New York and he said: "Do you want to test me, because I'm not a handsome guy." I said: "No, you're not going to look any different if you do a test."

On the Town was a great critics' favorite. Originally, they were looking for some backing for the show on Broadway. And they asked me to hear it. Comden and Green had written it and Leonard [Bernstein] had done the music. And they told me the idea of the Jerry Robbins ballet and the three sailors on one day's leave in New York. And I okayed it and the studio put up the money. So then we owned the property for pictures. Then, when I wanted to do it, Gene said: "I just did a sailor in *Anchors Aweigh!*"* I said: "But this is a different kind of a sailor." So we went ahead with it. [Stanley] Donen had been a chorus boy for me in *Best Foot Forward,* and then I gave him some second units to do. He wanted to become a director and I watched his work. And Gene thought a lot of him. They worked well together. *On the Town* was a very honest story. Three sailors meet three girls in New York, and then they've got to leave them. You don't know whether they're ever going to get together or not. So it had warmth. And I thought Betty and Adolph wrote great scenes in there for the film. And I brought Lenny Bernstein out to conduct the ballet music. That ballet was really a trial. It probably would have been better if the other two men had danced. See, Sinatra and [Jules] Munshin couldn't dance. We got by with it, but we could have had like *An American in Paris* ballet, where Caron and Kelly were both dancers.

For all of the film's success, Freed was aware that over the years a lot of people had compared the film to the stage original and complained about songs that had been dropped from the show in favor of new but not as good material by Roger Edens and others; and by the shift in character emphasis from the stage to the film.

---

*The first film to team Kelly with Frank Sinatra, it was produced by Joe Pasternak, but its spirit was very much in the Freed mold.

AF: You can't make your show a Bible. Otherwise you're not making a motion
picture. And, off the record, that's one of the problems with *My Fair Lady*. I
prefer to do original material. About the only times I did a stage play is when
Metro owned it . . . see, in *Silk Stockings, Ninotchka* was their property . . .
Kismet, which is not one of my favorites, MGM owned. . . . *Annie Get Your
Gun,* which was Irving Berlin, was different, and I bought it to give Judy a
kick, and that's when she got sick. She loved it so and wanted to do it. But
when you deal with a stage property, you have to change the dialogue if
you're making a film. There isn't as much dialogue in a picture, as a rule.
The picture gives you so much more visually than the stage does, and that
tells its own story. *The Band Wagon* opened with Fred just walking. And
when he walks, he dances. You know the man. You don't need dialogue for
that. But in *On the Town* we had other scenes in there that we needed other
songs for that Betty and Adolph did. I had compunctions about taking things
out, yeah . . . but I couldn't help it. But the thing for Sinatra and Betty
Garrett had to be written; there was nothing in the show for them. And they
worked well. And don't forget, Sinatra was a singer and not a dancer and he
had to have numbers he could do. Because everything in *On the Town* was
basically written for Jerry Robbins' dancing.

The film's great success led Kelly and Donen to *Singin' in the Rain,* a musical
with a plot going back to the early days when sound shook up the industry and
brought people like Freed into orbit.

AF: When I came to Metro, all the things with the diction lessons, all those
things were true. It was contemporary to the time I went in there, more than
autobiographical. But a lot of the things were based on things that happened
to us. For instance, shooting four pictures on one stage at the same time, you
could do that because they were silent. Then all of a sudden, when sound
came in, they were taking diction lessons. And some of those stars never did
make it. That's where the idea came from for dubbing the old stars. They
dubbed Richard Barthelmess over at Warner Brothers and then let people
think that that was him singing on the screen. The Jean Hagen character [the
immortal Lena "I cannnnnt staaaaannnn' it!" Lamont], that was the toughest
part to cast. I must have made five tests for that part. And she was just great.
She was a composite of a lot of silent stars . . . not Anita Page. Anita was
never that bad. Mae Murray was exactly it. Exactly. Jean never had a great
part after that film. Betty and Adolph wrote the script and we spent a lot of
time together, going over old stories, like trying to find a place for the microphone so you couldn't see it, and the diction lessons, and those things, yeah.

For Jerome Kern's *Show Boat,* Freed used a number of the stars associated with
Joe Pasternak films. Kathryn Grayson and Howard Keel played the lovers. It
also provided Ava Gardner with one of her finest roles in films, as Julie.

AF: That was a great cast. Kathryn Grayson was right, and Howard Keel was
perfect for that, he was just square enough for that part, which was a help,

and he had a good voice; and Marge and Gower [Champion] did a wonderful
cakewalk in there, and, you see, the great trick in that picture—you have this
great score of Kern's, one of the great scores in the American musical theater,
in fact, a revolution in the theater with Oscar Hammerstein's book—the big
trick was that "Ol' Man River" had been murdered to death. So I was trying
to find a great singer. And I finally heard of this fellow [William] Warfield,
who was in Australia, and he stopped the show singing "Ol' Man River."
Every song in *Show Boat* was one of Kern's great gems. But Ava Gardner
was the one that really made that part in there. I knew we had it made when
I finally got Ava into it. Ava was wonderful in that picture. It was the big start
of her career. I don't think any close-ups in any picture were as beautiful as
those she did in that picture. And I had a hell of a time with Dore Schary
because he wanted me to put Dinah Shore in that part. I had to make a test of
her. And Dinah was sending me flowers to the house and everything, and I
love Dinah, and she finally said: "Why don't you give me the part?" And I
said: "Because you're not a whore." And I said: "Ava is. When she sings
'Bill,' she's every streetwalker you ever saw."

Freed gives this exchange with swelling pride and an admiration which let you
know he didn't literally mean that Gardner was a prostitute at heart, but that she
could play the heart of a prostitute in a way that would rip everybody else's
heart out watching her. In the Kern "concert," *Till the Clouds Roll By,* the film
finished with a digest version of *Show Boat* which had a white-tuxedoed Frank
Sinatra singing "Ol' Man River," Dinah Shore singing Magnolia's songs (not
Julie's) and Lena Horne as Julie. Lena Horne has always claimed to have been
the victim of color prejudice for not being cast in the role when the film was
finally set to go, probably assuming that the trial run in an all-star musical
singalong-a-Kern made her a sure thing for the role. Freed dismisses that notion
out of hand.

AF: You couldn't pass Lena off as white. The girl that played the part had to
    look white, and had just that one drop of colored blood, which was the big-
    gest piece of injustice in the world against this girl. With Ava you could
    believe she had a drop of colored blood. That was another thing I had to
    overcome with the Code, because they didn't want any miscegenation. But
    Lena would have been pure Negro. I brought her here. I put Lena into *Cabin
    in the Sky.*

I wondered if he was sorry to be out of the business, since he had been talking
about his plans to work with Minnelli on *Say It with Music.*

AF: No. Because the whole business is in such a mess. I could have done a
    couple of pictures, but I didn't want to do them. You pick up the trades and
    read about MGM selling all the costumes. I went to Debbie Reynolds' house
    one night for dinner, and there's all the costumes she bought at the auction.
    She bought Fred Astaire's costume from the tramp number [*Easter Parade*]

and Judy's ruby slippers, and her [Debbie Reynolds'] costume from *Singin'
in the Rain*. At the moment I just want to relax a little. I don't want to do
anything that's going to spoil what I've done. I've been lucky. I had my
group. I had Alan Lerner, I had Fritz Loewe, I had Minnelli . . . I had all
these great talents. All these great people I worked with. Those are the great
moments.

1974

Tallulah Bankhead, photographed by Dorothy Wielding, 1931

TALLULAH
BANKHEAD

T ALLULAH HATED LIARS, phonies and bad manners. Being late was high up in the last category: delayed because of having stopped to pick up flowers on the way to her for dinner didn't wash. Forget the flowers—just be on time. She adored baseball with a zealot's passion. There are lots of funny stories about Tallulah rushing offstage as soon as she could to find out how her beloved Giants were scoring. She also had a slavish addiction to TV soap operas, so "Don't call me till after 4:30, dahling." She could sit and watch hoary tear-jerker movies like *Three Secrets,* with her legs drawn up beneath her on the sofa, a crimson muumuu hiding her body and giving her a shape like a flaming pyramid, the Scotch on the long coffee table within easy reach; all conversation restricted to commercial breaks and Tallulah sobbing brokenly. "You think it's really that good?" "Don't be *stupid,* DAHLING, it's terrible," and keep on crying.

She wore silky caftans or, for special occasions like the Truman Capote costume party or a dinner to honor Vivien Leigh, elegant but loosely cut evening gowns because, like so many excessive lifelong smokers, she suffered from emphysema. It was draining her energy. When she finally did give up cigarettes, it may have been on her doctor's orders, but Tallulah made it the occasion for a cause. It was 1966, still early days in America's unfolding disenchantment with the Vietnam war and Tallulah, anti-war, swore an oath to give up smoking "till our boys come back from Vietnam, dahling." But she didn't mind if anyone else smoked. She even encouraged it. "Help yourself, dahling," she said, pointing to the beautiful, filled cigarette case, "they're all yours. But would you mind, dahling . . . blowing your exhaust my way? Just what's left." And she shrugged away her addiction and the need for the sacrifice (if she was to live) with her famed barking laugh. One time, at Sardi's for an early dinner before the crowds would descend, we were sitting in a far corner and fell into our routine over coffee. I lit up, exhaled and she sucked it in; then I noticed people across from us not eating, just staring. Tallulah wasn't put off. "Don't mind them, dahling; they probably just think it's a new sex fad and they'll all be doing it tomorrow."

Tallulah was an actress who acquired more reputation by doing nothing than others had from a successful productive career. A bold, biting, spirited creature, she lived her defects as fully as her virtues. Jovial and outspoken, she

655

could blister a friend to his face with a thousand sarcasms, but, behind his back, she would defend him with courage and loyalty. She made fun of everything, herself included. Always claiming to be short of money, she nonetheless remained like a woman confident of a future before her, wallowing in idleness, condensing a whole book or a play into an epigram for the benefit of people who were incapable of putting one witticism into a whole book. In her youth she had made her fortune and reputation into a cushion on which she slept (when she slept), thus running the risk of waking up as an old woman in the poorhouse. With all that, keeping faith with her friends to the point of death, a sentimental fool, a swaggering clown and as simple-hearted as a child, she worked only by fits and starts or spurred by necessity.

She had tow-colored hair with gray streaks in it, and combed it the way it had been most of her life, long, with a parting on the left side, though no longer as thick and lustrous as in her youth. The hair style was a holdover from her film career, part of Hollywood's glamorization program to elongate her broad face and add mystery. She'd forgotten the reasons, but kept the style. When she turned her head sharply, the thinness and lightness of her hair made it lift up from her neck and about her cheeks, like the hair on a witch doctor's jou-jou sticks when they are being shaken and twirled at some cowering native. Her cheeks and her forehead were very broad, like sandstones, flat and smooth, and the skin very clear, hardly any lines; not knowing any better, you would have thought she was much younger and stronger than she was. She had the well-molded bones that had given her features their dramatic beauty in her youth, and later her glamour, though in an altered form. She looked like—but not quite like—the Tallulah one knew from photographs of her more than thirty years on the American stage and in films. Hers was not a personality built on repose, except when being photographed. "Where did you dredge up these perfectly horrible things, dahling? . . . That's not me! Is that me? Gawd . . . look at that nose . . . all rubber . . . I had no nose. Garbo had a *divine* nose." To prove it, she pushed her nose over against her cheek. Tallulah's glamour was not the stuff of rags and bones and hanks of hair (in fact, the sunken, hooded-eye look she affected was makeup, not nature, for her eyes were almost on an even plane with her forehead, though not as protrusive as Bette Davis'), but because she possessed these in some abandon, she was miscast in early talkies as an exotic '30s-style passive, a sort of American Garbo-Dietrich combo, instead of for her vibrant, larger-than-life presence. To paraphrase something Dorothy Parker once said: Tallulah, unlike Los Angeles, had her "there there." Failure to take off in films, due mostly to miscasting, derailed her interest in a film career, but this powerful wave of living and giving off energy and excitement was part of her until the end.

TB: I don't go to the theater or movies, only very rarely, as when you took me just recently. I'd never seen Richard Burton. I'd never seen Elizabeth Taylor except in something I didn't particularly care for. But I thought this picture, *Who's Afraid of Virginia Woolf?*, the whole picture was magnificent. And the man who directed, Mike Nichols, and I don't use the word carelessly, but for what he's done I think he's a genius. The last musical I saw was *Carousel* and I don't know how many years ago that was, and I *love* music, I listen to it all the time, I have my radio on all night: classical, jazz, Dixieland, all kinds of music. I love to watch rock and roll, except it makes me rather dizzy. And when people criticize it, I think they're crazy.

JK: When you went back to England to make *Die! Die! My Darling*, it was the first time for a long time. And when you were last in England during your greatest period, the period of Noel Coward and Somerset Maugham . . .

TB: I don't consider it their period, I consider it the Tallulah period! [Laughing.] I remember Max Beaverbrook [Britain's answer to William Randolph Hearst] saying that the only three interesting people to know in the British Empire were the Prince of Wales, George Bernard Shaw and Tallulah. So if you'll excuse me for being so modest . . . you may continue.

JK: Well, can you relate your first time in England, your period of Coward and Maugham, to your recent visit to do *Die! Die! My Darling*, which, after all, was a horror film?

TB: What a ridiculous title. . . . No. I can't possibly. It was done so quickly it just went past me. Although the play I enjoyed most, *Fallen Angels*, I only had four days rehearsal for, and Somerset Maugham did say it was the best comedy performance he'd ever seen. And that's rather ironic, because he'd just fired me from *Rain* after one day's rehearsal. And I thank Noel for that. Always. And then I did his *Private Lives* here as a revival, just for the summer, and I ended up playing in it for four years. So I admired those writers enormously. I didn't know Maugham very well,* but his wife, Syrie, who I think had great taste, furnished my house in London, and a lot of the furniture you see here is Syrie Maugham furniture. And that's Augustus John's portrait of me, and my Chagall and my Renoir, and that one I did myself, and a few other mementoes that I have, you know, for rainy days, as they say!

Now, my only claim to being an intellectual is that I hear that our very great President, Woodrow Wilson, and Winston Churchill and Franklin Roosevelt and I think my beloved Adlai Stevenson all love mystery books. And so I'm fascinated by anything like that, though I haven't read any of them for years. I never could be bothered to study at school. I had a very quick memory. And as I learned so quickly, I forgot it the next day. But now I read biographies more than novels. I adore Iris Murdoch, but my books pile up so. Even though I read a book a night sometimes.

---

*Later on she told me that she loathed Maugham, "a bitter little man," not for what he was or for what he did to her, but for the way he treated his wife, whom Tallulah counted as one of her dearest friends.

JK: Now, in terms of your own experience in summer stock or on Broadway, what do you think of the theater in America today?

TB: Well, I think comedy is the most creative and original thing. It isn't just the author, you've got to do something with your facial expressions, it's also timing. Everything is timing. You must create something out of yourself. And it makes me sick when nobody ever gets any award for a great comedy performance. Chaplin never got any award, although I cry more at his films than laugh, because they break your heart. I enjoy hearing people laugh. Particularly when you've had something to do with it. I've been in some very good plays and some very big hits and some very bad plays, and I've made some stupid choices, and I've turned down some very big hits which I won't go into because I'd have to mention other people who were second choices, so that's tactless and stupid and not very kind.

JK: Tallulah, you have said that you have three phobias: you hate to go to bed, you hate to get up and you hate to be alone.

TB: Well, no, I love to be alone, but I don't like to be alone in an empty house, if you know what I mean. But if I could go to sleep when I should, it would be marvelous. But I can't. If I could wake up and feel the way I feel when I'm supposed to go to sleep and I'm wide awake, and when I wake up I'm so sleepy but must get up because actors must never be late. And I'm a real pro like that, I'm never late, never miss a train, a plane, a rehearsal . . . and I cannot *bear* being kept waiting. And I've never been out alone in my life, so I'm never kept waiting . . . they come here and I'm at least comfortable while I'm waiting. Timing is everything.

JK: You never worked with John Barrymore?

TB: No, no, I haven't, but I knew him and adored him, and they were very, very wonderful to me when I first came to New York as a child and stayed at the Algonquin, which is quite the Mecca, if that's the right word for it, for the critics and the stars and all the great writers and the people from Europe and everything, and I met Tagore there, you know, and Galsworthy and so many of the English authors as well, and of course I adored Ethel Barrymore, who had the most beautiful voice. And the greatest wit, and she adored baseball, so naturally we became close friends. I don't know where people get the idea that I modeled my voice on hers. Hers was divine, the most beautiful thing. I was born with my croak, and now, with all that smoking, it's got even worse. I wish I'd had her voice. My Aunt Louise, who was chaperoning me at the time, took me there, and she went there just thinking it was a reasonable hotel. So just out of the blue I met everyone, in the first twenty-four hours I was in New York. Except when I had been to school here prior to that, you know.

JK: You've always been very pro-English.

TB: Oh, well, naturally, I adore . . . Well, before I ever went there, my family and everyone was very pro-English: pro-British, pro-Scotch, Irish, Welsh! And all my names are . . . Bankhead is a Scotch name.

JK: But Tallulah isn't . . .

TB: Tallulah is an Indian name. I'm named after my grandmother, and it means so many things that I, if I started telling you about it, would go on indefinitely. In Indian it means "love-maiden." Also, it means "terrible." "The Goddess of Vengeance." Tallulah Falls. Would this story take too long to tell you? It may be quite boring if I took so long, but my great-grandfather went from South Carolina down to Atlanta to look over this property he'd got there, and he passed through Georgia and these beautiful falls called Tallulah Falls. And these were apparently eighty feet taller than the Niagara Falls, the Indian pronunciation of which, by the way, is Algaro, which I think is much prettier than Niagara. And he wrote my great-grandmother in 1896, and I adored her and called her Granny (her last name was Macaulay), and he said, "If I have a child and it's a girl, I want her to be called Tallulah after these beautiful falls." Well, he never came back, he died of yellow fever, but my great-grandmother's first child was my grandmother Tallulah, her name was Tallulah James Brockman before she married Granddaddy, and then I of course was named after her. I had a photograph—I never keep scrapbooks—and she said: "To my beloved granddaughter who bears my full name." I always have TBB on my luggage because I didn't think TB would look too good—people might think, "I'll catch it." That's two of the names, but the other ones would be too complicated to go into.

JK: Tell me, how honest were you able to be in your autobiography?

TB: Well, I tried to be completely honest. Of course, one has to protect people who are dead and can't answer back, and you don't want to hit below the belt to those who can't hit back. But I wasn't bitchy about anyone who wasn't in a position . . . it's like being rude to a waiter, you don't snap your fingers to a waiter, you might snap them at someone who could tell you to be quiet. But there are certain things you don't tell out of good taste, so as not to offend or affront anyone. I don't mind shocking people, because to shock them doesn't necessarily mean that you offend them. Because some of the best theater is shock. And I don't mean this new theater that has things that are shocking in the old-fashioned sense of the word. But I don't go to the theater, so I don't know anything about all these angry, angry, angry, angry young or old men.

JK: You haven't seen Albee's play *Tiny Alice*?

TB: I adore him, we've played bridge quite a few times, but I'm afraid it closed too quickly. I saw *Virginia Woolf* . . . I went with him to see that. And I adored it.

JK: Did you feel that the character of Martha, the female lead, was a combination of Tallulah Bankhead and Bette Davis?

TB: Oh, good Lord, no, it couldn't possibly be. How could people, and I especially mean critics, be so stupid? How could it possibly have been? She was a college professor's wife who had this *idée fixe* about this child that never existed, and I never heard that before in my life. I'm always hearing the strangest things about me that have no basis in fact at all. There are some that *have*. No, I think most of his things are autobiographical. They say that *Malcolm* was—Albee was adopted, you know, when he was very young, I think maybe just a few days old. And there was some write-up about when someone came to a party and said, "Oh, I know your mother and father." And he said, "I wish I had." And apparently *Malcolm* is something to do with a boy of fifteen in search of his parents.

JK: I suppose the only out-and-out disaster that you ever had was *Antony and Cleopatra.**

TB: My dear, I've had *many* disasters. And very rarely do I get anything but controversial notices. Even some of my biggest hits—I mean by that, from the author's point of view—*Skin of Our Teeth* and *Little Foxes,* got absolutely controversial notices. In fact, I think the only play I've ever been in that got completely unanimous praise all around—for the direction, the author, the actors—was *They Knew What They Wanted,* which I did in England, and it was either just before or just after the terrible General Strike, and everyone from every economic background loved it. And it got absolute raves, and it was written by Sidney Howard. It got the Pulitzer Prize. As did *Skin of Our Teeth,* Thornton Wilder, who really is a genius, I love him. And Lillian Hellman's play *Little Foxes* got the Critics' Award. It was divided that year between that and *Abraham Lincoln* by that most divine man, Robert Sherwood.

JK: And you won the best-actress award.

TB: Yes, I won that in *Skin of Our Teeth,* and for *Little Foxes* . . . and in *Lifeboat.* I did love *Lifeboat,* and I liked my performance, thanks to Hitchcock. I read that script, and it was about forty pages. Now, that's nothing. That's not even half of a first act in a play. And I hadn't even met him. And he kept making my part like me, and I kept saying: "Don't make me say 'dahling,' they'll think I'm playing myself," but I did what he told me and I got the Critics' Award and everything else, and I was very proud of that. Thanks to Hitchcock. He understood me, and understood everybody. And he was so gentle. When he called actors cattle, he may have said it, but he doesn't mean it. It's a joke.

*A critic wrote of her Cleopatra, "Last night Miss Bankhead sailed up the Nile in a barge . . . and sank."

JK: Didn't it bother you when they made some of your plays into films, like *Little Foxes, Dark Victory** and *Jezebel*?

TB: I didn't do *Jezebel,* darling, I left it, Miriam Hopkins did it.

JK: Well, anyway . . .

TB: No, it didn't bother me in the least. It bothered Bette Davis, who was most generous and divine about it and was terribly upset. She said that no one but I should have played in *The Little Foxes*. But there was something political there, believe me.

JK: There was never any rivalry between you two?

TB: Oh, no, no . . . that was just a gag. You're too young to know this, but Fred Allen, one of our greatest wits on radio, and Jack Benny, they had this running feud which was absolutely nonexistent. It was just for fun. And Bette and I hardly ever met. It was just kidding on my [radio] show. *All About Eve* they said was all about me, and we'd kid and I'd say *All About Me,* and we begged Bette to come on the show and said she could even have approval of material, which we hardly ever gave to anyone, because the material would only be given to us on the Sunday. We did it an hour and a half before we went on the air, because you had to know who you were writing for. You couldn't write for Jimmy Durante the way you'd write for Judy Holliday or for me, or Judy Garland or Marlene—all these great stars who were on the show, there'd be eight or nine or ten of these stars on one evening. But oh, no, no . . . I admire Bette tremendously. Now, of course, pictures are like the theater, you go all over the world to make them. I might be in a play in Chicago and my best friends might be in San Francisco, Los Angeles, Detroit, Boston.

JK: So why, after such a long pause, did you decide to go back to films and do a horror film?

TB: Well, I don't know how to explain that, because it's absurd to think of the things I've turned down that were successful, and the things I've done that were not. No one knows if a racehorse might have won a race if it's scratched. And so I was in British Columbia visiting with a great friend of mine, Dola Cavendish, and I got this script from Joyce Selznick, who was working at Columbia, and it was quite interesting and I hadn't made a picture for a long time. . . . But don't ask me why I do anything. It's usually to keep the sheriff from breathing down my neck. Which I think most of us do. Because I'm from the South and I'm very lazy. So I would never do anything if I didn't have to. And then I wait until the very last moment.

---

*Besides Davis' version, it was remade as a film, *Stolen Hours,* starring Susan Hayward, and on TV with Lee Remick.

JK: Well, for a horror film, it turned out okay.

TB: Well, I must say . . . everything I do seems to turn out to be controversial
. . . but I was amazed at the marvelous notices I got. A great many, particularly the trade papers and *Life* magazine and *Time* and *Newsweek*. Of course
it got good and bad, but it's doing very well, I'm told. For a B picture, or a
C picture, whatever they call it!

JK: I came across a couple of titles which were made in 1918 in America, when
you must have been sixteen years old if that much. . . .

TB: I beg your pardon. [She does Mock Turtle anger—she's always some sort
of Alice creature drawn by Tenniel.] They were made in 1919—and I was
fifteen and a half years old. The only reason I can tell the truth about my age
is because my hair's never been touched. I've got divine little streaks of gray
which are so nicely set that people think I've got blond streaks in it. Because
I used to be a towhead, you know, and now you can see it's a sort of ash
blond. But I never had the patience to sit under a drier, and fortunately my
hair is very healthy—what's left of it, because it used to be very thick.

JK: I used to think you were a flaming redhead.

TB: Oh, no, no. In most of my photographs I look like a brunette; but even
when I was a very, very young girl I was a towhead. When I first went to
England I was very, very blond. . . . Well, I won a beauty contest when I
was at school run by *Picture Play* magazine. I sent a picture of myself, never
thinking for a second—because I was a little fatty, you know—and naturally
I didn't tell my family, and months passed, and one day I went down to the
drugstore and I was flipping through the magazines and there were the winners—ten girls and two boys—and there on the last page was my picture,
saying: "*Who* is she?" Because I'd never enclosed my name! Of course, I
nearly fainted, and dashed up the street knocking down several pedestrians,
saying: "I've won it! I've won it!" And of course the family thought I'd lost
my mind as usual—they probably thought I wasn't born with one anyway.
And then there was a family talk and they decided they'd have to let the child
do it or she'd never be happy. And my father, who was then in Congress (and
Granddad was in the Senate), wrote in on Congressional stationery saying it
was their daughter (they'd had 500 letters written in by others saying it was
their picture) and so they said would I send a duplicate. And it had been
taken at Harrison Ewing—a photographer there in Washington who took
everyone's photograph, you know—and so we sent a copy and that was that.
That's how that started. And so I did that picture—*Thirty a Week* [Goldwyn,
1918]. And then I went on the stage after that.

  I never kept anything, letters or anything. I can't be bothered. I can
hardly be bothered to open letters, let alone answering them! So don't ever
write me a letter, please—phone! I just am very, very naughty about things

like that. I did during the war, because I had two pictures, *Lifeboat* and *Royal Scandal* (it was called *Czarina* in England), and I did get thousands of letters then, which one never gets in the theater—no one does, it's a kind of mentality there, a different kind of people, they're more grownup, you know. By the time they could afford to go to the theater, they're no longer young enough to care about getting your picture. So I did religiously send to Private First Class So-and-So: "God Bless You, Tallulah." And then I did the most terrible thing that I'll never forgive myself for. When the war was over, I just threw hundreds of these letters away which were sent on to me by 20th Century— because I wasn't under contract, you see, I was just a freelance. And the studio stamped all theirs for the stars they had under contract and I had to do mine myself. I threw them away from all the poor kids who had God knows how many months left sitting around over there. That was sheer ignorance. But that's when I was very good about those things.

Lifeboat was the first film I'd done in, I think, twelve years. Hitchcock just wanted me to do it. I'd never even met him at the time. I was playing in *Skin of Our Teeth* and just about to go on tour with it, and I got this offer to do *Lifeboat*. And I admired his films so; and I'd seen his little daughter, Patricia, who was then only about eleven, give the most extraordinary performance for a child on the stage, and I just knew him from being a great fan of his. It was certainly the best picture I was in, and I liked it. It's the only time I don't mind watching myself on the screen!

JK: Why was there such a long pause, and why did you only make one film after that?

TB: Well, I turned down a lot, darling. I can't go into all those sordid details, but I did. And then I did a lot of plays. You see, the theater is the only thing where I felt my technique could be used. In the theater it's one dimension, and I'm a kind of a broad type of actress—you see, in the way I throw my arms out now—which may not be exaggerated on the stage, but in pictures I felt I was straitjacketed, and the camera coming up on me made me so nervous. I never did like that, even as a child. That goes back to being photographed once and not being allowed to go to the circus—I was so mad at not going to the circus . . . but then I went the next day! But it often happens that you have to turn down the best things because you're under contract to do a play. I won't go into all that because it's too gruesome and fascinating to think of all the things I didn't do!

JK: Well, except for *Milk Train*, you haven't done much on Broadway the last few years either.

TB: Because—I've told you, darling—I turned down, although I don't like to say it, I originally turned down *Auntie Mame*, I even suggested Rosalind Russell for it. It was an enormous hit for her, but I turned it down. I turned down *Oh Dad, Poor Dad*, which was done by this great choreographer-director Jerome Robbins. I turned down *Sweet Bird of Youth* by Tennessee Williams because I'd promised my friend to do *his* play and he said, "I'll release you from your contract," but I didn't think that was right, and it made Geraldine Page a star. So that's what I do. I usually make the wrong choices. A couple of them I didn't like to begin with, and some, like *The Eagle Has Two Heads*, I never should have done, but nobody held a gun to my head. That's what I mean, I have only myself to blame. And Mr. Brando, he may be a very fine actor, but every night, where he was supposed to land at my feet, he would end up somewhere else onstage, so you never knew where he was going to land. It was all that Method thing, but I thought it was a very unprofessional thing to do. It was a very important scene and I'd never know where he'd be from day to day.

I've never understood all that Method reasoning. I mean, you learn your lines, you listen for your cue and you come on and deliver your lines. All this nonsense about thinking yourself into a tree, or whatever. So those are some of the things I turned down, and some I shouldn't have done. I never saw *Auntie Mame* . . . but twenty-seven quick changes! You see, I've really survived, if you want to call it that, through the summer theaters, which pay much more than I'd make on Broadway unless you're on a profit basis. But you can make a lot of money being a guest on TV, even though they give you the most *awful* material, and I was absolutely amazed at all the laughs I got in that variety show. It took just two days to do and I was paid $7500, and now it's being shown again. But I don't think I'll ever act again, because I don't consider radio or TV acting.

JK: Before you went to Hollywood the first time, back in 1931, you made a film in England—or maybe two. Do you remember those?

TB (after a pause): Golly, how old are you? Yes, I did a silent film—of course, it was quite gruesome, but it had a most lovely line in the play, and it was by Pinero, called *His House in Order*. And the photography was so bad and so awful. . . .

JK: Well, let's skip *House in Order*. [She looks up from lighting up—at this point she still smoked a lot.] But how did your contract with Paramount come about? And once you signed, how much right did you have in selecting your roles or shaping your image?

TB: Well, that's the thing in pictures. You have no rights of any kind. I mean, it's all with the producer or the director, or in the cutting stage your best moment may end up as a line put over somebody else's face, or cut out, even if you're the star and all. I hate that word "star," it sounds so . . . but I mean the leading person. You have no say in it. In the theater you have some say. Of course, the author has the last word in America in the theater. If the author doesn't want a line changed, no matter if he's completely unknown, no matter who is in the play, the greatest draw of their time could not change a line if the author says no. But in pictures I don't know. I've always had the best associations in the movies I've made with the actors, the crew, the director; I mean, all this talk about Otto Preminger being such a tyrant . . . he was the kindest person in the world I ever worked with and one of my dearest friends, so I've never seen that side of him. I really mean it. In spite of what you may have heard, you know. But the movies is entirely the producer and the director.

JK: But at that time in the '30s Garbo had a certain amount of role approval.

TB: No, I don't think she did. She had no say. She never even saw rushes. She had no say in how it was cut. I don't think she even saw her own pictures.

JK: Well, I know in *Romance* [MGM, 1930] they took her voice and, because it was low, they decided to fool around with the sound level.

TB: They did that with me with Robert Montgomery [in *Faithless*], and I said: "What's happening to my voice?" And they said, "It sounds too low for his," and I said, "Well, *please!*" So they finally changed that. I don't mean that there was anything wrong with Robert Montgomery's voice—he was a very clever actor, a comedian, a serious actor too, but his voice was a high voice. Presumably that's what happened with John Gilbert when talkies came in. You started to ask me how I got into movies . . . Well, in the '30s, when I went there, you remember, talkies hadn't been in very long and it was difficult for some of the silent actresses, and actors too, to make that change to sound, because they didn't have that experience of expressing themselves through dialogue and all, which is two entirely different things, and what they [the studios] wanted to get was someone who was photogenic and who also could *act*—if I may modestly say so.

Tallulah was in full swing, riding on the back of her throaty, eminently personable voice, every so often hinting at more with a scrutinous stare, sucking in her cheeks all the while, her lips slightly apart in a mockery of her Hollywood glamour phase, and brushing a handful of hair from out of her face; being fine hair, like Veronica Lake's, it tended to fall over one eye a lot more than was needed for effect, but, unlike Veronica Lake, who kept chopping her hair off the moment it was long enough to fall into its old pattern, Tallulah had no unpleasant memories to brush aside; times were when she didn't even notice it was hanging over her eye while she was trying to peer through it. Her hair seemed to move with the heys and the hos of her sweeping, swooping, high-diving delivery. It was a voice with the legs and stamina her body no longer could muster, but listening to her gave you a pretty good idea of what a hell-raiser she must have been. While she talked, one could easily forget the inroads age and excess had made on her—a generation have tossed their fur coats over their shoulders in imitation of the way Tallulah threw a line over hers.

TB: So they took a test of me while I was still in England and I turned out to be very attractive photogenically, which was lucky, because it was just done at a studio there while I was doing *The Lady of the Camellias*—Glen Byam Shaw was my Armand. Most charming man, he's married to that lovely actress, Hermione Baddeley's sister . . . what's her name, Angela, and . . . where was I? What do you mean you don't know? Who am I talking for? Well, you're not here to get carried away. If we both get carried away, who's going to remember anything?

JK (some furious retracing of steps in my head): *Camille* . . .

TB (forgiving): I never will know why it's called *Camille*, do you? But anyway Sir Nigel Playfair produced it, and it was called what it was supposed to have been called because her name was Marguerite Gautier and his name was Armand, so where *Camille* came from? But, however. I did a scene from *The Lady of the Camellias*, then I did an ad-lib scene on the telephone with my shingled hair, which is how we wore it at that time. So I just did an ad-lib scene on the telephone and from that I got the contract. No agent. Nothing. It was very nice. I thought I'd make one picture, come back to England and finish paying for my Syrie Maugham furniture and for my Augustus John painting and be back. But they picked up my option and I stayed on more or less indefinitely.

JK: For *The Cheat, Faithless, Thunder Below, Tarnished Lady, My Sin, The Devil and the Deep* . . .

TB (in a voice that said, "Oh, woe is me, must we?"): Oh, yes.

The name B. P. Schulberg was still fresh in my mind.

TB: He was then one of the heads of Paramount, but, you see, those producers who were heads of the whole studio were different individuals from the producer on your film. Like Zanuck was the head of 20th Century–Fox, so he had a say in everything, but there'd also be special producers like Kenneth MacGowan, a very fine producer who was on *Lifeboat;* and Lubitsch—because Lubitsch had had a heart attack, he couldn't direct it, he'd written *A Royal Scandal* for me and only if I was going to do it would he do it. He'd done it originally as a silent film with Pola Negri and Rod La Rocque, you see [*Forbidden Paradise*] and . . . that's another time when I turned down two pictures while I was waiting for that. I was supposed to have done *The Woman in the Window* with Edward G. Robinson, and George Sand in *Song to Remember*, Merle Oberon did that because I was tied up. *Royal Scandal* was to have been ready in three months and it wasn't ready for eight months, you see. Now, things like that happen, those were two pictures I could have done in the meantime if we'd known. Then Lubitsch had a heart attack, but it was his picture. It was exactly as in the script; it was all laid out and Otto wouldn't even have his name on it, he didn't want to take any credit for it, although he was actually directing us during the whole thing, and Lubitsch would come down to see the takes, you know. He paid me a very great compliment. He said he thought it was the best comedy performance he had ever seen on the screen. I had one scene that was nine minutes long, and they never changed the camera, never took a close-up, anything, and that was quite unusual in those days because they'd cut and take about a minute for two or three lines and cut back and forth, but . . . the actor has no say, you know.

JK: But when you arrived at Paramount as a highly publicized import with this great reputation . . .

TB: I had no say about the stories or . . . Nothing. I knew nothing about making movies. I was ignorant. I was an amateur. I didn't know anything about lighting or photography. There are some stars, like Mary Pickford, who would light themselves; people who grew up on the screen and knew as much as the lighting man. I was a babe in arms by comparison. So who was I to say something? I had the loveliest relationship with people I was working with— they couldn't have been more divine, even if it used to kill me to get up at the crack of dawn. I didn't fight for things. If, as you say, a great many other actresses there did fight with the studio over their roles, well, they were just smarter than I was, that's all I can say. The famous story, which is completely untrue, is that I turned Adolph Zukor off the set, which was very much criticized. Because I wasn't like Garbo. I would see anybody. But I was very self-conscious acting with the cameras and the people so close to one, yet I know that Ruth Chatterton made a great success in movies at the same time because of the same thing, she'd come from the theater and spoke dialogue beautifully, and she would have about three rows of people there when she was acting. She wanted an audience, apart from the crew working on the picture. Now, what was my point?

JK: About Adolph Zukor . . .

TB: Ahhh! That I turned him off the set. Which was absolutely untrue. I had asked him would he *not* be on the set when I was doing this particular scene because it was my first or second picture and I was still very self-conscious and nervous. It was like going to Mars in a way. And he very kindly said yes. But I never ordered anyone off the set. *Order* is a word I don't use. I might request—"Darling, would you mind . . . ?" You know. It would have been discourteous to this older man who was head of this company, Famous Players it was called, and he had been responsible for a great deal of history of the movies, like Goldwyn, David Wark Griffith. But it made me out to be ill-mannered, which I just *don't* like. All I ask of anyone is to "cut my throat, but smile if you're going to." But that's what I was meaning about the things you hear which then go on to haunt you. But I never had any arguments because I didn't know what it was about. I still don't. But Paramount was then going through a very bad time, they were almost bankrupt. . . .

JK: It was Mae West who saved them.

TB: Well, she had just come out. I met her out there for the first time. Because all our dressing rooms were in one row of houses. Marlene dressed next to me, and we had the same makeup girl, Dot Parnell. She did Judy Garland for many years after that. And there was Claudette Colbert, and Carole Lombard, and Miriam Hopkins, and Helen Hayes was doing the Hemingway *Arms* thing with Gary Cooper, and then Mae West moved in. There were many many great stars, and in *The Devil and the Deep* we introduced Charles Laughton to American audiences. And he made an enormous success.

JK: Was he already hogging the cameras then?

TB: No, no. You can't control the camera. You can't do that like you can on the stage, where, if something goes wrong and the phone doesn't ring, you can turn your back to the audience and go BRRRRRRRRRRRRRR and pretend it's ringing, but on film you have no say over that. The only time I got annoyed with Charles Laughton—he wasn't actually very popular with the crew, I don't care if I do say this—but we worked at night a lot. The story took place in a submarine. We had a real submarine, with the advice of the Navy, but we had to shoot at nights because the top of the submarine had to be off because of the lights; and the dawn would come up and a bird would start singing and then we'd have to stop, because we couldn't have a bird singing in a submarine at the bottom of a sea.

I think script girls have the hardest job of all. We were doing this scene and she suddenly yawned, and Laughton boomed [Tallulah booms in imitation of a bombast with a mouthful of words]: "*How dare you yawn when I am doing a scene!*" And I got so angry, I said to him, "Don't you *dare* talk to her like that. We're all tired and exhausted." From then on he began calling everyone "darling." I don't think they liked that much either, because I call everyone "darling" because I can't remember their names, and he just thought that he was being amusing. But otherwise I admire him very much. And I think he was a very fine actor.

In those days there were three cameras on us—long shot, medium and close-up. There's a scene where Charles had to slap my face and I said, "Charles, do it. Hit me. I don't want to keep on doing this." Because in the movies you know it's coming up and you can always retake it, but on the stage you really hit somebody. I used to have to hit that divine Leslie Howard for months in *Cardboard Lover*. Only once did I hit him on the cheekbone, where it made his eye hurt, and he got angry. He didn't show it where I could see it, but it wasn't intentional. You have to hit somebody on the fleshy part of the cheek, because it's got to look and sound real. So I said, "Hit me hard, Charles. I know you're not going to hurt me, but let's get this over with, there are three cameras on us and maybe we can get it in one take." And then I had to pick up a cigarette and my hand was supposed to shake. Well, he really very nearly swiveled my head off, and when I picked up the cigarette, my hand was really shaking so that it looked as if I was overacting. But it really was quite a shock, and we only had to do it twice, but I had to see it six times in the rushes and every time I saw it I'd duck.

JK: Were you pleased with any of the films you made at that time?

TB: Well, I *adored* Gary, and I thought I looked better in that than any of the others, and that always pleases a woman, you know. And some of our scenes together, Gary's and mine, were very attractive. But Charles had the best part in it. Cary Grant had a small part in it. He didn't want to play it because he knew it wasn't a very good part, but I said I wanted him. Get *me* being so grand! But I had it in my contract that my name came first, that was the only thing I had to protect me. It was sheer impertinence, because I had no right to come first. Gary Cooper was *known* and a star. But it was Bankhead and Cooper in *Devil and the Deep,* introducing Charles Laughton. There was one scene where I finally lost my temper with Charles, and at the preview people saw that he was doing strange kinds of things, and they laughed in the wrong place because of this. And the studio asked me to redo it and I said no, I couldn't be bothered.

He had all these mannerisms—all stars have mannerisms that they are unaware of, and these antagonize as well as attract people, and they become a habit that you're not even aware of. That's the awful thing about the movies, you can see yourself and realize what you're doing, whereas on the stage you can merrily go along thinking how good you are because you *can't* see yourself and you can't really hear yourself. And you don't think you're good maybe when you are. If you get a laugh in the wrong place, you may be able to stop it. But once it's on the screen, you've had it. You can't put your hand through the screen and you can't kill everybody in the theater.

JK: Your film career seemed to have gotten derailed from the start by being shunted into the Garbo/Dietrich orbit, playing all those immoral, listless women in bad roles.

TB: What do you mean, bad? Morally bad?

JK: No, badly written, wrong for you.

TB (not listening to my explanation): You see, my darling, in England I had thrown off my wedding dress and stood there in my, what they called cami-knickers, or teddy-bears we called them in America—and which looks like an old-fashioned nightgown compared to bathing suits today. They were always having me undress onstage. I remember once with Bob Benchley, who is one of our great wits, and together with a few friends, we were coming back from a party and we all jumped into the swimming pool with our clothes on. Well, that was one of the biggest scandals in Hollywood, to jump in *with* your clothes on. Later they put it in a movie with Norma Shearer, but at the time it was quite a scandal, though what's so bad about that? It was daylight. Everything was under control.

Now, where were we? Dietrich and Garbo. Well, we share a certain bone structure . . . I'd give anything in the world for Garbo's nose. I think she would admire my hair because it's the only thing I've got that is better than any of them. Which is sheer luck, just one of those accidents of birth. That and my teeth. These [tugging at them for my benefit] are my own. Yes, they did have the battle of the exotics once in what they called the rotogravure section of the papers, with Garbo and Dietrich and me or I—I never know which it is. A few weeks later they had a big picture of me as the exotic of the exotics. You know, they had all that kind of nonsense. That was the whole trouble, to try and make someone different. My whole point was my vitality, which, if I showed it in pictures, looked as if I had St. Vitus' dance. Therefore, when I saw a test and saw what now looks like somebody doing the jitterbug, in calming myself down I lost a certain naturalness, part of my own personality which I had on the stage and which you either liked or disliked, but there it is, that is me.

JK: You knew Dietrich from your time at Paramount?

TB: Yes, that's when I first met her. She dined with me there. She said it was the first time she'd ever dined with anybody in Hollywood without Von Sternberg. She never stopped telephoning her daughter, Maria. I gave Maria her first part in the theater. Her very first part. And she weighed about 230 pounds then. Very beautiful, but very, very fat. She was in a play by Philip Barry, who wrote *Philadelphia Story,* which Katie [Hepburn] made such a big hit in, both on the stage and in the movies. And the next time I saw Maria was on *The Big Show* [Tallulah's radio program] and she was married and had two little boys. Marlene was on the show, and Maria came to see her during rehearsals, and she'd lost at least 150 pounds and was quite, quite lovely. She was an extraordinary child, but then of course Marlene had this awful fear about kidnaping . . . you remember the threats at the time, ohhhh, this all goes back so many years and it's hard for me to remember. And I'm the queen of non sequiturs, so it's hard for me to make much sense. You'd better ask me about somebody else now . . . but be careful, because I don't want to be indiscreet! Because I haven't said anything I haven't meant.

But there's a very funny story about Marlene, whom I adore, and I take no credit for her great success in the nightclub, but when I appeared at the Sands, I was the first so-called legitimate actress—why they call them that I'll never know—to appear in Las Vegas. I had wonderful material, I was very lucky, and I went back three or four times and made a great deal of money, more than it would take me to make in the theater in a year, and Marlene was out there for two or three weeks to sort of spy on me. We were great friends, very fond of each other, and we had a good time together, and so I introduced her for the first time she was ever in a nightclub. We arranged it, of course, and she rehearsed the orchestra, there's nothing she doesn't know or couldn't do herself, and she came on and looked beautiful and divine.

She was an amazing creature. She'd walk around at the swimming pool at the Sands with her hair up in curlers, no makeup at all, everyone could see her, and then that night she'd come into the casino with the white chiffon and the white fox furs and all the jewelry. [Tallulah melts the words "chiffon" and "fox" and "jewelry" in her mouth and blows them out to float in the air, so that you can almost imagine you are seeing Marlene.] She really is the most contradictory woman in real life to what you'd imagine. Once, still with the white chiffon dress on, she went into the Sands kitchen around 4:00 or 5:00 in the morning and cooked up scrambled eggs and tomatoes for me. It's really sad that the public never saw that side of her, for she is really a very witty, observing and amusing woman, and I'm sure could play comedy divinely.

Talking about movie stars, also a great friend of mine, though I don't see her very often, is Katharine Hepburn. I think Katie and Garbo have the two most interesting faces I've ever seen in the movies. As a child, of course, I adored women like Norma Talmadge, Pauline Frederick—all the vamps I used to love. Not the Mary Pickfords. Oh, even as a child I adored the "vamps." Nazimova. Oh, Nazimova I adored! But in the talkies Garbo and Hepburn were my favorites. They had such bone structure. Now, I only saw Marilyn Monroe once, in *Bus Stop*, and I think it was one of the greatest performances I've ever seen. Extraordinary. Almost transparent. And yet that was the only time I ever saw her. There are so many things I should see, but I get a bridge game going and they pile up on me. Katie and I used to go nearly every Sunday to George Cukor's for lunch, as nearly everyone did in Hollywood at one time or another. We were so different that it used to kill George. And yet I think we liked each other very much.

And Garbo has dined at my home. Miss Garbo. Greta. Whatever they want to call her. I always say Garbo, the way people say Tallulah. I've only seen her here and at Salka Viertel's about six times in my life, and that's over a long period of time. She loves to go "antiquing," as my little nephew calls it. She loves to go into shops. Before I sold my house to Huntington Hartford, I had this rather nice piece on the wall that I had bought from Guy Lombardo's brother, and he told me that Garbo had loved it but had said "zat I haf no vall to put it on." But I don't go antiquing. I have everything brought in to me because I can't be bothered. But the first time I met her, I had never seen anything so beautiful. She hadn't then started the suntan; her face was as white as snow. No lipstick, but her eyelashes, which are her own, made up very heavily. And her skin looked as if she had an electric light bulb inside, it was so transparent. And she laughed at everything I said, so I thought she had a marvelous sense of humor! And she was ingratiating and charming and poured wine for people, and the few times I've met her she never said, "I tink I go home" or whatever it is she's supposed to say.

JK: You made seven films out there?

TB: No, no, no, my dear child. I made three pictures in New York City at the Long Island studios. George Cukor directed my first, George Abbott the next two. That's when Lubitsch was out there making his pictures, but we didn't get together until twelve years later; and Chevalier was doing his pictures. Cukor had never directed a picture. Here was I, a stage actress with a stage director, stage writers . . . on my first film. I mean, we were all swimming without water wings and we had never been in the water before. I liked it because for the first time in my life I wasn't terrified about money because I was making so much, and it was during the Depression—everyone else seemed to be starving, but for the first time in my life I wasn't worried. Everything's always upside down with me. Of course, later on things backed up on me! There were hardly any taxes back then, in a sense. And I wasn't paying commission. In fact, I never have in the theater. I've never had a press agent; I've never taken an ad, and I've never endorsed anything.

JK: So after 1933 you left Hollywood and went back on the stage and you virtually remained there.

TB: Yes, I worked literally continuously.

Selznick wanted Tallulah for Belle Watling in *Gone With the Wind* and Tallulah wanted to play Scarlett and neither got their way, and a few other projects, like *The Little Foxes,* fell through, and except for the two films she had already spoken of in the mid-'40s, she went ahead and established a reputation for herself in the American theater much like the one she had had in England, as potentially one of its greatest actresses, but undoubtedly its most glamorous personality. Her acting reputation inevitably suffered as more and more she bowed to the public's demand for her personality. But then, her personality lifted her so high that, for an actress who had only two important roles on the stage, she was more loved and had more things written about her, and more plays influenced by her personality, than any of the so-called First Ladies of the American theater.

TB: I've never been temperamental in the theater in my life. And it's just an-other word for "temper." Now, I'll talk back to a *bully,* but I couldn't act with people who didn't help me. Every actor knows that if an understudy goes on, everyone is working for him or her, and he's better than the one who played it originally, because everyone is giving their all to help him, knowing the nervous tension and lack of preparation. Well, I don't know what my repu-tation is, except that I think I'm the dearest, kindest, sweetest person . . . I cry at the drop of an old man's hat. My sister and I sit here and watch TV in the most awful bathos. I give her a box of Kleenex, and I call us the Kleenex sisters. The music goes up and we start bawling.

JK: You and Tennessee Williams have been friends for a long time.

TB: Darling, you make *long* sound so ghastly. [She laughs.] Well, everything you've dredged up is long ago now. . . .

JK: Well, besides all the things you've turned down, I've always heard that a lot of American playwrights wrote plays with you in mind.

TB: Well, no. No good author writes a play for anybody except themselves.

JK: But I'm sure I've heard or read that Williams said that he's written plays, including *A Streetcar Named Desire,* with you in mind as the female lead.

TB: Gadge Kazan would say to me, and this divine Negro woman who later on became my friend, Gee Gee James, Tennessee would say to her, "Gee Gee, how would Tallulah say this?" But I was playing in a revival of *Private Lives* and I was under contract and ran for four years in that, so I couldn't have done it if I wanted to. They never even offered it because they knew I was under contract to John C. Wilson to do *Private Lives.* But I remember people coming backstage saying, "It's the greatest play for you, written for you." I said, "Well, it's a bit late." I never expected *Private Lives* to last that long.

JK: And what about Mary Chase? She supposedly wrote *Harvey* for you when it was still a play about a woman with a canary.

TB: A four-foot canary named Daisy. I didn't meet her till after *Harvey,* which, I think, had one of the greatest performances I've seen, given by Frank Fay. He was so great. But it wasn't written with me in mind. She never met me until years later at an agent's, when she said, "Oh, if I'd only known you, I wouldn't have changed the play, I would have kept it as a woman with a brother." It would have been amusing, the woman drank elderberry wine and wore velvet dresses with little spots all over them, and it would have been such an easy, lazy part, although it was a long part and I, think, a heartbreaking part. There is the long speech in the last act which just made me cry and which Frank Fay did brilliantly.

JK: But subsequently didn't Mary Chase* write *Mrs. McThing* for you, which Helen Hayes ended up playing?

TB: No, she did not write it for me. I was offered it first; and Mary Chase is a wonderful woman, but she makes you do these fantastic changes. In less than half a second you've got to change onstage. It was originally called *The Thing,* and that was the time when the Thing was one of these monsters, and

*Tallulah appeared in Mary Chase's play *Midgie Purvis* for a three-week run on Broadway in 1961.

I just didn't see myself in it. Although my great friends saw and adored it, I never saw it, so I don't know.

JK: What about you and Williams' play *Orpheus Descending*?

TB: *Battle of Angels* was the original title. It absolutely shocked me to death. I loathed it. And I turned it down. Like that horrible film you took me to see, what was it called? *Bust* . . .

JK: No, *Boom!*

TB (laughs): *Boom!*, bust, whatever . . . it was perfectly awful when I saw it onstage, and if I'd known that it was *Milk Train,* nothing on *earth* could have dragged me to see it, but you said it was Elizabeth Taylor and Richard Burton, who had been so wonderful in Albee's *Virginia Woolf* and you didn't warn me. And it [*Battle of Angels*] opened in Boston and—what has never happened in America—it was booed off the stage. They either walk out or don't applaud, but they never boo. It didn't even run a week. And I was playing summer theater between the run of *Little Foxes,* and my stage manager came back and said: "There's a man outside called Tennessee Williams to see you. He said he sent you a play." I said, "Well, send him in." And this little, bedraggled, dusty boy with a bicycle, who'd come from St. Louis to way up in Maine, came in and said, "Why didn't you do my play?" I said, "What play, darling?" He said: "*Battle of Angels.*" I said: "Because I thought it was repulsive and disgusting, that's why." And of course the next play he wrote was *Glass Menagerie,* which was beautiful and acted by the greatest actress I ever saw, Laurette Taylor—a tone poem more than anything else— and she gave it a magic which it had in reading it but not to that extent; and then came *Streetcar.* . . . Years later I was down in Key West with Tennessee and our friend James Herlihy [author of *Midnight Cowboy*] and we went to see a movie with Anna Magnani called *The Fugitive Kind,* which had been *Battle of Angels*. It was in this tiny little theater in this tiny little place called Key West, which is only about two miles by four, and when I came out, he asked me what I thought, and I told him I thought it was disgraceful. "They've turned a bad play into a terrible movie."

JK: How did Tennessee take that?

TB: Well, he roared with laughter. I mean, what else could he do? He knew it was probably true.

JK: But you must know that, while you may have turned down some duds, a lot of your friends have said that you rarely picked material worthy and you'd rather do an easy play on the summer circuit which pays a lot than a really good play.

TB: Well, that really isn't so. Because the summer circuit, which they don't have in England . . . I remember Sir Cedric Hardwicke and Dennis King, who were following me, were absolutely terrified. This divinely clever woman called Lillian Ross was writing for *The New Yorker* about the summer theaters and she ended up by asking Sir Cedric Hardwicke if they have summer theaters in England. He said: "Unhappily, no. We have no summers in England." But it's been a life-saver to actors in America. For young actors, it's a holiday at the same time as paying their living expenses; and for stars, they make a great deal of money . . . and I told you, I was lazy and if you can make $5000 a week and your house is given to you and your maid for ten weeks, why should I bother to do anything more? Now, I won't say I know a very great play when I see one, although I read avidly, and I think I read good books . . . But I hate to work. I'm lazy. I'm from the South. I'm just what they call "bone lazy" or "born lazy," either one of them! I was reared by my grandmother and grandfather and aunts because my mother died when I was born, and to exercise wasn't the right thing to do in those days. I wasn't allowed on a bicycle. Of course, I could be thrown off my horse every day and nearly be killed and they wouldn't have minded because that was all right. But a bicycle—no! We came from rather a small town, and we had everything in a way. We weren't rich, but we were well-to-do for the South; and Sister and I were sent from one aunt to the other. We led a gypsy life as a child, but loved by our aunts and uncles and all.

JK: Don't you really ever regret having passed up a good play?

TB: Darling, I never look over my shoulder.

JK: I remember you said that you "loathed" acting.

TB: I do.

JK: But you've been acting most of your life.

TB: Because you can't get off the merry-go-round, darling. And once you start, and you get used to living a certain way, you've got to keep making your living. I wouldn't be very happy living in a slum, and I can't put a key in the door, and I can't use a zip—I don't know *how* people zip themselves up in the back—I *have* to have someone looking after me, and that sounds *awfully* corny and snobbish and I *don't* mean it that way, but you know what I mean. I'd rather live in a poor bedroom with someone to help me than in the grandest home without anyone. Do you know, I couldn't use a dial for years because I didn't realize you had to pick up the phone to dial first? And I had to call for help and say I can't get anyone on this phone. Because I never observe anything, although I never forget anything I hear.

JK: Did you really mean it when you said that the humiliation of being in a bad play outrages all human dignity, and being caught in a long run is almost as bad?

TB: Well, there I think I was not quite honest. Everyone always asks you if you get tired of playing the same role. Well, not if it's a role you enjoy, and I've enjoyed some. And unless I've been frightfully ill, as I have been and played, I think it's really the most stupid thing in the world to say that "the show must go on," because I have nearly died playing with a fever of 106°, I've played with neuritis, gastric ulcers, nephritis, double pneumonia, you know. You might be crippled for life. I think it's absurd. Although I can understand it, because if the star doesn't play, the poor actors don't get paid. Not that I'm that noble—I want to get paid myself. That's why I do it. But, actually, a long run gives me a certain sense of security, and I think that's what we need, women particularly. And I've played every state in the Union except for Hawaii and Alaska, and I couldn't tell you about any of them. Because I used to go from the train to the hotel, from the hotel to the theater, and back to the hotel and the train. So I've played every state of the Union and yet I can't tell you anything about my country. Eighty-nine one-night stands I had in *The Little Foxes*. Always moving.

JK: But how could you say you loathed it?

TB: Well, you know, I use very *exaggerated* adjectives. I use the word "divine"—you know, "Isn't it divine?" Well, divine it isn't. And "terrific." Terrific really means terrifying. But a terrific hit isn't a terrifying hit. Or it isn't supposed to be. Or is it? So I'm very subject to using exaggeration in my speech. Well, my book was me, as much as I can tell, but . . . you know, I could tell a few tales, my dear, but . . . when they're dead, let them rest in peace, that's my motto.

What I'd like for the future is to have nice people around when I would like them around. And to be left alone when I don't. I don't look over my shoulder. I just live from day to day. For the future, I wouldn't mind if an atomic bomb hit me on the head, but only if it hit *me*—I wouldn't want it to hurt anybody else. I love lovely things, as almost everybody does. I take a bath in perfume, practically. I love beautiful flowers and I like lovely paintings. I like trees and reading and ball games and tennis . . . but I hate that awful game, what is it, that the English play—cricket? They don't even bother to run. They hit a ball and they just stand there. I don't understand it. I don't understand football, and they say it's the most marvelous spectator sport. I love to watch golf, particularly that putting bit.

Joe Louis, whom I worship, like Willie Mays, the great baseball player, they say he used to go to sleep just before a championship fight. And I couldn't sleep for three days before his fight, I couldn't bear him not to win! And apparently that is a form of nerves. I just get sleepy. But once I'm on . . . and, believe me, whether it's a one-night stand with only three people there or an opening night in the capital of the world, I do try to give as good a performance. It's just that I get sleepy. Ohhhhhh, if only I could get sleepy when I get home! When the show is over, I can't sleep at all. That's why I read so much. Read, read and read . . .

JK: Tallulah?

TB: I like the way you say Ta-*loo*-lah! You say it correctly, of course. So many people come up and say, "Oh, Miss Bankhead, would you give me an autograph of your stage name with your real name underneath!" Well, darling, you're very charming, and you haven't asked too many embarrassing questions, and if you had, you could always have stopped the tape.

JK: Thank you very much.

TB: Thank you . . . was it John, darling?

Everybody has stories about Tallulah, and so do I . . . the night she taught me how to smoke; the night she went to a Greenwich Village bar which ended up as a scene in the Broadway musical *Applause;* the night I made her forget baseball. . . . I thought it would be the last time I'd ever see her.

Tallulah hated liars. And it was a lie that got me into this situation. She was passionate about bridge and short of partners. I, eager to impress, casually said that I played. When she invited me to dinner and a game, I couldn't suddenly say: "No, no, I was bluffing." I figured it's just cards, and in the back of my mind was the hope that I'd learn to play or that the game would be canceled. But the day arrived. It was noon, and I asked Lillian Lang, a friend at the BBC, for a quick course on bridge. "It would take days, weeks, years to learn." "But I'm playing tonight. Just tell me something . . . how many cards do I get? How do I bid? I play Canasta, Hearts, Crazy 8's . . . would that help?" Lillian gave me a look that mixed concern with astonishment; but it was now too late to turn back. She gave me a few of the basic rules, which I tried to memorize, but panic is a great eraser. With each block I walked the situation only got worse. I had been trying to remember the rules and hoped for a pleasant accident that would enable me to call from a hospital, with a minor injury, to be sure, but enough to show I wasn't avoiding the game. If only I'd called the day before, told the truth in time for her to find a replacement. It's as clear now as it was then and I still feel the tightening in the pit of my stomach that went with it. When I arrived, late, the other players were already there and they were waiting dinner. Tallulah hated lateness, but tonight I didn't care.

Dinner was undoubtedly divine. Even though Tallulah, as was her wont, only picked at her food and my stomach fought every attempt to push anything down, the other two men ate well and with evident enjoyment. They were very nice, quite slim, youngish, casually stylish (three-button knit cardigans were all the rage). One of them worked with Tallulah's agency and looked after her, the other man was his friend and had wanted to meet "the legend." The talk was about goings-on at the office and an appearance of Tallulah's on a TV variety show on which, they both told her, she had looked magnificent. The conversation then turned to that evening's televised baseball game, which Tallulah planned to watch. We were going to play while TV was on, but she hoped we wouldn't mind, and they didn't.

Over dessert, while Maria, her cook, cleared the table, conversation turned to our game. Tallulah asked the man from the agency sitting on her right, "What convention do you like to play?" Panic began to mist me over with moisture. Convention? What's a convention? Lillian hadn't said anything about conventions. She must have told me about the wrong game! "Blackwood," he answered. My mind went blank. She then asked his friend. He said: "Stamen," I think, but what do I know? Then she asked me. I'd forgotten everything I'd been told. Everything. "You're the visitor, dahling, so you have first choice. What conventions do you like to play in England?" "I play by ear." There was an ungodly silence. A look crossed her face as if she'd been standing on a street corner and been splashed with mud from head to toe. Fast thinking: "I mean, I play anything you like. You pick." The moment for a clean breast of things had passed. We'd play as soon as she returned from the john.

Alone with two men I'd never seen before but for whose elegant ease I'd have given anything, I looked to them for a lifeline. I blurted out the truth: "I don't know how to play bridge. I've never played it. I just got some instructions at the office today. I forgot them. They didn't say anything about conventions." Knowing Tallulah and her towering rages when foul play was afoot, their *sang-froid* froze. It was now their turn to look horrified at the imminent disaster. Well, so much for their evening. They would take turns partnering me. Maybe it would turn out all right.

Tallulah came back. We moved to the card table already set up in the living room, the TV set turned so she could get a better view. When it came time to pick partners, both offered to play with me. Tallulah, who'd returned from the john with her own suspicions, looked pleased not to have to start with me. The cards were shuffled, dealt, and with her eyes on the TV, and talking about Edward Albee's new, critically panned play, she arranged her thirteen cards. It was clear that even while talking about one thing and watching another her concentration on her cards was intense. I was locked into position. There was no longer an outside world full of people, there was just north, south, east and me.

The opening bids were made. I have no idea what my partner opened with, or whether he passed, or whether it was a no-trump situation, since I had no idea what any of it meant. I simply counted the number of cards in each suit and if I had more clubs than whatever he said he had, I bid the number of clubs. I know Tallulah peered at me over the rim of her glasses as if she'd seen a leper, but she didn't know what to make of it . . . yet. She arrested a snort moving up her rubbery nose. My partner, whose game had just been blown, and his friend raised their cards to hide their thoughts. It turned out I was playing the hand when I would have given anything to have been the dummy. I would trump our own cards; I would fail to pick up one of our own tricks. We went down that round. We went down the next. We won when the cards were so good it was impossible to fail, but I had underbid, so we didn't have much to show for it. Without wanting to, I seemed forever to be playing my partner's hand. There is an inner reaction between players at bridge tables you never find elsewhere, so I have been told. You don't just signal your partner through your bids, but through raised eyebrows, scratching of chins, tugging at mustaches, puckering lips, flaring nostrils as if about to sneeze, even looks off into space. These meant nothing to me. My face was moving constantly, but that meant bewilderment to me and defeat to my partner.

The World Series was still going on, though now everybody, including Tallulah, was concentrating more and more on the game at hand. Tallulah was puzzled and showing signs of increasing dangerous restlessness. She and her partner were winning, and my partner wasn't complaining, so she couldn't say much, but she was snorting more and more.

Tallulah's mouth had now drawn down and set hard. The baseball game was going into extra innings and somebody suggested that maybe it was getting late and we should call it an evening. But Tallulah, looking squarely at me, would have none of it. It was her and me. "I suppose now it's *my* turn to lose." Her voice was absolutely flat when she said that. She was very angry, and she just grew angrier. I underbid on a good hand. I overbid with nothing to show. I did everything except throw in the towel. Now, as my partner and the victim of my playing, she no longer held back her feelings. Fury, frustration and puzzlement gathered in her face, pulling her features in around her eyes. They bored through her cards, through mine as if she could keep straight on and force her will into me and correct some of my worse excesses. But there was nothing there to correct.

Never had I heard such a gift for language used to lacerate somebody the way I was now being lacerated. This was Hecht and MacArthur, Kaufman and Hart, Broadway's finest at their most acidic. The tables were turned on the man who came to dinner. Clifton Webb in *Laura*? Fiddlesticks. I deserved it. I was actually relieved to be getting it. I didn't mind what she said, just let the game end. The others tried to stop her, but she only got furious with them, as if she sensed that they'd been holding out on her while playing with me, and I suspect the reason they got angry now was that they couldn't get angry when they had to put up with me as a partner, and they resented Tallulah behaving as if she were the only sufferer.

Then I started to laugh. It bubbled up out from under all that weight parked on top of it all day long. My body had inflated like a zeppelin full of laughing gas. First a helpless little splutter, then the eyes brimmed and flooded, and a first roar of laughter errupted. Then another. The laughter, increasingly uncontrollable, barely gave me pause for breath. Tallulah would look at the hand I might have laid down, scream with outrage, and I'd be off again in semi-hysterics. I was in great awe of Tallulah; I liked her so much. And now, on top of everything else, this! But I was helpless. My bones had turned to jelly. Twice I slid underneath the table.

"Sorry."

"Sorry? You're *sorry*?!" Sorry wasn't good enough, it was beyond sorry, but it had to do.

At one point, for no reason at all (not that any more reason was necessary) other than that a new hand had been dealt, one of the men started to giggle, and now three of us were hopelessly hysterical. It drowned Tallulah's thunder. She couldn't even maintain her anger, because as soon as she opened her mouth to chew my head off, I'd be off in gales. And then they'd be off, and we all would be saying: "Sorry," and I'd be telling them not to defend me because I deserved it all, but I don't think I ever finished a sentence.

Finally it was over. Tallulah said something like: "Well, I've never seen anything like this, and you will *never* do this again, or I will personally kill you." Laughter is devious. She tried to say it with some remaining semblance of seriousness, but even she found herself smiling against her will. So instead of tossing me out on my ear, she forgave. You don't stay angry with children and idiots, I suppose.

We became friends. Hardly an evening went by when I was in New York that I wouldn't go there for dinner. Often I would stay on until 2:00 or 3:00 a.m. Other times she'd send me off to enjoy myself. Frequently her oldest and dearest friend, Estelle Winwood, was there, looking even then, only eighty, frail and medieval, as though from a tattered tapestry. Estelle had the power to curb Tallulah's rantings with a soft, barely audible few words without ever dropping a stitch of her needlepoint. Tallulah adored her and was like a well-bred little Southern girl around her. Evenings were more raucous when another old drinking buddy, Patsy Kelly, was there. Then it was more like a scene from *Fallen Angels*.

Most of the time, though, we were alone, maybe had a few drinks, but she didn't drink much those last few years. A Scotch I poured early in the evening might get freshened once or twice. She left it to me to do, having shown me how, but it wasn't strong. There'd be TV, and lots of marvelous talk. Very ribald, very funny: politics, theater, films, books, her family, the South, her loves, her triumphs, childhood, England, all were stimulating grist to her conversation. But in all that time I never heard slander raise its fluty voice in her presence. And when I'd leave her company early in the morning, exhausted, in some of New York's muggiest summers, I would reenter the streets invigorated and looking forward to evening.

My interviews were done early on in our friendship, when I still blushed and fumbled. I even learned to talk back to her, to say enough is enough. Then she'd study me, and she was clearly amused and became very gracious and apologized for hurting my feelings. She wouldn't have to do much to win my affection back, but I saw her do it with absolute strangers. Taxi drivers who spoke to her as one of their own, somebody they loved and were proud of; couples in restaurants next to us who couldn't tear their eyes and ears away and would inevitably say: "Excuse me, but are you . . . ?" "Yes, dahling." "You don't remember me . . . ?" "Dahling, I have a terrible memory. I'm sure I *should* remember you." "We were sitting next to you on a plane, and you held our baby and she peed in your lap." "How could I forget that, dahlings!" she'd croak, and there would be that famous short burst of laughter like a growling stomach that made them feel like family. They'd talk, remember her in plays. She'd respond, charm them senseless, have them floating away, ready to tell all their friends about the night they had dinner next to Tallulah Bankhead.

Some nights she'd be telling old stories about herself, stories which she found funny but which had nothing to do with her, and others that were attributed to other personalities but which had in fact happened to her. There was the time she was in Washington for a Democratic Convention honoring her "divine friend, Adlai Stevenson," making him sound more like a Lothario than a legislator, so sexual and vital and adoring. And during a long speech by some senator she had to go to the john but found when she was settled in for the duration that there was no toilet paper at hand. "So I looked down and saw a pair of feet in the next stall. I knocked very politely and said: 'Excuse me, dahling, I don't have any toilet paper. Do you?' And this very proper Yankee voice said: 'No, I don't.' Well, dahling, I had to get back to the podium for Adlai's speech, so I asked her, very politely you understand, 'Excuse me, dahling, but do you have any Kleenex?' And this now quite chilly voice said: 'No, I don't.' So I said: 'Well then, dahling, do you happen to have two fives for a ten?'" And Tallulah finished the story, roaring with laughter. "Is that a true story?" I'd ask. "Of course not, dahling, but there are so many funny things that happened to me which they tell about others that I might as well take the ones that I like. After all, they're going to tell it about me anyway."

I think one of the best things about Tallulah was that she made you feel so alive, so much a part of things, filling you with her own experiences and waking you to your own. I couldn't imagine that incredible life force extinguished. "Now, you mustn't get serious, dahling," she'd say, seeing that I cared more than it was good to show. "Well, wherever you go, it'll be a damn sight funnier once you get there." She loved that. And I meant it.

Royal Scandal was on TV one night. The film was not a popular hit on the level of *Lifeboat,* but her performance was a comic jewel. Her timing, her sensitivity, her humor (as distinct from her wit) make it cherishable. She should have made more films after the success of *Lifeboat* gave her a whole new screen audience. But by then she belonged too much to the stage. It had first call. She went back to it. I'd never seen her onstage. If only . . . What must her Regina in *The Little Foxes* have been like?

It was early in the morning; we were both a little woozy from the drink and the smoke, and she was going to do her favorite moment from the play for me, her favorite speech. Tallulah went over to stand by the grand piano, beneath the full-size portrait of her by Augustus John, and started. And fumbled. Then swore, but at herself.

This play, this role had meant a very great deal to her. It had to do with a time in her life when everything had jelled. She stepped back and held herself very firmly, her eyes looking far away, outside her living room, beyond the present, somewhere where there was just herself and who she had been. Her red caftan hung from her shoulders to the floor, not catching on any part of her, as if she had no body with curves and bends to arrest it. In place of the pyramid was a crimson column, and her neck and head set upon it looked very white and separate, as though placed there moments before. Tallulah was not a young woman, and never a tall one, and she tended to slouch. But she now looked formidable and grand. And she started the speech from the top: "There must be a better place than this . . ." and did it all. Although it wasn't a sad speech, I listened deeply moved. Lillian Hellman, who wrote it, had little nice to say about Tallulah, who had given a well-written drawing-room melodrama the stature and significance of an American classic, something it's been trotted out as being but has never had since.

She flicked the hair back off her face and was back in the living room. "Dahling," she said very tenderly, "it's awfully late and you must be tired." She looked at me very solicitously. "You must get a taxi to take you home."

There were lots of other memories, though few that moved me as this had. When I first went to Hollywood, she phoned George Cukor and told him to look after me. When I got there, he did everything he could for a friend of Tallulah's. And when Hitchcock was in New York to promote *Torn Curtain,* I met him at a press breakfast in his honor. She had asked me to give her regards to him and a rather over-elaborately autographed photo of herself to his wife and daughter. When I arrived at her house later that night, every possible space was banked with flowers. "That divine Hitch," she barked when I asked where was the funeral. It was typical of the affection old friends held her in, even if they no longer had the energy to spend time with her.

I was in England when she died. Without her, New York was never the same to me. And though I later learned the game of bridge, I rarely play.

1964

K I M
S T A N L E Y

K IM STANLEY, the Jeanne Eagels of the American theater of the 1950s. Those who've seen her work in the plays with which she blazoned her talent across the stage—*Saint Joan, Bus Stop, Chéri, A Touch of the Poet, A Far Country* and the others—haven't forgotten her. Those who have seen her films—there are only four: *The Goddess, Seance on a Wet Afternoon, Frances* and *The Right Stuff*—can't forget her.

When I asked about her before going to meet with her, instead of information I got awe and envy. Say her name to people: a few will look puzzled and ask, "Who?" These are the same people who have never seen a Garbo film. Most, however, simply repeat her name, "Kim Stanley," quietly. She's like a sibyl, a high priestess . . . as solid, as authoritative, as absolute.

The day before I was to see her, I got a call from the press agent who'd set up the interview a month before. His voice on the other end of the line was somewhat breathless. He wanted to know, "Have you seen her in the theater?" "Why?" She had called him and said, "Look, I don't want to talk anymore about movies. I've hardly made any movies, they don't interest me. If he doesn't know my stage work, let's cancel." "You've seen her onstage, haven't you?" he finished. "No." "Oh, God." The press agent's voice was getting raspier, as though he'd jogged a mile in the smog. "Fake it, John. You can fake it." So now I was driving to see a woman who might chuck me out the moment she sensed that I was there under false colors.

The moment I saw her standing at the top of the steps at her rented aerie below the Hollywood sign, waiting while I parked my car, I knew there'd be no point in beating around the bush, not with the way she looked. I felt she'd see through me in an instant.

"I was terrified coming to see you."

"*You* were terrified," she laughs. "*I* was terrified. Why were *you* terrified?"

"I had better tell you right away," I said as I was going up the stairs to her, "I've never seen you on the stage, but I feel as if I know you, the way I know someone I've read about in a book." We were in her apartment: very simple, just a rental, evidently it wasn't going to be permanent. But I had struck a common chord with her.

683

There were a lot of surprises. Painfully, almost brutally honest about most things, she draws a very solid veil over any form of gossip or name-dropping. Her openness, her intensity and her palpable trust may be the reasons she makes it so difficult for interviewers to get to see her. But once you get to her, she is all country courtesy, she speaks clearly with passion, conviction, faith in the fairness of others.

JK: There are certain people who belong to their time. And the great thing about movies is that you can see it at once. I wondered why you weren't in films earlier, before *The Goddess,* because you were such an extraordinarily cinematic presence in the truest meaning of the word. As you were saying, Carole Lombard was—

KS: And usually she was not in terribly good films. But there was something about her, there was some kind of intelligence and guts in there that was not like the stars of her day. I was really heartsick when she died because she could do high comedy, she could do tragedy, she could do everything.

JK: You never saw Jeanne Eagels?

KS: No.

JK: You have a treat in store like you wouldn't believe.

KS: Where did you see her?

JK: Oh, I saw her in two films in London about eighteen years ago now. I went out of curiosity because I wanted to see John Gilbert [*Man, Woman and Sin,* MGM, 1927], and I like Monta Bell's work . . . he's an intriguing kind of a realistic director. But when you saw her on the screen, this woman long dead, this actress, you knew why the audiences went nuts. I say this only because I felt I knew you very well, I felt an instant rapport when I saw you on film. One knew more than the script gave one, I knew more than the story allowed. The camera caught your quality.

KS: It's amazing to get that out of *The Goddess,* because it's my least favorite out of any work I've ever done. I know why I did it, but they didn't really do the script I read. At that time, Paddy [Chayevsky, the author of the film] was really extraordinarily egotistical. He always was, but he did learn as he got older. And he didn't realize that editing is an art all its own. It's a craft and a discipline that really has nothing to do with playwriting. He edited it himself. That's the reason it's so strange, the way it is edited. And he left out all the comedic stuff, and it broke my heart because nobody doesn't try to laugh once in a while. I mean, *no fooling!* Little Orphan Annie in Hollywood is really not interesting. I was in London when I first saw it—it was horrible. I

Kim Stanley, photographed by Vandamm for *A Clearing in the Woods,* 1957

just crawled out of that theater. There were a couple of moments when I thought, "that's not bad"—but a couple of moments!

JK: But it was better about Hollywood and what it meant to become an overnight star than *The Barefoot Contessa,* God knows.

KS (laughs): Except she's so lovely and wonderful . . .

JK: But I always felt Mankiewicz knows more than we do and he's not going to tell us, and I don't like being talked down to. It lacks the humor and compassion and breadth of his film about the theater, *All About Eve.* Of course, Gardner had the quality of being real, as you do.

KS: That's the reason why I like the theater so much more. You can do it in sequence, in the context of the circumstances. That's such a lovely thing to do. And I've never done a film yet in sequence. The last scene of *The Goddess* was shot first. The very last scene was shot first. Then we jumped back to the car scene with the young girl. We jumped all over. It was a *terrible* experience, because I was an amateur in the medium. It was very difficult for me.

JK: Wasn't Cromwell [the director] much help?

KS: Oh, John was wonderful. John was the last of the great gentlemen. But Paddy didn't let him do his work. Until way into the film, when I would not act if Paddy was on the set. I couldn't, because he was really very disruptive and destructive to his own work. Later Paddy changed—much later on, but then . . . he would come in the morning to the makeup room and say—like, about the last scene, that wasn't an easy scene to do, and he'd say: "I saw the rushes of the last scene, and they were terrible." And I said: "When are we going to reshoot them?" He said: "We're not." And this was the beginning of the day at 5:30 in the morning. It's *terribly* stupid. Because you're gone for the day; you may as well be out to lunch. It's awfully hard with willpower to get *that* out of your head. And it's a fairly important scene, it's not walking down Hollywood Boulevard. I found it very difficult. After I saw it, I never wanted to do another film.

You see, you have *no* control, really, over what is seen on the screen. None. Graeme [Clifford] had to cut about forty-five to fifty minutes out of *Frances.* It was the forty-five or fifty minutes that Jessie [Jessica Lange] and I had done on why these two women are so inextricably linked. Because it doesn't quite make sense. Why should she be coming back to this woman?* You know, I'm not mad at Graeme himself, I'm damn mad at the studio who thinks the American public can sit still for five hours of football but can't sit still for a psychological study of—an emotional study of—a grown woman. And so it's constant *coitus interruptus.* You never know what is it she really

---

*Frances Farmer keeps going back home to the mother who keeps locking her up in hospitals.

wants. It leaves out all of the grace notes, all of the gristle, all of the muscle that goes between this and that; how she was formed; why; what is the hook between these two women. It was not in the script, and it was very difficult for both Jessie and me to find it, and we did find it before we hit that studio. Because we worked for a month and a half before we ever shot anything.

JK: She's divine in it. I love her. I love looking at her.

KS: Boy, she is some gal! She really is; she is such a good, hard worker. And very talented. You haven't seen the end of that yet. She is the *real* article, that lady. And I loved working with her. We're hoping to do something together. So that part of doing it was wonderful, but then to have it all cut . . . Because we did find what it was. And we found it without talking about it, because she's like I am, she doesn't want to sit down over coffee and talk about it. I find that very destructive to do, because once you've talked it all over, then nothing happens between you—because it's been pulped.

JK: But there is another way, of course. The other way was, when they used to make a lot of movies, they made so many, one after the other . . .

KS [laughs]: That you were bound to catch it somewhere? I didn't go to the movies much because my family was hardshell Baptist background, so to get to a movie was difficult. But when I got a little older, I learned to lie a lot. I spent a lot more time in libraries than I did in movies. There were a lot of them I hadn't seen when I was a young girl that I caught up with later. Like Marie Dressler; that's an actress who's just as good today as she was when she did it. In *Anna Christie,* Garbo is not too good—she's doing all that breast-beating and stuff, but Miss Dressler's performance is just as good now, just as real, just as protean . . . and she was just as good playing old dowagers, she's marvelous! And I always look for those replays of anything she does, and when I'm in New York I always go to the Modern Museum, because it's so refreshing to know the real article doesn't change all that much.

JK: Did you ever see Laurette Taylor on the screen?

KS: Thank the Lord! I didn't see her on the screen—but I did see her in the last play she did, *Glass Menagerie.* The first week I was there, in New York, I had gone to see Miss Cornell—most beautiful woman, my Lord!—in *Antigone,* because, coming from Texas, I thought, you know, Katharine Cornell is the greatest actress in America. And that was from the little bit of reading I had done—I had never heard of Laurette Taylor. And I cried afterwards, after seeing Cornell, and I thought, "That's it, I'm going to go home. If that's what they mean by the greatest actress, I want to go home." Because it was all singing, and posing; not at any moment was I moved. Now, I understand when she was younger that was not true. And I was just damnfool lucky that someone said to me at the end of that week: "Listen, you better go and see *Glass Menagerie;* I want you to see this actress." And she was a stranger to me; I mean, it was somebody I had just met—I was waiting on table—and she knew no more than I did about acting and actresses; who was great and who wasn't. And I was so lucky to see Laurette Taylor. Because otherwise I would not have become an actress. I was ready to go home.

I just hate to bad-mouth somebody that I haven't seen at their peak. But I was heartbroken at that. And then to see Laurette Taylor . . . I just couldn't believe that anybody could do that. I didn't believe that Tennessee—whom I now know very well—I didn't believe that Mr. Williams or any playwright had written down that part. There was no way that that could have been on a page. There was something about it that said to you: "Oh, well, if you can do *that, that's* something to aim at!" And, believe me, it was many years before I was able to do even one moment that well! But I knew the real thing when I saw it.

What I got out of books was that the world wasn't as small as the one I was in. And that there were people who thought the same kinds of things that I was feeling. That I wasn't out of my own world; and I was always so grateful to find someone.

JK: Were these books your parents approved of, or were you just reading everything?

KS: I don't think my parents really realized what I was really reading. But I was reading Henry Miller at a very early age. Because the library was very good there, and I had gone through all of my age books, and so I had a special pass to the adult section. And it was a way of escaping, it was like treading water until I could leave home. I knew that I did not belong where I was. I never thought I was stolen by gypsies—I'm too much a carbon copy of my father physically—but I just knew that I was waiting until I passed that time at home, and during that time I did meet someone, thank God, who taught me about music, and gave me some of the disciplines that are so intertwined, and that was my real education. It wasn't what was going on in school.

JK: I think I was in the same place. And nothing is as good as the forbidden. . . .

KS: Exactly. Because you know that there *is* that world. Suddenly it's open to you. And you know that you can get there. That there is a way. You're not an oddball, that there is somebody who will say, "Oh, hello . . ."

In my senior year in high school my father was doing his Ph.D. thesis in Taos, New Mexico, on what they now call Chicanos, and I chose to live with my father that year—my mother and father were divorced when I was three. Taos was really not a tourist place then, I fell in love with that part of the country. The mountains and the sky are just not to be believed. And he was on a foundation grant, and we lived in the foundation itself, and there was a wonderful library there—still is. And I used to steal his keys after he had gone to bed and go down to the library all by myself and read at night, sometimes till 2:00 or 3:00 in the morning—I managed to get by with very little sleep. And I spoke not a word of French—I spoke Spanish—at that time, but I would take out French books, and I didn't know what they were saying, but just the feel of the book and the look of the letters and the words, I could sit for hours just turning the pages as if I were reading. In my imagination I sure was someplace—I wasn't there. And that sounds really crazy.

JK: Do you remember what the first movie you saw was?

KS: The first movie I saw . . . in my life . . . was *King Kong*. The original *King Kong*. My brother snuck me out of the house and snuck me in to see it. For a very stupid brother reason, 'cause he knew when King Kong stepped on the pygmies I would just go crazy. I went to the bathroom and vomited and he had to take me home. I had three older brothers and they caught on very early to my receptivity to all things and they made hay out of it! My mother kept telling me if I wouldn't react they wouldn't do it! I couldn't understand how not reacting would change my inner . . . you know. The other thing was: "That's all in your head." And I remember thinking even when I was six: "Well, everything is, you know!" I mean, isn't everything? I mean, it's all connected to the shinbone down here, right? "It's all in your head!" Oh, well then, I'll just forget it, right? But my mother wasn't as strict about that as my father was. He still had a lot of the hardshell Baptist about him, and they were brought up that way to think that movies and dancing and listening to the radio was against God.

JK: That must have turned you against God for a long time after that.

KS: I did a *lot of work* to try and find a religion that fit. I mean, I did learn a lot about religions trying to find one that would allow me to do what I wanted to do! I did finally convert to Judaism. But really mostly because . . .

JK: So patriarchal . . .

KS: I don't mind that so much. I really don't mind patriarchal too much. Harold Clurman used to love to get me in front of people and say: "The reason that Kim is not interested in the feminist movement or Women's Lib or ERA or any of that jazz, except for the natural thing that people should get the same salaries for the same work, is because she thinks she's superior to men! And she doesn't want anybody to go around telling her she's equal!" I mean, he was exaggerating to make a point, but I'm afraid all that pigeonholing of things really matters very little to me. There's a lot that you could learn from patriarchal societies and religions. And if you notice who's strongest in Jewish families (and which can lead sometimes to horrible results), it's the mothers; but it's the reason that I've finally decided that all mothers are Jewish. It takes some will to try and go against that feeling of wanting to make the child some sort of an appendage of your own! And you have to really work at not doing that, for the good of the child and for the good of yourself, and because they're a separate human being. But I think all mothers have that impulse.

There are many things about Judaism that I really like a lot. I'm crazy about all the holidays. I think they have a purpose. So if I'm anything, that's pretty much what I am. But all the rules are ridiculous anyway. None of them come from the human being, the needs of the human being. And what sends me up the flute is all the wars that have been fought over God. And Jesus Christ. It's just terrible. Look at Ireland. All that "my book tells me so"—the Koran, or the Bible, or what have you.

JK: . . . And the whole foundation is such a dishonest lie to begin with. I happen to like the old religions best, because they at least were founded in something essential to the soil, to their livelihood, and they celebrate certain times because you have been working your back off. . . .

KS: What is as lovely as the harvest and the . . . you know. Most of the holidays I find a little difficult, since both my parents died this past year, but I now realize very very strongly that that has a real purpose. Because people say to you: "Well, they had such long lives." As if that is supposed to erase some of the . . . you know, some of the stuff that comes up. And it doesn't. It has nothing to do with it. It's one of those things where you put the salve over the thing before you clean the wound.

Both of my parents were farm people. My mother's father was a very learned man, a Greek scholar, but he was very misplaced as a hardshell Baptist and as a farmer—he didn't know bo-diddly about farming. But both of them came from—my mother would kill me if she heard me say this—peasant backgrounds. She always hated me to say that, but it's true. And to come out of that small Texas, Lampasas County, Lometa ranch farm, it took my father some time to get rid of that. He did get rid of a lot of it. But it took him a while. He was very concerned when I wanted to go into the theater. Actually, I didn't know what it meant to go into the theater. All I wanted to do was get out of Texas.

JK: You could have got out of Texas and become . . . anything.

KS: Well, I had found out by then that my writing was not superior. Because that was my first desire—to be a poet. Then I found out that it was pretty identifiable with Miss Emily Dickinson, and I could not be better than she. And when that came to my consciousness—in a flash, when you suddenly see yourself plain and true, I thought, well—you see, I didn't really study drama in school, but I had done some extracurricular stuff and it was the first time I was ever praised for anything that my brothers couldn't do better. They were all excellent students, and I was a good student, but it seemed to take a lot more work for me . . . also I found a lot of school very boring. The only real social event was the church. The Baptist church in Lometa. And so it's very u..derstandable, all this. But both of them did not stay there. My mother

was much more open to new things and ideas . . . especially after she made
the *horrible* thing of divorcing my father! You just don't do that! Her family
didn't speak to her. She broke a lot of the . . .

JK: Commandments . . .

KS: Yeah. She wanted me to do what I wanted to do. She was very, very helpful
to me always. But I don't think she took my acting terribly seriously.

Some guy saw me from some school that I don't care to mention, because I'm afraid that it's going to start up again and I don't want anybody to
go there and think they'll learn anything, but . . .

JK: Not Pasadena?

KS: Yeah. It was a drama school. And he was a teacher there, and he was
coming through town and saw me in a play, and I got a scholarship to go
there. Because teachers are poor, especially back then, and I suppose it's still
true now. So it was really—and I'm not joking—my ticket out of Texas.

JK: It certainly wasn't being on the screen?

KS: Not actually, as I started telling you before. Because I never thought I was
in any way good-looking enough to be in the movies. When I was growing
up, the people on the screen mostly were pretty. Except for Bette Davis. The
reason for the stage thing with me was, I think, because it was a little snobbish. Because I didn't think I was pretty enough to be a movie star, and plays
seemed to me to be more about something. And when I took the Greyhound
bus to New York, I didn't know anything. But I really had absolute confidence in myself. It didn't occur [to me] that they wouldn't give me a job in
New York. Because I knew you didn't have to be a raving beauty. And I knew
I could do everything else. I was in for a big *shock* . . . is what I was in for!

I went up to Kermit Bloomgarden's office, straight off the bus, and told
him he would have to replace Miss [Barbara] Bel Geddes in *Deep Are the
Roots* because I was right for the part! I knew more about the South and all
that stuff. I made a list of all the theatrical producers from the Yellow Pages,
and I went to see every one. I didn't know you had to please the secretary
first. I just saw the door and somebody else walk in, and I'd just walk in. It
was out of ignorance, so I just did it my way and I did those pieces. Of course
I never got a job from it. I was very bad. I did a little piece from *Saint Joan*,
of course, a little piece of Juliet and a little piece of Mary Queen of Scots.
Well, they were stunned, or they would have thrown me out, because you
just don't *do* that. Except in the movies. Walk in like that—unannounced.

JK: But didn't your innocence help you an awful lot?

KS: Well, I'll tell you what it did do for me. I don't think what I did there ever
helped me. Russel Crouse said to me: "You're such a nice girl, I think you
should go back to Texas!" Of course, I still had a Texas accent doing my

Saint Joan piece. But the inner thing that made me do that, that kind of strength has helped me. I guess all my life. I get that from both sides—my mother and my father, the most stubborn people in the world. And then I realized I had to change course, and somehow I had to get onstage. That was the only way I was going to be seen, and get jobs, and become a *wonderful* actress.

JK: Quote unquote. And you came there from Pasadena. That is where the whole Selznick group was—Dorothy McGuire, Gregory Peck . . .

KS: They weren't there when I was there, I think they had preceded me. I did one play there, and Sophie Rosenstein, who was also close to Frances Farmer—it's funny how life is—tested me at Warners. Which was a miserable experience. Not any fault of hers. They changed my face to look like a kewpie doll. . . . Even when I was young, skinny, adorable, and as pretty as I ever would be, I never *was* pretty. I had a kind of flair, but it certainly did not fit their idea, you know? And they tried to do that, and they even shaved the things off my teeth . . . it was terrible. The works . . . just for this test.

JK: It wasn't a test for something particular, just for a regular contract?

KS: Yes. And then I went in to see Michael Curtiz. And he said I had too many photographic problems. *Well,* that was mild compared to what Harry Cohn said!

JK: You mean, when you did *The Goddess*?

KS: No, that was long before I did *The Goddess*. The only movie role I ever wanted really badly was the girl in *From Here to Eternity*.

JK: The Donna Reed girl—the prostitute?

KS: The Donna *Reed* girl! Just because she got the Academy Award? That's *my* part! [Laughs.]

JK: Good for you! Oh, I wish you'd had it. You're going to love who I wish had also been in it, but I won't tell you.

KS: No, tell me.

JK: Well, the part that Deborah Kerr played. You know how everybody loves it if you're playing something you normally don't play?

KS: And shouldn't!

JK: They always think you're a great actor if you're playing the Hunchback of Notre Dame, which is a very good part, but the moment you're suffering, it's gotta be good. Well, you know Joan Crawford wanted that role. And also Rita Hayworth should have had it.

KS: Zinnemann had his hands tied by Cohn on that one. It was before Zinne-mann *was* Zinnemann. And it was because Harry Cohn was just . . . oh . . .

JK: You had a personal meeting with him?

KS: Yes, Monty [Clift] and I worked on a scene, even. And Zinnemann wanted me because he'd seen me in several plays. . . . But we'll skip the struggling years! The only reason I mention it is because I'm sure all these things have added up and had a lot to do with my not wanting to do films. And nobody was actually falling over my doorstep asking me to, either. But when they did ask me, I was very chary about it always.

I went in with Mr. Zinnemann, who's a lovely man—this was in New York—and he introduced me to Mr. Cohn. And staring right at me, not look-ing at Mr. Zinnemann, he said: "Why are you bringing me this girlie? She's not even pretty." Looking straight into my eyes. [Pause.] I wasn't ready for that! [Laughs.] I mean, I *knew* I wasn't pretty, but I wasn't ready for that kind of artillery at that close a range! To be fair about it—I don't remember too much, but I did call him a pig or something. And when I looked at Mr. Zinnemann, he was purple—with both rage and embarrassment for this strange man who didn't feel that he had to have any manners, I guess, be-cause when you have that much power, you don't have to. It could have gone unsaid, you know.

JK: Of course, he could never deal with people like Jean Arthur.

KS: I liked her a lot. Didn't you?

JK: Oh, very much, very much. This is an aside, but it's extraordinary: the three biggest stars he ever had—Jean Arthur, Rita Hayworth, Kim Novak—were all extremely introverted, painfully shy, hated to be confronted and couldn't deal with his kind of approach. For instance, Cohn would go and have a pee with the door open while Rita was sitting there where she couldn't miss it. She wouldn't know what to do, and would just sit and slowly petrify inside.

KS: Clifford [Odets] was always very fond of her, you know. She used to call him in the middle of the night when she was in trouble. He was kind of a father thing.

JK: Well, he finally wrote a film for her. *The Story on Page One.* He goes back to *Frances* as well—

KS: And to me. . . . He was the one that I didn't marry, however! But that was really because he was not good with children, but I loved him a lot. I really loved him.

JK: So that thing with the way he dropped Frances [Farmer] without telling her himself and letting someone else tell her, that's true?

KS: I know it's true.

But this brings us into the realm of gossip, and if it didn't happen to her, she drops it.

JK: I was curious why you . . . Okay. Here's this extraordinary theatrical star. Like Jeanne Eagels. Gone for a long time—I know you were teaching, but you were gone for a long time from Broadway. . . .

KS: I was forming a group theater is what I was doing, I wasn't *gone* anyplace. But I couldn't get any money to back it. I want to do the big shows, I don't want to do the little stuff. As [producer] Bob Whitehead said to me: "Kim, that's wonderful, but nobody will come." And Bob had five successes with me. [Pause.] Oh, well. Someday I'll have the money to do it, even if I do it in my old age.

JK: But your name was very strong. You were the thing of the '50s, the only one of a handful of tragediennes that the American theater has ever come up with. . . .

KS: Nobody ever remembers how funny I was in *Bus Stop* and *Picnic*. I always get those cryey parts and hysterical women. It's really very dumb.

JK: Why would that be? Because of *Cat on a Hot Tin Roof*?

Stanley had played Maggie in London. In 1984 Stanley played Big Mama, reuniting her with her friend Jessica Lange, playing Maggie the Cat in the made-for-TV film of the play.

KS: No, because the first thing I was seen in on Broadway was when I replaced Julie Harris in *Montserrat*. The little Indian girl who goes out to be killed. Well, there's a lot of laughs in that, right? Then the next thing was that marvelous play *House of Bernarda Alba* by Mr. [Garcia] Lorca, and that's where I made my big hit. And I did *Saint Joan*—a lot of people remember that. . . . And then they put my name above the title in *Traveling Lady*. But everybody forgets *Bus Stop*. . . . And *Picnic* I got a lot of laughs too. But they simply don't remember those things. And then there was [Arthur] Laurents' play *A Clearing in the Woods,* which is not a laugh a minute by any means, and then the wonderful book of the two *Chéri*'s by Colette. I wish the playwright had been up to the material, because Anita Loos just was not up to that material. Nobody further away from Colette than Anita Loos. That was too bad. But I did it because it was a big challenge to me. Because I can do Russian women much more easily—I'm much more akin to Russian. French women are real hard to do. Their quality is awfully hard to describe. All those experienced things that Colette describes, all those smells and tastes, a whole life . . . so yeasty. And at the same time having that other eye that is literally watching it. That is terribly difficult for an actress. One of the reasons I love Chekhov so much is because he's so funny. So funny.

JK: You had a very hard experience when the whole Actors Studio crew came to London with their production of Chekhov's *Three Sisters*.

KS (laughing without humor): Oh, do I remember! I've got the scars to show for it, baby! We all do. It's impossible really to describe what went wrong. Unfortunately, Geraldine [Page] couldn't go, and neither could Shirley Knight because she'd been crucified by the director. And she didn't want to go through that again.

JK: Who directed it?

KS: It's not just because he's dead, but because I'm tired of speaking against Lee [Strasberg]. Because Lee and I had our battles together, and we always had them face to face, and I don't need to use newspapers to clear the air. Lee and I loved each other, and we knew each other's work, and I also knew his faults and he knew mine.

JK: The reviews were very . . . I wondered whether it was a reaction to the whole Actors Studio thing?

KS: Well, in some ways I think the English think that they can do Chekhov better than the Russians can. But I can remember way back when I was doing *Cat on a Hot Tin Roof* in London and Kenneth Tynan had asked us to go on this show where he had asked us to argue with the top stars in London at the time about the Method. It was just nonsense. If you're an actor, it doesn't matter where you got it from or who helped you along the way. There's no big secret. You don't walk through the Actors Studio and come out with an aura. There are a lot of bad actors who come out of the Actors Studio, just as there are a lot of bad actors who come out of Birmingham Rep. And vice versa. And most of the reasons they're good they had when they walked into both places. *But* it can be freed, opened and *stretched* a good deal depending upon whom you're studying with, and we don't have Birmingham Rep in this country. And the Studio was that place for a lot of us, and I'm very grateful to Lee for all of that. Always shall be. But as a director he seems to go immediately against all his teachings and go straight for results. And it's very confusing for a cast who has worked for him for all of their productive lives. But I was not ashamed of what we did.

The opening night was a fiasco in London, but we should have never opened. None of us should have even been on the stage. We had completely new props that we had never touched, the lighting . . . George Scott, who was brilliant, a brilliant man, I love him, he took over one of the roles as a favor to me, because I needed all the support I could get. I can't tell you, it was just a fiasco. The stage was raked, so we all looked like we had peg-legs. I mean, I've worked on a raked stage, but *this* . . . We had not been *on* the stage, the lighting was all wrong, so we couldn't see each other, much less the audience see us. It was horrible. Just one of those things that happen. Just horrible. We begged Lee to postpone, just till we could get used . . . And they were still putting nails in the damn set! And when the curtain finally came down and then went up on the whole company, we were so used to hearing either tumultuous or even polite applause, and it went up to a roar of boos. And the stomping. [Laughs loudly, but not with humor.] And it takes longer than a second to realize what you're hearing, the shock is so incredible. It's like being pushed by this huge wall! And the stage manager, to whom the *Studio* was *God*—the *Studio* could do no wrong! He just kept raising this curtain. Again and again. Eight times. My God! We were being crucified and he kept raising the curtain. Finally, the eighth time, I stepped downward, turned to face the cast and bowed to them, and we left.

But I do think, regardless of how well prepared those very real things should have been—and weren't—that we got pot shots simply because we were the Actors Studio. Because later in the run the few people who did come back and see it were quite reasonable and complimentary. But I have to tell you that they had every right to boo. Even the next day I was grateful. Because that's something about the English that I like a lot. They let you know. I played up in Liverpool when I was doing *Cat on a Hot Tin Roof* and I loved it. They talk to you as a character: "Maggie, don't do that!" Or, if you're doing something they approve of: "That's right!"

JK: It doesn't throw you?

KS: Oh, no! I loved it! At first it was astonishing. But once you get used to it, they're right in there with you. [Laughs aloud.] I'm not talking so much about the West End kind of audience, they're usually quite polite. But in this case they had a real good reason. And if they've had any kind of expectation of how these American upstarts are going to teach us about Chekhov, then they certainly got such a poor opening night that it was like opening the floodgates of . . . of whatever suspicions they came with.

JK: Sometimes people like Chayefsky or Strasberg build up such a resistance to Hollywood that when finally it comes to them, they walk in there with such a resentment that they overdo the whole thing. It's as if he does a worse job just trying to pay them back for some earlier rejection.

KS: Also he [Chayefsky] had this other thing, which was the "I'm going to have a good time" thing. At that time [while making *The Goddess*], out of TV and things like *Marty,* he had a reputation for being a slice-of-life writer. Unquote. And it bugged the hell out of me. He wanted to prove that he was "an epic writer," and I am quoting now. These are words that I've heard from his mouth. And epic to Paddy meant EPIC, you know. That's why he cut all the scenes. And whether the character was taken from Rita Hayworth, or a combination of Marilyn and Rita and all the other people who were unfortunate in Hollywood in some ways, you can't tell me that those girls didn't try to have a good time! Don't tell me that! I know both of them had a terrific sense of humor, and forget it . . . you can't do that. It just looks stupid.

JK: What attracted you to *Frances*?

KS: The circumstances. I really do think most mothers of daughters and most daughters of mothers have one of the most complicated relationships in the world. I'm sure it may be true of sons and fathers. But it seems to be even more with women because they have so many layers of intuitive stuff—I don't mean men don't if they're allowed to, that's why I'm really for *Men's* Lib; little boys are taught from a very early age the way to behave because they're going to have to decide very soon what chute they're going to go down, they're going to be a lawyer, a doctor. And so a lot of intuitive stuff is almost cut off. I don't mean in every family. It's a generalization. But I think it's socially very true. As a result, that part of all of us that is intuitive and very alive when we're born is stopped.

I had a strict upbringing, but nobody ever said: "You stop that and get on with your homework." I was given a lot more leeway. And I'm very grateful for it. And I want to make it clear: I don't mean that women have this wonderful, intuitive, nebulous thing. It's because we're able—simply by the setup in most families, at least in my generation—to explore a lot of stuff that boys are not allowed to. They're aimed at something very early on. "Don't cry—that's not manly" . . . it dries up all the real stuff. It's very unfair, I think. Men have it much harder than women. Much harder. We have it much easier to get at our real selves. Women have so many more options.

JK: How did somebody get you to appear in *Frances*? What made you want to do it?

KS: Oh, I tried. I pleaded with Robert Whitehead to let me do some of the classics. I want to do Clytemnestra, I want to do *Ghosts,* I want to do *Medea,* but it's not anything that's selling on Broadway, if you've noticed what's happened in the American theater lately. All escape stuff. I can't tell you how many plays I've refused where the final scene is: "I'm leaving you, Charles, and I'm going out to find myself." Excuse *me*! At least in the '50s they all wrote from a different viewpoint. Tennessee and Bill Inge and Arthur Miller, all from their own viewpoint, were writing about something. Now I find that nobody's writing about what's really going on today. I haven't read even one passable play that has to do with the nuclear problem. But usually, doesn't art precede the social awareness of what is happening? Of course, what's going on now is too terrifying, and it immobilizes. Because one feels that there is *nothing* one can do.

JK: What was *Frances* a statement of? Was it meant to show us how bad Hollywood was, or how women were destroyed by Hollywood? I really didn't know what it was trying to tell me.

KS: You see, the fascinating thing about Frances Farmer—not about this particular film—was that her life seemed to encompass the politics of the '30s, the never-never land of Hollywood, and the psychiatric nonsense which is still going on in many parts of this country. . . . That made me do it.

I started writing about the way Harold [Clurman] was treated in the film. Because Harold was the great man of the theater in the 20th century. Not only was he a great critic, but he was a terrifically human, beautiful man. And the only person that I know that came out of the Group Theatre who never dropped the flag. And who couldn't be bought. He had no cruelty in him. Clifford had cruelty in him. He had also genius in him. He also had tenderness and lovely romanticism in him. He had a lot of things in him. But to disservice those two men, especially Harold, in that kind of way was, to me, an outrage. Well, it got so Graeme would run away when he saw me start, because if that was the only scene they were going to have Harold appear in, I said that they just had to get someone to play Harold who was so . . . I didn't know where they were going to find him, but someone who had such humanity and such grace and such real brilliance and passion—you see, these things don't go together—and this was what made him so unique in his time. He had such compassion for other people. He was a complete man.

JK: I don't know enough about Clurman from the film to know what he was supposed to have done to her, but then, Hollywood has never known how to treat its own on film. Once, all those bios were glossy. Now it's all shadows, which they think passes for realism. And neither are anywhere near the truth. I always thought that, unlike Farmer, Monroe was really a victim of her New York experience and not Hollywood. I mean, whatever Zanuck did to Monroe, she paid him back. As Jack Cole told me, Zanuck paid and paid where it really hurt a man like him. Monroe had beaten Hollywood at a game she understood. It was New York that beat her.

KS: I think you're right in some ways. But it must have hit that old note in the gut of hers. The insecurity of her childhood. Which would have come about in some kind of way later in life. But I don't think the New York experience was totally supportive of her.

When Monroe first came into the Actors Studio, though I was not part of the verbal way, I certainly harbored some doubts in my head. But thank God there were a number of us, like Maureen [Stapleton] and Geraldine [Page] . . . a lot of us . . . who had the guts to go and eat crow. Because she waited, she didn't do anything, for a long time she just sat and watched. Maureen got her to do the *Anna Christie* thing, in which Maureen was so frightened for Marilyn . . . and I think it's the only time that I've seen Maureen just unable to . . . because Maureen is always good, it's something about her—but that's the only time I've ever seen her when she just didn't know what she was doing at all. Because she was so nervous for Marilyn. And

Marilyn . . . was just wonderful. She was wonderful. We were taught never to clap at the Actors Studio, like we were in church and all that, but it was the first time I'd ever heard applause there. And some of us went to her privately and apologized. Even if some of us only had the attitude inside ourselves and never put her down vocally. I mean, you don't do that. To other people. I had to say to her, "I really admire you so much, because that's so hard to do. It's hard for all of us to work in front of each other." Which it was. You're not just working with your peers, you're working with the best people and in front of the best people. And it's very difficult. It's worse than any opening night. In terms of the hyperventilation that happens when you take a look at your partner. But she was uncanny in the way that she did it. There was nobody that didn't love her in that . . . anybody who had any largeness of spirit loved Marilyn. And she won us all. Not just the Studio, *but* what she went out to win, the intelligentsia, all those people, she won everybody. So in that matter I'm saying that the seed of the problem belonged someplace else. I'm not saying that we didn't help it, or that her marriage to Mr. [Arthur] Miller helped it, or that Lee's and Paula's [Strasberg] concentration on her helped it, but she actually had a thing about her that made you love her. And *that* experience could not have been a bad experience. Whatever seed of self-destructiveness was in her, I believe that seed belongs someplace else. I don't believe you can put it as late-dated as New York. Of course, Lee took advantage of her descent on the Studio.

JK: But then she goes back to Hollywood, and Hollywood is selling a product. And I was wondering how much it parallels Frances Farmer. And I also was wondering if you ever discussed the girl you played in *The Goddess* with Marilyn.

KS: I discussed it with her sister-in-law, who is in the film playing my aunt. Arthur Miller's sister. And Arthur wanted Marilyn to sue. I tell you, when I read the script, I did not think of Marilyn. Marilyn was not what occurred to me. Somebody more like Jayne Mansfield occurred to me. It might be any number of people like that, who've had tragic lives. Then when I got this message from Paddy saying it wasn't Marilyn, and he was so adamant about it, I wondered if it *was*! And I daresay he took a little from this, a little from that, a little from Carson McCullers . . . but it was a much better script than it was a movie. Only a fool would have turned it down.

I had no idea who was going to release the film, or that it would be Columbia. I just knew who was producing, and Paddy was going to be on the set every day, and I was promised three weeks' rehearsal, which turned out to be me standing in front of a camera . . . while they set positions, no other actors there. It really did shock me. This isn't rehearsing. What they were using it for was trying to make me look pretty on the screen. I wasn't plain.

JK: They might have known more what to do with you in Europe. Like Simone Signoret. That's very much your kind of face, really.

KS: She came backstage after the Colette play. I call it the Colette play because I can't bear to say the name of Anita Loos. And I said to her . . . she was complimenting me, saying how French I was—which I was, the last two weeks—and I said: "You know, Miss Signoret, you got all my reviews for this, at least all the ones I thought had any taste." They all said Miss Stanley was adorable, all that stuff, but too bad Signoret didn't play it! I said: "Did you know that?" She said: "No. But it is not true. It is not true because . . ." and this I thought was very kind of her, I really fell in love with her at that moment—she said: "In the movies, yes, I'd be better. But not on the stage." I thought that was very dear.

JK: Yes. She, of course, had that fiasco in England in *Macbeth.* Look, when Monroe did *Bus Stop,* you never spoke to her about it or *The Goddess*? Did you ever see her again?

KS: By that time she wasn't coming to the Studio regularly, and I wasn't either. When I was working, I didn't go because I had small children, you see. Sometimes we'd run across each other in Bloomingdale's, but we never discussed it [*Bus Stop*] at all.

JK: Was *Bus Stop* a part you would have wanted to play on the screen, or was it ever suggested?

KS: Well, I would be lying if I said I didn't want to film *Bus Stop,* but I certainly understand why Josh wanted her to do it.

JK: Who directed it on the stage?

KS: It was Harold Clurman. But Josh had directed me in *Picnic,* and he came backstage during the run of *Bus Stop* and said to me that he was going to do the movie. He was really a very decent, wonderful man, Josh, and he said: "I want to tell you before it's in the papers or anything that I'm going to use Marilyn Monroe." I said: "Of course." If I had been directing it, I would have used Marilyn Monroe . . . it was just too obvious not to! And also Josh's whole concept of it was so different from the play. Inge's play is a very small American primitive, and Josh of course went into the rodeo and the nightclub . . . it wasn't even the same genre, much less the same play. But it took me a long time to go and see it. There was someplace in there, I guess, I was afraid she'd be better than I. And he did ask me: "Would it bother you terribly if she came to see you in the play?" And it's well known that she did come quite often, but she used none of my stuff. I can tell you that absolutely truthfully. He evidently asked her to come to try and get my accent, which was authentic, because I grew up in that part of the country. I know Oklahoma and Arkansas and Texas . . . you just have to snap your finger and I'll go into it! But that was what he *said* he wanted her to come for, and she didn't even use that. So, except for some similarity in costume—which has nothing to do with anything—it was totally her own, just as mine was mine.

JK: Did she ever come backstage to see you?

KS: I think she probably was embarrassed to come backstage to see me. . . . I mean, I wouldn't come backstage if I were going to do the movie. But you know who did that who was really darling? When Elizabeth Taylor was married to Mike Todd and they'd asked her to do the movie of *Cat on a Hot Tin Roof,* she was in London and they came to see the play and she came back. And Mike Todd was carrying on: "Tell her she can't play *Cat . . .*" and he didn't realize he was giving me a back-handed insult, but because he was so charming he didn't really care. He said: "No one's going to believe that anybody wouldn't want to go to bed with her. Tell her she can't do that!"

JK: But if you're gay, you wouldn't want to, no matter how beautiful she was . . . that's the whole point!

KS (laughs): Well, I don't know. Tennessee and I argue about that a lot! About whether Brick is or is not. And about how many fences he wanted to straddle in that play. But she was charming. She said: "Now, listen. If I'm going to do it . . . Mike, shut up . . ." and it was the first time I'd met her, and when you get real close to her, she is fantastic-looking, and she said: "When I do it, I'm going to steal some things." I said: "Go ahead, be my guest. We all do."

JK: What made you do *Seance on a Wet Afternoon?* And also were you offered any other things? What were you offered?

KS: Oh, a lot of things I didn't really care for. The only thing I really liked was *From Here to Eternity.* No, the reason I did *Seance* was that I wanted to go to London, and because I had seen Bryan Forbes' *L-Shaped Room.* And because I had never before liked . . . Leslie Caron. And I thought, "God, if that director can do that to that cold fish, then that's a director I got to work with." Also I needed the money. I had three children to support. And a house I bought in the country and all those things.

JK: Don't husbands do anything?

KS: Well, I've been married four times, I'll put it that way. And all of them except the last are quite wonderful people and are still my friends! Even the one that's dead is still my friend. We were very close. And I'm very glad to have been associated with all of them except the last one, who was the only one to be from out of show business. I thought I was getting away from the crazy ones, going straight. . . . [Laughs loudly.]

I do an enormous amount of research. Not for television, which they shoot in five days. You can't. Not the way they do it now—on live television. You have to take a flying leap at a conclusion and hope that some of your instincts land. . . . But you really can't do that kind of research on TV, but I did it for that. I suppose it's all very self-indulgent, because I did the same thing on *Frances*. And *The Right Stuff*. And was able to use none of it, because the director already had it all chop . . . chop . . . chop.

JK: But back to *Seance*. You went asking for a seance?

KS: Oh, sure. As a civilian. It was interesting. But I'm an Aquarian and I have to be careful about getting into that stuff. There were two out of the fifteen— one woman and one man—that I researched . . . and that's when I stopped . . . and I thought, "This is no fake. There's something I don't know about, there's some kind of extrasensory something going on." If I didn't enjoy the idea of a group so much and love it so much, I would turn into one of those people who just research and pore over old stuff, you know. I love to research. It's the little girl in me. I'm always so comforted to go into a really large library and to know that, no matter how long I live, there would still be books that I hadn't read. It makes me very nervous when they have small stacks! I think, "Oh! I'm going to run out of books!" No, I felt the script itself didn't have much substance, but he's [Bryan Forbes] wonderful, and he edited that and made it look like what it was. . . .

I liked [Richard] Attenborough a lot, too. I mean, it became very clear that we work entirely differently as far as process is concerned. But you know that, and you work with it, and that's fine.

JK: Was working with Eric Portman [in *A Touch of the Poet*] a clue to how English actors work?

KS: No. Because, you know, Eric Portman was psychotic. Mr. Attenborough is not! I don't mean Portman wasn't a good actor.

JK: But I remember *A Touch of the Poet,* and reading about that, and Miss Helen Hayes, and the problems she had being in the middle, as it were.

KS: But she's really a lovely lady, really.

JK: It ran a long time, considering . . . some 200-odd performances.

KS: That's one of the reasons Bob [Whitehead] and I had a terrible fight over that . . . because I kept demanding, even out of town, and he promised me out of town that Eric would be replaced. Because Eric was beating me up onstage. It's not in the script.

JK (laughs): Well, he had a drinking problem.

KS: Tell *me* about it! But he wasn't so drunk that he hit Helen Hayes! You notice that, don't you? I mean, he knew who to hit!

JK: Was it because the two of you just didn't click together?

KS: It started at the first rehearsal is the truth. Not the first around-the-table thing, because that's where Harold [Clurman] did wonderful work. He always had such wonderful concepts, and if you really listen, it's really helpful. But the first time we were on our feet and he [Clurman] began to block, I was saying something to him [Portman], I'd done about two lines, and he turned to Harold and said: "Are you going to allow her to do that?" So it started right away. Then it didn't help that most of the bravos out of town were for me. I had an impacted wisdom tooth and I looked like a chipmunk half the time, because if he didn't slap both sides, he'd slap one for three nights and then the other. Now I have real jowls, but at that age I did not. . . . It was very painful, and that's the reason I left the show.

JK: I remember one very funny review about you on one side of the stage, Eric Portman on the other side, and Helen Hayes in the middle doing everything except a tap dance! It made me want to see it, because it sounded so extraordinary.

KS: It was very funny, because Harold was in London and we were going out to dinner. And we were in a taxicab, and I said: "I understand you're doing *A Touch of the Poet*." He said: "Yes. Helen Hayes and Eric Portman. I haven't cast the girl yet." And I said: "Well, what about me?" And he said: "Would you want to play it?" And I said: "Of course I would want to play it." A friend of mine in Germany had given it to me and I'd read it. He said: "Can you do sixteen?" I said: "Yeah, I can do sixteen. I can on the stage. I can't do it in the movies." And he said: "Well, if you say you can, you can." Because he did know me. And Miss Hayes gave part of her percentage up, and so did Mr. Portman, so I got my percentage of the gross and stuff. And it was all seemingly very friendly. But it turned into a very bad time with him, because by the time the fourth act came along he was so drunk that nobody could understand what he was saying, and he was a pitiful man in that sense, you felt sorry for him. But, on the other hand, he didn't make the mistake of slapping Miss Hayes' face.

JK: Let me return to something we spoke of earlier, when Harry Cohn said: "Why do you bring that little girl to me—she's not even pretty . . ."

KS: Let's get it straight; he didn't call me a girl, he called me a girlie! I mean, I realized the truth of it, but I didn't think I would hear it out of anybody's mouth. I don't remember exactly what I said; I remember using the word "pig" as I left, but I don't remember exactly how I said it. I just remember that word and Zinnemann's face.

JK: Did you ever encounter any other of these Hollywood types like Zanuck?

KS: No. That was the only experience. I never encountered anyone else like him. And I have never slept for my supper, I have never done any of those . . . I guess I was never cute enough, but I have never been propositioned to get a part or any of those things.

JK: Was there anybody besides Taylor who interested or impressed you? Like, for instance, did you ever see Tallulah Bankhead?

KS: You see, that was in her latter days, Miss Bankhead in *The Eagle Has Two Heads* . . .

JK: Which she loathed.

KS: I also think I didn't see her when she was at her best.

JK: Did you not see her as Blanche when she finally did *Streetcar*?

KS: There is no way I would have gone to see her as Blanche. By the time I saw her, she had that destructive kind of claque that thinks the more outrageous it is, it's okay. . . . I would just not have gone. Because I respect her too much. . . . I think what finally happened was she gave in to the audience. And the minute you let them lead you, you're in trouble. Because any actress can make that mistake. And let their wanting you to do something lead you to do it. It's almost as bad as believing your reviews. I really liked her very much as a person. I remember sitting next to her when I was still going out to nightclubs. Boy, that was a long time ago, and it was some kind of theatrical event, and Carol Channing imitated her doing "Bye Bye Blackbird," and Miss Bankhead was sitting at the next table just across from me. I mean, she was reachable. And I thought it was in poor taste, even if it was just for fun. There was something—I don't want to use an overdramatic word, but there was something tragic about the nature of what had happened to Miss Bankhead. Which I think that every young person even who hadn't seen her in her heyday was aware of, by some sort of thing that she emitted besides that camp stuff. And I thought it was a little vulgar. So I went over and just touched Miss Bankhead and said: "Nobody can do that song but you, and they should never try . . ." and she said: "Darling, I know that," and was very sweet.

JK: Did you ever see yourself, as others did, as a new type of American stage actress, a prototype for a '50s woman? I think of all those new faces who turned up in movies, after you'd made your mark on stage, like Joanne Woodward, Janice Rule, Eva Marie Saint, Lee Remick . . .

KS: I'm not sure I'd call myself that. It was just that I was responding to what was happening in the world out there. You see, I'm very in touch with not only Middle America, like Iowa and Texas and all that, I tell you those people who live on both coasts as I do and a lot of people in the theater and movies do, they are not in touch with that and have very strange ideas about what's going on. Because the truth is that people don't ask the same questions. It's now just seeping down to them about this atomic-nuclear crap that we're facing, and that if we don't face it now, it's . . . you know. What are we talking about! The minute I heard for the first time—it was about two years ago, I think it was on a news program where they're supposed to do it in depth, where they don't just give you the headline—and I heard the phrase "contained nuclear conflict." And I thought: "You misheard that." And then I heard it again. And I thought: "Oh-oh, are people beginning to buy this?"

You see, I think a writer like Doris Lessing is so brave, what she's doing, because so few writers are doing this. So few real writers are dealing with this.

Everybody's so immobilized that they just want to go see somebody tap dance, and do something that happened in 1930 or 1920 or 1928, or dress up and put the sequins on and please don't let me think about anything. And that certainly is not the function of a living art, is it? And, you know, I like *Guys and Dolls* and I like musicals and I liked *Chorus Line* . . . I like this and I like that, but you can get sick eating too much of that stuff. It sticks in our stomach. And the fact that so many thinking people are not writing about that is to me extraordinary. Doris Lessing wrote a play in the '50s—late '50s or early '60s, I'm not sure. I wanted to do that play so bad; I couldn't get anybody to do it with me.

JK: You've always gone your road. You did leave Broadway when you were the premiere actress of your time, and you just walked away. Or it seemed as if you vanished.

KS: Well, I had a nervous breakdown, but it wasn't because of *Three Sisters*. It may have contributed a little, because it was a harrowing experience to see people lashed before your eyes. I was not the butt of that and neither was Geraldine. We were left completely on our own. Unfortunately, you always need a third eye—everybody does. But we were left alone. But to see people that you care about really destroyed was a harrowing experience. Also, it was the end of my last marriage, which really threw me a terrible loop.

I tend to resent a lot the fact that I didn't spend more time with my children because I simply *had* to work—it wasn't always a matter of choice. And also, when I came out of the spin, I really had a lot of reassessment to do on my own self, and needed a quieter arena to do it in. Which is why I went to Santa Fe. And the combination of the mountains and that gorgeous sky and the horizon which goes on forever—makes some people nervous, that, but it's very comforting to me—and that's when I found out quite fortuitously—God had his hand on my shoulder in some way—that I'm extraordinarily good at teaching. . . . I would never have thought that I would be. The human exchange is fantastic. Much more interesting than acting. And especially the way acting is right now. I mean, there are so few things that I consider terribly worthwhile to say. Better not do anything, or do the *classics*.

Also I have a bee in my bonnet about doing . . . besides this project that Jessie and I want to do [that proved to be *Cat on a Hot Tin Roof*], but do you know a play called *Miss Margarida's Way*? See, that was something to say that I'd like to say. And I *loathe* the one-woman show! The whole idea of it has always made me say, "oh, really, forget it." But there's something about that play . . . well, your partner is however many people are out front. And that's some partner. And Estelle Parsons!—I went to see it thirteen times because I was so fascinated by what happens with that audience. A play that is really about fascism, you know, Miss Margarida. And the way the audience begins to believe they really are in school, and the kind of seductive thing that happens there. And then the audience becomes to one degree or another . . . the fascist. It just does something to me. Historically, I think it's also true. The oppressees become the oppressors in the revolutions, and there's something *so fascinating* to me about that, about human contact, and how one learns all of the wrong things from one's oppressors, and redoes them all in another way.

And they excuse it by the damn Bible. It's really horrendous. And horrendous on the other side too. But to open up that . . . because it's hard to do, it's so emotionally *battering,* you know, because it is a battlefield. And in the New York production—I saw it after it went to Broadway—but Estelle had to stay on during the *entr'actes.* Because otherwise the audience would come up and start tearing up her desk! And also in reading the play—I mean, there's no way I could do it the way Estelle did, she was wonderful in it— mine would be quite different because I'm a different person.

1983

EPILOGUE

"I wanted to be Irene Dunne, or Loretta Young. I wanted to be sunny."

—*Carol Burnett, April 1, 1985, CBS Morning News*

LIKE LORETTA AND IRENE, almost all the people in this book grew up, went to Hollywood, worked and established themselves before television was known outside the laboratories. They were among the first of a new breed of cross-cultural, mass-oriented, publicly ordained heroes.

The earliest stars and co-workers in this book—Gloria Swanson, Dorothy Gish, Colleen Moore, Anita Loos, Olga Baclanova among them—recall the time in California and New York before film idols (other than the ones they themselves became or grew up with) existed. Like pioneers in any field, they helped to dig the first ditch, build the first studios, define the basic ikons of the silver screen by laying the first tracks, and found, when they had time for reflection, that they had lived through and participated in an era written in lightning.

For a woman like Colleen Moore, a teenager when she arrived in Los Angeles in 1917, the strongest memories when she recounted them half a century later were not only of fabulous make-believe but of a hard-fought reality. Colleen had come from sophisticated Chicago to an industry booming in an undeveloped backwoods where the sort of people she might have read about in penny dreadfuls—*real* cowboys and *real* outlaws—played types like themselves on the screen. For Dorothy Gish there was the still-fresh memory of the tearful shock from her first public exposure to the adulation of a crowd of film fans. And Dagmar Godowsky, who had grown up in Europe and had tasted life from an emperor's lap, remembered Hollywood as a primitive community where people grew rich so fast that they could afford to eat food prepared for them by French chefs and served on silver and gold before they had time to learn the table manners to go with their new status.

If they are fascinating as storytellers now, it is not because they are keepers of the facts. They are the source and in some cases they were the catalysts for stories and facts that have become part of the legend of Hollywood. The dates they recall may be off ("Was I still in Berlin or in Hollywood?" "Was that before I had my daughter or after I had my son?" "Was I still married to Frank or Charlie, or Rudy, or Alla or Jane or . . . ?"). But it is in their recollection that a time lives. And along the way one hears of the real, ofttimes bitter, sometimes tragic cost that dreams exact when they are being realized, for imperfect table manners may not have been their only shortcomings as certifiable gods and goddesses.

More importantly, the creation of dreams would eventually exact a physical and mental toll few had the background, education and subsequently the stamina to cope with. In life, dreams can provide an escape from pressure. In the world of making make-believe believable, dreams can become the ultimate pressure. What fantasy world is there for people who make fantasy their livelihood and in the process have all their wildest dreams come true? For a man like Joel McCrea it was the physical reality of running a ranch. For women like Loretta Young and Irene Dunne it was their solidly grounded, sustaining religious faith. For some women it became marriage—once, twice or—as with Swanson, Crawford—four, five, sometimes even more times. Even when they didn't exceed the acceptable quota of husbands, it was assumed that they had.

The surest way to survive was to renounce dreams and keep working— work may prove back-breaking, but you stay sane, as Ida Lupino, Eleanor Powell, Stanwyck and others of that generation did. But they were stars of the '30s, a much more realistic era than those that had gone before, and they arrived by stepping around the first casualties and learned to keep their heads so they wouldn't end up the same way. There were those who pursued their destiny and scaled the heights while keeping their wits, their sanity and their wealth, like Mae West and Hepburn; whereas others, like Evelyn Brent and in a sense June Duprez, fell into fame as if by accident, then found themselves just as suddenly dropped back to the bottom, bruised, dizzied, disillusioned, apparently forgotten. A few, like Louise Brooks, were sought after, flirted with, acclaimed, cajoled, but wouldn't be bought and refused to play by the rules of the game and so found themselves thrown out and shunned. And there were those who could neither live down nor without their dreams, who ended up claiming to be her own younger sister; these were the real-life "Norma Desmonds" of Hollywood, afflicted with the leprosy of their vanity, for whom there was the ultimate refuge of self-delusion and sanitoriums.

But meanwhile their faces had gone up there on the screen, and they found immortality because of moments of time captured when they were young: moments which had survived by lying on a shelf in a basement, apparently forgotten, so completely neglected under the incessant spewing out of the new that an age of weekend anthropologists and treasure seekers were able to rummage without being warned off or hampered. But, surprise, surprise, not only the moments on screen were still there; these figures, ironically grown mythic, were alive, many still in their prime. Even some of the oldest were still working, and most were still amused and amusing. Recording them is history in the narrative tradition—stories of the "old days" of Hollywood handed down directly from participants, tales full of fact and fancy which constitute and finally define a time and place, a state of mind that is Hollywood.

This reclamation had already been begun before I got involved—by people like James Card, John Springer, Kevin Brownlow, Eileen Bowser, William Everson, Henri Langlois, to mention a few; and by the fans whose obsession had been deemed juvenile but who had much to do with keeping interest alive until it would flame up into today's respectable and culturally funded passion for curatorial restoration. And much more has been done since I stumbled in—done with more depth and closer scrutiny than I was interested in. For me the "movie star" was always the most remarkable thing about the movies. It was only natural that, in those first years of meeting these idols, from everything and everyone there emanated an indefinable poetic grace which exerted a powerful charm on the imagination of a young man used to living in emotional isolation.

The teens and the twenties of movies in America were the era of the Titans. Like the mythological Prometheans who first put shape to the world, they were big and often uncontrollable. Their size stamped the American film as the place to look for heroes. The changeover from the age of giants to the era of the studio was known as the coming of sound. The Titans were replaced by the gods.

The '30s were the years of Hollywood's gods, a decade of serene, sanely regulated omnipotence, when the industry was no longer arbitrarily shaped by the masses because it had learned to control a vital aspect of mass appeal via the institutionalization of awesome glamour. Glamour had been sparks thrown off by the giants in their play, and it was those electrical flashes that had made them fascinating. Now the sparks were gigantic flames, so bright, so powerful, that it is hard to believe they were manipulated. The individuals who were the source of the sparks could never be manufactured, but they had been harnessed to burn as a flame which was controlled by the studio. In a broad sense, then, the stars were the popular gods of the age, but the actual power—power being the financial control—lay with the high priests: the studio heads, the producers, the bankers, the majority stockholders, the moneylenders. To hear Olivia de Havilland tell it, the glamorous creatures of their heyday were little more than galley slaves on the barge of pleasure.

In the ritual presentation of the gods to their public, the movies they all expended their gifts on, the close-up became the highpoint of the proceedings. It had, of course, existed in the giant age, but in the '20s the close-up served a primarily dramatic function (Garbo taking a light for her cigarette from Gilbert's match in *Flesh and the Devil*); now the drama often functioned as an excuse for the close-up (Garbo in *Mata Hari,* in *Queen Christina,* etc.).

The age of the gods lasted through the next decade and even beyond. Hollywood studio power ceased to exert a major influence on the public seeking entertainment in self-identification, but the need for popular entertainment figures continued—only the venues changed. It is from the Hollywood of the '30s and '40s that we get our image of film stars, their heads and torsos revealed at a size commensurate with their powerful impact: like mighty Kong, first a tread, then a head, then a hand that lifts an awe-stricken maiden to behold his mighty face. Of course, in fact, unlike the mechanical Kong, a star's whole body was there, but so impressive were they that we preferred to take them in (comprehend them) in sections, a bit at a time—a mountain range that turns out to be a shoulder, a pair of majestic redwoods which on closer scrutiny turn out to be Rita's gams, a topographical view of a golden wheatfield that turns around to reveal Veronica Lake's face. When film stars were encountered in life by people not used to seeing their idols in person, the fans would often be disillusioned. "Oh dear," said an Ottawa matron waiting outside the hotel where Hollywood's blond, two-fisted hero Alan Ladd was staying while in Canada to make *Saskatchewan*, "he's so small!" Her disappointment was profound because of her emotional involvement with Alan Ladd on the screen.

Ultimately, the gods' attraction reached a peak and started to become old-hat. The displacement of movies and movie stars in the public's affection was not unlike the story of the giant Prometheus, who stole a spark of the divine fire with which the gods maintained dominion over man and gave it to mankind. Prometheus died a lingering death for his crime, but he had ended the reign of the gods. What happened to Hollywood and its gods was that the divine fire hit television.

Loretta Young recalls warnings and veiled threats she received from friends and studio heads when with her series she led the exodus of the big-time Hollywood stars to TV. In effect, because of TV, the old gods were displaced by Lilliputians. Soon the movie temples were deserted. But the film stars had left a legacy. Because of the great age of the movie star, and with the star as example, moviegoers had evolved and grown to realize and appreciate their own uniqueness. While this gave them a sense of their own worth, it also meant that they would not take the new idols of popular culture so seriously as before.

By the '60s, what had always been true was now clear to one and all: anybody could be a star.

But almost simultaneously it became clear that the old film stars had been even more significant than their original reign had suggested. When the old stars speak of their beginnings, one rarely hears talk of a role model, unless it's a mother, a father or D. W. Griffith, for their sort of fame had few precedents. But the second half of this century seems to model its idols on those of the first half.

During Hollywood's bewildered decline there was little talk of the past, no serious writing, no seminars, no college courses, no concerted effort at reclamation. In the mid-'60s, contemporary pop and TV idols, unburdening their souls on talk shows, cited the stars of the '30s and '40s as the formative source for the images they had modeled for themselves. Bogart lived on because of the children of the generation for whom he had been a star. These children had his movies not to look forward to, but to look back on and draw from. In yet one more neat little twist, TV, having assassinated the movies, ensured that the stars of the movies would never die: Hollywood's high priests, in their panic and scramble for money, unloaded their old films on-to TV.

We grew up in the '50s on stars like Rock Hudson in the movies and stars like Humphrey Bogart on TV. The new generation of moviegoers raced hot-rods, smoked pot and defied authority with the nonchalance of Bogart facing the Nazis and wiping the smirks off Peter Lorre, Mary Astor et al. Not only Bogart but also Rick; not only Rita Hayworth herself but also Gilda; stars and their characters became interchangeable.

To the '50s generation of moviegoers, a star like Doris Day was the equiv-alent of an Irene Dunne. To the critics writing in that era, Doris Day was a symptom of what was wrong with the films coming out of Hollywood. To the '80s generation, whose stars nearly all come from the rock-music scene, the opinions and ideals of the '50s are of little concern, but they find what Doris Day was about in a singer like Olivia Newton-John. Her hair may be unruly, and the only design evident in her wardrobe is in her jeans, but she has the same overlay of effervescence and the scrubbed-cheek wholesomeness. While the analogy gets a bit far-fetched, nevertheless entertainer Michael Jackson looks with awe to his idol, Fred Astaire. But then, fans have been dreaming of being Fred Astaire almost from the day he first danced across the screen fifty years ago. Baryshnikov dreamed of becoming Gene Kelly while still a boy in Russia. Tom Selleck finds his role model in mustachioed macho man Burt Reynolds, yet Reynolds himself, still a current big-screen hero, takes his slightly self-mocking, laid-back persona from the man who outlined those parameters back in the '30s, Clark Gable. I once asked Sophia Loren what had been her ambition when she set out on her career, and she unhesitatingly replied that she had wanted to be a film star like Rita Hayworth. That's the sort of star Raquel Welch hoped to become when she started in the '60s, and today Raquel Welch is a role model for dozens of current TV favorites.

The dress Jean Louis designed for Hayworth to wear in her ultimate screen incarnation as Gilda (the woman who was true to a man once, and look what happened), has taken on its own mythic status as the classic rag for a beautiful woman to wear while proclaiming her arrival as a sexually liberating love god-dess. In Madonna's rock video for the song "Material Girl," there is more of an air of dressing up than of actually laying claim to becoming the Monroe of the '80s; not only does she wear a carbon copy of the pink satin dress Monroe wore while singing "Diamonds Are a Girl's Best Friend" in the 1953 musical *Gentle-men Prefer Blondes,* but the choreography which Jack Cole created to illumi-nate Marilyn as the love goddess of the '50s has also been lifted *ad hoc* for Madonna's number. The effect is to further proclaim Monroe a star from a time when stars were still larger than life.

What this has done is to show, in the light given off by the fast-food idols of recent years, that the stars of the '20s, the '30s and the '40s had not merely been stars but had been the fondest of relatives, the dearest of memories, con-fessors, massive and benevolent idols whose influence outlasted the shift of decades.

INDEX